Praise for the Third Edition of *Spring in Action*

Continues to be the de-facto reference guide to Spring. Offers clear explanations of concepts with very good examples in an easy-to-read format.

—Dan Dobrin, CIBC

An indispensable guide to the large landscape of Spring.

—Mykel Alvis, Automaton Online

The one book you need on your desk when working with Spring.

—Josh Devins, Nokia

Covers both the fundamentals and the breadth of Spring.

—Chad Davis, Blackdog Software, Inc.

Using Spring is not difficult—but with this book it becomes much easier.

—Alberto Lagna, Biznology

One of my favorite technology books. Great content delivered by a great teacher.

—Robert Hanson, Author of Manning's *GWT in Action*

The right dose of humor with a load of technical wisdom is the perfect mix for learning Spring.

—Valentin Crettaz, Goomzee

Tremendous focus—and fun to read.

—Doug Warren, Java Web Services

Craig's witty examples make complex concepts easy to understand.

—Dan Alford

Spring in Action

FOURTH EDITION

CRAIG WALLS

MANNING
SHELTER ISLAND

For online information and ordering of this and other Manning books, please visit
www.manning.com. The publisher offers discounts on this book when ordered in quantity.
For more information, please contact

> Special Sales Department
> Manning Publications Co.
> 20 Baldwin Road
> PO Box 761
> Shelter Island, NY 11964
> Email: orders@manning.com

Manning Publications Co.
20 Baldwin Road
Shelter Island, NY 11964

Development editor: Cynthia Kane
Copyeditor: Andy Carroll
Proofreader: Alyson Brener
Typesetter: Dottie Marsico
Cover designer: Marija Tudor

ISBN 9781617291203
Printed in the United States of America
3 4 5 6 7 8 9 10 – EBM – 19 18 17 16 15

brief contents

contents

preface

The best keeps getting better. More than a dozen years ago, Spring entered the Java development scene with the ambitious goal of simplifying enterprise Java development. It challenged the heavyweight programming models of the time with a simpler and lighter programming model based on plain old Java objects.

Now, several years and many releases later, we see that Spring has had a tremendous impact on enterprise application development. It has become a de facto standard framework for countless Java projects and has had an impact on the evolution of some of the specifications and frameworks that it originally set out to replace. It'd be hard to deny that the current Enterprise JavaBeans (EJB) specification may have turned out very differently had Spring not challenged earlier versions of the EJB spec.

But Spring itself continues to evolve and improve upon itself, always seeking to make the difficult development tasks simpler and empower Java developers with innovative features. Where Spring had first set out to challenge the status quo, Spring now has leapt ahead and is paving trails in Java application development.

Therefore, it's time for an updated edition of this book to expose the current state of Spring. There's so much that has happened in the past few years since the previous edition of this book; it'd be impossible to cover everything in a single edition. Nevertheless, I still tried to pack this fourth edition of *Spring in Action* with as much as I could. Here are just a few of the exciting new things that have been added in this edition:

- An emphasis on Java-based Spring configuration with Java configuration options available for almost every area of Spring development
- Conditional configuration and profiles that make runtime decisions regarding what Spring configuration should be used or ignored

- Several enhancements and improvements to Spring MVC, especially with regard to creating REST services
- Using Thymeleaf with Spring web applications as an alternative to JSP
- Enabling Spring Security with Java-based configuration
- Using Spring Data to automatically generate repository implementations at runtime for JPA, MongoDB, and Neo4j
- Spring's new declarative caching support
- Asynchronous web messaging with WebSocket and STOMP
- Spring Boot, a game-changing new approach to working with Spring

If you're a seasoned Spring veteran, you'll find that these new elements will become valuable additions to your Spring toolkit. On the other hand, if you're new to Spring, you've picked a good time to learn Spring, and this book will help you get started.

This is, indeed, an exciting time to be working with Spring. It's been a blast to develop with Spring and write about it during the past 12 years. I can't wait to see what Spring does next!

acknowledgments

Before this book goes to press, before it is bound, before it is boxed, before it is shipped, and before you get your hands on it, there are many other hands that have touched it along the way. Even if you have an eBook copy that didn't go through that process, there were numerous hands on the bits and bytes that you downloaded—hands that edited it, reviewed it, typeset it, and proofread it. If it weren't for all of those hands, this book wouldn't exist.

First, a big thank you to everyone at Manning for working hard, for their patience when the writing wasn't moving as fast as it should have, and for prodding me along to get it done: Marjan Bace, Michael Stephens, Cynthia Kane, Andy Carroll, Benjamin Berg, Alyson Brener, Dottie Marisco, Mary Piergies, Janet Vail, and many others behind the scenes.

Getting feedback early and often is just as critical when writing a book as it is when developing software. While the pages of this book were still in a very rough form, there were several great reviewers who took the time to read the drafts and provide feedback that helped shape the final product. Thanks to the following: Bob Casazza, Chaoho Hsieh, Christophe Martini, Gregor Zurowski, James Wright, Jeelani Basha, Jens Richter, Jonathan Thoms, Josh Hart, Karen Christenson, Mario Arias, Michael Roberts, Paul Balogh, and Ricardo da Silva Lima. And special thanks to John Ryan for his thorough technical review of the manuscript shortly before it went into production.

Of course, I want to thank my beautiful wife for enduring yet another writing project and for her encouragement along the way. I love you more than you could possibly ever know.

To Maisy and Madi, the most awesome little girls in the world, thank you again for your hugs, laughs, and unusual insights into what should go into the book.

To my colleagues on the Spring team, what can I say? You guys ROCK! I'm humbled and grateful for being a part of the organization that drives Spring forward. I never cease to be amazed at the never-ending awesomeness that you crank out.

And many thanks to everyone I encounter as I travel the country speaking at user groups and No Fluff/Just Stuff conferences.

Finally, thank you to the Phoenicians. You (and Epcot fans) know what you did.

about this book

The Spring Framework was created with a very specific goal in mind—to make developing Java EE applications easier. Along the same lines, *Spring in Action, Fourth Edition* was written to make learning how to use Spring easier. My goal is not to give you a blow-by-blow listing of Spring APIs. Instead, I hope to present the Spring Framework in a way that is most relevant to a Java EE developer by providing practical code examples from real-world experiences. Since Spring is a modular framework, this book was written in the same way. I recognize that not all developers have the same needs. Some may want to learn the Spring Framework from the ground up, while others may want to pick and choose different topics and go at their own pace. That way, the book can act as a tool for learning Spring for the first time as well as a guide and reference for those wanting to dig deeper into specific features.

Spring in Action, *Fourth Edition* is for all Java developers, but enterprise Java developers will find it particularly useful. While I will guide you along gently through code examples that build in complexity throughout each chapter, the true power of Spring lies in its ability to make enterprise applications easier to develop. Therefore, enterprise developers will most fully appreciate the examples presented in this book. Because a vast portion of Spring is devoted to providing enterprise services, many parallels can be drawn between Spring and EJB.

Roadmap

Spring in Action, *Fourth Edition* is divided into four parts. The first part introduces you to the essentials of the Spring Framework. Part 2 expands on that by showing how to build web applications with Spring. Part 3 steps behind the front end and shows where

Spring fits in the back end of an application. The final part shows how Spring can be used to integrate with other applications and services.

In part 1, you'll explore the Spring container, dependency injection (DI), and aspect-oriented programming...the essentials of the Spring Framework. This will give you a foundation upon which the rest of the book will build.

- In chapter 1, you'll be given an overview of Spring, including some basic examples of DI and AOP. You'll also get an overview of the greater Spring ecosystem.
- Chapter 2 goes into more detail with DI, showing you various ways that the components in your application (the "beans") can be wired together. This includes wiring with XML, Java, and automatic wiring.
- With the basics of bean wiring down, chapter 3 presents several advanced wiring techniques. You won't need these techniques that often, but when you do need them this chapter will show you how to get the most power out of the Spring container.
- Chapter 4 explores how to use Spring AOP to decouple cross-cutting concerns from the objects that they service. This chapter also sets the stage for later chapters where you'll use AOP to provide declarative services such as transactions, security, and caching.

In part 2 you'll see how to use Spring to build web applications.

- Chapter 5 covers the basics of working with Spring MVC, the foundational web framework in Spring. You'll see how to write controllers to handle web requests and respond with model data.
- Once a controller is finished with its work, the model data must be rendered using a view. Chapter 6 will explore various view technologies that can be used with Spring, including JSP, Apache Tiles, and Thymeleaf.
- Chapter 7 goes beyond the basics of Spring MVC. In this chapter, you'll learn how to customize Spring MVC configuration, handle multipart file uploads, deal with exceptions that may occur in a controller, and pass data between requests with flash attributes.
- Chapter 8 explores Spring Web Flow, an extension to Spring MVC that enables development of conversational web applications. In this chapter, you'll learn how to build web applications that lead the user through a specific, guided flow.
- In chapter 9 you'll learn how to apply security to the web layer of your application using Spring Security.

Part 3 goes behind the front end of an application and looks at how data is processed and persisted.

- Data persistence is first tackled in chapter 10 using Spring's abstraction over JDBC to work with data stored in a relational database.
- Chapter 11 takes on data persistence from another angle, using the Java Persistence API (JPA) to store data in a relational database.

- Chapter 12 looks at how Spring works with non-relational databases, such as MongoDB and Neo4j. Regardless of where the data is stored, caching can help improve performance by not hitting the database any more than necessary.
- Chapter 13 introduces you to Spring's support for declarative caching.
- Chapter 14 revisits Spring Security, showing how to use AOP to apply security at the method level.

The final part looks at ways to integrate your Spring applications with other systems.

- Chapter 15 looks at how to create and consume remote services, including RMI, Hessian, Burlap, and SOAP-based services.
- In chapter 16, Spring MVC is revisited to see how to create RESTful services using the same programming model as described previously in chapter 5.
- Chapter 17 explores Spring support for asynchronous messaging. This chapter includes working with Java Message Service (JMS) as well as the Advanced Message Queuing Protocol (AMQP).
- Asynchronous messaging takes a different twist in chapter 18 where you'll see how to use Spring with WebSocket and STOMP for asynchronous communication between the server and a client.
- Chapter 19 looks at how to send emails with Spring.
- Chapter 20 highlights Spring's management support for Java Management Extensions (JMX), enabling you to monitor and modify runtime settings for a Spring application.
- Finally, in chapter 21 you'll be introduced to a game-changing and very new way to work with Spring called Spring Boot. You'll see how Spring Boot can take away much of the boilerplate configuration required in a Spring application, enabling you to focus on the business functionality.

Code conventions and downloads

There are many code examples throughout this book. These examples will always appear in a `fixed-width code font like this`. Any class name, method name, or XML fragment within the normal text of the book will appear in code font as well.

Many of Spring's classes and packages have exceptionally long (but expressive) names. Because of this, line-continuation markers (➡) may be included when necessary.

Not all code examples in this book will be complete. Often I only show a method or two from a class to focus on a particular topic. Complete source code for the applications found throughout the book can be downloaded from the publisher's website at www.manning.com/SpringinActionFourthEdition.

Author Online

Purchase of *Spring in Action, Fourth Edition* includes free access to a private web forum run by Manning Publications where you can make comments about the book, ask technical questions, and receive help from the author and from other users. To

access the forum and subscribe to it, point your web browser to www.manning.com/
SpringinActionFourthEdition. This page provides information on how to get on the
forum once you are registered, what kind of help is available, and the rules of con-
duct on the forum.

Manning's commitment to our readers is to provide a venue where a meaningful
dialogue between individual readers and between readers and the author can take
place. It is not a commitment to any specific amount of participation on the part of the
author, whose contribution to the book's forum remains voluntary (and unpaid). We
suggest you try asking the author some challenging questions, lest his interest stray!

The Author Online forum and the archives of previous discussions will be accessi-
ble from the publisher's website as long as the book is in print.

About the author

Craig Walls is a senior engineer with Pivotal as the project lead for Spring Social and
Spring Sync, and is the author of Manning's *Spring in Action* books, now updated in
this Fourth Edition. He's a zealous promoter of the Spring Framework, speaking frequently at local user groups and conferences and writing about Spring. When he's not
slinging code, Craig spends as much time as he can with his wife, two daughters, two
birds, and two dogs.

About the cover illustration

The figure on the cover of *Spring in Action, Fourth Edition*, is "Le Caraco," or an inhab-
itant of the province of Karak in southwest Jordan. Its capital is the city of Al-Karak,
which boasts an ancient hilltop castle with magnificent views of the Dead Sea and surrounding plains. The illustration is taken from a French travel book, *Encyclopédie des
Voyages* by J. G. St. Sauveur, published in 1796. Travel for pleasure was a relatively new
phenomenon at the time and travel guides such as this one were popular, introducing
both the tourist as well as the armchair traveler to the inhabitants of other regions of
France and abroad.

The diversity of the drawings in the *Encyclopédie des Voyages* speaks vividly of the dis-
tinctiveness and individuality of the world's towns and provinces just two hundred
years ago. This was a time when the dress codes of two regions separated by a few
dozen miles identified people uniquely as belonging to one or the other. The travel
guide brings to life a sense of isolation and distance of that period, and of every other
historic period except our own hyperkinetic present.

Dress codes have changed since then and the diversity by region, so rich at the
time, has faded away. It is now often hard to tell the inhabitants of one continent from
another. Perhaps, trying to view it optimistically, we have traded a cultural and visual
diversity for a more varied personal life—or a more varied and interesting intellectual
and technical life.

We at Manning celebrate the inventiveness, the initiative, and the fun of the com-
puter business with book covers based on the rich diversity of regional life two centu-
ries ago brought back to life by the pictures from this travel guide.

Part 1

Core Spring

Spring does a lot of things. But underneath all of the fantastic functionality it adds to enterprise development, its primary features are dependency injection (DI) and aspect-oriented programming (AOP).

Starting in chapter 1, "Springing into action," I'll give you a quick overview of the Spring Framework, including a quick overview of DI and AOP in Spring and show how they help with decoupling application components.

In chapter 2, "Wiring beans," we'll dive deeper into how to piece together the components of an application. We'll look at automatic configuration, Java-based configuration, and XML configuration options offered by Spring.

Chapter 3, "Advanced wiring," goes beyond the basics and shows you a few tricks and techniques that will help you get the most power out of Spring, including conditional configuration, dealing with ambiguity when autowiring, scoping, and the Spring Expression Language.

Chapter 4, "Aspect-oriented Spring," explores how to use Spring's AOP features to decouple system-wide services (such as security and auditing) from the objects they service. This chapter sets the stage for later chapters such as chapters 9, 13, and 14 where you'll see how to leverage Spring AOP for declarative security and caching.

Springing into action 1

This chapter covers

- Spring's bean container
- Exploring Spring's core modules
- The greater Spring ecosystem
- What's new in Spring

It's a good time to be a Java developer.

In its almost 20 year history, Java has seen some good times and some bad times. Despite a handful of rough spots, such as applets, Enterprise JavaBeans (EJB), Java Data Objects (JDO), and countless logging frameworks, Java has enjoyed a rich and diverse history as the platform on which much enterprise software has been built. And Spring has been a big part of that story.

In its early days, Spring was created as an alternative to heavier enterprise Java technologies, especially EJB. Spring offered a lighter and leaner programming model as compared to EJB. It empowered plain old Java objects (POJOs) with powers previously only available using EJB and other enterprise Java specifications.

Over time, EJB and the Java 2 Enterprise Edition (J2EE) evolved. EJB started offering a simple POJO-oriented programming model of its own. Now EJB employs ideas such as dependency injection (DI) and aspect-oriented programming (AOP), arguably inspired by the success of Spring.

Although J2EE (now known as JEE) was able to catch up with Spring, Spring never stopped moving forward. Spring has continued to progress in areas where, even now, JEE is just starting to explore or isn't innovating at all. Mobile development, social API integration, NoSQL databases, cloud computing, and big data are just a few areas where Spring has been and is innovating. And the future continues to look bright for Spring.

As I said, it's a good time to be a Java developer.

This book is an exploration of Spring. In this chapter, we'll examine Spring at a high level, providing you with a taste of what Spring is about. This chapter will give you a good idea of the types of problems Spring solves, and it will set the stage for the rest of the book.

1.1   *Simplifying Java development*

Spring is an open source framework, originally created by Rod Johnson and described in his book *Expert One-on-One: J2EE Design and Development* (Wrox, 2002, http://amzn.com/0764543857). Spring was created to address the complexity of enterprise application development and makes it possible to use plain-vanilla JavaBeans to achieve things that were previously only possible with EJB. But Spring's usefulness isn't limited to server-side development. Any Java application can benefit from Spring in terms of simplicity, testability, and loose coupling.

A bean by any other name... Although Spring uses the words *bean* and *JavaBean* liberally when referring to application components, this doesn't mean a Spring component must follow the JavaBeans specification to the letter. A Spring component can be any type of POJO. In this book, I assume a loose definition of *JavaBean*, which is synonymous with *POJO*.

As you'll see throughout this book, Spring does many things. But at the root of almost everything Spring provides are a few foundational ideas, all focused on Spring's fundamental mission: *Spring simplifies Java development.*

That's a bold statement! A lot of frameworks claim to simplify something or other. But Spring aims to simplify the broad subject of Java development. This begs for more explanation. How does Spring simplify Java development?

To back up its attack on Java complexity, Spring employs four key strategies:

- Lightweight and minimally invasive development with POJOs
- Loose coupling through DI and interface orientation
- Declarative programming through aspects and common conventions
- Eliminating boilerplate code with aspects and templates

Almost everything Spring does can be traced back to one or more of these four strategies. Throughout the rest of this chapter, I'll expand on each of these ideas, showing concrete examples of how Spring makes good on its promise to simplify Java development. Let's start with seeing how Spring remains minimally invasive by encouraging POJO-oriented development.

1.1.1 Unleashing the power of POJOs

If you've been doing Java development for long, you've probably seen (and may have even worked with) frameworks that lock you in by forcing you to extend one of their classes or implement one of their interfaces. The easy-target example of such an invasive programming model was EJB 2-era stateless session beans. But even though early EJBs were such an easy target, invasive programming could easily be found in earlier versions of Struts, WebWork, Tapestry, and countless other Java specifications and frameworks.

Spring avoids (as much as possible) littering your application code with its API. Spring almost never forces you to implement a Spring-specific interface or extend a Spring-specific class. Instead, the classes in a Spring-based application often have no indication that they're being used by Spring. At worst, a class may be annotated with one of Spring's annotations, but it's otherwise a POJO.

To illustrate, consider the `HelloWorldBean` class shown in the following listing.

> **Listing 1.1 Spring doesn't make any unreasonable demands on `HelloWorldBean`.**

```
package com.habuma.spring;
public class HelloWorldBean {
  public String sayHello() {          ⊲— This is all you need.
    return "Hello World";
  }
}
```

As you can see, this is a simple, garden-variety Java class—a POJO. Nothing special about it indicates that it's a Spring component. Spring's non-invasive programming model means this class could function equally well in a Spring application as it could in a non-Spring application.

Despite their simple form, POJOs can be powerful. One of the ways Spring empowers POJOs is by assembling them using DI. Let's see how DI can help keep application objects decoupled from each other.

1.1.2 Injecting dependencies

The phrase *dependency injection* may sound intimidating, conjuring up notions of a complex programming technique or design pattern. But as it turns out, DI isn't nearly as complex as it sounds. By applying DI in your projects, you'll find that your code will become significantly simpler, easier to understand, and easier to test.

HOW DI WORKS

Any nontrivial application (pretty much anything more complex than a Hello World example) is made up of two or more classes that collaborate with each other to perform some business logic. Traditionally, each object is responsible for obtaining its own references to the objects it collaborates with (its *dependencies*). This can lead to highly coupled and hard-to-test code.

For example, consider the `Knight` class shown next.

Listing 1.2   A `DamselRescuingKnight` can only embark on `RescueDamselQuests`.

```
package com.springinaction.knights;

public class DamselRescuingKnight implements Knight {

  private RescueDamselQuest quest;

  public DamselRescuingKnight() {
    this.quest = new RescueDamselQuest();     ◁┘ Tightly coupled to
  }                                                RescueDamselQuest

  public void embarkOnQuest() {
    quest.embark();
  }

}
```

As you can see, `DamselRescuingKnight` creates its own quest, a `RescueDamselQuest`, in the constructor. This makes a `DamselRescuingKnight` tightly coupled to a `Rescue-DamselQuest` and severely limits the knight's quest-embarking repertoire. If a damsel needs rescuing, this knight's there. But if a dragon needs slaying or a round table needs … well … rounding, then this knight's going to have to sit it out.

What's more, it'd be terribly difficult to write a unit test for `DamselRescuing-Knight`. In such a test, you'd like to be able to assert that the quest's `embark()` method is called when the knight's `embarkOnQuest()` method is called. But there's no clear way to accomplish that here. Unfortunately, `DamselRescuingKnight` will remain untested.

Coupling is a two-headed beast. On the one hand, tightly coupled code is difficult to test, difficult to reuse, and difficult to understand, and it typically exhibits "whack-a-mole" bug behavior (fixing one bug results in the creation of one or more new bugs). On the other hand, a certain amount of coupling is necessary—completely uncoupled code doesn't do anything. In order to do anything useful, classes need to know about each other somehow. Coupling is necessary but should be carefully managed.

With DI, objects are given their dependencies at creation time by some third party that coordinates each object in the system. Objects aren't expected to create or obtain their dependencies. As illustrated in figure 1.1, dependencies are injected into the objects that need them.

To illustrate this point, let's look at `BraveKnight` in the next listing: a knight who's not only brave, but also capable of embarking on any kind of quest that comes along.

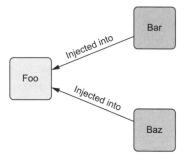

Figure 1.1   Dependency injection involves giving an object its dependencies as opposed to an object having to acquire those dependencies on its own.

Listing 1.3   A `BraveKnight` is flexible enough to take on any `Quest` he's given.

```
package com.springinaction.knights;

public class BraveKnight implements Knight {

  private Quest quest;

  public BraveKnight(Quest quest) {          ◁─────────── Quest is injected
    this.quest = quest;
  }

  public void embarkOnQuest() {
    quest.embark();
  }

}
```

As you can see, BraveKnight, unlike DamselRescuingKnight, doesn't create his own quest. Instead, he's given a quest at construction time as a constructor argument. This is a type of DI known as *constructor injection*.

What's more, the quest he's given is typed as Quest, an interface that all quests implement. So BraveKnight could embark on a RescueDamselQuest, a SlayDragonQuest, a MakeRoundTableRounderQuest, or any other Quest implementation he's given.

The point is that BraveKnight isn't coupled to any specific implementation of Quest. It doesn't matter to him what kind of quest he's asked to embark on, as long as it implements the Quest interface. That's the key benefit of DI—loose coupling. If an object only knows about its dependencies by their interface (not by their implementation or how they're instantiated), then the dependency can be swapped out with a different implementation without the depending object knowing the difference.

One of the most common ways a dependency is swapped out is with a mock implementation during testing. You were unable to adequately test DamselRescuingKnight due to tight coupling, but you can easily test BraveKnight by giving it a mock implementation of Quest, as shown next.

Listing 1.4   To test `BraveKnight`, inject it with a mock `Quest`.

```
package com.springinaction.knights;
import static org.mockito.Mockito.*;
import org.junit.Test;

public class BraveKnightTest {

  @Test
  public void knightShouldEmbarkOnQuest() {
    Quest mockQuest = mock(Quest.class);                  ◁── Create mock Quest
    BraveKnight knight = new BraveKnight(mockQuest);      ◁── Inject mock Quest
    knight.embarkOnQuest();
    verify(mockQuest, times(1)).embark();
  }

}
```

Here you use a mock object framework known as *Mockito* to create a mock implementation of the Quest interface. With the mock object in hand, you create a new instance of BraveKnight, injecting the mock Quest via the constructor. After calling the embarkOnQuest() method, you ask Mockito to verify that the mock Quest's embark() method was called exactly once.

INJECTING A QUEST INTO A KNIGHT

Now that the BraveKnight class is written in such a way that you can give a knight any quest you want, how can you specify which Quest to give him? Suppose, for instance, that you'd like for the BraveKnight to embark on a quest to slay a dragon. Perhaps SlayDragonQuest, shown in the following listing, would be appropriate.

Listing 1.5   SlayDragonQuest is a Quest to be injected into BraveKnight

```java
package com.springinaction.knights;

import java.io.PrintStream;

public class SlayDragonQuest implements Quest {

  private PrintStream stream;

  public SlayDragonQuest(PrintStream stream) {
    this.stream = stream;
  }

  public void embark() {
    stream.println("Embarking on quest to slay the dragon!");
  }

}
```

As you can see, SlayDragonQuest implements the Quest interface, making it a good fit for BraveKnight. You may also notice that rather than lean on System.out .println() like many small getting-started Java samples, SlayDragonQuest more generically asks for a PrintStream through its constructor. The big question here is, how can you give SlayDragonQuest to BraveKnight? And how can you give a Print-Stream to SlayDragonQuest?

The act of creating associations between application components is commonly referred to as *wiring*. In Spring, there are many ways to wire components together, but a common approach has always been via XML. The next listing shows a simple Spring configuration file, knights.xml, that wires a BraveKnight, a SlayDragonQuest, and a PrintStream together.

Listing 1.6   Injecting a SlayDragonQuest into a BraveKnight with Spring

```xml
<?xml version="1.0" encoding="UTF-8"?>
<beans xmlns="http://www.springframework.org/schema/beans"
  xmlns:xsi="http://www.w3.org/2001/XMLSchema-instance"
```

```
  xsi:schemaLocation="http://www.springframework.org/schema/beans
      http://www.springframework.org/schema/beans/spring-beans.xsd">

  <bean id="knight" class="com.springinaction.knights.BraveKnight">
    <constructor-arg ref="quest" />                  <-- Inject quest bean
  </bean>

  <bean id="quest" class="com.springinaction.knights.SlayDragonQuest">   <-- Create SlayDragonQuest
    <constructor-arg value="#{T(System).out}" />
  </bean>

</beans>
```

Here, `BraveKnight` and `SlayDragonQuest` are declared as beans in Spring. In the case of the `BraveKnight` bean, it's constructed, passing a reference to the `SlayDragonQuest` bean as a constructor argument. Meanwhile, the `SlayDragonQuest` bean declaration uses the Spring Expression Language to pass `System.out` (which is a `PrintStream`) to `SlayDragonQuest`'s constructor.

If XML configuration doesn't suit your tastes, you might like to know that Spring also allows you to express configuration using Java. For example, here you see a Java-based equivalent to listing 1.6.

Listing 1.7 Spring offers Java-based configuration as an alternative to XML.

```
package com.springinaction.knights.config;

import org.springframework.context.annotation.Bean;
import org.springframework.context.annotation.Configuration;

import com.springinaction.knights.BraveKnight;
import com.springinaction.knights.Knight;
import com.springinaction.knights.Quest;
import com.springinaction.knights.SlayDragonQuest;

@Configuration
public class KnightConfig {

  @Bean
  public Knight knight() {
    return new BraveKnight(quest());
  }

  @Bean
  public Quest quest() {
    return new SlayDragonQuest(System.out);
  }

}
```

Whether you use XML-based or Java-based configuration, the benefits of DI are the same. Although `BraveKnight` depends on a `Quest`, it doesn't know what type of `Quest` it will be given or where that `Quest` will come from. Likewise, `SlayDragonQuest` depends on a `PrintStream`, but it isn't coded with knowledge of how that `Print-Stream` comes to be. Only Spring, through its configuration, knows how all the pieces come together. This makes it possible to change those dependencies with no changes to the depending classes.

This example has shown a simple approach to wiring beans in Spring. Don't concern yourself too much with the details right now. We'll dig more into Spring configuration when we get to chapter 2. We'll also look at other ways that beans can be wired in Spring, including a way to let Spring automatically discover beans and create the relationships between them.

Now that you've declared the relationship between `BraveKnight` and a `Quest`, you need to load the XML configuration file and kick off the application.

SEEING IT WORK

In a Spring application, an *application context* loads bean definitions and wires them together. The Spring application context is fully responsible for the creation of and wiring of the objects that make up the application. Spring comes with several implementations of its application context, each primarily differing only in how it loads its configuration.

When the beans in knights.xml are declared in an XML file, an appropriate choice for application context might be `ClassPathXmlApplicationContext`.[1] This Spring context implementation loads the Spring context from one or more XML files located in the application's classpath. The `main()` method in the following listing uses `Class-PathXmlApplicationContext` to load knights.xml and to get a reference to the `Knight` object.

Listing 1.8   KnightMain.java loads the Spring context containing a `Knight`.

```java
package com.springinaction.knights;

import org.springframework.context.support.
                 ClassPathXmlApplicationContext;

public class KnightMain {

  public static void main(String[] args) throws Exception {      // Load Spring
    ClassPathXmlApplicationContext context =                     //   context
       new ClassPathXmlApplicationContext(
          "META-INF/spring/knight.xml");
    Knight knight = context.getBean(Knight.class);               // Get knight
    knight.embarkOnQuest();                    // Use knight     //   bean
     context.close();
  }

}
```

---

[1] For Java-based configurations, Spring offers `AnnotationConfigApplicationContext`.

Here the `main()` method creates the Spring application context based on the knights.xml file. Then it uses the application context as a factory to retrieve the bean whose ID is *knight*. With a reference to the `Knight` object, it calls the `embarkOnQuest()` method to have the knight embark on the quest he was given. Note that this class knows nothing about which type of `Quest` your hero has. For that matter, it's blissfully unaware of the fact that it's dealing with `BraveKnight`. Only the knights.xml file knows for sure what the implementations are.

And with that you have a quick introduction to dependency injection. You'll see a lot more DI throughout this book. But if you want even more DI, I encourage you to look at Dhanji R. Prasanna's *Dependency Injection* (Manning, 2009, www.manning.com/prasanna/), which covers DI in fine detail.

Now let's look at another of Spring's Java-simplifying strategies: declarative programming through aspects.

1.1.3 Applying aspects

Although DI makes it possible to tie software components together loosely, aspect-oriented programming (AOP) enables you to capture functionality that's used throughout your application in reusable components.

AOP is often defined as a technique that promotes separation of concerns in a software system. Systems are composed of several components, each responsible for a specific piece of functionality. But often these components also carry additional responsibilities beyond their core functionality. System services such as logging, transaction management, and security often find their way into components whose core responsibilities is something else. These system services are commonly referred to as *cross-cutting concerns* because they tend to cut across multiple components in a system.

By spreading these concerns across multiple components, you introduce two levels of complexity to your code:

- The code that implements the system-wide concerns is duplicated across multiple components. This means that if you need to change how those concerns work, you'll need to visit multiple components. Even if you've abstracted the concern to a separate module so that the impact to your components is a single method call, that method call is duplicated in multiple places.
- Your components are littered with code that isn't aligned with their core functionality. A method that adds an entry to an address book should only be concerned with how to add the address and not with whether it's secure or transactional.

Figure 1.2 illustrates this complexity. The business objects on the left are too intimately involved with the system services on the right. Not only does each object know that it's being logged, secured, and involved in a transactional context, but each object also is responsible for performing those services for itself.

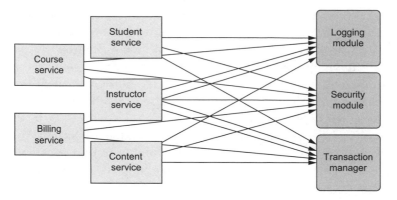

Figure 1.2   Calls to system-wide concerns such as logging and security are often scattered about in modules where those tasks are not their primary concern.

AOP makes it possible to modularize these services and then apply them declaratively to the components they should affect. This results in components that are more cohesive and that focus on their own specific concerns, completely ignorant of any system services that may be involved. In short, aspects ensure that POJOs remain plain.

It may help to think of aspects as blankets that cover many components of an application, as illustrated in figure 1.3. At its core, an application consists of modules that implement business functionality. With AOP, you can then cover your core application with layers of functionality. These layers can be applied declaratively throughout your application in a flexible manner without your core application even knowing they exist. This is a powerful concept, because it keeps the security, transaction, and logging concerns from littering the application's core business logic.

To demonstrate how aspects can be applied in Spring, let's revisit the knight example, adding a basic Spring aspect to the mix.

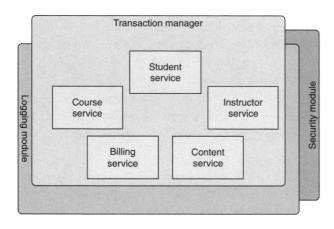

Figure 1.3   Using AOP, system-wide concerns blanket the components they impact. This leaves the application components to focus on their specific business functionality.

AOP IN ACTION

Anyone who knows anything about knights only knows about them because their deeds were chronicled in song by the musically inclined storytellers known as minstrels. Let's suppose that you want to record the comings and goings of your BraveKnight using the services of a minstrel. The following listing shows the Minstrel class you might use.

Listing 1.9   A `Minstrel` is a musically inclined logging system from medieval times.

```
package com.springinaction.knights;

import java.io.PrintStream;

public class Minstrel {

  private PrintStream stream;

  public Minstrel(PrintStream stream) {
    this.stream = stream;
  }

  public void singBeforeQuest() {                    ⟵ Called before quest
    stream.println("Fa la la, the knight is so brave!");
  }

  public void singAfterQuest() {                     ⟵ Called after quest
    stream.println("Tee hee hee, the brave knight " +
        "did embark on a quest!");
  }

}
```

As you can see, Minstrel is a simple class with two methods. The singBeforeQuest() method is intended to be invoked before a knight embarks on a quest, and the singAfterQuest() method should be invoked after the knight has completed a quest. In both cases, the Minstrel sings of the knight's deeds via a PrintStream injected through its constructor.

It should be simple to work this into your code—you can just inject it into BraveKnight, right? Let's make the appropriate tweaks to BraveKnight to use Minstrel. The next listing shows a first attempt at bringing BraveKnight and Minstrel together.

Listing 1.10   A `BraveKnight` that must call `Minstrel` methods

```
package com.springinaction.knights;

public class BraveKnight implements Knight {

  private Quest quest;
  private Minstrel minstrel;

  public BraveKnight(Quest quest, Minstrel minstrel) {
```

```
    this.quest = quest;
    this.minstrel = minstrel;
  }

  public void embarkOnQuest() throws QuestException {
    minstrel.singBeforeQuest();
    quest.embark();
    minstrel.singAfterQuest();
  }

}
```

Should a knight manage his own minstrel?

That should do the trick. Now all you need to do is go back to your Spring configuration to declare a `Minstrel` bean and inject it into the `BraveKnight` bean's constructor. But hold on...

Something doesn't seem right. Is it really within the knight's range of concern to manage his minstrel? It seems to me that minstrels should just do their job without having to be asked to do so. After all, that's a minstrel's job—to sing about the knight's endeavors. Why should the knight have to keep reminding the minstrel?

Furthermore, because the knight needs to know about the minstrel, you're forced to inject `Minstrel` into `BraveKnight`. This not only complicates the `BraveKnight` code but also makes me wonder if you'd ever want a knight who didn't have a minstrel. What if `Minstrel` is `null`? Should you introduce some `null`-checking logic to cover that case?

Your simple `BraveKnight` class is starting to get more complicated and would become more so if you were to handle the `nullMinstrel` scenario. But using AOP, you can declare that the minstrel should sing about a knight's quests and free the knight from having to deal with the `Minstrel` methods directly.

To turn `Minstrel` into an aspect, all you need to do is declare it as one in the Spring configuration file. Here's the updated knights.xml file, revised to declare `Minstrel` as an aspect.

Listing 1.11 Declaring the `Minstrel` as an aspect

```xml
<?xml version="1.0" encoding="UTF-8"?>>
<beans xmlns="http://www.springframework.org/schema/beans"
  xmlns:xsi="http://www.w3.org/2001/XMLSchema-instance"
  xmlns:aop="http://www.springframework.org/schema/aop"
  xsi:schemaLocation="http://www.springframework.org/schema/aop
      http://www.springframework.org/schema/aop/spring-aop-3.2.xsd
    http://www.springframework.org/schema/beans
      http://www.springframework.org/schema/beans/spring-beans.xsd">

  <bean id="knight" class="com.springinaction.knights.BraveKnight">
    <constructor-arg ref="quest" />
  </bean>

  <bean id="quest" class="com.springinaction.knights.SlayDragonQuest">
    <constructor-arg value="#{T(System).out}" />
  </bean>
```

```
<bean id="minstrel" class="com.springinaction.knights.Minstrel">  ⟵
  <constructor-arg value="#{T(System).out}" />
</bean>                                                     Declare Minstrel bean

<aop:config>
  <aop:aspect ref="minstrel">
    <aop:pointcut id="embark"                                        Define
        expression="execution(* *.embarkOnQuest(..))"/>  ⟵         pointcut

    <aop:before pointcut-ref="embark"        ⟵───────── Declare before advice
        method="singBeforeQuest"/>

    <aop:after pointcut-ref="embark"         ⟵───────── Declare after advice
        method="singAfterQuest"/>
  </aop:aspect>
</aop:config>
```

```
</beans>
```

Here you're using Spring's aop configuration namespace to declare that the Minstrel bean is an aspect. First you declare Minstrel as a bean. Then you refer to that bean in the <aop:aspect> element. Defining the aspect further, you declare (using <aop:before>) that before the embarkOnQuest() method is executed, the Minstrel's singBefore-Quest() should be called. This is called *before advice*. And you (using <aop:after>) declare that the singAfterQuest() method should be called after embarkOnQuest() has executed. This is known as *after advice*.

In both cases, the pointcut-ref attribute refers to a pointcut named *embark*. This pointcut is defined in the preceding <pointcut> element with an expression attribute set to select where the advice should be applied. The expression syntax is AspectJ's pointcut expression language.

Don't worry if you don't know AspectJ or the details of how AspectJ pointcut expressions are written. We'll talk more about Spring AOP later, in chapter 4. For now it's enough to know that you've asked Spring to call Minstrel's singBeforeQuest() and singAfterQuest() methods before and after BraveKnight embarks on a quest.

That's all there is to it! With a tiny bit of XML, you've turned Minstrel into a Spring aspect. Don't worry if this doesn't make complete sense yet—you'll see plenty more examples of Spring AOP in chapter 4 that should help clear this up. For now, there are two important points to take away from this example.

First, Minstrel is still a POJO—nothing about it indicates that it's to be used as an aspect. Instead, Minstrel became an aspect when you declared it as such in the Spring context.

Second, and most important, Minstrel can be applied to BraveKnight without BraveKnight needing to explicitly call on it. In fact, BraveKnight remains completely unaware of Minstrel's existence.

I should also point out that although you used some Spring magic to turn Minstrel into an aspect, it was declared as a Spring <bean> first. The point is that you can do anything with Spring aspects that you can do with other Spring beans, such as inject them with dependencies.

Using aspects to sing about knights can be fun. But Spring's AOP can be used for even more practical things. As you'll see later, Spring AOP can be employed to provide services such as declarative transactions and security (chapters 9 and 14).

But for now, let's look at one more way that Spring simplifies Java development.

1.1.4 *Eliminating boilerplate code with templates*

Have you ever written some code and then felt like you'd already written the same code before? That's not déjà vu, my friend. That's *boilerplate code*—the code that you often have to write over and over again to accomplish common and otherwise simple tasks.

Unfortunately, there are a lot of places where Java APIs involve a bunch of boilerplate code. A common example of boilerplate code can be seen when working with JDBC to query data from a database. If you've ever worked with JDBC, you've probably written something similar to the following.

Listing 1.12   Many Java APIs, such as JDBC, involve writing boilerplate code.

```java
public Employee getEmployeeById(long id) {
  Connection conn = null;
  PreparedStatement stmt = null;
  ResultSet rs = null;
  try {
    conn = dataSource.getConnection();
    stmt = conn.prepareStatement(
        "select id, firstname, lastname, salary from " +
        "employee where id=?");                    <--------- Select employee
    stmt.setLong(1, id);
    rs = stmt.executeQuery();
    Employee employee = null;
    if (rs.next()) {
      employee = new Employee();                   <--------- Create object from data
      employee.setId(rs.getLong("id"));
      employee.setFirstName(rs.getString("firstname"));
      employee.setLastName(rs.getString("lastname"));
      employee.setSalary(rs.getBigDecimal("salary"));
    }
    return employee;
  } catch (SQLException e) {                        <--------- What should be done here?
  } finally {
      if(rs != null) {                             <--------- Clean up mess
        try {
          rs.close();
        } catch(SQLException e) {}
      }
      if(stmt != null) {
        try {
        stmt.close();
        } catch(SQLException e) {}
      }
```

```
      if(conn != null) {
        try {
          conn.close();
        } catch(SQLException e) {}
      }
    }
    return null;
}
```

As you can see, this JDBC code queries the database for an employee's name and salary. But I'll bet you had to look hard to see that. That's because the small bit of code that's specific to querying for an employee is buried in a heap of JDBC ceremony. You first have to create a connection, then create a statement, and finally query for the results. And, to appease JDBC's anger, you must catch SQLException, a checked exception, even though there's not a lot you can do if it's thrown.

Finally, after all is said and done, you have to clean up the mess, closing down the connection, statement, and result set. This could also stir JDBC's anger, so you must catch SQLException here as well.

What's most notable about listing 1.12 is that much of it is the exact same code you'd write for pretty much any JDBC operation. Little of it has anything to do with querying for an employee, and much of it is JDBC boilerplate.

JDBC is not alone in the boilerplate code business. Many activities require similar boilerplate code. JMS, JNDI, and the consumption of REST services often involve a lot of commonly repeated code.

Spring seeks to eliminate boilerplate code by encapsulating it in templates. Spring's JdbcTemplate makes it possible to perform database operations without all the ceremony required by traditional JDBC.

For example, using Spring's SimpleJdbcTemplate (a specialization of Jdbc-Template that takes advantage of Java 5 features), the getEmployeeById() method can be rewritten so that its focus is on the task of retrieving employee data and not catering to the demands of the JDBC API. The following shows what such an updated getEmployeeById() method might look like.

> **Listing 1.13 Templates let your code focus on the task at hand.**

```
public Employee getEmployeeById(long id) {
  return jdbcTemplate.queryForObject(
          "select id, firstname, lastname, salary " +     ◁— SQL query
          "from employee where id=?",
          new RowMapper<Employee>() {
            public Employee mapRow(ResultSet rs,
                    int rowNum) throws SQLException {     ◁— Map results to object
              Employee employee = new Employee();
              employee.setId(rs.getLong("id"));
              employee.setFirstName(rs.getString("firstname"));
              employee.setLastName(rs.getString("lastname"));
              employee.setSalary(rs.getBigDecimal("salary"));
              return employee;
```

```
        }
    },
    id);    ◁─── Specify query parameter
}
```

As you can see, this new version of `getEmployeeById()` is much simpler and acutely focused on selecting an employee from the database. The template's `queryFor-Object()` method is given the SQL query, a `RowMapper` (for mapping result set data to a domain object), and zero or more query parameters. What you don't see in `get-EmployeeById()` is any of the JDBC boilerplate from before. Everything is handled inside the template.

I've shown you how Spring attacks complexity in Java development using POJO-oriented development, DI, aspects, and templates. Along the way, I showed you how to configure beans and aspects in XML-based configuration files. But how do those files get loaded? And what are they loaded into? Let's look at the Spring container, the place where your application's beans reside.

1.2 *Containing your beans*

In a Spring-based application, your application objects live in the Spring *container*. As illustrated in figure 1.4, the container creates the objects, wires them together, configures them, and manages their complete lifecycle from cradle to grave (or `new` to `finalize()`, as the case may be).

In the next chapter, you'll see how to configure Spring so it knows what objects it should create, configure, and wire together. First, though, it's important to get to know the container where your objects will be hanging out. Understanding the container will help you grasp how your objects will be managed.

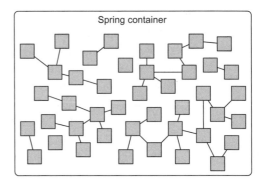

Figure 1.4   In a Spring application, objects are created, are wired together, and live in the Spring container.

The container is at the core of the Spring Framework. Spring's container uses DI to manage the components that make up an application. This includes creating associations between collaborating components. As such, these objects are cleaner and easier to understand, they support reuse, and they're easy to unit test.

There's no single Spring container. Spring comes with several container implementations that can be categorized into two distinct types. *Bean factories* (defined by the `org.springframework.beans.factory.BeanFactory` interface) are the simplest of containers, providing basic support for DI. *Application contexts* (defined by the `org.springframework.context.ApplicationContext` interface) build on the notion of a bean factory by providing application-framework services, such as the ability to resolve textual messages from a properties file and the ability to publish application events to interested event listeners.

Although it's possible to work with Spring using either bean factories or application contexts, bean factories are often too low-level for most applications. Therefore, application contexts are preferred over bean factories. We'll focus on working with application contexts and not spend any more time talking about bean factories.

1.2.1 Working with an application context

Spring comes with several flavors of application context. Here are a few that you'll most likely encounter:

- `AnnotationConfigApplicationContext`—Loads a Spring application context from one or more Java-based configuration classes
- `AnnotationConfigWebApplicationContext`—Loads a Spring web application context from one or more Java-based configuration classes
- `ClassPathXmlApplicationContext`—Loads a context definition from one or more XML files located in the classpath, treating context-definition files as classpath resources
- `FileSystemXmlApplicationContext`—Loads a context definition from one or more XML files in the filesystem
- `XmlWebApplicationContext`—Loads context definitions from one or more XML files contained in a web application

We'll talk more about `AnnotationConfigWebApplicationContext` and `XmlWebApplicationContext` in chapter 8 when we discuss web-based Spring applications. For now, let's load the application context from the filesystem using `FileSystemXmlApplicationContext` or from the classpath using `ClassPathXmlApplicationContext`.

Loading an application context from the filesystem or from the classpath is similar to how you load beans into a bean factory. For example, here's how you'd load a `FileSystemXmlApplicationContext`:

```
ApplicationContext context = new
        FileSystemXmlApplicationContext("c:/knight.xml");
```

Similarly, you can load an application context from the application's classpath using `ClassPathXmlApplicationContext`:

```
ApplicationContext context = new
        ClassPathXmlApplicationContext("knight.xml");
```

The difference between using `FileSystemXmlApplicationContext` and `ClassPathXmlApplicationContext` is that `FileSystemXmlApplicationContext` looks for knight.xml in a specific location within the filesystem, whereas `ClassPathXmlApplicationContext` looks for knight.xml anywhere in the classpath (including JAR files).

Alternatively, if you'd rather load your application context from a Java configuration, you can use AnnotationConfigApplicationContext:

```
ApplicationContext context = new AnnotationConfigApplicationContext(
    com.springinaction.knights.config.KnightConfig.class);
```

Instead of specifying an XML file from which to load the Spring application context, AnnotationConfigApplicationContext has been given a configuration class from which to load beans.

With an application context in hand, you can retrieve beans from the Spring container by calling the context's getBean() method.

Now that you know the basics of how to create a Spring container, let's take a closer look at the lifecycle of a bean in the bean container.

1.2.2   A bean's life

In a traditional Java application, the lifecycle of a bean is simple. Java's new keyword is used to instantiate the bean, and it's ready to use. Once the bean is no longer in use, it's eligible for garbage collection and eventually goes to the big bit bucket in the sky.

In contrast, the lifecycle of a bean in a Spring container is more elaborate. It's important to understand the lifecycle of a Spring bean, because you may want to take advantage of some of the opportunities that Spring offers to customize how a bean is created. Figure 1.5 shows the startup lifecycle of a typical bean as it's loaded into a Spring application context.

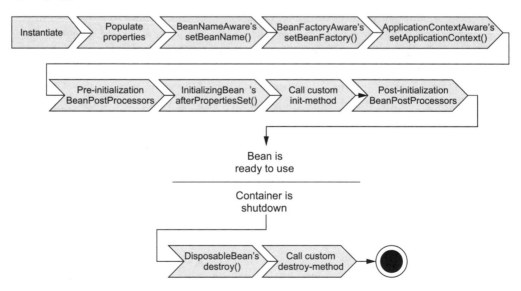

Figure 1.5   A bean goes through several steps between creation and destruction in the Spring container. Each step is an opportunity to customize how the bean is managed in Spring.

As you can see, a bean factory performs several setup steps before a bean is ready to use. Let's break down figure 1.5 in more detail:

1 Spring instantiates the bean.

2 Spring injects values and bean references into the bean's properties.

3 If the bean implements `BeanNameAware`, Spring passes the bean's ID to the `setBeanName()` method.

4 If the bean implements `BeanFactoryAware`, Spring calls the `setBeanFactory()` method, passing in the bean factory itself.

5 If the bean implements `ApplicationContextAware`, Spring calls the `setApplicationContext()` method, passing in a reference to the enclosing application context.

6 If the bean implements the `BeanPostProcessor` interface, Spring calls its `postProcessBeforeInitialization()` method.

7 If the bean implements the `InitializingBean` interface, Spring calls its `afterPropertiesSet()` method. Similarly, if the bean was declared with an `init-method`, then the specified initialization method is called.

8 If the bean implements `BeanPostProcessor`, Spring calls its `postProcessAfterInitialization()` method.

9 At this point, the bean is ready to be used by the application and remains in the application context until the application context is destroyed.

10 If the bean implements the `DisposableBean` interface, Spring calls its `destroy()` method. Likewise, if the bean was declared with a `destroy-method`, the specified method is called.

Now you know how to create and load a Spring container. But an empty container isn't much good by itself; it doesn't contain anything unless you put something in it. To achieve the benefits of Spring DI, you must wire your application objects into the Spring container. We'll go into bean wiring in more detail in chapter 2.

First, let's survey the modern Spring landscape to see what the Spring Framework is made up of and what the latest versions of Spring have to offer.

1.3 Surveying the Spring landscape

As you've seen, the Spring Framework is focused on simplifying enterprise Java development through DI, AOP, and boilerplate reduction. Even if that were all Spring did, it'd be worth using. But there's more to Spring than meets the eye.

Within the Spring Framework proper, you'll find several ways that Spring can ease Java development. But beyond the Spring Framework is a greater ecosystem of projects that build on the core framework, extending Spring into areas such as web services, REST, mobile, and NoSQL.

Let's first break down the core Spring Framework to see what it brings to the table. Then we'll expand our sights to review the other members of the greater Spring portfolio.

1.3.1 *Spring modules*

When you download the Spring distribution and dig into its libs folder, you'll find
several JAR files. As of Spring 4.0, there
are 20 distinct modules in the Spring
Framework distribution, with three JAR
files for each module (the binary class
library, the source JAR file, and a JavaDoc
JAR file). The complete list of library JAR
files is shown in figure 1.6.

These modules can be arranged into
six categories of functionality, as illustrated in figure 1.7.

Taken as a whole, these modules give
you everything you need to develop
enterprise-ready applications. But you
don't have to base your application fully
on the Spring Framework. You're free to
choose the modules that suit your application and look to other options when

**Figure 1.6   Spring 4.0 is made up of 20 distinct
modules.**

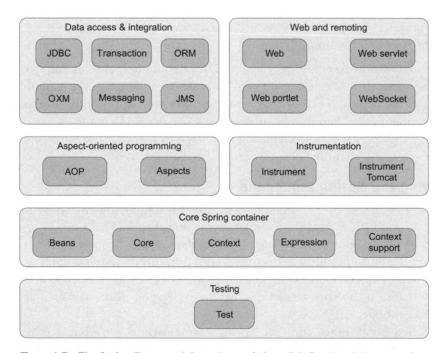

Figure 1.7   The Spring Framework is made up of six well-defined module categories.

Spring doesn't fit the bill. Spring even offers integration points with several other frameworks and libraries so that you don't have to write them yourself.

Let's look at each of Spring's modules, one at a time, to see how each fits in the overall Spring picture.

CORE SPRING CONTAINER

The centerpiece of the Spring Framework is a container that manages how the beans in a Spring-enabled application are created, configured, and managed. In this module is the Spring bean factory, which is the portion of Spring that provides DI. Building on the bean factory, you'll find several implementations of Spring's application context, each of which provides a different way to configure Spring.

In addition to the bean factory and application context, this module also supplies many enterprise services such as email, JNDI access, EJB integration, and scheduling.

All of Spring's modules are built on top of the core container. You'll implicitly use these classes when you configure your application. We'll discuss the core module throughout this book, starting in chapter 2 where we'll dig deep into Spring DI.

SPRING'S AOP MODULE

Spring provides rich support for aspect-oriented programming in its AOP module. This module serves as the basis for developing your own aspects for your Spring-enabled application. Like DI, AOP supports loose coupling of application objects. But with AOP, application-wide concerns (such as transactions and security) are decoupled from the objects to which they're applied.

We'll dig into Spring's AOP support in chapter 4.

DATA ACCESS AND INTEGRATION

Working with JDBC often results in a lot of boilerplate code that gets a connection, creates a statement, processes a result set, and then closes the connection. Spring's JDBC and *data-access objects* (DAO) module abstracts away the boilerplate code so that you can keep your database code clean and simple, and prevents problems that result from a failure to close database resources. This module also builds a layer of meaningful exceptions on top of the error messages given by several database servers. No more trying to decipher cryptic and proprietary SQL error messages!

For those who prefer using an *object-relational mapping* (ORM) tool over straight JDBC, Spring provides the ORM module. Spring's ORM support builds on the DAO support, providing a convenient way to build DAOs for several ORM solutions. Spring doesn't attempt to implement its own ORM solution but does provide hooks into several popular ORM frameworks, including Hibernate, Java Persistence API, Java Data Objects, and iBATIS SQL Maps. Spring's transaction management supports each of these ORM frameworks as well as JDBC.

You'll see how Spring's template-based JDBC abstraction can greatly simplify JDBC code when we look at Spring data access in chapter 10.

This module also includes a Spring abstraction over the Java Message Service (JMS) for asynchronous integration with other applications through messaging. And, as of

Spring 3.0, this module includes the object-to-XML mapping features that were originally part of the Spring Web Services project.

In addition, this module uses Spring's AOP module to provide transaction-management services for objects in a Spring application.

WEB AND REMOTING

The *Model-View-Controller* (MVC) paradigm is a commonly accepted approach to building web applications such that the user interface is separate from the application logic. Java has no shortage of MVC frameworks, with Apache Struts, JSF, WebWork, and Tapestry being among the most popular MVC choices.

Even though Spring integrates with several popular MVC frameworks, its web and remoting module comes with a capable MVC framework that promotes Spring's loosely coupled techniques in the web layer of an application. We'll look at Spring's MVC framework in chapters 5–7.

In addition to user-facing web applications, this module also provides several remoting options for building applications that interact with other applications. Spring's remoting capabilities include *Remote Method Invocation* (RMI), Hessian, Burlap, JAX-WS, and Spring's own HTTP invoker. Spring also offers first-class support for exposing and consuming REST APIs.

In chapter 15, we'll check out Spring remoting. And you'll learn how to create and consume REST APIs in chapter 16.

INSTRUMENTATION

Spring's instrumentation module includes support for adding agents to the JVM. Specifically, it provides a weaving agent for Tomcat that transforms class files as they're loaded by the classloader.

If that sounds like a lot to understand, don't worry too much about it. The instrumentation provided by this module has a narrow set of use cases and we won't be dealing with this module at all in this book.

TESTING

Recognizing the importance of developer-written tests, Spring provides a module dedicated to testing Spring applications.

In this module you'll find a collection of mock object implementations for writing unit tests against code that works with JNDI, servlets, and portlets. For integration-level testing, this module provides support for loading a collection of beans in a Spring application context and working with the beans in that context.

Throughout this book, many of the examples will be driven by tests, utilizing the testing facilities offered by Spring.

1.3.2 *The Spring portfolio*

When it comes to Spring, there's more than meets the eye. In fact, there's more than what comes in the Spring Framework download. If you stop at just the core Spring Framework, you'll miss out on a wealth of potential afforded by the larger Spring portfolio. The whole Spring portfolio includes several frameworks and libraries that build on the core Spring Framework and on each other. All together, the entire Spring portfolio brings the Spring programming model to almost every facet of Java development.

It would take several volumes to cover everything the Spring portfolio has to offer, and much of it is outside the scope of this book. But we'll look at some of the elements of the Spring portfolio; here's a taste of what lies beyond the core Spring Framework.

SPRING WEB FLOW

Spring Web Flow builds on Spring's core MVC framework to provide support for building conversational, flow-based web applications that guide users toward a goal (think wizards or shopping carts). We'll talk more about Spring Web Flow in chapter 8, and you can learn more about it at http://projects.spring.io/spring-webflow/.

SPRING WEB SERVICES

Although the core Spring Framework provides for declaratively publishing Spring beans as web services, those services are based on an arguably architecturally inferior contract-last model. The contract for the service is determined from the bean's interface. Spring Web Services offers a contract-first web services model where service implementations are written to satisfy the service contract.

I won't be talking about Spring-WS in this book, but you can read more about it at http://docs.spring.io/spring-ws/site/.

SPRING SECURITY

Security is a critical aspect of many applications. Implemented using Spring AOP, Spring Security offers a declarative security mechanism for Spring-based applications. You'll see how to add Spring Security to an application's web layer in chapter 9. We'll return to Spring Security again in chapter 14 to examine how to secure method invocations. For further exploration, Spring Security's home page is at http://projects.spring.io/spring-security/.

SPRING INTEGRATION

Many enterprise applications must interact with other enterprise applications. Spring Integration offers implementations of several common integration patterns in Spring's declarative style.

We won't cover Spring Integration in this book, but if you want more information, look at *Spring Integration in Action* by Mark Fisher, Jonas Partner, Marius Bogoevici, and Iwein Fuld (Manning, 2012, www.manning.com/fisher/). Or you can visit the Spring Integration home page at http://projects.spring.io/spring-integration/.

SPRING BATCH

When it's necessary to perform bulk operations on data, nothing beats batch processing. If you're going to be developing a batch application, you can use Spring's robust, POJO-oriented development model to do it using Spring Batch.

Spring Batch is beyond the scope of this book, but Arnaud Cogoluegnes, Thierry Templier, Gary Gregory, and Olivier Bazoud will enlighten you in their book, *Spring Batch in Action* (Manning, 2011, www.manning.com/templier/). You can also learn about Spring Batch from its home page at http://projects.spring.io/spring-batch/.

SPRING DATA

Spring Data makes it easy to work with all kinds of databases in Spring. Although the relational database has been ubiquitous in enterprise applications for many years, modern applications are recognizing that not all data is best served by columns and rows in a table. A new breed of databases, commonly referred to as *NoSQL databases*,[2] offer new ways of working with data that are more fitting than the traditional relational database.

Whether you're using a document database like MongoDB, a graph database such as Neo4j, or even a traditional relational database, Spring Data offers a simplified programming model for persistence. This includes, for many database types, an automatic repository mechanism that creates repository implementations for you.

We'll look at using Spring Data to simplify Java Persistence API (JPA) development in chapter 11 and then expand the discussion to include a few NoSQL databases in chapter 12.

SPRING SOCIAL

Social networking is a rising trend on the internet, and more and more applications are being outfitted with integration into social networking sites such as Facebook and Twitter. If this is the kind of thing that interests you, you'll want to look at Spring Social, a social networking extension to Spring.

But Spring Social is about more than just tweets and friends. Despite its name, Spring Social is less about the word *social* and more about the word *connect*. It helps you connect your Spring application with REST APIs, including many that may not have any social purpose to them.

Due to space constraints, we won't cover Spring Social in this book. But if you're interested in how Spring can help you connect with Facebook or Twitter, have a look at the Getting Started guides at https://spring.io/guides/gs/accessing-facebook/ and https://spring.io/guides/gs/accessing-twitter/.

SPRING MOBILE

Mobile applications are another significant area of software development. Smartphones and tablet devices are taking over as the preferred client for many users. Spring Mobile is a new extension to Spring MVC to support development of mobile web applications.

SPRING FOR ANDROID

Related to Spring Mobile is the Spring Android project. This project aims to bring some of the simplicity afforded by the Spring Framework to development of native

---

[2] I prefer the term *non-relational* or *schema-less* over *NoSQL*. Calling these databases *NoSQL* places the blame on the query language and not the database model.

applications for Android-based devices. Initially, this project is offering a version of Spring's `RestTemplate` that can be used in an Android application. It also works with Spring Social to enable native Android apps to connect with REST APIs.

I won't discuss Spring for Android in this book, but you can learn more about it at http://projects.spring.io/spring-android/.

SPRING BOOT

Spring greatly simplifies many programming tasks, reducing or even eliminating much of the boilerplate code you might normally be required to write without it. Spring Boot is an exciting new project that takes an opinionated view of developing with Spring to simplify Spring itself.

Spring Boot heavily employs automatic configuration techniques that can eliminate most (and in many cases, all) Spring configuration. It also provides several starter projects to help reduce the size of your Spring project build files, whether you're using Maven or Gradle.

We'll look at Spring Boot near the end of the book in chapter 21.

1.4 What's new in Spring

When the third edition of this book went to press, the latest version of Spring was version 3.0.5. That was around three years ago, and a lot has changed since then. The Spring Framework has seen three significant releases—3.1, 3.2, and now 4.0—each bringing new features and improvements to ease application development. And several of the other members of the Spring portfolio have undergone major changes.

This edition of *Spring in Action* has been updated to cover many of the most exciting and useful features in these releases. But for now, let's briefly size up what's new in Spring.

1.4.1 What was new in Spring 3.1?

Spring 3.1 had several useful new features and improvements, many of which were focused on simplifying and improving configuration. In addition, Spring 3.1 provided declarative caching support as well as many improvements to Spring MVC. Here's a brief list of some of the highlights of Spring 3.1:

- To address the common issue of selecting distinct configurations for various environments (such as development, test, and production), Spring 3.1 introduced environment profiles. Profiles make it possible, for instance, to select a different data source bean depending on which environment the application is deployed in.
- Building on Spring 3.0's Java-based configuration, Spring 3.1 added several *enable* annotations to switch on certain features of Spring with a single annotation.
- Declarative caching support made its way into Spring, making it possible to declare caching boundaries and rules with simple annotations, similar to how you could already declare transaction boundaries.

- A new `c` namespace brought constructor injection the same succinct attribute-oriented style as Spring 2.0's `p` namespace brought to property injection.
- Spring began to support Servlet 3.0, including the ability to declare servlets and filters in Java-based configuration instead of web.xml.
- Improvements to Spring's JPA support made it possible to completely configure JPA in Spring without needing a persistence.xml file.

Spring 3.1 also included several enhancements to Spring MVC:

- Automatic binding of path variables to model attributes
- `@RequestMapping` `produces` and `consumes` attributes, for matching against a request's `Accept` and `Content-Type` headers
- A `@RequestPart` annotation that enables binding parts of a multipart request to handler method parameters
- Support for flash attributes (attributes that survive a redirect) and a `Redirect-Attributes` type to carry the flash attributes between requests

Just as important as what was new in Spring 3.1 is what was no longer available in Spring as of Spring 3.1. Specifically, Spring's `JpaTemplate` and `JpaDaoSupport` classes were deprecated in favor of native `EntityManager` usage. Even though they were deprecated, they were still around in Spring 3.2. But you shouldn't use them, because they weren't upgraded to support JPA 2.0 and have been removed in Spring 4.

Now let's look at what was new in Spring 3.2.

1.4.2 *What was new in Spring 3.2?*

Whereas Spring 3.1 was largely focused on configuration improvements with a small set of other enhancements, including Spring MVC enhancements, Spring 3.2 was primarily a Spring MVC-focused release. Spring MVC 3.2 boasted the following improvements:

- Spring 3.2 controllers can take advantage of Servlet 3's asynchronous requests to spin off request processing in separate threads, freeing up the servlet thread to process more requests.
- Although Spring MVC controllers have been easily testable as POJOs since Spring 2.5, Spring 3.2 included a Spring MVC test framework for writing richer tests against controllers, asserting their behavior as controllers, but without a servlet container.
- In addition to improved controller testing, Spring 3.2 included support for testing `RestTemplate`-based clients without sending requests to the real REST endpoint.
- An `@ControllerAdvice` annotation enables common `@ExceptionHandler`, `@InitBinder`, and `@ModelAttributes` methods to be collected in a single class and applied to all controllers.
- Prior to Spring 3.2, full content negotiation support was only available via `ContentNegotiatingViewResolver`. But in Spring 3.2, full content negotiation

became available throughout Spring MVC, even on controller methods relying on message converters for content consumption and production.

- Spring MVC 3.2 included a new `@MatrixVariable` annotation for binding a request's matrix variables to handler method parameters.
- The abstract base class `AbstractDispatcherServletInitializer` can be used for conveniently configuring `DispatcherServlet` without web.xml. Likewise, a subclass named `AbstractAnnotationConfigDispatcherServletInitializer` can be used when you wish to configure Spring with Java-based configuration.
- The `ResponseEntityExceptionHandler` class was added to be used as an alternative to `DefaultHandlerExceptionResolver`. `ResponseEntityException-Handler` methods return `ResponseEntity<Object>` instead of `ModelAndView`.
- `RestTemplate` and `@RequestBody` arguments support generic types.
- `RestTemplate` and `@RequestMapping` methods support the HTTP `PATCH` method.
- Mapped interceptors support URL patterns to be excluded from interceptor processing.

Although Spring MVC was the main story of Spring 3.2, a few other non-MVC improvements were added as well. Here are a few of the most interesting new features in Spring 3.2:

- `@Autowired`, `@Value`, and `@Bean` annotations can be used as meta-annotations to create custom injection and bean-declaration annotations.
- The `@DateTimeFormat` annotation no longer has a hard dependency on Joda-Time. If JodaTime is present, it is used. Otherwise, `SimpleDateFormat` is used.
- Spring's declarative caching support has initial support for JCache 0.5.
- You can define global formats for parsing and rendering dates and times.
- Integration tests can configure and load a `WebApplicationContext`.
- Integration tests can test against request- and session-scoped beans.

You'll see a lot of Spring 3.2's features across several chapters in this book, especially in the web and REST chapters.

1.4.3 What's new in Spring 4.0?

Spring 4.0 is the freshest release of Spring available. There are a lot of exciting new features in Spring 4.0, including the following:

- Spring now includes support for WebSocket programming, including support for JSR-356: Java API for WebSocket.
- Recognizing that WebSocket offers a low-level API, screaming for a higher-level abstraction, Spring 4.0 includes a higher level message-oriented programming model on top of WebSocket that's based on SockJS and includes STOMP sub-protocol support.

- A new messaging module with many types carried over from the Spring Integration project. This messaging module supports Spring's SockJS/STOMP support. It also includes template-based support for publishing messages.

- Spring 4.0 is one of the first (if not *the* first) Java frameworks to support Java 8 features, including lambdas. Among other things, this makes working with certain callback interfaces (such as `RowMapper` with `JdbcTemplate`) much cleaner and easier to read.

- Along with Java 8 support comes support for JSR-310: Data and Time API, offering the opportunity for developers to work with dates and times in a richer API than that offered with `java.util.Date` or `java.util.Calendar`.

- A smooth programming experience for applications developed in Groovy has also been added, essentially enabling a Spring application to be developed easily entirely in Groovy. With this comes the BeanBuilder from Grails, enabling Spring applications to be configured with Groovy.

- Generalized support for conditional bean creation has been added, wherein beans can be declared to be created only if a developer-defined condition is met.

- Spring 4.0 also includes a new asynchronous implementation of Spring's `RestTemplate` that returns immediately but allows for callbacks once the operation completes.

- Support for many JEE specs has been added, including JMS 2.0, JTA 1.2, JPA 2.1, and Bean Validation 1.1.

As you can see, a lot of exciting new stuff has found its way into the latest versions of the Spring Framework. Throughout this book, we'll look at many of these new features as well as many of the long-standing features of Spring.

1.5   *Summary*

You should now have a good idea of what Spring brings to the table. Spring aims to make enterprise Java development easier and to promote loosely coupled code. Vital to this are dependency injection and aspect-oriented programming.

In this chapter, you got a taste of DI in Spring. DI is a way of associating application objects such that the objects don't need to know where their dependencies come from or how they're implemented. Rather than acquiring dependencies on their own, dependent objects are given the objects that they depend on. Because dependent objects often only know about their injected objects through interfaces, coupling is kept low.

In addition to DI, you also saw a glimpse of Spring's AOP support. AOP enables you to centralize in one place—an aspect—logic that would normally be scattered throughout an application. When Spring wires your beans together, these aspects can be woven in at runtime, effectively giving the beans new behavior.

DI and AOP are central to everything in Spring. Thus you must understand how to use these principal functions of Spring to be able to use the rest of the framework. In this chapter, we've just scratched the surface of Spring's DI and AOP features. Over the next few chapters, we'll dig deeper into DI and AOP.

Without further ado, let's move on to chapter 2 to learn how to wire objects together in Spring using DI.

Wiring beans

2

Have you ever stuck around long enough after a movie to watch the credits? It's incredible how many different people it takes to pull together a major motion picture. In addition to the obvious participants—the actors, scriptwriters, directors, and producers—there are the not-so-obvious—the musicians, special effects crew, and art directors. And that's not to mention the key grip, sound mixer, costumers, makeup artists, stunt coordinators, publicists, first assistant to the cameraperson, second assistant to the cameraperson, set designers, gaffer, and (perhaps most important) caterers.

Now imagine what your favorite movie would've been like had none of these people talked to one another. Let's say that they all showed up at the studio and started doing their own thing without any coordination of any kind. If the director keeps to himself and doesn't say "Roll 'em," then the cameraperson wouldn't start shooting. It probably wouldn't matter anyway, because the lead actress would still be in her trailer and the lighting wouldn't work because the gaffer wouldn't have been hired. Maybe you've seen a movie where it looks like this is what happened.

But most movies (the good ones, anyway) are the product of thousands of people working together toward the common goal of making a blockbuster film.

In this respect, a great piece of software isn't much different. Any nontrivial application is made up of several objects that must work together to meet some business goal. These objects must be aware of one another and communicate with one another to get their jobs done. In an online shopping application, for instance, an order-manager component may need to work with a product-manager component and a credit-card authorization component. All of these will likely need to work with a data-access component to read from and write to a database.

But as you saw in chapter 1, the traditional approach to creating associations between application objects (via construction or lookup) leads to complicated code that's difficult to reuse and unit-test. At best, these objects do more work than they should. At worst, they're highly coupled to one another, making them hard to reuse and hard to test.

In Spring, objects aren't responsible for finding or creating the other objects that they need to do their jobs. Instead, the container gives them references to the objects that they collaborate with. An order-manager component, for example, may need a credit-card authorizer—but it doesn't have to create the credit-card authorizer. It just needs to show up empty-handed, and it's given a credit-card authorizer to work with.

The act of creating these associations between application objects is the essence of dependency injection (DI) and is commonly referred to as *wiring*. In this chapter, we'll explore the basics of bean wiring using Spring. DI is the most elemental thing Spring does, so these are techniques you'll use almost every time you develop Spring-based applications.

There are many ways to wire beans in Spring. To begin, let's take a moment to get a feel for the three most common approaches for configuring the Spring container.

2.1 *Exploring Spring's configuration options*

As mentioned in chapter 1, the Spring container is responsible for creating the beans in your application and coordinating the relationships between those objects via DI. But it's your responsibility as a developer to tell Spring which beans to create and how to wire them together. When it comes to expressing a bean wiring specification, Spring is incredibly flexible, offering three primary wiring mechanisms:

- Explicit configuration in XML
- Explicit configuration in Java
- Implicit bean discovery and automatic wiring

At first glance, it may seem that offering these three configuration options complicates Spring. There is some overlap in what each configuration technique offers, and it can be overwhelming to decide which technique is most applicable for a given situation. But don't be distressed—in many cases, the choice is largely a matter of personal taste, and you're welcome to choose the approach that feels best for you.

It's great that you have many choices about how to wire beans in Spring, but at some point you must select one.

There's no single right answer here. Any choice you make must be suitable for you and your project. And who says that you must make one choice? Spring's configuration styles are mix-and-match, so you could choose XML to wire up some beans, use Spring's Java-based configuration (JavaConfig) for other beans, and let other beans be automatically discovered by Spring.

Even so, my recommendation is to lean on automatic configuration as much as you can. The less configuration you have to do explicitly, the better. When you must explicitly configure beans (such as when you're configuring beans for which you don't maintain the source code), I'd favor the type-safe and more powerful JavaConfig over XML. Finally, fall back on XML only in situations where there's a convenient XML namespace you want to use that has no equivalent in JavaConfig.

We'll explore all three of these techniques in detail in this chapter and apply them throughout the book. At this point, let's test-taste each one to get an idea of what they're like. For your first sampling of Spring configuration, let's look at Spring's automatic configuration.

2.2   *Automatically wiring beans*

A little bit later in this chapter, you'll see how to express Spring wiring in both Java and XML. Even though you'll find a lot of use for those explicit wiring techniques, nothing beats Spring's automatic configuration for ease of use. Why bother explicitly wiring beans together if Spring can be configured to automatically do it for you?

Spring attacks automatic wiring from two angles:

- *Component scanning*—Spring automatically discovers beans to be created in the application context.
- *Autowiring*—Spring automatically satisfies bean dependencies.

Working together, component scanning and autowiring are a powerful force and can help keep explicit configuration to a minimum.

To demonstrate component scanning and autowiring, you're going to create a few beans that represent some of the components in a stereo system. You'll start by creating a `CompactDisc` class that Spring will discover and create as a bean. Then you'll create a `CDPlayer` class and have Spring discover it and inject it with the `CompactDisc` bean.

2.2.1   *Creating discoverable beans*

In this age of MP3 files and streaming music, the compact disc may seem a bit quaint and archaic. Not as much as cassette tapes, eight-tracks, or vinyl records, of course, but CDs are becoming more and more scarce as the last remnant of physical music delivery.

In spite of that, the CD provides a nice illustration of how DI works. CD players are of little value unless you insert (or inject) a CD into them. You could say that a CD player depends on a CD to do its job.

To bring this illustration to life in Spring, let's establish the concept of a CD in Java. The following listing shows `CompactDisc`, an interface that defines a CD.

Listing 2.1   The `CompactDisc` interface defines the concept of a CD in Java.

```
package soundsystem;

public interface CompactDisc {
  void play();
}
```

The specifics of the `CompactDisc` interface aren't important. What is important is that you've defined it as an interface. As an interface, it defines the contract through which a CD player can operate on the CD. And it keeps the coupling between any CD player implementation and the CD itself to a minimum.

You still need an implementation of `CompactDisc`, though. In fact, you could have several `CompactDisc` implementations. In this case, you'll start with one: the `SgtPeppers` class, as shown in the next listing.

Listing 2.2   @`CompactDisc`-annotated `SgtPeppers` implements `CompactDisc`

```
package soundsystem;
import org.springframework.stereotype.Component;

@Component
public class SgtPeppers implements CompactDisc {

  private String title = "Sgt. Pepper's Lonely Hearts Club Band";
  private String artist = "The Beatles";

  public void play() {
    System.out.println("Playing " + title + " by " + artist);
  }

}
```

As with the `CompactDisc` interface, the specifics of `SgtPeppers` aren't important to this discussion. What you should take note of is that `SgtPeppers` is annotated with @`Component`. This simple annotation identifies this class as a component class and serves as a clue to Spring that a bean should be created for the class. There's no need to explicitly configure a `SgtPeppers` bean; Spring will do it for you because this class is annotated with @`Component`.

Component scanning isn't turned on by default, however. You'll still need to write an explicit configuration to tell Spring to seek out classes annotated with @`Component` and to create beans from them. The configuration class in the following listing shows the minimal configuration to make this possible.

Listing 2.3 @ComponentScan enables component scanning

```
package soundsystem;
import org.springframework.context.annotation.ComponentScan;
import org.springframework.context.annotation.Configuration;

@Configuration
@ComponentScan
public class CDPlayerConfig {
}
```

The CDPlayerConfig class defines a Spring wiring specification, expressed in Java. We'll look at Java-based Spring configuration more in section 2.3. But for now, observe that CDPlayerConfig doesn't explicitly define any beans itself. Instead, it's annotated with @ComponentScan to enable component scanning in Spring.

With no further configuration, @ComponentScan will default to scanning the same package as the configuration class. Therefore, because CDPlayerConfig is in the soundsystem package, Spring will scan that package and any subpackages underneath it, looking for classes that are annotated with @Component. It should find the Compact-Disc class and automatically create a bean for it in Spring.

If you'd rather turn on component scanning via XML configuration, then you can use the <context:component-scan> element from Spring's context namespace. Here is a minimal XML configuration to enable component scanning.

Listing 2.4 Enabling component scanning in XML

```
<?xml version="1.0" encoding="UTF-8"?>
<beans xmlns="http://www.springframework.org/schema/beans"
  xmlns:xsi="http://www.w3.org/2001/XMLSchema-instance"
  xmlns:context="http://www.springframework.org/schema/context"
  xsi:schemaLocation="http://www.springframework.org/schema/beans
    http://www.springframework.org/schema/beans/spring-beans.xsd
    http://www.springframework.org/schema/context
    http://www.springframework.org/schema/context/spring-context.xsd">

  <context:component-scan base-package="soundsystem" />

</beans>
```

Even though XML is an option for enabling component scanning, I'm going to focus on using the preferred Java-based configuration for the remainder of this discussion. If XML is more your style, though, you'll be happy to know that the <context:component-scan> element has attributes and sub-elements that mirror the attributes you'll use when working with @ComponentScan.

Believe it or not, with only two classes created, you already have something that you can try out. To test that component scanning works, let's write a simple JUnit test that creates a Spring application context and asserts that the CompactDisc bean is, in fact, created. CDPlayerTest in the next listing does precisely that.

Listing 2.5 Testing that a `CompactDisc` was found by component scanning

```java
package soundsystem;

import static org.junit.Assert.*;

import org.junit.Test;
import org.junit.runner.RunWith;
import org.springframework.beans.factory.annotation.Autowired;
import org.springframework.test.context.ContextConfiguration;
import org.springframework.test.context.junit4.SpringJUnit4ClassRunner;

@RunWith(SpringJUnit4ClassRunner.class)
@ContextConfiguration(classes=CDPlayerConfig.class)
public class CDPlayerTest {

  @Autowired
  private CompactDisc cd;

  @Test
  public void cdShouldNotBeNull() {
    assertNotNull(cd);
  }

}
```

CDPlayerTest takes advantage of Spring's SpringJUnit4ClassRunner to have a Spring application context automatically created when the test starts. And the @Context-Configuration annotation tells it to load its configuration from the CDPlayerConfig class. Because that configuration class includes @ComponentScan, the resulting application context should include the CompactDisc bean.

To prove that, the test has a property of type CompactDisc that is annotated with @Autowired to inject the CompactDisc bean into the test. (I'll talk more about @Autowired in a moment.) Finally, a simple test method asserts that the cd property isn't null. If it's not null, that means Spring was able to discover the CompactDisc class, automatically create it as a bean in the Spring application context, and inject it into the test.

The test should pass with flying colors (or, hopefully, the color green in your test runner). Your first simple component-scanning exercise was a success! Even though you've only used it to create a single bean, that same small amount of configuration is good for discovering and creating any number of beans. Any classes in or under the soundsystem package that are annotated with @Component will also be created as beans. One line with @ComponentScan in exchange for countless automatically created beans is a good trade-off.

Now let's dig a bit deeper into @ComponentScan and @Component and see what else you can do with component scanning.

2.2.2   *Naming a component-scanned bean*

All beans in a Spring application context are given an ID. What may not have been apparent from the previous example is that although you didn't explicitly give the SgtPeppers bean an ID, it was given one derived from its class name. Specifically, the bean was given an ID of sgtPeppers by lowercasing the first letter of the class name.

If you'd rather give the bean a different ID, all you have to do is pass the desired ID as a value to the @Component annotation. For example, if you wanted to identify the bean as lonelyHeartsClub, then you'd annotate the SgtPeppers class with @Component like this:

```
@Component("lonelyHeartsClub")
public class SgtPeppers implements CompactDisc {
  ...
}
```

Another way to name a bean is to not use the @Component annotation at all. Instead, you can use the @Named annotation from the Java Dependency Injection specification (JSR-330) to provide a bean ID:

```
package soundsystem;
import javax.inject.Named;

@Named("lonelyHeartsClub")
public class SgtPeppers implements CompactDisc {
  ...
}
```

Spring supports the @Named annotation as an alternative to @Component. There are a few subtle differences, but in most common cases they're interchangeable.

With that said, I have a strong preference for the @Component annotation, largely because @Named is ... well ... poorly named. It doesn't describe what it does as well as @Component. Therefore, I won't use @Named any further in this book or its examples.

2.2.3   *Setting a base package for component scanning*

Thus far, you've used @ComponentScan with no attributes. That means it will default to the configuration class's package as its base package to scan for components. But what if you want to scan a different package? Or what if you want to scan multiple base packages?

One common reason for explicitly setting the base package is so that you can keep all of your configuration code in a package of its own, separate from the rest of your application's code. In that case, the default base package won't do.

No problem. To specify a different base package, you only need to specify the package in @ComponentScan's value attribute:

```
@Configuration
@ComponentScan("soundsystem")
public class CDPlayerConfig {}
```

Or, if you'd rather it be clear that you're setting the base package, you can do so with the `basePackages` attribute:

```
@Configuration
@ComponentScan(basePackages="soundsystem")
public class CDPlayerConfig {}
```

You probably noticed that `basePackages` is plural. If you're wondering whether that means you can specify multiple base packages, you can. All you need to do is set `basePackages` to an array of packages to be scanned:

```
@Configuration
@ComponentScan(basePackages={"soundsystem", "video"})
public class CDPlayerConfig {}
```

The one thing about setting the base packages as shown here is that they're expressed as `String` values. That's fine, I suppose, but it's not very type-safe. If you were to refactor the package names, the specified base packages would be wrong.

Rather than specify the packages as simple `String` values, `@ComponentScan` also offers you the option of specifying them via classes or interfaces that are in the packages:

```
@Configuration
@ComponentScan(basePackageClasses={CDPlayer.class, DVDPlayer.class})
public class CDPlayerConfig {}
```

As you can see, the `basePackages` attribute has been replaced with `basePackageClasses`. And instead of identifying the packages with `String` names, the array given to `basePackageClasses` includes classes. Whatever packages those classes are in will be used as the base package for component scanning.

Although I've specified component classes for `basePackageClasses`, you might consider creating an empty marker interface in the packages to be scanned. With a marker interface, you can still have a refactor-friendly reference to an interface, but without references to any actual application code (that could later be refactored out of the package you intended to component-scan).

If all the objects in your applications were standalone and had no dependencies, like the `SgtPeppers` bean, then component scanning would be everything you need. But many objects lean on other objects for help to get their job done. You need a way to wire up your component-scanned beans with any dependencies they have. To do that, we'll need to look at autowiring, the other side of automatic Spring configuration.

2.2.4 *Annotating beans to be automatically wired*

Put succinctly, autowiring is a means of letting Spring automatically satisfy a bean's dependencies by finding other beans in the application context that are a match to the bean's needs. To indicate that autowiring should be performed, you can use Spring's `@Autowired` annotation.

For example, consider the `CDPlayer` class in the following listing. Its constructor is annotated with `@Autowired`, indicating that when Spring creates the `CDPlayer` bean, it should instantiate it via that constructor and pass in a bean that is assignable to `CompactDisc`.

> **Listing 2.6   Injecting a `CompactDisc` into a `CDPlayer` bean using autowiring**

```
package soundsystem;
import org.springframework.beans.factory.annotation.Autowired;
import org.springframework.stereotype.Component;

@Component
public class CDPlayer implements MediaPlayer {
  private CompactDisc cd;

  @Autowired
  public CDPlayer(CompactDisc cd) {
    this.cd = cd;
  }

  public void play() {
    cd.play();
  }

}
```

The `@Autowired` annotation's use isn't limited to constructors. It can also be used on a property's setter method. For example, if `CDPlayer` had a `setCompactDisc()` method, you might annotate it for autowiring like this:

```
@Autowired
public void setCompactDisc(CompactDisc cd) {
  this.cd = cd;
}
```

After Spring has instantiated the bean, it will try to satisfy the dependencies expressed through methods such as the `setCompactDisc()` method that are annotated with `@Autowired`.

Actually, there's nothing special about setter methods. `@Autowired` can also be applied on any method on the class. Pretending that `CDPlayer` has an `insertDisc()` method, `@Autowired` would work equally well there as on `setCompactDisc()`:

```
@Autowired
public void insertDisc(CompactDisc cd) {
  this.cd = cd;
}
```

Whether it's a constructor, a setter method, or any other method, Spring will attempt to satisfy the dependency expressed in the method's parameters. Assuming that one and only one bean matches, that bean will be wired in.

If there are no matching beans, Spring will throw an exception as the application context is being created. To avoid that exception, you can set the `required` attribute on `@Autowired` to `false`:

```
@Autowired(required=false)
public CDPlayer(CompactDisc cd) {
  this.cd = cd;
}
```

When `required` is `false`, Spring will attempt to perform autowiring; but if there are no matching beans, it will leave the bean unwired. You should be careful setting `required` to `false`, however. Leaving the property unwired could lead to `NullPointer-Exceptions` if you don't check for `null` in your code.

In the event that multiple beans can satisfy the dependency, Spring will throw an exception indicating ambiguity in selecting a bean for autowiring. We'll talk more about managing ambiguity in autowiring later, in chapter 3.

`@Autowired` is a Spring-specific annotation. If it troubles you to be scattering Spring-specific annotations throughout your code for autowiring, you might consider using the `@Inject` annotation instead:

```
package soundsystem;
import javax.inject.Inject;
import javax.inject.Named;

@Named
public class CDPlayer {

  ...

  @Inject
  public CDPlayer(CompactDisc cd) {
    this.cd = cd;
  }


  ...

}
```

`@Inject` comes from the Java Dependency Injection specification, the same specification that gave us `@Named`. Spring supports the `@Inject` annotation for autowiring alongside its own `@Autowired`. Although there are some subtle differences between `@Inject` and `@Autowired`, they're interchangeable in many cases.

I have no strong preference between `@Autowired` and `@Inject`. In fact, I sometimes find myself using both in a given project. For the purposes of the examples in this book, however, I'll consistently use `@Autowired`. You're welcome to use whichever one suits you best.

2.2.5 *Verifying automatic configuration*

Now that you've annotated `CDPlayer`'s constructor with `@Autowired`, you can be assured that Spring will automatically inject it with a bean assignable to `CompactDisc`. To be certain, let's change `CDPlayerTest` to play the compact disc through the `CDPlayer` bean:

```
package soundsystem;
import static org.junit.Assert.*;
```

```
import org.junit.Rule;
import org.junit.Test;
import org.junit.contrib.java.lang.system.StandardOutputStreamLog;
import org.junit.runner.RunWith;
import org.springframework.beans.factory.annotation.Autowired;
import org.springframework.test.context.ContextConfiguration;
import org.springframework.test.context.junit4.SpringJUnit4ClassRunner;

@RunWith(SpringJUnit4ClassRunner.class)
@ContextConfiguration(classes=CDPlayerConfig.class)
public class CDPlayerTest {

  @Rule
  public final StandardOutputStreamLog log =
                          new StandardOutputStreamLog();

  @Autowired
  private MediaPlayer player;

  @Autowired
  private CompactDisc cd;

  @Test
  public void cdShouldNotBeNull() {
    assertNotNull(cd);
  }

  @Test
  public void play() {
    player.play();
    assertEquals(
        "Playing Sgt. Pepper's Lonely Hearts Club Band" +
        " by The Beatles\n",
        log.getLog());
  }

}
```

Now, in addition to injecting CompactDisc, you're injecting the CDPlayer bean into the test's player member variable (as the more generic MediaPlayer type). In the play() test method, you call the play() method on the CDPlayer and assert that it does what you expect.

Testing code that uses System.out.println() is a tricky business. Therefore, this example uses StandardOutputStreamLog, a JUnit rule from the System Rules library (http://stefanbirkner.github.io/system-rules/index.html) that lets you make assertions against whatever is written to the console. Here it's asserting that the message from the SgtPeppers.play() method was sent to the console.

Now you know the basics of component scanning and autowiring. We'll revisit component scanning in chapter 3 when we look at ways to address autowiring ambiguity.

But at this point, let's set aside component scanning and autowiring and see how you can explicitly wire beans in Spring. We'll start with Spring's facility for expressing configuration in Java.

2.3   *Wiring beans with Java*

Although automatic Spring configuration with component scanning and automatic wiring is preferable in many cases, there are times when automatic configuration isn't an option and you must configure Spring explicitly. For instance, let's say that you want to wire components from some third-party library into your application. Because you don't have the source code for that library, there's no opportunity to annotate its classes with @Component and @Autowired. Therefore, automatic configuration isn't an option.

In that case, you must turn to explicit configuration. You have two choices for explicit configuration: Java and XML. In this section, we'll look at how to use Java-Config. We'll then follow up in the next section on Spring's XML configuration.

As I mentioned earlier, JavaConfig is the preferred option for explicit configuration because it's more powerful, type-safe, and refactor-friendly. That's because it's just Java code, like any other Java code in your application.

At the same time, it's important to recognize that JavaConfig code isn't just any other Java code. It's conceptually set apart from the business logic and domain code in your application. Even though it's expressed in the same language as those components, JavaConfig is configuration code. This means it shouldn't contain any business logic, nor should JavaConfig invade any code where business logic resides. In fact, although it's not required, JavaConfig is often set apart in a separate package from the rest of an application's logic so there's no confusion as to its purpose.

Let's see how to explicitly configure Spring with JavaConfig.

2.3.1   *Creating a configuration class*

Earlier in this chapter, in listing 2.3, you got your first taste of JavaConfig. Let's revisit CDPlayerConfig from that example:

```
package soundsystem;
import org.springframework.context.annotation.Configuration;

@Configuration
public class CDPlayerConfig {
}
```

The key to creating a JavaConfig class is to annotate it with @Configuration. The @Configuration annotation identifies this as a configuration class, and it's expected to contain details on beans that are to be created in the Spring application context.

So far, you've relied on component scanning to discover the beans that Spring should create. Although there's no reason you can't use component scanning and explicit configuration together, we're focusing on explicit configuration in this section, so I've removed the @ComponentScan annotation from CDPlayerConfig.

With @ComponentScan gone, the CDPlayerConfig class is ineffective. If you were to run CDPlayerTest now, the test would fail with a BeanCreationException. The test expects to be injected with CDPlayer and CompactDisc, but those beans are never created because they're never discovered by component scanning.

To make the test happy again, you could put @ComponentScan back in. Keeping the focus on explicit configuration, however, let's see how you can wire the CDPlayer and CompactDisc beans in JavaConfig.

2.3.2   *Declaring a simple bean*

To declare a bean in JavaConfig, you write a method that creates an instance of the desired type and annotate it with @Bean. For example, the following method declares the CompactDisc bean:

```
@Bean
public CompactDisc sgtPeppers() {
  return new SgtPeppers();
}
```

The @Bean annotation tells Spring that this method will return an object that should be registered as a bean in the Spring application context. The body of the method contains logic that ultimately results in the creation of the bean instance.

By default, the bean will be given an ID that is the same as the @Bean-annotated method's name. In this case, the bean will be named compactDisc. If you'd rather it have a different name, you can either rename the method or prescribe a different name with the name attribute:

```
@Bean(name="lonelyHeartsClubBand")
public CompactDisc sgtPeppers() {
  return new SgtPeppers();
}
```

No matter how you name the bean, this bean declaration is about as simple as they come. The body of the method returns a new instance of SgtPeppers. But because it's expressed in Java, it has every capability afforded it by the Java language to do almost anything to arrive at the CompactDisc that is returned.

Unleashing your imagination a bit, you might do something crazy like randomly selecting a CompactDisc from a selection of choices:

```
@Bean
public CompactDisc randomBeatlesCD() {
  int choice = (int) Math.floor(Math.random() * 4);
  if (choice == 0) {
    return new SgtPeppers();
  } else if (choice == 1) {
    return new WhiteAlbum();
  } else if (choice == 2) {
    return new HardDaysNight();
  } else {
    return new Revolver();
  }
}
```

I'll let you daydream a bit about all the ways you can exploit the power of Java to produce a bean from an @Bean-annotated method. When you're done, we'll pick it back up and look at how you can inject the CompactDisc bean into the CDPlayer in JavaConfig.

2.3.3   *Injecting with JavaConfig*

The CompactDisc bean you declared was simple and had no dependencies of its own. But now you must declare the CDPlayer bean, which depends on a CompactDisc. How can you wire that up in JavaConfig?

The simplest way to wire up beans in JavaConfig is to refer to the referenced bean's method. For example, here's how you might declare the CDPlayer bean:

```
@Bean
public CDPlayer cdPlayer() {
  return new CDPlayer(sgtPeppers());
}
```

The cdPlayer() method, like the sgtPeppers() method, is annotated with @Bean to indicate that it will produce an instance of a bean to be registered in the Spring application context. The ID of the bean will be cdPlayer, the same as the method's name.

The body of the cdPlayer() method differs subtly from that of the sgtPeppers() method. Rather than construct an instance via its default method, the CDPlayer instance is created by calling its constructor that takes a CompactDisc.

It appears that the CompactDisc is provided by calling sgtPeppers, but that's not exactly true. Because the sgtPeppers() method is annotated with @Bean, Spring will intercept any calls to it and ensure that the bean produced by that method is returned rather than allowing it to be invoked again.

For example, suppose you were to introduce another CDPlayer bean that is just like the first:

```
@Bean
public CDPlayer cdPlayer() {
  return new CDPlayer(sgtPeppers());
}

@Bean
public CDPlayer anotherCDPlayer() {
  return new CDPlayer(sgtPeppers());
}
```

If the call to sgtPeppers() was treated like any other call to a Java method, then each CDPlayer would be given its own instance of SgtPeppers. That would make sense if we were talking about real CD players and compact discs. If you have two CD players, there's no physical way for a single compact disc to simultaneously be inserted into two CD players.

In software, however, there's no reason you couldn't inject the same instance of SgtPeppers into as many other beans as you want. By default, all beans in Spring are singletons, and there's no reason you need to create a duplicate instance for the second CDPlayer bean. So Spring intercepts the call to sgtPeppers() and makes sure that what is returned is the Spring bean that was created when Spring itself called sgtPeppers() to create the CompactDisc bean. Therefore, both CDPlayer beans will be given the same instance of SgtPeppers.

I can see how referring to a bean by calling its method can be confusing. There's another way that might be easier to digest:

```
@Bean
public CDPlayer cdPlayer(CompactDisc compactDisc) {
  return new CDPlayer(compactDisc);
}
```

Here, the `cdPlayer()` method asks for a `CompactDisc` as a parameter. When Spring calls `cdPlayer()` to create the `CDPlayer` bean, it autowires a `CompactDisc` into the configuration method. Then the body of the method can use it however it sees fit. With this technique, the `cdPlayer()` method can still inject the `CompactDisc` into the `CDPlayer`'s constructor without explicitly referring to the `CompactDisc`'s `@Bean` method.

This approach to referring to other beans is usually the best choice because it doesn't depend on the `CompactDisc` bean being declared in the same configuration class. In fact, there's nothing that says the `CompactDisc` bean even needs to be declared in JavaConfig; it could have been discovered by component scanning or declared in XML. You could break up your configuration into a healthy mix of configuration classes, XML files, and automatically scanned and wired beans. No matter how the `CompactDisc` was created, Spring will be happy to hand it to this configuration method to create the `CDPlayer` bean.

In any event, it's important to recognize that although you're performing DI via the `CDPlayer`'s constructor, there's no reason you couldn't apply other styles of DI here. For example, if you wanted to inject a `CompactDisc` via a setter method, it might look like this:

```
@Bean
public CDPlayer cdPlayer(CompactDisc compactDisc) {
  CDPlayer cdPlayer = new CDPlayer(compactDisc);
  cdPlayer.setCompactDisc(compactDisc);
  return cdPlayer;
}
```

Once again, it bears repeating that the body of an `@Bean` method can utilize whatever Java is necessary to produce the bean instance. Constructor and setter injection just happen to be two simple examples of what you can do in an `@Bean`-annotated method. The possibilities are limited only by the capabilities of the Java language.

2.4   *Wiring beans with XML*

So far, you've seen how to let Spring automatically discover and wire beans. And you've seen how to step in and explicitly wire beans using JavaConfig. But there's another option for bean wiring that, although less desirable, has a long history with Spring.

Since the beginning of Spring, XML has been the primary way of expressing configuration. Countless lines of XML have been created in the name of Spring. And for many, Spring has become synonymous with XML configuration.

Although it's true that Spring has long been associated with XML, let's be clear that XML isn't the only option for configuring Spring. And now that Spring has strong support for automatic configuration and Java-based configuration, XML should not be your first choice.

Nevertheless, because so much XML-based Spring configuration has already been written, it's important to understand how to use XML with Spring. I hope, however, that this section will only serve to help you work with existing XML configuration, and that you'll lean on automatic configuration and JavaConfig for any new Spring work you do.

2.4.1 Creating an XML configuration specification

Before you can start using XML to wire together beans in Spring, you'll need to create the empty configuration specification. With JavaConfig, that meant creating a class annotated with `@Configuration`. For XML configuration, that means creating an XML file rooted with a `<beans>` element.

The simplest possible Spring XML configuration looks like this:

```
<?xml version="1.0" encoding="UTF-8"?>
<beans xmlns="http://www.springframework.org/schema/beans"
  xmlns:xsi="http://www.w3.org/2001/XMLSchema-instance"
  xsi:schemaLocation="http://www.springframework.org/schema/beans
    http://www.springframework.org/schema/beans/spring-beans.xsd
    http://www.springframework.org/schema/context">

  <!-- configuration details go here -->

</beans>
```

It doesn't take much to see that this basic XML configuration is already much more complex than an equivalent JavaConfig class. Whereas JavaConfig's `@Configuration` annotation was all you needed to get started, the XML elements for configuring Spring are defined in several XML schema (XSD) files that must be declared in the preamble of the XML configuration file.

> **CREATING XML CONFIGURATIONS WITH SPRING TOOL SUITE** An easy way to create and manage Spring XML configuration files is to use Spring Tool Suite (https://spring.io/tools/sts). Select File > New > Spring Bean Configuration File from Spring Tool Suite's menu to create a Spring XML configuration file, and select from one of the available configuration namespaces.

The most basic XML elements for wiring beans are contained in the `spring-beans` schema, which is declared as the root namespace of this XML file. The `<beans>` element, the root element of any Spring configuration file, is one of the elements in this schema.

Several other schemas are available for configuring Spring in XML. Although I'm going to focus on automatic and Java configuration throughout this book, I'll at least keep you informed along the way when some of these other schemas might come into play.

As it is, you have a perfectly valid Spring XML configuration. It's also a perfectly useless configuration, because it doesn't (yet) declare any beans. To give it some life, let's re-create the CD example, this time using XML configuration instead of Java-Config or automatic configuration.

2.4.2   Declaring a simple <bean>

To declare a bean in Spring's XML-based configuration, you're going to use another element from the `spring-beans` schema: the `<bean>` element. The `<bean>` element is the XML analogue to JavaConfig's `@Bean` annotation. You can use it to declare the `CompactDisc` bean like this:

```
<bean class="soundsystem.SgtPeppers" />
```

Here you declare a very simple bean. The class used to create this bean is specified in the `class` attribute and is expressed as the fully qualified class name.

For lack of an explicitly given ID, the bean will be named according to the fully qualified class name. In this case, the bean's ID will be `soundsystem.SgtPeppers#0`. The `#0` is an enumeration used to differentiate this bean from any other bean of the same type. If you were to declare another `SgtPeppers` bean without explicitly identifying it, it would automatically be given an ID of `soundsystem.SgtPeppers#1`.

Even though it's convenient to have beans named automatically for you, the generated names will be less useful if you need to refer to them later. Therefore, it's usually a good idea to give each bean a name of your own choosing via the `id` attribute:

```
<bean id="compactDisc" class="soundsystem.SgtPeppers" />
```

You'll use this explicit name in a moment when you wire this bean into the `CDPlayer` bean.

> **REDUCING VERBOSITY**   To cut down on XML verbosity, only explicitly name a bean if you'll need to refer to it by name (such as if you were to inject a reference to it into another bean).

But before we go any further, let's take a moment to examine some of the characteristics of this simple bean declaration.

The first thing to notice is that you aren't directly responsible for creating an instance of `SgtPeppers` as you were when using JavaConfig. When Spring sees this `<bean>` element, it will create a `SgtPeppers` bean for you by calling its default constructor. Bean creation is much more passive with XML configuration. But it's also less powerful than JavaConfig, where you can do almost anything imaginable to arrive at the bean instance.

Another notable thing about this simple `<bean>` declaration is that you express the type of the bean as a string set to the `class` attribute. Who's to say that the value given to `class` even refers to a real class? Spring's XML configuration doesn't benefit from compile-time verification of the Java types being referred to. And even if it does refer to an actual type, what will happen if you rename the class?

CHECK XML VALIDITY WITH AN IDE   Using a Spring-aware IDE such as Spring Tool Suite can help a lot to ensure the validity of your Spring XML configuration.

These are just a few of the reasons why JavaConfig is preferable over XML configuration. I encourage you to be mindful of these shortcomings of XML configuration when choosing the configuration style for your application. Nevertheless, let's continue this study of Spring's XML configuration to see how you can inject your SgtPeppers bean into the CDPlayer.

2.4.3 *Initializing a bean with constructor injection*

There's only one way to declare a bean in Spring XML configuration: use the <bean> element, and specify a class attribute. Spring takes it from there.

But when it comes to declaring DI in XML, there are several options and styles. With specific regard to constructor injection, you have two basic options to choose from:

- The <constructor-arg> element
- Using the c-namespace introduced in Spring 3.0

The difference between these two choices is largely one of verbosity. As you'll see, the <constructor-arg> element is generally more verbose than using the c-namespace and results in XML that is more difficult to read. On the other hand, <constructor-arg> can do a few things that the c-namespace can't.

As we look at constructor injection in Spring XML, we'll stack these two options side by side. First, let's see how each fares at injecting bean references.

INJECTING CONSTRUCTORS WITH BEAN REFERENCES

As currently defined, the CDPlayer bean has a constructor that accepts a Compact-Disc. This makes it a perfect candidate for injection with a bean reference.

Because you've already declared a SgtPeppers bean, and because the SgtPeppers class implements the CompactDisc interface, you have a bean to inject into a CDPlayer bean. All you need to do is declare the CDPlayer bean in XML and reference the SgtPeppers bean by its ID:

```
<bean id="cdPlayer" class="soundsystem.CDPlayer">
  <constructor-arg ref="compactDisc" />
</bean>
```

When Spring encounters this <bean> element, it will create an instance of CDPlayer. The <constructor-arg> element tells it to pass a reference to the bean whose ID is compactDisc to the CDPlayer's constructor.

Alternatively, you can use Spring's c-namespace. The c-namespace was introduced in Spring 3.0 as a more succinct way of expressing constructor args in XML. To use it, you must declare its schema in the preamble of the XML, like this:

```
<?xml version="1.0" encoding="UTF-8"?>
<beans xmlns="http://www.springframework.org/schema/beans"
  xmlns:c="http://www.springframework.org/schema/c"
  xmlns:xsi="http://www.w3.org/2001/XMLSchema-instance"
  xsi:schemaLocation="http://www.springframework.org/schema/beans
  http://www.springframework.org/schema/beans/spring-beans.xsd">

  ...

</beans>
```

With the c-namespace and schema declared, you can use it to declare a constructor argument like this:

```
<bean id="cdPlayer" class="soundsystem.CDPlayer"
    c:cd-ref="compactDisc" />
```

Here you're using the c-namespace to declare the constructor argument as an attribute of the <bean> element. And it's a rather odd-looking attribute name. Figure 2.1 illustrates how the pieces of the attribute name come together.

The attribute name starts with c:, the namespace prefix. Following that is the name of the constructor argument being wired. After that is -ref, a naming convention that indicates to Spring that you're wiring a reference to a bean named compactDisc and not the literal String value "compactDisc".

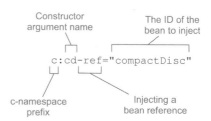

Figure 2.1   Injecting a bean reference into a constructor argument with Spring's c-namespace

It's clear that using c-namespace attributes is much more terse than using the <constructor-arg> element. That's one of the reasons that I like it a lot. Aside from being slightly easier to read, c-namespace attributes are especially helpful when I have to write code samples that fit neatly within the margins of a book.

But one thing that bugs me about the c-namespace as I've used it in the previous example is that it directly refers to the name of the constructor argument. Referring to a parameter name seems a bit flaky to me. Referring to a parameter by name requires that you compile your code with debug symbols stored in the class code. If you optimize your builds to leave out debug symbols, then this probably won't work.

Instead, you could refer to the parameter's position in the parameter list:

```
<bean id="cdPlayer" class="soundsystem.CDPlayer"
    c:_0-ref="compactDisc" />
```

This c-namespace attribute looks even more bizarre than the last one. I've replaced the name of the parameter with 0, the parameter index. But because XML doesn't allow digits as the first character of an attribute, I had to add an underscore as a prefix.

Using an index to identify the constructor argument feels better than referencing it by its name. Even if debug symbols are excluded from the build, the parameters will still be in the same order. And if there were multiple constructor arguments, it would certainly be useful. But because you have only one constructor argument, you have one more option—don't identify the parameter at all:

```
<bean id="cdPlayer" class="soundsystem.CDPlayer"
    c:_-ref="compactDisc" />
```

This is by far the most peculiar c-namespace attribute. There's no parameter index or parameter name. There's just an underscore placeholder followed by -ref to indicate that you're wiring a reference.

Now that you've tried wiring a reference to other beans, let's see how to wire literal values into constructors.

INJECTING CONSTRUCTORS WITH LITERAL VALUES

Although DI often refers to the type of wiring you've done thus far—wiring references to objects into other objects that depend on them—sometimes all you need to do is configure an object with a literal value. To illustrate, suppose you were to create a new implementation of CompactDisc, as shown here:

```
package soundsystem;

public class BlankDisc implements CompactDisc {

  private String title;
  private String artist;

  public BlankDisc(String title, String artist) {
    this.title = title;
    this.artist = artist;
  }

  public void play() {
    System.out.println("Playing " + title + " by " + artist);
  }

}
```

Unlike SgtPeppers, which was hard-coded with a title and artist, this implementation of CompactDisc is considerably more flexible. Much like a real-world blank disc, it can be set to contain any artist and title you want. Now you can change the existing SgtPeppers bean to use this class instead:

```
<bean id="compactDisc"
      class="soundsystem.BlankDisc">
  <constructor-arg value="Sgt. Pepper's Lonely Hearts Club Band" />
  <constructor-arg value="The Beatles" />
</bean>
```

Once again, the <constructor-arg> element is used to inject into constructor arguments. But this time, instead of using the ref attribute to reference another bean, you use the value attribute to indicate that the given value is to be taken literally and injected into the constructor.

How would this look if you were to use c-namespace attributes instead? One possible rendition might reference the constructor arguments by name:

```
<bean id="compactDisc"
    class="soundsystem.BlankDisc"
    c:_title="Sgt. Pepper's Lonely Hearts Club Band"
    c:_artist="The Beatles" />
```

As you can see, wiring literal values via the c-namespace differs from wiring references in that the -ref suffix is left off the attribute name. Similarly, you could wire the same literal values using parameter indexes, like this:

```
<bean id="compactDisc"
    class="soundsystem.BlankDisc"
    c:_0="Sgt. Pepper's Lonely Hearts Club Band"
    c:_1="The Beatles" />
```

XML doesn't allow more than one attribute on a given element to share the same name. Therefore, you can't use the simple underscore when you have two or more constructor arguments. But you can use it when there's only one constructor argument. For the sake of completeness, let's pretend that BlankDisc has a single-argument constructor that takes the album's title. In that case, you could declare it in Spring like this:

```
<bean id="compactDisc" class="soundsystem.BlankDisc"
    c:_="Sgt. Pepper's Lonely Hearts Club Band" />
```

When it comes to wiring bean reference and literal values, both <constructor-arg> and the c-namespace attributes are equally capable. But there's one thing that <constructor-arg> can do that the c-namespace can't do. Let's look at how to wire collections to constructor arguments.

WIRING COLLECTIONS

Up until now, we've assumed that CompactDisc was defined by merely a title and an artist name. But if that's all that came with a real-world CD, the technology would've never taken off. What makes CDs worth buying is that they carry music on them. Most CDs carry roughly a dozen tracks, each holding a song.

If CompactDisc is to truly model a real-world CD, then it must also have the notion of a list of tracks. Consider the new BlankDisc shown here:

```
package soundsystem.collections;
import java.util.List;
import soundsystem.CompactDisc;

public class BlankDisc implements CompactDisc {

  private String title;
  private String artist;
  private List<String> tracks;

  public BlankDisc(String title, String artist, List<String> tracks) {
    this.title = title;
    this.artist = artist;
    this.tracks = tracks;
  }
```

```
  public void play() {
    System.out.println("Playing " + title + " by " + artist);
    for (String track : tracks) {
      System.out.println("-Track: " + track);
    }
  }

}
```

This change has implications for how you configure the bean in Spring. You must provide a list of tracks when declaring the bean.

The simplest thing you could do is leave the list `null`. Because it's a constructor argument, you must specify it, but you can still pass `null` like this:

```
<bean id="compactDisc" class="soundsystem.BlankDisc">
  <constructor-arg value="Sgt. Pepper's Lonely Hearts Club Band" />
  <constructor-arg value="The Beatles" />
  <constructor-arg><null/></constructor-arg>
</bean>
```

The `<null/>` element does as you'd expect: it passes `null` into the constructor. It's a dirty fix, but it will work at injection time. You'll get a `NullPointerException` when the `play()` method is called, so it's far from ideal.

A better fix would be to supply a list of track names. For that you have a couple of options. First, you could specify it as a list, using the `<list>` element:

```
<bean id="compactDisc" class="soundsystem.BlankDisc">
  <constructor-arg value="Sgt. Pepper's Lonely Hearts Club Band" />
  <constructor-arg value="The Beatles" />
  <constructor-arg>
    <list>
      <value>Sgt. Pepper's Lonely Hearts Club Band</value>
      <value>With a Little Help from My Friends</value>
      <value>Lucy in the Sky with Diamonds</value>
      <value>Getting Better</value>
      <value>Fixing a Hole</value>
      <!-- ...other tracks omitted for brevity... -->
    </list>
  </constructor-arg>
</bean>
```

The `<list>` element is a child of `<constructor-arg>` and indicates that a list of values is to be passed into the constructor. The `<value>` element is used to specify each element of the list.

Similarly, a list of bean references could be wired using the `<ref>` element instead of `<value>`. For example, suppose you have a `Discography` class with the following constructor:

```
public Discography(String artist, List<CompactDisc> cds) { ... }
```

You can then configure a `Discography` bean like this:

```
<bean id="beatlesDiscography"
      class="soundsystem.Discography">
```

```
    <constructor-arg value="The Beatles" />
    <constructor-arg>
      <list>
        <ref bean="sgtPeppers" />
        <ref bean="whiteAlbum" />
        <ref bean="hardDaysNight" />
        <ref bean="revolver" />
        ...
      </list>
    </constructor-arg>
</bean>
```

It makes sense to use `<list>` when wiring a constructor argument of type `java.util.List`. Even so, you could also use the `<set>` element in the same way:

```
<bean id="compactDisc" class="soundsystem.BlankDisc">
  <constructor-arg value="Sgt. Pepper's Lonely Hearts Club Band" />
  <constructor-arg value="The Beatles" />
  <constructor-arg>
    <set>
      <value>Sgt. Pepper's Lonely Hearts Club Band</value>
      <value>With a Little Help from My Friends</value>
      <value>Lucy in the Sky with Diamonds</value>
      <value>Getting Better</value>
      <value>Fixing a Hole</value>
      <!-- ...other tracks omitted for brevity... -->
    </set>
  </constructor-arg>
</bean>
```

There's little difference between `<set>` and `<list>`. The main difference is that when Spring creates the collection to be wired, it will create it as either a `java.util.Set` or a `java.util.List`. If it's a `Set`, then any duplicate values will be discarded and the ordering may not be honored. But in either case, either a `<set>` or a `<list>` can be wired into a `List`, a `Set`, or even an array.

Wiring collections is one place where the `<constructor-arg>` has an advantage over the c-namespace attributes. There's no obvious way to wire collections like this via c-namespace attributes.

There are a handful of other nuances to using both `<constructor-arg>` and the c-namespace for constructor injection. But what we've covered here should carry you quite far, especially considering my earlier advice to favor Java configuration over XML configuration. Therefore, rather than belabor the topic of constructor injection in XML, let's move on to see how to wire properties in XML.

2.4.4   *Setting properties*

Up to this point, the `CDPlayer` and `BlankDisc` classes have been configured entirely through constructor injection and don't have any property setter methods. In contrast, let's examine how property injection works in Spring XML. Suppose that your new property-injected `CDPlayer` looks like this:

```
package soundsystem;
import org.springframework.beans.factory.annotation.Autowired;
import soundsystem.CompactDisc;
import soundsystem.MediaPlayer;

public class CDPlayer implements MediaPlayer {
  private CompactDisc compactDisc;

  @Autowired
  public void setCompactDisc(CompactDisc compactDisc) {
    this.compactDisc = compactDisc;
  }

  public void play() {
    compactDisc.play();
  }
}
```

CHOOSING BETWEEN CONSTRUCTOR INJECTION AND PROPERTY INJECTION As a general rule, I favor constructor injection for hard dependencies and property injection for any optional dependencies. In light of that rule, we could argue that the title, artist, and track list are hard dependencies for a `Blank-Disc` and that constructor injection was the right choice. It's debatable, however, whether a `CompactDisc` is a hard or optional dependency for a `CDPlayer`. I stand by that choice, but you could say that a `CDPlayer` might still have some limited functionality even without a `CompactDisc` being injected into it.

Now that `CDPlayer` doesn't have any constructors (aside from the implicit default constructor), it also doesn't have any hard dependencies. Therefore, you could declare it as a Spring bean like this:

```
<bean id="cdPlayer"
      class="soundsystem.CDPlayer" />
```

Spring will have absolutely no problem creating that bean. Your `CDPlayerTest` would fail with a `NullPointerException`, however, because you never injected `CDPlayer`'s `compactDisc` property. But you can fix that with the following change to the XML:

```
<bean id="cdPlayer"
      class="soundsystem.CDPlayer">
  <property name="compactDisc" ref="compactDisc" />
</bean>
```

The `<property>` element does for property setter methods what the `<constructor-arg>` element does for constructors. In this case, it references (with the `ref` attribute) the bean whose ID is `compactDisc` to be injected into the `compactDisc` property (via the `setCompactDisc()` method). Now if you run your test, it should pass.

You may also like to know that just as Spring offers the c-namespace as an alternative to the `<constructor-arg>` element, Spring also offers a succinct p-namespace as an alternative to the `<property>` element. To enable the p-namespace, you must declare it among the other namespaces in the XML file:

```
<?xml version="1.0" encoding="UTF-8"?>
<beans xmlns="http://www.springframework.org/schema/beans"
  xmlns:p="http://www.springframework.org/schema/p"
  xmlns:xsi="http://www.w3.org/2001/XMLSchema-instance"
  xsi:schemaLocation="http://www.springframework.org/schema/beans
    http://www.springframework.org/schema/beans/spring-beans.xsd">
  ...
</bean>
```

Using the p-namespace, you can wire the `compactDisc` property like this:

```
<bean id="cdPlayer"
      class="soundsystem.CDPlayer"
      p:compactDisc-ref="compactDisc" />
```

The p-namespace attributes follow a naming convention similar to that of the c-namespace attributes. Figure 2.2 illustrates how this p-namespace attribute name breaks down.

First, the attribute name is prefixed with `p:` to indicate that you're setting a property. Next up is the name of the property to be injected. Finally, the name ends with `-ref` as a clue to Spring that you're wiring a reference to a bean and not a literal value.

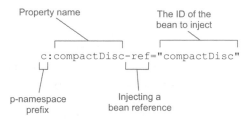

Figure 2.2   Injecting a bean reference into a property with Spring's p-namespace

INJECTING PROPERTIES WITH LITERAL VALUES

Properties can be injected with literal values in much the same way as constructor arguments. As an example, let's revisit the `BlankDisc` bean. This time, however, `BlankDisc`s will be configured entirely by property injection, not constructor injection. The new `BlankDisc` class looks like this:

```
package soundsystem;
import java.util.List;
import soundsystem.CompactDisc;

public class BlankDisc implements CompactDisc {

  private String title;
  private String artist;
  private List<String> tracks;

  public void setTitle(String title) {
    this.title = title;
  }

  public void setArtist(String artist) {
    this.artist = artist;
  }
```

```
public void setTracks(List<String> tracks) {
  this.tracks = tracks;
}

public void play() {
  System.out.println("Playing " + title + " by " + artist);
  for (String track : tracks) {
    System.out.println("-Track: " + track);
  }
}

}
```

Now you're no longer obligated to wire any of these properties. You could create a BlankDisc bean in its most blank form as follows:

```
<bean id="reallyBlankDisc"
    class="soundsystem.BlankDisc" />
```

Of course, wiring the bean without setting those properties wouldn't play out well at runtime. The play() method would claim that it's playing null by null just before a NullPointerException is thrown because there are no tracks. Therefore, you probably should wire up those properties. You can do that using the value attribute of the <property> element:

```
<bean id="compactDisc"
    class="soundsystem.BlankDisc">
  <property name="title"
              value="Sgt. Pepper's Lonely Hearts Club Band" />
  <property name="artist" value="The Beatles" />
  <property name="tracks">
    <list>
      <value>Sgt. Pepper's Lonely Hearts Club Band</value>
      <value>With a Little Help from My Friends</value>
      <value>Lucy in the Sky with Diamonds</value>
      <value>Getting Better</value>
      <value>Fixing a Hole</value>
      <!-- ...other tracks omitted for brevity... -->
    </list>
  </property>
</bean>
```

Aside from using the <property> element's value attribute to set the title and artist properties, notice how you set the tracks property with a nested <list> element, the same as before when wiring the tracks through <constructor-arg>.

Optionally, you can accomplish the same thing using p-namespace attributes:

```
<bean id="compactDisc"
    class="soundsystem.BlankDisc"
    p:title="Sgt. Pepper's Lonely Hearts Club Band"
    p:artist="The Beatles">
  <property name="tracks">
    <list>
      <value>Sgt. Pepper's Lonely Hearts Club Band</value>
```

```
            <value>With a Little Help from My Friends</value>
            <value>Lucy in the Sky with Diamonds</value>
            <value>Getting Better</value>
            <value>Fixing a Hole</value>
            <!-- ...other tracks omitted for brevity... -->
        </list>
    </property>
</bean>
```

As with c-namespace attributes, the only difference between wiring a bean reference and wiring a literal value is the presence or absence of a `-ref` suffix. Without the `-ref` suffix, you're wiring literal values.

Notice, however, that you can't use the p-namespace when wiring a collection. Unfortunately, there's no convenient way to specify a list of values (or bean references) with the p-namespace. But you can take advantage of something from Spring's util-namespace to simplify the `BlankDisc` bean.

First, you need to declare the util-namespace and its schema in the XML:

```
<?xml version="1.0" encoding="UTF-8"?>
<beans xmlns="http://www.springframework.org/schema/beans"
  xmlns:xsi="http://www.w3.org/2001/XMLSchema-instance"
  xmlns:p="http://www.springframework.org/schema/p"
  xmlns:util="http://www.springframework.org/schema/util"
  xsi:schemaLocation="http://www.springframework.org/schema/beans
    http://www.springframework.org/schema/beans/spring-beans.xsd
    http://www.springframework.org/schema/util
    http://www.springframework.org/schema/util/spring-util.xsd">

    ...

</beans>
```

One of the things that the util-namespace offers is the `<util:list>` element, which creates a list bean. Using `<util:list>`, you can shift the track list out of the Blank-Disc bean and into a bean of its own, like this:

```
<util:list id="trackList">
    <value>Sgt. Pepper's Lonely Hearts Club Band</value>
    <value>With a Little Help from My Friends</value>
    <value>Lucy in the Sky with Diamonds</value>
    <value>Getting Better</value>
    <value>Fixing a Hole</value>
    <!-- ...other tracks omitted for brevity... -->
</util:list>
```

Now you can wire the track-list bean into the `BlankDisc` bean's `tracks` property just like any other bean:

```
<bean id="compactDisc"
      class="soundsystem.BlankDisc"
      p:title="Sgt. Pepper's Lonely Hearts Club Band"
      p:artist="The Beatles"
      p:tracks-ref="trackList" />
```

The `<util:list>` element is just one of several elements in the `util`-namespace. Table 2.1 lists everything the `util`-namespace has to offer.

Table 2.1 Elements in Spring's `util-namespace`

Element	Description
`<util:constant>`	References a `public static` field on a type and exposes it as a bean
`<util:list>`	Creates a bean that is a `java.util.List` of values or references
`<util:map>`	Creates a bean that is a `java.util.Map` of values or references
`<util:properties>`	Creates a bean that is a `java.util.Properties`
`<util:property-path>`	References a bean property (or nested property) and exposes it as a bean
`<util:set>`	Creates a bean that is a `java.util.Set` of values or references

You'll occasionally call on members of the `util`-namespace as you need them. For now, though, let's wrap up this chapter by seeing how you can mix and match automatic configuration, JavaConfig, and XML configuration.

2.5 *Importing and mixing configurations*

In a typical Spring application, you're likely to need to use both automatic and explicit configuration. And even if you favor JavaConfig for explicit configuration, there may be times when XML configuration is the best choice.

Fortunately, none of the configuration options available in Spring are mutually exclusive. You're free to mix component scanning and autowiring with JavaConfig and/or XML configuration. In fact, as you saw in section 2.2.1, you'll need at least a little explicit configuration to enable component scanning and autowiring.

The first thing to know about mixing configuration styles is that when it comes to autowiring, it doesn't matter where the bean to be wired comes from. Autowiring considers all beans in the Spring container, regardless of whether they were declared in JavaConfig or XML or picked up by component scanning.

That leaves you with how to reference beans when doing explicit configuration, either with XML configuration or with Java configuration. Let's start by seeing how to reference XML-configured beans from JavaConfig.

2.5.1 *Referencing XML configuration in JavaConfig*

Pretend for a moment that `CDPlayerConfig` is getting unwieldy and you want to split it apart. Sure, it only declares two beans, which is a far cry from a complex Spring configuration. Nevertheless, let's pretend that two beans is two beans too many.

What you could do is break out the `BlankDisc` bean from `CDPlayerConfig` into its own `CDConfig` class, like this:

```
package soundsystem;
import org.springframework.context.annotation.Bean;
```

```
import org.springframework.context.annotation.Configuration;

@Configuration
public class CDConfig {
  @Bean
  public CompactDisc compactDisc() {
    return new SgtPeppers();
  }
}
```

Now that the `compactDisc()` method is gone from `CDPlayerConfig`, you need a way to bring the two configuration classes together. One way is to import `CDConfig` from `CDPlayerConfig` using the `@Import` annotation:

```
package soundsystem;
import org.springframework.context.annotation.Bean;
import org.springframework.context.annotation.Configuration;
import org.springframework.context.annotation.Import;

@Configuration
@Import(CDConfig.class)
public class CDPlayerConfig {

  @Bean
  public CDPlayer cdPlayer(CompactDisc compactDisc) {
    return new CDPlayer(compactDisc);
  }

}
```

Or, better yet, you can leave `@Import` out of `CDPlayerConfig` and instead create a higher-level `SoundSystemConfig` that uses `@Import` to bring both configurations together:

```
package soundsystem;
import org.springframework.context.annotation.Configuration;
import org.springframework.context.annotation.Import;

@Configuration
@Import({CDPlayerConfig.class, CDConfig.class})
public class SoundSystemConfig {
}
```

Either way, you've separated the configuration of `CDPlayer` from the configuration of `BlankDisc`. Now let's suppose that (for whatever reason) you want to configure the `BlankDisc` bean in XML like this:

```
<bean id="compactDisc"
      class="soundsystem.BlankDisc"
      c:_0="Sgt. Pepper's Lonely Hearts Club Band"
      c:_1="The Beatles">
  <constructor-arg>
    <list>
      <value>Sgt. Pepper's Lonely Hearts Club Band</value>
      <value>With a Little Help from My Friends</value>
```

```
      <value>Lucy in the Sky with Diamonds</value>
      <value>Getting Better</value>
      <value>Fixing a Hole</value>
      <!-- ...other tracks omitted for brevity... -->
    </list>
  </constructor-arg>
</bean>
```

With `BlankDisc` being declared in XML, how can you have Spring load it in along with the rest of your Java-based configuration?

The answer lies with the `@ImportResource` annotation. Assuming that the `Blank-Disc` bean is declared in a file named cd-config.xml that can be found at the root of the classpath, you can change `SoundSystemConfig` to use `@ImportResource` like this:

```
package soundsystem;
import org.springframework.context.annotation.Configuration;
import org.springframework.context.annotation.Import;
import org.springframework.context.annotation.ImportResource;

@Configuration
@Import(CDPlayerConfig.class)
@ImportResource("classpath:cd-config.xml")
public class SoundSystemConfig {
}
```

Both beans—`CDPlayer` configured in JavaConfig and `BlankDisc` configured in XML—will be loaded into the Spring container. And because `CDPlayer`'s `@Bean` method accepts a `CompactDisc` as a parameter, the `BlankDisc` bean will be wired into it, even though it's configured in XML.

Let's run through this exercise again. But this time, you'll reference a JavaConfig-declared bean from XML.

2.5.2 *Referencing JavaConfig in XML configuration*

Suppose you're working with Spring's XML-based configuration and you've decided that the XML is getting out of hand. As before, you're only dealing with two beans, and things could be worse. But before you're inundated with a flood of angle brackets, you decide to break the XML configuration file apart.

With JavaConfig, I showed you how to use `@Import` and `@ImportResource` to split up your JavaConfig classes. In XML, you can use the `<import>` element to split up the XML configuration.

For example, suppose you were to split out the `BlankDisc` bean into its own configuration file called cd-config.xml, as you did when working with `@ImportResource`. You can reference that file from the XML configuration file using `<import>`:

```
<?xml version="1.0" encoding="UTF-8"?>
<beans xmlns="http://www.springframework.org/schema/beans"
  xmlns:xsi="http://www.w3.org/2001/XMLSchema-instance"
  xmlns:c="http://www.springframework.org/schema/c"
  xsi:schemaLocation="http://www.springframework.org/schema/beans
    http://www.springframework.org/schema/beans/spring-beans.xsd">
```

```
<import resource="cd-config.xml" />

<bean id="cdPlayer"
      class="soundsystem.CDPlayer"
      c:cd-ref="compactDisc" />
```

```
</beans>
```

Now, suppose that instead of configuring `BlankDisc` in XML, you want to configure it in XML while leaving the `CDPlayer` configuration in JavaConfig. How can your XML-based configuration reference a JavaConfig class?

As it turns out, the answer isn't intuitive. The `<import>` element only works to import other XML configuration files, and there isn't an XML element whose job it is to import JavaConfig classes.

There is, however, an element you already know that can be used to bring a Java configuration into an XML configuration: the `<bean>` element. To import a JavaConfig class into an XML configuration, you declare it as a bean like this:

```
<?xml version="1.0" encoding="UTF-8"?>
<beans xmlns="http://www.springframework.org/schema/beans"
  xmlns:xsi="http://www.w3.org/2001/XMLSchema-instance"
  xmlns:c="http://www.springframework.org/schema/c"
  xsi:schemaLocation="http://www.springframework.org/schema/beans
    http://www.springframework.org/schema/beans/spring-beans.xsd">

  <bean class="soundsystem.CDConfig" />

  <bean id="cdPlayer"
        class="soundsystem.CDPlayer"
        c:cd-ref="compactDisc" />

</beans>
```

And just like that, the two configurations—one expressed in XML and one expressed in Java—have been brought together. Similarly, you might consider creating a higher-level configuration file that doesn't declare any beans but that brings two or more configurations together. For example, you could leave the `CDConfig` bean out of the previous XML configuration and instead have a third configuration file that joins them:

```
<?xml version="1.0" encoding="UTF-8"?>
<beans xmlns="http://www.springframework.org/schema/beans"
  xmlns:xsi="http://www.w3.org/2001/XMLSchema-instance"
  xmlns:c="http://www.springframework.org/schema/c"
  xsi:schemaLocation="http://www.springframework.org/schema/beans
    http://www.springframework.org/schema/beans/spring-beans.xsd">

  <bean class="soundsystem.CDConfig" />

  <import resource="cdplayer-config.xml" />

</beans>
```

Whether I'm using JavaConfig or XML wiring, I often create a *root configuration*, as I've shown here, that brings together two or more wiring classes and/or XML files. It's in this root configuration that I'll also usually turn on component scanning (with either `<context:component-scan>` or `@ComponentScan`). You'll see this technique employed for many of the examples in this book.

2.6 *Summary*

At the core of the Spring Framework is the Spring container. This container manages the lifecycle of the components of an application, creating those components and ensuring that their dependencies are met so that they can do their job.

In this chapter, we've looked at three primary ways of wiring beans together in Spring: automatic configuration, explicit Java-based configuration, and explicit XML-based configuration. No matter which you choose, these techniques describe the components in a Spring application and the relationships between those components.

I've also strongly recommended that you favor automatic configuration as much as possible to avoid the maintenance costs involved with explicit configuration. But when you must explicitly configure Spring, you should favor Java-based configuration—which is more powerful, type-safe, and refactorable—over XML configuration. This preference will guide my choice of wiring techniques as I present the examples throughout this book.

Because dependency injection is an essential part of working with Spring, the techniques shown in this chapter will play a role in almost everything else you do in this book. Building on this foundation, the next chapter will present some more advanced bean-wiring techniques that will help you make the most of the Spring container.

Advanced wiring 3

This chapter covers

- Spring profiles
- Conditional bean declaration
- Autowiring and ambiguity
- Bean scoping
- The Spring Expression Language

In the previous chapter, we looked at some essential bean-wiring techniques. You're likely to find a lot of use for what you learned in that chapter. But there's more to bean wiring than what we explored in chapter 2. Spring has several other tricks up its sleeve for more advanced bean wiring.

In this chapter, we'll dig in to some of these advanced techniques. You won't get as much day-to-day use out of the techniques in this chapter, but that doesn't mean they're any less valuable.

3.1 Environments and profiles

One of the most challenging things about developing software is transitioning an application from one environment to another. Certain environment-specific choices made for development aren't appropriate or won't work when the application transitions from development to production. Database configuration, encryption algorithms, and integration with external systems are just a few examples of things that are likely to vary across deployment environments.

Consider database configuration, for instance. In a development environment, you're likely to use an embedded database preloaded with test data. For example, in a Spring configuration class, you might use `EmbeddedDatabaseBuilder` in an `@Bean` method like this:

```
@Bean(destroyMethod="shutdown")
public DataSource dataSource() {
    return new EmbeddedDatabaseBuilder()
        .addScript("classpath:schema.sql")
        .addScript("classpath:test-data.sql")
        .build();
}
```

This will create a bean of type `javax.sql.DataSource`. But it's *how* that bean is created that's most interesting. Using `EmbeddedDatabaseBuilder` sets up an embedded Hypersonic database whose schema is defined in schema.sql and loaded with test data from test-data.sql.

This `DataSource` is useful in a development environment when you're running integration tests or firing up an application for manual testing. You can count on your database being in a given state every time you start it.

Although that makes an `EmbeddedDatabaseBuilder`-created `DataSource` perfect for development, it makes it a horrible choice for production. In a production setting, you may want to retrieve a `DataSource` from your container using JNDI. In that case, the following `@Bean` method is more appropriate:

```
@Bean
public DataSource dataSource() {
  JndiObjectFactoryBean jndiObjectFactoryBean =
      new JndiObjectFactoryBean();
  jndiObjectFactoryBean.setJndiName("jdbc/myDS");
  jndiObjectFactoryBean.setResourceRef(true);
  jndiObjectFactoryBean.setProxyInterface(javax.sql.DataSource.class);
  return (DataSource) jndiObjectFactoryBean.getObject();
}
```

Retrieving a `DataSource` from JNDI allows your container to make decisions about how it's created, including handing off a `DataSource` from a container-managed connection pool. Even so, using a JNDI-managed `DataSource` is more fitting for production and unnecessarily complicated for a simple integration test or developer test.

Meanwhile, in a QA environment you could select a completely different `DataSource` configuration. You might choose to configure a Commons DBCP connection pool like this:

```
@Bean(destroyMethod="close")
public DataSource dataSource() {
  BasicDataSource dataSource = new BasicDataSource();
  dataSource.setUrl("jdbc:h2:tcp://dbserver/~/test");
  dataSource.setDriverClassName("org.h2.Driver");
```

```
    dataSource.setUsername("sa");
    dataSource.setPassword("password");
    dataSource.setInitialSize(20);
    dataSource.setMaxActive(30);
    return dataSource;
}
```

Clearly, all three versions of the `dataSource()` method presented here are different from each other. They all produce a bean whose type is `javax.sql.DataSource`, but that's where the similarities end. Each applies a completely different strategy for producing the `DataSource` bean.

Again, this discussion isn't about how to configure a `DataSource` (we'll talk more about that in chapter 10). But certainly the seemingly simple `DataSource` bean isn't so simple. It's a good example of a bean that might vary across different environments. You must find a way to configure a `DataSource` bean so that the most appropriate configuration is chosen for each environment.

One way of doing this is to configure each bean in a separate configuration class (or XML file) and then make a build-time decision (perhaps using Maven profiles) about which to compile into the deployable application. The problem with this solution is that it requires that the application be rebuilt for each environment. A rebuild might not be that big a problem when going from development to QA. But requiring a rebuild between QA and production has the potential to introduce bugs and cause an epidemic of ulcers among the members of your QA team.

Fortunately, Spring has a solution that doesn't require a rebuild.

3.1.1 *Configuring profile beans*

Spring's solution for environment-specific beans isn't much different from build-time solutions. Certainly, an environment-specific decision is made as to which beans will and won't be created. But rather than make that decision at build time, Spring waits to make the decision at runtime. Consequently, the same deployment unit (perhaps a WAR file) will work in all environments without being rebuilt.

In version 3.1, Spring introduced bean profiles. To use profiles, you must gather all the varying bean definitions into one or more profiles and then make sure the proper profile is active when your application is deployed in each environment.

In Java configuration, you can use the `@Profile` annotation to specify which profile a bean belongs to. For example, the embedded database `DataSource` bean might be configured in a configuration class like this:

```
package com.myapp;
import javax.activation.DataSource;
import org.springframework.context.annotation.Bean;
import org.springframework.context.annotation.Configuration;
import org.springframework.context.annotation.Profile;
import
   org.springframework.jdbc.datasource.embedded.EmbeddedDatabaseBuilder;
import
```

```
org.springframework.jdbc.datasource.embedded.EmbeddedDatabaseType;

@Configuration
@Profile("dev")
public class DevelopmentProfileConfig {

  @Bean(destroyMethod="shutdown")
  public DataSource dataSource() {
      return new EmbeddedDatabaseBuilder()
          .setType(EmbeddedDatabaseType.H2)
          .addScript("classpath:schema.sql")
          .addScript("classpath:test-data.sql")
          .build();
  }

}
```

The main thing I want to draw your attention to is the @Profile annotation applied at the class level. It tells Spring that the beans in this configuration class should be created only if the dev profile is active. If the dev profile isn't active, then the @Bean methods will be ignored.

Meanwhile, you may have another configuration class for production that looks like this:

```
package com.myapp;
import javax.activation.DataSource;
import org.springframework.context.annotation.Bean;
import org.springframework.context.annotation.Configuration;
import org.springframework.context.annotation.Profile;
import org.springframework.jndi.JndiObjectFactoryBean;

@Configuration
@Profile("prod")
public class ProductionProfileConfig {

  @Bean
  public DataSource dataSource() {
    JndiObjectFactoryBean jndiObjectFactoryBean =
        new JndiObjectFactoryBean();
    jndiObjectFactoryBean.setJndiName("jdbc/myDS");
    jndiObjectFactoryBean.setResourceRef(true);
    jndiObjectFactoryBean.setProxyInterface(
        javax.sql.DataSource.class);
    return (DataSource) jndiObjectFactoryBean.getObject();
  }

}
```

In this case, the bean won't be created unless the prod profile is active.

In Spring 3.1, you could only use the @Profile annotation at the class level. Starting with Spring 3.2, however, you can use @Profile at the method level, alongside the @Bean annotation. This makes it possible to combine both bean declarations into a single configuration class, as shown in the following listing.

Listing 3.1   The @Profile annotation wires beans based on active files

```
package com.myapp;
import javax.activation.DataSource;
import org.springframework.context.annotation.Bean;
import org.springframework.context.annotation.Configuration;
import org.springframework.context.annotation.Profile;
import
  org.springframework.jdbc.datasource.embedded.EmbeddedDatabaseBuilder;
import
  org.springframework.jdbc.datasource.embedded.EmbeddedDatabaseType;
import org.springframework.jndi.JndiObjectFactoryBean;

@Configuration
public class DataSourceConfig {

  @Bean(destroyMethod="shutdown")
  @Profile("dev")                        ◁─────────────── Wired for "dev" profile
  public DataSource embeddedDataSource() {
      return new EmbeddedDatabaseBuilder()
          .setType(EmbeddedDatabaseType.H2)
          .addScript("classpath:schema.sql")
          .addScript("classpath:test-data.sql")
          .build();
  }

  @Bean
  @Profile("prod")                       ◁─────────────── Wired for "prod" profile
  public DataSource jndiDataSource() {
    JndiObjectFactoryBean jndiObjectFactoryBean =
        new JndiObjectFactoryBean();
    jndiObjectFactoryBean.setJndiName("jdbc/myDS");
    jndiObjectFactoryBean.setResourceRef(true);
    jndiObjectFactoryBean.setProxyInterface(javax.sql.DataSource.class);
    return (DataSource) jndiObjectFactoryBean.getObject();
  }

}
```

What's not apparent here is that although each of the DataSource beans is in a profile and will only be created if the prescribed profile is active, there are probably other beans that aren't defined in the scope of a given profile. Any bean that isn't given a profile will always be created, regardless of what profile is active.

CONFIGURING PROFILES IN XML

You can also configure profiled beans in XML by setting the profile attribute of the <beans> element. For example, to define the embedded database DataSource bean for development in XML, you can create a configuration XML file that looks like this:

```
<?xml version="1.0" encoding="UTF-8"?>
<beans xmlns="http://www.springframework.org/schema/beans"
  xmlns:xsi="http://www.w3.org/2001/XMLSchema-instance"
  xmlns:jdbc="http://www.springframework.org/schema/jdbc"
  xsi:schemaLocation="
```

```
    http://www.springframework.org/schema/jdbc
    http://www.springframework.org/schema/jdbc/spring-jdbc.xsd
    http://www.springframework.org/schema/beans
    http://www.springframework.org/schema/beans/spring-beans.xsd"
  profile="dev">

  <jdbc:embedded-database id="dataSource">
    <jdbc:script location="classpath:schema.sql" />
    <jdbc:script location="classpath:test-data.sql" />
  </jdbc:embedded-database>

</beans>
```

Likewise, you could create another configuration file, with `profile` set to `prod` for the production-ready JNDI-obtained `DataSource` bean. And you could create yet another XML file for the connection pool–defined `DataSource` bean specified by the `qa` profile. All the configuration XML files are collected into the deployment unit (likely a WAR file), but only those whose `profile` attribute matches the active profile will be used.

Rather than creating a proliferation of XML files for each environment, you also have the option of defining `<beans>` elements embedded in the root `<beans>` element. This helps to collect all profiled bean definitions into a single XML file, as shown next.

Listing 3.2 `<beans>` elements can be repeated to specify multiple profiles

```
<?xml version="1.0" encoding="UTF-8"?>
<beans xmlns="http://www.springframework.org/schema/beans"
  xmlns:xsi="http://www.w3.org/2001/XMLSchema-instance"
  xmlns:jdbc="http://www.springframework.org/schema/jdbc"
  xmlns:jee="http://www.springframework.org/schema/jee"
  xmlns:p="http://www.springframework.org/schema/p"
  xsi:schemaLocation="
    http://www.springframework.org/schema/jee
    http://www.springframework.org/schema/jee/spring-jee.xsd
    http://www.springframework.org/schema/jdbc
    http://www.springframework.org/schema/jdbc/spring-jdbc.xsd
    http://www.springframework.org/schema/beans
    http://www.springframework.org/schema/beans/spring-beans.xsd">

  <beans profile="dev">                    ⊲──────────── "dev" profile beans
    <jdbc:embedded-database id="dataSource">
      <jdbc:script location="classpath:schema.sql" />
      <jdbc:script location="classpath:test-data.sql" />
    </jdbc:embedded-database>
  </beans>

  <beans profile="qa">                     ⊲──────────── "qa" profile beans
    <bean id="dataSource"
          class="org.apache.commons.dbcp.BasicDataSource"
          destroy-method="close"
          p:url="jdbc:h2:tcp://dbserver/~/test"
          p:driverClassName="org.h2.Driver"
          p:username="sa"
          p:password="password"
```

```
            p:initialSize="20"
            p:maxActive="30" />
    </beans>

    <beans profile="prod">                    ⟵──────────── "prod" profile beans
        <jee:jndi-lookup id="dataSource"
                    jndi-name="jdbc/myDatabase"
                    resource-ref="true"
                    proxy-interface="javax.sql.DataSource" />
    </beans>
</beans>
```

Aside from the fact that all these beans are now defined in the same XML file, the effect is the same as if they were defined in separate XML files. There are three beans, all of type `javax.sql.DataSource` and all with an ID of `dataSource`. But at runtime, only one bean will be created, depending on which profile is active.

That raises the question: how do you make a profile active?

3.1.2 Activating profiles

Spring honors two separate properties when determining which profiles are active: `spring.profiles.active` and `spring.profiles.default`. If `spring.profiles.active` is set, then its value determines which profiles are active. But if `spring.profiles.active` isn't set, then Spring looks to `spring.profiles.default`. If neither `spring.profiles.active` nor `spring.profiles.default` is set, then there are no active profiles, and only those beans that aren't defined as being in a profile are created.

There are several ways to set these properties:

- As initialization parameters on `DispatcherServlet`
- As context parameters of a web application
- As JNDI entries
- As environment variables
- As JVM system properties
- Using the `@ActiveProfiles` annotation on an integration test class

I'll leave it to you to choose the best combination of `spring.profiles.active` and `spring.profiles.default` to suit your needs.

One approach that I like is to set `spring.profiles.default` to the development profile using parameters on `DispatcherServlet` and in the servlet context (for the sake of `ContextLoaderListener`). For example, a web application's web.xml file might set `spring.profiles.default` as shown in the next listing.

> **Listing 3.3   Setting default profiles in a web application's web.xml file**

```
<?xml version="1.0" encoding="UTF-8"?>
<web-app version="2.5"
  xmlns="http://java.sun.com/xml/ns/javaee"
  xmlns:xsi="http://www.w3.org/2001/XMLSchema-instance"
  xsi:schemaLocation="http://java.sun.com/xml/ns/javaee
     http://java.sun.com/xml/ns/javaee/web-app_2_5.xsd">
```

```
<context-param>
  <param-name>contextConfigLocation</param-name>
  <param-value>/WEB-INF/spring/root-context.xml</param-value>
</context-param>

<context-param>
  <param-name>spring.profiles.default</param-name>          Set default profile
  <param-value>dev</param-value>                             for context
</context-param>

<listener>
  <listener-class>
    org.springframework.web.context.ContextLoaderListener
  </listener-class>
</listener>

<servlet>
  <servlet-name>appServlet</servlet-name>
  <servlet-class>
    org.springframework.web.servlet.DispatcherServlet
  </servlet-class>
  <init-param>
    <param-name>spring.profiles.default</param-name>        Set default profile
    <param-value>dev</param-value>                           for servlet
  </init-param>
  <load-on-startup>1</load-on-startup>
</servlet>

<servlet-mapping>
  <servlet-name>appServlet</servlet-name>
  <url-pattern>/</url-pattern>
</servlet-mapping>

</web-app>
```

With `spring.profiles.default` set this way, any developer can retrieve the application code from source control and run it using development settings (such as an embedded database) without any additional configuration.

Then, when the application is deployed in a QA, production, or other environment, the person responsible for deploying it can set `spring.profiles.active` using system properties, environment variables, or JNDI as appropriate. When `spring.profiles.active` is set, it doesn't matter what `spring.profiles.default` is set to; the profiles set in `spring.profiles.active` take precedence.

You've probably noticed that the word *profiles* is plural in `spring.profiles.active` and `spring.profiles.default`. This means you can activate multiple profiles at the same time by listing the profile names, separated by commas. Of course, it probably doesn't make much sense to enable both `dev` and `prod` profiles at the same time, but you could enable multiple orthogonal profiles simultaneously.

TESTING WITH PROFILES

When running an integration test, you'll often want to test using the same configuration (or some subset thereof) you'd use in production. But if your configuration references beans that are in profiles, you need a way to enable the appropriate profile when running those tests.

Spring offers the `@ActiveProfiles` annotation to let you specify which profile(s) should be active when a test is run. Often it's the development profile that you'll want to activate during an integration test. For example, here's a snippet of a test class that uses `@ActiveProfiles` to activate the dev profile:

```
@RunWith(SpringJUnit4ClassRunner.class)
@ContextConfiguration(classes={PersistenceTestConfig.class})
@ActiveProfiles("dev")
public class PersistenceTest {
  ...
}
```

Spring profiles are a great way to conditionally define beans where the condition is based on which profile is active. But Spring 4 offers a more general-purpose mechanism for conditional bean definitions where the condition is up to you. Let's see how to define conditional beans using Spring 4 and the `@Conditional` annotation.

3.2   *Conditional beans*

Suppose you want one or more beans to be configured if and only if some library is available in the application's classpath. Or let's say you want a bean to be created only if a certain other bean is also declared. Maybe you want a bean to be created if and only if a specific environment variable is set.

Until Spring 4, it was difficult to achieve this level of conditional configuration, but Spring 4 introduced a new `@Conditional` annotation that can be applied to `@Bean` methods. If the prescribed condition evaluates to `true`, then the bean is created. Otherwise the bean is ignored.

For example, suppose you have a class named `MagicBean` that you only want Spring to instantiate if a `magic` environment property has been set. If the environment has no such property, then the `MagicBean` should be ignored. The following listing shows a configuration that conditionally configures the `MagicBean` using `@Conditional`.

> **Listing 3.4   Conditionally configuring a bean**

```
@Bean
@Conditional(MagicExistsCondition.class)      ◁———— Conditionally create bean
public MagicBean magicBean() {
  return new MagicBean();
}
```

As you can see, `@Conditional` is given a `Class` that specifies the condition—in this case, `MagicExistsCondition`. `@Conditional` comes paired with a `Condition` interface:

```
public interface Condition {
    boolean matches(ConditionContext ctxt,
                AnnotatedTypeMetadata metadata);
}
```

The class given to @Conditional can be any type that implements the Condition interface. As you can see, it's a straightforward interface to implement, requiring only that you provide an implementation for the matches() method. If the matches() method returns true, then the @Conditional-annotated beans are created. If matches() returns false, then those beans aren't created.

For this example, you need to create an implementation of Condition that hinges its decision on the presence of a magic property in the environment. The next listing shows MagicExistsCondition, an implementation of Condition that does the trick.

Listing 3.5 Checking for the presence of magic in a Condition

```
package com.habuma.restfun;
import org.springframework.context.annotation.Condition;
import org.springframework.context.annotation.ConditionContext;
import org.springframework.core.type.AnnotatedTypeMetadata;
import org.springframework.util.ClassUtils;

public class MagicExistsCondition implements Condition {

  public boolean matches(
          ConditionContext context, AnnotatedTypeMetadata metadata) {
    Environment env = context.getEnvironment();
    return env.containsProperty("magic");          ◁———— Check for "magic" property
  }

}
```

The matches() method in this listing is simple but powerful. It uses the Environment obtained from the given ConditionContext object to check for the presence of an environment property named magic. For this example, the value of the property is irrelevant; it only needs to exist. This results in true being returned from matches(). Consequently, the condition is met, and any beans whose @Conditional annotation refers to MagicExistsCondition will be created.

On the other hand, if the property doesn't exist, the condition will fail, false will be returned from matches(), and none of those beans will be created.

MagicExistsCondition only uses the Environment from the ConditionContext, but there's much more that a Condition implementation can consider. The matches() method is given a ConditionContext and an AnnotatedTypeMetadata to use in making its decision.

ConditionContext is an interface that looks something like this:

```
public interface ConditionContext {
  BeanDefinitionRegistry getRegistry();
  ConfigurableListableBeanFactory getBeanFactory();
  Environment getEnvironment();
  ResourceLoader getResourceLoader();
  ClassLoader getClassLoader();
}
```

From the `ConditionContext`, you can do the following:

- Check for bean definitions via the `BeanDefinitionRegistry` returned from `getRegistry()`.
- Check for the presence of beans, and even dig into bean properties via the `ConfigurableListableBeanFactory` returned from `getBeanFactory()`.
- Check for the presence and values of environment variables via the `Environment` retrieved from `getEnvironment()`.
- Read and inspect the contents of resources loaded via the `ResourceLoader` returned from `getResourceLoader()`.
- Load and check for the presence of classes via the `ClassLoader` returned from `getClassLoader()`.

As for the `AnnotatedTypeMetadata`, it offers you a chance to inspect annotations that may also be placed on the `@Bean` method. Like `ConditionContext`, `Annotated-TypeMetadata` is an interface. It looks like this:

```
public interface AnnotatedTypeMetadata {
  boolean isAnnotated(String annotationType);
  Map<String, Object> getAnnotationAttributes(String annotationType);
  Map<String, Object> getAnnotationAttributes(
          String annotationType, boolean classValuesAsString);
  MultiValueMap<String, Object> getAllAnnotationAttributes(
          String annotationType);
  MultiValueMap<String, Object> getAllAnnotationAttributes(
          String annotationType, boolean classValuesAsString);
}
```

Using the `isAnnotated()` method, you can check to see if the `@Bean` method is annotated with any particular annotation type. Using the other methods, you can check on the attributes of any annotation applied to the `@Bean` method.

Interestingly, starting with Spring 4, the `@Profile` annotation has been refactored to be based on `@Conditional` and the `Condition` interface. As another example of how to work with `@Conditional` and `Condition`, let's look at how `@Profile` is implemented in Spring 4.

The `@Profile` annotation looks like this:

```
@Retention(RetentionPolicy.RUNTIME)
@Target({ElementType.TYPE, ElementType.METHOD})
@Documented
@Conditional(ProfileCondition.class)
public @interface Profile {
  String[] value();
}
```

Notice that `@Profile` is itself annotated with `@Conditional` and refers to `Profile-Condition` as the `Condition` implementation. As shown next, `ProfileCondition` implements `Condition` and considers several factors from both `ConditionContext` and `AnnotatedTypeMetadata` in making its decision.

Listing 3.6 `ProfileCondition` checking whether a bean profile is acceptable

```
class ProfileCondition implements Condition {
  public boolean matches(
      ConditionContext context, AnnotatedTypeMetadata metadata) {
    if (context.getEnvironment() != null) {
      MultiValueMap<String, Object> attrs =
          metadata.getAllAnnotationAttributes(Profile.class.getName());
      if (attrs != null) {
        for (Object value : attrs.get("value")) {
          if (context.getEnvironment()
                    .acceptsProfiles(((String[]) value))) {
            return true;
          }
        }
        return false;
      }
    }
    return true;
  }
}
```

As you can see, `ProfileCondition` fetches all the annotation attributes for the
`@Profile` annotation from `AnnotatedTypeMetadata`. With that, it checks explicitly for
the `value` attribute, which contains the name of the bean's profile. It then consults
with the `Environment` retrieved from the `ConditionContext` to see whether the profile is active (by calling the `acceptsProfiles()` method).

3.3 *Addressing ambiguity in autowiring*

In chapter 2, you saw how to use autowiring to let Spring do all the work when injecting bean references into constructor arguments or properties. Autowiring is a huge
help because it reduces the amount of explicit configuration necessary to assemble
application components.

But autowiring only works when exactly one bean matches the desired result.
When there's more than one matching bean, the ambiguity prevents Spring from
autowiring the property, constructor argument, or method parameter.

To illustrate autowiring ambiguity, suppose you've annotated the following `set-
Dessert()` method with `@Autowired`:

```
@Autowired
public void setDessert(Dessert dessert) {
    this.dessert = dessert;
}
```

In this example, `Dessert` is an interface and is implemented by three classes: `Cake`,
`Cookies`, and `IceCream`:

```
@Component
public class Cake implements Dessert { ... }

@Component
public class Cookies implements Dessert { ... }
```

```
@Component
public class IceCream implements Dessert { ... }
```

Because all three implementations are annotated by `@Component`, they're all picked up during component-scanning and created as beans in the Spring application context. Then, when Spring tries to autowire the `Dessert` parameter in `setDessert()`, it doesn't have a single, unambiguous choice. Although most people wouldn't have any problem making choices when faced with multiple dessert options, Spring can't choose. Spring has no option but to fail and throw an exception. To be precise, Spring throws a `NoUniqueBeanDefinitionException`:

```
nested exception is
    org.springframework.beans.factory.NoUniqueBeanDefinitionException:
No qualifying bean of type [com.desserteater.Dessert] is defined:
    expected single matching bean but found 3: cake,cookies,iceCream
```

Of course, this dessert-eating example is contrived to illustrate how autowiring can run into trouble with ambiguity. In reality, autowiring ambiguity is more rare than you'd expect. Even though such ambiguity is a real problem, more often than not there's only one implementation of a given type, and autowiring works perfectly.

For those times when ambiguity does happen, however, Spring offers a couple of options. You can declare one of the candidate beans as the primary choice, or you can use qualifiers to help Spring narrow its choices to a single candidate.

3.3.1   *Designating a primary bean*

If you're like me, you enjoy all kinds of desserts. Cake … cookies … ice cream … it's all good. But if you were forced to choose only a single dessert, which is your favorite?

When declaring beans, you can avoid autowiring ambiguity by designating one of the candidate beans as a primary bean. In the event of any ambiguity, Spring will choose the primary bean over any other candidate beans. Essentially, you're declaring your "favorite" bean.

Let's say that ice cream is your favorite dessert. You can express that favorite choice in Spring using the `@Primary` annotation. `@Primary` can be used either alongside `@Component` for beans that are component-scanned or alongside `@Bean` for beans declared in Java configuration. For example, here's how you might declare the `@Component`-annotated `IceCream` bean as the primary choice:

```
@Component
@Primary
public class IceCream implements Dessert { ... }
```

Or, if you're declaring the `IceCream` bean explicitly in Java configuration, the `@Bean` method might look like this:

```
@Bean
@Primary
public Dessert iceCream() {
    return new IceCream();
}
```

If you're configuring your beans in XML, you're not left out. The <bean> element has a primary attribute to specify a primary bean:

```
<bean id="iceCream"
      class="com.desserteater.IceCream"
      primary="true" />
```

No matter how you designate a primary bean, the effect is the same. You're telling Spring that it should choose the primary bean in the case of ambiguity.

This works well right up to the point where you designate two or more primary beans. For example, suppose the Cake class looks like this:

```
@Component
@Primary
public class Cake implements Dessert { ... }
```

Now there are two primary Dessert beans: Cake and IceCream. This poses a new ambiguity issue. Just as Spring couldn't choose among multiple candidate beans, it can't choose among multiple primary beans. Clearly, when more than one bean is designated as primary, there are no primary candidates.

For a more powerful ambiguity-busting mechanism, let's look at qualifiers.

3.3.2 *Qualifying autowired beans*

The limitation of primary beans is that @Primary doesn't limit the choices to a single unambiguous option. It only designates a preferred option. When there's more than one primary, there's not much else you can do to narrow the choices further.

In contrast, Spring's qualifiers apply a narrowing operation to all candidate beans, ultimately arriving at the single bean that meets the prescribed qualifications. If ambiguity still exists after applying all qualifiers, you can always apply more qualifiers to narrow the choices further.

The @Qualifier annotation is the main way to work with qualifiers. It can be applied alongside @Autowired or @Inject at the point of injection to specify which bean you want to be injected. For example, let's say you want to ensure that the IceCream bean is injected into setDessert():

```
@Autowired
@Qualifier("iceCream")
public void setDessert(Dessert dessert) {
    this.dessert = dessert;
}
```

This is a prime example of qualifiers in their simplest form. The parameter given to @Qualifier is the ID of the bean that you want to inject. All @Component-annotated classes will be created as beans whose ID is the uncapitalized class name. Therefore, @Qualifier("iceCream") refers to the bean created when component-scanning created an instance of the IceCream class.

Actually, there's a bit more to the story than that. To be more precise, @Qualifier ("iceCream") refers to the bean that has the String "iceCream" as a qualifier. For lack of having specified any other qualifiers, all beans are given a default qualifier that's the same as their bean ID. Therefore, the setDessert() method will be injected with the bean that has "iceCream" as a qualifier. That just happens to be the bean whose ID is iceCream, created when the IceCream class was component-scanned.

Basing qualification on the default bean ID qualifier is simple but can pose some problems. What do you suppose would happen if you refactored the IceCream class, renaming it Gelato? In that case, the bean's ID and default qualifier would be gelato, which doesn't match the qualifier on setDessert(). Autowiring would fail.

The problem is that you specified a qualifier on setDessert() that is tightly coupled to the class name of the bean being injected. Any change to that class name will render the qualifier ineffective.

CREATING CUSTOM QUALIFIERS

Instead of relying on the bean ID as the qualifier, you can assign your own qualifier to a bean. All you need to do is place the @Qualifier annotation on the bean declaration. For example, it can be applied alongside @Component like this:

```
@Component
@Qualifier("cold")
public class IceCream implements Dessert { ... }
```

In this case, a qualifier of cold is assigned to the IceCream bean. Because it's not coupled to the class name, you can refactor the name of the IceCream class all you want without worrying about breaking autowiring. It will work as long as you refer to the cold qualifier at the injection point:

```
@Autowired
@Qualifier("cold")
public void setDessert(Dessert dessert) {
    this.dessert = dessert;
}
```

It's worth noting that @Qualifier can also be used alongside the @Bean annotation when explicitly defining beans with Java configuration:

```
@Bean
@Qualifier("cold")
public Dessert iceCream() {
    return new IceCream();
}
```

When defining custom @Qualifier values, it's a good practice to use a trait or descriptive term for the bean, rather than using an arbitrary name. In this case, I've described the IceCream bean as a "cold" bean. At the injection point, it reads as "give me the cold dessert," which happens to describe IceCream. Similarly, I might describe Cake as "soft" and Cookies as "crispy."

DEFINING CUSTOM QUALIFIER ANNOTATIONS

Trait-oriented qualifiers are better than those based on the bean ID. But they still run into trouble when you have multiple beans that share common traits. For example, imagine what would happen if you introduced this new `Dessert` bean:

```
@Component
@Qualifier("cold")
public class Popsicle implements Dessert { ... }
```

Oh no! Now you have two "cold" desserts. Once again you're faced with ambiguity in autowiring dessert beans. You need more qualifiers to narrow the selection to a single bean.

Perhaps the solution is to tack on another `@Qualifier` at both the injection point and at the bean definition. Maybe the `IceCream` class could look like this:

```
@Component
@Qualifier("cold")
@Qualifier("creamy")
public class IceCream implements Dessert { ... }
```

Perhaps the `Popsicle` class could also use another `@Qualifier`:

```
@Component
@Qualifier("cold")
@Qualifier("fruity")
public class Popsicle implements Dessert { ... }
```

And at the injection point, you could narrow it down to `IceCream` like this:

```
@Autowired
@Qualifier("cold")
@Qualifier("creamy")
public void setDessert(Dessert dessert) {
    this.dessert = dessert;
}
```

There's only one small problem: Java doesn't allow multiple annotations of the same type to be repeated on the same item.[1] The compiler will complain with errors if you try this. There's no way you can use `@Qualifier` (at least not directly) to narrow the list of autowiring candidates to a single choice.

What you can do, however, is create custom qualifier annotations to represent the traits you want your beans to be qualified with. All you have to do is create an annotation that is itself annotated with `@Qualifier`. Rather than use `@Qualifier("cold")`, you can use a custom `@Cold` annotation that's defined like this:

```
@Target({ElementType.CONSTRUCTOR, ElementType.FIELD,
        ElementType.METHOD, ElementType.TYPE})
@Retention(RetentionPolicy.RUNTIME)
@Qualifier
public @interface Cold { }
```

---

[1] Java 8 allows repeated annotations, as long as the annotation is annotated with `@Repeatable`. Even so, Spring's `@Qualifier` annotation isn't annotated with `@Repeatable`.

Likewise, you can create a new `@Creamy` annotation as a replacement for `@Qualifier` ("creamy"):

```
@Target({ElementType.CONSTRUCTOR, ElementType.FIELD,
        ElementType.METHOD, ElementType.TYPE})
@Retention(RetentionPolicy.RUNTIME)
@Qualifier
public @interface Creamy { }
```

And, similarly, you can create `@Soft`, `@Crispy`, and `@Fruity` annotations to use wherever you'd otherwise use the `@Qualifier` annotation. By annotating these annotations with `@Qualifier`, they take on the characteristics of `@Qualifier`. They are, in fact, qualifier annotations in their own right.

Now you can revisit `IceCream` and annotate it with `@Cold` and `@Creamy`, like this:

```
@Component
@Cold
@Creamy
public class IceCream implements Dessert { ... }
```

Similarly, the `Popsicle` class can be annotated with `@Cold` and `@Fruity`:

```
@Component
@Cold
@Fruity
public class Popsicle implements Dessert { ... }
```

Finally, at the injection point, you can use any combination of qualifier annotations necessary to narrow the selection to the one bean that meets your specifications. To arrive at the `IceCream` bean, the `setDessert()` method can be annotated like this:

```
@Autowired
@Cold
@Creamy
public void setDessert(Dessert dessert) {
    this.dessert = dessert;
}
```

By defining custom qualifier annotations, you're able to use multiple qualifiers together with no limitations or complaints from the Java compiler. Also, your custom annotations are more type-safe than using the raw `@Qualifier` annotation and specifying the qualifier as a `String`.

Take a closer look at the `setDessert()` method and how it's annotated. Nowhere do you explicitly say that you want that method to be autowired with the `IceCream` bean. Instead, you identify the desired bean by its traits, `@Cold` and `@Creamy`. Thus `set-Dessert()` remains decoupled from any specific `Dessert` implementation. Any bean that satisfies those traits will do fine. It just so happens that in your current selection of `Dessert` implementations, the `IceCream` bean is the single matching candidate.

In this section and the previous section, we explored a couple of ways to extend Spring with custom annotations. To create a custom conditional annotation, you create a new annotation and annotate it with `@Conditional`. And to create a custom qualifier annotation, you can create a new annotation and annotate it with `@Qualifier`. This technique can be applied using many of Spring's annotations, composing them into custom special-purpose annotations.

Now let's take a moment to see how you can declare beans to be created in different scopes.

3.4 Scoping beans

By default, all beans created in the Spring application context are created as singletons. That is to say, no matter how many times a given bean is injected into other beans, it's always the same instance that is injected each time.

Most of the time, singleton beans are ideal. The cost of instantiating and garbage-collecting instances of objects that are only used for small tasks can't be justified when an object is stateless and can be reused over and over again in an application.

But sometimes you may find yourself working with a mutable class that does maintain some state and therefore isn't safe for reuse. In that case, declaring the class as a singleton bean probably isn't a good idea because that object can be tainted and create unexpected problems when reused later.

Spring defines several scopes under which a bean can be created, including the following:

- *Singleton*—One instance of the bean is created for the entire application.
- *Prototype*—One instance of the bean is created every time the bean is injected into or retrieved from the Spring application context.
- *Session*—In a web application, one instance of the bean is created for each session.
- *Request*—In a web application, one instance of the bean is created for each request.

Singleton scope is the default scope, but as we've discussed, it isn't ideal for mutable types. To select an alternative type, you can use the @Scope annotation, either in conjunction with the @Component annotation or with the @Bean annotation.

For example, if you're relying on component-scanning to discover and declare a bean, then you can annotate the bean class with @Scope to make it a prototype bean:

```
@Component
@Scope(ConfigurableBeanFactory.SCOPE_PROTOTYPE)
public class Notepad { ... }
```

Here, you specify prototype scope by using the SCOPE_PROTOTYPE constant from the ConfigurableBeanFactory class. You could also use @Scope("prototype"), but using the SCOPE_PROTOTYPE constant is safer and less prone to mistakes.

Alternatively, if you're configuring the Notepad bean as a prototype in Java configuration, you can use @Scope along with @Bean to specify the desired scoping:

```
@Bean
@Scope(ConfigurableBeanFactory.SCOPE_PROTOTYPE)
public Notepad notepad() {
  return new Notepad();
}
```

And, in the event that you're configuring the bean in XML, you can set the scope using the `scope` attribute of the `<bean>` element:

```
<bean id="notepad"
      class="com.myapp.Notepad"
      scope="prototype" />
```

Regardless of how you specify prototype scope, an instance of the bean will be created each and every time it's injected into or retrieved from the Spring application context. Consequently, everyone gets their own instance of `Notepad`.

3.4.1 *Working with request and session scope*

In a web application, it may be useful to instantiate a bean that's shared within the scope of a given request or session. For instance, in a typical e-commerce application, you may have a bean that represents the user's shopping cart. If the shopping cart bean is a singleton, then all users will be adding products to the same cart. On the other hand, if the shopping cart is prototype-scoped, then products added to the cart in one area of the application may not be available in another part of the application where a different prototype-scoped shopping cart was injected.

In the case of a shopping cart bean, session scope makes the most sense, because it's most directly attached to a given user. To apply session scope, you can use the `@Scope` annotation in a way similar to how you specified prototype scope:

```
@Component
@Scope(
    value=WebApplicationContext.SCOPE_SESSION,
    proxyMode=ScopedProxyMode.INTERFACES)
public ShoppingCart cart() { ... }
```

Here you're setting the `value` attribute to the `SCOPE_SESSION` constant from `WebApplicationContext` (which has a value of `session`). This tells Spring to create an instance of the `ShoppingCart` bean for each session in a web application. There will be multiple instances of the `ShoppingCart` bean, but only one will be created for a given session and it will essentially be a singleton as far as that session is concerned.

Notice that `@Scope` also has a `proxyMode` attribute set to `ScopedProxyMode.INTERFACES`. This attribute addresses a problem encountered when injecting a session- or request-scoped bean into a singleton-scoped bean. But before I explain `proxyMode`, let's look at a scenario that presents the problem that `proxyMode` addresses.

Suppose you want to inject the `ShoppingCart` bean into the following setter method on a singleton `StoreService` bean:

```
@Component
public class StoreService {

  @Autowired
  public void setShoppingCart(ShoppingCart shoppingCart) {
    this.shoppingCart = shoppingCart;
  }

  ...
}
```

Because `StoreService` is a singleton bean, it will be created as the Spring application context is loaded. As it's created, Spring will attempt to inject `ShoppingCart` into the `setShoppingCart()` method. But the `ShoppingCart` bean, being session scoped, doesn't exist yet. There won't be an instance of `ShoppingCart` until a user comes along and a session is created.

Moreover, there will be many instances of `ShoppingCart`: one per user. You don't want Spring to inject just any single instance of `ShoppingCart` into `StoreService`. You want `StoreService` to work with the `ShoppingCart` instance for whichever session happens to be in play when `StoreService` needs to work with the shopping cart.

Instead of injecting the actual `ShoppingCart` bean into `StoreService`, Spring should inject a proxy to the `ShoppingCart` bean, as illustrated in listing 3.2. This proxy will expose the same methods as `ShoppingCart` so that for all `StoreService` knows, it *is* the shopping cart. But when `StoreService` calls methods on `ShoppingCart`, the proxy will lazily resolve it and delegate the call to the actual session-scoped `Shopping-Cart` bean. See figure 3.1.

Now let's take this understanding of scoped proxies and discuss the `proxyMode` attribute. As configured, `proxyMode` is set to `ScopedProxyMode.INTERFACES`, indicating that the proxy should implement the `ShoppingCart` interface and delegate to the implementation bean.

This is fine (and the most ideal proxy mode) as long as `ShoppingCart` is an interface and not a class. But if `ShoppingCart` is a concrete class, there's no way Spring can create an interface-based proxy. Instead, it must use CGLib to generate a class-based proxy. So, if the bean type is a concrete class, you must set `proxyMode` to `ScopedProxy-Mode.TARGET_CLASS` to indicate that the proxy should be generated as an extension of the target class.

Although I've focused on session scope, know that request-scoped beans pose the same wiring challenges as session-scoped beans. Therefore, request-scoped beans should also be injected as scoped proxies.

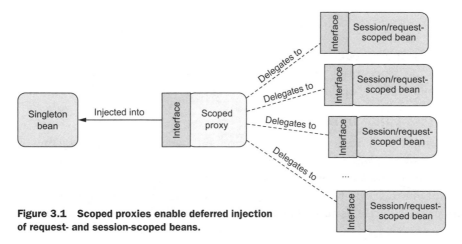

Figure 3.1 Scoped proxies enable deferred injection of request- and session-scoped beans.

3.4.2 *Declaring scoped proxies in XML*

If you're declaring your session-scoped or request-scoped beans in XML, then you can't use the @Scope annotation or its proxyMode attribute. The scope attribute of the <bean> element lets you set the bean scope, but how can you specify the proxy mode?

To set the proxy mode, you must use a new element from Spring's aop namespace:

```
<bean id="cart"
      class="com.myapp.ShoppingCart"
      scope="session">
  <aop:scoped-proxy />
</bean>
```

<aop:scoped-proxy> is the Spring XML configuration's counterpart to the @Scope annotation's proxyMode attribute. It tells Spring to create a scoped proxy for the bean. By default, it uses CGLib to create a target class proxy. But you can ask it to generate an interface-based proxy by setting the proxy-target-class attribute to false:

```
<bean id="cart"
      class="com.myapp.ShoppingCart"
      scope="session">
  <aop:scoped-proxy proxy-target-class="false" />
</bean>
```

In order to use the <aop:scoped-proxy> element, you must declare Spring's aop namespace in your XML configuration:

```
<?xml version="1.0" encoding="UTF-8"?>
<beans xmlns="http://www.springframework.org/schema/beans"
  xmlns:xsi="http://www.w3.org/2001/XMLSchema-instance"
  xmlns:aop="http://www.springframework.org/schema/aop"
  xsi:schemaLocation="
    http://www.springframework.org/schema/aop
    http://www.springframework.org/schema/aop/spring-aop.xsd
    http://www.springframework.org/schema/beans
    http://www.springframework.org/schema/beans/spring-beans.xsd">

  ...

</beans>
```

We'll talk more about Spring's aop namespace in chapter 4 when you work with Spring and aspect-oriented programming. For now, let's wrap up this chapter by looking at one more of Spring's advanced wiring options: Spring Expression Language.

3.5 *Runtime value injection*

When we talk about dependency injection and wiring, we're often talking about wiring a bean reference into a property or constructor argument of another bean. It's often about associating one object with another object.

But another side to bean wiring is when you wire a value into a bean property or into its constructor as an argument. You did a lot of value wiring in chapter 2, such as wiring the name of an album into the constructor or `title` property of a `BlankDisc` bean. For example, you might have wired up a `BlankDisc` like this:

```
@Bean
public CompactDisc sgtPeppers() {
  return new BlankDisc(
      "Sgt. Pepper's Lonely Hearts Club Band",
      "The Beatles");
}
```

Although this accomplished what you needed, setting the title and artist for the `BlankDisc` bean, it did so with values hard-coded in the configuration class. Likewise, if you had done this in XML, the values would have also been hard-coded:

```
<bean id="sgtPeppers"
      class="soundsystem.BlankDisc"
      c:_title="Sgt. Pepper's Lonely Hearts Club Band"
      c:_artist="The Beatles" />
```

Sometimes hard-coded values are fine. Other times, however, you may want to avoid hard-coded values and let the values be determined at runtime. For those cases, Spring offers two ways of evaluating values at runtime:

- Property placeholders
- The Spring Expression Language (SpEL)

You'll soon see that the application of these two techniques is similar, although their purposes and behavior are different. Let's start with a look at property placeholders, the simpler of the two, and then dig into the more powerful SpEL.

3.5.1 Injecting external values

The simplest way to resolve external values in Spring is to declare a property source and retrieve the properties via the Spring `Environment`. For example, the following listing shows a basic Spring configuration class that uses external properties to wire up a `BlankDisc` bean.

> **Listing 3.7 Using the @PropertySource annotation and Environment**

```
package com.soundsystem;
import org.springframework.beans.factory.annotation.Autowired;
import org.springframework.context.annotation.Bean;
import org.springframework.context.annotation.Configuration;
import org.springframework.context.annotation.PropertySource;
import org.springframework.core.env.Environment;

@Configuration
@PropertySource("classpath:/com/soundsystem/app.properties")    ◁── Declare a
 public class ExpressiveConfig {                                       property
                                                                      source
    @Autowired
    Environment env;

    @Bean
```

```
public BlankDisc disc() {
  return new BlankDisc(
      env.getProperty("disc.title"),          ◁— Retrieve property values
        env.getProperty("disc.artist"));
  }

}
```

In this example, @PropertySource references a file named app.properties in the classpath. It might look something like this:

```
disc.title=Sgt. Peppers Lonely Hearts Club Band
disc.artist=The Beatles
```

This properties file is loaded into Spring's Environment, from which it can be retrieved later. Meanwhile, in the disc() method, a new BlankDisc is created; its constructor arguments are resolved from the properties file by calling getProperty().

DIGGING INTO SPRING'S ENVIRONMENT

While we're on the subject of Environment, you might find it helpful to know that the getProperty() method shown in listing 3.7 isn't the only method you can use to fetch a property value. getProperty() is overloaded into four variations:

- String getProperty(String key)
- String getProperty(String key, String defaultValue)
- T getProperty(String key, Class<T> type)
- T getProperty(String key, Class<T> type, T defaultValue)

The first two forms of getProperty() always return a String value. You saw how to use the first form in listing 3.7. But you can tweak the @Bean method slightly to work with default values if the specified properties don't exist:

```
@Bean
public BlankDisc disc() {
return new BlankDisc(
    env.getProperty("disc.title", "Rattle and Hum"),
    env.getProperty("disc.artist", "U2"));
}
```

The second two forms of getProperty() work much like the first two, but they recognize that not all values may be Strings. For example, suppose you're retrieving a value representing the number of connections to maintain in a connection pool. If you receive a String value from the properties file, then you'll need to convert it to an Integer before you can use it. But using one of the overloaded getProperty() methods handles that conversion for you:

```
int connectionCount =
    env.getProperty("db.connection.count", Integer.class, 30);
```

A few more property-related methods are offered by Environment. If you use either of the getProperty() methods without specifying a default value, you'll receive null if the property isn't defined. If you want to require that the property be defined, you can use getRequiredProperty() like this:

```
@Bean
public BlankDisc disc() {
return new BlankDisc(
    env.getRequiredProperty("disc.title"),
    env.getRequiredProperty("disc.artist"));
}
```

Here, if either the disc.title property or the disc.artist property is undefined, an IllegalStateException will be thrown.

If you want to check for the existence of a property, you can call contains-Property() on Environment:

```
boolean titleExists = env.containsProperty("disc.title");
```

Finally, if you need to resolve a property into a Class, you can use the getProperty-AsClass() method:

```
Class<CompactDisc> cdClass =
    env.getPropertyAsClass("disc.class", CompactDisc.class);
```

Digressing a bit from the subject of properties, Environment also offers some methods for checking which profiles are active:

- String[] getActiveProfiles()—Returns an array of active profile names
- String[] getDefaultProfiles()—Returns an array of default profile names
- boolean acceptsProfiles(String... profiles)—Returns true if the environment supports the given profile(s)

You saw how to use the acceptsProfiles() method in listing 3.6. In that case, Environment was retrieved from ConditionContext, and the acceptsProfiles() method was used to ensure that a given bean's profile was in play before allowing the bean to be created. You often won't need the profile-focused methods from Environment, but it's good to know that they're available.

Retrieving properties directly from Environment is handy, especially when you're wiring beans in Java configuration. But Spring also offers the option of wiring properties with placeholder values that are resolved from a property source.

RESOLVING PROPERTY PLACEHOLDERS

Spring has always supported the option of externalizing properties into a properties file and then plugging them into Spring beans using placeholder values. In Spring wiring, placeholder values are property names wrapped with ${ ... }. As an example, you can resolve the constructor arguments for a BlankDisc in XML like this:

```
<bean id="sgtPeppers"
    class="soundsystem.BlankDisc"
    c:_title="${disc.title}"
    c:_artist="${disc.artist}" />
```

As shown here, the `title` constructor argument is given a value that's resolved from the property whose name is `disc.title`. And the `artist` argument is wired with the value of the property whose name is `disc.artist`. In this way, the XML configuration doesn't use any hard-coded values. Instead, the values are resolved from a source external to the configuration file. (We'll talk about how those properties are resolved in a moment.)

When relying on component-scanning and autowiring to create and initialize your application components, there's no configuration file or class where you can specify the placeholders. Instead, you can use the `@Value` annotation in much the same way as you might use the `@Autowired` annotation. In the `BlankDisc` class, for example, the constructor might be written like this:

```
public BlankDisc(
      @Value("${disc.title}") String title,
      @Value("${disc.artist}") String artist) {
  this.title = title;
  this.artist = artist;
}
```

In order to use placeholder values, you must configure either a `PropertyPlaceholder-Configurer` bean or a `PropertySourcesPlaceholderConfigurer` bean. Starting with Spring 3.1, `PropertySourcesPlaceholderConfigurer` is preferred because it resolves placeholders against the Spring `Environment` and its set of property sources.

The following `@Bean` method configures `PropertySourcesPlaceholderConfigurer` in Java configuration:

```
@Bean
public
static PropertySourcesPlaceholderConfigurer placeholderConfigurer() {
  return new PropertySourcesPlaceholderConfigurer();
}
```

If you'd rather use XML configuration, the `<context:property-placeholder>` element from Spring's `context` namespace will give you a `PropertySourcesPlaceholder-Configurer` bean:

```
<?xml version="1.0" encoding="UTF-8"?>
<beans xmlns="http://www.springframework.org/schema/beans"
  xmlns:xsi="http://www.w3.org/2001/XMLSchema-instance"
  xmlns:context="http://www.springframework.org/schema/context"
  xsi:schemaLocation="
    http://www.springframework.org/schema/beans
    http://www.springframework.org/schema/beans/spring-beans.xsd
    http://www.springframework.org/schema/context
    http://www.springframework.org/schema/context/spring-context.xsd">

  <context:property-placeholder />

</beans>
```

Resolving external properties is one way to defer value resolution until runtime, but its focus is finely tuned on resolving properties, by name, from Spring's `Environment` and property sources. Spring Expression Language, on the other hand, offers a more general way of calculating values for injection at runtime.

3.5.2 *Wiring with the Spring Expression Language*

Spring 3 introduced Spring Expression Language (SpEL), a powerful yet succinct way of wiring values into a bean's properties or constructor arguments using expressions that are evaluated at runtime. Using SpEL, you can pull off amazing feats of bean wiring that would be much more difficult (or in some cases impossible) using other wiring techniques.

SpEL has a lot of tricks up its sleeves, including the following:

- The ability to reference beans by their IDs
- Invoking methods and accessing properties on objects
- Mathematical, relational, and logical operations on values
- Regular expression matching
- Collection manipulation

As you'll see later in this book, SpEL can also be used for purposes other than dependency injection. Spring Security, for example, supports defining security constraints using SpEL expressions. And if you're using Thymeleaf templates as the views in your Spring MVC application, those templates can use SpEL expressions to reference model data.

To get started, let's consider a few examples of SpEL expressions and see how to wire them into beans. Then we'll take a deeper dive into some of SpEL's primitive expressions that can be pieced together into more powerful expressions.

A FEW SpEL EXAMPLES

SpEL is such a flexible expression language that it would be impossible to show you all the ways it can be used in the space allowed in this book. But there is enough room to show you a few basic examples from which you can draw inspiration for your own expressions.

The first thing to know is that SpEL expressions are framed with #{ ... }, much as property placeholders are framed with ${ ... }. What follows is possibly one of the simplest SpEL expressions you can write:

```
#{1}
```

Stripping away the #{ ... } markers, what's left is the body of a SpEL expression, which is a numeric constant. It probably won't surprise you much to learn that this expression evaluates to the numeric value of 1.

Of course, you're not likely to use such a simple expression in a real application. You're more likely to build up more interesting expressions, such as this one:

```
#{T(System).currentTimeMillis()}
```

Ultimately this expression evaluates to the current time in milliseconds at the moment when the expression is evaluated. The `T()` operator evaluates `java.lang.System` as a type so that the `staticcurrentTimeMillis()` method can be invoked.

SpEL expressions can also refer to other beans or properties on those beans. For example, the following expression evaluates to the value of the `artist` property on a bean whose ID is `sgtPeppers`:

```
#{sgtPeppers.artist}
```

You can also refer to system properties via the `systemProperties` object:

```
#{systemProperties['disc.title']}
```

These are just a few basic examples of SpEL. You'll see more before this chapter ends. But first, let's consider how you might use these expressions during bean wiring.

When injecting properties and constructor arguments on beans that are created via component-scanning, you can use the `@Value` annotation, much as you saw earlier with property placeholders. Rather than use a placeholder expression, however, you use a SpEL expression. For example, here's what the `BlankDisc` constructor might look like, drawing the album title and artist from system properties:

```
public BlankDisc(
      @Value("#{systemProperties['disc.title']}") String title,
      @Value("#{systemProperties['disc.artist']}") String artist) {
  this.title = title;
  this.artist = artist;
}
```

In XML configuration, you can pass in the SpEL expression to the `value` attribute of `<property>` or `<constructor-arg>`, or as the value given to a p-namespace or c-namespace entry. For example, here's the XML declaration of the `BlankDisc` bean that has its constructor arguments set from a SpEL expression:

```
<bean id="sgtPeppers"
      class="soundsystem.BlankDisc"
      c:_title="#{systemProperties['disc.title']}"
      c:_artist="#{systemProperties['disc.artist']}" />
```

Now that we've looked at a few simple examples and how to inject values resolved from SpEL expressions, let's go over some of the primitive expressions supported in SpEL.

EXPRESSING LITERAL VALUES

You've already seen an example of using SpEL to express a literal integer value. But it can also be used for floating-point numbers, `String` values, and Boolean values.

Here's an example of a SpEL expression that is a floating-point value:

```
#{3.14159}
```

Numbers can also be expressed in scientific notation. For example, the following expression evaluates to 98,700:

```
#{9.87E4}
```

A SpEL expression can also evaluate literal `String` values, such as

```
#{'Hello'}
```

Finally, Boolean literals `true` and `false` are evaluated to their Boolean value. For example,

```
#{false}
```

Working with literal values in SpEL is mundane. After all, you don't need SpEL to set an integer property to 1 or a Boolean property to `false`. I admit there's not much use in SpEL expressions that only contain literal values. But remember that more interesting SpEL expressions are composed of simpler expressions, so it's good to know how to work with literal values in SpEL. You'll eventually need them as you compose more complex expressions.

REFERENCING BEANS, PROPERTIES, AND METHODS

Another basic thing that a SpEL expression can do is reference another bean by its ID. For example, you could use SpEL to wire one bean into another bean's property by using the bean ID as the SpEL expression (in this case, a bean whose ID is `sgtPeppers`):

```
#{sgtPeppers}
```

Now let's say that you want to refer to the `artist` property of the `sgtPeppers` bean in an expression:

```
#{sgtPeppers.artist}
```

The first part of the expression body refers to the bean whose ID is `sgtPeppers`. What follows the period delimiter is a reference to the `artist` property.

In addition to referencing a bean's properties, you can also call methods on a bean. For example, suppose you have another bean whose ID is `artistSelector`. You can call that bean's `selectArtist()` method in a SpEL expression like this:

```
#{artistSelector.selectArtist()}
```

You can also call methods on the value returned from the invoked method. For example, if `selectArtist()` returns a `String`, you can call `toUpperCase()` to make the entire artist name uppercase lettering:

```
#{artistSelector.selectArtist().toUpperCase()}
```

This will work fine, as long as `selectArtist()` doesn't return `null`. To guard against a `NullPointerException`, you can use the type-safe operator:

```
#{artistSelector.selectArtist()?.toUpperCase()}
```

Instead of a lonely dot (.) to access the `toUpperCase()` method, now you're using the `?.` operator. This operator makes sure the item to its left isn't `null` before accessing the thing on its right. So, if `selectArtist()` returns `null`, then SpEL won't even try to invoke `toUpperCase()`. The expression will evaluate to `null`.

WORKING WITH TYPES IN EXPRESSIONS

The key to working with class-scoped methods and constants in SpEL is to use the `T()` operator. For example, to express Java's `Math` class in SpEL, you need to use the `T()` operator like this:

```
T(java.lang.Math)
```

The result of the `T()` operator, as shown here, is a `Class` object that represents `java.lang.Math`. You can even wire it into a bean property of type `Class`, if you want. But the real value of the `T()` operator is that it gives you access to static methods and constants on the evaluated type.

For example, suppose you need to wire the value of pi into a bean property. The following SpEL expression does the trick:

```
T(java.lang.Math).PI
```

Similarly, static methods can be invoked in the type resolved with the `T()` operator. You've seen an example of using `T()` to make a call to `System.currentTimeMillis()`. Here's another example that evaluates to a random value between 0 and 1:

```
T(java.lang.Math).random()
```

SpEL OPERATORS

SpEL offers several operators that you can apply on values in SpEL expressions. Table 3.1 summarizes these operators.

Table 3.1 SpEL operators for manipulating expression values

Operator type	Operators
Arithmetic	+, -, *, /, %, ^
Comparison	<, lt, >, gt, ==, eq, <=, le, >=, ge
Logical	and, or, not, |
Conditional	?: (ternary), ?: (Elvis)
Regular expression	`matches`

As a simple example of using one of these operators, consider the following SpEL expression:

```
#{2 * T(java.lang.Math).PI * circle.radius}
```

Not only is this a great example of using SpEL's multiplication operator (`*`), but it also shows how you can compose simpler expressions into a more complex expression. Here the value of pi is multiplied by 2, and that result is multiplied by the value of the `radius` property of a bean whose ID is `circle`. Essentially, it evaluates to the circumference of the circle defined in the `circle` bean.

Similarly, you can use the carat symbol (^) in an expression to calculate a circle's area:

```
#{T(java.lang.Math).PI * circle.radius ^ 2}
```

The carat symbol is the power-of operator. In this case, it's used to calculate the square of the circle's radius.

When working with `String` values, the + operator performs concatenation, just as in Java:

```
#{disc.title + ' by ' + disc.artist}
```

SpEL also offers comparison operators for comparing values in an expression. Notice in table 3.1 that the comparison operators come in two forms: symbolic and textual. For the most part, the symbolic operators are equivalent to their textual counterparts, and you're welcome to use whichever one suits you best.

For example, to compare two numbers for equality, you can use the double-equal (==) operator:

```
#{counter.total == 100}
```

Or you can use the textual `eq` operator:

```
#{counter.total eq 100}
```

Either way, the result is the same. The expression evaluates to a Boolean: `true` if `counter.total` is equal to `100` or `false` if it's not.

SpEL also offers a ternary operator that works much like Java's ternary operator. For example, the following expression evaluates to the `String` "Winner!" if `scoreboard.score > 1000` or "Loser" if not:

```
#{scoreboard.score > 1000 ? "Winner!" : "Loser"}
```

A common use of the ternary operator is to check for a `null` value and offer a default value in place of the `null`. For example, the following expression evaluates to the value of `disc.title` if it isn't `null`. If `disc.title` is `null`, then the expression evaluates to "Rattle and Hum".

```
#{disc.title ?: 'Rattle and Hum'}
```

This expression is commonly referred to as the *Elvis* operator. This strange name comes from using the operator as an emoticon, where the question mark appears to form the shape of Elvis Presley's hair style.[2]

EVALUATING REGULAR EXPRESSIONS

When working with text, it's sometimes useful to check whether that text matches a certain pattern. SpEL supports pattern matching in expressions with its `matches` operator. The `matches` operator attempts to apply a regular expression (given as its right-side argument) against a `String` value (given as the left-side argument). The result of

---

[2] Don't blame me. I didn't come up with that name. But you gotta admit—it does kinda look like Elvis's hair.

a `matches` evaluation is a Boolean value: `true` if the value matches the regular expression, and `false` otherwise.

To demonstrate, suppose you want to check whether a `String` contains a valid email address. In that case, you can apply `matches` like this:

```
#{admin.email matches '[a-zA-Z0-9._%+-]+@[a-zA-Z0-9.-]+\\.com'}
```

Exploring the mysteries of the enigmatic regular-expression syntax is outside the scope of this book. And I realize that the regular expression given here isn't robust enough to cover all scenarios. But for the purposes of showing off the `matches` operator, it'll have to suffice.

EVALUATING COLLECTIONS

Some of SpEL's most amazing tricks involve working with collections and arrays. The most basic thing you can do is reference a single element from a list:

```
#{jukebox.songs[4].title}
```

This evaluates to the `title` property of the fifth (zero-based) element from the `songs` collection property on the bean whose ID is `jukebox`.

To spice things up a bit, I suppose you could randomly select a song from the jukebox:

```
#{jukebox.songs[T(java.lang.Math).random() *
                     jukebox.songs.size()].title}
```

As it turns out, the `[]` operator used to fetch an indexed element from a collection or array can also be used to fetch a single character from a `String`. For example,

```
#{'This is a test'[3]}
```

This references the fourth (zero-based) character in the `String`, or *s*.

SpEL also offers a selection operator (`.?[]`) to filter a collection into a subset of the collection. As a demonstration, suppose you want a list of all songs in the jukebox where the `artist` property is `Aerosmith`. The following expression uses the selection operator to arrive at the list of available Aerosmith songs:

```
#{jukebox.songs.?[artist eq 'Aerosmith']}
```

As you can see, the selection operator accepts another expression within its square brackets. As SpEL iterates over the list of songs, it evaluates that expression for each entry in the songs collection. If the expression evaluates to `true`, then the entry is carried over into the new collection. Otherwise it's left out of the new collection. In this case, the inner expression checks to see if the song's `artist` property equals `Aerosmith`.

SpEL also offers two other selection operations: `.^[]` for selecting the first matching entry and `.$[]` for selecting the last matching entry. To demonstrate, consider this expression, which finds the first song in the list whose `artist` property is `Aerosmith`:

```
#{jukebox.songs.^[artist eq 'Aerosmith']}
```

Finally, SpEL offers a projection operator (`.![]`) to project properties from the elements in the collection onto a new collection. As an example, suppose you don't want a collection of the song objects, but a collection of all the song titles. The following expression projects the `title` property into a new collection of `Strings`:

```
#{jukebox.songs.![title]}
```

Naturally, the projection operator can be combined with any of SpEL's other operators, including the selection operator. For example, you could use this expression to obtain a list of all of Aerosmith's songs:

```
#{jukebox.songs.?[artist eq 'Aerosmith'].![title]}
```

We've only scratched the surface of what SpEL can do. There will be more opportunities to tinker with SpEL throughout this book, especially when defining security constraints.

For now, however, let me wrap up this discussion of SpEL with a warning. SpEL expressions are handy and powerful ways to dynamically inject values into Spring beans. It can be tempting to get crafty and write very involved expressions. But take care not to get *too* clever with your expressions. The more clever your expressions become, the more important it will be to test them. Ultimately, SpEL expressions are given as `String` values and can be difficult to test. For that reason, I encourage you to keep your expressions simple so that testing isn't as big a concern.

3.6 Summary

We've covered a lot of ground in this chapter. In doing so, we've built on the foundational bean-wiring techniques explored in chapter 2 with some powerful advanced wiring tricks.

We started by using Spring profiles to address a common problem where Spring beans must vary across deployment environments. By resolving environment-specific beans at runtime by matching them against one or more active profiles, Spring makes it possible to deploy the same deployment unit across multiple environments without rebuilding.

Profiled beans are one way to conditionally create beans at runtime, but Spring 4 offers a more generic way to declare beans that are created (or not created) depending on the outcome of a given condition. The `@Conditional` annotation, paired with an implementation of Spring's `Condition` interface, offers developers a powerful and flexible mechanism for conditionally creating beans.

We also looked at two techniques for resolving autowiring ambiguity: primary beans and qualifiers. Although designating a bean as a primary bean is simple, it's also limited, so we discussed using qualifiers to narrow the list of autowire candidates to a single bean. In addition, you saw how to create custom qualifier annotations that describe a bean by its traits.

Although most Spring beans are created as singletons, there are times when other creation strategies are more appropriate. Out of the box, Spring allows beans to be created as singletons, prototypes, request-scoped, or session-scoped. When declaring request- or session-scoped beans, you also learned how to control the way scoped proxies are created, either as class-based proxies or interface-based proxies.

Finally, we looked at the Spring Expression Language, which gives you a way to resolve values to be injected into bean properties at runtime.

With a strong foundation in bean wiring established, we'll now turn our attention to aspect-oriented programming (AOP). Much as dependency injection helps decouple components from the other components they collaborate with, AOP helps decouple your application components from tasks that span multiple components in an application. In the next chapter, we'll dig into creating and working with aspects in Spring.

Aspect-oriented Spring

4

This chapter covers

- Basics of aspect-oriented programming
- Creating aspects from POJOs
- Using `@AspectJ` annotations
- Injecting dependencies into AspectJ aspects

As I'm writing this chapter, summertime is upon Texas (where I reside). And in Texas, it's very common to go through several days of record-high temperatures. It's hot. In weather like this, air conditioning is a must. But the downside of air conditioning is that it uses electricity, and electricity costs money. There's little we can do to avoid paying for a cool and comfortable home. That's because every home has a meter that measures every kilowatt, and once a month someone comes by to read that meter so that the electric company knows how much to bill us.

Now imagine what would happen if the meter went away and nobody came by to measure our electricity usage. Suppose it was up to each homeowner to contact the electric company and report their electricity usage. Although it's possible that some obsessive homeowners would keep careful records of how much they used their lights, televisions, and air conditioning, most wouldn't bother. Electricity on the honor system might be great for consumers, but it would be less than ideal for the electric companies.

Monitoring electricity consumption is an important function, but it isn't foremost in most homeowners' minds. Mowing the lawn, vacuuming the carpet, and cleaning the bathroom are the kinds of things that homeowners are actively involved in. Monitoring the amount of electricity used by their house is a passive event from the homeowner's point of view. (Although it'd be great if mowing the lawn was also a passive event—especially on these hot days.)

Some functions of software systems are like the electric meters on our homes. The functions need to be applied at multiple points within the application, but it's undesirable to explicitly call them at every point. Logging, security, and transaction management are important, but should they be activities that your application objects are actively participating in? Or would it be better for your application objects to focus on the business domain problems they're designed for, and to leave certain aspects to be handled by someone else?

In software development, functions that span multiple points of an application are called *cross-cutting concerns*. Typically, these cross-cutting concerns are conceptually separate from (but often embedded directly within) the application's business logic. Separating these cross-cutting concerns from the business logic is where aspect-oriented programming (AOP) goes to work.

In chapter 2, you learned how to use dependency injection to manage and configure application objects. Whereas DI helps you decouple application objects from each other, AOP helps you decouple cross-cutting concerns from the objects they affect.

Logging is a common example of the application of aspects, but it's not the only thing aspects are good for. Throughout this book, you'll see several practical applications of aspects, including declarative transactions, security, and caching.

This chapter explores Spring's support for aspects, including how to declare regular classes to be aspects and how to use annotations to create aspects. In addition, you'll see how AspectJ—another popular AOP implementation—can complement Spring's AOP framework. But first, before we get carried away with transactions, security, and caching, let's see how aspects are implemented in Spring, starting with a primer on a few of AOP's fundamentals.

4.1   *What is aspect-oriented programming?*

As stated earlier, aspects help to modularize cross-cutting concerns. In short, a cross-cutting concern can be described as any functionality that affects multiple points of an application. Security, for example, is a cross-cutting concern, in that many methods in an application can have security rules applied to them. Figure 4.1 gives a visual depiction of cross-cutting concerns.

This figure represents a typical application that's broken down into modules. Each module's main concern is to provide services for its particular domain. But each module also requires similar ancillary functionality, such as security and transaction management.

A common object-oriented technique for reusing common functionality is to apply inheritance or delegation. But inheritance can lead to a brittle object hierarchy if the same base class is used throughout an application, and delegation can be cumbersome because complicated calls to the delegate object may be required.

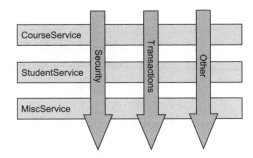

Aspects offer an alternative to inheritance and delegation that can be cleaner in many circumstances. With AOP, you still define the common functionality in one

Figure 4.1 Aspects modularize cross-cutting concerns, applying logic that spans multiple application objects.

place, but you can declaratively define how and where this functionality is applied without having to modify the class to which you're applying the new feature. Cross-cutting concerns can now be modularized into special classes called *aspects*. This has two benefits. First, the logic for each concern is in one place, as opposed to being scattered all over the code base. Second, your service modules are cleaner because they only contain code for their primary concern (or core functionality), and secondary concerns have been moved to aspects.

4.1.1 Defining AOP terminology

Like most technologies, AOP has its own jargon. Aspects are often described in terms of advice, pointcuts, and join points. Figure 4.2 illustrates how these concepts are tied together.

Unfortunately, many of the terms used to describe AOP features aren't intuitive. Nevertheless, they're now part of the AOP idiom, and in order to understand AOP, you must know these terms. Before you walk the walk, you have to learn to talk the talk.

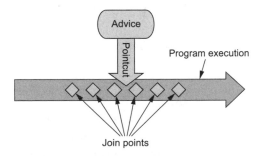

Figure 4.2 An aspect's functionality (advice) is woven into a program's execution at one or more join points.

ADVICE

When a meter reader shows up at your house, his purpose is to report the number of kilowatt hours back to the electric company. Sure, he has a list of houses that he must visit, and the information he reports is important. But the actual act of recording electricity usage is the meter reader's main job.

Likewise, aspects have a purpose—a job they're meant to do. In AOP terms, the job of an aspect is called *advice*.

Advice defines both the *what* and the *when* of an aspect. In addition to describing the job that an aspect will perform, advice addresses the question of when to perform the job. Should it be applied before a method is invoked? After the method is invoked? Both before and after method invocation? Or should it be applied only if a method throws an exception?

Spring aspects can work with five kinds of advice:

- *Before*—The advice functionality takes place before the advised method is invoked.
- *After*—The advice functionality takes place after the advised method completes, regardless of the outcome.
- *After-returning*—The advice functionality takes place after the advised method successfully completes.
- *After-throwing*—The advice functionality takes place after the advised method throws an exception.
- *Around*—The advice wraps the advised method, providing some functionality before and after the advised method is invoked.

JOIN POINTS

An electric company services several houses, perhaps even an entire city. Each house has an electric meter that needs to be read, so each house is a potential target for the meter reader. The meter reader could potentially read all kinds of devices, but to do her job, she needs to target electric meters that are attached to houses.

In the same way, your application may have thousands of opportunities for advice to be applied. These opportunities are known as join points. A *join point* is a point in the execution of the application where an aspect can be plugged in. This point could be a method being called, an exception being thrown, or even a field being modified. These are the points where your aspect's code can be inserted into the normal flow of your application to add new behavior.

POINTCUTS

It's not possible for any one meter reader to visit all houses serviced by the electric company. Instead, each one is assigned a subset of all the houses to visit. Likewise, an aspect doesn't necessarily advise all join points in an application. *Pointcuts* help narrow down the join points advised by an aspect.

If advice defines the *what* and *when* of aspects, then pointcuts define the *where*. A pointcut definition matches one or more join points at which advice should be woven. Often you specify these pointcuts using explicit class and method names or through regular expressions that define matching class and method name patterns. Some AOP frameworks allow you to create dynamic pointcuts that determine whether to apply advice based on runtime decisions, such as the value of method parameters.

ASPECTS

When a meter reader starts his day, he knows both what he's supposed to do (report electricity usage) and which houses to collect that information from. Thus he knows everything he needs to know to get his job done.

An *aspect* is the merger of advice and pointcuts. Taken together, advice and pointcuts define everything there is to know about an aspect—what it does and where and when it does it.

INTRODUCTIONS

An *introduction* allows you to add new methods or attributes to existing classes. For example, you could create an `Auditable` advice class that keeps the state of when an object was last modified. This could be as simple as having one method, `setLast-Modified(Date)`, and an instance variable to hold this state. The new method and instance variable can then be introduced to existing classes without having to change them, giving them new behavior and state.

WEAVING

Weaving is the process of applying aspects to a target object to create a new proxied object. The aspects are woven into the target object at the specified join points. The weaving can take place at several points in the target object's lifetime:

- *Compile time*—Aspects are woven in when the target class is compiled. This requires a special compiler. AspectJ's weaving compiler weaves aspects this way.
- *Class load time*—Aspects are woven in when the target class is loaded into the JVM. This requires a special `ClassLoader` that enhances the target class's byte-code before the class is introduced into the application. AspectJ 5's *load-time weaving* (LTW) support weaves aspects this way.
- *Runtime*—Aspects are woven in sometime during the execution of the application. Typically, an AOP container dynamically generates a proxy object that delegates to the target object while weaving in the aspects. This is how Spring AOP aspects are woven.

That's a lot of new terms to get to know. Revisiting figure 4.1, you can now see how advice contains the cross-cutting behavior that needs to be applied to an application's objects. The join points are all the points within the execution flow of the application that are candidates to have advice applied. The pointcut defines where (at what join points) that advice is applied. The key concept you should take from this is that pointcuts define which join points get advised.

Now that you're familiar with some basic AOP terminology, let's see how these core AOP concepts are implemented in Spring.

4.1.2 *Spring's AOP support*

Not all AOP frameworks are created equal. They may differ in how rich their join point models are. Some allow you to apply advice at the field-modification level, whereas others only expose the join points related to method invocations. They may also differ in how and when they weave the aspects. Whatever the case, the ability to create pointcuts that define the join points at which aspects should be woven is what makes it an AOP framework.

Because this is a Spring book, we'll focus on Spring AOP. Even so, there's a lot of synergy between the Spring and AspectJ projects, and the AOP support in Spring borrows a lot from the AspectJ project.

Spring's support for AOP comes in four styles:

- Classic Spring proxy-based AOP
- Pure-POJO aspects
- `@AspectJ` annotation-driven aspects
- Injected AspectJ aspects (available in all versions of Spring)

The first three styles are all variations on Spring's own AOP implementation. Spring AOP is built around dynamic proxies. Consequently, Spring's AOP support is limited to method interception.

The term *classic* usually carries a good connotation. Classic cars, classic golf tournaments, and classic Coca-Cola are all good things. But Spring's classic AOP programming model isn't so great. Oh, it was good in its day. But now Spring supports much cleaner and easier ways to work with aspects. When held up against simple declarative AOP and annotation-based AOP, Spring's classic AOP seems bulky and overcomplicated. Therefore, I won't be covering *classic* Spring AOP.

With Spring's `aop` namespace, you can turn pure POJOs into aspects. In truth, those POJOs will only supply methods that are called in reaction to a pointcut. Unfortunately, this technique requires XML configuration, but it's an easy way to declaratively turn any object into an aspect.

Spring borrows AspectJ's aspects to enable annotation-driven AOP. Under the covers, it's still Spring's proxy-based AOP, but the programming model is almost identical to writing full-blown AspectJ annotated aspects. The perk of this AOP style is that it can be done without any XML configuration.

If your AOP needs exceed simple method interception (constructor or property interception, for example), you'll want to consider implementing aspects in AspectJ. In that case, the fourth style listed will enable you to inject values into AspectJ-driven aspects.

We'll explore more of these Spring AOP techniques in this chapter. But before we get started, it's important to understand a few key points of Spring's AOP framework.

SPRING ADVICE IS WRITTEN IN JAVA

All the advice you create in Spring is written in a standard Java class. That way, you get the benefit of developing your aspects in the same integrated development environment (IDE) you'd use for normal Java development. The pointcuts that define where advice should be applied may be specified with annotations or configured in a Spring XML configuration, but either will be familiar to Java developers.

Contrast this with AspectJ. Although AspectJ now supports annotation-based aspects, it also comes as a language extension to Java. This approach has benefits and drawbacks. By having an AOP-specific language, you get more power and fine-grained control, as well as a richer AOP toolset. But you're required to learn a new tool and syntax to accomplish this.

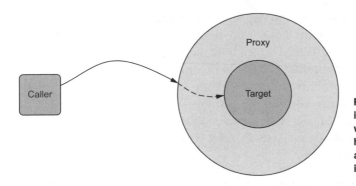

Figure 4.3 Spring aspects are implemented as proxies that wrap the target object. The proxy handles method calls, performs additional aspect logic, and then invokes the target method.

SPRING ADVISES OBJECTS AT RUNTIME

In Spring, aspects are woven into Spring-managed beans at runtime by wrapping them with a proxy class. As illustrated in figure 4.3, the proxy class poses as the target bean, intercepting advised method calls and forwarding those calls to the target bean. Between the time when the proxy intercepts the method call and the time when it invokes the target bean's method, the proxy performs the aspect logic.

Spring doesn't create a proxied object until that proxied bean is needed by the application. If you're using an `ApplicationContext`, the proxied objects will be created when it loads all the beans from the `BeanFactory`. Because Spring creates proxies at runtime, you don't need a special compiler to weave aspects in Spring's AOP.

SPRING ONLY SUPPORTS METHOD JOIN POINTS

As mentioned earlier, multiple join-point models are available through various AOP implementations. Because it's based on dynamic proxies, Spring only supports method join points. This is in contrast to some other AOP frameworks, such as AspectJ and JBoss, which provide field and constructor join points in addition to method pointcuts. Spring's lack of field pointcuts prevents you from creating very fine-grained advice, such as intercepting updates to an object's field. And without constructor pointcuts, there's no way to apply advice when a bean is instantiated.

But method interception should suit most, if not all, of your needs. If you find yourself in need of more than method interception, you'll want to complement Spring AOP with AspectJ.

Now you have a general idea of what AOP does and how it's supported by Spring. It's time to get your hands dirty creating aspects in Spring. Let's start with Spring's declarative AOP model.

4.2   *Selecting join points with pointcuts*

As mentioned before, pointcuts are used to pinpoint where an aspect's advice should be applied. Along with an aspect's advice, pointcuts are among the most fundamental elements of an aspect. Therefore, it's important to know how to write pointcuts.

In Spring AOP, pointcuts are defined using AspectJ's pointcut expression language. If you're already familiar with AspectJ, then defining pointcuts in Spring should feel natural. But in case you're new to AspectJ, this section will serve as a quick lesson on writing AspectJ-style pointcuts. For a more detailed discussion of AspectJ and AspectJ's pointcut expression language, I strongly recommend Ramnivas Laddad's *AspectJ in Action, Second Edition* (Manning, 2009, www.manning.com/laddad2/).

The most important thing to know about AspectJ pointcuts as they pertain to Spring AOP is that Spring only supports a subset of the pointcut designators available in AspectJ. Recall that Spring AOP is proxy-based, and certain pointcut expressions aren't relevant to proxy-based AOP. Table 4.1 lists the AspectJ pointcut designators that are supported in Spring AOP.

Table 4.1   Spring uses AspectJ's pointcut expression language to define Spring aspects.

AspectJ designator	Description
args()	Limits join-point matches to the execution of methods whose arguments are instances of the given types
@args()	Limits join-point matches to the execution of methods whose arguments are annotated with the given annotation types
execution()	Matches join points that are method executions
this()	Limits join-point matches to those where the bean reference of the AOP proxy is of a given type
target()	Limits join-point matches to those where the target object is of a given type
@target()	Limits matching to join points where the class of the executing object has an annotation of the given type
within()	Limits matching to join points within certain types
@within()	Limits matching to join points within types that have the given annotation (the execution of methods declared in types with the given annotation when using Spring AOP)
@annotation	Limits join-point matches to those where the subject of the join point has the given annotation

Attempting to use any of AspectJ's other designators will result in an `IllegalArgument-Exception` being thrown.

As you browse through the supported designators, note that the `execution` designator is the only one that actually performs matches. The other designators are used to limit those matches. This means `execution` is the primary designator you'll use in every pointcut definition you write. You'll use the other designators to constrain the pointcut's reach.

4.2.1   *Writing pointcuts*

To demonstrate aspects in Spring, you need something to be the subject of the aspect's pointcuts. For that purpose, let's define a `Performance` interface:

```
package concert;

public interface Performance {
  public void perform();
}
```

Performance represents any kind of live performance, such as a stage play, a movie, or a concert. Let's say that you want to write an aspect that triggers off Performance's perform() method. Figure 4.4 shows a pointcut expression that can be used to apply advice whenever the perform() method is executed.

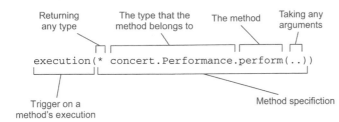

Figure 4.4 Selecting Performance's perform() method with an AspectJ pointcut expression

You use the execution() designator to select Performance's perform() method. The method specification starts with an asterisk, which indicates that you don't care what type the method returns. Then you specify the fully qualified class name and the name of the method you want to select. For the method's parameter list, you use the double dot (..), indicating that the pointcut should select any perform() method, no matter what the argument list is.

Now let's suppose that you want to confine the reach of that pointcut to only the concert package. In that case, you can limit the match by tacking on a within() designator, as shown in figure 4.5.

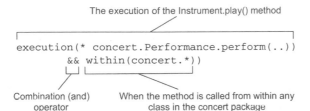

Figure 4.5 Limiting a pointcut's reach by using the within() designator

Note that you use the && operator to combine the execution() and within() designators in an "and" relationship (where both designators must match for the pointcut to match). Similarly, you could use the || operator to indicate an "or" relationship. And the ! operator can be used to negate the effect of a designator.

Because ampersands have special meaning in XML, you're free to use and in place of && when specifying pointcuts in a Spring XML-based configuration. Likewise, or and not can be used in place of || and !, respectively.

4.2.2 *Selecting beans in pointcuts*

In addition to the designators listed in table 4.1, Spring adds a `bean()` designator that lets you identify beans by their ID in a pointcut expression. `bean()` takes a bean ID or name as an argument and limits the pointcut's effect to that specific bean.

For example, consider the following pointcut:

```
execution(* concert.Performance.perform())
      and bean('woodstock')
```

Here you're saying that you want to apply aspect advice to the execution of `Performance`'s `perform()` method, but limited to the bean whose ID is `woodstock`.

Narrowing a pointcut to a specific bean may be valuable in some cases, but you can also use negation to apply an aspect to all beans that don't have a specific ID:

```
execution(* concert.Performance.perform())
      and !bean('woodstock')
```

In this case, the aspect's advice will be woven into all beans whose ID isn't `woodstock`.

Now that we've covered the basics of writing pointcuts, let's see how to write the advice and declare the aspects that use those pointcuts.

4.3 *Creating annotated aspects*

A key feature introduced in AspectJ 5 is the ability to use annotations to create aspects. Prior to AspectJ 5, writing AspectJ aspects involved learning a Java language extension. But AspectJ's annotation-oriented model makes it simple to turn any class into an aspect by sprinkling a few annotations around.

You've already defined the `Performance` interface as the subject of your aspect's pointcuts. Now let's use AspectJ annotations to create an aspect.

4.3.1 *Defining an aspect*

A performance isn't a performance without an audience. Or is it? When you think about it from the perspective of a performance, an audience is important but isn't central to the function of the performance itself; it's a separate concern. Therefore, it makes sense to define the audience as an aspect that's applied to a performance.

The following listing shows the `Audience` class that defines the aspect you'll need.

Listing 4.1 Audience class: an aspect that watches a performance

```
package concert;
import org.aspectj.lang.annotation.AfterReturning;
import org.aspectj.lang.annotation.AfterThrowing;
import org.aspectj.lang.annotation.Aspect;
import org.aspectj.lang.annotation.Before;

@Aspect
public class Audience {

  @Before("execution(** concert.Performance.perform(..))")    ◁┘ Before
  public void silenceCellPhones() {                              performance
```

```
    System.out.println("Silencing cell phones");
  }

  @Before("execution(** concert.Performance.perform(..))")   ◁─┐  Before
  public void takeSeats() {                                       performance
    System.out.println("Taking seats");
  }

  @AfterReturning("execution(** concert.Performance.perform(..))")   ◁─┐
  public void applause() {                                              After
    System.out.println("CLAP CLAP CLAP!!!");                            performance
  }

  @AfterThrowing("execution(** concert.Performance.perform(..))")   ◁─┐
  public void demandRefund() {                                          After bad
    System.out.println("Demanding a refund");                           performance
  }

}
```

Notice how the `Audience` class is annotated with `@Aspect`. This annotation indicates that `Audience` isn't just any POJO—it's an aspect. And throughout the `Audience` class are methods that are annotated to define the specifics of the aspect.

`Audience` has four methods that define things an audience might do as it observes a performance. Before the performance, the audience should take their seats (`takeSeats()`) and silence their cell phones (`silenceCellPhones()`). If the performance goes well, the audience should applaud (`applause()`). But if the performance fails to meet the audience's expectations, then the audience should demand a refund (`demandRefund()`).

As you can see, those methods are annotated with advice annotations to indicate when those methods should be called. AspectJ provides five annotations for defining advice, as listed in table 4.2.

Table 4.2 Spring uses AspectJ annotations to declare advice methods.

Annotation	Advice
`@After`	The advice method is called after the advised method returns or throws an exception.
`@AfterReturning`	The advice method is called after the advised method returns.
`@AfterThrowing`	The advice method is called after the advised method throws an exception.
`@Around`	The advice method wraps the advised method.
`@Before`	The advice method is called before the advised method is called.

The `Audience` class makes use of three out of the five advice annotations. The `takeSeats()` and `silenceCellPhones()` methods are both annotated with `@Before`, indicating that they should be called before a performance is performed. The `applause()` method is annotated with `@AfterReturning` so that it will be called after a performance returns successfully. And the @AfterThrowing annotation is placed on demandRefund() so that it will be called if any exceptions are thrown during a performance.

You've probably noticed that all of these annotations are given a pointcut expression as a value. And you may have noticed that it's the same pointcut expression on all four methods. They could each be given a different pointcut expression, but this particular pointcut suits your needs for all the advice methods. Taking a closer look at the pointcut expression given to the advice annotations, you'll see that it triggers on the execution of the perform() method on a Performance.

It's a shame that you had to repeat that same pointcut expression four times. Duplication like this doesn't feel right. It'd be nice if you could define the pointcut once and then reference it every time you need it.

Fortunately, there's a way: the @Pointcut annotation defines a reusable pointcut within an @AspectJ aspect. The next listing shows the Audience aspect, updated to use @Pointcut.

Listing 4.2 Declaring a frequently used pointcut expression with @Pointcut

```java
package concert;
import org.aspectj.lang.annotation.AfterReturning;
import org.aspectj.lang.annotation.AfterThrowing;
import org.aspectj.lang.annotation.Aspect;
import org.aspectj.lang.annotation.Before;
import org.aspectj.lang.annotation.Pointcut;

@Aspect
public class Audience {

  @Pointcut("execution(** concert.Performance.perform(..))")    ← Define named pointcut
  public void performance() {}

  @Before("performance()")                          ←
  public void silenceCellPhones() {                      Before performance
    System.out.println("Silencing cell phones");
  }

  @Before("performance()")                          ←
  public void takeSeats() {
    System.out.println("Taking seats");
  }

  @AfterReturning("performance()")        ←————————— After performance
  public void applause() {
    System.out.println("CLAP CLAP CLAP!!!");
  }

  @AfterThrowing("performance()")         ←————————— After bad performance
  public void demandRefund() {
    System.out.println("Demanding a refund");
  }

}
```

In `Audience`, the `performance()` method is annotated with `@Pointcut`. The value given to the `@Pointcut` annotation is a pointcut expression, just like the ones you used previously with the advice annotations. By annotating `performance()` with `@Pointcut` in this way, you essentially extend the pointcut expression language so that you can use `performance()` in your pointcut expressions anywhere you'd otherwise use the longer expression. As you can see, you replace the longer expression in all the advice annotations with `performance()`.

The body of the `performance()` method is irrelevant and, in fact, should be empty. The method itself is just a marker, giving the `@Pointcut` annotation something to attach itself to.

Note that aside from the annotations and the no-op `performance()` method, the `Audience` class is essentially a POJO. Its methods can be called just like methods on any other Java class. Its methods can be individually unit-tested just as in any other Java class. `Audience` is just another Java class that happens to be annotated to be used as an aspect.

And, just like any other Java class, it can be wired as a bean in Spring:

```
@Bean
public Audience audience() {
    return new Audience();
}
```

If you were to stop here, `Audience` would only be a bean in the Spring container. Even though it's annotated with AspectJ annotations, it wouldn't be treated as an aspect without something that interpreted those annotations and created the proxies that turn it into an aspect.

If you're using JavaConfig, you can turn on auto-proxying by applying the `@EnableAspectJAutoProxy` annotation at the class level of the configuration class. The following configuration class shows how to enable auto-proxying in JavaConfig.

Listing 4.3 Enabling auto-proxying of AspectJ annotations in JavaConfig

```
package concert;

import org.springframework.context.annotation.Bean;
import org.springframework.context.annotation.ComponentScan;
import org.springframework.context.annotation.Configuration;
import org.springframework.context.annotation.EnableAspectJAutoProxy;

@Configuration
@EnableAspectJAutoProxy          ◁─────┐  Enable AspectJ
@ComponentScan                         │  auto-proxying
public class ConcertConfig {

  @Bean
  public Audience audience() {   ◁───┐  Declare
    return new Audience();           │  Audience bean
  }

}
```

If, however, you're using XML to wire your beans in Spring, then you need to use the `<aop:aspectj-autoproxy>` element from Spring's `aop` namespace. The XML configuration in the following listing shows how this is done.

Listing 4.4   Enabling AspectJ auto-proxying in XML using Spring's `aop` namespace

```xml
<?xml version="1.0" encoding="UTF-8"?>
<beans xmlns="http://www.springframework.org/schema/beans"
  xmlns:xsi="http://www.w3.org/2001/XMLSchema-instance"
  xmlns:context="http://www.springframework.org/schema/context"
  xmlns:aop="http://www.springframework.org/schema/aop"
  xsi:schemaLocation="http://www.springframework.org/schema/aop
    http://www.springframework.org/schema/aop/spring-aop.xsd
    http://www.springframework.org/schema/beans
    http://www.springframework.org/schema/beans/spring-beans.xsd
    http://www.springframework.org/schema/context
    http://www.springframework.org/schema/context/spring-context.xsd">

  <context:component-scan base-package="concert" />

  <aop:aspectj-autoproxy />

  <bean class="concert.Audience" />

</beans>
```

Declare Spring's aop namespace

Enable AspectJ auto-proxying

Declare the Audience bean

Whether you use JavaConfig or XML, AspectJ auto-proxying uses the `@Aspect`-annotated bean to create a proxy around any other beans for which the aspect's pointcuts are a match. In this case, a proxy will be created for the `Concert` bean, with the advice methods in `Audience` being applied before and after the `perform()` method.

It's important to understand that Spring's AspectJ auto-proxying only uses `@AspectJ` annotations as a guide for creating proxy-based aspects. Under the covers, it's still Spring's proxy-based aspects. This is significant because it means that although you're using `@AspectJ` annotations, you're still limited to proxying method invocations. If you want to be able to exploit the full power of AspectJ, you'll have to use the AspectJ runtime and not rely on Spring to create proxy-based aspects.

At this point, your aspect is defined using distinct advice methods for before and after advice. But table 4.2 mentions another kind of advice: *around advice*. Around advice is just different enough from the other advice types that it's worth spending a moment seeing how to write it.

4.3.2   *Creating around advice*

Around advice is the most powerful advice type. It allows you to write logic that completely wraps the advised method. It's essentially like writing both before advice and after advice in a single advice method.

To illustrate around advice, let's rewrite the `Audience` aspect. This time you'll use a single around advice method instead of distinct before and after advice methods.

Listing 4.5   Reimplementing the `Audience` aspect using around advice

```
package concert;
import org.aspectj.lang.ProceedingJoinPoint;
import org.aspectj.lang.annotation.Around;
import org.aspectj.lang.annotation.Aspect;
import org.aspectj.lang.annotation.Pointcut;

@Aspect
public class Audience {

  @Pointcut("execution(** concert.Performance.perform(..))")
  public void performance() {}

  @Around("performance()")
  public void watchPerformance(ProceedingJoinPoint jp) {
    try {
      System.out.println("Silencing cell phones");
      System.out.println("Taking seats");
      jp.proceed();
      System.out.println("CLAP CLAP CLAP!!!");
    } catch (Throwable e) {
      System.out.println("Demanding a refund");
    }

  }

}
```

Declare named pointcut →

Around advice method →

Here the `@Around` annotation indicates that the `watchPerformance()` method is to be applied as around advice to the `performance()` pointcut. In this advice, the audience will silence their cell phones and take their seats before the performance and will applaud after the performance. And just like before, if an exception is thrown during the performance, the audience will ask for their money back.

As you can see, the effect of this advice is identical to what you did earlier with before and after advice. But here it's all in a single advice method, whereas before it was spread across four distinct advice methods.

The first thing you'll notice about this new advice method is that it's given a `ProceedingJoinPoint` as a parameter. This object is necessary because it's how you can invoke the advised method from within your advice. The advice method will do everything it needs to do; and when it's ready to pass control to the advised method, it will call `ProceedingJoinPoint`'s `proceed()` method.

Note that it's crucial that you remember to include a call to the `proceed()` method. If you don't, then your advice will effectively block access to the advised method. Maybe that's what you want, but chances are good that you do want the advised method to be executed at some point.

What's also interesting is that just as you can omit a call to the `proceed()` method to block access to the advised method, you can also invoke it multiple times from within the advice. One reason for doing this may be to implement retry logic to perform repeated attempts on the advised method should it fail.

4.3.3   *Handling parameters in advice*

So far, your aspects have been simple, taking no parameters. The only exception is that the watchPerformance() method you wrote for the around advice example took a ProceedingJoinPoint as a parameter. Other than that, the advice you've written hasn't bothered to look at any parameters passed to the advised methods. That's been okay, though, because the perform() method you were advising didn't take any parameters.

But what if your aspect was to advise a method that does take parameters? Could the aspect access the parameters that are passed into the method and use them?

To illustrate, let's revisit the BlankDisc class from section 2.4.4. As it is, the play() method cycles through all the tracks and calls playTrack() for each track. But you could call the playTrack() method directly to play an individual track.

Suppose you want to keep a count of how many times each track is played. One way to do this is to change the playTrack() method to directly keep track of that count each time it's called. But track-counting logic is a separate concern from playing a track and therefore doesn't belong in the playTrack() method. This looks like a job for an aspect.

To keep a running count of how many times a track is played, let's create Track-Counter, an aspect that advises playTrack(). The following listing shows just such an aspect.

Listing 4.6   Using parameterized advice to count how many times a track is played

```
package soundsystem;
import java.util.HashMap;
import java.util.Map;
import org.aspectj.lang.annotation.Aspect;
import org.aspectj.lang.annotation.Before;
import org.aspectj.lang.annotation.Pointcut;

@Aspect
public class TrackCounter {

  private Map<Integer, Integer> trackCounts =
      new HashMap<Integer, Integer>();

  @Pointcut(                                                       ◁─┐ Advise the
     "execution(* soundsystem.CompactDisc.playTrack(int)) " +     ◁─┤ playTrack()
     "&& args(trackNumber)")                                         │ method
  public void trackPlayed(int trackNumber) {}

  @Before("trackPlayed(trackNumber)")                    ◁──────────┐ Count a track
  public void countTrack(int trackNumber) {                         │ before it's played
    int currentCount = getPlayCount(trackNumber);
    trackCounts.put(trackNumber, currentCount + 1);
  }

  public int getPlayCount(int trackNumber) {
    return trackCounts.containsKey(trackNumber)
        ? trackCounts.get(trackNumber) : 0;
  }
}
```

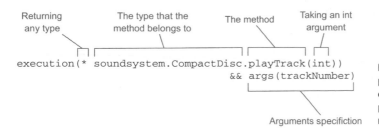

Figure 4.6 **Declaring a parameter in a pointcut expression that's to be passed into an advice method**

As with the other aspects you've created so far, this aspect uses @Pointcut to define a named pointcut and @Before to declare a method as supplying before advice. What's different here, however, is that the pointcut also declares parameters to be supplied to the advice method. Figure 4.6 breaks down the pointcut expression to show where the parameter is specified.

The thing to focus on in the figure is the args(trackNumber) qualifier in the pointcut expression. This indicates that any int argument that is passed into the execution of playTrack() should also be passed into the advice. The parameter name, trackNumber, also matches the parameter in the pointcut method signature.

That carries over into the advice method where the @Before annotation is defined with the named pointcut, trackPlayed(trackNumber). The parameter in the pointcut aligns with the parameter of the same name in the pointcut method, completing the path of the parameter from the named pointcut to the advice method.

Now you can configure BlankDisc and TrackCounter as beans in the Spring configuration and enable AspectJ auto-proxying, as shown next.

Listing 4.7 Configuring `TrackCounter` to count the number of times a track is played

```
package soundsystem;
import java.util.ArrayList;
import java.util.List;
import org.springframework.context.annotation.Bean;
import org.springframework.context.annotation.Configuration;
import org.springframework.context.annotation.EnableAspectJAutoProxy;

@Configuration
@EnableAspectJAutoProxy            <----  Enable AspectJ auto-proxying
public class TrackCounterConfig {

  @Bean
  public CompactDisc sgtPeppers() {      <----  CompactDisc bean
    BlankDisc cd = new BlankDisc();
    cd.setTitle("Sgt. Pepper's Lonely Hearts Club Band");
    cd.setArtist("The Beatles");
    List<String> tracks = new ArrayList<String>();
    tracks.add("Sgt. Pepper's Lonely Hearts Club Band");
    tracks.add("With a Little Help from My Friends");
    tracks.add("Lucy in the Sky with Diamonds");
    tracks.add("Getting Better");
    tracks.add("Fixing a Hole");
```

```
    // ...other tracks omitted for brevity...
    cd.setTracks(tracks);
    return cd;
  }

  @Bean
  public TrackCounter trackCounter() {        ◁——— TrackCounter bean
    return new TrackCounter();
  }

}
```

Finally, to prove that this all works, you can write the following simple test. It plays a few tracks and then asserts the play count through the TrackCounter bean.

Listing 4.8 Testing the TrackCounter aspect

```
package soundsystem;
import static org.junit.Assert.*;
import org.junit.Assert;
import org.junit.Rule;
import org.junit.Test;
import org.junit.contrib.java.lang.system.StandardOutputStreamLog;
import org.junit.runner.RunWith;
import org.springframework.beans.factory.annotation.Autowired;
import org.springframework.test.context.ContextConfiguration;
import org.springframework.test.context.junit4.SpringJUnit4ClassRunner;

@RunWith(SpringJUnit4ClassRunner.class)
@ContextConfiguration(classes=TrackCounterConfig.class)
public class TrackCounterTest {

  @Rule
  public final StandardOutputStreamLog log =
                                    new StandardOutputStreamLog();

  @Autowired
  private CompactDisc cd;

  @Autowired
  private TrackCounter counter;

  @Test
  public void testTrackCounter() {
    cd.playTrack(1);                 ◁——————— Play some tracks
    cd.playTrack(2);
    cd.playTrack(3);
    cd.playTrack(3);
    cd.playTrack(3);
    cd.playTrack(3);
    cd.playTrack(7);
    cd.playTrack(7);

    assertEquals(1,  counter.getPlayCount(1));    ◁— Assert the expected counts
    assertEquals(1,  counter.getPlayCount(2));
    assertEquals(4,  counter.getPlayCount(3));
    assertEquals(0,  counter.getPlayCount(4));
```

```
    assertEquals(0,  counter.getPlayCount(5));
    assertEquals(0,  counter.getPlayCount(6));
    assertEquals(2,  counter.getPlayCount(7));
  }

}
```

The aspects you've worked with thus far wrap existing methods on the advised object. But method wrapping is just one of the tricks that aspects can perform. Let's see how to write aspects that introduce completely new functionality into an advised object.

4.3.4 *Annotating introductions*

Some languages, such as Ruby and Groovy, have the notion of open classes. They make it possible to add new methods to an object or class without directly changing the definition of those objects or classes. Unfortunately, Java isn't that dynamic. Once a class has been compiled, there's little you can do to append new functionality to it.

But if you think about it, isn't that what you've been doing in this chapter with aspects? Sure, you haven't added any new methods to objects, but you're adding new functionality around the methods that the objects already have. If an aspect can wrap existing methods with additional functionality, why not add new methods to the object? In fact, using an AOP concept known as *introduction*, aspects can attach new methods to Spring beans.

Recall that in Spring, aspects are proxies that implement the same interfaces as the beans they wrap. What if, in addition to implementing those interfaces, the proxy is also exposed through some new interface? Then any bean that's advised by the aspect will appear to implement the new interface, even if its underlying implementation class doesn't. Figure 4.7 illustrates how this works.

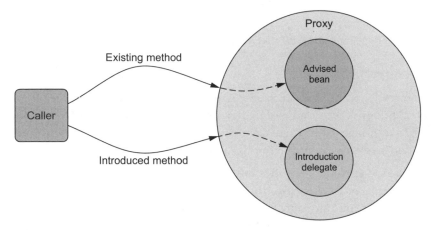

Figure 4.7   With Spring AOP, you can introduce new methods to a bean. A proxy intercepts the calls and delegates to a different object that provides the implementation.

Notice that when a method on the introduced interface is called, the proxy delegates the call to some other object that provides the implementation of the new interface. Effectively, this gives you one bean whose implementation is split across multiple classes.

Putting this idea to work, let's say you want to introduce the following `Encoreable` interface to any implementation of `Performance`:

```
package concert;

public interface Encoreable {
    void performEncore();
}
```

Setting aside any debates as to whether *Encoreable* is a real word, you need a way to apply this interface to your `Performance` implementations. I suppose you could visit all implementations of `Performance` and change them so that they also implement `Encoreable`. But from a design standpoint, that may not be the best move. Not all `Performance`s will necessarily be `Encoreable`. Moreover, it may not be possible to change all implementations of `Performance`, especially if you're working with third-party implementations and don't have the source code.

Fortunately, AOP introductions can help you without compromising design choices or requiring invasive changes to the existing implementations. To pull it off, you create a new aspect:

```
package concert;

import org.aspectj.lang.annotation.Aspect;
import org.aspectj.lang.annotation.DeclareParents;

@Aspect
public class EncoreableIntroducer {

  @DeclareParents(value="concert.Performance+",
                defaultImpl=DefaultEncoreable.class)
  public static Encoreable encoreable;

}
```

As you can see, `EncoreableIntroducer` is an aspect. But unlike the aspects you've created so far, it doesn't provide before, after, or around advice. Instead, it introduces the `Encoreable` interface to `Performance` beans using the `@DeclareParents` annotation.

The `@DeclareParents` annotation is made up of three parts:

- The `value` attribute identifies the kinds of beans that should be introduced with the interface. In this case, that's anything that implements the `Performance` interface. (The plus sign at the end specifies any subtype of `Performance`, as opposed to `Performance` itself.)
- The `defaultImpl` attribute identifies the class that will provide the implementation for the introduction. Here you're saying that `DefaultEncoreable` will provide that implementation.

- The static property that is annotated by @DeclareParents specifies the interface that's to be introduced. In this case, you're introducing the Encoreable interface.

As with any aspect, you need to declare EncoreableIntroducer as a bean in the Spring application context:

```
<bean class="concert.EncoreableIntroducer" />
```

Spring auto-proxying will take it from there. When Spring discovers a bean annotated with @Aspect, it will automatically create a proxy that delegates calls to either the proxied bean or to the introduction implementation, depending on whether the method called belongs to the proxied bean or to the introduced interface.

Annotations and auto-proxying provide a convenient programming model for creating aspects in Spring. It's simple and involves only minimal Spring configuration. But annotation-oriented aspect declaration has one clear disadvantage: you must be able to annotate the advice class. And to do that, you must have the source code.

When you don't have the source code, or if you don't want to place AspectJ annotations in your code, Spring offers another option for aspects. Let's see how you can declare aspects in a Spring XML configuration file.

4.4 Declaring aspects in XML

Early in this book, I established a preference for annotation-based configuration over Java-based configuration, and Java-based configuration over XML configuration. But if you need to declare aspects without annotating the advice class, then you must turn to XML configuration.

Spring's aop namespace offers several elements that are useful for declaring aspects in XML, as described in table 4.3.

Table 4.3   Spring's AOP configuration elements enable non-invasive declaration of aspects.

AOP configuration element	Purpose
<aop:advisor>	Defines an AOP advisor.
<aop:after>	Defines an AOP after advice (regardless of whether the advised method returns successfully).
<aop:after-returning>	Defines an AOP after-returning advice.
<aop:after-throwing>	Defines an AOP after-throwing advice.
<aop:around>	Defines an AOP around advice.
<aop:aspect>	Defines an aspect.
<aop:aspectj-autoproxy>	Enables annotation-driven aspects using @AspectJ.
<aop:before>	Defines an AOP before advice.

Table 4.3 Spring's AOP configuration elements enable non-invasive declaration of aspects. *(continued)*

AOP configuration element	Purpose
`<aop:config>`	The top-level AOP element. Most `\<aop:\*\>` elements must be contained within `\<aop:config\>`.
`<aop:declare-parents>`	Introduces additional interfaces to advised objects that are transparently implemented.
`<aop:pointcut>`	Defines a pointcut.

You've already seen the `<aop:aspectj-autoproxy>` element and how it can enable auto-proxying of AspectJ-annotated advice classes. But the other elements in the `aop` namespace let you declare aspects directly in your Spring configuration without using annotations.

For example, let's have another look at the `Audience` class. This time, let's remove all of those AspectJ annotations:

```
package concert;

public class Audience {

  public void silenceCellPhones() {
    System.out.println("Silencing cell phones");
  }

  public void takeSeats() {
    System.out.println("Taking seats");
  }

  public void applause() {
    System.out.println("CLAP CLAP CLAP!!!");
  }

  public void demandRefund() {
    System.out.println("Demanding a refund");
  }

}
```

As you can see, without the AspectJ annotations, there's nothing remarkable about the `Audience` class. It's a basic Java class with a handful of methods. And you can register it as a bean in the Spring application context like any other class.

Despite its unassuming appearance, what's remarkable about `Audience` is that it has all the makings of AOP advice. It just needs a little help to become the advice it's meant to be.

4.4.1 *Declaring before and after advice*

You could put back all the AspectJ annotations, but that isn't the point of this section. Instead, you'll use some of the elements from Spring's `aop` namespace to turn the annotation-free `Audience` into an aspect. The next listing shows the XML you need.

Listing 4.9 Annotation-free `Audience` class, declared in XML as an aspect

```
<aop:config>
  <aop:aspect ref="audience">          <─── Reference audience bean

    <aop:before                                                   ◁─┐
      pointcut="execution(** concert.Performance.perform(..))"      │ Before
      method="silenceCellPhones"/>                                  │ performance
                                                                    │
    <aop:before                                                  ◁─┘
      pointcut="execution(** concert.Performance.perform(..))"
      method="takeSeats"/>

    <aop:after-returning               ◁─────────────── After performance
      pointcut="execution(** concert.Performance.perform(..))"
      method="applause"/>

    <aop:after-throwing                ◁─────────────── After bad performance
      pointcut="execution(** concert.Performance.perform(..))"
      method="demandRefund"/>

  </aop:aspect>
</aop:config>
```

The first thing to notice about the Spring AOP configuration elements is that most of them must be used in the context of the `<aop:config>` element. There are a few exceptions to this rule, but when it comes to declaring beans as aspects, you'll always start with `<aop:config>`.

In `<aop:config>`, you may declare one or more advisers, aspects, or pointcuts. In listing 4.9, you declare a single aspect using the `<aop:aspect>` element. The `ref` attribute references the POJO bean that will be used to supply the functionality of the aspect—in this case, `audience`. The bean that's referenced by the `ref` attribute will supply the methods called by any advice in the aspect.

It's worth noting that the referenced advice bean can be any type that provides methods to be called at the designated pointcuts. This makes Spring's XML configuration for AOP a handy way to use types defined in third-party libraries as advice, even though you can't annotate them with AspectJ aspects.

The aspect has four different bits of advice. The two `<aop:before>` elements define before advice that will call the `takeSeats()` and `silenceCellPhones()` methods (declared by the `method` attribute) of the `Audience` bean before any methods matching the pointcut are executed. The `<aop:after-returning>` element defines after-returning advice to call the `applause()` method after the pointcut. Meanwhile, the `<aop:after-throwing>` element defines an after-throwing advice to call the `demandRefund()` method if any exceptions are thrown. Figure 4.8 shows how the advice logic is woven into the business logic.

In all advice elements, the `pointcut` attribute defines the pointcut where the advice will be applied. The value given to the `pointcut` attribute is a pointcut defined in AspectJ's pointcut expression syntax.

Figure 4.8 The `Audience` aspect includes four bits of advice that weave advice logic around methods that match the aspect's pointcut.

You've probably noticed that the value of the `pointcut` attribute is the same for all the advice elements. That's because all the advice is being applied to the same pointcut.

When you found the same kind of duplication in your AspectJ-annotated advice, you eliminated it by using the `@Pointcut` annotation. For XML-based aspect declarations, however, you'll need to use the `<aop:pointcut>` element. The following XML shows how to extract the common pointcut expression into a single pointcut declaration that can be used across all advice elements.

Listing 4.10 Defining a named pointcut with `<aop:pointcut>`

```
<aop:config>
  <aop:aspect ref="audience">
    <aop:pointcut                        ⟵———————— Define pointcut
        id="performance"
        expression="execution(** concert.Performance.perform(..))" />

    <aop:before                          ⟵┐
        pointcut-ref="performance"        │
        method="silenceCellPhones"/>      │
                                          ├ Reference
    <aop:before                          ⟵┤ pointcut
        pointcut-ref="performance"        │
        method="takeSeats"/>              │
                                          │
    <aop:after-returning                 ⟵┘
        pointcut-ref="performance"
        method="applause"/>
```

```
    <aop:after-throwing                    <─── Reference pointcut
      pointcut-ref="performance"
      method="demandRefund"/>
  </aop:aspect>
</aop:config>
```

Now the pointcut is defined in a single location and is referenced across multiple advice elements. The `<aop:pointcut>` element defines the pointcut to have an `id` of `performance`. Meanwhile, all the advice elements have been changed to reference the named pointcut with the `pointcut-ref` attribute.

As used in listing 4.10, the `<aop:pointcut>` element defines a pointcut that can be referenced by all advice in the same `<aop:aspect>` element. But you can also define pointcuts that can be used across multiple aspects by placing the `<aop:pointcut>` elements within the scope of the `<aop:config>` element.

4.4.2 Declaring around advice

The current implementation of `Audience` works great. But basic before and after advice have some limitations. Specifically, it's tricky to share information between before advice and after advice without resorting to storing that information in member variables.

For example, suppose that in addition to putting away cell phones and applauding at the end, you also want the audience to keep their eyes on their watches and report how long the performance takes. The only way to accomplish this with before and after advice is to note the start time in before advice and report the length of time in after advice. But you'd have to store the start time in a member variable. Because `Audience` is a singleton, it wouldn't be thread-safe to retain state like that.

Around advice has an advantage over before and after advice in this regard. With around advice, you can accomplish the same thing you could with distinct before and after advice, but you can do it in a single method. Because the entire set of advice takes place in a single method, there's no need to retain state in a member variable.

For example, consider the new annotation-free `Audience` class with a single `watch-Performance()` method.

Listing 4.11 Providing around advice with the `watchPerformance()` method

```
package concert;

import org.aspectj.lang.ProceedingJoinPoint;

public class Audience {

  public void watchPerformance(ProceedingJoinPoint jp) {
    try {

      System.out.println("Silencing cell phones");     ┐  Before performance
      System.out.println("Taking seats");              ┘

      jp.proceed();              <─────────────── Proceed to advised method
```

```
        System.out.println("CLAP CLAP CLAP!!!");        ◁───── After performance
    } catch (Throwable e) {

        System.out.println("Demanding a refund");       ◁── After bad performance

    }
  }

}
```

In the case of the audience aspect, the `watchPerformance()` method contains all the functionality of the previous four advice methods. But all of it is contained in this single method, and this method is responsible for its own exception handling.

Declaring around advice isn't dramatically different from declaring other types of advice. All you need to do is use the `<aop:around>` element, as shown next.

Listing 4.12   Declaring around advice in XML with the `<aop:around>` element

```
<aop:config>
  <aop:aspect ref="audience">
    <aop:pointcut
        id="performance"
        expression="execution(** concert.Performance.perform(..))" />

    <aop:around                        ◁───────────── Declare around advice
        pointcut-ref="performance"
        method="watchPerformance"/>
  </aop:aspect>
</aop:config>
```

As with the other advice XML elements, `<aop:around>` is given a pointcut and the name of an advice method. Here you're using the same pointcut as before, but you set the `method` attribute to point to the new `watchPerformance()` method.

4.4.3   *Passing parameters to advice*

In section 4.3.3, you used AspectJ annotations to create an aspect that kept a running count of the number of times tracks were played on a `CompactDisc`. Now that you're configuring your aspects in XML, let's see how you can accomplish the same thing.

First, let's strip all the @AspectJ annotations out of the `TrackCounter`.

Listing 4.13   Annotation-free `TrackCounter`

```
package soundsystem;
import java.util.HashMap;
import java.util.Map;

public class TrackCounter {

  private Map<Integer, Integer> trackCounts =
      new HashMap<Integer, Integer>();
                                                         Method to be declared
  public void countTrack(int trackNumber) {        ◁──┐ as before advice
    int currentCount = getPlayCount(trackNumber);
    trackCounts.put(trackNumber, currentCount + 1);
  }
```

```
  public int getPlayCount(int trackNumber) {
    return trackCounts.containsKey(trackNumber)
        ? trackCounts.get(trackNumber) : 0;
  }

}
```

Without the AspectJ annotations, `TrackCounter` seems kind of bare. And as it stands now, `TrackCounter` won't count any tracks unless you explicitly call the `countTrack()` method. But with a little XML Spring configuration, you can reinstate `TrackCounter`'s status as an aspect.

The following listing shows the complete Spring configuration that declares both the `TrackCounter` bean and the `BlankDisc` bean and enables `TrackCounter` as an aspect.

Listing 4.14 Configuring `TrackCounter` as a parameterized aspect in XML

```xml
<?xml version="1.0" encoding="UTF-8"?>
<beans xmlns="http://www.springframework.org/schema/beans"
  xmlns:xsi="http://www.w3.org/2001/XMLSchema-instance"
  xmlns:aop="http://www.springframework.org/schema/aop"
  xsi:schemaLocation=
    "http://www.springframework.org/schema/aop
    http://www.springframework.org/schema/aop/spring-aop.xsd
    http://www.springframework.org/schema/beans
    http://www.springframework.org/schema/beans/spring-beans.xsd">

  <bean id="trackCounter"
        class="soundsystem.TrackCounter" />          <!-- ← TrackCounter bean -->

  <bean id="cd"
        class="soundsystem.BlankDisc">               <!-- ← BlankDisc bean -->
    <property name="title"
              value="Sgt. Pepper's Lonely Hearts Club Band" />
    <property name="artist" value="The Beatles" />
    <property name="tracks">
      <list>
        <value>Sgt. Pepper's Lonely Hearts Club Band</value>
        <value>With a Little Help from My Friends</value>
        <value>Lucy in the Sky with Diamonds</value>
        <value>Getting Better</value>
        <value>Fixing a Hole</value>
        <!-- ...other tracks omitted for brevity... -->
      </list>
    </property>
  </bean>

  <aop:config>                                       <!-- Declare TrackCounter -->
    <aop:aspect ref="trackCounter">                  <!-- ← as an aspect -->
      <aop:pointcut id="trackPlayed" expression=
          "execution(* soundsystem.CompactDisc.playTrack(int))
              and args(trackNumber)" />

      <aop:before
          pointcut-ref="trackPlayed"
```

```
            method="countTrack"/>
    </aop:aspect>
  </aop:config>
</beans>
```

As you can see, you're using the same XML elements from the aop namespace as before; they declare a POJO to be treated as an aspect. The only significant difference is that your pointcut expression now includes a parameter to be passed into the advice method. If you compare this expression with the one from listing 4.6, you'll see that they're almost identical. The only real difference is that here you use the and keyword instead of && (because ampersands are interpreted as the beginning of an entity in XML).

Now that you've exercised Spring's aop namespace to declare a few basic aspects in XML, let's see how the aop namespace can help you declare introduction aspects.

4.4.4   *Introducing new functionality with aspects*

Earlier, in section 4.3.4, I showed you how to use AspectJ's @DeclareParents annotation to magically introduce a new method into an advised bean. But AOP introductions aren't exclusive to AspectJ. Using the <aop:declare-parents> element from Spring's aop namespace, you can do similar magic in XML.

The following snippet of XML is equivalent to the AspectJ-based introduction you created earlier:

```
<aop:aspect>
  <aop:declare-parents
    types-matching="concert.Performance+"
    implement-interface="concert.Encoreable"
    default-impl="concert.DefaultEncoreable"
    />
</aop:aspect>
```

As its name implies, <aop:declare-parents> declares that the beans it advises will have new parents in its object hierarchy. Specifically, in this case you're saying that the beans whose type matches the Performance interface (per the types-matching attribute) should have Encoreable in their parentage (per the implement-interface attribute). The final matter to settle is where the implementation of the Encoreable's methods will come from.

There are two ways to identify the implementation of the introduced interface. In this case, you're using the default-impl attribute to explicitly identify the implementation by its fully qualified class name. Alternatively, you could identify it using the delegate-ref attribute:

```
<aop:aspect>
  <aop:declare-parents
    types-matching="concert.Performance+"
    implement-interface="concert.Encoreable"
    delegate-ref="encoreableDelegate"
    />
</aop:aspect>
```

The `delegate-ref` attribute refers to a Spring bean as the introduction delegate. This assumes that a bean with an ID of `encoreableDelegate` exists in the Spring context:

```
<bean id="encoreableDelegate"
      class="concert.DefaultEncoreable" />
```

The difference between directly identifying the delegate using `default-impl` and indirectly using `delegate-ref` is that the latter will be a Spring bean that itself may be injected, advised, or otherwise configured through Spring.

4.5   *Injecting AspectJ aspects*

Although Spring AOP is sufficient for many applications of aspects, it's a weak AOP solution when contrasted with AspectJ. AspectJ offers many types of pointcuts that aren't possible with Spring AOP.

Constructor pointcuts, for example, are convenient when you need to apply advice on the creation of an object. Unlike constructors in some other object-oriented languages, Java constructors are different from normal methods. This makes Spring's proxy-based AOP woefully inadequate for advising the creation of an object.

For the most part, AspectJ aspects are independent of Spring. Although they can be woven into any Java-based application, including Spring applications, there's little involvement on Spring's part in applying AspectJ aspects.

But any well-designed and meaningful aspect will likely depend on other classes to assist in its work. If an aspect depends on one or more classes when executing its advice, you can instantiate those collaborating objects with the aspect itself. Or, better yet, you can use Spring's dependency injection to inject beans into AspectJ aspects.

To illustrate, let's create a new aspect for performances. Specifically, let's create an aspect that plays the role of a critic who watches a performance and provides a critical review afterward. `CriticAspect` is such an aspect.

> **Listing 4.15   Implementing a performance critic using AspectJ**

```
package concert;
public aspect CriticAspect {
  public CriticAspect() {}

  pointcut performance() : execution(* perform(..));

  afterReturning() : performance() {
    System.out.println(criticismEngine.getCriticism());
  }                                                             Inject
                                                          CriticismEngine
  private CriticismEngine criticismEngine;

  public void setCriticismEngine(CriticismEngine criticismEngine) {
    this.criticismEngine = criticismEngine;
  }
}
```

The chief responsibility for `CriticAspect` is to comment on a performance after the performance has completed. The `performance()` pointcut in listing 4.15 matches the

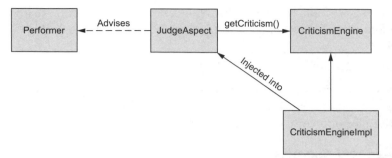

Figure 4.9 Aspects need injection, too. Spring can inject AspectJ aspects with dependencies just as if they were another bean.

perform() method. When it's married with the afterReturning() advice, you get an aspect that reacts to the completion of a performance.

What makes listing 4.15 interesting is that the critic doesn't make commentary on its own. Instead, CriticAspect collaborates with a CriticismEngine object, calling its getCriticism() method, to produce critical commentary after a performance. To avoid unnecessary coupling between CriticAspect and CriticismEngine, Critic-Aspect is given a reference to CriticismEngine through setter injection. This relationship is illustrated in figure 4.9.

CriticismEngine is an interface that declares a simple getCriticism() method. The next listing shows the implementation of CriticismEngine.

Listing 4.16 `CriticismEngine` to be injected into `CriticAspect`

```
package com.springinaction.springidol;
public class CriticismEngineImpl implements CriticismEngine {
  public CriticismEngineImpl() {}

  public String getCriticism() {
    int i = (int) (Math.random() * criticismPool.length);
    return criticismPool[i];
  }

  // injected
  private String[] criticismPool;
  public void setCriticismPool(String[] criticismPool) {
    this.criticismPool = criticismPool;
  }
}
```

CriticismEngineImpl implements the CriticismEngine interface by randomly choosing a critical comment from a pool of injected criticisms. This class can be declared as a Spring <bean> using the following XML:

```
<bean id="criticismEngine"
    class="com.springinaction.springidol.CriticismEngineImpl">
  <property name="criticisms">
    <list>
      <value>Worst performance ever!</value>
      <value>I laughed, I cried, then I realized I was at the
          wrong show.</value>
```

```
        <value>A must see show!</value>
      </list>
    </property>
</bean>
```

So far, so good. You now have a `CriticismEngine` implementation to give to `Critic-Aspect`. All that's left is to wire `CriticismEngineImpl` into `CriticAspect`.

Before I show you how to do the injection, you should know that AspectJ aspects can be woven into your application without involving Spring at all. But if you want to use Spring's dependency injection to inject collaborators into an AspectJ aspect, you'll need to declare the aspect as a `<bean>` in Spring's configuration. The following `<bean>` declaration injects the `criticismEngine` bean into `CriticAspect`:

```
<bean class="com.springinaction.springidol.CriticAspect"
    factory-method="aspectOf">
  <property name="criticismEngine" ref="criticismEngine" />
</bean>
```

For the most part, this `<bean>` declaration isn't much different from any other `<bean>` you may find in Spring. The big difference is the use of the `factory-method` attribute. Normally, Spring beans are instantiated by the Spring container, but AspectJ aspects are created by the AspectJ runtime. By the time Spring gets a chance to inject `CriticismEngine` into `CriticAspect`, `CriticAspect` has already been instantiated.

Because Spring isn't responsible for the creation of `CriticAspect`, it isn't possible to declare `CriticAspect` as a bean in Spring. Instead, you need a way for Spring to get a handle to the `CriticAspect` instance that has already been created by AspectJ so that you can inject it with a `CriticismEngine`. Conveniently, all AspectJ aspects provide a static `aspectOf()` method that returns the singleton instance of the aspect. So to get an instance of the aspect, you must use `factory-method` to invoke the `aspectOf()` method instead of trying to call `CriticAspect`'s constructor.

In short, Spring doesn't use the `<bean>` declaration from earlier to create an instance of the `CriticAspect`—it has already been created by the AspectJ runtime. Instead, Spring retrieves a reference to the aspect through the `aspectOf()` factory method and then performs dependency injection on it as prescribed by the `<bean>` element.

4.6   *Summary*

AOP is a powerful complement to object-oriented programming. With aspects, you can group application behavior that was once spread throughout your applications into reusable modules. You can then declare exactly where and how this behavior is applied. This reduces code duplication and lets your classes focus on their main functionality.

Spring provides an AOP framework that lets you insert aspects around method executions. You've learned how to weave advice before, after, and around a method invocation, as well as to add custom behavior for handling exceptions.

You have several choices in how you can use aspects in your Spring applications. Wiring advice and pointcuts in Spring is much easier with the addition of @AspectJ annotation support and a simplified configuration schema.

Finally, there are times when Spring AOP isn't enough, and you must turn to AspectJ for more powerful aspects. For those situations, we looked at how to use Spring to inject dependencies into AspectJ aspects.

At this point, we've covered the basics of the Spring Framework. You've seen how to configure the Spring container and how to apply aspects to Spring-managed objects. These core techniques offer you a great opportunity to create applications composed of loosely coupled objects.

Now we'll move past the essentials and look at what it takes to build real applications in Spring. Starting in the next chapter, you'll see how to build web applications using Spring.

Part 2

Spring on the web

Spring is often used to develop web applications. Therefore, in part 2 you'll see how to use Spring's MVC framework to add a web front end to your application.

In chapter 5, "Building Spring web applications," you'll learn the basics of Spring MVC, a web framework built on the principles of the Spring Framework. You'll discover how to write controllers to handle web requests and see how to transparently bind request parameters and payload to your business objects while providing validation and error handling at the same time.

Chapter 6, "Rendering web views," continues what chapter 5 started by showing you how to take model data produced in Spring MVC controllers and render it as HTML to be served to a user's browser. This chapter includes discussions of JavaServer Pages (JSP), Apache Tiles, and Thymeleaf templates.

In Chapter 7, "Advanced Spring MVC," you'll learn a few more advanced techniques to use when building web applications, including custom Spring MVC configuration options, handling multipart file uploads, dealing with exceptions, and passing data across requests using flash attributes.

Chapter 8, "Working with Spring Web Flow," will show you how to build conversation, flow-based web applications using the Spring Web Flow framework.

As security is an important aspect of many applications, chapter 9, "Securing Spring," will show you how to use Spring Security to secure your web application and protect the information it serves.

Building Spring
web applications

5

This chapter covers

- Mapping requests to Spring controllers
- Transparently binding form parameters
- Validating form submissions

As an enterprise Java developer, you've likely developed a web-based application or two. For many Java developers, web-based applications are their primary focus. If this is your experience, then you're well aware of the challenges that come with these systems. Specifically, state management, workflow, and validation are all important features that need to be addressed. None of these is made any easier given the HTTP protocol's stateless nature.

Spring's web framework is designed to help you address these concerns. Based on the Model-View-Controller (MVC) pattern, Spring MVC helps you build web-based applications that are as flexible and as loosely coupled as the Spring Framework itself.

In this chapter, we'll explore the essentials of Spring's MVC web framework. We'll focus on using annotations to create controllers that handle various kinds of web requests, parameters, and form input. Before we go too deep with the specifics of Spring MVC, let's start with a high-level view and set up the basic plumbing needed to make Spring MVC work.

5.1   *Getting started with Spring MVC*

Have you ever seen the children's game Mousetrap? It's crazy. The goal is to send a small steel ball through a series of wacky contraptions in order to trigger a mousetrap. The ball navigates all kinds of intricate gadgets, from rolling down a curvy ramp to springing off a teeter-totter to spinning on a miniature Ferris wheel to being kicked out of a bucket by a rubber boot. It goes through all this to spring a trap on a poor, unsuspecting plastic mouse.

At first glance, you may think that Spring's MVC framework is a lot like Mousetrap. Instead of moving a ball through various ramps, teeter-totters, and wheels, Spring moves requests between a dispatcher servlet, handler mappings, controllers, and view resolvers. But don't draw too strong a comparison between Spring MVC and the Rube Goldberg-esque game of Mousetrap. Each of the components in Spring MVC performs a specific purpose. And it's really not that complex.

Let's take a look at how a request makes its way from the client through the components in Spring MVC, ultimately resulting in a request that goes back to the client.

5.1.1   *Following the life of a request*

Every time a user clicks a link or submits a form in their web browser, a request goes to work. A request's job description is that of a courier. Just like a postal carrier or a FedEx delivery person, a request lives to carry information from one place to another.

The request is a busy creature. From the time it leaves the browser until it returns with a response, it makes several stops, each time dropping off a bit of information and picking up some more. Figure 5.1 shows all the stops the request makes as it travels through Spring MVC.

When the request leaves the browser ❶, it carries information about what the user is asking for. At the least, the request will be carrying the requested URL. But it may also carry additional data, such as the information submitted in a form by the user.

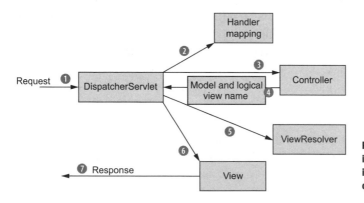

Figure 5.1 **A request couriers information to several stops on its way to producing the desired results.**

The first stop in the request's travels is at Spring's `DispatcherServlet`. Like most Java-based web frameworks, Spring MVC funnels requests through a single front controller servlet. A *front controller* is a common web application pattern where a single servlet delegates responsibility for a request to other components of an application to perform actual processing. In the case of Spring MVC, `DispatcherServlet` is the front controller.

The `DispatcherServlet`'s job is to send the request on to a Spring MVC controller. A *controller* is a Spring component that processes the request. But a typical application may have several controllers, and `DispatcherServlet` needs some help deciding which controller to send the request to. So the `DispatcherServlet` consults one or more handler mappings ❷ to figure out where the request's next stop will be. The handler mapping pays particular attention to the URL carried by the request when making its decision.

Once an appropriate controller has been chosen, `DispatcherServlet` sends the request on its merry way to the chosen controller ❸. At the controller, the request drops off its payload (the information submitted by the user) and patiently waits while the controller processes that information. (Actually, a well-designed controller performs little or no processing itself and instead delegates responsibility for the business logic to one or more service objects.)

The logic performed by a controller often results in some information that needs to be carried back to the user and displayed in the browser. This information is referred to as the *model*. But sending raw information back to the user isn't sufficient—it needs to be formatted in a user-friendly format, typically HTML. For that, the information needs to be given to a view, typically a JavaServer Page (JSP).

One of the last things a controller does is package up the model data and identify the name of a view that should render the output. It then sends the request, along with the model and view name, back to the `DispatcherServlet` ❹.

So that the controller doesn't get coupled to a particular view, the view name passed back to `DispatcherServlet` doesn't directly identify a specific JSP. It doesn't even necessarily suggest that the view is a JSP. Instead, it only carries a logical name that will be used to look up the actual view that will produce the result. The `DispatcherServlet` consults a view resolver ❺ to map the logical view name to a specific view implementation, which may or may not be a JSP.

Now that `DispatcherServlet` knows which view will render the result, the request's job is almost over. Its final stop is at the view implementation ❻, typically a JSP, where it delivers the model data. The request's job is finally done. The view will use the model data to render output that will be carried back to the client by the (not-so-hardworking) response object ❼.

As you can see, a request goes through several steps along its way to producing a response for the client. Most of these steps take place within the Spring MVC framework, in the components shown in figure 5.1. Although the bulk of this chapter will focus on writing controllers, let's take a moment to set up the essential components of Spring MVC.

5.1.2 Setting up Spring MVC

Based on figure 5.1, it looks like there are a lot of moving parts to be configured. Fortunately, thanks to some advancements in the most recent versions of Spring, it's easy to get started with Spring MVC. For now, you'll take the simplest approach to configuring Spring MVC: you'll do just enough configuring to be able to run the controllers you create. In chapter 7, we'll look at some additional setup options.

CONFIGURING DISPATCHERSERVLET

`DispatcherServlet` is the centerpiece of Spring MVC. It's where the request first hits the framework, and it's responsible for routing the request through all the other components.

Historically, servlets like `DispatcherServlet` have been configured in a web.xml file that's carried in the web application's WAR file. Certainly that's one option for configuring `DispatcherServlet`. But thanks to recent advances in the Servlet 3 specification and in Spring 3.1, it's not the only option. And it's not the option we'll go with in this chapter.

Instead of a web.xml file, you're going to use Java to configure `DispatcherServlet` in the servlet container. The following listing shows the Java class you'll need.

Listing 5.1   Configuring `DispatcherServlet`

```java
package spittr.config;
import org.springframework.web.servlet.support.
            AbstractAnnotationConfigDispatcherServletInitializer;

public class SpittrWebAppInitializer
      extends AbstractAnnotationConfigDispatcherServletInitializer {

  @Override
  protected String[] getServletMappings() {          <─── Map DispatcherServlet to /
    return new String[] { "/" };
  }

  @Override
  protected Class<?>[] getRootConfigClasses() {
    return new Class<?>[] { RootConfig.class };
  }

  @Override
  protected Class<?>[] getServletConfigClasses() {   <─── Specify configuration class
    return new Class<?>[] { WebConfig.class };
  }

}
```

Before we dive into the details of listing 5.1, you may wonder what the word *spittr* has to do with anything. The class is named `SpittrWebAppInitializer`, and it's in a package named spittr.config. I'll explain that in a moment (in section 5.1.3), but for now, suffice it to say that the application you'll create is named Spittr.

To understand how listing 5.1 works, it's probably sufficient to know that any class that extends `AbstractAnnotationConfigDispatcherServletInitializer` will automatically be used to configure `DispatcherServlet` and the Spring application context in the application's servlet context.

AbstractAnnotationConfigDispatcherServletInitializer exposed

If you insist on the more detailed explanation, here it is. In a Servlet 3.0 environment, the container looks for any classes in the classpath that implement the `javax.servlet.ServletContainerInitializer` interface; if any are found, they're used to configure the servlet container.

Spring supplies an implementation of that interface called `SpringServletContainerInitializer` that, in turn, seeks out any classes that implement `WebApplicationInitializer` and delegates to them for configuration. Spring 3.2 introduced a convenient base implementation of `WebApplicationInitializer` called `AbstractAnnotationConfigDispatcherServletInitializer`. Because your `SpittrWebAppInitializer` extends `AbstractAnnotationConfigDispatcherServletInitializer` (and thus implements `WebApplicationInitializer`), it will be automatically discovered when deployed in a Servlet 3.0 container and be used to configure the servlet context.

Even though its name is extremely long, `AbstractAnnotationConfigDispatcherServletInitializer` is a snap to use. Looking at listing 5.1, you can see that `SpittrWebAppInitializer` overrides three methods.

The first method, `getServletMappings()`, identifies one or more paths that `DispatcherServlet` will be mapped to. In this case, it's mapped to /, indicating that it will be the application's default servlet. It will handle all requests coming into the application.

In order to understand the other two methods, you must first understand the relationship between `DispatcherServlet` and a servlet listener known as `ContextLoaderListener`.

A TALE OF TWO APPLICATION CONTEXTS

When `DispatcherServlet` starts up, it creates a Spring application context and starts loading it with beans declared in the configuration files or classes that it's given. With the `getServletConfigClasses()` method in listing 5.1, you've asked that `DispatcherServlet` load its application context with beans defined in the `WebConfig` configuration class (using Java configuration).

But in Spring web applications, there's often another application context. This other application context is created by `ContextLoaderListener`.

Whereas `DispatcherServlet` is expected to load beans containing web components such as controllers, view resolvers, and handler mappings, `ContextLoaderListener` is expected to load the other beans in your application. These beans are typically the middle-tier and data-tier components that drive the back end of the application.

Under the covers, `AbstractAnnotationConfigDispatcherServletInitializer` creates both a `DispatcherServlet` and a `ContextLoaderListener`. The `@Configuration` classes returned from `getServletConfigClasses()` will define beans for `Dispatcher-Servlet`'s application context. Meanwhile, the `@Configuration` class's returned `get-RootConfigClasses()` will be used to configure the application context created by `ContextLoaderListener`.

In this case, your root configuration is defined in `RootConfig`, whereas `Dispatcher-Servlet`'s configuration is declared in `WebConfig`. You'll see what those two configuration classes look like in a moment.

It's important to realize that configuring `DispatcherServlet` via `Abstract-AnnotationConfigDispatcherServletInitializer` is an alternative to the traditional web.xml file. Although you can include a web.xml file alongside a subclass of `AbstractAnnotationConfigDispatcherServletInitializer` if you like, it's not necessary.

The only gotcha with configuring `DispatcherServlet` in this way, as opposed to in a web.xml file, is that it will only work when deploying to a server that supports Servlet 3.0, such as Apache Tomcat 7 or higher. The Servlet 3.0 specification has been final since December 2009, and the odds are good that you'll be deploying your applications to a servlet container that supports Servlet 3.0.

If you're not yet working with a Servlet 3.0-capable server, then configuring `DispatcherServlet` in a subclass of `AbstractAnnotationConfigDispatcherServlet-Initializer` won't work for you. You'll have no choice but to configure `Dispatcher-Servlet` in web.xml. We'll look at web.xml and other configuration options in chapter 7. For now, though, let's look at `WebConfig` and `RootConfig`, the two configuration classes referred to in listing 5.1, and see how to enable Spring MVC.

ENABLING SPRING MVC

Just as there are several ways of configuring `DispatcherServlet`, there's more than one way to enable Spring MVC components. Historically, Spring has been configured using XML, and there's an `<mvc:annotation-driven>` element that you can use to enable annotation-driven Spring MVC.

We'll talk about `<mvc:annotation-driven>`, among other Spring MVC configuration options, in chapter 7. But for now, you'll keep your Spring MVC setup simple and Java-based.

The *very* simplest Spring MVC configuration you can create is a class annotated with `@EnableWebMvc`:

```
package spittr.config;
import org.springframework.context.annotation.Configuration;
import org.springframework.web.servlet.config.annotation.EnableWebMvc;

@Configuration
@EnableWebMvc
public class WebConfig {
}
```

This will work, and it will enable Spring MVC. But it leaves a lot to be desired:

- No view resolver is configured. As such, Spring will default to using `Bean-NameViewResolver`, a view resolver that resolves views by looking for beans whose ID matches the view name and whose class implements the `View` interface.
- Component-scanning isn't enabled. Consequently, the only way Spring will find any controllers is if you declare them explicitly in the configuration.
- As it is, `DispatcherServlet` is mapped as the default servlet for the application and will handle *all* requests, including requests for static resources, such as images and stylesheets (which is probably not what you want in most cases).

Therefore, you need to add a bit more configuration in `WebConfig` on top of this bare minimum Spring MVC configuration to make it useful. The new `WebConfig` in the next listing addresses these concerns.

Listing 5.2   A minimal yet useful configuration for Spring MVC

```
package spittr.config;
import org.springframework.context.annotation.Bean;
import org.springframework.context.annotation.ComponentScan;
import org.springframework.context.annotation.Configuration;
import org.springframework.web.servlet.ViewResolver;
import org.springframework.web.servlet.config.annotation.
                                    DefaultServletHandlerConfigurer;
import org.springframework.web.servlet.config.annotation.EnableWebMvc;
import org.springframework.web.servlet.config.annotation.
                                    WebMvcConfigurerAdapter;
import org.springframework.web.servlet.view.
                                    InternalResourceViewResolver;

@Configuration
@EnableWebMvc                          ⟵── Enable Spring MVC
@ComponentScan("spitter.web")               ⟵── Enable component-scanning
public class WebConfig
        extends WebMvcConfigurerAdapter {

  @Bean
  public ViewResolver viewResolver() {          ⎫ Configure a JSP
    InternalResourceViewResolver resolver =     ⎬ view resolver
            new InternalResourceViewResolver(); ⎭
    resolver.setPrefix("/WEB-INF/views/");
    resolver.setSuffix(".jsp");
    resolver.setExposeContextBeansAsAttributes(true);
    return resolver;
  }

  @Override                                         ⎫ Configure static
  public void configureDefaultServletHandling(      ⎬ content handling
        DefaultServletHandlerConfigurer configurer) {
    configurer.enable();
  }

}
```

The first thing to notice in listing 5.2 is that `WebConfig` is now annotated with `@ComponentScan` so that the spitter.web package will be scanned for components. As you'll soon see, the controllers you write will be annotated with `@Controller`, which will make them candidates for component-scanning. Consequently, you won't have to explicitly declare any controllers in the configuration class.

Next, you add a `ViewResolver` bean. More specifically, it's an `Internal-ResourceViewResolver`. We'll talk more about view resolvers in chapter 6. For now, just know that it's configured to look for JSP files by wrapping view names with a specific prefix and suffix (for example, a view name of home will be resolved as /WEB-INF/views/home.jsp).

Finally, this new `WebConfig` class extends `WebMvcConfigurerAdapter` and overrides its `configureDefaultServletHandling()` method. By calling `enable()` on the given `DefaultServletHandlerConfigurer`, you're asking `DispatcherServlet` to forward requests for static resources to the servlet container's default servlet and not to try to handle them itself.

With `WebConfig` settled, what about `RootConfig`? Because this chapter is focused on web development, and web configuration is done in the application context created by `DispatcherServlet`, you'll keep `RootConfig` relatively simple for now:

```
package spittr.config;

import org.springframework.context.annotation.ComponentScan;
import org.springframework.context.annotation.ComponentScan.Filter;
import org.springframework.context.annotation.Configuration;
import org.springframework.context.annotation.FilterType;
import org.springframework.web.servlet.config.annotation.EnableWebMvc;

@Configuration
@ComponentScan(basePackages={"spitter"},
    excludeFilters={
        @Filter(type=FilterType.ANNOTATION, value=EnableWebMvc.class)
    })
public class RootConfig {
}
```

The only significant thing to note in `RootConfig` is that it's annotated with `@Component-Scan`. There will be plenty of opportunities throughout this book to flesh out `Root-Config` with non-web components.

You're almost ready to start building a web application with Spring MVC. The big question at this point is what application you'll build.

5.1.3 *Introducing the Spittr application*

In an attempt to get in on the online social networking game, you're going to develop a simple microblogging application. In many ways, your application will be much like the original microblogging application, Twitter. You'll add some little twists on the idea along the way. And, of course, you'll develop it using Spring.

Borrowing some ideas from Twitter and implementing them in Spring gives the application a working title: Spitter. Taking it a step further and applying a naming pattern that's popular with sites like Flickr, let's drop the *e* and call the app Spittr. This name will also be helpful in differentiating the application name from a domain type you'll create called `Spitter`.

The Spittr application has two essential domain concepts: *spitters* (the users of the application) and *spittles* (the brief status updates that users publish). We'll draw primarily on these two domain concepts throughout this book as we flesh out the functionality of the Spittr application. Initially, in this chapter, you'll build out the web layer of the application, create controllers that display spittles, and process forms where users register as spitters.

The stage is now set. You've configured `DispatcherServlet`, enabled essential Spring MVC components, and established a target application. Let's turn to the meat of the chapter: handling web requests with Spring MVC controllers.

5.2 *Writing a simple controller*

In Spring MVC, controllers are just classes with methods that are annotated with `@RequestMapping` to declare the kind of requests they'll handle.

Starting simple, let's imagine a controller class that handles requests for / and renders the application's home page. `HomeController`, shown in the following listing, is an example of what might be the simplest possible Spring MVC controller class.

> **Listing 5.3 `HomeController`: an example of an extremely simple controller**

```
package spittr.web;
import static org.springframework.web.bind.annotation.RequestMethod.*;
import org.springframework.stereotype.Controller;
import org.springframework.web.bind.annotation.RequestMapping;
import org.springframework.web.bind.annotation.RequestMethod;

@Controller                          ⟵── Declared to be a controller
public class HomeController {

  @RequestMapping(value="/", method=GET)     ⟵── Handle GET requests for /
  public String home() {
    return "home";                   ⟵── View name is home
  }

}
```

The first thing you'll notice about `HomeController` is that it's annotated with `@Controller`. Although it's clear that this annotation declares a controller, the annotation has little to do with Spring MVC.

`@Controller` is a stereotype annotation, based on the `@Component` annotation. Its purpose here is entirely for the benefit of component-scanning. Because `Home-Controller` is annotated with `@Controller`, the component scanner will automatically pick up `HomeController` and declare it as a bean in the Spring application context.

You could have annotated HomeController with @Component, and it would have had the same effect, but it would have been less expressive about what type of component HomeController is.

HomeController's only method, the home() method, is annotated with @Request-Mapping. The value attribute specifies the request path that this method will handle, and the method attribute details the HTTP method that it can handle. In this case, whenever an HTTP GET request comes in for /, the home() method will be called.

As you can see, the home() method doesn't do much: it returns a String value of "home". This String will be interpreted by Spring MVC as the name of the view that will be rendered. DispatcherServlet will ask the view resolver to resolve this logical view name into an actual view.

Given the way you configured InternalResourceViewResolver, the view name "home" will be resolved as a JSP at /WEB-INF/views/home.jsp. For now, you'll keep the Spittr application's home page rather basic, as shown next.

Listing 5.4   Spittr home page, defined as a simple JSP

```
<%@ taglib uri="http://java.sun.com/jsp/jstl/core" prefix="c" %>
<%@ page session="false" %>
<html>
  <head>
    <title>Spittr</title>
    <link rel="stylesheet"
          type="text/css"
          href="<c:url value="/resources/style.css" />" >
  </head>
  <body>
    <h1>Welcome to Spittr</h1>

    <a href="<c:url value="/spittles" />">Spittles</a> |
    <a href="<c:url value="/spitter/register" />">Register</a>
  </body>
</html>
```

There's nothing noteworthy about this JSP. It merely welcomes the user to the application and offers two links: one to view a Spittle list and another to register with the application. Figure 5.2 shows what the home page looks like at this point.

Before this chapter is complete, you'll have implemented the controller methods to handle those requests. But for now, let's throw some requests at this controller and see if it works. The obvious way to test a controller may be to build and deploy the application and poke at it with a web browser, but an automated test will give you quicker feedback and more consistent hands-off results. So, let's cover HomeController with a test.

5.2.1 *Testing the controller*

Take another look at HomeController. If you squint really hard—so hard that you can't see the annotations—you'll see that what's left is a simple POJO. And you know

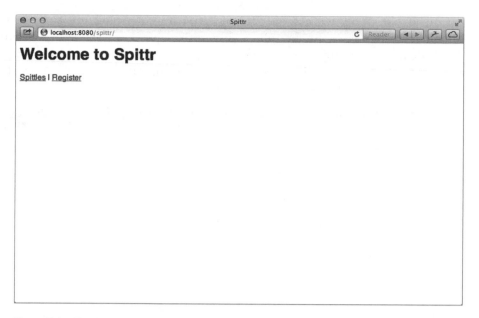

Figure 5.2   The Spittr home page in action

it's easy to test POJOs. Therefore, you can test `HomeController` by writing a simple test like the following.

Listing 5.5   `HomeControllerTest`: tests `HomeController`

```
package spittr.web;
import static org.junit.Assert.assertEquals;
import org.junit.Test;
import spittr.web.HomeController;

public class HomeControllerTest {
  @Test
  public void testHomePage() throws Exception {
    HomeController controller = new HomeController();
    assertEquals("home", controller.home());
  }
}
```

Although the test in listing 5.5 is straightforward, it only tests what happens in the `home()` method. It calls `home()` directly and asserts that a `String` containing the value "home" is returned. It completely fails to test what makes that method a Spring MVC controller method. Nothing about the test asserts that `home()` will be called when a GET request for / comes in. And just because it returns "home", there's nothing to truly test that home is the name of the view.

Starting with Spring 3.2, however, you have a way to test Spring MVC controllers as controllers, not merely as POJOs. Spring now includes a mechanism for mocking all the mechanics of Spring MVC and executing HTTP requests against controllers. This will enable you to test your controllers without firing up a web server or web browser.

To demonstrate proper testing of a Spring MVC controller, you can rewrite Home-ControllerTest to take advantage of the new Spring MVC testing features. The following listing shows the new HomeControllerTest.

Listing 5.6   Revised `HomeControllerTest`

```
package spittr.web;
import static
  org.springframework.test.web.servlet.request.MockMvcRequestBuilders.*;
import static
  org.springframework.test.web.servlet.result.MockMvcResultMatchers.*;
import static
  org.springframework.test.web.servlet.setup.MockMvcBuilders.*;
import org.junit.Test;
import org.springframework.test.web.servlet.MockMvc;
import spittr.web.HomeController;

public class HomeControllerTest {
  @Test
  public void testHomePage() throws Exception {
    HomeController controller = new HomeController();
    MockMvc mockMvc =                                    ←— Set up MockMvc
        standaloneSetup(controller).build();

    mockMvc.perform(get("/"))                   ←— Perform GET /
          .andExpect(view().name("home"));      ←— Expect home view
  }
}
```

Even though this new version of the test is a few lines longer than its predecessor, it more completely tests HomeController. Rather than call home() directly and test its return value, this test issues a GET request for / and asserts that the resulting view is named home. It starts by passing an instance of HomeController to MockMvcBuilders .standaloneSetup() and calling build() to set up the MockMvc instance. Then it asks the MockMvc instance to perform a GET request for / and sets an expectation for the view name.

5.2.2   *Defining class-level request handling*

Now that you have a test around HomeController, you can do a bit of refactoring to be certain that nothing breaks. One thing you can do is split up @RequestMapping by placing the path-mapping portion of it at the class level. The next listing shows how this is done.

Listing 5.7   Splitting the `@RequestMapping` in `HomeController`

```
package spittr.web;
import static org.springframework.web.bind.annotation.RequestMethod.*;
import org.springframework.stereotype.Controller;
import org.springframework.web.bind.annotation.RequestMapping;
```

```
import org.springframework.web.bind.annotation.RequestMethod;

@Controller
@RequestMapping("/")                          <—— Map controller to /
public class HomeController {

  @RequestMapping(method=GET)                 <—— Handle GET requests
  public String home() {
    return "home";              <—— View name is home
  }

}
```

In this new version of HomeController, the path has been moved up to a new class-level @RequestMapping, whereas the HTTP method is still mapped at the method level. Any time there's a class-level @RequestMapping on a controller class, it applies to all handler methods in the controller. Then any @RequestMapping annotations on handler methods will complement the class-level @RequestMapping.

In the case of HomeController, there's only one handler method. Its @RequestMapping, when taken together with the class-level @RequestMapping, indicates that the home() method will handle GET requests for /.

In other words, you really haven't changed anything. You've moved a few things around, but HomeController still does the same thing as before. Because you have a test, you can be sure you haven't broken anything along the way.

While you're tinkering with the @RequestMapping annotations, you can make another tweak to HomeController. The value attribute of @RequestMapping accepts an array of String. So far, you've only given it a single String value of "/". But you can also map it to requests whose path is /homepage by changing the class-level @RequestMapping to look like this:

```
@Controller
@RequestMapping({"/", "/homepage"})
public class HomeController {
...
}
```

Now HomeController's home() method is mapped to handle GET requests for both / and /homepage requests.

5.2.3 *Passing model data to the view*

As it stands now, HomeController is a great example of how to write an extremely simple controller. But most controllers aren't this simple. In the Spittr application, you'll need a page that displays a list of the most recent spittles that have been submitted. Therefore, you'll need a new method to serve such a page.

First you need to define a repository for data access. For decoupling purposes, and so you don't get bogged down in database specifics, you'll define the repository as an interface now and create an implementation of it later (in chapter 10). At the moment, you only need a repository that can fetch a list of the spittles. Spittle-Repository, as defined here, is a sufficient start:

```
package spittr.data;
import java.util.List;
import spittr.Spittle;

public interface SpittleRepository {
  List<Spittle> findSpittles(long max, int count);
}
```

The findSpittles() method takes two parameters. The max parameter is a Spittle ID that represents the maximum ID of any Spittle that should be returned. As for the count parameter, it indicates how many Spittle objects to return. In order to get the 20 most recent Spittle objects, you can call findSpittles() like this:

```
List<Spittle> recent =
        spittleRepository.findSpittles(Long.MAX_VALUE, 20);
```

You'll keep the Spittle class fairly simple for now, as shown next. It will have properties to carry a message, a timestamp, and the latitude/longitude of the location from which the spittle was posted.

Listing 5.8 Spittle class: carries a message, a timestamp, and a location

```
package spittr;
import java.util.Date;

public class Spittle {
  private final Long id;
  private final String message;
  private final Date time;
  private Double latitude;
  private Double longitude;

  public Spittle(String message, Date time) {
    this(message, time, null, null);
  }

  public Spittle(
      String message, Date time, Double longitude, Double latitude) {
    this.id = null;
    this.message = message;
    this.time = time;
    this.longitude = longitude;
    this.latitude = latitude;
  }

  public long getId() {
    return id;
  }

  public String getMessage() {
    return message;
  }

  public Date getTime() {
    return time;
  }
```

```
public Double getLongitude() {
    return longitude;
}

public Double getLatitude() {
    return latitude;
}

@Override
public boolean equals(Object that) {
    return EqualsBuilder.reflectionEquals(this, that, "id", "time");
}

@Override
public int hashCode() {
    return HashCodeBuilder.reflectionHashCode(this, "id", "time");
}
}
```

For the most part, `Spittle` is a basic POJO data object—nothing complicated. The only thing to note is that you're using Apache Commons Lang for easy implementation of the `equals()` and `hashCode()` methods. Aside from the general utility value of those methods, they'll be valuable in writing a test for the controller handler method.

While we're on the subject of testing, let's go ahead and write a test for the new controller method. The following listing uses Spring's `MockMvc` to assert the behavior you want in the new handler method.

Listing 5.9 Testing that `SpittleController` handles `GET` requests for `/spittles`

```
@Test
public void shouldShowRecentSpittles() throws Exception {
  List<Spittle> expectedSpittles = createSpittleList(20);
  SpittleRepository mockRepository =                    <-- Mock repository
      mock(SpittleRepository.class);
  when(mockRepository.findSpittles(Long.MAX_VALUE, 20))
      .thenReturn(expectedSpittles);

  SpittleController controller =
        new SpittleController(mockRepository);

  SpittleController controller =
        new SpittleController(mockRepository);
  MockMvc mockMvc = standaloneSetup(controller)         <-- Mock Spring MVC
      .setSingleView(
        new InternalResourceView("/WEB-INF/views/spittles.jsp"))
      .build();

  mockMvc.perform(get("/spittles"))                     <-- GET /spittles
    .andExpect(view().name("spittles"))
    .andExpect(model().attributeExists("spittleList"))
    .andExpect(model().attribute("spittleList",         <-- Assert expectations
      hasItems(expectedSpittles.toArray()))));
}

...
```

```
private List<Spittle> createSpittleList(int count) {
  List<Spittle> spittles = new ArrayList<Spittle>();
  for (int i=0; i < count; i++) {
    spittles.add(new Spittle("Spittle " + i, new Date()));
  }
  return spittles;
}
```

This test starts by creating a mock implementation of the `SpittleRepository` interface that will return a list of 20 `Spittle` objects from its `findSpittles()` method. It then injects that repository into a new `SpittleController` instance and sets up `Mock-Mvc` to use that controller.

Notice that unlike `HomeControllerTest`, this test calls `setSingleView()` on the `MockMvc` builder. This is so the mock framework won't try to resolve the view name coming from the controller on its own. In many cases, this is unnecessary. But for this controller method, the view name will be similar to the request's path; left to its default view resolution, `MockMvc` will fail because the view path will be confused with the controller's path. The actual path given when constructing the `Internal-ResourceView` is unimportant in this test, but you set it to be consistent with how you've configured `InternalResourceViewResolver`.

The test wraps up by performing a `GET` request for /spittles and asserting that the view name is `spittles` and that the model has an attribute named `spittleList` with the expected contents.

Of course, if you ran the test at this point, it would fail. It wouldn't just fail to run; it would fail to compile. That's because you haven't yet written the `Spittle-Controller`. Let's create a `SpittleController` so that it satisfies the expectations of the test in listing 5.9. Here's an implementation of `SpittleController` that should satisfy the test.

> **Listing 5.10   `SpittleController`: places a list of recent spittles in the model**

```
package spittr.web;
import java.util.List;
import org.springframework.beans.factory.annotation.Autowired;
import org.springframework.stereotype.Controller;
import org.springframework.web.bind.annotation.RequestMapping;
import org.springframework.web.bind.annotation.RequestMethod;
import spittr.Spittle;
import spittr.data.SpittleRepository;

@Controller
@RequestMapping("/spittles")
public class SpittleController {

  private SpittleRepository spittleRepository;

  @Autowired
  public SpittleController(                        <─── Inject SpittleRepository
      SpittleRepository spittleRepository) {
    this.spittleRepository = spittleRepository;
```

```
  }

  @RequestMapping(method=RequestMethod.GET)
  public String spittles(Model model) {
    model.addAttribute(                          <—  Add spittles to model
        spittleRepository.findSpittles(
            Long.MAX_VALUE, 20));
    return "spittles";                           <—  Return view name
  }

}
```

As you can see, `SpittleController` has a constructor that's annotated with
`@Autowired` to be given a `SpittleRepository`. That `SpittleRepository` is then used
in the `spittles()` method to fetch a list of recent spittles.

Notice that the `spittles()` method is given a `Model` as a parameter. This is so that
`spittles()` can populate the model with the `Spittle` list it retrieves from the repository. The `Model` is essentially a map (that is, a collection of key-value pairs) that will be
handed off to the view so that the data can be rendered to the client. When `add-
Attribute()` is called without specifying a key, the key is inferred from the type of
object being set as the value. In this case, because it's a `List<Spittle>`, the key will be
inferred as `spittleList`.

The last thing `spittles()` does is return `spittles` as the name of the view that will
render the model.

If you'd prefer to be explicit about the model key, you're welcome to specify it. For
example, the following version of `spittles()` is equivalent to the one in listing 5.10:

```
@RequestMapping(method=RequestMethod.GET)
public String spittles(Model model) {
  model.addAttribute("spittleList",
      spittleRepository.findSpittles(Long.MAX_VALUE, 20));
  return "spittles";
}
```

Likewise, if you'd prefer to work with a non-Spring type, you can ask for a `java
.util.Map` instead of `Model`. Here's another version of `spittles()` that's functionally
equivalent to the others:

```
@RequestMapping(method=RequestMethod.GET)
public String spittles(Map model) {
  model.put("spittleList",
          spittleRepository.findSpittles(Long.MAX_VALUE, 20));
  return "spittles";
}
```

And while we're on the subject of alternate implementations, here's another way to
write the `spittles()` method:

```
@RequestMapping(method=RequestMethod.GET)
public List<Spittle> spittles() {
  return spittleRepository.findSpittles(Long.MAX_VALUE, 20));
}
```

This version is quite a bit different from the others. Rather than return a logical view name and explicitly setting the model, this method returns the `Spittle` list. When a handler method returns an object or a collection like this, the value returned is put into the model, and the model key is inferred from its type (`spittleList`, as in the other examples).

As for the logical view name, it's inferred from the request path. Because this method handles `GET` requests for /spittles, the view name is `spittles` (chopping off the leading slash).

No matter which way you choose to write the `spittles()` method, the result is the same. A list of `Spittle` objects is stored in the model with a key of `spittleList` and given to the view whose name is `spittles`. Given the way you've configured `InternalResourceViewResolver`, that view is a JSP at /WEB-INF/views/spittles.jsp.

Now that there's data in the model, how does the JSP access it? As it turns out, when the view is a JSP, the model data is copied into the request as request attributes. Therefore, the spittles.jsp file can use JavaServer Pages Standard Tag Library's (JSTL) `<c:forEach>` tag to render the list of spittles:

```
<c:forEach items="${spittleList}" var="spittle" >
  <li id="spittle_<c:out value="spittle.id"/>">
    <div class="spittleMessage">
      <c:out value="${spittle.message}" />
    </div>
    <div>
      <span class="spittleTime"><c:out value="${spittle.time}" /></span>
      <span class="spittleLocation">
          (<c:out value="${spittle.latitude}" />,
          <c:out value="${spittle.longitude}" />)</span>
    </div>
  </li>
</c:forEach>
```

Figure 5.3 will help you visualize how this might look in your web browser.

Although `SpittleController` is simple, it's still a step up from what you wrote in `HomeController`. One thing that neither `HomeController` nor `SpittleController` does, however, is handle any form of input. Let's expand on `SpittleController` to take some input from the client.

5.3   *Accepting request input*

Some web applications are read-only. Humans poke about on the website in their web browser, reading whatever content the server sends to the browser.

The good news is that it doesn't have to be that way. Many web applications give the user an opportunity to chime in and send data back to the server. Without this capability, the web would be a very different place.

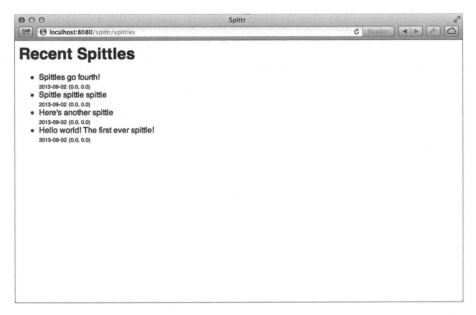

Figure 5.3 Spittle model data from a controller is made available as request parameters and rendered as a list on a web page.

Spring MVC provides several ways that a client can pass data into a controller's handler method. These include

- Query parameters
- Form parameters
- Path variables

You'll see how to write controllers to handle input using all of these mechanisms. For a start, let's look at handling requests with query parameters, the simplest and most straightforward way to send data from the client to the server.

5.3.1 Taking query parameters

One thing that your Spittr application will need to do is display a paged list of spittles. As it is, `SpittleController` only displays the most recent spittles; it offers no way to page back through the history of the spittles that have been written. If you're going to let users go through spittle history a page at a time, you'll need to offer a way for them to pass in parameters that determine which set of spittles to display.

In deciding how to do this, consider that if you're viewing a page of spittles, it's ordered with the most recent spittle first. Therefore, the first spittle on the next page should have an ID that is *before* the ID of the last spittle on the current page. So, in order to display the next page of spittles, you should be able to pass in a spittle ID that is just less than the ID of the last spittle on the current page. You can also pass in a parameter saying how many spittles to display.

To implement this paging solution, you'll need to write a handler method that accepts the following:

- A `before` parameter (which indicates the ID of the `Spittle` that all `Spittle` objects in the results are before)
- A `count` parameter (which indicates how many spittles to include in the result)

To achieve this, let's replace the `spittles()` method you created in listing 5.10 with a new `spittles()` method that works with the `before` and `count` parameters. You'll start by adding a test to reflect the functionality you want to see from the new `spittles()` method.

Listing 5.11 New method to test for a paged list of spittles

```
@Test
public void shouldShowPagedSpittles() throws Exception {
  List<Spittle> expectedSpittles = createSpittleList(50);
  SpittleRepository mockRepository = mock(SpittleRepository.class);
  when(mockRepository.findSpittles(238900, 50))
      .thenReturn(expectedSpittles);                       ◁─┐ Expect max and
                                                             │ count parameters
  SpittleController controller =
      new SpittleController(mockRepository);
  MockMvc mockMvc = standaloneSetup(controller)
      .setSingleView(
          new InternalResourceView("/WEB-INF/views/spittles.jsp"))
      .build();

  mockMvc.perform(get("/spittles?max=238900&count=50"))    ◁─┐ Pass max and
    .andExpect(view().name("spittles"))                      │ count
    .andExpect(model().attributeExists("spittleList"))       │ parameters
    .andExpect(model().attribute("spittleList",
                hasItems(expectedSpittles.toArray())));
}
```

The key difference between this test method and the one in listing 5.9 is that it performs a GET request against /spittles, passing in values for the max and count parameters. This tests the handler method when those parameters are present; the other test method tests for when those parameters are absent. With both tests in place, you can be assured that no matter what changes you make to the controller, it will still be able to handle both kinds of requests:

```
@RequestMapping(method=RequestMethod.GET)
public List<Spittle> spittles(
    @RequestParam("max") long max,
    @RequestParam("count") int count) {
  return spittleRepository.findSpittles(max, count);
}
```

If the handler method in `SpittleController` is going to handle requests with or without the max and count parameters, you'll need to change it to accept those parameters but still default to `Long.MAX_VALUE` and `20` if those parameters are absent on the request. The `defaultValue` attribute of `@RequestParam` will do the trick:

```
@RequestMapping(method=RequestMethod.GET)
public List<Spittle> spittles(
    @RequestParam(value="max",
                  defaultValue=MAX_LONG_AS_STRING) long max,
    @RequestParam(value="count", defaultValue="20") int count) {
  return spittleRepository.findSpittles(max, count);
}
```

Now, if the `max` parameter isn't specified, it will default to the maximum value of `Long`. Because query parameters are always of type `String`, the `defaultValue` attribute requires a `String` value. Therefore, `Long.MAX_VALUE` won't work. Instead, you can capture `Long.MAX_VALUE` in a `String` constant named `MAX_LONG_AS_STRING`:

```
private static final String MAX_LONG_AS_STRING =
        Long.toString(Long.MAX_VALUE);
```

Even though the `defaultValue` is given as a `String`, it will be converted to a `Long` when bound to the method's `max` parameter.

The `count` parameter will default to 20 if the request doesn't have a `count` parameter.

Query parameters are a common way to pass information to a controller in a request. Another way that's popular, especially in a discussion of building resource-oriented controllers, is to pass parameters as part of the request path. Let's see how to use path variables to take input as part of the request path.

5.3.2 *Taking input via path parameters*

Let's say your application needs to support the display of a single `Spittle`, given its ID. One option you have is to write a handler method that accepts the ID as a query parameter using `@RequestParam`:

```
@RequestMapping(value="/show", method=RequestMethod.GET)
public String showSpittle(
    @RequestParam("spittle_id") long spittleId,
    Model model) {
  model.addAttribute(spittleRepository.findOne(spittleId));
  return "spittle";
}
```

This handler method would handle requests such as /spittles/show?spittle_id=12345. Although this could be made to work, it's not ideal from a resource-orientation perspective. Ideally, the resource being identified (the `Spittle`) would be identified by the URL path, not by query parameters. As a general rule, query parameters should not be used to identify a resource. A `GET` request for /spittles/12345 is better than one for /spittles/show?spittle_id=12345. The former identifies a resource to be retrieved. The latter describes an operation with a parameter—essentially RPC over HTTP.

With the goal of resource-oriented controllers in mind, let's capture this require-ment in a test. The following listing shows a new test method to assert resource-oriented request handling in `SpittleController`.

Listing 5.12   Testing a request for a `Spittle` with ID specified in a path variable

```
@Test
public void testSpittle() throws Exception {
  Spittle expectedSpittle = new Spittle("Hello", new Date());
  SpittleRepository mockRepository = mock(SpittleRepository.class);
  when(mockRepository.findOne(12345)).thenReturn(expectedSpittle);

  SpittleController controller = new SpittleController(mockRepository);
  MockMvc mockMvc = standaloneSetup(controller).build();

  mockMvc.perform(get("/spittles/12345"))                ◁─────────  Request resource
    .andExpect(view().name("spittle"))                              via path
    .andExpect(model().attributeExists("spittle"))
    .andExpect(model().attribute("spittle", expectedSpittle));
}
```

As you can see, this test sets up a mock repository, a controller, and `MockMvc`, much like the other tests you've written in this chapter. The most important part of the test is in the last few lines, where it performs a GET request for /spittles/12345 and asserts that the view name is `spittle` and that the expected `Spittle` object is placed in the model. Because you haven't yet implemented the handler method for that kind of request, the request will fail. But you can fix that by adding a new method to `Spittle-Controller`.

Up to this point, all of your controller methods have been mapped (via `@Request-Mapping`) to a statically defined path. But if you're going to make this test pass, you'll need to write an `@RequestMapping` that has a variable portion of the path that repre-sents the `Spittle` ID.

To accommodate these path variables, Spring MVC allows for placeholders in an `@RequestMapping` path. The placeholders are names surrounded by curly braces (`{` and `}`). Although all the other parts of the path need to match exactly for the request to be handled, the placeholder can carry any value.

Here's a handler method that uses placeholders to accept a `Spittle` ID as part of the path:

```
@RequestMapping(value="/{spittleId}", method=RequestMethod.GET)
public String spittle(
    @PathVariable("spittleId") long spittleId,
    Model model) {
  model.addAttribute(spittleRepository.findOne(spittleId));
  return "spittle";
}
```

For example, it can handle requests for /spittles/12345, the path being tested for in listing 5.12.

As you can see, spittle() has a spittleId parameter that is annotated with @PathVariable("spittleId"). This indicates that whatever value is at the placeholder position in the request path will be passed into the handler method's spittleId parameter. If the request is a GET request for /spittles/54321, then 54321 will be passed in as the value of spittleId.

Notice that the phrase spittleId is repeated a few times in the example: in the @RequestMapping path, as the value attribute of @PathVariable, and again as a method parameter name. Because the method parameter name happens to be the same as the placeholder name, you can optionally omit the value parameter on @PathVariable:

```
@RequestMapping(value="/{spittleId}", method=RequestMethod.GET)
public String spittle(@PathVariable long spittleId, Model model) {
  model.addAttribute(spittleRepository.findOne(spittleId));
  return "spittle";
}
```

If no value attribute is given for @PathVariable, it assumes the placeholder's name is the same as the method parameter name. This can make the code a little cleaner by not duplicating the placeholder name any more than necessary. But be cautioned: if you decide to rename the parameter, you must also change the placeholder name to match.

The spittle() method will pass the parameter along to the findOne() method on the SpittleRepository to find a single Spittle object and will add that Spittle to the model. The model key will be spittle, inferred by the type passed in to add-Attribute().

The data in the Spittle object can then be rendered in the view by referring to the request attribute whose key is spittle (the same as the model key). Here's a snippet of a JSP view that renders the Spittle:

```
<div class="spittleView">
  <div class="spittleMessage"><c:out value="${spittle.message}" /></div>
  <div>
    <span class="spittleTime"><c:out value="${spittle.time}" /></span>
  </div>
</div>
```

There's nothing flashy about this view, as you can see from the screenshot in figure 5.4.

Query parameters and path parameters are fine for passing small amounts of data on a request. But often you need to pass a lot of data (perhaps data coming from a form submission), and query parameters are too awkward and limited for that. Let's see how you can write controller methods that handle form submissions.

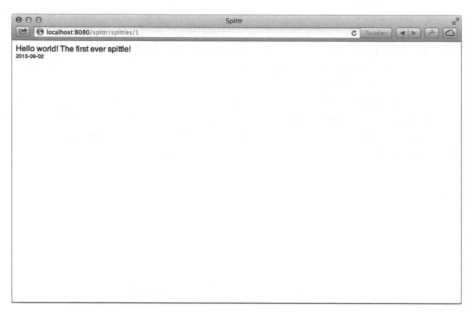

Figure 5.4   Displaying a spittle in the browser

5.4   *Processing forms*

Web applications typically do more than just push content out to the user. Most also let users participate in the conversation by filling out forms and submitting data back into the application. Spring MVC controllers are well-suited for form processing as well as serving content.

There are two sides to working with forms: displaying the form and processing the data the user submits from the form. In the Spittr application, you'll need a form for new users to register with the application. `SpitterController` is a new controller with a single request-handling method for displaying the registration form.

Listing 5.13   `SpitterController`: displays a form for users to sign up with the app

```
package spittr.web;
import static org.springframework.web.bind.annotation.RequestMethod.*;
import org.springframework.beans.factory.annotation.Autowired;
import org.springframework.stereotype.Controller;
import org.springframework.ui.Model;
import org.springframework.web.bind.annotation.PathVariable;
import org.springframework.web.bind.annotation.RequestMapping;
import org.springframework.web.bind.annotation.RequestMethod;
import spittr.Spitter;
import spittr.data.SpitterRepository;

@Controller
@RequestMapping("/spitter")
public class SpitterController {
```

```
@RequestMapping(value="/register", method=GET)          ◁─┐ Handle GET requests
public String showRegistrationForm() {                     │ for /spitter/register
  return "registerForm";
}

}
```

The showRegistrationForm() method's @RequestMapping annotation, along with the class-level @RequestMapping annotation, declares that it will handle HTTP GET requests for /spitter/register. It's a simple method, taking no input and only returning a logical view named registerForm. Given how you've configured InternalResourceView-Resolver, that means the JSP at /WEB-INF/views/registerForm.jsp will be called on to render the registration form.

As simple as showRegistrationForm() is, it still deserves to be covered by a test. Because it's a simple method, its test will be equally simple.

Listing 5.14 Testing a form-displaying controller method

```
@Test
public void shouldShowRegistration() throws Exception {
  SpitterController controller = new SpitterController();
  MockMvc mockMvc = standaloneSetup(controller).build();      ◁─ Set up MockMvc

  mockMvc.perform(get("/spitter/register"))
         .andExpect(view().name("registerForm"));      ◁─ Assert registerForm view
}
```

This test method is very similar to the test for the home page controller method. It performs a GET request for /spitter/register and then asserts that the resulting view is named registerForm.

Now let's get back to the view. Because the view name is registerForm, you'll need a JSP named registerForm.jsp. This JSP must include an HTML <form> where the user will enter information to sign up with the application. Here's the JSP you'll use for now.

Listing 5.15 JSP to render a registration form

```
<%@ taglib uri="http://java.sun.com/jsp/jstl/core" prefix="c" %>
<%@ page session="false" %>
<html>
  <head>
    <title>Spittr</title>
    <link rel="stylesheet" type="text/css"
          href="<c:url value="/resources/style.css" />" >
  </head>
  <body>
    <h1>Register</h1>

    <form method="POST">
      First Name: <input type="text" name="firstName" /><br/>
      Last Name: <input type="text" name="lastName" /><br/>
      Username: <input type="text" name="username" /><br/>
      Password: <input type="password" name="password" /><br/>
```

```
        <input type="submit" value="Register" />
      </form>
   </body>
</html>
```

As you can see, this JSP is fairly basic. It has HTML form fields to capture the user's first name, last name, a username, and a password, as well as a button to submit the form. Rendered in the browser, it looks a little something like figure 5.5.

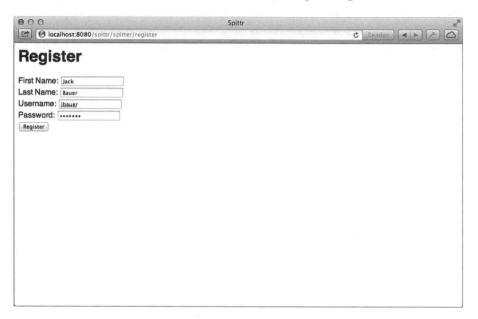

Figure 5.5   The registration page offers a form that will be processed by `SpitterController` to add a new user to the application.

Notice that the `<form>` tag doesn't have an `action` parameter set. Because of that, when this form is submitted, it will be posted back to the same URL path that displayed it. That is, it will be posted back to /spitters/register.

That means you'll need something back on the server to handle the HTTP POST request. Let's add another method to `SpitterController` to handle form submission.

5.4.1   *Writing a form-handling controller*

When processing the POST request from the registration form, the controller needs to accept the form data and save the form data as a `Spitter` object. Finally, in order to prevent a duplicate submission (such as might happen if the user clicked their browser's Refresh button), it should redirect the browser to the newly created user's profile page. This behavior is captured and tested in `shouldProcessRegistration()`.

Listing 5.16 Testing form-handling controller methods

```
@Test
public void shouldProcessRegistration() throws Exception {
  SpitterRepository mockRepository =
          mock(SpitterRepository.class);      ◁— Set up mock repository
  Spitter unsaved =
          new Spitter("jbauer", "24hours", "Jack", "Bauer");
  Spitter saved =
          new Spitter(24L, "jbauer", "24hours", "Jack", "Bauer");
  when(mockRepository.save(unsaved)).thenReturn(saved);

  SpitterController controller =
          new SpitterController(mockRepository);
  MockMvc mockMvc = standaloneSetup(controller).build();     ◁— Set up MockMvc

  mockMvc.perform(post("/spitter/register")        ◁— Perform request
          .param("firstName", "Jack")
          .param("lastName", "Bauer")
          .param("username", "jbauer")
          .param("password", "24hours"))
          .andExpect(redirectedUrl("/spitter/jbauer"));

  verify(mockRepository, atLeastOnce()).save(unsaved);       ◁— Verify save
}
```

Clearly, this test is more involved than the test for displaying the registration form. After setting up a mock implementation of SpitterRepository and creating a controller and MockMvc setup to execute against, shouldProcessRegistration() performs a POST request against /spitter/register. As part of that POST request, user information is passed as parameters on the request to simulate a form being submitted.

When handling a POST request, it's usually a good idea to send a redirect after the POST has completed processing so that a browser refresh won't accidentally submit the form a second time. This test expects that the request will end in a redirect to /spitter /jbauer, the URL path of the new user's profile page.

Finally, the test verifies that the mocked SpitterRepository was actually used to save the data coming in on the form.

Now let's implement the controller method that will handle this form submission test. shouldProcessRegistration() may have left you with the impression that a chunk of work is required to satisfy the test. But as you can see in the new Spitter-Controller in this listing, there's not much to it.

Listing 5.17 Handling form submission to register a new user

```
package spittr.web;

import static org.springframework.web.bind.annotation.RequestMethod.*;

import org.springframework.beans.factory.annotation.Autowired;
import org.springframework.stereotype.Controller;
import org.springframework.ui.Model;
import org.springframework.web.bind.annotation.PathVariable;
import org.springframework.web.bind.annotation.RequestMapping;
```

```
import spittr.Spitter;
import spittr.data.SpitterRepository;

@Controller
@RequestMapping("/spitter")
public class SpitterController {
  private SpitterRepository spitterRepository;

  @Autowired
  public SpitterController(                       <-- Inject SpitterRepository
      SpitterRepository spitterRepository) {
    this.spitterRepository = spitterRepository;
  }

  @RequestMapping(value="/register", method=GET)
  public String showRegistrationForm() {
    return "registerForm";
  }

  @RequestMapping(value="/register", method=POST)
  public String processRegistration(Spitter spitter) {
    spitterRepository.save(spitter);              <-- Save a Spitter

    return "redirect:/spitter/" +          <-- Redirect to profile page
           spitter.getUsername();
  }
}
```

The `showRegistrationForm()` method is still in place. But notice the new `process-Registration()` method: it's given a `Spitter` object as a parameter. This object has `firstName`, `lastName`, `username`, and `password` properties that will be populated from the request parameters of the same name.

Once it's called with the `Spitter` object, `processRegistration()` calls the `save()` method on the `SpitterRepository` that is now injected into `SpitterController` in the constructor.

The last thing that `processRegistration()` does is return a `String` specifying the view. But this view specification is different from what you've seen before. Rather than just return a view name and let the view resolver sort it out, here you're returning a redirect specification.

When `InternalResourceViewResolver` sees the `redirect:` prefix on the view specification, it knows to interpret it as a redirect specification instead of as a view name. In this case, it will redirect to the path for a user's profile page. For example, if the `Spitter` `.username` property is jbauer, then the view will redirect to /spitter/jbauer.

It's worth noting that in addition to `redirect:`, `InternalResourceViewResolver` also recognizes the `forward:` prefix. When it sees a view specification prefixed with `forward:`, the request is forwarded to the given URL path instead of redirected.

Perfect! At this point, the test in listing 5.16 should pass. But you're not finished yet. Because you're redirecting to the user's profile page, you should probably add a handler method to `SpitterController` to handle requests for the profile page. Here's a `showSpitterProfile()` method that will do the trick:

```
@RequestMapping(value="/{username}", method=GET)
```

```
public String showSpitterProfile(
      @PathVariable String username, Model model) {
  Spitter spitter = spitterRepository.findByUsername(username);
  model.addAttribute(spitter);
  return "profile";
}
```

showSpitterProfile() fetches a Spitter object from the SpitterRepository by the username. It adds the Spitter to the model and then returns profile, the logical view name for the profile view. Like all the other views presented in this chapter, you'll keep the profile view simple for now:

```
<h1>Your Profile</h1>
<c:out value="${spitter.username}" /><br/>
<c:out value="${spitter.firstName}" />
    <c:out value="${spitter.lastName}" />
```

Figure 5.6 shows the profile page as rendered in a web browser.

What will happen if the form doesn't send a username or password parameter? Or what if the firstName or lastName value is empty or too long? Let's look at how to add validation to the form submission to prevent inconsistencies in the data presented.

5.4.2 Validating forms

If the user were to leave the username or password field empty when submitting the form, it could result in the creation of a new Spitter object whose username and password were empty Strings. At the very least, this is odd behavior. But left

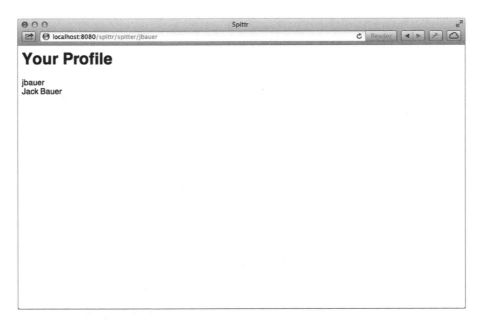

Figure 5.6 The Spittr profile page displays a user's information, as populated into the model by SpitterController.

unchecked, it could present a security concern where anyone could sign in to the application by submitting an empty login form.

Also, you should take steps to prevent the user from submitting an empty first-Name and/or lastName in an effort to maintain some level of anonymity. And it's probably a good idea to limit the length of the values given in those fields, keeping them at a reasonable size and avoiding misuse of the fields.

One way to handle validation, albeit naive, is to add code to the process-Registration() method to check for invalid values and send the user back to the registration form unless the data is valid. It's a short method, so tossing in a few extra if statements won't do much harm. Right?

Rather than litter your handler methods with validation logic, however, you can take advantage of Spring's support for the Java Validation API (a.k.a. JSR-303). Starting with Spring 3.0, Spring supports the Java Validation API in Spring MVC. No extra configuration is required to make Java Validation work in Spring MVC. You just need to make sure an implementation of the Java API, such as Hibernate Validator, is in the project's classpath.

The Java Validation API defines several annotations that you can put on properties to place constraints on the values of those properties. All of these annotations are in the javax.validation.constraints package. Table 5.1 lists these validation annotations.

Table 5.1 Validation annotations provided by the Java Validation API

Annotation	Description
@AssertFalse	The annotated element must be a Boolean type and be false.
@AssertTrue	The annotated element must be a Boolean type and be true.
@DecimalMax	The annotated element must be a number whose value is less than or equal to a given BigDecimalString value.
@DecimalMin	The annotated element must be a number whose value is greater than or equal to a given BigDecimalString value.
@Digits	The annotated element must be a number whose value has a specified number of digits.
@Future	The value of the annotated element must be a date in the future.
@Max	The annotated element must be a number whose value is less than or equal to a given value.
@Min	The annotated element must be a number whose value is greater than or equal to a given value.
@NotNull	The value of the annotated element must not be null.
@Null	The value of the annotated element must be null.
@Past	The value of the annotated element must be a date in the past.
@Pattern	The value of the annotated element must match a given regular expression.

Table 5.1   Validation annotations provided by the Java Validation API *(continued)*

Annotation	Description
@Size	The value of the annotated element must be either a `String`, a collection, or an array whose length fits within the given range.

In addition to the annotations in table 5.1, Java Validation API implementations may provide additional validation annotations. And it's also possible to define your own constraints. But for our purposes, we'll focus on a couple of the core constraint validations from the table.

Thinking over the constraints you need to apply to the fields in Spitter, it seems you'll probably need the @NotNull and @Size annotations. All you need to do is toss those annotations around on the properties of Spitter. The next listing shows Spitter with its properties annotated for validation.

Listing 5.18   `SpittleForm`: carries only fields submitted in a `SpittlePOST` request

```
package spittr;
import javax.validation.constraints.NotNull;
import javax.validation.constraints.Size;
import org.apache.commons.lang3.builder.EqualsBuilder;
import org.apache.commons.lang3.builder.HashCodeBuilder;

public class Spitter {

  private Long id;

  @NotNull
  @Size(min=5, max=16)          Not null, from 5
  private String username;      to 16 characters

  @NotNull
  @Size(min=5, max=25)          Not null, from 5
  private String password;      to 25 characters


  @NotNull
  @Size(min=2, max=30)          Not null, from 2
  private String firstName;     to 30 characters

  @NotNull
  @Size(min=2, max=30)          Not null, from 2
  private String lastName;      to 30 characters

  ...

}
```

All the properties of Spitter are now annotated with @NotNull to ensure that they aren't left null. Similarly, the @Size annotation is placed on the properties to constrain them between minimum and maximum lengths. What this means in the Spittr application is that the user must completely fill out the registration form with values that fit within the size constraints.

Now that you have annotated `Spitter` with validation constraints, you need to change the `processRegistration()` method to apply validation. The new validation-enabled `processRegistration()` is shown next.

Listing 5.19   `processRegistration()`: ensures that data submitted is valid

```
@RequestMapping(value="/register", method=POST)
public String processRegistration(
    @Valid Spitter spitter,          ◁— Validate Spitter input
    Errors errors) {

  if (errors.hasErrors()) {                    Return to form on
    return "registerForm";           ◁┘       validation errors
  }

  spitterRepository.save(spitter);
  return "redirect:/spitter/" + spitter.getUsername();
}
```

A lot has changed since the original `processRegistration()` in listing 5.17. The `Spitter` parameter is now annotated with `@Valid` to indicate to Spring that the command object has validation constraints that should be enforced.

Just having validation constraints on the `Spitter`'s properties won't prevent the form from being submitted. Even if the user fails to fill in a field on the form or gives a value whose length exceeds the maximum length, the `processRegistration()` method will still be called. This gives you a chance to deal with the validation problems however you see fit in `processRegistration()`.

If there are any validation errors, they're available in the `Errors` object that you're now asking for as a parameter to `processRegistration()`. (Note that it's important that the `Errors` parameter immediately follow the `@Valid`-annotated parameter that's being validated.) The first thing `processRegistration()` does is call `Errors.has-Errors()` to check for any errors.

If there are errors, `Errors.hasErrors()` returns `registerForm`, the view name for the registration form. This will take the user's browser back to the registration form so they can correct any problems and try again. For now, the blank form will be displayed, but in the next chapter, you'll adapt the form to show the values that were originally submitted and communicate validation problems to the user.

If there are no errors, the `Spitter` is saved via the repository, and the controller redirects to the profile page as before.

5.5   *Summary*

In this chapter, you've made a good start on the web portion of your application. As you've seen, Spring comes with a powerful and flexible web framework. Employing annotations, Spring MVC offers a near-POJO development model, making simple work of developing controllers that handle requests and are easy to test.

When it comes to writing controller handler methods, Spring MVC is extremely flexible. As a rule of thumb, if your handler method needs something, then it should ask for that object as a parameter. Likewise, anything it doesn't need should be left out of the parameter list. This leads to infinite possibilities in request handling, while maintaining a simple programming model.

Although much of this chapter focused on request handling with controllers, response rendering is also important. We briefly looked at how to write views for your controllers using JSPs. But there's more to Spring MVC views than the basic JSPs you wrote in this chapter.

Coming up in chapter 6, we'll dig deeper into Spring views, expanding on how you can take advantage of Spring tag libraries in JSP. You'll also see how to add consistent layouts to your views using Apache Tiles. And we'll look at Thymeleaf, an exciting alternative to JSP that comes with built-in Spring support.

Rendering web views

This chapter covers

- Rendering model data as HTML
- Using JSP views
- Defining view layout with tiles
- Working with Thymeleaf views

In the previous chapter, we primarily focused on writing the controllers that handle web requests. You also created some simple views to render the model data produced by those controllers, but we didn't spend too much time discussing the views or what happens between the time a controller finishes handling a request and the time the results are displayed in the user's web browser. That's the topic of this chapter.

6.1 Understanding view resolution

None of the methods in the controllers you wrote in chapter 5 directly produce the HTML that is rendered in the browser. Instead, they populate the model with some data and then pass the model off to a view for rendering. Those methods return a `String` value that is the logical name of the view but that doesn't directly refer to a specific view implementation. Although you wrote a few simple JavaServer Page (JSP) views, nothing in the controllers is aware of that fact.

Decoupling request-handling logic in the controller from the view-rendering of a view is an important feature of Spring MVC. If the controller methods were directly responsible for producing HTML, it would be difficult to maintain and update the view without getting your hands dirty in request-handling logic. At most, the controller methods and view implementations should agree on the contents of the model; apart from that, they should keep an arms-length distance from each other.

But if the controller only knows about the view by a logical view name, how does Spring determine which actual view implementation it should use to render the model? That's a job for Spring's view resolvers.

In chapter 5, you used a view resolver known as `InternalResourceViewResolver`. It was configured to apply a prefix of /WEB-INF/views/ and a suffix of .jsp to a view name to arrive at the physical location of the JSP that would render the model. Now let's take a step back and look at view resolution in general and some of the other view resolvers that Spring offers.

Spring MVC defines an interface named `ViewResolver` that looks a little something like this:

```
public interface ViewResolver {
  View resolveViewName(String viewName, Locale locale)
                     throws Exception;
}
```

The `resolveViewName()` method, when given a view name and a `Locale`, returns a `View` instance. `View` is another interface that looks like this:

```
public interface View {
  String getContentType();
  void render(Map<String, ?> model,
           HttpServletRequest request,
           HttpServletResponse response) throws Exception;
}
```

The `View` interface's job is to take the model, as well as the servlet request and response objects, and render output into the response.

It looks simple enough. All you need to do is start writing implementations of `ViewResolver` and `View` to render content into the response to be displayed in your users' browsers. Right?

Not necessarily. Although you can write your own custom implementations of `ViewResolver` and `View`, and although there are some special cases where that's necessary, typically you needn't worry yourself with these interfaces. I only mention them to give you some insight into how view resolution works. Fortunately, Spring provides several out-of-the-box implementations, listed in table 6.1, that fit most circumstances.

Table 6.1 Spring comes with 13 view resolvers to translate logical view names into physical view implementations.

View resolver	Description
BeanNameViewResolver	Resolves views as beans in the Spring application context whose ID is the same as the view name.
ContentNegotiatingViewResolver	Resolves views by considering the content type desired by the client and delegating to another view resolver that can produce that type.
FreeMarkerViewResolver	Resolves views as FreeMarker templates.
InternalResourceViewResolver	Resolves views as resources internal to the web application (typically JSPs).
JasperReportsViewResolver	Resolves views as JasperReports definitions.
ResourceBundleViewResolver	Resolves views from a resource bundle (typically a properties file).
TilesViewResolver	Resolves views as Apache Tile definitions, where the tile ID is the same as the view name. Note that there are two different TilesViewResolver implementations, one each for Tiles 2.0 and Tiles 3.0.
UrlBasedViewResolver	Resolves views directly from the view name, where the view name matches the name of a physical view definition.
VelocityLayoutViewResolver	Resolves views as Velocity layouts to compose pages from different Velocity templates.
VelocityViewResolver	Resolves views as Velocity templates.
XmlViewResolver	Resolves views as bean definitions from a specified XML file. Similar to BeanNameViewResolver.
XsltViewResolver	Resolves views to be rendered as the result of an XSLT transformation.

Note that all the view resolvers in table 6.1 are available in both Spring 4 and Spring 3.2. And all but one of them (the Tiles 3 TilesViewResolver) are supported by Spring 3.1.

We don't have room in this book to cover all 13 view resolvers offered by Spring. But that's okay, because there are only a handful of them that you'll ever need in most applications.

For the most part, each of the view resolvers in table 6.1 corresponds to a specific view technology available for Java web applications. InternalResourceViewResolver is typically used for JSP, TilesViewResolver is for Apache Tiles views, and FreeMarker-ViewResolver and VelocityViewResolver map to FreeMarker and Velocity template views respectively.

In this chapter, we'll focus our attention on the view technologies that are most relevant to the majority of Java developers. Because most Java web applications use JSP, we'll start by looking at `InternalResourceViewResolver`, the view resolver that's typically used to resolve JSP views. Then we'll try out `TilesViewResolver` to achieve layout control over JSP pages.

To wrap up this chapter, we'll look at a view-resolver option that isn't listed in table 6.1. Thymeleaf is a compelling alternative to JSP that offers a view resolver for working with Thymeleaf's *natural templates*: templates that have more in common with the HTML they produce than with the Java code that drives them. Thymeleaf is such an exciting view option that I wouldn't blame you if you flipped a few pages ahead to section 6.4 to see how to use it with Spring.

If you're still on this page, it's probably because you know that JSP has been, and still is, the dominant view technology for Java. You've probably used JSP on several projects before and are likely to need it again. So let's start with a look at how you can use JSP views with Spring MVC.

6.2 Creating JSP views

Believe it or not, JavaServer Pages has been the go-to view technology for Java-based web applications for almost 15 years. Although it started out as an ugly, Java-centric twist on similar templating technologies (such as Microsoft's Active Server Pages), JSP has evolved over the years to include support for an expression language and custom tag libraries.

Spring supports JSP views in two ways:

- `InternalResourceViewResolver` can be used to resolve view names into JSP files. Moreover, if you're using JavaServer Pages Standard Tag Library (JSTL) tags in your JSP pages, `InternalResourceViewResolver` can resolve view names into JSP files fronted by `JstlView` to expose JSTL locale and resource bundle variables to JSTL's formatting and message tags.
- Spring provides two JSP tag libraries, one for form-to-model binding and one providing general utility features.

Whether or not you use JSTL or intend to use Spring's JSP tag libraries, it's important to configure a view resolver to resolve JSP views. Although a few of Spring's other view resolvers could be used to map view names to JSP files, `InternalResourceView-Resolver` is the simplest and most commonly used view resolver for this task. We touched on configuring `InternalResourceViewResolver` in chapter 5. But that was done in haste just so you could exercise your controllers in a web browser. Let's take a closer look at `InternalResourceViewResolver` and see how to tweak it to do your bidding.

6.2.1 Configuring a JSP-ready view resolver

Whereas some view resolvers, such as `ResourceBundleViewResolver`, directly map a logical view name to a specific implementation of the `View` interface, `Internal-ResourceViewResolver` takes a more indirect approach. It follows a convention whereby a prefix and a suffix are attached to the view name to determine the physical path to a view resource in the same web application.

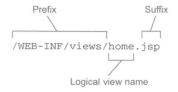

Figure 6.1 `InternalResourceViewResolver` resolves views by adding a prefix and a suffix to the view name.

As an example, consider the simple case where the logical view name is home. It's a common practice to place JSP files under the web application's WEB-INF folder to prevent direct access. If you were to keep all your JSP files in /WEB-INF/views/, and if your home page JSP is named home.jsp, then you could derive the physical view path by prefixing the logical view name home with /WEB-INF/views/ and adding a suffix of .jsp. This is illustrated in figure 6.1.

You can configure `InternalResourceViewResolver` to apply this convention when resolving views by configuring it with this @Bean-annotated method:

```
@Bean
public ViewResolver viewResolver() {
  InternalResourceViewResolver resolver =
      new InternalResourceViewResolver();
  resolver.setPrefix("/WEB-INF/views/");
  resolver.setSuffix(".jsp");
  return resolver;
}
```

Optionally, if you prefer to use Spring's XML-based configuration, you can configure `InternalResourceViewResolver` like this:

```
<bean id="viewResolver"
      class="org.springframework.web.servlet.view.
                         InternalResourceViewResolver"
      p:prefix="/WEB-INF/views/"
      p:suffix=".jsp" />
```

With this configuration of `InternalResourceViewResolver` in place, you can expect it to resolve logical view names into JSP files such as this:

- home resolves to /WEB-INF/views/home.jsp
- productList resolves to /WEB-INF/views/productList.jsp
- books/detail resolves to /WEB-INF/views/books/detail.jsp

Let me call particular attention to that last example. When a logical view name has a slash in it, that slash is carried over into the resource path name. Therefore, it maps to a JSP file that's in a subdirectory of whatever directory is referenced by the `prefix` property. This offers a handy way of organizing your view templates under a hierarchy of directories rather than keeping them all in a single directory.

RESOLVING JSTL VIEWS

So far you've configured the basic, garden-variety `InternalResourceViewResolver`. It ultimately resolves logical view names into instances of `InternalResourceView` that reference JSP files. But if those JSP files are using JSTL tags for formatting or messages, then you may want to configure `InternalResourceViewResolver` to resolve a `JstlView` instead.

JSTL's formatting tags need a `Locale` to properly format locale-specific values such as dates and money. And its message tags can use a Spring message source and a `Locale` to properly choose messages to render in HTML. By resolving `JstlView`, the JSTL tags will be given the `Locale` and any message source configured in Spring.

All that's needed to have `InternalResourceViewResolver` resolve `JstlView` instead of `InternalResourceView` is to set its `viewClass` property:

```
@Bean
public ViewResolver viewResolver() {
  InternalResourceViewResolver resolver =
      new InternalResourceViewResolver();
  resolver.setPrefix("/WEB-INF/views/");
  resolver.setSuffix(".jsp");
  resolver.setViewClass(
      org.springframework.web.servlet.view.JstlView.class);
  return resolver;
}
```

Again, you can accomplish the same thing with XML:

```
<bean id="viewResolver"
      class="org.springframework.web.servlet.view.
                        InternalResourceViewResolver"
      p:prefix="/WEB-INF/views/"
      p:suffix=".jsp"
      p:viewClass="org.springframework.web.servlet.view.JstlView" />
```

Whether you use Java configuration or XML, this will ensure that JSTL's formatting and message tags will get the `Locale` and message sources configured in Spring.

6.2.2 *Using Spring's JSP libraries*

Tag libraries are a powerful way to bring functionality to a JSP template without resorting to writing Java code directly in scriptlet blocks. Spring offers two JSP tag libraries to help define the view of your Spring MVC web views. One tag library renders HTML form tags that are bound to a `model` attribute. The other has a hodgepodge of utility tags that come in handy from time to time.

You're likely to find the form-binding tag library to be the more useful of the two tag libraries. So that's where you'll start with Spring's JSP tags. You'll see how to bind the Spittr application's registration form to the model so that the form will be prepopulated and validation errors can be displayed after a failed form submission.

BINDING FORMS TO THE MODEL

Spring's form-binding JSP tag library includes 14 tags, most of which render HTML form tags. But what makes these different from the raw HTML tags is that they're bound to an object in the model and can be populated with values from the model object's properties. The tag library also includes a tag that can be used to communicate errors to the user by rendering them into the resulting HTML.

To use the form-binding tag library, you'll need to declare it in the JSP pages that will use it:

```
<%@ taglib uri="http://www.springframework.org/tags/form" prefix="sf" %>
```

Notice that I specified a prefix of `sf`, but it's also common to use a prefix of `form`. You may specify any prefix you'd like. I chose `sf` because it's succinct, easy to type, and an abbreviation for *Spring forms*. Throughout this book, I'll assume a prefix of `sf` whenever the form-binding library is used.

Once you declare the form-binding tag library, you're afforded 14 tags. These are listed in table 6.2.

Table 6.2   Spring's form-binding tag library includes tags to bind model objects to and from rendered HTML forms.

JSP tag	Description
`<sf:checkbox>`	Renders an HTML `<input>` tag with `type` set to `checkbox`.
`<sf:checkboxes>`	Renders multiple HTML `<input>` tags with `type` set to `checkbox`.
`<sf:errors>`	Renders field errors in an HTML `<span>` tag.
`<sf:form>`	Renders an HTML `<form>` tag and exposed binding path to inner tags for data-binding.
`<sf:hidden>`	Renders an HTML `<input>` tag with `type` set to `hidden`.
`<sf:input>`	Renders an HTML `<input>` tag with `type` set to `text`.
`<sf:label>`	Renders an HTML `<label>` tag.
`<sf:option>`	Renders an HTML `<option>` tag. The `selected` attribute is set according to the bound value.
`<sf:options>`	Renders a list of HTML `<option>` tags corresponding to the bound collection, array, or map.
`<sf:password>`	Renders an HTML `<input>` tag with `type` set to `password`.
`<sf:radiobutton>`	Renders an HTML `<input>` tag with `type` set to `radio`.
`<sf:radiobuttons>`	Renders multiple HTML `<input>` tags with `type` set to `radio`.
`<sf:select>`	Renders an HTML `<select>` tag.
`<sf:textarea>`	Renders an HTML `<textarea>` tag.

It would be hard to cook up an example to demonstrate all of these tags, and any attempt would certainly be contrived. For the Spittr example, you'll only use the tags that are fitting for the Spittr application's registration form. Specifically, you'll start by using `<sf:form>`, `<sf:input>`, and `<sf:password>`. Applying those tags to the registration JSP, you get the following:

```
<sf:form method="POST" commandName="spitter">
  First Name: <sf:input path="firstName" /><br/>
  Last Name: <sf:input path="lastName" /><br/>
  Email: <sf:input path="email" /><br/>
  Username: <sf:input path="username" /><br/>
  Password: <sf:password path="password" /><br/>
  <input type="submit" value="Register" />
</sf:form>
```

The `<sf:form>` tag renders an HTML `<form>` tag. But it also sets some context around a model object designated in the `commandName` attribute. Properties on the model object will be referenced in the other form-binding tags you use.

In the preceding code, you set `commandName` to `spitter`. Therefore, there must be an object in the model whose key is `spitter`, or else the form won't be able to render (and you'll get JSP errors). That means you need to make a small change to `Spitter-Controller` to ensure that a `Spitter` object is in the model under the `spitter` key:

```
@RequestMapping(value="/register", method=GET)
public String showRegistrationForm(Model model) {
  model.addAttribute(new Spitter());
  return "registerForm";
}
```

This tweak to `showRegistrationForm()` now has that method adding a new `Spitter` instance to the model. The model key will be inferred from the object type to be `spitter`—exactly what you need it to be.

Going back to the form, the first three fields have had their HTML `<input>` tag replaced with `<sf:input>`. This tag renders an HTML `<input>` tag with the `type` attribute set to `text`. Its `value` attribute will be set to the value of the model object's property specified in the `path` attribute. For instance, if the `Spitter` object in the model has `Jack` as the value of its `firstName` property, then `<sf:input path="firstName"/>` will render an `<input>` tag with `value="Jack"`.

The `password` field uses `<sf:password>` instead of `<sf:input>`. `<sf:password>` is similar to `<sf:input>` but renders an HTML `<input>` whose `type` attribute is set to `password` so that the value will be masked as it's typed.

To help you visualize what the resulting HTML will look like, suppose that a user has already submitted the form with invalid values for all the fields. After validation fails and the user is forwarded back to the registration form, the resulting HTML `<form>` element looks like this:

```
<form id="spitter" action="/spitter/spitter/register" method="POST">
  First Name:
      <input id="firstName"
             name="firstName" type="text" value="J"/><br/>
  Last Name:
      <input id="lastName"
             name="lastName" type="text" value="B"/><br/>
  Email:
      <input id="email"
             name="email" type="text" value="jack"/><br/>
```

```
Username:
    <input id="username"
           name="username" type="text" value="jack"/><br/>
Password:
    <input id="password"
           name="password" type="password" value=""/><br/>
<input type="submit" value="Register" />
</form>
```

It's worth noting that starting with Spring 3.1, the `<sf:input>` tag allows you to specify a `type` attribute so that you can declare HTML 5–specific type text fields such as `data`, `range`, and `email`, among other options. For example, you could declare the `email` field like this:

```
Email: <sf:input path="email" type="email" /><br/>
```

This is rendered to HTML as

```
Email:
    <input id="email" name="email" type="email" value="jack"/><br/>
```

Using Spring's form-binding tags gives you a slight improvement over using standard HTML tags—the form is prepopulated with the previously entered values after failed validation. But it still fails to tell the user what they did wrong. To guide the user in fixing their mistakes, you'll need the `<sf:errors>` tag.

DISPLAYING ERRORS
When there are validation errors, the details of those errors are carried in the request along with model data. All you need to do is dig into the model and extract the errors to display to the user. The `<sf:errors>` tag makes this a simple task.

For example, look at how `<sf:errors>` is used in this snippet from register-Form.jsp:

```
<sf:form method="POST" commandName="spitter">
  First Name: <sf:input path="firstName" />
    <sf:errors path="firstName" /><br/>
...
</sf:form>
```

Even though I'm only showing you `<sf:errors>` as applied to the First Name field, it's just as easy to use on all the fields in the registration form. Here its `path` attribute is set to `firstName`, the name of the `Spitter` model object property for which errors should be displayed. If there are no errors for the `firstName` property, then `<sf:errors>` won't render anything. But if there is a validation error, it will render that error message in an HTML `<span>` tag.

For example, if the user submits `J` as the first name, the following HTML is rendered for the First Name field:

```
First Name: <input id="firstName"
                   name="firstName" type="text" value="J"/>
<span id="firstName.errors">size must be between 2 and 30</span>
```

Now you're communicating the error to the user, and they have a chance to fix it. You can take this a step further by changing the style of the error so that it stands out. To do that, set the `cssClass` attribute:

```
<sf:form method="POST" commandName="spitter" >
  First Name: <sf:input path="firstName" />
    <sf:errors path="firstName" cssClass="error" /><br/>
...
</sf:form>
```

Again, for brevity's sake, I've only shown how to set the `cssClass` attribute for the `<sf:errors>` tag whose path is `firstName`. You can certainly apply it to the other fields as well.

Now the errors`<span>` has a `class` attribute set to `error`. All that's left is to define a CSS style for that class. Here's a simple CSS style that renders the error in red:

```
span.error {
  color: red;
}
```

Figure 6.2 shows how the form might look in a web browser at this point.

Displaying validation errors next to the fields that have errors is a nice way to draw the user's attention to problems they need to fix. But it could be problematic with regard to layout. Another way to handle validation errors is to display them all together. To do this, you can remove the `<sf:errors>` element from each field and place it at the top of the form like this:

```
<sf:form method="POST" commandName="spitter" >
  <sf:errors path="*" element="div" cssClass="errors" />

...
</sf:form>
```

What's noticeably different about this `<sf:errors>` as compared to the ones you've used before is that its `path` is set to `*`. This is a wildcard selector that tells `<sf:errors>` to render all errors for all properties.

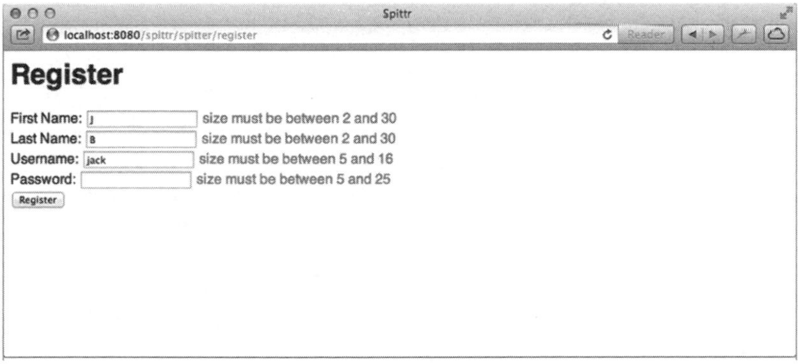

Figure 6.2   Displaying validation errors next to form fields

Also notice that you set the element attribute to div. By default, errors are rendered in an HTML <span> tag, which is fine when there's only one error to display. But when you're rendering errors for all fields, there could easily be more than one error to display, and a <span> tag (an inline tag) is not ideal. A block tag such as <div> would be better. Therefore, you can set the element attribute to div so that errors render in a <div> tag.

As before, cssClass is set to errors so that you can style the <div>. Here's some CSS to style the <div> with a red border and a light red background:

```
div.errors {
  background-color: #ffcccc;
  border: 2px solid red;
}
```

Now you've shoved all the errors to the top of the form, which may make laying out the page easier. But you've lost the ability to highlight the fields that need to be corrected. That's easily addressed by setting the cssErrorClass attribute on each field. You can also wrap each label with <sf:label> and set its cssErrorClass. Here's the First Name field with the necessary changes applied:

```
<sf:form method="POST" commandName="spitter" >
  <sf:label path="firstName"
      cssErrorClass="error">First Name</sf:label>:
    <sf:input path="firstName" cssErrorClass="error" /><br/>
...
</sf:form>
```

The <sf:label> tag, much like the other form-binding tags, has a path attribute to indicate which property of the model object it belongs to. In this case, it's set to firstName so it will be bound to the Spitter object's firstName property. Assuming there are no validation errors, this will render an HTML <label> element like this:

```
<label for="firstName">First Name</label>
```

On its own, setting the path attribute on <sf:label> doesn't accomplish much. But you're also setting cssErrorClass. If the bound property has any errors, the rendered <label> element's class attribute will be set to error like this:

```
<label for="firstName" class="error">First Name</label>
```

Similarly, the <sf:input> tag now has its cssErrorClass set to error. If there's a validation error, the rendered <input> tag's class attribute will be set to error. Now you can style the label and the fields so that the user's attention is drawn to them if there are any errors. For example, the following CSS renders the label in red and the input field with a light red background:

```
label.error {
  color: red;
}

input.error {
  background-color: #ffcccc;
}
```

Now you have a fairly nice way of presenting validation errors to the user. There's one more thing you can do to make those errors friendlier to read. Revisiting the `Spitter` class, you can set the `message` attribute on the validation annotations to reference a friendly message that you'll define in a properties file:

```
@NotNull
@Size(min=5, max=16, message="{username.size}")
private String username;

@NotNull
@Size(min=5, max=25, message="{password.size}")
private String password;

@NotNull
@Size(min=2, max=30, message="{firstName.size}")
private String firstName;

@NotNull
@Size(min=2, max=30, message="{lastName.size}")
private String lastName;

@NotNull
@Email(message="{email.valid}")
private String email;
```

For each of the fields, the `@Size` annotation has `message` set to a string whose value is wrapped in curly braces. If you left the curly braces out, the value given to `message` would be the error message displayed to the user. But by using curly braces, you designate a property in a properties file that contains the actual message.

All that's left to do is to create a file named ValidationMessages.properties at the root of the classpath:

```
firstName.size=
    First name must be between {min} and {max} characters long.
lastName.size=
    Last name must be between {min} and {max} characters long.
username.size=
    Username must be between {min} and {max} characters long.
password.size=
    Password must be between {min} and {max} characters long.
email.valid=The email address must be valid.
```

Notice how the key for each message in ValidationMessages.properties corresponds to the placeholder values in the `message` attributes. Also, so that the minimum and maximum lengths aren't hard-coded in ValidationMessages.properties, the friendly messages have placeholders of their own—{min} and {max}—that reference the `min` and `max` attributes given on the `@Size` annotation.

When the user submits a registration form that fails validation, they might see something like figure 6.3 in their browser.

What's nice about extracting the error messages to a properties file is that you can display language- and locale-specific messages by creating a locale-specific properties file. For example, to display the errors in Spanish if the user's browser has its language

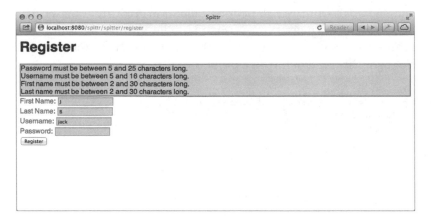

Figure 6.3   Validation errors displayed with friendly error messages pulled from a properties file

set to Spanish, you can create a file named ValidationErrors_es.properties with the following content:

```
firstName.size=
    Nombre debe ser entre {min} y {max} caracteres largo.
lastName.size=
    El apellido debe ser entre {min} y {max} caracteres largo.
username.size=
    Nombre de usuario debe ser entre {min} y {max} caracteres largo.
password.size=
    Contraseña debe estar entre {min} y {max} caracteres largo.
email.valid=La dirección de email no es válida
```

You can create as many renditions of ValidationMessages.properties as necessary to cover all the languages and locales your application will support.

SPRING'S GENERAL TAG LIBRARY

In addition to the form-binding tag library, Spring also offers a more general JSP tag library. In fact, this tag library was the first JSP tag library available in Spring. It has grown a bit over the years, but it was available in the earliest versions of Spring.

To use Spring's general tag library, you must declare it in the pages that will use it:

```
<%@ taglib uri="http://www.springframework.org/tags" prefix="s" %>
```

As with any JSP tag library, the `prefix` can be anything you want. Commonly, `spring` is given as the prefix for this tag library. But I prefer to use `s` because it's much more succinct and easier to type and read.

With the tag library declared, you can now use the 10 JSP tags listed in table 6.3.

Table 6.3 Spring's *other* JSP tag library offers a handful of convenient utility tags in addition to some legacy data-binding tags.

JSP tag	Description
`<s:bind>`	Exports a bound property status to a page-scoped `status` property. Used along with `<s:path>` to obtain a bound property value.
`<s:escapeBody>`	HTML and/or JavaScript escapes the content in the body of the tag.
`<s:hasBindErrors>`	Conditionally renders content if a specified model object (in a request attribute) has bind errors.
`<s:htmlEscape>`	Sets the default HTML escape value for the current page.
`<s:message>`	Retrieves the message with the given code and either renders it (default) or assigns it to a page-, request-, session-, or application-scoped variable (when using the `var` and `scope` attributes).
`<s:nestedPath>`	Sets a nested path to be used by `<s:bind>`.
`<s:theme>`	Retrieves a theme message with the given code and either renders it (default) or assigns it to a page-, request-, session-, or application-scoped variable (when using the `var` and `scope` attributes).
`<s:transform>`	Transforms properties not contained in a command object using a command object's property editors.
`<s:url>`	Creates context-relative URLs with support for URI template variables and HTML/XML/JavaScript escaping. Can either render the URL (default) or assign it to a page-, request-, session-, or application-scoped variable (when using the `var` and `scope` attributes).
`<s:eval>`	Evaluates Spring Expression Language (SpEL) expressions, rendering the result (default) or assigning it to a page-, request-, session-, or application-scoped variable (when using the `var` and `scope` attributes).

Several of the tags in table 6.3 have been made obsolete by Spring's form-binding tag library. The `<s:bind>` tag, for instance, was Spring's original form-binding tag, and it was much more complex than the tags covered in the previous section.

Because this tag library sees a lot less action than the form-binding tags, I won't cover each tag in detail. Instead, I'll quickly go over a handful of the most valuable tags and leave it to you to explore the others on your own. (Odds are good that you won't need them often—if at all.)

DISPLAYING INTERNATIONALIZED MESSAGES

As it stands, your JSP templates contain a lot of hard-coded text. There's nothing horribly wrong with that, but it doesn't lend itself to easily changing the text. Moreover, there's no way to internationalize the text so it's tailored to the user's language settings.

For instance, consider the welcome message on the home page:

```
<h1>Welcome to Spittr!</h1>
```

The only way to modify that message is to open home.jsp and change it. Not a big deal, I suppose. But spreading your application's text across multiple templates means changing a lot of JSP files for large-scale changes of the application's messaging.

A more significant issue is that no matter what text you choose for the welcome message, all users see the same message. The web is a global network, and the applications you build for it are likely to have a global audience. Therefore, it's wise to communicate to your users in their language and not force them to use a single language.

The <s:message> tag is perfect for rendering text that's externalized in one or more properties files. Using <s:message>, you can replace the hard-coded welcome message with the following:

```
<h1><s:message code="spittr.welcome" /></h1>
```

As used here, <s:message> will render the text available from a message source where the key is spittr.welcome. Therefore, you'll need to configure such a message source if you expect <s:message> to be able to do its job.

Spring has a handful of message-source classes, all implementing the Message-Source interface. One of the more common and useful implementations is Resource-BundleMessageSource. It loads messages from a properties file whose name is derived from a base name. The following @Bean method configures ResourceBundleMessage-Source:

```
@Bean
public MessageSource messageSource() {
  ResourceBundleMessageSource messageSource =
          new ResourceBundleMessageSource();
  messageSource.setBasename("messages");
  return messageSource;
}
```

The key thing in this bean declaration is the setting of the basename property. You can set it to any value you'd like, but here I've chosen to set it to messages. By setting it to messages, you can expect ResourceBundleMessageResolver to resolve messages from properties files at the root of the classpath whose names are derived from that base name.

Optionally, you may choose ReloadableResourceBundleMessageSource, which works much like ResourceBundleMessageSource, but it has the ability to reload message properties without recompiling or restarting the application. Here's a sample configuration for ReloadableResourceBundleMessageSource:

```
@Bean
public MessageSource messageSource() {
  ReloadableResourceBundleMessageSource messageSource =
     new ReloadableResourceBundleMessageSource();
  messageSource.setBasename("file:///etc/spittr/messages");
  messageSource.setCacheSeconds(10);
  return messageSource;
}
```

The key difference here is that the basename property is configured to look outside of the application (not in the classpath, like ResourceBundleMessageSource). The basename property can be set to look for messages in the classpath (with a classpath: prefix), in the filesystem (with a file: prefix), or at the root of the web application (with no prefix). Here, it's configured to look for messages in properties files in the /etc/spittr directory of the server's filesystem and with a base filename of "messages".

Now let's create those properties files. To start, you'll create the default properties file named messages.properties. It will be located either at the root of the classpath (if you're using ResourceBundleMessageSource) or at the path specified in the basename property (if you're using ReloadableResourceBundleMessageSource). It needs the following entry for the spittr.welcome message:

```
spittr.welcome=Welcome to Spittr!
```

If you create no other messages files, then all you've accomplished is extracting the hard-coded message from the JSP into a properties file as a hard-coded message. It does give you one-stop editing for all of your application's messages, but little more than that.

Nevertheless, the essential pieces are in place to start internationalizing the message. If, for example, you wanted to show the welcome message in Spanish for anyone whose language settings are set to Spanish, you'd need to create another properties file named messages_es.properties with this entry:

```
spittr.welcome=Bienvenidos a Spittr!
```

Now you've accomplished something big. Your application is only a few more <s:message> tags and language-specific properties files away from being an international success! I'll leave it to you to internationalize the rest of the application.

CREATING URLS

The <s:url> tag is a modest little tag. Its main job is to create a URL and either assign it to a variable or render it in the response. It's a drop-in replacement for JSTL's <c:url> tag, but with a few new tricks up its sleeve.

In its simplest form, <s:url> takes a servlet-context-relative URL and renders it with the servlet context path prepended. For example, consider this basic use of <s:url>:

```
<a href="<s:url href="/spitter/register" />">Register</a>
```

If the application's servlet context is named spittr, then the following HTML will be rendered in the response:

```
<a href="/spittr/spitter/register">Register</a>
```

This enables you to create URLs without worrying about what the servlet context path will be. The <s:url> tag takes care of it for you.

Optionally, you can have <s:url> construct the URL and assign it to a variable to be used later in the template:

```
<s:url href="/spitter/register" var="registerUrl" />

<a href="${registerUrl}">Register</a>
```

By default, URL variables are created in page scope. But you can have `<s:url>` create them in application, session, or request scope instead by setting the `scope` attribute:

```
<s:url href="/spitter/register" var="registerUrl" scope="request" />
```

If you'd like to add parameters to the URL, you can do so with the `<s:param>` tag. For instance, here's a `<s:url>` tag with two nested `<s:param>` tags to set the `max` and `count` parameters for /spittles:

```
<s:url href="/spittles" var="spittlesUrl">
  <s:param name="max" value="60" />
  <s:param name="count" value="20" />
</s:url>
```

So far, you've seen nothing that `<s:url>` can do that JSTL's `<c:url>` can't do. But what if you need to create a URL with a `path` parameter? How can you write the `href` value such that it has a replaceable `path` parameter?

For instance, suppose you need to create a URL for a particular user's profile page. No problem. Once again, the `<s:param>` tag is up to the task:

```
<s:url href="/spitter/{username}" var="spitterUrl">
  <s:param name="username" value="jbauer" />
</s:url>
```

When the `href` value is a placeholder that matches a parameter specified by `<s:param>`, the parameter is inserted into the placeholder's spot. If the `<s:param>` parameter doesn't match any placeholders in `href`, then the parameter is used as a query parameter.

The `<s:url>` tag can also address any escaping needs for the URL. For example, if you intend to render the URL to be displayed as part of the content on a web page (as opposed to being used as a hypertext link), you may want to ask `<s:url>` to do HTML escaping on the URL by setting the `htmlEscape` attribute to `true`. For example, the following `<s:url>` tag renders an HTML-escaped URL:

```
<s:url value="/spittles" htmlEscape="true">
  <s:param name="max" value="60" />
  <s:param name="count" value="20" />
</s:url>
```

This results in the URL being rendered like this:

```
/spitter/spittles?max=60&amp;count=20
```

On the other hand, if you intend to use the URL in JavaScript code, you may want to set the `javaScriptEscape` attribute to `true`:

```
<s:url value="/spittles" var="spittlesJSUrl" javaScriptEscape="true">
  <s:param name="max" value="60" />
  <s:param name="count" value="20" />
</s:url>
```

```
<script>
  var spittlesUrl = "${spittlesJSUrl}"
</script>
```

This renders the following to the response:

```
<script>
  var spittlesUrl = "\/spitter\/spittles?max=60&count=20"
</script>
```

Speaking of escaping, there's another tag for escaping content other than tags. Let's have a look.

ESCAPING CONTENT

The `<s:escapeBody>` tag is a general-purpose escaping tag. It renders any content nested in its body, escaping as necessary.

For example, suppose you want to display a snippet of HTML code on a page. In order for it to be displayed properly, the < and > characters need to be replaced with < and > or the browser will interpret the HTML as any other HTML in the page.

Nothing's stopping you from putting in < and > escaping by hand, but it's cumbersome and doesn't read well. Instead, you can use `<s:escapeBody>` and let Spring take care of it for you:

```
<s:escapeBody htmlEscape="true">
<h1>Hello</h1>
</s:escapeBody>
```

This renders the following to the body of the response:

```
&lt;h1&gt;Hello&lt;/h1&gt;
```

Of course, even though it looks horrible in its escaped form, the browser is happy to render it as the un-escaped HTML you want the user to see.

The `<s:escapeBody>` tag also supports JavaScript escaping with the `javaScript-Escape` attribute:

```
<s:escapeBody javaScriptEscape="true">
<h1>Hello</h1>
</s:escapeBody>
```

`<s:escapeBody>` does one job and does it well. Unlike `<s:url>`, it only renders content and doesn't let you assign that content to a variable.

Now that you've seen how to use JSP to define Spring views, let's consider what would be required to make them aesthetically appealing. There's a lot you can do by adding common elements to the pages, such as inserting a header with a site logo, applying a stylesheet, and maybe even showing a copyright in the footer. But rather than do that in each of the JSP files in the Spittr application, let's see how to employ Apache Tiles to bring some common and reusable layouts to your templates.

6.3 *Defining a layout with Apache Tiles views*

At this point, you've done very little with regard to the layout of your application's web pages. Each JSP is fully responsible for defining its own layout, and they're not doing much in that regard.

Suppose you want to add a common header and footer to all pages in the application. The naive way to do this is to visit every JSP template and add the HTML for the header and footer. But that approach doesn't scale well with regard to maintenance. There's an initial cost of adding those elements to each and every page, and any future changes will incur a similar cost.

A better approach is to use a layout engine such as Apache Tiles to define a common page layout that will be applied to all pages. Spring MVC provides support for Apache Tiles in the form of a view resolver that can resolve logical view names into tile definitions.

6.3.1 *Configuring a Tiles view resolver*

In order to use Tiles with Spring, you'll have to configure a couple of beans. You need a `TilesConfigurer` bean whose job is to locate and load tile definitions and generally coordinate Tiles. In addition, you need a `TilesViewResolver` bean to resolve logical view names to tile definitions.

This pair of components comes in two forms: a pair for Apache Tiles 2 and another pair for Apache Tiles 3. The most significant difference between the two sets of Tiles components is in their package names. The `TilesConfigurer/TilesViewResolver` pair for Apache Tiles 2 comes in the `org.springframework.web.servlet` `.view.tiles2` package, whereas the Tiles 3 variety comes in the `org.springframework` `.web.servlet.view.tiles3` package. For our purposes, I'll assume that you're using Tiles 3.

First, let's add the `TilesConfigurer` bean as shown in the following listing.

Listing 6.1   Configuring `TilesConfigurer` to resolve tile definitions

```
@Bean
public TilesConfigurer tilesConfigurer() {
  TilesConfigurer tiles = new TilesConfigurer();       Specify tile
  tiles.setDefinitions(new String[] {            ◁─┘   definition locations
      "/WEB-INF/layout/tiles.xml"
  });
  tiles.setCheckRefresh(true);     ◁── Enable refresh
  return tiles;
}
```

When configuring a `TilesConfigurer`, the most important property you set is `definitions`. This property takes an array of `Strings` where each entry specifies the location of tile-definition XML files. For the Spittr application, you'll have it look for a file named tiles.xml in the /WEB-INF/layout/ directory.

Although you're not taking advantage of it here, it's also possible to specify multiple tile-definition files and even use wildcards in the location path. For example, you could ask that `TilesConfigurer` look for any file named tiles.xml anywhere under the /WEB-INF/ directory by setting the `definitions` property like this:

```
tiles.setDefinitions(new String[] {
    "/WEB-INF/**/tiles.xml"
});
```

In this case, you're using Ant-style wildcards (`**`) so that `TilesConfigurer` will recursively dig under all subdirectories in /WEB-INF/ in its search for tile definitions.

Next, let's configure `TilesViewResolver`. As you can see, it's a rather basic bean definition, with no properties to set:

```
@Bean
public ViewResolver viewResolver() {
  return new TilesViewResolver();
}
```

Optionally, if you prefer working with XML configuration, you may choose to configure `TilesConfigurer` and `TilesViewResolver` like this:

```
<bean id="tilesConfigurer" class=
    "org.springframework.web.servlet.view.tiles3.TilesConfigurer">
  <property name="definitions">
    <list>
      <value>/WEB-INF/layout/tiles.xml.xml</value>
      <value>/WEB-INF/views/**/tiles.xml</value>
    </list>
  </property>
</bean>

<bean id="viewResolver" class=
    "org.springframework.web.servlet.view.tiles3.TilesViewResolver" />
```

Whereas `TilesConfigurer` loads tile definitions and coordinates with Apache Tiles, `TilesViewResolver` resolves logical view names to views that reference tile definitions. It does this by looking for a tile definition whose name matches the logical view name. You'll need to create a few tile definitions to see how this works.

DEFINING TILES

Apache Tiles provides a document type definition (DTD) for specifying tile definitions in an XML file. Each definition consists of a `<definition>` element that generally has one or more `<put-attribute>` elements. For example, the following XML document defines several tiles for the Spittr application.

Listing 6.2 Defining tiles for the Spittr application

```
<?xml version="1.0" encoding="ISO-8859-1" ?>
<!DOCTYPE tiles-definitions PUBLIC
        "-//Apache Software Foundation//DTD Tiles Configuration 3.0//EN"
        "http://tiles.apache.org/dtds/tiles-config_3_0.dtd">
<tiles-definitions>

  <definition name="base"                         ⟵— **Define a base tile**
            template="/WEB-INF/layout/page.jsp">
```

```
    <put-attribute name="header"
                   value="/WEB-INF/layout/header.jsp" />
    <put-attribute name="footer"
                   value="/WEB-INF/layout/footer.jsp" />      ⟵─ Set an attribute
  </definition>

  <definition name="home" extends="base">                     ⟵─ Extend the base tile
    <put-attribute name="body"
                   value="/WEB-INF/views/home.jsp" />
  </definition>

  <definition name="registerForm" extends="base">
    <put-attribute name="body"
                   value="/WEB-INF/views/registerForm.jsp" />
  </definition>

  <definition name="profile" extends="base">
    <put-attribute name="body"
                   value="/WEB-INF/views/profile.jsp" />
  </definition>

  <definition name="spittles" extends="base">
    <put-attribute name="body"
                   value="/WEB-INF/views/spittles.jsp" />
  </definition>

  <definition name="spittle" extends="base">
    <put-attribute name="body"
                   value="/WEB-INF/views/spittle.jsp" />
  </definition>

</tiles-definitions>
```

Each <definition> element defines a tile that ultimately references a JSP template. In the case of the tile whose name is base, the template referenced is at /WEB-INF/layout/page.jsp. A tile may also reference other JSP templates to be embedded in the main template. For the base tile, it references a header JSP template and a footer JSP template.

The page.jsp template referenced by the base tile is shown next.

Listing 6.3 Main layout template: references other templates to create a view

```
<%@ taglib uri="http://www.springframework.org/tags" prefix="s" %>
<%@ taglib uri="http://tiles.apache.org/tags-tiles" prefix="t" %>
<%@ page session="false" %>
<html>
  <head>
    <title>Spittr</title>
    <link rel="stylesheet"
          type="text/css"
          href="<s:url value="/resources/style.css" />" >
  </head>
  <body>
    <div id="header">
      <t:insertAttribute name="header" />                     ⟵─ Insert the header
    </div>
```

```
    <div id="content">
      <t:insertAttribute name="body" />                    ⟵— Insert the body
    </div>
    <div id="footer">
      <t:insertAttribute name="footer" />                  ⟵— Insert the footer
    </div>
  </body>
</html>
```

The key thing to observe in listing 6.3 is how it uses the `<t:insertAttribute>` JSP tag from the Tiles tag library to insert other templates. It's used to insert the attributes named header, body, and footer. Ultimately, this gives you a layout that somewhat resembles figure 6.4.

The header and footer attributes were set in the base tile definition to point at /WEB-INF/layout/header.jsp and /WEB-INF/layout/footer.jsp respectively. But what about the body attribute? Where is it set?

The base tile is never expected to be used on its own. It serves as a base definition (thus the meaning behind its name) for other tile definitions to extend. Throughout the rest of listing 6.2, you can see that the other tile definitions all extend base. This means they inherit its settings for the header and footer attributes (although they could choose to override them). But each also sets a body attribute to reference a JSP template specific to that tile.

Focusing on the home tile, notice that it extends base. Because it extends base, it inherits the template and all the attributes from base. Even though the home tile definition is relatively simple, it has the following effective definition:

```
<definition name="home" template="/WEB-INF/layout/page.jsp">
  <put-attribute name="header" value="/WEB-INF/layout/header.jsp" />
  <put-attribute name="footer" value="/WEB-INF/layout/footer.jsp" />
  <put-attribute name="body" value="/WEB-INF/views/home.jsp" />
</definition>
```

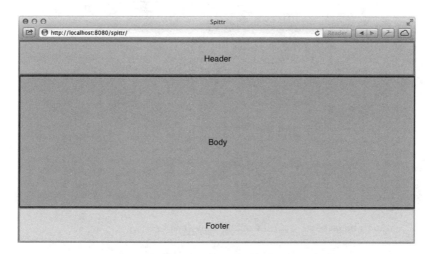

Figure 6.4   A general layout defining a header, a body, and a footer

The individual templates referenced by the attributes are simple. Here's the header.jsp template:

```
<%@ taglib uri="http://www.springframework.org/tags" prefix="s" %>
<a href="<s:url value="/" />"><img
    src="<s:url value="/resources" />/images/spittr_logo_50.png"
    border="0"/></a>
```

The footer.jsp template is even simpler:

```
Copyright &copy; Craig Walls
```

Each tile that extends base defines its own body template, so each will differ from the others. But to complete the picture for the home tile, here's home.jsp:

```
<%@ taglib uri="http://java.sun.com/jsp/jstl/core" prefix="c" %>
<%@ page session="false" %>
<h1>Welcome to Spittr</h1>

<a href="<c:url value="/spittles" />">Spittles</a> |
<a href="<c:url value="/spitter/register" />">Register</a>
```

The key point here is that the common elements of a page are captured in page.jsp, header.jsp, and footer.jsp and are absent in each of the other tile templates. This makes them reusable across all pages and simplifies maintenance of those elements.

To see how this all comes together, look at figure 6.5. As you can see, the page includes some styling and imagery to increase the application's aesthetics. These weren't pertinent to the discussion of page layout with Tiles, so I chose not to cover the details in this section. Nevertheless, you can see how the various components of the page are brought together by the tile definitions to render the Spittr home page.

Figure 6.5   The Spittr home page, laid out using Apache Tiles

JSP has long been the go-to option for templating in Java web applications. But there's a new contender for the job, known as Thymeleaf. Let's see how to use Thymeleaf templates with a Spring MVC application.

6.4 Working with Thymeleaf

Even though JSP has been around for a long time and is ubiquitous among Java web servers, it has a few unfortunate flaws. One significant issue with JSP is that it appears to be a form of HTML or XML, but it's really neither. Most JSP templates take the form of HTML, littered with tags from various JSP tag libraries. Although these tag libraries bring dynamic rendering power to JSP in a succinct form, they break any hope of authoring a well-formed document. As an extreme example, consider that a JSP tag can even be used as the value of an HTML parameter:

```
<input type="text" value="<c:out value="${thing.name}"/>" />
```

A side effect of tag libraries and JSP's lack of good form is that a JSP template often only coincidentally resembles the HTML it produces. Indeed, viewing an unrendered JSP template in a web browser or an HTML editor gives some puzzling and ugly results. The results aren't just incompletely rendered—they're a visual disaster! Because JSP isn't truly HTML, many web browsers and editors struggle to display anything that aesthetically approximates what the template will render.

Also, JSP is a specification that's tightly coupled to the servlet specification. This means it can only be used for web views in a servlet-based web application. JSP templates aren't an option for general-purpose templating (such as formatted emails) or in web applications that aren't based on servlets.

Several attempts have been made over the years to supplant JSP as the dominant view technology for Java applications. The most recent contender, Thymeleaf, shows some real promise and is an exciting choice to consider. Thymeleaf templates are natural and don't rely on tag libraries. They can be edited and rendered anywhere that raw HTML is welcome. And because they're not coupled to the servlet specification, Thymeleaf templates can go places JSPs dare not tread. Let's look at how to use Thymeleaf with Spring MVC.

6.4.1 Configuring a Thymeleaf view resolver

In order to use Thymeleaf with Spring, you'll need to configure three beans that enable Thymeleaf-Spring integration:

- A `ThymeleafViewResolver` that resolves Thymeleaf template views from logical view names
- A `SpringTemplateEngine` to process the templates and render the results
- A `TemplateResolver` that loads Thymeleaf templates

Here's the Java configuration that declares those beans.

Listing 6.4   Configuring Thymeleaf support for Spring in Java configuration

```
@Bean
public ViewResolver viewResolver(                    ←— Thymeleaf view resolver
      SpringTemplateEngine templateEngine) {
  ThymeleafViewResolver viewResolver = new ThymeleafViewResolver();
  viewResolver.setTemplateEngine(templateEngine);
  return viewResolver;
}

@Bean
public TemplateEngine templateEngine(                ←— Template engine
      TemplateResolver templateResolver) {
  SpringTemplateEngine templateEngine = new SpringTemplateEngine();
  templateEngine.setTemplateResolver(templateResolver);
  return templateEngine;
}

@Bean
public TemplateResolver templateResolver() {         ←— Template resolver
  TemplateResolver templateResolver =
        new ServletContextTemplateResolver();
  templateResolver.setPrefix("/WEB-INF/templates/");
  templateResolver.setSuffix(".html");
  templateResolver.setTemplateMode("HTML5");
  return templateResolver;
}
```

If you'd prefer to configure the beans in XML, the following <bean> declarations will do the trick.

Listing 6.5   Configuring Thymeleaf support for Spring in XML

```
<bean id="viewResolver"                              ←— Thymeleaf view resolver
      class="org.thymeleaf.spring3.view.ThymeleafViewResolver"
      p:templateEngine-ref="templateEngine" />

<bean id="templateEngine"                            ←— Template engine
      class="org.thymeleaf.spring3.SpringTemplateEngine"
      p:templateResolver-ref="templateResolver" />

<bean id="templateResolver" class=                   ←— Template resolver
   "org.thymeleaf.templateresolver.ServletContextTemplateResolver"
      p:prefix="/WEB-INF/templates/"
      p:suffix=".html"
      p:templateMode="HTML5" />
```

No matter which configuration style you use, Thymeleaf is now ready to render its templates in response to requests handled by Spring MVC controllers.

ThymeleafViewResolver is an implementation of Spring MVC's ViewResolver. Just like any view resolver, it takes a logical view name and resolves a view. But in this case, that view is ultimately a Thymeleaf template.

Notice that the ThymeleafViewResolver bean is injected with a reference to the SpringTemplateEngine bean. SpringTemplateEngine is a Spring-enabled Thymeleaf engine for parsing templates and rendering results based on those templates. As you can see, it's injected with a reference to the `TemplateResolver` bean.

`TemplateResolver` is what ultimately locates the templates. It's configured much as you previously configured `InternalResourceViewResolver` with `prefix` and `suffix` properties. The prefix and suffix are applied to the logical view name to locate the Thymeleaf template. Its `templateMode` property is also set to HTML5, indicating that the templates resolved are expected to render HTML5 output.

Now that all the Thymeleaf beans have been configured, it's time to create a few of those templates.

6.4.2 Defining Thymeleaf templates

Thymeleaf templates are primarily just HTML files. There are no special tags or tag libraries as with JSP. What makes Thymeleaf tick, however, is that it adds Thymeleaf attributes to the standard set of HTML tags via a custom namespace. The following listing shows home.html, the home page template that uses the Thymeleaf namespace.

Listing 6.6   home.html: home page template using the Thymeleaf namespace

```
<html xmlns="http://www.w3.org/1999/xhtml"
    xmlns:th="http://www.thymeleaf.org">        <--- Declare Thymeleaf namespace
  <head>
    <title>Spittr</title>
    <link rel="stylesheet"
        type="text/css"
        th:href="@{/resources/style.css}"></link>   <--- th:href link to stylesheet
  </head>
  <body>
    <h1>Welcome to Spittr</h1>

    <a th:href="@{/spittles}">Spittles</a> |        <--- th:href links to pages
    <a th:href="@{/spitter/register}">Register</a>
  </body>
</html>
```

The home page template is relatively simple and only takes advantage of the `th:href` attribute. This attribute greatly resembles its native HTML counterpart, the `href` attribute, and can be used the same way. What makes `th:href` special is that its value can contain Thymeleaf expressions to evaluate dynamic values. It will render a standard `href` attribute containing a value that's dynamically created at render time. This is how many of the attributes in the Thymeleaf namespace work: they mirror the standard HTML attribute that they share a name with, to render some computed value. In this case, all three uses of the `th:href` attribute use the `@{}` expressions to calculate context-sensitive URL paths (much as you might use JSTL's `<c:url>` tag or Spring's `<s:url>` tag in a JSP page).

Even though home.html is a rather basic specimen of a Thymeleaf template, it's still remarkable in that it's a near-pure HTML template. The only thing that stands out is the `th:href` attribute. Otherwise, it's your basic, garden-variety HTML file.

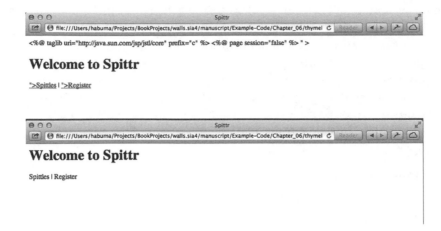

Figure 6.6   Thymeleaf templates, unlike JSPs, are HTML and can be rendered and edited just like HTML.

This means Thymeleaf templates, unlike JSPs, can be edited and even rendered naturally, without going through any sort of processor. Sure, you'll need Thymeleaf to process the templates to fully render the desired output. But as is, without any special processing, home.html can be loaded into a web browser and will appear much as it will when fully rendered. To illustrate, figure 6.6 shows a comparison of home.jsp (top) and home.html (bottom) when viewed in a web browser.

As you can see, the JSP template renders poorly in the web browser. Although you can see familiar elements, the JSP tag library declarations are also displayed. And there's some odd unfinished markup just before the links, the result of the `<s:url>` tag not being properly interpreted by the web browser.

In contrast, the Thymeleaf template renders almost flawlessly. The only things that aren't quite right are the links. The web browser doesn't treat the `th:href` attribute like `href`, so the links aren't rendered as links. Aside from that minor issue, the template renders exactly as you'd expect.

Simple templates like home.html are a nice introduction to Thymeleaf. But form binding is something that Spring's JSP tags excel at. If you're abandoning JSP, must you abandon form binding as well? Fear not. Thymeleaf has a little something up its sleeve.

FORM BINDING WITH THYMELEAF

Form binding is an important feature of Spring MVC. It makes it possible for controllers to receive command objects populated with data submitted in a form and for the form to be prepopulated with values from the command object when displaying the form. Without proper form binding, you'd have to ensure that the HTML form fields were properly named to map to the backing command object's properties. And you'd also be responsible for ensuring that the fields' values were set to the command object's properties when redisplaying a form after validation failure.

But with form binding, this is taken care of for you. As a reminder of how form binding works, here's the First Name field from registration.jsp:

```
<sf:label path="firstName"
    cssErrorClass="error">First Name</sf:label>:
  <sf:input path="firstName" cssErrorClass="error" /><br/>
```

Here the `<sf:input>` tag from Spring's form-binding tag library is called on to render an HTML `<input>` tag with its `value` attribute set to the value of the backing object's `firstName` property. It also uses Spring's `<sf:label>` and its `cssErrorClass` to render the label in red if there are any validation errors.

But in this section we're not talking about JSP. On the contrary, we're talking about replacing JSP with Thymeleaf. So instead of using Spring's JSP tags to achieve form binding, you'll take advantage of features of Thymeleaf's Spring dialect.

As a demonstration, consider this snippet of a Thymeleaf template that renders the First Name field:

```
<label th:class="${#fields.hasErrors('firstName')}? 'error'">
    First Name</label>:
<input type="text" th:field="*{firstName}"
        th:class="${#fields.hasErrors('firstName')}? 'error'" /><br/>
```

Instead of using the `cssClassName` attribute as you did with Spring's JSP tags, here you use Thymeleaf's `th:class` attribute on standard HTML tags. The `th:class` attribute renders a `class` attribute with a value calculated from the given expression. In both uses of `th:class`, it directly checks to see if there are any field errors for the `first-Name` field. If so, the `class` attribute is rendered with a value of `error`. If there are no field errors, the `class` attribute isn't rendered at all.

The `<input>` tag uses the `th:field` attribute to reference the `firstName` field from the backing object. This may be slightly different than you expected. Many times in a Thymeleaf template, you'll use a Thymeleaf attribute that mirrors a standard HTML attribute, so it might seem appropriate to use the `th:value` attribute to set the `<input>` tag's `value` attribute.

Instead, because you're binding the field to the backing object's `firstName` property, you use the `th:field` attribute, referring to the `firstName` field. By using `th:field`, you get both a `value` attribute set to the value of `firstName` and also a `name` attribute set to `firstName`.

To demonstrate Thymeleaf data binding in action, the following listing shows the complete registration form template.

> **Listing 6.7 Registration page, using Thymeleaf to bind a form to a command object**

```
                  <form method="POST" th:object="${spitter}">
Display    ┌──▷  <div class="errors" th:if="${#fields.hasErrors('*')}">
errors     │        <ul>
                       <li th:each="err : ${#fields.errors('*')}"
                           th:text="${err}">Input is incorrect</li>
                     </ul>
```

```
            </div>
First name  ──▷   <label th:class="${#fields.hasErrors('firstName')}? 'error'">
                First Name</label>:
              <input type="text" th:field="*{firstName}"
                  th:class="${#fields.hasErrors('firstName')}? 'error'" /><br/>
Last name   ──▷   <label th:class="${#fields.hasErrors('lastName')}? 'error'">
                Last Name</label>:
              <input type="text" th:field="*{lastName}"
                  th:class="${#fields.hasErrors('lastName')}? 'error'" /><br/>
Email       ──▷   <label th:class="${#fields.hasErrors('email')}? 'error'">
                Email</label>:
              <input type="text" th:field="*{email}"
                  th:class="${#fields.hasErrors('email')}? 'error'" /><br/>
Username    ──▷   <label th:class="${#fields.hasErrors('username')}? 'error'">
                Username</label>:
              <input type="text" th:field="*{username}"
                  th:class="${#fields.hasErrors('username')}? 'error'" /><br/>
Password    ──▷   <label th:class="${#fields.hasErrors('password')}? 'error'">
                Password</label>:
              <input type="password" th:field="*{password}"
                  th:class="${#fields.hasErrors('password')}? 'error'" /><br/>

            <input type="submit" value="Register" />
          </form>
```

Listing 6.7 shows that all the form fields use the same Thymeleaf attributes and the
*{} expression to bind to the backing object. This repeats what you already did with
the First Name field.

But also notice that Thymeleaf is used near the top of the form to render all errors.
The <div> element has a th:if attribute that checks to see if there are any errors. If
there are, the <div> will be rendered. Otherwise, it won't be rendered.

In the <div> is an unordered list to display each of the errors. The th:each attribute on the <li> tag instructs Thymeleaf to render the <li> one time for each error,
assigning the current error in each iteration to a variable named err.

The <li> tag also has a th:text attribute. This attribute instructs Thymeleaf to
evaluate an expression (in this case, the value of the err variable) and render its value
as the body of the <li> tag. In effect, there will be one <li> for each error, displaying
the text of that error.

You may be wondering about the difference between the expressions wrapped with
${} and those wrapped with *{}. The ${} expressions (such as ${spitter}) are vari-
able expressions. Normally, these are Object-Graph Navigation Language (OGNL)
expressions (http://commons.apache.org/proper/commons-ognl/). But when used
with Spring, they're SpEL expressions. In the case of ${spitter}, it resolves to the
model property whose key is spitter.

As for *{} expressions, they're selection expressions. Whereas variable expressions
are evaluated against the entire SpEL context, selection expressions are evaluated on
a selected object. In the case of the form, the selected object is the one given in the

`<form>` tag's `th:object` attribute: a `Spitter` object from the model. Therefore the `*{firstName}` expression evaluates to the `firstName` property on the `Spitter` object.

6.5 *Summary*

Processing requests is only half of the story of Spring MVC. If the results coming from the controllers you write are ever to be seen, the model data they produce needs to be rendered into views and displayed in the user's web browser. Spring is flexible with regard to view rendering and offers several out-of-the-box options, including conventional JavaServer Pages and the popular Apache Tiles layout engine.

In this chapter, you've had a quick look at all the view and view-resolution options offered by Spring. We also took a deeper dive to show how you can use JSP and Apache Tiles with Spring MVC.

You also saw how to use Thymeleaf, an alternative to JSP, as the view layer of a Spring MVC application. Thymeleaf is a compelling option because it enables the creation of natural templates that are still pure HTML and can be edited and viewed *in the raw* as if they were static HTML, but still render dynamic model data at runtime. Moreover, Thymeleaf templates are largely decoupled from servlets, enabling them to be used in places where JSPs can't.

With the view of the Spittr application defined, you have a small but deployable and functional web application written with Spring MVC. We still need to flesh out some other concerns like data persistence and security, and we'll get to those in due time. But the application is starting to take shape nicely.

Before we dive deeper into the application stack, the next chapter continues our discussion of Spring MVC, looking at some of the more useful and advanced capabilities in the framework.

Advanced Spring MVC

This chapter covers

- Alternate Spring MVC configuration options
- Handling file uploads
- Handling exceptions in controllers
- Working with flash attributes

But wait! There's more!

You've probably heard those words before if you've ever seen one of those "as seen on TV" ads for some gizmo or gadget. Just about the time the ad has completely described the product and made initial claims about what it can do, you hear, "But wait! There's more!" and the ad continues to tell you just how much more amazing the product can be.

In many ways, Spring MVC (and, indeed, every part of Spring) has that feel of "There's more!" Just about the time you think you've got your head around what Spring MVC can do, you find out there's even more that you can do with it.

In chapter 5, we looked at essential Spring MVC and how to write controllers to handle various kinds of requests. Then you built on that in chapter 6 to create the JSP and Thymeleaf views that present model data to the user. You might think you know everything about Spring MVC. But wait! There's more!

In this chapter, we'll continue with the Spring MVC topic by covering a handful of features that exceed the basics covered in chapters 5 and 6. We'll look at how to write controllers that accept file uploads, how to handle exceptions thrown from controllers, and how to pass data around in the model such that it survives a redirect.

But first, I have a promise to keep. In chapter 5, I quickly showed you how to use `AbstractAnnotationConfigDispatcherServletInitializer` to set up Spring MVC, and I promised that I'd show you some alternate setup options. So before we look at file uploads and exception handling, let's take a moment to explore some of the other ways you can set up `DispatcherServlet` and `ContextLoaderListener`.

7.1 *Alternate Spring MVC configuration*

In chapter 5, we took a quick path toward setting up Spring MVC by extending `AbstractAnnotationConfigDispatcherServletInitializer`. That convenient base class assumes that you want a basic `DispatcherServlet` and `ContextLoaderListener` setup and that your Spring configuration will be in Java instead of XML.

Although that is a safe assumption for many Spring applications, it may not always fit what you need. You may need servlets and filters in addition to `DispatcherServlet`. Maybe you need to do some additional configuration on `DispatcherServlet` itself. Or, if you're deploying your application to a pre-Servlet 3.0 container, you may need to configure `DispatcherServlet` in a traditional web.xml file.

Fortunately, there are several ways that Spring returns some control to you when the garden-variety `AbstractAnnotationConfigDispatcherServletInitializer` configuration doesn't fit your needs. Let's start by looking at a few ways to customize how `DispatcherServlet` is configured.

7.1.1 *Customizing DispatcherServlet configuration*

It isn't apparent from the looks of the class in listing 7.1, but there's more to `AbstractAnnotationConfigDispatcherServletInitializer` than meets the eye. The three methods you wrote in `SpittrWebAppInitializer` were the only `abstract` ones you were required to override. But there are more methods that can be overridden to apply additional configuration.

One such method is `customizeRegistration()`. After `AbstractAnnotation-ConfigDispatcherServletInitializer` registers `DispatcherServlet` with the servlet container, it calls the `customizeRegistration()` method, passing in the `Servlet-Registration.Dynamic` that resulted from the servlet registration. By overriding `customizeRegistration()`, you can apply additional configuration to `Dispatcher-Servlet`.

For instance, a little later in this chapter (in section 7.2) you'll see how to handle multipart requests and file uploads with Spring MVC. If you plan to use Servlet 3.0 support for multipart configuration, you need to enable `DispatcherServlet`'s registration to enable multipart requests. You can override the `customizeRegistration()` method to set a `MultipartConfigElement` like this:

```
@Override
protected void customizeRegistration(Dynamic registration) {
```

```
registration.setMultipartConfig(
    new MultipartConfigElement("/tmp/spittr/uploads"));
}
```

With the `ServletRegistration.Dynamic` that's given to `customizeRegistration()`, you can do several things, including set the load-on-startup priority by calling `set-LoadOnStartup()`, set an initialization parameter by calling `setInitParameter()`, and call `setMultipartConfig()` to configure Servlet 3.0 multipart support. In the preceding example, you're setting up multipart support to temporarily store uploaded files at /tmp/spittr/uploads.

7.1.2 *Adding additional servlets and filters*

Given the way that `AbstractAnnotationConfigDispatcherServletInitializer` is defined, it will create a `DispatcherServlet` and a `ContextLoaderListener`. But what if you want to register additional servlets, filters, or listeners?

One of the nice things about working with a Java-based initializer is that (unlike with web.xml) you can define as many initializer classes as you want. Therefore, if you need to register any additional components into the web container, you need only create a new initializer class. The easiest way to do this is by implementing Spring's `WebApplicationInitializer` interface.

For example, the following listing shows how to create an implementation of `WebApplicationInitializer` that registers a servlet.

Listing 7.1 Implementing `WebApplicationInitializer` to register a servlet

```
package com.myapp.config;
import javax.servlet.ServletContext;
import javax.servlet.ServletException;
import javax.servlet.ServletRegistration.Dynamic;
import org.springframework.web.WebApplicationInitializer;
import com.myapp.MyServlet;

public class MyServletInitializer implements WebApplicationInitializer {

  @Override
  public void onStartup(ServletContext servletContext)
      throws ServletException {

    Dynamic myServlet =                                      Register the
        servletContext.addServlet("myServlet", MyServlet.class);   servlet

    myServlet.addMapping("/custom/**");              ⟵  Map the servlet
  }

}
```

Listing 7.1 is a rather basic servlet-registering initializer class. It registers a servlet and maps it to a single path. You could use this approach to register `DispatcherServlet` manually. (But there's no need, because `AbstractAnnotationConfigDispatcher-ServletInitializer` does a fine job without as much code.)

Similarly, you can register listeners and filters by creating a new implementation of WebApplicationInitializer. For example, the next listing shows how to register a filter.

Listing 7.2 A `WebApplicationInitializer` that can also register filters

```
@Override
public void onStartup(ServletContext servletContext)
      throws ServletException {

  javax.servlet.FilterRegistration.Dynamic filter =                 Register
    servletContext.addFilter("myFilter", MyFilter.class);           filter

  filter.addMappingForUrlPatterns(null, false, "/custom/*");        Add filter
}                                                                   mapping
```

WebApplicationInitializer is a fine general-purpose way of registering servlets, filters, and listeners in Java when deploying to a Servlet 3.0 container. But if you're registering a filter and only need to map that filter to DispatcherServlet, then there's a shortcut in AbstractAnnotationConfigDispatcherServletInitializer.

To register one or more filters and map them to DispatcherServlet, all you need to do is override the getServletFilters() method of AbstractAnnotationConfig-DispatcherServletInitializer. For example, the following getServletFilters() method overrides the one from AbstractAnnotationConfigDispatcherServlet-Initializer to register a filter:

```
@Override
protected Filter[] getServletFilters() {
  return new Filter[] { new MyFilter() };
}
```

As you can see, this method returns an array of javax.servlet.Filter. Here it only returns a single filter, but it could return as many filters as you need. There's no need to declare the mapping for the filters; any filter returned from getServletFilters() will automatically be mapped to DispatcherServlet.

When deploying to a Servlet 3.0 container, Spring offers several ways of registering servlets (including DispatcherServlet), filters, and listeners *without* creating a web.xml file. But you don't have to use any of those if you don't want to. If you aren't deploying your application to a Servlet 3.0 container (or if you just like working with web.xml), then there's no reason you can't configure Spring MVC in a legacy manner with web.xml. Let's see how.

7.1.3 *Declaring DispatcherServlet in web.xml*

In a typical Spring MVC application, you need a DispatcherServlet and a Context-LoaderListener. AbstractAnnotationConfigDispatcherServletInitializer will register these automatically for you, but if you're registering them in web.xml, you'll need to do all the work.

Here's a basic web.xml file with a typical setup for `DispatcherServlet` and `ContextLoaderListener`.

Listing 7.3   Setting up Spring MVC in web.xml

```xml
<?xml version="1.0" encoding="UTF-8"?>
<web-app version="2.5"
  xmlns="http://java.sun.com/xml/ns/javaee"
  xmlns:xsi="http://www.w3.org/2001/XMLSchema-instance"
  xsi:schemaLocation="http://java.sun.com/xml/ns/javaee
      http://java.sun.com/xml/ns/javaee/web-app_2_5.xsd">

  <context-param>                                                    Set root
    <param-name>contextConfigLocation</param-name>                  context
    <param-value>/WEB-INF/spring/root-context.xml</param-value>  ◁┘ location
  </context-param>

  <listener>
    <listener-class>
      org.springframework.web.context.ContextLoaderListener     ◁┐
    </listener-class>                                              Register
  </listener>                                           ContextLoaderListener

  <servlet>
    <servlet-name>appServlet</servlet-name>
    <servlet-class>
      org.springframework.web.servlet.DispatcherServlet          ◁┐
    </servlet-class>                                               Register
    <load-on-startup>1</load-on-startup>                  DispatcherServlet
  </servlet>

  <servlet-mapping>
    <servlet-name>appServlet</servlet-name>             ◁┐ Map
    <url-pattern>/</url-pattern>                            DispatcherServlet
  </servlet-mapping>                                        to /

</web-app>
```

As I mentioned in chapter 5, `ContextLoaderListener` and `DispatcherServlet` each load a Spring application context. The `contextConfigLocation` context parameter specifies the location of the XML file that defines the root application context loaded by `ContextLoaderListener`. As defined in listing 7.3, the root context is loaded with bean definitions in /WEB-INF/spring/root-context.xml.

`DispatcherServlet` loads its application context with beans defined in a file whose name is based on the servlet name. In listing 7.3, the servlet is named `appServlet`. Therefore, `DispatcherServlet` loads its application context from an XML file at /WEB-INF/appServlet-context.xml.

If you'd rather specify the location of the `DispatcherServlet` configuration file, you can set a `contextConfigLocation` initialization parameter on the servlet. For example, the following `DispatcherServlet` configuration has `DispatcherServlet` loading its beans from /WEB-INF/spring/appServlet/servlet-context.xml:

```
<servlet>
  <servlet-name>appServlet</servlet-name>
  <servlet-class>
    org.springframework.web.servlet.DispatcherServlet
  </servlet-class>
  <init-param>
    <param-name>contextConfigLocation</param-name>
    <param-value>
      /WEB-INF/spring/appServlet/servlet-context.xml
    </param-value>
  </init-param>
  <load-on-startup>1</load-on-startup>
</servlet>
```

Of course, that's how you'd have `DispatcherServlet` and `ContextLoaderListener` load their respective application contexts from XML. But throughout much of this book, we'll favor Java configuration over XML configuration. Therefore you'll need to set up Spring MVC to load the configuration from `@Configuration`-annotated classes.

To use Java-based configuration in Spring MVC, you need to tell `DispatcherServlet` and `ContextLoaderListener` to use `AnnotationConfigWebApplicationContext`, an implementation of `WebApplicationContext` that loads Java configuration classes instead of XML. You can do that by setting the `contextClass` context parameter and initialization parameter for `DispatcherServlet`. The next listing shows a new web.xml file that sets up Spring MVC for Java-based Spring configuration.

Listing 7.4   Configuring web.xml to use Java configuration

```
<?xml version="1.0" encoding="UTF-8"?>
<web-app version="2.5"
  xmlns="http://java.sun.com/xml/ns/javaee"
  xmlns:xsi="http://www.w3.org/2001/XMLSchema-instance"
  xsi:schemaLocation="http://java.sun.com/xml/ns/javaee
      http://java.sun.com/xml/ns/javaee/web-app_2_5.xsd">

  <context-param>                                              ← Use Java
    <param-name>contextClass</param-name>                        configuration
    <param-value>
      org.springframework.web.context.support.
                            ↳ AnnotationConfigWebApplicationContext
    </param-value>
  </context-param>

  <context-param>
    <param-name>contextConfigLocation</param-name>
    <param-value>com.habuma.spitter.config.RootConfig</param-value>  ←
  </context-param>                                              Specify root
                                                                configuration class
  <listener>
    <listener-class>
      org.springframework.web.context.ContextLoaderListener
    </listener-class>
  </listener>
```

```
<servlet>
  <servlet-name>appServlet</servlet-name>
  <servlet-class>
    org.springframework.web.servlet.DispatcherServlet
  </servlet-class>
  <init-param>                                              ┌─ Use Java
    <param-name>contextClass</param-name>       ◁──────────┘   configuration
    <param-value>
      org.springframework.web.context.support.
                          ⮕ AnnotationConfigWebApplicationContext
    </param-value>
  </init-param>
  <init-param>
    <param-name>contextConfigLocation</param-name>     ◁─┐ Specify
    <param-value>                                         │ DispatcherServlet
      com.habuma.spitter.config.WebConfigConfig           │ configuration class
    </param-value>
  </init-param>
  <load-on-startup>1</load-on-startup>
</servlet>

<servlet-mapping>
  <servlet-name>appServlet</servlet-name>
  <url-pattern>/</url-pattern>
</servlet-mapping>
```

`</web-app>`

Now that we've looked at a variety of ways to set up Spring MVC, let's examine how to use Spring MVC to handle file uploads.

7.2 *Processing multipart form data*

It's common for a web application to enable its users to upload content. On sites like Facebook and Flickr, it's normal for users to upload photos and videos to share with their family and friends. There are also several services that allow users to upload photos to be printed on paper the old-fashioned way or to be applied to T-shirts and coffee mugs.

The Spittr application calls for file uploads in two places. When a new user registers with the application, you'd like them to be able to provide a picture to associate with their profile. And when a user posts a new Spittle, they may want to upload a photo to go along with their message.

The request resulting from a typical form submission is simple and takes the form of multiple name-value pairs separated by ampersands. For example, when submitting the registration form from the Spittr application, the request might look like this:

```
firstName=Charles&lastName=Xavier&email=professorx%40xmen.org
&username=professorx&password=letmein01
```

Although this encoding scheme is simple and sufficient for typical text-based form submissions, it isn't robust enough to carry binary data such as an uploaded image. In contrast, multipart form data breaks a form into individual parts, with one part per field. Each part can have its own type. Typical form fields have textual data in their parts, but when something is being uploaded, the part can be binary, as shown in the following multipart request body:

```
------WebKitFormBoundaryqgkaBn8IHJCuNmiW
Content-Disposition: form-data; name="firstName"

Charles
------WebKitFormBoundaryqgkaBn8IHJCuNmiW
Content-Disposition: form-data; name="lastName"

Xavier
------WebKitFormBoundaryqgkaBn8IHJCuNmiW
Content-Disposition: form-data; name="email"

charles@xmen.com
------WebKitFormBoundaryqgkaBn8IHJCuNmiW
Content-Disposition: form-data; name="username"

professorx
------WebKitFormBoundaryqgkaBn8IHJCuNmiW
Content-Disposition: form-data; name="password"

letmein01
------WebKitFormBoundaryqgkaBn8IHJCuNmiW
Content-Disposition: form-data; name="profilePicture"; filename="me.jpg"
Content-Type: image/jpeg

  [[ Binary image data goes here ]]
------WebKitFormBoundaryqgkaBn8IHJCuNmiW--
```

In this multipart request, the `profilePicture` part is noticeably different from the other parts. Among other things, it has its own `Content-Type` header indicating that it's a JPEG image. And although it may not be obvious, the body of the `profile-Picture` part is binary data instead of simple text.

Even though multipart requests look complex, handling them in a Spring MVC controller is easy. But before you can write controller methods to handle file uploads, you must configure a multipart resolver to tell `DispatcherServlet` how to read multipart requests.

7.2.1 *Configuring a multipart resolver*

`DispatcherServlet` doesn't implement any logic for parsing the data in a multipart request. Instead, it delegates to an implementation of Spring's `MultipartResolver` strategy interface to resolve the content in a multipart request. Since Spring 3.1, Spring comes with two out-of-the-box implementations of `MultipartResolver` to choose from:

- `CommonsMultipartResolver`—Resolves multipart requests using Jakarta Commons FileUpload
- `StandardServletMultipartResolver`—Relies on Servlet 3.0 support for multipart requests (since Spring 3.1)

Generally speaking, `StandardServletMultipartResolver` should probably be your first choice of these two. It uses existing support in your servlet container and doesn't require any additional project dependencies. But you might choose `Commons-MultipartResolver` if you'll be deploying your application to a pre-Servlet 3.0 container or if you aren't using Spring 3.1 or higher yet.

RESOLVING MULTIPART REQUESTS WITH SERVLET 3.0

The Servlet 3.0-compatible `StandardServletMultipartResolver` has no constructor arguments or properties to be set. This makes it extremely simple to declare as a bean in your Spring configuration, as shown here:

```
@Bean
public MultipartResolver multipartResolver() throws IOException {
  return new StandardServletMultipartResolver();
}
```

As easy as that `@Bean` method is, you might be wondering how you can place constraints on the way `StandardServletMultipartResolver` works. What if you want to limit the maximum size of file that a user can upload? Or what if you'd like to specify the location where the uploaded files are temporarily written while they're being uploaded? With no properties and no constructor arguments, `StandardServlet-MultipartResolver` seems limiting.

On the contrary, it's possible to configure constraints on `StandardServlet-MultipartResolver`. But instead of configuring `StandardServletMultipartResolver` in your Spring configuration, you must specify multipart configuration in the servlet configuration. At the very least, you must specify the temporary file path where the file will be written during the upload. `StandardServletMultipartResolver` won't work unless you configure this minimum detail. More specifically, you must configure multipart details as part of `DispatcherServlet`'s configuration in web.xml or in the servlet initializer class.

If you're configuring `DispatcherServlet` in a servlet initializer class that implements `WebApplicationInitializer`, you can configure multipart details by calling `setMultipartConfig()` on the servlet registration, passing an instance of `Multipart-ConfigElement`. Here's a minimal multipart configuration for `DispatcherServlet` that sets the temporary location to /tmp/spittr/uploads:

```
DispatcherServlet ds = new DispatcherServlet();
Dynamic registration = context.addServlet("appServlet", ds);
registration.addMapping("/");
registration.setMultipartConfig(
    new MultipartConfigElement("/tmp/spittr/uploads"));
```

If you've configured `DispatcherServlet` in a servlet initializer class that extends `AbstractAnnotationConfigDispatcherServletInitializer` or `AbstractDispatcher-ServletInitializer`, you don't create the instance of `DispatcherServlet` or register it with the servlet context directly. Consequently, there's no handy reference to the `Dynamic` servlet registration to work with. But you can override the `customize-Registration()` method (which is given a `Dynamic` as a parameter) to configure multipart details:

```
@Override
protected void customizeRegistration(Dynamic registration) {
  registration.setMultipartConfig(
      new MultipartConfigElement("/tmp/spittr/uploads"));
}
```

The single-argument constructor for `MultipartConfigElement` that you've been using thus far takes the absolute path to a directory in the filesystem where the uploaded file will be written temporarily. But there's another constructor that lets you set a few constraints on the size of the file being uploaded. In addition to the temporary location path, the other constructor accepts the following:

- The maximum size (in bytes) of any file uploaded. By default there is no limit.
- The maximum size (in bytes) of the entire multipart request, regardless of how many parts or how big any of the parts are. By default there is no limit.
- The maximum size (in bytes) of a file that can be uploaded without being written to the temporary location. The default is 0, meaning that all uploaded files will be written to disk.

For example, suppose you want to limit files to no more than 2 MB, to limit the entire request to no more than 4 MB, and to write all files to disk. The following use of `MultipartConfigElement` sets those thresholds:

```
@Override
protected void customizeRegistration(Dynamic registration) {
  registration.setMultipartConfig(
      new MultipartConfigElement("/tmp/spittr/uploads",
          2097152, 4194304, 0));
}
```

If you're configuring `DispatcherServlet` in a more traditional way in web.xml, you can specify multipart configuration using the `<multipart-config>` element in the `<servlet>` element, like this:

```
<servlet>
  <servlet-name>appServlet</servlet-name>
  <servlet-class>
    org.springframework.web.servlet.DispatcherServlet
  </servlet-class>
  <load-on-startup>1</load-on-startup>
  <multipart-config>
    <location>/tmp/spittr/uploads</location>
    <max-file-size>2097152</max-file-size>
    <max-request-size>4194304</max-request-size>
  </multipart-config>
</servlet>
```

The defaults for `<multipart-config>` are the same as for `MultipartConfigElement`. And just as with `MultipartConfigElement`, you must configure the `<location>`.

CONFIGURING A JAKARTA COMMONS FILEUPLOAD MULTIPART RESOLVER

`StandardServletMultipartResolver` is usually the best choice, but if you're not deploying your application to a Servlet 3.0 container, you'll need an alternative. You can write your own implementation of the `MultipartResolver` interface if you'd like. But unless you need to perform some special handling during multipart request handling, there's no reason to do that. Spring offers `CommonsMultipartResolver` as an out-of-the-box alternative to `StandardServletMultipartResolver`.

The simplest way to declare `CommonsMultipartResolver` as a Spring bean is like this:

```
@Bean
public MultipartResolver multipartResolver() {
  return new CommonsMultipartResolver();
}
```

Unlike `StandardServletMultipartResolver`, there's no need to configure a temporary file location with `CommonsMultipartResolver`. By default, the location is the servlet container's temporary directory. But you can specify a different location by setting the `uploadTempDir` property:

```
@Bean
public MultipartResolver multipartResolver() throws IOException {
  CommonsMultipartResolver multipartResolver =
      new CommonsMultipartResolver();
  multipartResolver.setUploadTempDir(
      new FileSystemResource("/tmp/spittr/uploads"));
  return multipartResolver;
}
```

In fact, you can specify other multipart upload details directly in the Spring configuration in the same way, by setting properties on `CommonsMultipartResolver`. For example, the following configuration is roughly equivalent to how you configured `StandardServletMultipartResolver` via `MultipartConfigElement` earlier:

```
@Bean
public MultipartResolver multipartResolver() throws IOException {
  CommonsMultipartResolver multipartResolver =
          new CommonsMultipartResolver();
  multipartResolver.setUploadTempDir(
      new FileSystemResource("/tmp/spittr/uploads"));
  multipartResolver.setMaxUploadSize(2097152);
  multipartResolver.setMaxInMemorySize(0);
  return multipartResolver;
}
```

Here you're setting the maximum file size to 2 MB and the maximum in-memory size to 0 bytes. These two properties directly correspond to `MultipartConfigElement`'s second and fourth constructor arguments, indicating that no files larger than 2 MB may be uploaded and that all files will be written to disk no matter what size. Unlike `MultipartConfigElement`, however, there's no way to specify the maximum multipart request size.

7.2.2 *Handling multipart requests*

Now that you've configured multipart support in Spring (and perhaps in the servlet container), you're ready to write controller methods to accept the uploaded files. The most common way of doing that is to annotate a controller method parameter with @RequestPart.

Suppose you want to offer people the opportunity to upload an image when they register as users of the Spittr application. You need to update the registration form so that the user can select a picture to be uploaded, and you need to tweak the process-Registration() method in SpitterController to accept the uploaded file. The following snippet from the Thymeleaf registration form view (registrationForm.html) highlights the necessary changes to the form:

```
<form method="POST" th:object="${spitter}"
      enctype="multipart/form-data">

...

  <label>Profile Picture</label>:
    <input type="file"
           name="profilePicture"
           accept="image/jpeg,image/png,image/gif" /><br/>

...

</form>
```

The <form> tag now has its enctype attribute set to multipart/form-data. This tells the browser to submit the form as multipart data instead of form data. Each field has its own part in the multipart request.

In addition to all the existing fields on the registration form, you've added a new <input> field whose type is file. This lets the user select an image file to upload. The accept attribute is set to limit file types to JPEG, PNG, and GIF images. And according to its name attribute, the image data will be sent in the multipart request in the profilePicture part.

Now you just need to change the processRegistration() method to accept the uploaded image. One way to do that is to add a byte array parameter that's annotated with @RequestPart. Here's an example:

```
@RequestMapping(value="/register", method=POST)
public String processRegistration(
    @RequestPart("profilePicture") byte[] profilePicture,
    @Valid Spitter spitter,
    Errors errors) {
  ...
}
```

When the registration form is submitted, the profilePicture attribute is given an array of byte containing the data from the request part (as specified by @Request-Part). If the user submits the form without selecting a file, then the array will be empty (but not null). With the image data in hand, all that's left is for process-Registration() to save the file somewhere.

We'll discuss how to save the image data more in a bit. But first, consider what you know about the image data that was submitted. Or, more important, what do you *not* know? Although you have the image data as an array of byte and from that you can derive the size of the image, there's little else you know about it. You have no idea what type of file it is or even what the name of the original file was. And it's up to you to figure out how to turn that byte array into a file you can save.

RECEIVING A MULTIPARTFILE

Working with the uploaded file's raw bytes is simple but limiting. Therefore, Spring also offers MultipartFile as a way to get a richer object for processing multipart data. The following listing shows what the MultipartFile interface looks like.

> **Listing 7.5   Spring's `MultipartFile` interface for working with uploaded files**

```
package org.springframework.web.multipart;
import java.io.File;
import java.io.IOException;
import java.io.InputStream;

public interface MultipartFile {
  String getName();
  String getOriginalFilename();
  String getContentType();
  boolean isEmpty();
  long getSize();
  byte[] getBytes() throws IOException;
  InputStream getInputStream() throws IOException;
  void transferTo(File dest) throws IOException;
}
```

As you can see, MultipartFile offers a way to get at the bytes for the uploaded file. But it offers much more, including the original filename, size, and content type. It also offers an InputStream for reading the file data as a stream.

What's more, MultipartFile offers a convenient transferTo() method to help you write the uploaded file to the filesystem. For example, you could add the following lines to processRegistration() to write the uploaded image file to the filesystem:

```
profilePicture.transferTo(
    new File("/data/spittr/" + profilePicture.getOriginalFilename()));
```

Saving a file to the local filesystem like this is simple enough, but it leaves the management of the file up to you. You're responsible for ensuring that there's plenty of space. It's up to you to make sure the file is backed up in case of a hardware failure. And it's your job to deal with synchronizing the image files across multiple servers in a cluster.

SAVING FILES TO AMAZON S3

Another option is to hand that responsibility off to someone else. With only a bit more code, you can save the images to the cloud. The following listing, for example, shows saveImage(), a method you can call from processRegistration() to save the uploaded image to Amazon S3.

Listing 7.6 Saving a `MultipartFile` to Amazon S3

```
private void saveImage(MultipartFile image)
    throws ImageUploadException {
  try {
    AWSCredentials awsCredentials =
        new AWSCredentials(s3AccessKey, s2SecretKey);
    S3Service s3 = new RestS3Service(awsCredentials);

    S3Bucket bucket = s3.getBucket("spittrImages");
    S3Object imageObject =
        new S3Object(image.getOriginalFilename());

    imageObject.setDataInputStream(
        image.getInputStream());
    imageObject.setContentLength(image.getSize());
    imageObject.setContentType(image.getContentType());

    AccessControlList acl = new AccessControlList();
    acl.setOwner(bucket.getOwner());
    acl.grantPermission(GroupGrantee.ALL_USERS,
        Permission.PERMISSION_READ);
    imageObject.setAcl(acl);

    s3.putObject(bucket, imageObject);
  } catch (Exception e) {
    throw new ImageUploadException("Unable to save image", e);
  }
}
```

Annotations:
- **Set up S3 service** → `S3Service s3 = new RestS3Service(awsCredentials);`
- **Create S3 bucket and object** ← `S3Bucket bucket = s3.getBucket("spittrImages");`
- **Set image data** ← `imageObject.setDataInputStream(`
- **Set permissions** ← `AccessControlList acl = new AccessControlList();`
- **Save image** ← `s3.putObject(bucket, imageObject);`

The first thing that saveImage() does is set up Amazon Web Service (AWS) credentials. For this, you'll need an S3 access key and an S3 secret access key. These will be given to you by Amazon when you sign up for S3 service. They're provided to SpitterController via value injection.

With the AWS credentials in hand, saveImage() creates an instance of JetS3t's RestS3Service, through which it operates on the S3 filesystem. It gets a reference to the spitterImages bucket, creates an S3Object to contain the image, and then fills that S3Object with image data.

Just before calling the putObject() method to write the image data to S3, save-Image() sets the permissions on the S3Object to allow all users to view it. This is important—without it, the images wouldn't be visible to your application's users. Finally, if anything goes wrong, an ImageUploadException will be thrown.

RECEIVING THE UPLOADED FILE AS A PART

If you're deploying your application to a Servlet 3.0 container, you have an alternative to MultipartFile. Spring MVC will also accept a javax.servlet.http.Part as a controller method parameter. Using Part instead of MultipartFile leaves the process-Registration() method signature looking like this:

```
@RequestMapping(value="/register", method=POST)
public String processRegistration(
    @RequestPart("profilePicture") Part profilePicture,
    @Valid Spitter spitter,
    Errors errors) {
  ...
}
```

For the most part (no pun intended), the `Part` interface isn't much different from `MultipartFile`. As you can see in the next listing, the `Part` interface has several methods that mirror the methods in `MultipartFile`.

Listing 7.7   Part interface: an alternative to Spring's `MultipartFile`

```
package javax.servlet.http;
import java.io.*;
import java.util.*;

public interface Part {
  public InputStream getInputStream() throws IOException;
  public String getContentType();
  public String getName();
  public String getSubmittedFileName();
  public long getSize();
  public void write(String fileName) throws IOException;
  public void delete() throws IOException;
  public String getHeader(String name);
  public Collection<String> getHeaders(String name);
  public Collection<String> getHeaderNames();
}
```

In many cases, the `Part` methods are named exactly the same as the `MultipartFile` methods. A few have similar but different names; `getSubmittedFileName()`, for example, corresponds to `getOriginalFilename()`. Likewise, `write()` corresponds to `transferTo()`, making it possible to write the uploaded file like this:

```
profilePicture.write("/data/spittr/" +
        profilePicture.getOriginalFilename());
```

It's worth noting that if you write your controller handler methods to accept file uploads via a `Part` parameter, then you don't need to configure the `StandardServletMultipartResolver` bean. `StandardServletMultipartResolver` is required only when you're working with `MultipartFile`.

7.3   *Handling exceptions*

Up to this point, we've been assuming that everything will always work in the Spittr application. But what if something goes wrong? What if, while handling a request, an exception is thrown? What response will be sent to the client when thing go awry?

No matter what happens, good or bad, the outcome of a servlet request is a servlet response. If an exception occurs during request processing, the outcome is still a servlet response. Somehow, the exception must be translated into a response.

Spring offers a handful of ways to translate exceptions to responses:

- Certain Spring exceptions are automatically mapped to specific HTTP status codes.
- An exception can be annotated with @ResponseStatus to map it to an HTTP status code.
- A method can be annotated with @ExceptionHandler to handle the exception.

The simplest way to handle an exception is to map it to the HTTP status code to be placed on the response. Let's see how to map exceptions to HTTP status codes.

7.3.1 *Mapping exceptions to HTTP status codes*

Out of the box, Spring automatically maps a dozen of its own exceptions to appropriate status codes. Table 7.1 shows those mappings.

Table 7.1 Some Spring exceptions are mapped by default to HTTP status codes.

Spring exception	HTTP status code
BindException	400 - Bad Request
ConversionNotSupportedException	500 - Internal Server Error
HttpMediaTypeNotAcceptableException	406 - Not Acceptable
HttpMediaTypeNotSupportedException	415 - Unsupported Media Type
HttpMessageNotReadableException	400 - Bad Request
HttpMessageNotWritableException	500 - Internal Server Error
HttpRequestMethodNotSupportedException	405 - Method Not Allowed
MethodArgumentNotValidException	400 - Bad Request
MissingServletRequestParameterException	400 - Bad Request
MissingServletRequestPartException	400 - Bad Request
NoSuchRequestHandlingMethodException	404 - Not Found
TypeMismatchException	400 - Bad Request

The exceptions in table 7.1 are usually thrown by Spring itself as the result of something going wrong in DispatcherServlet or while performing validation. For example, if DispatcherServlet can't find a controller method suitable to handle a request, a NoSuchRequestHandlingMethodException will be thrown, resulting in a response with a status code of 404 (Not Found).

Although these built-in mappings are helpful, they do no good for any application exceptions that may be thrown. Fortunately, Spring offers a way to map exceptions to HTTP status codes via the @ResponseStatus annotation.

To demonstrate, consider the following request-handling method from Spittle-Controller that could result in an HTTP 404 status (but doesn't):

```
@RequestMapping(value="/{spittleId}", method=RequestMethod.GET)
public String spittle(
    @PathVariable("spittleId") long spittleId,
    Model model) {
  Spittle spittle = spittleRepository.findOne(spittleId);
  if (spittle == null) {
    throw new SpittleNotFoundException();
  }
  model.addAttribute(spittle);
  return "spittle";
}
```

Here, a Spittle is retrieved by its ID from the SpittleRepository. If findOne() returns a Spittle object, that Spittle is put into the model, and the view whose name is spittle is tasked with rendering it in the response. But if findOne() returns null, then a SpittleNotFoundException is thrown. For now, SpittleNotFound-Exception is a simple unchecked exception that looks like this:

```
package spittr.web;
public class SpittleNotFoundException extends RuntimeException {
}
```

If the spittle() method is called on to handle a request, and the given ID comes up empty, the SpittleNotFoundException will (by default) result in a response with a 500 (Internal Server Error) status code. In fact, in the event of any exception that isn't otherwise mapped, the response will always have a 500 status code. But you can change that by mapping SpittleNotFoundException otherwise.

When SpittleNotFoundException is thrown, it's a situation where a requested resource isn't found. The HTTP status code of 404 is precisely the appropriate response status code when a resource isn't found. So, let's use @ResponseStatus to map SpittleNotFoundException to HTTP status code 404.

Listing 7.8   @ResponseStatus annotation: maps exceptions to a specified status code

```
package spittr.web;
import org.springframework.http.HttpStatus;
import org.springframework.web.bind.annotation.ResponseStatus;

@ResponseStatus(value=HttpStatus.NOT_FOUND,                     ◁——  Map exception
                reason="Spittle Not Found")                          to HTTP Status
public class SpittleNotFoundException extends RuntimeException {      404
}
```

After introducing this @ResponseStatus annotation, if a SpittleNotFoundException were to be thrown from a controller method, the response would have a status code of 404 and a reason of Spittle Not Found.

7.3.2 *Writing exception-handling methods*

Mapping exceptions to status codes is simple and sufficient for many cases. But what if you want the response to carry more than just a status code that represents the error that occurred? Rather than treat the exception generically as some HTTP error, maybe you'd like to handle the exception the same way you might handle the request itself.

As an example, suppose that SpittleRepository's save() method throws a DuplicateSpittleException if a user attempts to create a Spittle with text identical to one they've already created. That means the saveSpittle() method of Spittle-Controller might need to deal with that exception. As shown in the following listing, saveSpittle() could directly handle the exception.

Listing 7.9 Handling an exception directly in a request-handling method

```
@RequestMapping(method=RequestMethod.POST)
public String saveSpittle(SpittleForm form, Model model) {
  try {
    spittleRepository.save(
        new Spittle(null, form.getMessage(), new Date(),
            form.getLongitude(), form.getLatitude()));
    return "redirect:/spittles";
  } catch (DuplicateSpittleException e) {        ⟵┘ Catch the
    return "error/duplicate";                          exception
  }
}
```

There's nothing particularly outstanding about listing 7.9. It's a basic example of Java exception handling. Nothing more.

It works fine, but the method is a bit complex. Two paths can be taken, each with a different outcome. It'd be simpler if saveSpittle() could focus on the happy path and let some other method deal with the exception.

First, let's rip the exception-handling code out of saveSpittle():

```
@RequestMapping(method=RequestMethod.POST)
public String saveSpittle(SpittleForm form, Model model) {
  spittleRepository.save(
      new Spittle(null, form.getMessage(), new Date(),
          form.getLongitude(), form.getLatitude()));
  return "redirect:/spittles";
}
```

As you can see, saveSpittle() is now much simpler. Because it's written to only be concerned with the successful saving of a Spittle, it has only one path and is easy to follow (and test).

Now let's add a new method to SpittleController that will handle the case where DuplicateSpittleException is thrown:

```
@ExceptionHandler(DuplicateSpittleException.class)
public String handleDuplicateSpittle() {
  return "error/duplicate";
}
```

The `@ExceptionHandler` annotation has been applied to the `handleDuplicate-Spittle()` method, designating it as the go-to method when a `DuplicateSpittle-Exception` is thrown. It returns a `String`, which, just as with the request-handling method, specifies the logical name of the view to render, telling the user that they attempted to create a duplicate entry.

What's especially interesting about `@ExceptionHandler` methods is that they handle their exceptions from *any* handler method in the same controller. So although you created the `handleDuplicateSpittle()` method from the code extracted from `saveSpittle()`, it will handle a `DuplicateSpittleException` thrown from any method in `SpittleController`. Rather than duplicate exception-handling code in every method that has the potential for throwing a `DuplicateSpittleException`, this one method covers them all.

If `@ExceptionHandler` methods can handle exceptions thrown from any handler method in the same controller class, you might be wondering if there's a way they can handle exceptions thrown from handler methods in *any* controller. As of Spring 3.2 they certainly can, but only if they're defined in a controller advice class.

What's a controller advice class? I'm glad you asked, because that's what we'll look at next.

7.4   *Advising controllers*

Certain aspects of controller classes might be handier if they could be applied broadly across all controllers in a given application. `@ExceptionHandler` methods, for instance, could prove useful in handling exceptions across multiple controllers. If a particular exception is thrown from multiple controller classes, you might find yourself duplicating the same `@ExceptionHandler` method in all of those controllers. Or, to avoid the duplication, you might create a base controller class that all of your controllers could extend to inherit the common `@ExceptionHandler` method.

Spring 3.2 brings another option to the table: controller advice. A *controller advice* is any class that's annotated with `@ControllerAdvice` and has one or more of the following kinds of methods:

- `@ExceptionHandler`-annotated
- `@InitBinder`-annotated
- `@ModelAttribute`-annotated

Those methods in an `@ControllerAdvice`-annotated class are applied globally across all `@RequestMapping`-annotated methods on all controllers in an application.

The `@ControllerAdvice` annotation is itself annotated with `@Component`. Therefore, an `@ControllerAdvice`-annotated class will be picked up by component-scanning, just like an `@Controller`-annotated class.

One of the most practical uses for `@ControllerAdvice` is to gather all `@Exception-Handler` methods in a single class so that exceptions from all controllers are handled consistently in one place. For example, suppose you want to apply the `Duplicate-SpittleException`-handling method across all controllers in your application. The next listing shows `AppWideExceptionHandler`, a `@ControllerAdvice`-annotated class that does just that.

Listing 7.10 Using `@ControllerAdvice` to handle exception for all controllers

```
package spitter.web;
import org.springframework.web.bind.annotation.ControllerAdvice;
import org.springframework.web.bind.annotation.ExceptionHandler;

@ControllerAdvice                                              ◁── Declare
public class AppWideExceptionHandler {                              controller advice

  @ExceptionHandler(DuplicateSpittleException.class)          ◁── Define exception-
  public String duplicateSpittleHandler() {                        handler method
    return "error/duplicate";
  }

}
```

Now, if a `DuplicateSpittleException` is thrown from *any* controller method, no matter which controller it's in, this `duplicateSpittleHandler()` method will be called to handle the exception. The `@ExceptionHandler`-annotated method can be written much like an `@RequestMapping`-annotated method. As shown in listing 7.10, it returns `error/duplicate` as the logical view name so that a friendly error page is displayed to the user.

7.5   *Carrying data across redirect requests*

As mentioned in section XREF _writing_a_form_handling_controller, it's generally a good practice to perform a redirect after handling a `POST` request. Among other things, this prevents the client from reissuing a dangerous `POST` request if the user clicks the Refresh or back-arrow button in their browser.

In chapter 5, you used the power of the `redirect:` prefix in the view names returned from controller methods. When a controller method returns a `String` whose value starts with `redirect:`, that `String` isn't used to look up a view, but is instead used as a path to redirect the browser to. Looking back at listing XREF ex_SpitterController_processRegistration_validation, you'll see that the last line of the `processRegistration()` method returns a `redirect:String` like this:

```
return "redirect:/spitter/" + spitter.getUsername();
```

The `redirect:` prefix makes working with redirects plain and simple. You'd think there's nothing more that Spring could do to make working with redirects any simpler. But wait: Spring has a bit more to offer to help with redirects.

Specifically, how can a redirecting method send data to the method that handles the redirect? Typically, when a handler method completes, any model data specified

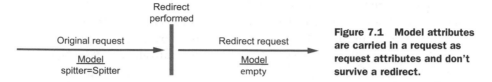

Figure 7.1 Model attributes are carried in a request as request attributes and don't survive a redirect.

in the method is copied into the request as request attributes, and the request is forwarded to the view for rendering. Because it's the same request that's handled by both the controller method and the view, the request attributes survive the forward.

But as illustrated in figure 7.1, when a controller method results in a redirect, the original request ends and a new HTTP GET request begins. Any model data carried in the original request dies with the request. The new request is devoid of any model data in its attributes and has to figure it out on its own.

Clearly, the model isn't going to help you carry data across a redirect. But there are a couple of options to get the data from the redirecting method to the redirect-handling method:

- Passing data as path variables and/or query parameters using URL templates
- Sending data in flash attributes

First we'll look at how Spring can help you send data in path variables and/or query parameters.

7.5.1 *Redirecting with URL templates*

Passing data in path variables and query parameters seems simple enough. In listing XREF ex_SpitterController_processRegistration_validation, for example, the newly created `Spitter`'s username is passed as a path variable. But as it's currently written, the username value is concatenated to the redirect `String`. That works, but it's far from bulletproof. `String` concatenation is dangerous business when constructing things like URLs and SQL queries.

Instead of concatenating your way to a redirect URL, Spring offers the option of using templates to define redirect URLs. For example, the last line of process-Registration() in listing XREF ex_SpitterController_processRegistration_validation could be written like this:

```
return "redirect:/spitter/{username}";
```

All you need to do is set the value in the model. To do that, the processRegistration() needs to be written to accept a Model as a parameter and populate it with the username. Here's how it can set the username value in the model so that it can fill in the placeholder in the redirect path:

```
@RequestMapping(value="/register", method=POST)
public String processRegistration(
    Spitter spitter, Model model) {
  spitterRepository.save(spitter);
```

```
model.addAttribute("username", spitter.getUsername());
return "redirect:/spitter/{username}";
}
```

Because it's filled into the placeholder in the URL template instead of concatenated into the redirect `String`, any unsafe characters in the `username` property are escaped. This is safer than allowing the user to type in whatever they want for the username and then appending it to the path.

What's more, any other primitive values in the model are also added to the redirect URL as query parameters. Suppose, for the sake of example, that in addition to the username, the model also contained the newly created `Spitter` object's `id` property. The `processRegistration()` method could be written like this:

```
@RequestMapping(value="/register", method=POST)
public String processRegistration(
    Spitter spitter, Model model) {
  spitterRepository.save(spitter);
  model.addAttribute("username", spitter.getUsername());
  model.addAttribute("spitterId", spitter.getId());
  return "redirect:/spitter/{username}";
}
```

Not much has changed with regard to the redirect `String` being returned. But because the `spitterId` attribute from the model doesn't map to any URL placeholders in the redirect, it's tacked on to the redirect automatically as a query parameter.

If the `username` attribute is `habuma` and the `spitterId` attribute is `42`, then the resulting redirect path will be `/spitter/habuma?spitterId=42`.

Sending data across a redirect via path variables and query parameters is easy and straightforward, but it's also somewhat limiting. It's only good for sending simple values, such as `String` and numeric values. There's no good way to send anything more complex in a URL. But that's where flash attributes come in to help.

7.5.2 *Working with flash attributes*

Let's say that instead of sending a username or ID in the redirect, you want to send the actual `Spitter` object. If you send just the ID, then the method that handles the redirect has to turn around and look up the `Spitter` from the database. But before the redirect, you already have the `Spitter` object in hand. Why not send it to the redirect-handling method to display?

A `Spitter` object is a bit more complex than a `String` or an `int`. Therefore, it can't easily be sent as a path variable or a query parameter. It can, however, be set as an attribute in the model.

But as we've already discussed, model attributes are ultimately copied into the request as request attributes and are lost when the redirect takes place. Therefore, you need to put the `Spitter` object somewhere that will survive the redirect.

One option is to put the `Spitter` into the session. A session is long-lasting, spanning multiple requests. So you could put the `Spitter` into the session before the redirect and then retrieve it from the session after the redirect. Of course, you're also responsible for cleaning it up from the session after the redirect.

As it turns out, Spring agrees that putting data into the session is a great way to pass information that survives a redirect. But Spring doesn't think you should be responsible for managing that data. Instead, Spring offers the capability of sending the data as *flash attributes*. Flash attributes, by definition, carry data until the next request; then they go away.

Spring offers a way to set flash attributes via `RedirectAttributes`, a sub-interface of `Model` added in Spring 3.1. `RedirectAttributes` offers everything that `Model` offers, plus a few methods for setting flash attributes.

Specifically, `RedirectAttributes` provides a couple of `addFlashAttribute()` methods for adding a flash attribute. Revisiting the `processRegistration()` method once more, you can use `addFlashAttribute()` to add the `Spitter` object to the model:

```
@RequestMapping(value="/register", method=POST)
public String processRegistration(
    Spitter spitter, RedirectAttributes model) {
  spitterRepository.save(spitter);
  model.addAttribute("username", spitter.getUsername());
  model.addFlashAttribute("spitter", spitter);
  return "redirect:/spitter/{username}";
}
```

Here, you're calling `addFlashAttribute()`, giving it `spitter` as the key and the `Spitter` object as a value. Optionally, you can leave the `key` parameter out and let the key be inferred from the value type:

```
model.addFlashAttribute(spitter);
```

Because you're passing a `Spitter` object to `addFlashAttribute()`, the key is inferred to be `spitter`.

Before the redirect takes place, all flash attributes are copied into the session. After the redirect, the flash attributes stored in the session are moved out of the session and into the model. The method that handles the redirect request can then access the `Spitter` from the model, just like any other model object. Figure 7.2 illustrates how this works.

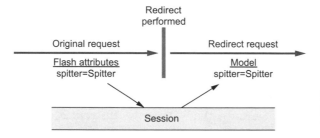

Figure 7.2 Flash attributes are stored in the session and then retrieved into the model, surviving a redirect.

To complete the flash attribute story, here's a slightly updated version of show-SpitterProfile() that checks for a Spitter in the model before going to the trouble of looking it up from the database:

```
@RequestMapping(value="/{username}", method=GET)
public String showSpitterProfile(
        @PathVariable String username, Model model) {
  if (!model.containsAttribute("spitter")) {
    model.addAttribute(
        spitterRepository.findByUsername(username));
  }
  return "profile";
}
```

As you can see, the first thing showSpitterProfile() does is check to see if there's a model attribute whose key is spitter. If the model contains a spitter attribute, then there's nothing to do. The Spitter object contained therein will be carried forward to the view for rendering. But if the model doesn't contain a spitter attribute, then showSpitterProfile() will look up the Spitter from the repository and store it in the model.

7.6 *Summary*

When it comes to Spring, there's always more: more features, more choices, and more ways to achieve your development goals. Spring MVC has a lot of capabilities and many tricks up its sleeves.

Spring MVC setup is certainly one area where you have a lot of choices. In this chapter, we started by looking at various ways to set up Spring MVC's Dispatcher-Servlet and ContextLoaderListener. You saw how to tweak DispatcherServlet's registration and how to register additional servlets and filters. And, in case you're deploying your application to an older application server, we took a quick look at how to declare DispatcherServlet and ContextLoaderListener in web.xml.

Then we took a look at how to handle exceptions thrown from Spring MVC controllers. Although an @RequestMapping method could handle exceptions itself, your controller code is much cleaner when you extract the exception handling into a separate method.

To consistently handle common tasks, including exception handling, across all controllers in your application, Spring 3.2 introduced @ControllerAdvice to create classes that collect common controller behavior in one place.

Finally, we looked at how to carry data across redirects, including Spring's support for flash attributes: model-like attributes that will survive a redirect. This enables you to properly respond to POST requests with a redirect, but to still carry model data obtained while handling a POST request and use it or display it after the redirect.

In case you're wondering—yes, there's more! We still haven't discussed everything Spring MVC can do. We'll pick up the discussion of Spring MVC again in chapter 16, when you see how to use it to create REST APIs.

But for now, we'll set aside Spring MVC and look at Spring Web Flow, a flow framework built on top of Spring MVC for creating applications that walk a user through a series of guided steps.

Working with
Spring Web Flow

8

This chapter covers
- Creating conversational web applications
- Defining flow states and actions
- Securing web flows

One of the strangely wonderful things about the internet is that it's so easy to get lost. There are so many things to see and read. The hyperlink is at the core of the internet's power. But at the same time, it's no wonder they call it *the web*. Just like webs built by spiders, it traps anyone who happens to crawl across it. I'll confess: one reason it took me so long to write this book is because I once got lost in an endless path of Wikipedia links.

There are times when a web application must take control of a web surfer's voyage, leading the user step by step through the application. The quintessential example of such an application is the checkout process on an e-commerce site. Starting with the shopping cart, the application leads you through a process of entering shipping details and billing information, and ultimately it displays an order confirmation.

Spring Web Flow is a web framework that enables the development of elements following a prescribed flow. In this chapter, we'll explore Spring Web Flow and see how it fits into the Spring web framework landscape.

It's possible to write a flowed application with any web framework. I've even seen a Struts application that had a certain flow built into it. But without a way to separate the flow from the implementation, you'll find that the definition of the flow is scattered across the various elements that make up the flow. There's no one place to go to fully understand the flow.

Spring Web Flow is an extension to Spring MVC that enables development of flow-based web applications. It does this by separating the definition of an application's flow from the classes and views that implement the flow's behavior.

As you get to know Spring Web Flow, you'll take a break from the Spittr example and work on a new web application for taking pizza orders. You'll use Spring Web Flow to define the order process.

The first step in working with Spring Web Flow is to install it in your project. Let's start there.

8.1   Configuring Web Flow in Spring

Spring Web Flow is built on a foundation of Spring MVC. That means all requests to a flow first go through Spring MVC's `DispatcherServlet`. From there, a handful of special beans in the Spring application context must be configured to handle the flow request and execute the flow.

At this time, there's no support for configuring Spring Web Flow in Java, so you have no choice but to configure it in XML. Several of the web flow beans are declared using elements from Spring Web Flow's Spring configuration XML namespace. Therefore, you'll need to add the namespace declaration to the context definition XML file:

```
<?xml version="1.0" encoding="UTF-8"?>
<beans xmlns="http://www.springframework.org/schema/beans"
 xmlns:xsi="http://www.w3.org/2001/XMLSchema-instance"
 xmlns:flow="http://www.springframework.org/schema/webflow-config"
 xsi:schemaLocation=
   "http://www.springframework.org/schema/webflow-config
   http://www.springframework.org/schema/webflow-config/[CA]
   spring-webflow-config-2.3.xsd
http://www.springframework.org/schema/beans
http://www.springframework.org/schema/beans/spring-beans.xsd">
```

With the namespace declaration in place, you're ready to start wiring up web flow beans, starting with the flow executor.

8.1.1   Wiring a flow executor

As its name implies, the *flow executor* drives the execution of a flow. When a user enters a flow, the flow executor creates and launches an instance of the flow execution for that user. When the flow pauses (such as when a view is presented to the user), the flow executor also resumes the flow once the user has taken some action.

The `<flow:flow-executor>` element creates a flow executor in Spring:

```
<flow:flow-executor id="flowExecutor" />
```

Although the flow executor is responsible for creating and executing flows, it's not responsible for loading flow definitions. That responsibility falls to a flow registry, which you'll create next.

8.1.2 Configuring a flow registry

A *flow registry*'s job is to load flow definitions and make them available to the flow executor. You can configure a flow registry in the Spring configuration with the `<flow:flow-registry>` element like this:

```
<flow:flow-registry id="flowRegistry" base-path="/WEB-INF/flows">
   <flow:flow-location-pattern value="*-flow.xml" />
</flow:flow-registry>
```

As declared here, the flow registry will look for flow definitions under the /WEB-INF/flows directory, as specified in the `base-path` attribute. Per the `<flow:flow-location-pattern>` element, any XML file whose name ends with *-flow.xml* will be considered a flow definition.

All flows are referred to by their IDs. Using `<flow:flow-location-pattern>` as you have, the flow ID is the directory path relative to the `base-path`—or the part of the path represented with the double asterisk. Figure 8.1 shows how the flow ID is calculated in this scenario.

Alternatively, you can leave off the `base-path` attribute and explicitly identify the flow definition file's location:

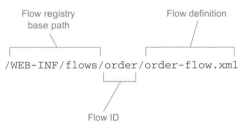

Figure 8.1   When using a flow location pattern, the path to the flow definition file relative to the base path is used as the flow's ID.

```
<flow:flow-registry id="flowRegistry">
   <flow:flow-location path="/WEB-INF/flows/springpizza.xml" />
</flow:flow-registry>
```

Here, the `<flow:flow-location>` element is used instead of `<flow:flow-location-pattern>`. The `path` attribute directly points at the /WEB-INF/flows/springpizza.xml file as the flow definition. When configured this way, the flow's ID is derived from the base name of the flow definition file, *springpizza* in this case.

If you'd like to be even more explicit about the flow's ID, you can set it with the `id` attribute of the `<flow:flow-location>` element. For example, to specify `pizza` as the flow's ID, configure `<flow:flow-location>` like this:

```
<flow:flow-registry id="flowRegistry">
   <flow:flow-location id="pizza"
        path="/WEB-INF/flows/springpizza.xml" />
</flow:flow-registry>
```

8.1.3   *Handling flow requests*

As you saw in the previous chapter, DispatcherServlet typically dispatches requests to controllers. But for flows, you need a FlowHandlerMapping to help Dispatcher-Servlet know that it should send flow requests to Spring Web Flow. The FlowHandler-Mapping is configured in the Spring application context like this:

```
<bean class=
       "org.springframework.webflow.mvc.servlet.FlowHandlerMapping">
  <property name="flowRegistry" ref="flowRegistry" />
</bean>
```

As you can see, the FlowHandlerMapping is wired with a reference to the flow registry so it knows when a request's URL maps to a flow. For example, if you have a flow whose ID is pizza, then FlowHandlerMapping will know to map a request to that flow if the request's URL pattern (relative to the application context path) is /pizza.

Whereas the FlowHandlerMapping's job is to direct flow requests to Spring Web Flow, it's the job of a FlowHandlerAdapter to answer that call. A FlowHandlerAdapter is equivalent to a Spring MVC controller in that it handles requests coming in for a flow and processes those requests. The FlowHandlerAdapter is wired as a Spring bean like this:

```
<bean class=
       "org.springframework.webflow.mvc.servlet.FlowHandlerAdapter">
  <property name="flowExecutor" ref="flowExecutor" />
</bean>
```

This handler adapter is the bridge between DispatcherServlet and Spring Web Flow. It handles flow requests and manipulates the flow based on those requests. Here, it's wired with a reference to the flow executor to execute the flows for which it handles requests.

You've configured all the beans and components that are needed for Spring Web Flow to work. What's left is to define a flow. You'll do that soon enough. But first, let's get to know the elements that are put together to make up a flow.

8.2   *The components of a flow*

In Spring Web Flow, a flow is defined by three primary elements: states, transitions, and flow data. *States* are points in a flow where something happens. If you imagine a flow as being like a road trip, then states are the towns, truck stops, and scenic stops along the way. Instead of picking up a bag of Doritos and a Diet Coke, a state in a flow is where some logic is performed, some decision is made, or some page is presented to the user.

If flow states are like the points on a map where you might stop during a road trip, then *transitions* are the roads that connect those points. In a flow, you get from one state to another by way of a transition.

As you travel from town to town, you may pick up some souvenirs, memories, and empty snack bags along the way. Similarly, as a flow progresses, it collects some data:

the current condition of the flow. I'm tempted to refer to it as the state of the flow, but the word *state* already has another meaning when talking about flows.

Let's take a closer look at how these three elements are defined in Spring Web Flow.

8.2.1 States

Spring Web Flow defines five different kinds of state, as shown in table 8.1. This selection of states makes it possible to construct virtually any arrangement of functionality into a conversational web application. Although not all flows require all the states described in the table, you'll probably end up using most of them at one time or another.

Table 8.1   Spring Web Flow's selections of states

State type	What it's for
Action	Action states are where the logic of a flow takes place.
Decision	Decision states branch the flow in two directions, routing the flow based on the outcome of evaluating flow data.
End	The end state is the last stop for a flow. Once a flow has reached its end state, the flow is terminated.
Subflow	A subflow state starts a new flow in the context of a flow that is already underway.
View	A view state pauses the flow and invites the user to participate in the flow.

In a moment, you'll see how to piece these different kinds of states together to form a complete flow. But first, let's get to know how these flow elements are manifested in a Spring Web Flow definition.

VIEW STATES

View states are used to display information to the user and to offer the user an opportunity to play an active role in the flow. The actual view implementation could be any of the views supported by Spring MVC but is often implemented in JSP.

In the flow definition XML file, the `<view-state>` element is used to define a view state:

```
<view-state id="welcome" />
```

In this simple example, the `id` attribute serves a dual purpose. First, it identifies the state in the flow. Also, because no view has been specified otherwise, it specifies `welcome` as the logical name of the view to be rendered when the flow reaches this state.

If you'd rather explicitly identify another view name, then you can do so with the `view` attribute:

```
<view-state id="welcome" view="greeting" />
```

If a flow presents a form to the user, you may want to specify the object to which the form will be bound. To do that, set the `model` attribute:

```
<view-state id="takePayment" model="flowScope.paymentDetails"/>
```

Here you specify that the form in the `takePayment` view will be bound to the flow-scoped `paymentDetails` object. (We'll talk more about flow scopes and data in a moment.)

ACTION STATES

Whereas view states involve the users of the application in the flow, action states are where the application itself goes to work. Action states typically invoke some method on a Spring-managed bean and then transition to another state depending on the outcome of the method call.

In the flow definition XML, action states are expressed with the `<action-state>` element. Here's an example:

```
<action-state id="saveOrder">
  <evaluate expression="pizzaFlowActions.saveOrder(order)" />
  <transition to="thankYou" />
</action-state>
```

Although it's not strictly required, `<action-state>` elements usually have an `<evaluate>` element as a child. The `<evaluate>` element gives an action state something to do. The `expression` attribute is given an expression that's evaluated when the state is entered. In this case, `expression` is given a SpEL expression indicating that the `saveOrder()` method should be called on a bean whose ID is `pizzaFlowActions`.

> ### Spring Web Flow and expression languages
>
> Spring Web Flow has been fickle in its choice of expression languages over the years. In version 1.0, Spring Web Flow used the Object-Graph Navigation Language (OGNL). It then flirted with the Unified Expression Language (Unified EL) starting in version 2.0. Now, starting with version 2.1, Spring Web Flow's loyalties are with SpEL.
>
> Although it's possible to configure Spring Web Flow to use any of these expression languages, SpEL is the default and recommended expression language. Therefore, I'll focus on SpEL when defining flows and disregard the other options.

DECISION STATES

It's possible for a flow to be purely linear, stepping from one state to another without taking any alternate routes. But more often, a flow branches at one point or another, depending on the flow's current circumstances.

Decision states enable a binary branch in a flow execution. A decision state evaluates a Boolean expression and takes one of two transitions, depending on whether the expression evaluates to `true` or `false`. In the XML flow definition, decision states are defined by the `<decision-state>` element. A typical example of a decision state might look like this:

```
<decision-state id="checkDeliveryArea">
  <if test="pizzaFlowActions.checkDeliveryArea(customer.zipCode)"
      then="addCustomer"
      else="deliveryWarning" />
</decision-state>
```

As you can see, the `<decision-state>` element doesn't work alone. The `<if>` element is the heart of a decision state. It's where the expression is evaluated. If the expression evaluates to `true`, then the flow transitions to the state identified by the `then` attribute. But if it's `false`, the flow transitions to the state named in the `else` attribute.

SUBFLOW STATES

You probably wouldn't write all of your application's logic in a single method. Instead, you'll break it up into multiple classes, methods, and other structures.

In the same way, it's a good idea to break flows down into discrete parts. The `<subflow-state>` element lets you call another flow from within an executing flow. It's analogous to calling a method from within another method.

A `<subflow-state>` might be declared as follows:

```
<subflow-state id="order" subflow="pizza/order">
  <input name="order" value="order"/>
  <transition on="orderCreated" to="payment" />
</subflow-state>
```

Here, the `<input>` element is used to pass the order object as input to the subflow. And if the subflow ends with an `<end-state>` whose ID is `orderCreated`, then the flow will transition to the state whose ID is `payment`.

But I'm getting ahead of myself. I haven't talked about the `<end-state>` element or transitions yet. We'll look at transitions soon, in section 8.2.2. As for end states, that's what we'll look at next.

END STATES

Eventually, all flows must come to an end. And that's what they do when they transition to an end state. The `<end-state>` element designates the end of a flow and typically appears like this:

```
<end-state id="customerReady" />
```

When the flow reaches an `<end-state>`, the flow ends. What happens next depends on a few factors:

- If the flow that's ending is a subflow, the calling flow will proceed from the `<subflow-state>`. The `<end-state>`'s ID will be used as an event to trigger the transition away from the `<subflow-state>`.
- If the `<end-state>` has its `view` attribute set, the specified view will be rendered. The view may be a flow-relative path to a view template, prefixed with

`externalRedirect:` to redirect to some page external to the flow, or prefixed with `flowRedirect:` to redirect to another flow.

- If the ending flow isn't a subflow and no `view` is specified, the flow ends. The browser lands on the flow's base URL, and, with no current flow active, a new instance of the flow begins.

It's important to realize that a flow may have more than one end state. Because the end state's ID determines the event fired from a subflow, you may want to end the flow through multiple end states to trigger different events in the calling flow. Even in flows that aren't subflows, there may be several landing pages that follow the completion of a flow, depending on the course that the flow took.

Now that we've looked at the various kinds of states in a flow, we should take a moment to examine how the flow travels between states. Let's look at how you can pave some roads in a flow by defining transitions.

8.2.2   Transitions

As I've already mentioned, transitions connect the states within a flow. Every state in a flow, with the exception of end states, should have at least one transition so that the flow will know where to go once that state has completed. A state may have multiple transitions, each one representing a different path that could be taken on completion of the state.

A transition is defined by the `<transition>` element, a child of the various state elements (`<action-state>`, `<view-state>`, and `<subflow-state>`). In its simplest form, the `<transition>` element identifies the next state in the flow:

```
<transition to="customerReady" />
```

The `to` attribute is used to specify the next state in the flow. When `<transition>` is declared with only a `to` attribute, the transition is the default transition for that state and will be taken if no other transitions are applicable.

More commonly, transitions are defined to take place on some event being fired. In a view state, the event is usually an action taken by the user. In an action state, the event is the result of evaluating an expression. In the case of a subflow state, the event is determined by the ID of the subflow's end state. In any event (no pun intended), you can specify the event to trigger the transition in the on attribute:

```
<transition on="phoneEntered" to="lookupCustomer"/>
```

In this example, the flow will transition to the state whose ID is `lookupCustomer` if a `phoneEntered` event is fired.

The flow can also transition to another state in response to some exception being thrown. For example, if a customer record can't be found, you may want the flow to transition to a view state that presents a registration form. The following snippet shows that kind of transition:

```
<transition
    on-exception=
        "com.springinaction.pizza.service.CustomerNotFoundException"
    to="registrationForm" />
```

The on-exception attribute is much like the on attribute, except that it specifies an exception to transition on instead of an event. In this case, a CustomerNotFound-Exception will cause the flow to transition to the registrationForm state.

GLOBAL TRANSITIONS

After you've created a flow, you may find that several states share some common transitions. For example, I wouldn't be surprised to find the following <transition> sprinkled all over a flow:

```
<transition on="cancel" to="endState" />
```

Rather than repeat common transitions in multiple states, you can define them as global transitions by placing the <transition> element as a child of a <global-transitions> element. For example,

```
<global-transitions>
  <transition on="cancel" to="endState" />
</global-transitions>
```

With this global transition in place, all states in the flow will have an implicit cancel transition.

We've talked about states and transitions. Before we get busy writing flows, let's look at flow data, the remaining member of the web flow triad.

8.2.3 *Flow data*

If you've ever played one of those old text-based adventure games, you know that as you move from location to location, you occasionally find objects lying around that you can pick up and carry with you. Sometimes you need an object right away. Other times, you may carry an object through the entire game without knowing what it's for—until you get to that final puzzle and find that it's useful after all.

In many ways, flows are like those adventure games. As the flow progresses from one state to another, it picks up data. Sometimes that data is only needed for a little while (maybe just long enough to display a page to the user). Other times, that data is carried through the entire flow and is ultimately used as the flow completes.

DECLARING VARIABLES

Flow data is stored in variables that can be referenced at various points in the flow. It can be created and accumulated in several ways. The simplest way to create a variable in a flow is by using the <var> element:

```
<var name="customer" class="com.springinaction.pizza.domain.Customer"/>
```

Here, a new instance of a Customer object is created and placed into the variable whose name is customer. This variable is available to all states in a flow.

As part of an action state or on entry to a view state, you may also create variables using the <evaluate> element. For example,

```
<evaluate result="viewScope.toppingsList"
   expression="T(com.springinaction.pizza.domain.Topping).asList()" />
```

In this case, the <evaluate> element evaluates an expression (a SpEL expression) and places the result in a variable named toppingsList that's view-scoped. (We'll talk more about scopes in a moment.)

Similarly, the <set> element can set a variable's value:

```
<set name="flowScope.pizza"
   value="new com.springinaction.pizza.domain.Pizza()" />
```

The <set> element works much the same as the <evaluate> element, setting a variable to the resulting value from an evaluated expression. Here, you're setting a flow-scoped pizza variable to a new instance of a Pizza object.

You'll see more specifics on how these elements are used in an actual flow when you get to section 8.3 and start building a real working web flow. But first, let's see what it means for a variable to be flow-scoped, be view-scoped, or use some other scope.

SCOPING FLOW DATA

The lifespan and visibility of data carried in a flow will vary depending on the scope of the variable it's kept in. Spring Web Flow defines five scopes, as described in table 8.2.

Table 8.2   Spring Web Flow's selections of scopes

Scope	Lifespan and visibility
Conversation	Created when a top-level flow starts, and destroyed when the top-level flow ends. Shared by a top-level flow and all of its subflows.
Flow	Created when a flow starts, and destroyed when the flow ends. Only visible in the flow it was created by.
Request	Created when a request is made into a flow, and destroyed when the flow returns.
Flash	Created when a flow starts, and destroyed when the flow ends. It's also cleared out after a view state renders.
View	Created when a view state is entered, and destroyed when the state exits. Visible only in the view state.

When you declare a variable using the <var> element, the variable is always flow-scoped in the flow defining the variable. When you use <set> or <evaluate>, the scope is specified as a prefix for the name or result attribute. For example, here's how you would assign a value to a flow-scoped variable named theAnswer:

```
<set name="flowScope.theAnswer" value="42"/>
```

Now that you've seen all the raw materials of a web flow, it's time to piece them together into a full-blown, fully functional web flow. As you do, keep your eyes peeled for examples of how to store data in scoped variables.

8.3 Putting it all together: the pizza flow

As I mentioned earlier in this chapter, we're taking a break from the Spittr application. Instead, you've been asked to build out an online pizza-ordering application where hungry web visitors can order their favorite Italian pie.

As it turns out, the process of ordering a pizza can be defined nicely in a flow. You'll start by building a high-level flow that defines the overall process of ordering a pizza. Then you'll break that flow down into subflows that define the details at a lower level.

8.3.1 Defining the base flow

A new pizza chain, Spizza, has decided to relieve the load on its stores' telephones by allowing customers to place orders online. When a customer visits the Spizza website, they'll identify themselves, select one or more pizzas to add to their order, provide payment information, and then submit the order and wait for their pizza to arrive, hot and fresh. Figure 8.2 illustrates this flow.

The boxes in the diagram represent states, and the arrows represent transitions. As you can see, the overall pizza flow is simple and linear. It should be easy to express this flow in Spring Web Flow. The only thing that makes it interesting is that the first three states can be more involved than suggested by a simple box.

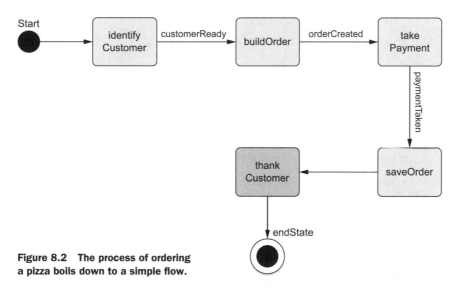

Figure 8.2 The process of ordering a pizza boils down to a simple flow.

The following listing shows the high-level pizza order flow as defined using Spring Web Flow's XML-based flow definition.

> **Listing 8.1 Pizza order flow, defined as a Spring Web Flow**

```xml
<?xml version="1.0" encoding="UTF-8"?>
<flow xmlns="http://www.springframework.org/schema/webflow"
  xmlns:xsi="http://www.w3.org/2001/XMLSchema-instance"
  xsi:schemaLocation="http://www.springframework.org/schema/webflow
  http://www.springframework.org/schema/webflow/spring-webflow-2.3.xsd">
  <var name="order"
       class="com.springinaction.pizza.domain.Order"/>
  <subflow-state id="identifyCustomer" subflow="pizza/customer">
    <output name="customer" value="order.customer"/>
    <transition on="customerReady" to="buildOrder" />
  </subflow-state>
  <subflow-state id="buildOrder" subflow="pizza/order">
    <input name="order" value="order"/>
    <transition on="orderCreated" to="takePayment" />
  </subflow-state>
  <subflow-state id="takePayment" subflow="pizza/payment">
    <input name="order" value="order"/>
    <transition on="paymentTaken" to="saveOrder"/>
  </subflow-state>
  <action-state id="saveOrder">
    <evaluate expression="pizzaFlowActions.saveOrder(order)" />
    <transition to="thankCustomer" />
  </action-state>
  <view-state id="thankCustomer">
    <transition to="endState" />
  </view-state>
  <end-state id="endState" />
  <global-transitions>
    <transition on="cancel" to="endState" />
  </global-transitions>
</flow>
```

Annotations (left): **Call customer subflow** → `<subflow-state id="identifyCustomer" ...>`

Annotations (right):
- **Call order subflow** → `<subflow-state id="buildOrder" ...>`
- **Call payment subflow** → `<subflow-state id="takePayment" ...>`
- **Save order** → `<action-state id="saveOrder">`
- **Thank customer** → `<view-state id="thankCustomer">`
- **Global cancel transition** → `<transition on="cancel" to="endState" />`

The first thing you see in the flow definition is the declaration of the `order` variable. Each time the flow starts, a new instance of `Order` is created. The `Order` class has properties for carrying all the information about an order, including the customer information, the list of pizzas ordered, and the payment details.

> **Listing 8.2 `Order`: carries all the details pertaining to a pizza order**

```java
package com.springinaction.pizza.domain;
import java.io.Serializable;
import java.util.ArrayList;
import java.util.List;
public class Order implements Serializable {
  private static final long serialVersionUID = 1L;
  private Customer customer;
  private List<Pizza> pizzas;
  private Payment payment;
```

```
   public Order() {
      pizzas = new ArrayList<Pizza>();
      customer = new Customer();
   }
   public Customer getCustomer() {
      return customer;
   }
   public void setCustomer(Customer customer) {
      this.customer = customer;
   }
   public List<Pizza> getPizzas() {
      return pizzas;
   }
   public void setPizzas(List<Pizza> pizzas) {
      this.pizzas = pizzas;
   }
   public void addPizza(Pizza pizza) {
      pizzas.add(pizza);
   }
   public float getTotal() {
      return 0.0f;
   }
   public Payment getPayment() {
      return payment;
   }
   public void setPayment(Payment payment) {
      this.payment = payment;
   }
}
```

The main portion of the flow definition is made up of the flow states. By default, the first state in the flow definition file is also the first state that will be visited in the flow. In this case, that's the identifyCustomer state (a subflow state). But if you'd like, you can explicitly identify any state as the starting state by setting the start-state attribute in the <flow> element:

```
<?xml version="1.0" encoding="UTF-8"?>
<flow xmlns="http://www.springframework.org/schema/webflow"
  xmlns:xsi="http://www.w3.org/2001/XMLSchema-instance"
  xsi:schemaLocation="http://www.springframework.org/schema/webflow
  http://www.springframework.org/schema/webflow/spring-webflow-2.3.xsd"
  start-state="identifyCustomer">
...
</flow>
```

Identifying a customer, building a pizza order, and taking payment are activities that are too complex to be crammed into a single state. That's why you'll define them later in more detail as flows in their own right. But for the purposes of the high-level pizza flow, these activities are expressed with the <subflow-state> element.

The order flow variable will be populated by the first three states and then saved in the fourth state. The identifyCustomer subflow state uses the <output> element to populate the order's customer property, setting it to the output received from calling the customer subflow. The `buildOrder` and `takePayment` states take a different approach, using `<input>` to pass the `order` flow variable as input so that those sub-flows can populate the `order` internally.

After the order has been given a customer, some pizzas, and payment details, it's time to save it. The `saveOrder` state is an action state that handles that task. It uses `<evaluate>` to make a call to the `saveOrder()` method on the bean whose ID is `pizza-FlowActions`, passing in the order to be saved. When it's finished saving the order, it transitions to `thankCustomer`.

The `thankCustomer` state is a simple view state, backed by the JSP file at /WEB-INF/flows/pizza/thankCustomer.jsp, as shown next.

Listing 8.3   JSP view that thanks the customer for their order

```html
<html xmlns:jsp="http://java.sun.com/JSP/Page">
  <jsp:output omit-xml-declaration="yes"/>
  <jsp:directive.page contentType="text/html;charset=UTF-8" />
  <head><title>Spizza</title></head>
  <body>
    <h2>Thank you for your order!</h2>
    <![CDATA[
    <a href='${flowExecutionUrl}&_eventId=finished'>Finish</a>    ⟵── Fire finished
    ]]>                                                                   event
    </body>
</html>
```

The "thank you" page thanks the customer for their order and gives a link for the customer to finish the flow. This link is the most interesting thing on the page, because it shows one way that a user can interact with the flow.

Spring Web Flow provides a `flowExecutionUrl` variable, which contains the URL for the flow, for use in the view. The Finish link attaches an `_eventId` parameter to the URL to fire a `finished` event back to the web flow. That event sends the flow to the end state.

At the end state, the flow ends. Because there are no further details on where to go after the flow ends, the flow will start over again at the `identifyCustomer` state, ready to take another pizza order.

That covers the general flow for ordering a pizza. But there's more to the flow than what you see in listing 8.1. You still need to define the subflows for the `identify-Customer`, `buildOrder`, and `takePayment` states. Let's build those flows next, starting with the one that identifies the customer.

8.3.2   *Collecting customer information*

If you've ordered a pizza before, you probably know the drill. The first thing you're asked for is your phone number. Aside from giving the pizza shop a way to call you if the delivery driver can't find your house, the phone number also serves as your identification. If you're a repeat customer, the shop can use that phone number to look up your address so that it will know where to deliver your order.

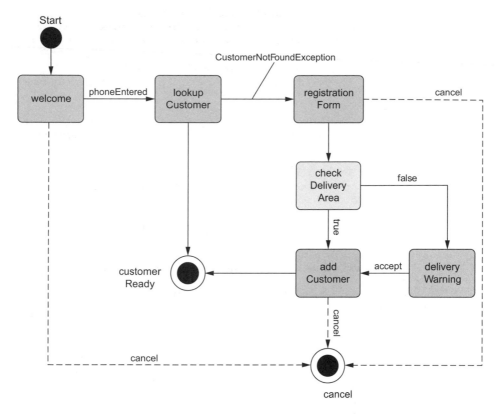

Figure 8.3 The flow for identifying a customer has a few more twists than the pizza flow.

For a new customer, the phone number won't turn up any results, so the next information the shop will ask for is your address. At this point, the pizzeria knows who you are and where to deliver your pizzas. But before you're asked what kind of pizza you want, the shop needs to check to make sure your address falls within its delivery area. If not, you'll have to go pick up the pizza yourself.

The initial question-and-answer period that begins every pizza order can be illustrated with the flow diagram in figure 8.3.

This flow is more interesting than the top-level pizza flow. It isn't linear, and it branches in a couple of places depending on different conditions. For example, after looking up the customer, the flow could either end (if the customer was found) or transition to a registration form (if the customer was not found). Also, at the `check-DeliveryArea` state, the customer may or may not be warned that their address isn't in the delivery area.

The following listing shows the flow definition for identifying the customer.

Listing 8.4 Identifying the hungry pizza customer with a web flow

```
<?xml version="1.0" encoding="UTF-8"?>
<flow xmlns="http://www.springframework.org/schema/webflow"
```

```
xmlns:xsi="http://www.w3.org/2001/XMLSchema-instance"
xsi:schemaLocation="http://www.springframework.org/schema/webflow
http://www.springframework.org/schema/webflow/spring-webflow-2.3.xsd">
<var name="customer"
     class="com.springinaction.pizza.domain.Customer"/>
<view-state id="welcome">                        ⟵ Welcome customer
   <transition on="phoneEntered" to="lookupCustomer"/>
</view-state>
<action-
   state id="lookupCustomer">                    ⟵ Look up customer
   <evaluate result="customer" expression=
 "pizzaFlowActions.lookupCustomer(requestParameters.phoneNumber)" />
   <transition to="registrationForm" on-exception=
       "com.springinaction.pizza.service.CustomerNotFoundException" />
   <transition to="customerReady" />
</action-state>
<view-state id="registrationForm" model="customer">  ⟵ Register new customer
   <on-entry>
    <evaluate expression=
        "customer.phoneNumber = requestParameters.phoneNumber" />
   </on-entry>
   <transition on="submit" to="checkDeliveryArea" />       Check
</view-state>                                               delivery
<decision-state id="checkDeliveryArea">                    area
   <if test="pizzaFlowActions.checkDeliveryArea(customer.zipCode)"
       then="addCustomer"
       else="deliveryWarning"/>                            Show
</decision-state>                                           delivery
<view-state id="deliveryWarning">                          warning
   <transition on="accept" to="addCustomer" />
</view-state>                                               Add customer
<action-state id="addCustomer">
   <evaluate expression="pizzaFlowActions.addCustomer(customer)" />
   <transition to="customerReady" />
</action-state>
<end-state id="cancel" />
<end-state id="customerReady">
  <output name="customer" />
</end-state>
<global-transitions>
  <transition on="cancel" to="cancel" />
</global-transitions>
</flow>
```

This flow introduces a few new tricks, including your first use of the `<decision-state>` element. Also, because it's a subflow of the `pizza` flow, it expects to receive an `Order` object as input.

As before, let's break down this flow definition state by state, starting with the `welcome` state.

ASKING FOR A PHONE NUMBER

The `welcome` state is a fairly straightforward view state that welcomes the customer to the Spizza website and asks them to enter their phone number. The state itself isn't particularly interesting. It has two transitions: one that directs the flow to the `lookup-Customer` state if a `phoneEntered` event is fired from the view, and another `cancel` transition, defined as a global transition, that reacts to a `cancel` event.

Where the `welcome` state gets interesting is in the view. The `welcome` view is defined in /WEB-INF/flows/pizza/customer/welcome.jspx, as shown next.

Listing 8.5 Welcoming the customer and asking for their phone number

```
<html xmlns:jsp="http://java.sun.com/JSP/Page"
    xmlns:form="http://www.springframework.org/tags/form">
  <jsp:output omit-xml-declaration="yes"/>
  <jsp:directive.page contentType="text/html;charset=UTF-8" />
  <head><title>Spizza</title></head>
  <body>
    <h2>Welcome to Spizza!!!</h2>
    <form:form>
      <input type="hidden" name="_flowExecutionKey"
            value="${flowExecutionKey}"/>              <⎯ Flow execution key
       <input type="text" name="phoneNumber"/><br/>
      <input type="submit" name="_eventId_phoneEntered"
            value="Lookup Customer" />                 <⎯ Fire
    </form:form>                                            phoneEntered
  </body>                                                   event
</html>
```

This simple form prompts the user to enter their phone number. But the form has two special ingredients that enable it to drive the flow.

First, note the hidden `_flowExecutionKey` field. When a view state is entered, the flow pauses and waits for the user to take some action. The flow execution key is given to the view as a sort of claim ticket for the flow. When the user submits the form, the flow execution key is sent along with it in the `_flowExecutionKey` field, and the flow resumes where it left off.

Also pay special attention to the submit button's name. The `_eventId_` portion of the button's name is a clue to Spring Web Flow that what follows is an event that should be fired. When the form is submitted by clicking that button, a `phoneEntered` event is fired, triggering a transition to `lookupCustomer`.

LOOKING UP THE CUSTOMER

After the welcome form has been submitted, the customer's phone number is among the request parameters and is ready to be used to look up a customer. The `lookup-Customer` state's `<evaluate>` element is where that happens. It pulls the phone number off the request parameters and passes it to the `lookupCustomer()` method on the `pizzaFlowActions` bean.

The implementation of `lookupCustomer()` isn't important right now. It's sufficient to know that it will either return a `Customer` object or throw a `CustomerNotFound-Exception`.

In the former case, the `Customer` object is assigned to the `customer` variable (per the `result` attribute) and the default transition takes the flow to the `customerReady` state. But if the customer can't be found, then a `CustomerNotFoundException` will be thrown, and the flow will transition to the `registrationForm` state.

REGISTERING A NEW CUSTOMER

The `registrationForm` state is where the user is asked for their delivery address. Like other view states you've seen, it renders a JSP view. The JSP file is shown next.

Listing 8.6   Registering a new customer

```
<html xmlns:c="http://java.sun.com/jsp/jstl/core"
      xmlns:jsp="http://java.sun.com/JSP/Page"
      xmlns:spring="http://www.springframework.org/tags"
      xmlns:form="http://www.springframework.org/tags/form">
  <jsp:output omit-xml-declaration="yes"/>
  <jsp:directive.page contentType="text/html;charset=UTF-8" />
  <head><title>Spizza</title></head>
  <body>
    <h2>Customer Registration</h2>
    <form:form commandName="customer">
      <input type="hidden" name="_flowExecutionKey"
             value="${flowExecutionKey}"/>
      <b>Phone number: </b><form:input path="phoneNumber"/><br/>
      <b>Name: </b><form:input path="name"/><br/>
      <b>Address: </b><form:input path="address"/><br/>
      <b>City: </b><form:input path="city"/><br/>
      <b>State: </b><form:input path="state"/><br/>
      <b>Zip Code: </b><form:input path="zipCode"/><br/>
      <input type="submit" name="_eventId_submit"
             value="Submit" />
      <input type="submit" name="_eventId_cancel"
             value="Cancel" />
    </form:form>
    </body>
</html>
```

This isn't the first form you've seen in your flow. The `welcome` view state also displays a form to the customer. That form is simple and has only a single field. It's easy enough to pull that field's value from the request parameters. The registration form, on the other hand, is more involved.

Instead of dealing with the fields one at a time through the request parameters, it makes more sense to bind the form to a `Customer` object and let the framework do all the hard work.

CHECKING THE DELIVERY AREA

After the customer has given their address, you need to be sure that they live in the delivery area. If Spizza can't deliver to them, you should let them know and advise them that they'll need to come in and pick up the pizzas themselves.

To make that decision, you use a decision state. The `checkDeliveryArea` decision state has an `<if>` element that passes the customer's ZIP code in to the `checkDelivery-Area()` method on the `pizzaFlowActions` bean. That method returns a Boolean value: `true` if the customer is in the delivery area, and `false` otherwise.

If the customer is in the delivery area, the flow transitions to the addCustomer state. If not, the customer is taken to the deliveryWarning view state. The view behind the deliveryWarning is /WEB-INF/flows/pizza/customer/deliveryWarning.jspx, shown next.

Listing 8.7 Warning a customer that pizza can't be delivered to their address

```
<html xmlns:jsp="http://java.sun.com/JSP/Page">
  <jsp:output omit-xml-declaration="yes"/>
  <jsp:directive.page contentType="text/html;charset=UTF-8" />
  <head><title>Spizza</title></head>
  <body>
        <h2>Delivery Unavailable</h2>
        <p>The address is outside of our delivery area. You may
        still place the order, but you will need to pick it up
        yourself.</p>
        <![CDATA[
        <a href="${flowExecutionUrl}&_eventId=accept">
                              Continue, I'll pick up the order</a> |
        <a href="${flowExecutionUrl}&_eventId=cancel">Never mind</a>
        ]]>
  </body>
</html>
```

The key flow-related items in deliveryWarning.jspx are the two links that offer the customer a chance to continue with the order or to cancel. Using the same flow-ExecutionUrl variable that you use in the welcome state, these links trigger either an accept event or a cancel event in the flow. If an accept event is sent, the flow will transition to the addCustomer state. Otherwise, the global cancel transition will be followed, and the subflow will transition to the cancel end state.

We'll talk about the end states in a moment. First, let's take a quick look at the addCustomer state.

STORING THE CUSTOMER DATA

By the time the flow arrives at the addCustomer state, the customer has entered their address. For future reference, that address needs to be stored (probably in a database). The addCustomer state has an <evaluate> element that calls the add-Customer() method on the pizzaFlowActions bean, passing in the customer flow variable.

Once the evaluation is complete, the default transition will be taken, and the flow will transition to the end state whose ID is customerReady.

ENDING THE FLOW

Normally, a flow's end state isn't that interesting. But in this flow, there's not just one end state, but two. When a subflow ends, it fires a flow event that's equivalent to its end state's ID. If the flow only has one end state, then it always fires the same event. But with two or more end states, a flow can influence the direction of the calling flow.

When the customer flow goes down any of the normal paths, it ultimately lands on the end state whose ID is customerReady. When the calling pizza flow resumes, it receives a customerReady event, which results in a transition to the buildOrder state.

Note that the customerReady end state includes an <output> element. This element is a flow's equivalent of Java's return statement. It passes back some data from a subflow to the calling flow. In this case, <output> returns the customer flow variable so that the identifyCustomer subflow state in the pizza flow can assign it to the order. On the other hand, if a cancel event is triggered at any time during the customer flow, it exits the flow through the end state whose ID is cancel. That triggers a cancel event in the pizza flow and results in a transition (via the global transition) to the pizza flow's end state.

8.3.3   *Building an order*

After the customer has been identified, the next step in the main flow is to figure out what kind of pizzas they want. The order subflow, as illustrated in figure 8.4, is where the user is prompted to create pizzas and add them to the order.

As you can see, the showOrder state is the centerpiece of the order subflow. It's the first state the user sees on entering the flow, and it's the state to which the user is sent after adding a new pizza to the order. It displays the current state of the order and offers the user a chance to add another pizza to the order.

When the user chooses to add a pizza to the order, the flow transitions to the createPizza state. This is another view state

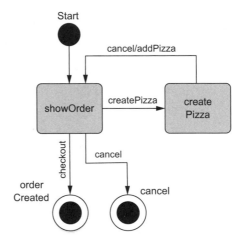

Figure 8.4   Pizzas are added via the order subflow.

that gives the user a selection of pizza sizes and toppings with which to build a pizza. From here, the user may add a pizza or cancel. In either event, the flow transitions back to the showOrder state.

From the showOrder state, the user may choose to either submit the order or cancel the order. Either choice ends the order subflow, but the main flow will go down different paths depending on which choice is made.

The following listing shows how the diagram translates into a Spring Web Flow definition.

Listing 8.8   Order subflow view shows states to display the order and create a pizza

```xml
<?xml version="1.0" encoding="UTF-8"?>
<flow xmlns="http://www.springframework.org/schema/webflow"
  xmlns:xsi="http://www.w3.org/2001/XMLSchema-instance"
```

```
    xsi:schemaLocation="http://www.springframework.org/schema/webflow
    http://www.springframework.org/schema/webflow/spring-webflow-2.3.xsd">

    <input name="order" required="true" />          ⟵  Accept order as input

    <view-state id="showOrder">                     ⟵  Order display state
        <transition on="createPizza" to="createPizza" />
      <transition on="checkout" to="orderCreated" />
      <transition on="cancel" to="cancel" />
    </view-state>

    <view-
       state id="createPizza" model="flowScope.pizza">   ⟵  Pizza creation state
       <on-entry>
        <set name="flowScope.pizza"
            value="new com.springinaction.pizza.domain.Pizza()" />
        <evaluate result="viewScope.toppingsList"  expression=
            "T(com.springinaction.pizza.domain.Topping).asList()" />
       </on-entry>
       <transition on="addPizza" to="showOrder">
         <evaluate expression="order.addPizza(flowScope.pizza)" />
       </transition>
       <transition on="cancel" to="showOrder" />
    </view-state>

    <end-state id="cancel" /            ⟵————————  Cancel end state

    <end-state id="orderCreated" />     ⟵————————  Create order end state

</flow>
```

This subflow operates on the Order object created in the main flow. Therefore, you need a way of passing the Order from the main flow to the subflow. As you'll recall from listing 8.1, you use the <input> element to pass the Order in to the flow. Here you're using it to accept that Order object. If you think of this subflow as being analogous to a method in Java, the <input> element used here is effectively defining the subflow's signature. This flow requires a single parameter called order.

Next you find the showOrder state, a basic view state with three different transitions: one for creating a pizza, one for submitting the order, and another to cancel the order.

The createPizza state is more interesting. Its view is a form that submits a new Pizza object to be added to the order. The <on-entry> element adds a new Pizza object to flow scope to be populated when the form is submitted. Note that the model of this view state references the same flow-scoped Pizza object. That Pizza object is bound to the Create Pizza form, shown next.

Listing 8.9   Adding pizzas with an HTML form bound to a flow-scoped object

```
<div xmlns:form="http://www.springframework.org/tags/form"
     xmlns:jsp="http://java.sun.com/JSP/Page">
  <jsp:output omit-xml-declaration="yes"/>
  <jsp:directive.page contentType="text/html;charset=UTF-8" />
    <h2>Create Pizza</h2>
    <form:form commandName="pizza">
      <input type="hidden" name="_flowExecutionKey"
```

```
            value="${flowExecutionKey}"/>
        <b>Size: </b><br/>
   <form:radiobutton path="size"
                      label="Small (12-inch)" value="SMALL"/><br/>
   <form:radiobutton path="size"
                      label="Medium (14-inch)" value="MEDIUM"/><br/>
   <form:radiobutton path="size"
                      label="Large (16-inch)" value="LARGE"/><br/>
   <form:radiobutton path="size"
                      label="Ginormous (20-inch)" value="GINORMOUS"/>
        <br/>
        <br/>
        <b>Toppings: </b><br/>
        <form:checkboxes path="toppings" items="${toppingsList}"
                         delimiter="&lt;br/&gt;"/><br/><br/>
        <input type="submit" class="button"
            name="_eventId_addPizza" value="Continue"/>
        <input type="submit" class="button"
            name="_eventId_cancel" value="Cancel"/>
    </form:form>
</div>
```

When the form is submitted via the Continue button, the size and topping selections are bound to the `Pizza` object, and the `addPizza` transition is taken. The `<evaluate>` element associated with that transition indicates that the flow-scoped `Pizza` object should be passed in a call to the order's `addPizza()` method before transitioning to the `showOrder` state.

There are two ways to end the flow. The user can either click the Cancel button on the `showOrder` view or click the Checkout button. Either way, the flow transitions to an `<end-state>`. But the `id` of the end state chosen determines the event triggered on the way out of this flow and ultimately determines the next step in the main flow. The main flow will either transition on `cancel` or transition on `orderCreated`. In the former case, the outer flow ends; in the latter case, it transitions to the `takePayment` subflow, which we'll look at next.

8.3.4   *Taking payment*

It's not common to get a free pizza, and the Spizza pizzeria wouldn't stay in business long if it let customers order pizzas without providing some form of payment. As the pizza flow nears an end, the final subflow prompts the user to enter payment details. This simple flow is illustrated in figure 8.5.

Like the order subflow, the payment subflow accepts an `Order` object as input using the `<input>` element.

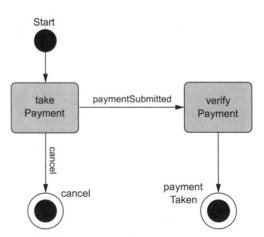

Figure 8.5   The final step in placing a pizza order is to take payment from the customer through the payment subflow.

As you can see, on entering the payment subflow, the user arrives at the take-Payment state. This is a view state where the user can indicate that they'll pay by credit card, check, or cash. On submitting their payment information, they're taken to the verifyPayment state, an action state that verifies that their payment information is acceptable.

The payment subflow is defined in XML as shown next.

Listing 8.10 Payment subflow, with one view state and one action state

```xml
<?xml version="1.0" encoding="UTF-8"?>
<flow xmlns="http://www.springframework.org/schema/webflow"
  xmlns:xsi="http://www.w3.org/2001/XMLSchema-instance"
  xsi:schemaLocation="http://www.springframework.org/schema/webflow
  http://www.springframework.org/schema/webflow/spring-webflow-2.3.xsd">
  <input name="order" required="true"/>
  <view-state id="takePayment" model="flowScope.paymentDetails">
    <on-entry>
      <set name="flowScope.paymentDetails"
 value="new com.springinaction.pizza.domain.PaymentDetails()" />
      <evaluate result="viewScope.paymentTypeList" expression=
"T(com.springinaction.pizza.domain.PaymentType).asList()" />
    </on-entry>
    <transition on="paymentSubmitted" to="verifyPayment" />
    <transition on="cancel" to="cancel" />
  </view-state>
  <action-state id="verifyPayment">
    <evaluate result="order.payment" expression=
        "pizzaFlowActions.verifyPayment(flowScope.paymentDetails)" />
    <transition to="paymentTaken" />
  </action-state>

  <end-state id="cancel" />
  <end-state id="paymentTaken" />
</flow>
```

As the flow enters the takePayment view state, the <on-entry> element sets up the payment form by first using a SpEL expression to create a new PaymentDetails instance in flow scope. This is effectively the backing object for the form. It also sets the view-scoped paymentTypeList variable to a list containing the values of the PaymentType enum (shown in the next listing). SpEL's T() operator is used to get the PaymentType class so that the static toList() method can be invoked.

Listing 8.11 PaymentType enumeration: defines customer choices for payment

```java
package com.springinaction.pizza.domain;
import static org.apache.commons.lang.WordUtils.*;
import java.util.Arrays;
import java.util.List;
public enum PaymentType {
  CASH, CHECK, CREDIT_CARD;
  public static List<PaymentType> asList() {
    PaymentType[] all = PaymentType.values();
```

```
      return Arrays.asList(all);
    }
    @Override
    public String toString() {
      return capitalizeFully(name().replace('_', ' '));
    }
}
```

On being presented with the payment form, the user may either submit a payment or cancel. Depending on the choice made, the payment subflow ends through either the paymentTaken <end-state> or the cancel <end-state>. As with other subflows, either <end-state> will end the subflow and return control to the main flow. But the id of the <end-state> taken determines the transition taken next in the main flow.

Now we've stepped all the way through the pizza flow and its subflows. You've seen a lot of what Spring Web Flow is capable of. Before we finish with the Web Flow topic, let's take a quick look at what's involved in securing access to a flow or any of its states.

8.4   *Securing web flows*

In the next chapter, you'll see how to secure Spring web applications using Spring Security. But while we're on the subject of Spring Web Flow, let's quickly look at how it supports flow-level security when used along with Spring Security.

States, transitions, and entire flows can be secured in Spring Web Flow by using the <secured> element as a child of those elements. For example, to secure access to a view state, you might use <secured> like this:

```
<view-state id="restricted">
  <secured attributes="ROLE_ADMIN" match="all"/>
</view-state>
```

As configured here, access to the view state will be restricted to only users who are granted ROLE_ADMIN access (per the attributes attribute). The attributes attribute takes a comma-separated list of authorities that the user must have to gain access to the state, transition, or flow. The match attribute can be set to either any or all. If it's set to any, then the user must be granted at least one of the authorities listed in attributes. If it's set to all, then the user must have been granted all the authorities. You may be wondering how a user is granted the authorities checked for by the <secured> element. For that matter, how does the user log in to the application in the first place? The answers to those questions will be addressed in the next chapter.

8.5   *Summary*

Not all web applications are freely navigable. Sometimes a user must be guided along, asked appropriate questions, and led to specific pages based on their responses. In these situations, an application feels less like a menu of options and more like a conversation between the application and the user.

In this chapter, we've explored Spring Web Flow, a web framework that enables development of conversational applications. Along the way, you built a flow-based application to take pizza orders. You started by defining the overall path the application should take, beginning with gathering customer information and concluding with the order being saved in the system.

A flow is made up of several states and transitions that define how the conversation traverses from state to state. The states themselves come in several varieties: action states that perform business logic, view states that involve the user in the flow, decision states that dynamically direct the flow, and end states that signify the end of a flow. In addition, there are subflow states, which are themselves defined by a flow.

Finally, you saw hints about how access to a flow, state, or transition can be restricted to users who are granted specific authorities. But we deferred conversation of how the user authenticates to the application and how the user is granted those authorities. That's where Spring Security comes in, and Spring Security is what we'll explore in the next chapter.

Securing web applications

This chapter covers

- Introducing Spring Security
- Securing web applications using servlet filters
- Authentication against databases and LDAP

Have you ever noticed that most people in television sitcoms don't lock their doors? It happens all the time. On *Seinfeld*, Kramer frequently let himself into Jerry's apartment to help himself to the goodies in Jerry's refrigerator. On *Friends*, the various characters often entered one another's apartments without warning or hesitation. Once, while in London, Ross even burst into Chandler's hotel room, narrowly missing Chandler in a compromising situation with Ross's sister.

In the days of *Leave it to Beaver*, it wasn't so unusual for people to leave their doors unlocked. But it seems crazy that in a day when we're concerned with privacy and security, we see television characters enabling unhindered access to their apartments and homes.

Information is probably the most valuable item we now have; crooks are looking for ways to steal our data and identities by sneaking into unsecured applications. As software developers, we must take steps to protect the information that resides in our applications. Whether it's an email account protected with a username/password pair or a brokerage account protected with a trading PIN, security is a crucial *aspect* of most applications.

It's no accident that I chose to describe application security with the word "aspect." Security is a concern that transcends an application's functionality. For the most part, an application should play no part in securing itself. Although you could write security functionality directly into your application's code (and that's not uncommon), it's better to keep security concerns separate from application concerns.

If you're thinking that it's starting to sound as if security is accomplished using aspect-oriented techniques, you're right. In this chapter we're going to explore ways to secure your applications with aspects. But you won't have to develop those aspects yourself—we're going to look at Spring Security, a security framework implemented with Spring AOP and servlet filters.

9.1 *Getting started with Spring Security*

Spring Security is a security framework that provides declarative security for your Spring-based applications. Spring Security provides a comprehensive security solution, handling authentication and authorization at both the web request level and at the method invocation level. Based on the Spring Framework, Spring Security takes full advantage of dependency injection (DI) and aspect-oriented techniques.

Spring Security got its start as Acegi Security. Acegi was a powerful security framework, but it had one big turn-off: it required a *lot* of XML configuration. I'll spare you the intricate details of what such a configuration may have looked like. Suffice it to say that it was common for a typical Acegi configuration to grow to several hundred lines of XML.

With version 2.0, Acegi Security became Spring Security. But the 2.0 release brought more than just a superficial name change. Spring Security 2.0 introduced a new security-specific XML namespace for configuring security in Spring. The new namespace, along with annotations and reasonable defaults, slimmed typical security configuration from hundreds of lines to only a dozen or so lines of XML. Spring Security 3.0 added SpEL to the mix, simplifying security configuration even more.

Now at version 3.2, Spring Security tackles security from two angles. To secure web requests and restrict access at the URL level, Spring Security uses servlet filters. Spring Security can also secure method invocations using Spring AOP, proxying objects and applying advice to ensure that the user has the proper authority to invoke secured methods.

We'll focus on web-layer security with Spring Security in this chapter. Later, in chapter 14, we'll revisit Spring Security and see how it can be used to secure method invocations.

9.1.1   *Understanding Spring Security modules*

No matter what kind of application you want to secure using Spring Security, the first thing you need to do is to add the Spring Security modules to the application's classpath. Spring Security 3.2 is divided into eleven modules, as listed in table 9.1.

Table 9.1   Spring Security is partitioned into eleven modules

Module	Description
ACL	Provides support for domain object security through access control lists (ACLs).
Aspects	A small module providing support for AspectJ-based aspects instead of standard Spring AOP when using Spring Security annotations.
CAS Client	Support for single sign-on authentication using Jasig's Central Authentication Service (CAS).
Configuration	Contains support for configuring Spring Security with XML and Java. (Java configuration support introduced in Spring Security 3.2.)
Core	Provides the essential Spring Security library.
Cryptography	Provides support for encryption and password encoding.
LDAP	Provides support for LDAP-based authentication.
OpenID	Contains support for centralized authentication with OpenID.
Remoting	Provides integration with Spring Remoting.
Tag Library	Spring Security's JSP tag library.
Web	Provides Spring Security's filter-based web security support.

At the least, you'll want to include the Core and Configuration modules in your application's classpath. Spring Security is often used to secure web applications, and that's certainly the case with the Spittr application, so you'll also need to add the Web module. We'll also be taking advantage of Spring Security's JSP tag library, so you'll need to add that module to the mix.

9.1.2   *Filtering web requests*

Spring Security employs several servlet filters to provide various aspects of security. You might be thinking that means you'll need to configure several filters in a web.xml file, or perhaps in a `WebApplicationInitializer` class. But thanks to a little Spring magic, you'll only need to configure one of those filters.

    `DelegatingFilterProxy` is a special servlet filter that, by itself, doesn't do much. Instead, it delegates to an implementation of `javax.servlet.Filter` that's registered as a <bean> in the Spring application context, as illustrated in figure 9.1.

Figure 9.1 `DelegatingFilterProxy` **proxies filter handling to a delegate filter bean in the Spring application context.**

If you like configuring servlets and filters in the traditional web.xml file, you can do that with the `<filter>` element, like this:

```
<filter>
    <filter-name>springSecurityFilterChain</filter-name>
    <filter-class>
        org.springframework.web.filter.DelegatingFilterProxy
    </filter-class>
</filter>
```

The most important thing here is that the `<filter-name>` be set to `springSecurity-FilterChain`. That's because you'll soon be configuring Spring Security for web security, and there will be a filter bean named `springSecurityFilterChain` that `DelegatingFilterProxy` will need to delegate to.

If you'd rather configure `DelegatingFilterProxy` in Java with a `WebApplication-Initializer`, then all you need to do is create a new class that extends `Abstract-SecurityWebApplicationInitializer`:

```
package spitter.config;
import org.springframework.security.web.context.
                        AbstractSecurityWebApplicationInitializer;

public class SecurityWebInitializer
        extends AbstractSecurityWebApplicationInitializer {}
```

`AbstractSecurityWebApplicationInitializer` implements `WebApplication-Initializer`, so it will be discovered by Spring and be used to register `Delegating-FilterProxy` with the web container. Although you can override its `appendFilters()` or `insertFilters()` methods to register filters of your own choosing, you need not override anything to register `DelegatingFilterProxy`.

Whether you configure `DelegatingFilterProxy` in web.xml or by subclassing `AbstractSecurityWebApplicationInitializer`, it will intercept requests coming into the application and delegate them to a bean whose ID is `springSecurityFilter-Chain`.

As for the `springSecurityFilterChain` bean itself, it's another special filter known as `FilterChainProxy`. It's a single filter that chains together one or more additional filters. Spring Security relies on several servlet filters to provide different security features, but you should almost never need to know these details, as you likely won't need to explicitly declare the `springSecurityFilterChain` bean or any of the filters it chains together. Those filters will be created when you enable web security.

To get the ball rolling with web security, let's create the simplest possible security configuration.

9.1.3 *Writing a simple security configuration*

In the early days of Spring Security (way back when it was known as Acegi Security), you'd need to write hundreds of lines of XML configuration just to enable simple security in a web application. Spring Security 2.0 made things better by offering a security-specific XML configuration namespace.

Spring 3.2 introduced a new Java configuration option, altogether eliminating the need for XML security configuration. The following listing shows the simplest possible Java configuration for Spring Security.

Listing 9.1   The simplest configuration class to enable web security for Spring MVC

```
package spitter.config;
import org.springframework.context.annotation.Configuration;
import org.springframework.security.config.annotation.web.
                                    configuration.EnableWebSecurity;
import org.springframework.security.config.annotation.web.
                              configuration.WebSecurityConfigurerAdapter;

@Configuration
@EnableWebSecurity
public class SecurityConfig extends WebSecurityConfigurerAdapter {
}
```

Enable web security ⟶ @EnableWebSecurity

As its name suggests, the @EnableWebSecurity annotation enables web security. It is useless on its own, however. Spring Security must be configured in a bean that implements WebSecurityConfigurer or (for convenience) extends WebSecurityConfigurer-Adapter. Any bean in the Spring application context that implements WebSecurity-Configurer can contribute to Spring Security configuration, but it's often most convenient for the configuration class to extend WebSecurityConfigurerAdapter, as shown in listing 9.1.

@EnableWebSecurity is generally useful for enabling security in any web application. But if you happen to be developing a Spring MVC application, you should consider using @EnableWebMvcSecurity instead, as shown in the following listing.

Listing 9.2   The simplest configuration class to enable web security for Spring MVC

```
package spitter.config;
import org.springframework.context.annotation.Configuration;
import org.springframework.security.config.annotation.web.
                              configuration.WebSecurityConfigurerAdapter;
import org.springframework.security.config.annotation.web.servlet.
                              configuration.EnableWebMvcSecurity;

@Configuration
@EnableWebMvcSecurity
 public class SecurityConfig extends WebSecurityConfigurerAdapter {
}
```

Enable Spring MVC security ⟶ @EnableWebMvcSecurity

Among other things, the @EnableWebMvcSecurity annotation configures a Spring MVC argument resolver so that handler methods can receive the authenticated user's principal (or username) via @AuthenticationPrincipal-annotated parameters. It also configures a bean that automatically adds a hidden cross-site request forgery (CSRF) token field on forms using Spring's form-binding tag library.

It may not look like much, but the security configuration class in listings 9.1 and 9.2 packs quite a punch. Either one will lock down an application so tightly that nobody can get in!

Although it's not strictly required, you'll probably want to specify the finer points of web security by overriding one or more of the methods from WebSecurityConfigurerAdapter. You can configure web security by overriding WebSecurityConfigurerAdapter's three configure() methods and setting behavior on the parameter passed in. Table 9.2 describes these three methods.

Table 9.2 Overriding WebSecurityConfigurerAdapter's configure() methods

Method	Description
configure(WebSecurity)	Override to configure Spring Security's filter chain.
configure(HttpSecurity)	Override to configure how requests are secured by interceptors.
configure(AuthenticationManagerBuilder)	Override to configure user-details services.

Looking back to listing 9.2, you can see that it doesn't override any of these three configure() methods, and that explains why the application is now locked down tight. Although the default filter chain is fine for our needs, the default configure(HttpSecurity) effectively looks like this:

```
protected void configure(HttpSecurity http) throws Exception {
  http
    .authorizeRequests()
      .anyRequest().authenticated()
      .and()
    .formLogin().and()
    .httpBasic();
}
```

This simple default configuration specifies how HTTP requests should be secured and what options a client has for authenticating the user. The call to authorizeRequests() and anyRequest().authenticated() demands that all HTTP requests coming into the application be authenticated. It also configures Spring Security to support authentication via a form-based login (using a predefined login page) as well as HTTP Basic.

Meanwhile, because you haven't overridden the configure(AuthenticationManagerBuilder) method, there's no user store backing the authentication process.

With no user store, there are effectively no users. Therefore, all requests require authentication, but there's nobody who can log in.

You're going to need to add a bit more configuration to bend Spring Security to fit your application's needs. Specifically, you'll need to…

- Configure a user store
- Specify which requests should and should not require authentication, as well as what authorities they require
- Provide a custom login screen to replace the plain default login screen

In addition to these facets of Spring Security, you may also want to selectively render certain content in your web views based on security constraints.

First things first, however. Let's see how to configure user services to access user data during the authentication process.

9.2 *Selecting user details services*

Suppose you were to go out for a nice dinner at an exclusive restaurant. Of course, you made the reservation several weeks in advance to be assured that you have a table. As you enter the restaurant, you give the host your name. Unfortunately, there's no record of your reservation. Your special evening is in jeopardy. Not one to give up so easily, you ask the host to check the reservation list again. That's when things get weird.

The host says that there isn't a reservation list. Your name isn't on the list—nobody's name is on the list—because there isn't a list. That would explain why you can't get in the door, despite the fact that the place is empty. Weeks later, you'll realize that it also explains why the restaurant ended up closing and being replaced with a taqueria.

That's the scenario you have with your application at this point. There's no way to get into the application because even if the user thinks they should be allowed in, there's no record of them having access to the application. For lack of a user store, the application is so exclusive that it's completely unusable.

What you need is a user store—some place where usernames, passwords, and other data can be kept and retrieved from when making authentication decisions.

Fortunately, Spring Security is extremely flexible and is capable of authenticating users against virtually any data store. Several common user store situations—such as in-memory, relational database, and LDAP—are provided out of the box. But you can also create and plug in custom user store implementations.

Spring Security's Java configuration makes it easy to configure one or more data store options. We'll start with the simplest user store: one that maintains its user store in memory.

9.2.1   *Working with an in-memory user store*

Since your security configuration class extends `WebSecurityConfigurerAdapter`, the easiest way to configure a user store is to override the `configure()` method that takes an `AuthenticationManagerBuilder` as a parameter. `AuthenticationManagerBuilder` has several methods that can be used to configure Spring Security's authentication support. With the `inMemoryAuthentication()` method, you can enable and configure and optionally populate an in-memory user store.

For example, in the following listing, `SecurityConfig` overrides `configure()` to configure an in-memory user store with two users.

Listing 9.3   Configuring Spring Security to use an in-memory user store

```
package spitter.config;

import org.springframework.beans.factory.annotation.Autowired;
import org.springframework.context.annotation.Configuration;
import org.springframework.security.config.annotation.
                  authentication.builders.AuthenticationManagerBuilder;
import org.springframework.security.config.annotation.web.
                               configuration.WebSecurityConfigurerAdapter;
import org.springframework.security.config.annotation.web.servlet.
                               configuration.EnableWebMvcSecurity;

@Configuration
@EnableWebMvcSecurity
public class SecurityConfig extends WebSecurityConfigurerAdapter {

  @Override
  protected void configure(AuthenticationManagerBuilder auth)
                                                    throws Exception {
    auth
    .inMemoryAuthentication()
       .withUser("user").password("password").roles("USER").and()
       .withUser("admin").password("password").roles("USER", "ADMIN");
  }

}
```

Enable an in-memory user store. ⊳ (annotation pointing to `.inMemoryAuthentication()`)

As you can see, the `AuthenticationManagerBuilder` given to `configure()` employs a builder-style interface to build up authentication configuration. Simply calling `inMemoryAuthentication()` will enable an in-memory user store. But you'll also need some users in there, or else it's as if you have no user store at all.

Therefore, you need to call the `withUser()` method to add a new user to the in-memory user store. The parameter given is the username. `withUser()` returns a `User-DetailsManagerConfigurer.UserDetailsBuilder`,which has several methods for further configuration of the user, including `password()` to set the user's password and `roles()` to give the user one or more role authorities.

In listing 9.3, you're adding two users, "user" and "admin", both with "password" for a password. The "user" user has the USER role, while the "admin" user has both

USER and ADMIN roles. As you can see, the `and()` method is used to chain together multiple user configurations.

In addition to `password()`, `roles()`, and `and()`, there are several other methods for configuring user details for in-memory user stores. Table 9.3 describes all of the methods available from `UserDetailsManagerConfigurer.UserDetailsBuilder`.

Table 9.3   Methods for configuring user details

Module	Description
`accountExpired(boolean)`	Defines if the account is expired or not
`accountLocked(boolean)`	Defines if the account is locked or not
`and()`	Used for chaining configuration
`authorities(GrantedAuthority…)`	Specifies one or more authorities to grant to the user
`authorities(List<? extends GrantedAuthority>)`	Specifies one or more authorities to grant to the user
`authorities(String…)`	Specifies one or more authorities to grant to the user
`credentialsExpired(boolean)`	Defines if the credentials are expired or not
`disabled(boolean)`	Defines if the account is disabled or not
`password(String)`	Specifies the user's password
`roles(String…)`	Specifies one or more roles to assign to the user

Note that the `roles()` method is a shortcut for the `authorities()` methods. Any values given to `roles()` are prefixed with `ROLE_` and assigned as authorities to the user. In effect, the following user configuration is equivalent to that in listing 9.3:

```
auth
.inMemoryAuthentication()
  .withUser("user").password("password")
                        .authorities("ROLE_USER").and()
  .withUser("admin").password("password")
                        .authorities("ROLE_USER", "ROLE_ADMIN");
```

Although an in-memory user store is very useful for debugging and developer testing purposes, it's probably not the most ideal choice for a production application. For production-ready purposes, it's usually better to maintain user data in a database of some sort.

9.2.2   *Authenticating against database tables*

It's quite common for user data to be stored in a relational database, accessed via JDBC. To configure Spring Security to authenticate against a JDBC-backed user store, you can use the `jdbcAuthentication()` method. The minimal configuration required is as follows:

```
@Autowired
DataSource dataSource;

@Override
protected void configure(AuthenticationManagerBuilder auth)
                                                   throws Exception {
  auth
    .jdbcAuthentication()
      .dataSource(dataSource);
}
```

The only thing you must configure is a DataSource so that it's able to access the relational database. The DataSource is provided here via the magic of autowiring.

OVERRIDING THE DEFAULT USER QUERIES

Although this minimal configuration will work, it makes some assumptions about your database schema. It expects that certain tables exist where user data will be kept. More specifically, the following snippet of code from Spring Security's internals shows the SQL queries that will be performed when looking up user details:

```
public static final String DEF_USERS_BY_USERNAME_QUERY =
        "select username,password,enabled " +
        "from users " +
        "where username = ?";
public static final String DEF_AUTHORITIES_BY_USERNAME_QUERY =
        "select username,authority " +
        "from authorities " +
        "where username = ?";
public static final String DEF_GROUP_AUTHORITIES_BY_USERNAME_QUERY =
        "select g.id, g.group_name, ga.authority " +
        "from groups g, group_members gm, group_authorities ga " +
        "where gm.username = ? " +
        "and g.id = ga.group_id " +
        "and g.id = gm.group_id";
```

The first query retrieves a user's username, password, and whether or not they're enabled. This information is used to authenticate the user. The next query looks up the user's granted authorities for authorization purposes, and the final query looks up authorities granted to a user as a member of a group.

If you're okay with defining and populating tables in your database that satisfy those queries, then there's not much else for you to do. But chances are your database doesn't look anything like this, and you'll want more control over the queries. In that case, you can configure your own queries like this:

```
@Override
protected void configure(AuthenticationManagerBuilder auth)
                                                   throws Exception {
  auth
    .jdbcAuthentication()
      .dataSource(dataSource)
      .usersByUsernameQuery(
        "select username, password, true " +
```

```
        "from Spitter where username=?")
    .authoritiesByUsernameQuery(
        "select username, 'ROLE_USER' from Spitter where username=?");
}
```

In this case, you're only overriding the authentication and basic authorization queries. But you can also override the group authorities query by calling `group-AuthoritiesByUsername()` with a custom query.

When replacing the default SQL queries with those of your own design, it's important to adhere to the basic contract of the queries. All of them take the username as their only parameter. The authentication query selects the username, password, and enabled status. The authorities query selects zero or more rows containing the username and a granted authority. And the group authorities query selects zero or more rows each with a group ID, group name, and an authority.

WORKING WITH ENCODED PASSWORDS

Focusing on the authentication query, you can see that user passwords are expected to be stored in the database. The only problem with that is that if the passwords are stored in plain text, they're subject to the prying eyes of a hacker. But if you encode the password in the database, then authentication will fail because it won't match the plain text password submitted by the user.

To remedy this problem, you need to specify a password encoder by calling the `passwordEncoder()` method:

```
@Override
protected void configure(AuthenticationManagerBuilder auth)
                                                throws Exception {
  auth
    .jdbcAuthentication()
      .dataSource(dataSource)
      .usersByUsernameQuery(
        "select username, password, true " +
        "from Spitter where username=?")
      .authoritiesByUsernameQuery(
        "select username, 'ROLE_USER' from Spitter where username=?")
      .passwordEncoder(new StandardPasswordEncoder("53cr3t"));
}
```

The `passwordEncoder` method accepts any implementation of Spring Security's `PasswordEncoder` interface. Spring Security's cryptography module includes three such implementations: `BCryptPasswordEncoder`, `NoOpPasswordEncoder`, and `StandardPasswordEncoder`.

The preceding code uses `StandardPasswordEncoder`. But you can always provide your own custom implementation if none of the out-of-the-box implementations meet your needs. The `PasswordEncoder` interface is rather simple:

```
public interface PasswordEncoder {
  String encode(CharSequence rawPassword);
  boolean matches(CharSequence rawPassword, String encodedPassword);
}
```

No matter which password encoder you use, it's important to understand that the password in the database is never decoded. Instead, the password that the user enters at login is encoded using the same algorithm and is then compared with the encoded password in the database. That comparison is performed in the `PasswordEncoder`'s `matches()` method.

Relational databases are just one storage option for user data. Another very common choice is to keep user data in an LDAP repository.

9.2.3 *Applying LDAP-backed authentication*

To configure Spring Security for LDAP-based authentication, you can use the `ldap-Authentication()` method. This method is the LDAP analog to `jdbcAuthentication()`. The following `configure()` method shows a simple configuration for LDAP authentication:

```
@Override
protected void configure(AuthenticationManagerBuilder auth)
                                                 throws Exception {
  auth
    .ldapAuthentication()
      .userSearchFilter("(uid={0})")
      .groupSearchFilter("member={0}");
}
```

The `userSearchFilter()` and `groupSearchFilter()` methods are used to provide a filter for the base LDAP queries, which are used to search for users and groups. By default, the base queries for both users and groups are empty, indicating that the search will be done from the root of the LDAP hierarchy. But you can change that by specifying a query base:

```
@Override
protected void configure(AuthenticationManagerBuilder auth)
                                                 throws Exception {
  auth
    .ldapAuthentication()
      .userSearchBase("ou=people")
      .userSearchFilter("(uid={0})")
      .groupSearchBase("ou=groups")
      .groupSearchFilter("member={0}");
}
```

The `userSearchBase()` method provides a base query for finding users. Likewise, the `groupSearchBase()` specifies the base query for finding groups. Rather than search from the root, this example specifies that users be searched for where the organization unit is `people`. And groups should be searched for where the organizational unit is `groups`.

CONFIGURING PASSWORD COMPARISON

The default strategy for authenticating against LDAP is to perform a bind operation, authenticating the user directly to the LDAP server. Another option is to perform a comparison operation. This involves sending the entered password to the LDAP directory and asking the server to compare the password against a user's password attribute. Because the comparison is done within the LDAP server, the actual password remains secret.

If you'd rather authenticate by doing a password comparison, you can declare so with the passwordCompare() method:

```
@Override
protected void configure(AuthenticationManagerBuilder auth)
                                                    throws Exception {
  auth
    .ldapAuthentication()
      .userSearchBase("ou=people")
      .userSearchFilter("(uid={0})")
      .groupSearchBase("ou=groups")
      .groupSearchFilter("member={0}")
      .passwordCompare();
}
```

By default, the password given in the login form will be compared with the value of the userPassword attribute in the user's LDAP entry. If the password is kept in a different attribute, you can specify the password attribute's name with passwordAttribute():

```
@Override
protected void configure(AuthenticationManagerBuilder auth)
                                                    throws Exception {
  auth
    .ldapAuthentication()
      .userSearchBase("ou=people")
      .userSearchFilter("(uid={0})")
      .groupSearchBase("ou=groups")
      .groupSearchFilter("member={0}")
      .passwordCompare()
      .passwordEncoder(new Md5PasswordEncoder())
      .passwordAttribute("passcode");
}
```

In this example, you specify that the "passcode" attribute is what should be compared with the given password. Moreover, you also specify a password encoder. It's nice that the actual password is kept secret on the server when doing server-side password comparison. But the attempted password is still passed across the wire to the LDAP server and could be intercepted by a hacker. To prevent that, you can specify an encryption strategy by calling the passwordEncoder() method.

In the example, passwords are encrypted using MD5. This assumes that the passwords are also encrypted using MD5 in the LDAP server.

REFERRING TO A REMOTE LDAP SERVER

The one thing I've left out until now is where the LDAP server and data actually reside. You've happily been configuring Spring to authenticate against an LDAP server, but where is that server?

By default, Spring Security's LDAP authentication assumes that the LDAP server is listening on port 33389 on localhost. But if your LDAP server is on another machine, you can use the contextSource() method to configure the location:

```
@Override
protected void configure(AuthenticationManagerBuilder auth)
        throws Exception {
  auth
  .ldapAuthentication()
    .userSearchBase("ou=people")
    .userSearchFilter("(uid={0})")
    .groupSearchBase("ou=groups")
    .groupSearchFilter("member={0}")
    .contextSource()
      .url("ldap://habuma.com:389/dc=habuma,dc=com");
}
```

The contextSource() method returns a ContextSourceBuilder, which, among other things, offers the url() method that lets you specify the location of the LDAP server.

CONFIGURING AN EMBEDDED LDAP SERVER

If you don't happen to have an LDAP server lying around waiting to be authenticated against, Spring Security can provide an embedded LDAP server for you. Instead of setting the URL to a remote LDAP server, you can specify the root suffix for the embedded server via the root() method:

```
@Override
protected void configure(AuthenticationManagerBuilder auth)
        throws Exception {
  auth
  .ldapAuthentication()
    .userSearchBase("ou=people")
    .userSearchFilter("(uid={0})")
    .groupSearchBase("ou=groups")
    .groupSearchFilter("member={0}")
    .contextSource()
      .root("dc=habuma,dc=com");
}
```

When the LDAP server starts, it will attempt to load data from any LDIF files that it can find in the classpath. LDIF (LDAP Data Interchange Format) is a standard way of representing LDAP data in a plain text file. Each record is composed of one or more lines, each containing a name:value pair. Records are separated from each other by blank lines.

If you'd rather that Spring not rummage through your classpath looking for just any LDIF files it can find, you can be more explicit about which LDIF file gets loaded by calling the ldif() method:

```
@Override
protected void configure(AuthenticationManagerBuilder auth)
        throws Exception {
  auth
```

```
    .ldapAuthentication()
      .userSearchBase("ou=people")
      .userSearchFilter("(uid={0})")
      .groupSearchBase("ou=groups")
      .groupSearchFilter("member={0}")
      .contextSource()
        .root("dc=habuma,dc=com")
        .ldif("classpath:users.ldif");
}
```

Here you specifically ask the LDAP server to load its content from the users.ldif file at
the root of the classpath. In case you're curious, here's an LDIF file that you could use
to load the embedded LDAP server with user data:

```
dn: ou=groups,dc=habuma,dc=com
objectclass: top
objectclass: organizationalUnit
ou: groups
dn: ou=people,dc=habuma,dc=com
objectclass: top
objectclass: organizationalUnit
ou: people
dn: uid=habuma,ou=people,dc=habuma,dc=com
objectclass: top
objectclass: person
objectclass: organizationalPerson
objectclass: inetOrgPerson
cn: Craig Walls
sn: Walls
uid: habuma
userPassword: password
dn: uid=jsmith,ou=people,dc=habuma,dc=com
objectclass: top
objectclass: person
objectclass: organizationalPerson
objectclass: inetOrgPerson
cn: John Smith
sn: Smith
uid: jsmith
userPassword: password
dn: cn=spittr,ou=groups,dc=habuma,dc=com
objectclass: top
objectclass: groupOfNames
cn: spittr
member: uid=habuma,ou=people,dc=habuma,dc=com
```

Spring Security's built-in user stores are convenient and cover the most common use
cases. But if your authentication needs are of the uncommon variety, you may need to
create and configure a custom user-details service.

9.2.4 *Configuring a custom user service*

Suppose that you need to authenticate against users in a non-relational database such as Mongo or Neo4j. In that case, you'll need to implement a custom implementation of the `UserDetailsService` interface.

The `UserDetailsService` interface is rather straightforward:

```
public interface UserDetailsService {
  UserDetails loadUserByUsername(String username)
                              throws UsernameNotFoundException;
}
```

All you need to do is implement the `loadUserByUsername()` method to find a user given the user's username. `loadUserByUsername()` then returns a `UserDetails` object representing the given user. The following listing shows an implementation of `UserDetailsService` that looks up a user from a given implementation of `Spitter-Repository`.

Listing 9.4   Retrieve a UserDetails object from a SpitterRepository

```
package spittr.security;
import org.springframework.security.core.GrantedAuthority;
import org.springframework.security.core.authority.
                                     SimpleGrantedAuthority;
import org.springframework.security.core.userdetails.User;
import org.springframework.security.core.userdetails.UserDetails;
import org.springframework.security.core.userdetails.
                                     UserDetailsService;
import org.springframework.security.core.userdetails.
                                     UsernameNotFoundException;
import spittr.Spitter;
import spittr.data.SpitterRepository;

public class SpitterUserService implements UserDetailsService {

  private final SpitterRepository spitterRepository;

  public SpitterUserService(SpitterRepository spitterRepository) {       ⟵┐ Inject
    this.spitterRepository = spitterRepository;                            SpitterRepository
  }

  @Override
  public UserDetails loadUserByUsername(String username)
    throws UsernameNotFoundException {                                    ┌ Look up
    Spitter spitter = spitterRepository.findByUsername(username);   ⟵──┘ Spitter
    if (spitter != null) {
      List<GrantedAuthority> authorities =                                ┌ Create
          new ArrayList<GrantedAuthority>();                               authorities
      authorities.add(new SimpleGrantedAuthority("ROLE_SPITTER"));  ⟵──┘ list

      return new User(                        ⟵┐ Return a
          spitter.getUsername(),                User
          spitter.getPassword(),
          authorities);
    }
```

```
    throw new UsernameNotFoundException(
        "User '" + username + "' not found.");
  }

}
```

What's interesting about SpitterUserService is that it has no idea how the user data is persisted. The SpitterRepository it's given could look up the Spitter from a relational database, from a document database, from a graph database, or it could just make it up. SpitterUserService doesn't know or care what underlying data storage is used. It just fetches the Spitter object and uses it to create a User object. (User is a concrete implementation of UserDetails.)

To use SpitterUserService to authenticate users, you can configure it in your security configuration with the userDetailsService() method:

```
@Autowired
SpitterRepository spitterRepository;

@Override
protected void configure(AuthenticationManagerBuilder auth)
                                                    throws Exception {
  auth
    .userDetailsService(new SpitterUserService(spitterRepository));
}
```

The userDetailsService() method (like jdbcAuthentication(), ldapAuthentication(), and inMemoryAuthentication()) configures a configuration store. But instead of using one of Spring's provided user stores, it takes any implementation of UserDetailsService.

Another option worth considering is that you could change Spitter so that it implements UserDetailsService. By doing that, you could return the Spitter directly from the loadUserByUsername() method without copying its values into a User object.

9.3   *Intercepting requests*

Earlier, in section 9.1.3, you saw an extremely simple Spring Security configuration and learned how it falls back to a default configuration where all requests require authentication. Some may argue that too much security is better than too little. But there's also something to be said about applying the appropriate amount of security.

In any given application, not all requests should be secured equally. Some may require authentication; some may not. Some requests may only be available to users with certain authorities and unavailable to those without those authorities.

For example, consider the requests served by the Spittr application. Certainly, the home page is public and doesn't need to be secured. Likewise, since all Spittle objects are essentially public, the pages that display Spittles don't require security. Requests that create a Spittle, however, should only be performed by an authenticated user. Similarly, although user profile pages are public and don't require authentication, if you were to handle a request for /spitters/me to display the current user's profile, then authentication is required to know whose profile to show.

The key to fine-tuning security for each request is to override the `configure (HttpSecurity)` method. The following code snippet shows how you might override `configure(HttpSecurity)` to selectively apply security to different URL paths.

```
@Override
protected void configure(HttpSecurity http) throws Exception {
  http
    .authorizeRequests()
      .antMatchers("/spitters/me").authenticated()
      .antMatchers(HttpMethod.POST, "/spittles").authenticated()
      .anyRequest().permitAll();
}
```

The `HttpSecurity` object given to `configure()` can be used to configure several aspects of HTTP security. Here you're calling `authorizeRequests()` and then calling methods on the object it returns to indicate that you want to configure request-level security details. The first call to `antMatchers()` specifies that requests whose path is /spitters/me should be authenticated. The second call to `antMatchers()` is even more specific, saying that any HTTP POST request to /spittles must be authenticated. Finally, a call to `anyRequests()` says that all other requests should be permitted, not requiring authentication or any authorities.

The path given to `antMatchers()` supports Ant-style wildcarding. Although we're not using it here, you could specify a path with a wildcard like this:

```
.antMatchers("/spitters/**").authenticated();
```

You could also specify multiple paths in a single call to `antMatchers()`:

```
.antMatchers("/spitters/**", "/spittles/mine").authenticated();
```

Whereas the `antMatchers()` method works with paths that may contain Ant-style wildcards, there's also a `regexMatchers()` method that accepts regular expressions to define request paths. For example, the following snippet uses a regular expression that's equivalent to /spitters/** (Ant-style):

```
.regexMatchers("/spitters/.*").authenticated();
```

Aside from path selection, we've also used `authenticated()` and `permitAll()` to define how the paths should be secured. The `authenticated()` method demands that the user have logged into the application to perform the request. If the user isn't authenticated, Spring Security's filters will capture the request and redirect the user to the application's login page. Meanwhile, the `permitAll()` method allows the requests without any security demands.

In addition to `authenticated()` and `permitAll()`, there are other methods that can be used to define how a request should be secured. Table 9.4 describes all of the options available.

Table 9.4   Configuration methods to define how a path is to be secured

Method	What it does
access(String)	Allows access if the given SpEL expression evaluates to true
anonymous()	Allows access to anonymous users
authenticated()	Allows access to authenticated users
denyAll()	Denies access unconditionally
fullyAuthenticated()	Allows access if the user is fully authenticated (not remembered)
hasAnyAuthority(String…)	Allows access if the user has any of the given authorities
hasAnyRole(String…)	Allows access if the user has any of the given roles
hasAuthority(String)	Allows access if the user has the given authority
hasIpAddress(String)	Allows access if the request comes from the given IP address
hasRole(String)	Allows access if the user has the given role
not()	Negates the effect of any of the other access methods
permitAll()	Allows access unconditionally
rememberMe()	Allows access for users who are authenticated via remember-me

Using methods from table 9.4, you can configure security to require more than just an authenticated user. For example, you could change the previous configure() method to require that the user not only be authenticated, but also have ROLE_SPITTER authority:

```
@Override
protected void configure(HttpSecurity http) throws Exception {
  http
    .authorizeRequests()
      .antMatchers("/spitters/me").hasAuthority("ROLE_SPITTER")
      .antMatchers(HttpMethod.POST, "/spittles")
                                  .hasAuthority("ROLE_SPITTER")
      .anyRequest().permitAll();
}
```

Optionally, you can use the hasRole() method to have the ROLE_ prefix applied automatically:

```
@Override
protected void configure(HttpSecurity http) throws Exception {
  http
    .authorizeRequests()
      .antMatchers("/spitter/me").hasRole("SPITTER")
      .antMatchers(HttpMethod.POST, "/spittles").hasRole("SPITTER")
      .anyRequest().permitAll();
}
```

You can chain as many calls to `antMatchers()`, `regexMatchers()`, and `anyRequest()` as you need to fully establish the security rules around your web application. You should know, however, that they'll be applied in the order given. For that reason, it's important to configure the most specific request path patterns first and the least specific ones (such as `anyRequest()`) last. If not, then the least specific paths will trump the more specific ones.

9.3.1 Securing with Spring Expressions

Most of the methods in table 9.4 are one-dimensional. That is, you can use `hasRole()` to require a certain role, but you can't also use `hasIpAddress()` to require a specific IP address on the same path.

Moreover, there's no way to work in any conditions that aren't defined by the methods in table 9.4. What if you wanted to restrict access to certain roles only on Tuesday?

In chapter 3, you saw how to use the Spring Expression Language (SpEL) as an advanced technique for wiring bean properties. Using the `access()` method, you can also use SpEL as a means for declaring access requirements. For example, here's how you could use a SpEL expression to require ROLE_SPITTER access for the /spitter/me URL pattern:

```
.antMatchers("/spitter/me").access("hasRole('ROLE_SPITTER')")
```

This security constraint placed on /spitter/me is equivalent to the one we started with, except that now it uses SpEL to express the security rules. The `hasRole()` expression evaluates to `true` if the current user has been granted the given authority.

What makes SpEL a more powerful option here is that `hasRole()` is only one of the security-specific expressions supported. Table 9.5 lists all of the SpEL expressions available in Spring Security.

Table 9.5 Spring Security extends the Spring Expression Language with several security-specific expressions

Security expression	What it evaluates to
`authentication`	The user's authentication object
`denyAll`	Always evaluates to false
`hasAnyRole(list of roles)`	True if the user has any of the given roles
`hasRole(role)`	True if the user has the given role
`hasIpAddress(IP address)`	True if the request comes from the given IP address
`isAnonymous()`	True if the user is anonymous
`isAuthenticated()`	True if the user is authenticated
`isFullyAuthenticated()`	True if the user is fully authenticated (not authenticated with remember-me)

Table 9.5   Spring Security extends the Spring Expression Language with several security-specific expressions *(continued)*

Security expression	What it evaluates to
`isRememberMe()`	True if the user was authenticated via remember-me
`permitAll`	Always evaluates to true
`principal`	The user's principal object

With Spring Security's SpEL expressions at your disposal, you can do more than just limit access based on a user's granted authorities. For example, if you wanted to lock down the /spitter/me URLs to not only require ROLE_SPITTER, but to also only be allowed from a given IP address, you might call the `access()` method like this:

```
.antMatchers("/spitter/me")
  .access("hasRole('ROLE_SPITTER') and hasIpAddress('192.168.1.2')")
```

With SpEL-based security constraints, the possibilities are virtually endless. I'll bet that you're already dreaming up interesting security constraints based on SpEL.

But for now, let's look at another way that Spring Security intercepts requests to enforce channel security.

9.3.2   *Enforcing channel security*

Submitting data across HTTP can be a risky proposition. It may not be a big deal to send a spittle message in the clear over HTTP. But if you're passing sensitive information such as passwords and credit card numbers across HTTP, then you're asking for trouble. Data is sent over HTTP unencrypted, leaving an open opportunity for a hacker to intercept the request and see information you don't want them to see. That's why sensitive information should be sent encrypted over HTTPS.

Working with HTTPS seems simple enough. All you have to do is add an s after the `http` in a URL and you're set. Right?

That's true, but it places responsibility for using the HTTPS channel in the wrong place. Just as it's easy to make a page secure by adding an s, it's just as easy to forget to add that s. If you have several links in your app that require HTTPS, chances are good that you'll forget to add an s or two.

On the other hand, you might overcorrect and use HTTPS in places where it's unnecessary.

In addition to the `authorizeRequests()` method, the `HttpSecurity` object passed into `configure()` has a `requiresChannel()` method that lets you declare channel requirements for various URL patterns.

For example, consider the Spittr application's registration form. Although Spittr doesn't ask for credit card numbers or social security numbers or anything terribly sensitive, users may want their registration information to be kept private. To ensure that the registration form is sent over HTTPS, you can add `requiresChannel()` to the configuration, as in the following listing.

Listing 9.5 The `requiresChannel()` method enforces HTTPS for select URLs

```
@Override
protected void configure(HttpSecurity http) throws Exception {
  http
    .authorizeRequests()
      .antMatchers("/spitter/me").hasRole("SPITTER")
      .antMatchers(HttpMethod.POST, "/spittles").hasRole("SPITTER")
      .anyRequest().permitAll();
    .and()
    .requiresChannel()
      .antMatchers("/spitter/form").requiresSecure();      ⊲— Require HTTPS
}
```

Any time a request comes in for /spitter/form, Spring Security will see that it requires a secure channel (per the call to `requiresSecure()`) and automatically redirect the request to go over HTTPS.

Conversely, some pages don't need to be sent over HTTPS. The home page, for example, doesn't carry any sensitive information and should be sent over HTTP. You can declare that the home page always be sent over HTTP by using `requires-Insecure()` instead of `requiresSecure`:

```
.antMatchers("/").requiresInecure();
```

If a request for / comes in over HTTPS, Spring Security will redirect the request to flow over the insecure HTTP.

Notice that the path selection options for channel enforcement are the same as for `authorizeRequests()`. In listing 9.5 you're using `antMatches()`, but `regexMatchers()` is also available for selecting path patterns with regular expressions.

9.3.3 Preventing cross-site request forgery

As you'll recall, our `SpittleController` will create a new `Spittle` for a user when a POST request is submitted to /spittles. But what if that POST request comes from another website? And what if that POST request is the result of submitting the following form on that other site?

```
<form method="POST" action="http://www.spittr.com/spittles">
  <input type="hidden" name="message" value="I'm stupid!" />
  <input type="submit" value="Click here to win a new car!" />
</form>
```

Let's say that you're tempted by the offer of winning a new car and you click the button—you'll submit the form to http://www.spittr.com/spittles. If you're already logged in to spittr.com, you'll be broadcasting a message that tells everyone that you made a bad decision.

This is a simple example of a cross-site request forgery (CSRF). Basically, a CSRF attack happens when one site tricks a user into submitting a request to another server, possibly having a negative outcome. Although posting "I'm stupid!" to a microblogging site is hardly the worst example of CSRF, you can easily imagine more serious exploits, perhaps performing some undesired operation on your bank account.

Starting with Spring Security 3.2, CSRF protection is enabled by default. In fact, unless you take steps to work with CSRF protection or disable it, you'll probably have trouble getting the forms in your application to submit successfully.

Spring Security implements CSRF protection with a synchronizer token. State-changing requests (for example, any request that is not GET, HEAD, OPTIONS, or TRACE) will be intercepted and checked for a CSRF token. If the request doesn't carry a CSRF token, or if the token doesn't match the token on the server, the request will fail with a CsrfException.

This means that any forms in your application must submit a token in a _csrf field. And that token must be the same as the one calculated and stored by the server so that it matches up when the form is submitted.

Fortunately, Spring Security makes this easy for you by putting the token into the request under the request attributes. If you're using Thymeleaf for your page template, you'll get the hidden _csrf field automatically, as long as the `<form>` tag's `action` attribute is prefixed to come from the Thymeleaf namespace:

```
<form method="POST" th:action="@{/spittles}">
  ...
</form>
```

If you're using JSP for page templates, you can do something very similar:

```
<input type="hidden"
       name="${_csrf.parameterName}"
       value="${_csrf.token}" />
```

Even better, if you're using Spring's form-binding tag library, the `<sf:form>` tag will automatically add the hidden CSRF token tag for you.

Another way of dealing with CSRF is to not deal with it at all. You can disable Spring Security's CSRF protection by calling `csrf().disable()` in the configuration, as shown in the next listing.

Listing 9.6   You can disable Spring Security's CSRF protection

```
@Override
protected void configure(HttpSecurity http) throws Exception {
  http
    ...
    .csrf()
      .disable();          ⟵— Disable CSRF protection
  }
```

Be warned that it's generally not a good idea to disable CSRF protection. If you do, you leave your application open to a CSRF attack. Use the configuration in listing 9.6 only after careful deliberation.

Now that you've configured a user store and configured Spring Security to intercept requests, you should turn your attention to prompting the user for their credentials.

9.4 Authenticating users

When you were still using the extremely simple Spring Security configuration in listing 9.1, you got a login page for free. In fact, up until you overrode `configure(Http-Security)`, you could count on a plain-vanilla, yet fully functional login page. But as soon as you override `configure(HttpSecurity)`, you lose that simple login page.

Fortunately, it's easy enough to get it back. All you need to do is call `formLogin()` in the `configure(HttpSecurity)` method, as shown in the following listing.

Listing 9.7 The `formLogin()` method enables a basic login page

```
@Override
protected void configure(HttpSecurity http) throws Exception {
  http
    .formLogin()                          ←— Enable default login page
    .and()
    .authorizeRequests()
      .antMatchers("/spitter/me").hasRole("SPITTER")
      .antMatchers(HttpMethod.POST, "/spittles").hasRole("SPITTER")
      .anyRequest().permitAll();
    .and()
    .requiresChannel()
      .antMatchers("/spitter/form").requiresSecure();
}
```

Notice that, as before, `and()` is called to chain together different configuration instructions.

If you link to /login in the application, or if the user navigates to a page that requires authentication, then the login page will be shown in the browser. As you can see in figure 9.2, the page isn't very exciting aesthetically, but it does the job it needs to do.

I'll bet you'd prefer that your application's login page look nicer than the default login page. It'd be a shame to have such a plain login page ruin your otherwise beautifully designed website. No problem. Let's see how you can add a custom login page to your application.

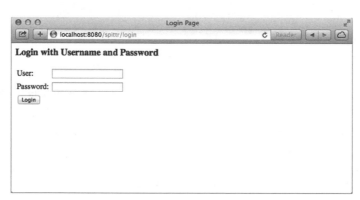

Figure 9.2 The default login page is simple aesthetically, but fully functional

9.4.1 *Adding a custom login page*

The first step toward creating a custom login page is knowing what you need to include in the login form. Look no further than the HTML source of the default login page to see what's required:

```html
<html>
<head><title>Login Page</title></head>
<body onload='document.f.username.focus();'>
<h3>Login with Username and Password</h3>
<form name='f' action='/spittr/login' method='POST'>
 <table>
    <tr><td>User:</td><td>
        <input type='text' name='username' value=''></td></tr>
    <tr><td>Password:</td>
        <td><input type='password' name='password'/></td></tr>
    <tr><td colspan='2'>
        <input name="submit" type="submit" value="Login"/></td></tr>
    <input name="_csrf" type="hidden"
           value="6829b1ae-0a14-4920-aac4-5abbd7eeb9ee" />
  </table>
</form>
</body>
</html>
```

The key thing to note is where the `<form>` submits to. And make note of the username and password fields; you'll need those same fields on your login page. Finally, assuming that you've not disabled CSRF, you'll need to be sure to include a `_csrf` field with the CSRF token.

The following listing shows a Thymeleaf template that provides a login page within the style of the Spittr application.

Listing 9.8   A custom login page for the Spittr application (as a Thymeleaf template)

```html
<html xmlns="http://www.w3.org/1999/xhtml"
      xmlns:th="http://www.thymeleaf.org">
  <head>
    <title>Spitter</title>
    <link rel="stylesheet"
          type="text/css"
          th:href="@{/resources/style.css}"></link>
  </head>
  <body onload='document.f.username.focus();'>
    <div id="header" th:include="page :: header"></div>

<div id="content">
<form name='f' th:action='@{/login}' method='POST'>          ⟵── Submit to /login
    <table>
    <tr><td>User:</td><td>
        <input type='text' name='username' value='' /></td></tr>
    <tr><td>Password:</td>
        <td><input type='password' name='password'/></td></tr>
    <tr><td colspan='2'>
        <input name="submit" type="submit" value="Login"/></td></tr>
```

```
      </table>
    </form>
  </div>
  <div id="footer" th:include="page :: copy"></div>
  </body>
</html>
```

Notice that the Thymeleaf template has both username and password fields, just like the default login page. It also submits to the context-relative /login page. And since this is a Thymeleaf template, the hidden _csrf field will automatically be added to the form.

9.4.2 Enabling HTTP Basic authentication

Form-based authentication is ideal for human users of an application. But in chapter 16, you'll see how to turn some of your web application's pages into a RESTful API. When the user of the application is another application, prompting for login with a form just won't do.

HTTP Basic authentication is one way to authenticate a user to an application directly in the HTTP request itself. You may have seen HTTP Basic authentication before. When encountered by a web browser, it prompts the user with a plain modal dialog box.

But that's just how it's manifested in a web browser. In reality, it's an HTTP 401 response, indicating that a username and password must be presented with the request. This makes it suitable as a means for REST clients to authenticate against the services they're consuming.

Enabling HTTP Basic authentication is as simple as calling httpBasic() on the HttpSecurity object passed into configure(). Optionally, you can specify a realm by calling realmName(). Here's a rather typical example of Spring Security configuration to enable HTTP Basic:

```
@Override
protected void configure(HttpSecurity http) throws Exception {
  http
    .formLogin()
      .loginPage("/login")
    .and()
    .httpBasic()
      .realmName("Spittr")
    .and()
  ...
}
```

Notice that once again the and() method is used to chain together different configuration directives in configure().

Not much customization is available or even required with httpBasic(). HTTP Basic authentication is either turned on or it's not. So rather than dwell on the topic any further, let's move on to see how to have a user automatically authenticated via remember-me functionality.

9.4.3   *Enabling remember-me functionality*

It's important for an application to be able to authenticate users. But from the user's perspective, it'd be nice if the application didn't always prompt them with a login every time they use it. That's why many websites offer remember-me functionality, so that you can log in once and then be remembered by the application when you come back to it later.

Spring Security makes it easy to add remember-me functionality to an application. To turn on remember-me support, all you need to do is call `rememberMe()` on the `HttpSecurity` passed into `configure()`:

```
@Override
  protected void configure(HttpSecurity http) throws Exception {
    http
      .formLogin()
        .loginPage("/login")
      .and()
      .rememberMe()
        .tokenValiditySeconds(2419200)
        .key("spittrKey")
  ...
}
```

Here, in addition to turning on remember-me functionality, a bit of special configuration has also been added. By default, a remember-me token is stored in a cookie that's valid for up to two weeks. But this example specifies that the token should stay valid for up to four weeks (2,419,200 seconds).

The token that's stored in the cookie is made up of the username, password, an expiration date, and a private key—all encoded in an MD5 hash before being written to the cookie. By default, the private key is `SpringSecured`, but this example sets it to `spitterKey` to make it specific to the Spittr application.

Simple enough. Now that the remember-me functionality is enabled, you'll need a way for users to indicate that they'd like the application to remember them. For that, the login request will need to include a `remember-me` parameter. A simple check box in the login form ought to do the job:

```
<input id="remember_me" name="remember-me" type="checkbox"/>
<label for="remember_me" class="inline">Remember me</label>
```

Just as important as being able to log in to an application is the ability to log out. This is especially true if you've enabled remember-me; otherwise the user would be logged into the application forever. Let's see how you can add the ability to log out.

9.4.4   *Logging out*

As it turns out, logout capability is already enabled by your configuration without you having to do anything else. All you need to do is add a link that uses it.

Logout is implemented as a servlet filter that (by default) intercepts requests to /logout. Therefore, adding logout to an application is as easy as adding the following link (shown here as a Thymeleaf snippet):

```
<a th:href="@{/logout}">Logout</a>
```

When the user clicks on the link, the request for /logout will be handled by Spring Security's `LogoutFilter`. The user will be logged out and any remember-me tokens cleared. After the logout is complete, the user's browser will be redirected to /login?logout to give the user an opportunity to log in again.

If you'd like to have the user redirected to some other page, such as the application's home page, you can configure that in `configure()` like this:

```
@Override
protected void configure(HttpSecurity http) throws Exception {
  http
    .formLogin()
      .loginPage("/login")
    .and()
    .logout()
      .logoutSuccessUrl("/")
  ...
}
```

Here, as before, `and()` chains a call to `logout()`. The `logout()` method offers methods for configuring logout behavior. In this case, the call to `logoutSuccessUrl()` indicates that the browser should be redirected to / after a successful logout.

In addition to `logoutSuccessUrl()`, you may want to also override the default path that `LogoutFilter` intercepts. You can do that with a call to `logoutUrl()`:

```
.logout()
  .logoutSuccessUrl("/")
  .logoutUrl("/signout")
```

So far you've seen how to secure web applications as requests are made. The assumption has been that security would involve stopping a user from accessing a URL that they're not authorized to use. But it's also a good idea to never show links that a user won't be able to follow. Let's see how to add view layer security.

9.5 Securing the view

When rendering HTML to be served in the browser, you may want the view to reflect the security constraints and information. A simple example may be that you want to render the authenticated user's principal (for example, "You are logged in as…"). Or you may want to conditionally render certain view elements, depending on what authorities have been granted to the user.

In chapter 6, we looked at two significant options for rendering views in a Spring MVC application: JSP and Thymeleaf. It doesn't matter which of these options you choose, there's a way to work with security in the view. Spring Security itself provides a JSP tag library, whereas Thymeleaf offers Spring Security integration through a special dialect.

Let's see how to work Spring Security into our views, starting with Spring Security's JSP tag library.

9.5.1   *Using Spring Security's JSP tag library*

Spring Security's JSP tag library is small and includes only three tags, listed in table 9.6.

Table 9.6   Spring Security supports security in the view layer with a JSP tag library

JSP tag	What it does
`<security:accesscontrollist>`	Conditionally renders its body content if the user is granted authorities by an access control list
`<security:authentication>`	Renders details about the current authentication
`<security:authorize>`	Conditionally renders its body content if the user is granted certain authorities or if a SpEL expression evaluates to `true`

To use the JSP tag library, we'll need to declare it in any JSP file where it will be used:

```
<%@ taglib prefix="security"
           uri="http://www.springframework.org/security/tags" %>
```

Once the tag library has been declared in the JSP file, you're ready to use it. Let's look at each of the three JSP tags that come with Spring Security and see how they work.

ACCESSING AUTHENTICATION DETAILS

One of the simplest things that the Spring Security JSP tag library can do is provide convenient access to the user's authentication information. For example, it's common for websites to display a "welcome" or "hello" message in the page header, identifying the user by their username. That's precisely the kind of thing that `<security:authentication>` can do for us. Here's an example:

```
Hello <security:authentication property="principal.username" />!
```

The `property` attribute identifies a property of the user's authentication object. The properties available will vary depending on how the user was authenticated, but you can count on a few common properties being available, including those listed in table 9.7.

In our example, the property being rendered is actually the nested `username` property of the `principal` property.

Table 9.7   You can access several of the user's authentication details using the `<security:authentication>` JSP tag

Authentication property	Description
`authorities`	A collection of `GrantedAuthority` objects that represent the privileges granted to the user

Table 9.7 You can access several of the user's authentication details using the `<security:authentication>` JSP tag

Authentication property	Description
`credentials`	The credentials that were used to verify the principal (commonly, this is the user's password)
`details`	Additional information about the authentication (IP address, certificate serial number, session ID, and so on)
`principal`	The user's principal

When used as shown in the previous example, `<security:authentication>` will render the property's value in the view. But if you'd rather assign it to a variable, then simply specify the name of the variable in the `var` attribute. For example, here's how you could assign it to a property named `loginId`:

```
<security:authentication property="principal.username"
        var="loginId"/>
```

The variable is created in page scope by default. But if you'd rather create it in some other scope, such as request or session (or any of the scopes available from `javax.servlet.jsp.PageContext`), you can specify it via the `scope` attribute. For example, to create the variable in request scope, use the `<security:authentication>` tag like this:

```
<security:authentication property="principal.username"
        var="loginId" scope="request" />
```

The `<security:authentication>` tag is useful, but it's just the start of what Spring Security's JSP tag library can do. Let's see how to conditionally render content depending on the user's privileges.

CONDITIONAL RENDERING

Sometimes portions of the view should or shouldn't be rendered, depending on what the user is privileged to see. There's no point in showing a login form to a user who's already logged in or in showing a personalized greeting to a user who's not logged in.

Spring Security's `<security:authorize>` JSP tag conditionally renders a portion of the view depending on the user's granted authorities. For example, in the Spittr application you don't want to show the form for adding a new spittle unless the user has the ROLE_SPITTER role. Listing 9.9 shows how to use the `<security:authorize>` tag to display the spittle form if the user has ROLE_SPITTER authority.

Listing 9.9 `<sec:authorize>` conditionally renders content based on SpEL

```
<sec:authorize access="hasRole('ROLE_SPITTER')">          ⟵   Only with
 <s:url value="/spittles" var="spittle_url" />                ROLE_SPITTER
  <sf:form modelAttribute="spittle"                           authority
            action="${spittle_url}">
```

```
    <sf:label path="text"><s:message code="label.spittle"
                    text="Enter spittle:"/></sf:label>
    <sf:textarea path="text" rows="2" cols="40" />
       <sf:errors path="text" />

    <br/>
    <div class="spitItSubmitIt">
      <input type="submit" value="Spit it!"
           class="status-btn round-btn disabled" />
    </div>
  </sf:form>
</sec:authorize>
```

The access attribute is given a SpEL expression whose result determines whether `<security:authorize>`'s body is rendered. Here you're using the `hasRole ('ROLE_SPITTER')` expression to ensure that the user has the `ROLE_SPITTER` role. But you have the full power of SpEL at your disposal when setting the `access` attribute, including the Spring Security-provided expressions listed in table 9.5.

With these expressions available, you can cook up some interesting security constraints. For example, imagine that the application has some administrative functions that are only available to the user whose username is "habuma". Maybe you'd use the `isAuthenticated()` and `principal` expressions like this:

```
<security:authorize
   access="isAuthenticated() and principal.username=='habuma'">
  <a href="/admin">Administration</a>
</security:authorize>
```

I'm sure you can dream up even more interesting expressions than that. I'll leave it up to your imagination to concoct more security constraints. The options are virtually limitless with SpEL.

But one thing about the example that I dreamt up still bugs me. Though I might want to restrict the administrative functions to "habuma", perhaps doing it with a JSP tag isn't ideal. Sure, it'll keep the link from being rendered in the view. But nothing's stopping anyone from manually entering the /admin URL in the browser's address line.

Drawing on what you learned earlier in this chapter, that should be an easy thing to fix. Adding a new call to the `antMatchers()` method in the security configuration will tighten security around the /admin URL:

```
.antMatchers("/admin")
  .access("isAuthenticated() and principal.username=='habuma'");
```

Now the admin functionality is locked down. The URL is secured and the link to the URL won't appear unless the user is authorized to use it. But to do that, you had to declare the SpEL expression in two places—in the security configuration and in the `<security:authorize>` tag's `access` attribute. Is there any way to eliminate that duplication and still prevent the link to the administrative functions from being rendered unless the rule is met?

That's what the `<security:authorize>` tag's `url` attribute is for. Unlike the `access` attribute where the security constraint is explicitly declared, the `url` attribute indirectly refers to the security constraints for a given URL pattern. Since you've already declared security constraints for /admin in the Spring Security configuration, you can use the url attribute like this:

```
<security:authorize url="/admin">
  <spring:url value="/admin" var="admin_url" />
  <br/><a href="${admin_url}">Admin</a>
</security:authorize>
```

Since the /admin URL is restricted to only authenticated users whose principal's username is "habuma", the body of the `<security:authorize>` tag will only be rendered if those same conditions are met. The expression was configured in one place (in the security configuration), but used in two places.

Spring Security's JSP tag library comes in very handy, especially when it comes to conditionally rendering view elements to only those users who are allowed to see them. But if you've chosen Thymeleaf instead of JSP for your views, then you're not out of luck. You've already seen how Thymeleaf's Spring dialect will automatically add a hidden CSRF token field to your forms. Now let's look at how Thymeleaf supports Spring Security.

9.5.2 *Working with Thymeleaf's Spring Security dialect*

Much like Spring Security's JSP tag library, Thymeleaf's security dialect offers conditional rendering and the ability to render authentication details. Table 9.8 lists the attributes provided by the security dialect.

Table 9.8   Thymeleaf's security dialect offers attributes that mirror much of Spring Security's tag library

Attribute	What it does
sec:authentication	Renders properties of the authentication object. Similar to Spring Security's `<sec:authentication/>` JSP tag.
sec:authorize	Conditionally renders content based on evaluation of an expression. Similar to Spring Security's `<sec:authorize/>` JSP tag.
sec:authorize-acl	Conditionally renders content based on evaluation of an expression. Similar to Spring Security's `<sec:accesscontrollist/>` JSP tag.
sec:authorize-expr	An alias for the sec:authorize attribute.
sec:authorize-url	Conditionally renders content based on evaluation of security rules associated with a given URL path. Similar to Spring Security's `<sec:authorize/>` JSP tag when using the url attribute.

In order to use the security dialect, you'll need to make sure that the Thymeleaf Extras Spring Security module is in your application's classpath. Then you'll need to register the SpringSecurityDialect with the SpringTemplateEngine in your configuration. Listing 9.10 shows the @Bean method that declares the SpringTemplate-Engine bean, including the SpringSecurityDialect.

Listing 9.10   Registering Thymeleaf's Spring Security dialect

```
@Bean
public SpringTemplateEngine templateEngine(
                                TemplateResolver templateResolver) {
  SpringTemplateEngine templateEngine = new SpringTemplateEngine();
  templateEngine.setTemplateResolver(templateResolver);
  templateEngine.addDialect(new SpringSecurityDialect());   ◁─┐ Register the
   return templateEngine;                                      │ security dialect
}
```

With the security dialect, you're almost ready to start using its attributes in your Thymeleaf templates. First, declare the security namespace in the templates where you'll be using those attributes:

```
<!DOCTYPE html>
<html xmlns="http://www.w3.org/1999/xhtml"
      xmlns:th="http://www.thymeleaf.org"
      xmlns:sec=
         "http://www.thymeleaf.org/thymeleaf-extras-springsecurity3">
  ...
</html>
```

Here the standard Thymeleaf dialect is assigned to the `th` prefix as before, and the security dialect is assigned to the `sec` prefix.

Now you can use the Thymeleaf attributes however you see fit. For example, suppose that you want to render text saying "Hello" to the user if the user is authenticated. The following snippet from a Thymeleaf template will do the trick:

```
<div sec:authorize="isAuthenticated()">
  Hello <span sec:authentication="name">someone</span>
</div>
```

The `sec:authorize` attribute takes a SpEL expression. If that expression evaluates to `true`, then the body of the element will be rendered. In this case, the expression is `isAuthenticated()`, so the body of the `<div>` tag will be rendered only if the user is authenticated. With regard to the body, it says "Hello" to the authentication's `name` property.

As you'll recall, Spring Security's `<sec:authorize>` JSP tag has a `url` attribute that causes its body to be conditionally rendered based on the authorizations associated with a given URL path. With Thymeleaf, you can accomplish the same thing with the `sec:authorize-url` attribute. For example, the following Thymeleaf snippet accomplishes the same thing you previously used the `<sec:authorize>` JSP tag and `url` attribute for:

```
<span sec:authorize-url="/admin">
  <br/><a th:href="@{/admin}">Admin</a>
</span>
```

Assuming that the user has authorization to access /admin, then a link to the admin page will be rendered; otherwise it won't.

9.6   *Summary*

Security is a crucial aspect of many applications. Spring Security provides a mechanism for securing your application that's simple, flexible, and powerful.

Using a series of servlet filters, Spring Security can control access to web resources, including Spring MVC controllers. But thanks to Spring Security's Java configuration model, you don't need to deal with those filters directly. Web security can be declared concisely.

When it comes to authenticating users, Spring Security offers several options. You saw how to configure authentication against an in-memory user store, a relational database, and LDAP directory servers. And when your authentication needs don't fit any of those options, you saw how to create and configure a custom user-details service.

Over the past few chapters, you've seen how Spring fits into the front end of an application. Coming up in the next section, we'll move a bit deeper down the stack and see how Spring plays a part in the back end. That exploration will start in the next chapter with a look at Spring's JDBC abstraction.

Part 3

Spring in the back end

Although the web pages served by a web application are all your users ever see, the real work happens behind the scenes on the back end server where data is processed and persisted. Part 3 will look at how Spring can help you work with data in the back end.

Relational databases have been the workhorse of enterprise applications for decades. In chapter 10, "Hitting the database with Spring and JDBC," you'll see how to use Spring's JDBC abstraction to query relational databases in a way that is far simpler than native JDBC.

If JDBC is not your style, perhaps you'd rather work with an object-relational mapping (ORM) framework. Chapter 11, "Persisting data with object-relational mapping," will show you how Spring integrates with ORM frameworks such as Hibernate and other implementations of the Java Persistence API (JPA). In addition, you'll see how to work magic with Spring Data JPA, automatically generating repository implementations on the fly at runtime.

Relational databases aren't always a perfect fit. Therefore, chapter 12, "Working with NoSQL databases," looks at other Spring data projects useful for persisting data in a variety of nonrelational databases, including MongoDB, Neo4j, and Redis.

Chapter 13, "Caching data," layers the previous persistence chapters with caching, to improve application performance by avoiding the database altogether if the data needed is readily available.

Security is an important aspect in the back end as well as the front end. In Chapter 14, "Securing methods," you'll see how to apply Spring Security in the back end, intercepting method calls and ensuring that the caller has been granted proper authority.

Hitting the database
with Spring and JDBC

This chapter covers

- Defining Spring's data-access support
- Configuring database resources
- Working with Spring's JDBC template

With the core of the Spring container now under your belt, it's time to put it to work in real applications. A perfect place to start is with a requirement of nearly any enterprise application: persisting data. You have probably dealt with database access in an application in the past. In practice, you'll know that data access has many pitfalls. You have to initialize your data-access framework, open connections, handle various exceptions, and close connections. If you get any of this wrong, you could potentially corrupt or delete valuable company data. In case you haven't experienced the consequences of mishandled data access, it's a *Bad Thing*.

Because we strive for *Good Things*, we turn to Spring. Spring comes with a family of data-access frameworks that integrate with a variety of data-access technologies. Whether you're persisting your data via direct JDBC or an object-relational mapping (ORM) framework such as Hibernate, Spring removes the tedium of data access from your persistence code. Instead, you can lean on Spring to handle the low-level data-access work for you so that you can turn your attention to managing your application's data.

As you develop the persistence layer of the Spittr application, you're faced with some choices. You could use JDBC, Hibernate, the Java Persistence API (JPA), or any of a number of persistence frameworks. Or you might consider one of the new breed of NoSQL databases (or schemaless databases, as I prefer to call them) that are popular these days.

No matter what choice you make, it's good to know that there's probably support for it in Spring. In this chapter, we'll focus on Spring's support for JDBC. But first, let's lay some groundwork by getting familiar with Spring's persistence philosophy.

10.1 *Learning Spring's data-access philosophy*

From the previous chapters, you know that one of Spring's goals is to allow you to develop applications following the sound object-oriented (OO) principle of coding to interfaces. Spring's data-access support is no exception.

Like many applications, your Spittr application needs to read data from and write data to some kind of database. To avoid scattering persistence logic across all components in the application, it's good to factor database access into one or more components that are focused on that task. Such components are commonly called data-access objects (DAOs) or repositories.

To avoid coupling the application to any particular data-access strategy, properly written repositories should expose their functionality through interfaces. Figure 10.1 shows the proper approach to designing your data-access tier.

As you can see, the service objects access the repositories through interfaces. This has a couple of positive consequences. First, it makes your service objects easily testable, because they're not coupled to a specific data-access implementation. In fact, you could create mock implementations of these data-access interfaces. That would allow you to test your service object without ever having to connect to the database, which would significantly speed up your unit tests and rule out the chance of a test failure due to inconsistent data.

In addition, the data-access tier is accessed in a persistence technology–agnostic manner. The chosen persistence approach is isolated to the repository, and only the

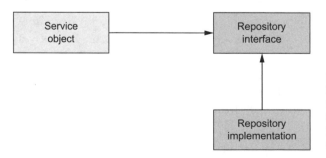

Figure 10.1 Service objects don't handle their own data access. Instead, they delegate data access to repositories. The repository's interface keeps it loosely coupled to the service object.

relevant data-access methods are exposed through the interface. This makes for a flexible application design and allows the chosen persistence framework to be swapped out with minimal impact on the rest of the application. If the implementation details of the data-access tier were to leak into other parts of the application, the entire application would become coupled with the data-access tier, leading to a rigid application design.

> **INTERFACES AND SPRING**   If, after reading the last couple of paragraphs, you feel that I have a strong bias toward hiding the persistence layer behind interfaces, then I'm happy I was able to get that point across. I believe that interfaces are key to writing loosely coupled code and that they should be used at all layers of an application, not just at the data-access layer. That said, it's also important to note that though Spring encourages the use of interfaces, Spring doesn't require them—you're welcome to use Spring to wire a bean (repository or otherwise) directly into a property of another bean without an interface between them.

One way Spring helps you insulate your data-access tier from the rest of your application is by providing a consistent exception hierarchy that's used across all of its supported persistence options.

10.1.1 *Getting to know Spring's data-access exception hierarchy*

There's an old joke about a skydiver who's blown off course and ends up landing in a tree, dangling above the ground. After a while, someone walks by, and the skydiver asks where he is. The passerby answers, "You're about 20 feet off the ground." The skydiver replies, "You must be a software analyst." "You're right. How did you know?" asks the passerby. "Because what you told me was 100% accurate but completely worthless."

That story has been told several times, with the profession or nationality of the passerby different each time. But the story reminds me of JDBC's SQLException. If you've ever written JDBC code (without Spring), you're probably keenly aware that you can't do anything with JDBC without being forced to catch SQLException. SQLException means something went wrong while trying to access a database. But there's little about that exception that tells you what went wrong or how to deal with it.

Some common problems that might cause a SQLException to be thrown include these:

- The application is unable to connect to the database.
- The query being performed has errors in its syntax.
- The tables and/or columns referred to in the query don't exist.
- An attempt was made to insert or update values that violate a database constraint.

The big question surrounding SQLException is how it should be handled when it's caught. As it turns out, many of the problems that trigger a SQLException can't be remedied in a catch block. Most SQLExceptions that are thrown indicate a fatal condition. If the application can't connect to the database, that usually means the application will be unable to continue. Likewise, if there are errors in the query, little can be done about it at runtime.

If nothing can be done to recover from a SQLException, why are you forced to catch it?

Even if you have a plan for dealing with some SQLExceptions, you'll have to catch the SQLException and dig around in its properties for more information about the nature of the problem. That's because SQLException is treated as a one-size-fits-all exception for problems related to data access. Rather than have a different exception type for each possible problem, SQLException is the exception that's thrown for all data-access problems.

Some persistence frameworks offer a richer hierarchy of exceptions. Hibernate, for example, offers almost two dozen different exceptions, each targeting a specific data-access problem. This makes it possible to write catch blocks for the exceptions that you want to deal with.

Even so, Hibernate's exceptions are specific to Hibernate. As stated before, we'd like to isolate the specifics of the persistence mechanism to the data-access layer. If Hibernate-specific exceptions are being thrown, then the fact that you're dealing with Hibernate will leak into the rest of the application. Either that, or you'll be forced to catch persistence platform exceptions and rethrow them as platform-agnostic exceptions.

On one hand, JDBC's exception hierarchy is too generic—it's not much of a hierarchy at all. On the other hand, Hibernate's exception hierarchy is proprietary to Hibernate. What we need is a hierarchy of data-access exceptions that are descriptive but not directly associated with a specific persistence framework.

SPRING'S PERSISTENCE PLATFORM–AGNOSTIC EXCEPTIONS

Spring JDBC provides a hierarchy of data-access exceptions that solve both problems. In contrast to JDBC, Spring provides several data-access exceptions, each descriptive of the problem for which they're thrown. Table 10.1 shows some of Spring's data-access exceptions lined up against the exceptions offered by JDBC.

As you can see, Spring has an exception for virtually anything that could go wrong when reading from or writing to a database. And the list of Spring's data-access exceptions is more vast than what's shown in table 10.1. (I would have listed them all, but I didn't want JDBC to get an inferiority complex.)

Even though Spring's exception hierarchy is far richer than JDBC's simple SQLException, it isn't associated with any particular persistence solution. This means you can count on Spring to throw a consistent set of exceptions, regardless of which persistence provider you choose. This helps to keep your persistence choice confined to the data-access layer.

Table 10.1 JDBC's exception hierarchy versus Spring's data-access exceptions

JDBC's exceptions	Spring's data-access exceptions
BatchUpdateException DataTruncation SQLException SQLWarning	BadSqlGrammarException CannotAcquireLockException CannotSerializeTransactionException CannotGetJdbcConnectionException CleanupFailureDataAccessException ConcurrencyFailureException DataAccessException DataAccessResourceFailureException DataIntegrityViolationException DataRetrievalFailureException DataSourceLookupApiUsageException DeadlockLoserDataAccessException DuplicateKeyException EmptyResultDataAccessException IncorrectResultSizeDataAccessException IncorrectUpdateSemanticsDataAccessException InvalidDataAccessApiUsageException InvalidDataAccessResourceUsageException InvalidResultSetAccessException JdbcUpdateAffectedIncorrectNumberOfRowsException LobRetrievalFailureException NonTransientDataAccessResourceException OptimisticLockingFailureException PermissionDeniedDataAccessException PessimisticLockingFailureException QueryTimeoutException RecoverableDataAccessException SQLWarningException SqlXmlFeatureNotImplementedException TransientDataAccessException TransientDataAccessResourceException TypeMismatchDataAccessException UncategorizedDataAccessException UncategorizedSQLException

LOOK, MA! NO CATCH BLOCKS!

What isn't evident from table 10.1 is that all of those exceptions are rooted with
DataAccessException. What makes DataAccessException special is that it's an
unchecked exception. In other words, you don't have to catch any of the data-access
exceptions thrown from Spring (although you're welcome to if you'd like).

DataAccessException is just one example of Spring's across-the-board philosophy
of checked versus unchecked exceptions. Spring takes the stance that many exceptions are the result of problems that can't be addressed in a catch block. Instead of
forcing developers to write catch blocks (which are often left empty), Spring promotes the use of unchecked exceptions. This leaves the decision of whether or not to
catch an exception in your hands.

To take advantage of Spring's data-access exceptions, you must use one of Spring's supported data-access templates. Let's look at how Spring templates can greatly simplify data access.

10.1.2   *Templating data access*

You've probably traveled by plane before. If so, you'll surely agree that one of the most important parts of traveling is getting your luggage from point A to point B. There are many steps to this process: When you arrive at the terminal, your first stop is at the counter to check your luggage. Next, security scans it to ensure the safety of the flight. Then it takes a ride on the luggage train on its way to being placed on the plane. If you need to catch a connecting flight, your luggage needs to be moved, as well. When you arrive at your final destination, the luggage has to be removed from the plane and placed on the carousel. Finally, you go down to the baggage claim area and pick it up.

Even though there are many steps to this process, you're actively involved in only a couple of them. The carrier is responsible for driving the process. You're involved only when you need to be; the rest is taken care of. This mirrors a powerful design pattern: the template method pattern.

A template method defines the skeleton of a process. In the example, the process is moving luggage from departure city to arrival city. The process itself is fixed; it never changes. The overall sequence of events for handling luggage occurs the same way every time: luggage is checked in, luggage is loaded onto the plane, and so forth. Some steps of the process are fixed as well—they happen the same way every time. When the plane arrives at its destination, every piece of luggage is unloaded one at a time and placed on a carousel to be taken to baggage claim.

At certain points, the process delegates its work to a subclass to fill in some implementation-specific details. This is the variable part of the process. For example, the handling of luggage starts with a passenger checking in the luggage at the counter. This part of the process always has to happen at the beginning, so its sequence in the process is fixed. Because each passenger's luggage check-in is different, the implementation of this part of the process is determined by the passenger. In software terms, a template method delegates the implementation-specific portions of the process to an interface. Different implementations of this interface define specific implementations of this portion of the process.

This is the same pattern that Spring applies to data access. No matter what technology you're using, certain data-access steps are required. For example, you always need to obtain a connection to your data store and clean up resources when you're done. These are the fixed steps in a data-access process. But each data-access method you write is slightly different. You query for different objects and update the data in different ways. These are the variable steps in the data-access process.

Spring separates the fixed and variable parts of the data-access process into two distinct classes: *templates* and *callbacks*. Templates manage the fixed part of the process, whereas your custom data-access code is handled in callbacks. Figure 10.2 shows the responsibilities of both classes.

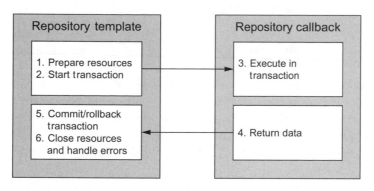

Figure 10.2 Spring's data-access template classes take responsibility for common data-access duties. For application-specific tasks, it calls back into a custom callback object.

As you can see, Spring's template classes handle the fixed parts of data access—controlling transactions, managing resources, and handling exceptions. Meanwhile, the specifics of data access as they pertain to your application—creating statements, binding parameters, and marshaling result sets—are handled in the callback implementation. In practice, this makes for an elegant framework, because all you have to worry about is your data-access logic.

Spring comes with several templates to choose from, depending on your persistence platform choice. If you're using straight JDBC, then you'll want to use `Jdbc-Template`. But if you favor one of the object-relational mapping frameworks, perhaps `HibernateTemplate` or `JpaTemplate` is more suitable. Table 10.2 lists all of Spring's data-access templates and their purposes.

Table 10.2 Spring comes with several data-access templates, each suitable for a different persistence mechanism.

Template class (`org.springframework.*`)	Used to template . . .
`jca.cci.core.CciTemplate`	JCA CCI connections
`jdbc.core.JdbcTemplate`	JDBC connections
`jdbc.core.namedparam.NamedParameterJdbcTemplate`	JDBC connections with support for named parameters
`jdbc.core.simple.SimpleJdbcTemplate`	JDBC connections, simplified with Java 5 constructs (deprecated in Spring 3.1)
`orm.hibernate3.HibernateTemplate`	Hibernate 3.x+ sessions
`orm.ibatis.SqlMapClientTemplate`	iBATIS SqlMap clients
`orm.jdo.JdoTemplate`	Java Data Object implementations
`orm.jpa.JpaTemplate`	Java Persistence API entity managers

Spring provides support for several persistence frameworks, and there isn't enough space to cover them all in this chapter. Therefore, I'm going to focus on what I believe are the most beneficial persistence options and the ones you'll most likely be using.

We'll start with basic JDBC access in this chapter, because it's the simplest way to read data from and write data to a database. Then, in chapter 11, we'll look at Hibernate and JPA, two of the most popular POJO-based ORM solutions. We'll wrap up our exploration of Spring persistence in chapter 12 by looking at how the Spring Data project brings the world of schemaless data to Spring.

But first things first. Most of Spring's persistence support options depend on a data source, so before you can get started with declaring templates and repositories, you need to configure Spring with a data source to be able to connect to the database.

10.2 Configuring a data source

Regardless of which form of Spring-supported data access you use, you'll likely need to configure a reference to a data source. Spring offers several options for configuring data-source beans in your Spring application, including these:

- Data sources that are defined by a JDBC driver
- Data sources that are looked up by JNDI
- Data sources that pool connections

For production-ready applications, I recommend using a data source that draws its connections from a connection pool. When possible, I prefer to retrieve the pooled data source from an application server via JNDI. With that preference in mind, let's start by looking at how to configure Spring to retrieve a data source from JNDI.

10.2.1 Using JNDI data sources

Spring applications are often deployed to run in a Java EE application server such as WebSphere or JBoss, or even a web container like Tomcat. These servers allow you to configure data sources to be retrieved via JNDI. The benefit of configuring data sources in this way is that they can be managed completely external to the application, allowing the application to ask for a data source when it's ready to access the database. Moreover, data sources managed in an application server are often pooled for greater performance and can be hot-swapped by system administrators.

With Spring, you can configure a reference to a data source that's kept in JNDI and wire it into the classes that need it as if it were just another Spring bean. The `<jee:jndi-lookup>` element from Spring's `jee` namespace makes it possible to retrieve any object, including data sources, from JNDI and make it available as a Spring bean. For example, if your application's data source were configured in JNDI, you might use `<jee:jndi-lookup>` like this to wire it into Spring:

```
<jee:jndi-lookup id="dataSource"
    jndi-name="/jdbc/SpitterDS"
resource-ref="true" />
```

The `jndi-name` attribute is used to specify the name of the resource in JNDI. If only the `jndi-name` property is set, then the data source will be looked up using the name given as is. But if the application is running in a Java application server, you'll want to set the `resource-ref` property to `true` so that the value given in `jndi-name` will be prepended with `java:comp/env/`.

Alternatively, if you're using Java configuration, you can use `JndiObjectFactory-Bean` to look up the `DataSource` from JNDI:

```
@Bean
public JndiObjectFactoryBean dataSource() {
  JndiObjectFactoryBean jndiObjectFB = new JndiObjectFactoryBean();
  jndiObjectFB.setJndiName("jdbc/SpittrDS");
  jndiObjectFB.setResourceRef(true);
  jndiObjectFB.setProxyInterface(javax.sql.DataSource.class);
  return jndiObjectFB;
}
```

Clearly, the Java configuration for JNDI-fetched beans is more involved. Many times, Java configuration is simpler than XML configuration, but this is one time when you might write more code in Java. Even so, it's easy to see how this Java configuration parallels the XML equivalent. And it isn't that much more Java configuration.

10.2.2 *Using a pooled data source*

If you're unable to retrieve a data source from JNDI, the next best thing is to configure a pooled data source directly in Spring. Although Spring doesn't provide a pooled data source, plenty of suitable ones are available, including the following open source options:

- Apache Commons DBCP (http://jakarta.apache.org/commons/dbcp)
- c3p0 (http://sourceforge.net/projects/c3p0/)
- BoneCP (http://jolbox.com/)

Most of these connection pools can be configured as a data source in Spring in a way that resembles Spring's own `DriverManagerDataSource` or `SingleConnectionData-Source` (which we'll talk about next). For example, here's how you might configure DBCP's `BasicDataSource`:

```
<bean id="dataSource" class="org.apache.commons.dbcp.BasicDataSource"
  p:driverClassName="org.h2.Driver"
  p:url="jdbc:h2:tcp://localhost/~/spitter"
  p:username="sa"
  p:password=""
  p:initialSize="5"
  p:maxActive="10" />
```

Or, if you prefer Java configuration, the pooled `DataSource` bean can be declared like this:

```
@Bean
public BasicDataSource dataSource() {
```

```
    BasicDataSource ds = new BasicDataSource();
    ds.setDriverClassName("org.h2.Driver");
    ds.setUrl("jdbc:h2:tcp://localhost/~/spitter");
    ds.setUsername("sa");
    ds.setPassword("");
    ds.setInitialSize(5);
    ds.setMaxActive(10);
    return ds;
}
```

The first four properties are elemental to configuring a `BasicDataSource`. The `driverClassName` property specifies the fully qualified name of the JDBC driver class. Here you configure it with the JDBC driver for the H2 database. The `url` property is where you set the complete JDBC URL for the database. Finally, the `username` and `password` properties are used to authenticate when you're connecting to the database.

Those four basic properties define connection information for `BasicDataSource`. In addition, you can use several properties to configure the data source pool. Table 10.3 lists a few of the most useful pool-configuration properties of DBCP's `BasicDataSource`.

In this case, you've configured the pool to start with five connections. Should more connections be needed, `BasicDataSource` is allowed to create them, up to a maximum of 10 active connections.

Table 10.3   `BasicDataSource`'s pool-configuration properties

Pool-configuration property	What it specifies
`initialSize`	The number of connections created when the pool is started.
`maxActive`	The maximum number of connections that can be allocated from the pool at the same time. If 0, there's no limit.
`maxIdle`	The maximum number of connections that can be idle in the pool without extras being released. If 0, there's no limit.
`maxOpenPreparedStatements`	The maximum number of prepared statements that can be allocated from the statement pool at the same time. If 0, there's no limit.
`maxWait`	How long the pool will wait for a connection to be returned to the pool (when there are no available connections) before an exception is thrown. If 1, wait indefinitely.
`minEvictableIdleTimeMillis`	How long a connection can remain idle in the pool before it's eligible for eviction.
`minIdle`	The minimum number of connections that can remain idle in the pool without new connections being created.
`poolPreparedStatements`	Whether or not to pool prepared statements (Boolean).

10.2.3 *Using JDBC driver-based data sources*

The simplest data source you can configure in Spring is one that's defined through a JDBC driver. Spring offers three such data-source classes to choose from (all in the `org.springframework.jdbc.datasource` package):

- `DriverManagerDataSource`—Returns a new connection every time a connection is requested. Unlike DBCP's `BasicDataSource`, the connections provided by `DriverManagerDataSource` aren't pooled.

- `SimpleDriverDataSource`—Works much the same as `DriverManagerData-Source` except that it works with the JDBC driver directly to overcome class loading issues that may arise in certain environments, such as in an OSGi container.

- `SingleConnectionDataSource`—Returns the same connection every time a connection is requested. Although `SingleConnectionDataSource` isn't exactly a pooled data source, you can think of it as a data source with a pool of exactly one connection.

Configuring any of these data sources is similar to how you configured DBCP's `Basic-DataSource`. For example, here's how you'd configure a `DriverManagerDataSource` bean:

```
@Bean
public DataSource dataSource() {
  DriverManagerDataSource ds = new DriverManagerDataSource();
  ds.setDriverClassName("org.h2.Driver");
  ds.setUrl("jdbc:h2:tcp://localhost/~/spitter");
  ds.setUsername("sa");
  ds.setPassword("");
  return ds;
}
```

In XML, the `DriverManagerDataSource` can be configured as follows:

```
<bean id="dataSource"
  class="org.springframework.jdbc.datasource.DriverManagerDataSource"
  p:driverClassName="org.h2.Driver"
  p:url="jdbc:h2:tcp://localhost/~/spitter"
  p:uscrname="sa"
  p:password="" />
```

The only significant difference with these data-source beans as compared to the pooling data-source beans is that because they don't provide a connection pool, there are no pool configuration properties to set.

Although these data sources are great for small applications and running in development, you should seriously consider the implications of using them in a production application. Because `SingleConnectionDataSource` has one and only one database connection to work with, it doesn't work well in multithreaded applications and is best limited to use in testing. At the same time, even though `DriverManager-DataSource` and `SimpleDriverDataSource` are both capable of supporting multiple threads, they incur a performance cost for creating a new connection each time a connection is requested. Because of these limitations, I strongly recommend using pooled data sources.

10.2.4 *Using an embedded data source*

There's one more data source I want to tell you about: the embedded database. An embedded database runs as part of your application instead of as a separate database server that your application connects to. Although it's not very useful in production settings, an embedded database is a perfect choice for development and testing purposes. That's because it allows you to populate your database with test data that's reset every time you restart your application or run your tests.

Spring's `jdbc` namespace makes configuring an embedded database simple. For example, the following listing shows how to use the `jdbc` namespace to configure an embedded H2 database that's preloaded with a set of test data.

Listing 10.1   Configuring an embedded database using the `jdbc` namespace

```
<?xml version="1.0" encoding="UTF-
    8"?> <beans xmlns="http://www.springframework.org/schema/beans"
  xmlns:xsi="http://www.w3.org/2001/XMLSchema-instance"
  xmlns:jdbc="http://www.springframework.org/schema/jdbc"
  xmlns:c="http://www.springframework.org/schema/c"
  xsi:schemaLocation="http://www.springframework.org/schema/jdbc
    http://www.springframework.org/schema/jdbc/spring-jdbc-3.1.xsd
      http://www.springframework.org/schema/beans
      http://www.springframework.org/schema/beans/spring-beans.xsd">
...

  <jdbc:embedded-
     database id="dataSource" type="H2">     <jdbc:script location="com/habum
     a/spitter/db/jdbc/schema.sql"/>     <jdbc:script location="com/habuma/sp
     itter/db/jdbc/test-data.sql"/>    </jdbc:embedded-database>
...

</beans>
```

The `<jdbc:embedded-database>`'s `type` property is set to `H2` to indicate that the embedded database should be an H2 database. (Be sure to have H2 in your application's classpath.) Alternatively, you may set `type` to `DERBY` to use an embedded Apache Derby database.

In `<jdbc:embedded-database>`, you may configure zero or more `<jdbc:script>` elements to set up the database. Listing 10.1 includes two `<jdbc:script>` elements: the first references schema.sql, which contains SQL to create the tables in the database; the second references test-data.sql, to populate the database with test data.

In addition to setting up an embedded database, the `<jdbc:embedded-database>` element also exposes a data source that can be used like any of the other data-source beans you've seen. The `id` attribute is set to `dataSource`, which will be the ID of the exposed data-source bean. Therefore, anywhere you need a `javax.sql.DataSource`, you can inject the `dataSource` bean.

When you configure an embedded database in Java configuration, there isn't the convenience of the `jdbc` namespace. Instead, you can use `EmbeddedDatabaseBuilder` to construct the `DataSource`:

```java
@Bean
public DataSource dataSource() {
  return new EmbeddedDatabaseBuilder()
      .setType(EmbeddedDatabaseType.H2)
      .addScript("classpath:schema.sql")
      .addScript("classpath:test-data.sql")
      .build();
}
```

As you can see, the `setType()` method is the equivalent to the `<jdbc:embedded-database>` element's `type` attribute. And instead of using the `<jdbc:script>` element to specify initialization SQL, you can call `addScript()`.

10.2.5 *Using profiles to select a data source*

You've seen a handful of different ways to configure data sources in Spring, and I'll bet you've identified one or two of them that seem appropriate for your application. In fact, you probably see a need for one of those data-source beans in one environment and a different one in another environment.

For example, the `<jdbc:embedded-database>` element is great for development time. But you may want to use DBCP's `BasicDataSource` in your QA environment. And perhaps you need to use `<jee:jndi-lookup>` in your production deployment.

Spring's bean-profiles feature that we discussed in chapter 3 is perfect here. All you need to do is configure each of these data sources in different profiles, as shown next.

Listing 10.2 Spring profiles enabling selection of a data source at runtime

```java
package com.habuma.spittr.config;
import org.apache.commons.dbcp.BasicDataSource;
import javax.sql.DataSource;
import org.springframework.context.annotation.Bean;
import org.springframework.context.annotation.Configuration;
import org.springframework.context.annotation.Profile;
import
  org.springframework.jdbc.datasource.embedded.EmbeddedDatabaseBuilder;
import
  org.springframework.jdbc.datasource.embedded.EmbeddedDatabaseType;
import org.springframework.jndi.JndiObjectFactoryBean;

@Configuration
public class DataSourceConfiguration {

  @Profile("development")                    // Development
  @Bean                                      // data source
  public DataSource embeddedDataSource() {
    return new EmbeddedDatabaseBuilder()
```

```
      .setType(EmbeddedDatabaseType.H2)
      .addScript("classpath:schema.sql")
      .addScript("classpath:test-data.sql")
      .build();
  }

  @Profile("qa")                              <─── QA data source
  @Bean
  public DataSource Data() {
    BasicDataSource ds = new BasicDataSource();
    ds.setDriverClassName("org.h2.Driver");
    ds.setUrl("jdbc:h2:tcp://localhost/~/spitter");
    ds.setUsername("sa");
    ds.setPassword("");
    ds.setInitialSize(5);
    ds.setMaxActive(10);
    return ds;
  }

  @Profile("production")                      <─── Production data source
  @Bean
  public DataSource dataSource() {
    JndiObjectFactoryBean jndiObjectFactoryBean
                                = new JndiObjectFactoryBean();
    jndiObjectFactoryBean.setJndiName("jdbc/SpittrDS");
    jndiObjectFactoryBean.setResourceRef(true);
    jndiObjectFactoryBean.setProxyInterface(javax.sql.DataSource.class);
    return (DataSource) jndiObjectFactoryBean.getObject();
  }
}
```

Using profiles, the data source is chosen at runtime, based on which profile is active. As configured in listing 10.2, the embedded database is created if and only if the development profile is active. Similarly, the DBCP BasicDataSource is created if and only if the qa profile is active. And the data source is retrieved from JNDI if and only if the production profile is active.

For the sake of completeness, the following listing shows the same profile-driven configuration using Spring XML configuration instead of Java configuration.

> **Listing 10.3 Configuring profile-selected data sources in XML**

```
<?xml version="1.0" encoding="UTF-
    8"?> <beans xmlns="http://www.springframework.org/schema/beans"
  xmlns:xsi="http://www.w3.org/2001/XMLSchema-instance"
  xmlns:jdbc="http://www.springframework.org/schema/jdbc"
  xmlns:jee="http://www.springframework.org/schema/jee"
  xmlns:p="http://www.springframework.org/schema/p"
  xsi:schemaLocation="http://www.springframework.org/schema/jdbc
    http://www.springframework.org/schema/jdbc/spring-jdbc-3.1.xsd
  http://www.springframework.org/schema/jee
  http://www.springframework.org/schema/jee/spring-jee-3.1.xsd
  http://www.springframework.org/schema/beans
    http://www.springframework.org/schema/beans/spring-beans.xsd">
```
Development
data source └─▷ `<beans profile="development">`

```
    <jdbc:embedded-
      database id="dataSource" type="H2">        <jdbc:script location="com/hab
    uma/spitter/db/jdbc/schema.sql"/>          <jdbc:script location="com/habum
    a/spitter/db/jdbc/test-data.sql"/>         </jdbc:embedded-
    database>     </beans>
  <beans profile="qa">                          ⟵── QA data source
    <bean id="dataSource"
          class="org.apache.commons.dbcp.BasicDataSource"
      p:driverClassName="org.h2.Driver"
      p:url="jdbc:h2:tcp://localhost/~/spitter"
      p:username="sa"
      p:password=""
      p:initialSize="5"
      p:maxActive="10" />    </beans>
  <beans profile="production">                  ⟵── Production data source
    <jee:jndi-lookup id="dataSource"
                     jndi-name="/jdbc/SpitterDS"
                     resource-ref="true" />    </beans>
</beans>
```

Now that you've established a connection to the database through a data source, you're ready to access the database. As I've already mentioned, Spring affords you several options for working with relational databases, including JDBC, Hibernate, and the Java Persistence API (JPA). In the next section, you'll see how to build the persistence layer of a Spring application using Spring's support for JDBC. But if Hibernate or JPA is more your style, feel free to jump ahead to the next chapter where those are the topics.

10.3 *Using JDBC with Spring*

There are many persistence technologies. Hibernate, iBATIS, and JPA are just a few. Despite this, a good number of applications write Java objects to a database the old-fashioned way: they earn it. No, wait—that's how people make money. The tried-and-true method for persisting data is with good old JDBC.

And why not? JDBC doesn't require mastering another framework's query language. It's built on top of SQL, which is the data-access language. Plus, you can more finely tune the performance of your data access when you use JDBC than with practically any other technology. And JDBC allows you to take advantage of your database's proprietary features, where other frameworks may discourage or flat-out prohibit this.

What's more, JDBC lets you work with data at a much lower level than the persistence frameworks. You're in full control of how your application reads and manipulates data. This includes allowing you to access and manipulate individual columns in a database. This fine-grained approach to data access comes in handy in applications, such as reporting applications, where it doesn't make sense to organize the data into objects just to then unwind it back into raw data.

But all is not sunny in the world of JDBC. With its power, flexibility, and other niceties also come some not-so-niceties.

10.3.1 *Tackling runaway JDBC code*

Although JDBC gives you an API that works closely with your database, you're responsible for handling everything related to accessing the database. This includes managing database resources and handling exceptions. If you've ever written JDBC that inserts data into the database, the following code shouldn't be too alien to you.

Listing 10.4   Using JDBC to insert a row into a database

```
private static final String SQL_INSERT_SPITTER =
 "insert into spitter (username, password, fullname) values (?, ?, ?)";
private DataSource dataSource;
public void addSpitter(Spitter spitter) {
  Connection conn = null;
  PreparedStatement stmt = null;
  try {
    conn = dataSource.getConnection();                           ⟵  Get
                                                                     connection
    stmt = conn.prepareStatement(SQL_INSERT_SPITTER);     ⟵  Create statement
    stmt.setString(1, spitter.getUsername());              ⟵  Bind
    stmt.setString(2, spitter.getPassword());                 parameters
    stmt.setString(3, spitter.getFullName());
    stmt.execute();
  } catch (SQLException e) {
    // do something...not sure what, though              ⟵  Handle
  } finally {                                                  exceptions
    try {                                                      (somehow)
      if (stmt != null) {            ⟵  Clean up
        stmt.close();
      }
      if (conn != null) {
        conn.close();
      }
    } catch (SQLException e) {
      // I'm even less sure about what to do here
    }
  }
}
```

Execute statement → `stmt.execute();`

Holy runaway code, Batman! That's more than 20 lines of code to insert an object into a database. As far as JDBC operations go, this is about as simple as it gets. So why does it take this many lines to do something so straightforward? Actually, it doesn't. Only a handful of lines do the insert. But JDBC requires that you properly manage connections and statements and somehow handle the SQLException that may be thrown.

Speaking of that SQLException, not only is it not clear how you should handle it (because it's not clear what went wrong), but you're forced to catch it twice! You must catch it if something goes wrong while inserting a record, and you have to catch it again if something goes wrong when closing the statement and connection. Seems like a lot of work to handle something that usually can't be handled programmatically.

Now look at the next listing, where you use traditional JDBC to update a row in the `Spitter` table in the database.

Listing 10.5 Using JDBC to update a row in a database

```
private static final String SQL_UPDATE_SPITTER =
        "update spitter set username = ?, password = ?, fullname = ?"
        + "where id = ?";
public void saveSpitter(Spitter spitter) {
  Connection conn = null;
  PreparedStatement stmt = null;
  try {
    conn = dataSource.getConnection();                      ◁─┐  Get
                                                               │  connection
    stmt = conn.prepareStatement(SQL_UPDATE_SPITTER);     ◁──  Create statement
    stmt.setString(1, spitter.getUsername());             ◁─┐  Bind
    stmt.setString(2, spitter.getPassword());                │  parameters
    stmt.setString(3, spitter.getFullName());
    stmt.setLong(4, spitter.getId());
    stmt.execute();
  } catch (SQLException e) {
    // Still not sure what I'm supposed to do here           ◁─┐  Handle
  } finally {                                                   │  exceptions
    try {                                                       │  (somehow)
      if (stmt != null) {            ◁──  Clean up
        stmt.close();
      }
      if (conn != null) {
        conn.close();
      }
    } catch (SQLException e) {
      // or here
    }
  }
}
```

Execute statement └▷ `stmt.execute();`

At first glance, listing 10.5 may appear to be identical to listing 10.4. In fact, disregarding the SQL `String` and the line where the statement is created, they're identical. Again, that's a lot of code to do something as simple as update a single row in a database. What's more, that's a lot of repeated code. Ideally, you'd only have to write the lines that are specific to the task at hand. After all, those are the only lines that distinguish listing 10.5 from listing 10.4. The rest is boilerplate code.

To round out our tour of conventional JDBC, let's see how you might retrieve data from the database. As you can see here, that's not pretty, either.

Listing 10.6   Using JDBC to query a row from a database

```
private static final String SQL_SELECT_SPITTER =
    "select id, username, fullname from spitter where id = ?";
public Spitter findOne(long id) {
  Connection conn = null;
  PreparedStatement stmt = null;
  ResultSet rs = null;
  try {
    conn = dataSource.getConnection();                  ⟵┐ Get connection
    stmt = conn.prepareStatement(SQL_SELECT_SPITTER);   ⟵ Create statement
    stmt.setLong(1, id)            ⟵┐
    rs = stmt.executeQuery();         Bind parameters
    Spitter spitter = null;
    if (rs.next()) {               ⟵ Process results
      spitter = new Spitter();
      spitter.setId(rs.getLong("id"));
      spitter.setUsername(rs.getString("username"));
      spitter.setPassword(rs.getString("password"));
      spitter.setFullName(rs.getString("fullname"));
    }
    return spitter;
  } catch (SQLException e) {        ⟵ Handle exceptions (somehow)
  } finally {
    if(rs != null) {
      try {
        rs.close();
      } catch(SQLException e) {}
    }

    if(stmt != null) {
      try {
      stmt.close();                              Clean up
      } catch(SQLException e) {}
    }

    if(conn != null) {
      try {
        conn.close();
      } catch(SQLException e) {}
    }
  }
  return null;
}
```

Execute query points to `rs = stmt.executeQuery();`

That's almost as verbose as the insert and update examples—maybe more. It's like the Pareto principle flipped on its head: 20% of the code is needed to query a row, whereas 80% is boilerplate.

By now you should see that much of JDBC code is boilerplate for creating connections and statements and handling exceptions. With my point made, I'll end the torture and not make you look at any more of this nasty code.

The fact is that all that JDBC boilerplate code is important. Cleaning up resources and handling errors is what makes data access robust. Without it, errors would go undetected and resources would be left open, leading to unpredictable code and resource leaks. So not only do you need this code, but you also need to make sure it's correct. This is all the more reason to let a framework deal with the boilerplate so you know that it's written once and written right.

10.3.2 *Working with JDBC templates*

Spring's JDBC framework will clean up your JDBC code by shouldering the burden of resource management and exception handling. This leaves you free to write only the code necessary to move data to and from the database.

As I explained in the previous section, Spring abstracts away the boilerplate data-access code behind template classes. For JDBC, Spring comes with three template classes to choose from:

- `JdbcTemplate`—The most basic of Spring's JDBC templates, this class provides simple access to a database through JDBC and indexed-parameter queries.
- `NamedParameterJdbcTemplate`—This JDBC template class enables you to perform queries where values are bound to named parameters in SQL, rather than indexed parameters.
- `SimpleJdbcTemplate`—This version of the JDBC template takes advantage of Java 5 features such as autoboxing, generics, and variable parameter lists to simplify how a JDBC template is used.

At one time, you had to weigh your choice of JDBC template carefully. But starting with Spring 3.1, the decision became easier. `SimpleJdbcTemplate` has been deprecated and its Java 5 features have been rolled into `JdbcTemplate`. Moreover, you only need `NamedParameterJdbcTemplate` when you want to work with named parameters in queries. That leaves good ol' `JdbcTemplate` as your go-to option for most JDBC work—that's the option I'll focus on in this section.

INSERTING DATA USING JDBCTEMPLATE

All that a `JdbcTemplate` needs in order to do its work is a `DataSource`. This makes it easy enough to configure a `JdbcTemplate` bean in Spring with the following `@Bean` method:

```
@Bean
public JdbcTemplate jdbcTemplate(DataSource dataSource) {
  return new JdbcTemplate(dataSource);
}
```

Here, the `DataSource` is injected via constructor injection. The `dataSource` bean being referenced can be any implementation of `javax.sql.DataSource`, including those you created in section 10.2.

Now you can wire the `jdbcTemplate` bean into your repository and use it to access the database. For example, suppose the Spitter repository is written to use `JdbcTemplate`:

```
@Repository
public class JdbcSpitterRepository implements SpitterRepository {

  private JdbcOperations jdbcOperations;

  @Inject
  public JdbcSpitterRepository(JdbcOperations jdbcOperations) {
    this.jdbcOperations = jdbcOperations;
  }

  ...

}
```

Here JdbcSpitterRepository is annotated with @Repository, which qualifies it to be automatically created by component-scanning. And its constructor is annotated with @Inject so that when it's created, it will be given a JdbcOperations object. Jdbc-Operations is an interface defining operations implemented by JdbcTemplate. By injecting a JdbcOperations instead of the concrete JdbcTemplate, JdbcSpitter-Repository is able to remain loosely coupled to JdbcTemplate via the Jdbc-Operations interface.

As an alternative to component-scanning and autowiring, you could explicitly declare JdbcSpitterRepository as a bean in Spring, like this:

```
@Bean
public SpitterRepository spitterRepository(JdbcTemplate jdbcTemplate) {
  return new JdbcSpitterRepository(jdbcTemplate);
}
```

With a JdbcTemplate at your repository's disposal, you can greatly simplify the addSpitter() method from listing 10.4. The new JdbcTemplate-based addSpitter() method is as follows.

Listing 10.7 JdbcTemplate-based addSpitter() method

```
public void addSpitter(Spitter spitter) {
    jdbcOperations.update(INSERT_SPITTER,          ⟵── Insert Spitter

        spitter.getUsername(),
        spitter.getPassword(),
        spitter.getFullName(),
        spitter.getEmail(),
        spitter.isUpdateByEmail());
}
```

I think you'll agree that this version of addSpitter() is significantly simpler. There's no more connection or statement-creation code—and no more exception-handling code. There's nothing but pure data-insertion goodness.

Just because you don't see a lot of boilerplate code doesn't mean it's not there. It's cleverly hidden in the JDBC template class. When the update() method is called, JdbcTemplate gets a connection, creates a statement, and executes the insert SQL.

What you also don't see is how the SQLException is handled. Internally, Jdbc-Template catches any SQLExceptions that may be thrown. It then translates the generic SQLException into one of the more specific data-access exceptions from table 10.1 and rethrows it. Because Spring's data-access exceptions are all runtime exceptions, you don't have to catch them in the addSpitter() method.

READING DATA WITH JDBCTEMPLATE

Reading data is also simplified with JdbcTemplate. Listing 10.8 shows a new version of findOne() that uses JdbcTemplate callbacks to query for a Spitter by ID and map the result set to a Spitter object.

> **Listing 10.8 Querying for a Spitter using JdbcTemplate**

```
public Spitter findOne(long id) {
    return jdbcOperations.queryForObject(          ⟵— Query for Spitter
            SELECT_SPITTER_BY_ID, new SpitterRowMapper(),
            id            ⟵┐
            );                    │ Map results
}                                 │ to object
...

private static final class SpitterRowMapper
                    implements RowMapper<Spitter> {
  public Spitter mapRow(ResultSet rs, int rowNum)
                                    throws SQLException {
    return new Spitter(              ⟵┐
        rs.getLong("id"),           │ Bind
        rs.getString("username"),   │ parameters
        rs.getString("password"),
        rs.getString("fullName"),
        rs.getString("email"),
        rs.getBoolean("updateByEmail"));
  }
}
```

This findOne() method uses JdbcTemplate's queryForObject() method to query for a Spitter from the database. The queryForObject() method takes three parameters:

- A String containing the SQL to be used to select the data from the database
- A RowMapper object that extracts values from a ResultSet and constructs a domain object (in this case, a Spitter)
- A variable argument list of values to be bound to indexed parameters of the query

The real magic happens in the SpitterRowMapper object, which implements the Row-Mapper interface. For every row that results from the query, JdbcTemplate calls the mapRow() method of the RowMapper, passing in a ResultSet and an integer carrying the row number. In SpitterRowMapper's mapRow() method is the code that creates a Spitter object and populates it with values from the ResultSet.

Just like addSpitter(), the findOne() method is free of JDBC boilerplate code. Unlike traditional JDBC, there's no resource-management or exception-handling code. Methods that use JdbcTemplate are laser focused on retrieving a Spitter object from the database.

USING JAVA 8 LAMBDAS WITH JDBCTEMPLATE

Because the RowMapper interface only declares the addRow() method, it fits the bill for a *functional interface*. This means that if you're developing your application using Java 8, you can express the RowMapper implementation with a lambda instead of with a concrete class implementation.

For example, the findOne() method in listing 10.8 can be rewritten using Java 8 lambdas like this:

```
public Spitter findOne(long id) {
  return jdbcOperations.queryForObject(
    SELECT_SPITTER_BY_ID,
    (rs, rowNum) -&gt; {
      return new Spitter(
        rs.getLong("id"),
        rs.getString("username"),
        rs.getString("password"),
        rs.getString("fullName"),
        rs.getString("email"),
        rs.getBoolean("updateByEmail"));
    },
    id);
}
```

As you can see, the lambda is easier on the eyes than a full-blown RowMapper implementation, but it's just as effective. Java coerces the lambda into a RowMapper for the sake of satisfying the parameter it's being passed into.

Alternatively, you can use Java 8 method references to define the mapping in a separate method:

```
public Spitter findOne(long id) {
  return jdbcOperations.queryForObject(
    SELECT_SPITTER_BY_ID, this::mapSpitter, id);
}

private Spitter mapSpitter(ResultSet rs, int row) throws SQLException {
    return new Spitter(
      rs.getLong("id"),
      rs.getString("username"),
      rs.getString("password"),
      rs.getString("fullName"),
      rs.getString("email"),
      rs.getBoolean("updateByEmail"));
}
```

In either event, you don't have to explicitly implement the RowMapper interface. You must provide a lambda or method that takes the same parameters and returns the same type as if you had implemented RowMapper.

USING NAMED PARAMETERS

The addSpitter() method in listing 10.7 uses indexed parameters. This means you have to notice the order of the parameters in the query and list the values in the correct order when passing them to the update() method. If you ever changed the SQL in such a way that the order of the parameters changed, you'd also need to change the order of the values.

Optionally, you could use named parameters. Named parameters let you give each parameter in the SQL an explicit name and refer to the parameter by that name when binding values to the statement. For example, suppose the SQL_INSERT_SPITTER query were defined as follows:

```
private static final String SQL_INSERT_SPITTER =
    "insert into spitter (username, password, fullname) " +
    "values (:username, :password, :fullname)";
```

With named-parameter queries, the order of the bound values isn't important. You can bind each value by name. If the query changes and the order of the parameters is no longer the same, you won't have to change the binding code.

Spring's NamedParameterJdbcTemplate is a special JDBC template class that supports working with named parameters. NamedParameterJdbcTemplate can be declared in Spring in much the same way as the regular JdbcTemplate:

```
@Bean
public NamedParameterJdbcTemplate jdbcTemplate(DataSource dataSource) {
  return new NamedParameterJdbcTemplate(dataSource);
}
```

Had you injected a NamedParameterJdbcOperations (the interface that Named-ParameterJdbcTemplate implements) into your repository instead of JdbcOperations, your addSpitter() method might look like this.

Listing 10.9 Using named parameters with Spring JDBC templates

```
private static final String INSERT_SPITTER =
    "insert into Spitter " +
    "    (username, password, fullname, email, updateByEmail) " +
    "values " +
    "    (:username, :password, :fullname, :email, :updateByEmail)";

public void addSpitter(Spitter spitter) {
    Map<String, Object> paramMap = new HashMap<String, Object>();
    paramMap.put("username", spitter.getUsername());     ⟵ Bind parameters
    paramMap.put("password", spitter.getPassword());
    paramMap.put("fullname", spitter.getFullName());
    paramMap.put("email", spitter.getEmail());
    paramMap.put("updateByEmail", spitter.isUpdateByEmail());

    jdbcOperations.update(INSERT_SPITTER, paramMap);     ⟵ Perform insert
}
```

The first thing you'll notice is that this version of addSpitter() is longer than the previous version. That's because named parameters are bound through a java.util.Map.

Nevertheless, every line is focused on the goal of inserting a `Spitter` object into the database. There's still no resource-management or exception-handling code cluttering up the chief purpose of the method.

10.4   Summary

Data is the lifeblood of an application. Some of the data-centric among you may even contend that data *is* the application. With such significance placed on data, it's important that you develop the data-access portion of your applications in a way that's robust, simple, and clear.

JDBC is the most basic way to work with relational data in Java. But as defined in the specification, JDBC can be somewhat unwieldy. Spring takes much of the pain out of working with JDBC, eliminating boilerplate code and simplifying JDBC exception handling, leaving you little more to deal with than writing the SQL that should be performed.

In this chapter, we looked at Spring's support for data persistence. We also looked at Spring's template-based abstraction for JDBC, which greatly simplifies working with JDBC.

Coming up in the next chapter, we'll continue our survey of Spring's data-persistence support by looking at Spring's facilities for the Java Persistence API.

Persisting data with object-relational mapping

11

> ## This chapter covers
> - Working with Spring and Hibernate
> - Writing Spring-free repositories with contextual sessions
> - Using JPA with Spring
> - Automatic JPA repositories with Spring Data

When we were kids, riding a bike was fun, wasn't it? We'd ride to school in the mornings. When school let out, we'd cruise to our best friend's house. When it got late and our parents were yelling at us for staying out past dark, we'd peddle home for the night. Gee, those days were fun.

Then we grew up, and now we need more than a bike. Sometimes we have to travel a long distance to work. Groceries have to be hauled, and our kids need to get to soccer practice. And if we live in Texas, air conditioning is a must! Our needs have outgrown our bikes.

JDBC is the bike of the persistence world. It's great for what it does, and for some jobs it works fine. But as applications become more complex, so do our persistence requirements. We need to be able to map object properties to database columns

305

and have our statements and queries created for us, freeing us from typing an endless string of question marks. We also need features that are more sophisticated:

- *Lazy loading*—As object graphs become more complex, you sometimes don't want to fetch entire relationships immediately. To use a typical example, suppose you're selecting a collection of `PurchaseOrder` objects, and each of these objects contains a collection of `LineItem` objects. If you're only interested in `PurchaseOrder` attributes, it makes no sense to grab the `LineItem` data. That could be expensive. Lazy loading allows you to grab data only as it's needed.

- *Eager fetching*—This is the opposite of lazy loading. Eager fetching allows you to grab an entire object graph in one query. In the cases where you know you need a `PurchaseOrder` object and its associated `LineItems`, eager fetching lets you get this from the database in one operation, saving you from costly round-trips.

- *Cascading*—Sometimes changes to a database table should result in changes to other tables as well. Going back to the purchase order example, when an `Order` object is deleted, you also want to delete the associated `LineItems` from the database.

Several frameworks are available that provide these services. The general name for these services is *object-relational mapping* (ORM). Using an ORM tool for your persistence layer can save you literally thousands of lines of code and hours of development time. This lets you switch your focus from writing error-prone SQL code to addressing your application's requirements.

Spring provides support for several persistence frameworks, including Hibernate, iBATIS, Java Data Objects (JDO), and the Java Persistence API (JPA). As with Spring's JDBC support, Spring's support for ORM frameworks provides integration points to the frameworks as well as some additional services:

- Integrated support for Spring declarative transactions
- Transparent exception handling
- Thread-safe, lightweight template classes
- DAO support classes
- Resource management

I don't have enough space in this chapter to cover all the ORM frameworks that are supported by Spring. But that's okay, because Spring's support for one ORM solution is similar to the next. Once you get the hang of using one ORM framework with Spring, you'll find it easy to switch to another.

In this chapter, we'll look at how Spring integrates with two of the most commonly used ORM solutions: Hibernate and JPA. You'll also get your first look at the Spring Data project by looking at Spring Data JPA. In doing so, you'll not only learn how Spring Data JPA can take away a lot of the boilerplate code in your JPA repositories, but you'll also have a foundation to build on in the next chapter when we look at using Spring Data for schemaless storage options.

Let's get started by exploring Spring's support for Hibernate.

11.1 Integrating Hibernate with Spring

Hibernate is an open source persistence framework that has gained significant popularity in the developer community. It provides not only basic object-relational mapping but also all the other sophisticated features you'd expect from a full-featured ORM tool, such as caching, lazy loading, eager fetching, and distributed caching.

In this section, we'll focus on how Spring integrates with Hibernate, without dwelling too much on the intricate details of using Hibernate. If you need to learn more about working with Hibernate, I recommend either *Java Persistence with Hibernate, Second Edition* by Christian Bauer, Gavin King, and Gary Gregory (Manning, 2014, www.manning.com/bauer3/) or the Hibernate website at www.hibernate.org.

11.1.1 Declaring a Hibernate session factory

Natively, the main interface for working with Hibernate is `org.hibernate.Session`. The `Session` interface provides basic data-access functionality such as the ability to save, update, delete, and load objects from the database. Through the Hibernate `Session`, an application's repository performs all of its persistence needs.

The standard way to get a reference to a Hibernate `Session` object is through an implementation of Hibernate's `SessionFactory` interface. Among other things, `SessionFactory` is responsible for opening, closing, and managing Hibernate `Session`s.

In Spring, the way to get a Hibernate `SessionFactory` is through one of Spring's Hibernate session-factory beans. As of version 3.1, Spring comes with three session-factory beans to choose from:

- `org.springframework.orm.hibernate3.LocalSessionFactoryBean`
- `org.springframework.orm.hibernate3.annotation.AnnotationSession-FactoryBean`
- `org.springframework.orm.hibernate4.LocalSessionFactoryBean`

These session-factory beans are implementations of Spring's `FactoryBean` interface that produce a Hibernate `SessionFactory` when wired into any property of type `SessionFactory`. This makes it possible to configure your Hibernate session factory alongside the other beans in your application's Spring context.

Choosing which of these session factory beans to use comes down to which version of Hibernate you're using and whether you'll be defining your object-to-database mapping in XML or using annotations. If you're using Hibernate 3.2 or higher (up to but not including Hibernate 4.0) and doing the mapping in XML, you'll need to configure `LocalSessionFactoryBean` from the `org.springframework.orm.hibernate3` package in Spring:

```
@Bean
public LocalSessionFactoryBean sessionFactory(DataSource dataSource) {
  LocalSessionFactoryBean sfb = new LocalSessionFactoryBean();
  sfb.setDataSource(dataSource);
  sfb.setMappingResources(new String[] { "Spitter.hbm.xml" });
  Properties props = new Properties();
```

```
props.setProperty("dialect", "org.hibernate.dialect.H2Dialect");
sfb.setHibernateProperties(props);
return sfb;
}
```

`LocalSessionFactoryBean` is configured here with three properties. The `dataSource` property is wired with a reference to a `DataSource` bean. The `mappingResources` property lists one or more Hibernate mapping files that define the persistence strategy for the application. Finally, `hibernateProperties` is where you configure the minutia of how Hibernate should operate. In this case, you're saying that Hibernate will be working with an H2 database and should use the `H2Dialect` to construct SQL accordingly.

If annotation-oriented persistence is more your style, and if you're not yet using Hibernate 4, then you'll want to use `AnnotationSessionFactoryBean` instead of `LocalSessionFactoryBean`:

```
@Bean
public AnnotationSessionFactoryBean sessionFactory(DataSource ds) {
  AnnotationSessionFactoryBean sfb = new AnnotationSessionFactoryBean();
  sfb.setDataSource(ds);
  sfb.setPackagesToScan(new String[] { "com.habuma.spittr.domain" });
  Properties props = new Properties();
  props.setProperty("dialect", "org.hibernate.dialect.H2Dialect");
  sfb.setHibernateProperties(props);
  return sfb;
}
```

Or, if you're using Hibernate 4, you should use the `LocalSessionFactoryBean` from the `org.springframework.orm.hibernate4` package. Although it shares a name with the `LocalSessionFactoryBean` from the Hibernate 3 package, this new session factory bean added in Spring 3.1 is like a mashup of the Hibernate 3 `LocalSessionFactory-Bean` and `AnnotationSessionFactoryBean`. It has many of the same properties and can be configured for either XML-based mapping or annotation-based mapping. Here's how you'd configure it for annotation-based mapping:

```
@Bean
public LocalSessionFactoryBean sessionFactory(DataSource dataSource) {
  LocalSessionFactoryBean sfb = new LocalSessionFactoryBean();
  sfb.setDataSource(dataSource);
  sfb.setPackagesToScan(new String[] { "com.habuma.spittr.domain" });
  Properties props = new Properties();
  props.setProperty("dialect", "org.hibernate.dialect.H2Dialect");
  sfb.setHibernateProperties(props);
  return sfb;
}
```

In either case, the `dataSource` and `hibernateProperties` properties specify where to find a database connection and what kind of database you'll be dealing with. But instead of listing Hibernate mapping files, you can use the `packagesToScan` property to tell Spring to scan one or more packages, looking for domain classes that are annotated for persistence with Hibernate. This includes classes that are annotated with JPA's `@Entity` or `@MappedSuperclass` and Hibernate's own `@Entity` annotation.

If you'd prefer, you may also explicitly list all of your application's persistent classes by specifying a list of fully qualified class names in the `annotatedClasses` property:

```
sfb.setAnnotatedClasses(
  new Class<?>[] { Spitter.class, Spittle.class }
);
```

The `annotatedClasses` property is fine for hand-picking a few domain classes. But `packagesToScan` is more appropriate if you have a lot of domain classes and don't want to list them all or if you want the freedom to add or remove domain classes without revisiting the Spring configuration.

With a Hibernate session factory bean declared in the Spring application context, you're ready to start creating your repository classes.

11.1.2 Building Spring-free Hibernate

In the early days of Spring and Hibernate, writing a repository class would involve working with Spring's `HibernateTemplate`. `HibernateTemplate` would ensure that only one Hibernate session would be used per transaction. The downside of this approach is that your repository implementation would be directly coupled to Spring.

The best practice now, however, is to take advantage of Hibernate contextual sessions and not use `HibernateTemplate` at all. This can be done by wiring a Hibernate `SessionFactory` directly into your repository and using it to obtain a session, as shown in the following listing.

Listing 11.1 Spring-free Hibernate repositories, enabled by Hibernate sessions

```
public HibernateSpitterRepository(SessionFactory sessionFactory) {
      this.sessionFactory = sessionFactory;                      ◁─┐ Inject
  }                                                                │ SessionFactory

  private Session currentSession() {
      return sessionFactory.getCurrentSession();   ◁─┐ Retrieve current
  }                                                  │ Session from
                                                     │ SessionFactory
  public long count() {
      return findAll().size();
  }

  public Spitter save(Spitter spitter) {
      Serializable id = currentSession().save(spitter);   ◁─┐ Use current
                                                            │ Session
      return new Spitter((Long) id,
              spitter.getUsername(),
              spitter.getPassword(),
              spitter.getFullName(),
              spitter.getEmail(),
              spitter.isUpdateByEmail());
  }
```

```
public Spitter findOne(long id) {
    return (Spitter) currentSession().get(Spitter.class, id);
}

public Spitter findByUsername(String username) {
    return (Spitter) currentSession()
            .createCriteria(Spitter.class)
            .add(Restrictions.eq("username", username))
            .list().get(0);
}

public List<Spitter> findAll() {
    return (List<Spitter>) currentSession()
            .createCriteria(Spitter.class).list();
}

}
```

There are several things to take note of in listing 11.1. First, you're using the `@Inject` annotation to have Spring automatically inject a `SessionFactory` into `Hibernate-SpitterRepository`'s sessionFactory property. Then, in the `currentSession()` method, you use that `SessionFactory` to get the current transaction's session.

Also note that you annotate the class with `@Repository`. This accomplishes two things. First, `@Repository` is another one of Spring's stereotype annotations that, among other things, are scanned by Spring component-scanning. This means you won't have to explicitly declare a `HibernateSpitterRepository` bean, as long as the repository class is in a package covered by component-scanning.

In addition to helping to reduce explicit configuration, `@Repository` serves another purpose. Recall that one of the jobs of a template class is to catch platform-specific exceptions and rethrow them as one of Spring's unified unchecked exceptions. But if you're using Hibernate contextual sessions and not a Hibernate template, how can the exception translation take place?

To add exception translation to a template-less Hibernate repository, you just need to add a `PersistenceExceptionTranslationPostProcessor` bean to the Spring application context:

```
@Bean
public BeanPostProcessor persistenceTranslation() {
  return new PersistenceExceptionTranslationPostProcessor();
}
```

`PersistenceExceptionTranslationPostProcessor` is a bean post-processor that adds an adviser to any bean that's annotated with `@Repository` so that any platform-specific exceptions are caught and then rethrown as one of Spring's unchecked data-access exceptions.

Now the Hibernate version of your repository is complete. And you were able to develop it without directly depending on any Spring-specific classes (aside from the `@Repository` annotation). That same template-less approach can be applied when developing a pure JPA-based repository. Let's take one more stab at developing a `SpitterRepository` implementation, this time using JPA.

11.2 *Spring and the Java Persistence API*

The Java Persistence API (JPA) emerged out of the rubble of EJB 2's entity beans as the next-generation Java persistence standard. JPA is a POJO-based persistence mechanism that draws ideas from both Hibernate and Java Data Objects (JDO) and mixes Java 5 annotations in for good measure.

With the Spring 2.0 release came the premiere of Spring integration with JPA. The irony is that many blame (or credit) Spring with the demise of EJB. But now that Spring provides support for JPA, many developers are recommending JPA for persistence in Spring-based applications. In fact, some say that Spring-JPA is the dream team for POJO development.

The first step toward using JPA with Spring is to configure an entity manager factory as a bean in the Spring application context.

11.2.1 *Configuring an entity manager factory*

In a nutshell, JPA-based applications use an implementation of `EntityManager-Factory` to get an instance of an `EntityManager`. The JPA specification defines two kinds of entity managers:

- *Application-managed*—Entity managers are created when an application directly requests one from an entity manager factory. With application-managed entity managers, the application is responsible for opening or closing entity managers and involving the entity manager in transactions. This type of entity manager is most appropriate for use in standalone applications that don't run in a Java EE container.

- *Container-managed*—Entity managers are created and managed by a Java EE container. The application doesn't interact with the entity manager factory at all. Instead, entity managers are obtained directly through injection or from JNDI. The container is responsible for configuring the entity manager factories. This type of entity manager is most appropriate for use by a Java EE container that wants to maintain some control over JPA configuration beyond what's specified in persistence.xml.

Both kinds of entity manager implement the same `EntityManager` interface. The key difference isn't in the `EntityManager` itself, but rather in how the `EntityManager` is created and managed. Application-managed `EntityManagers` are created by an `Entity-ManagerFactory` obtained by calling the `createEntityManagerFactory()` method of the `PersistenceProvider`. Meanwhile, container-managed `EntityManagerFactorys` are obtained through `PersistenceProvider`'s `createContainerEntityManager-Factory()` method.

What does this all mean for Spring developers wanting to use JPA? Not much. Regardless of which variety of `EntityManagerFactory` you want to use, Spring will take responsibility for managing `EntityManagers` for you. If you're using an application-managed entity manager, Spring plays the role of an application and transparently deals with the `EntityManager` on your behalf. In the container-managed scenario, Spring plays the role of the container.

Each flavor of entity manager factory is produced by a corresponding Spring factory bean:

- `LocalEntityManagerFactoryBean` produces an application-managed `Entity-ManagerFactory`.
- `LocalContainerEntityManagerFactoryBean` produces a container-managed `EntityManagerFactory`.

It's important to point out that the choice made between an application-managed `EntityManagerFactory` and a container-managed `EntityManagerFactory` is completely transparent to a Spring-based application. When you're working with Spring and JPA, the intricate details of dealing with either form of `EntityManagerFactory` are hidden, leaving your data-access code to focus on its true purpose: data access.

The only real difference between application-managed and container-managed entity manager factories, as far as Spring is concerned, is how each is configured in the Spring application context. Let's start by looking at how to configure the application-managed `LocalEntityManagerFactoryBean` in Spring. Then you'll see how to configure a container-managed `LocalContainerEntityManagerFactoryBean`.

CONFIGURING APPLICATION-MANAGED JPA

Application-managed entity-manager factories derive most of their configuration information from a configuration file called persistence.xml. This file must appear in the META-INF directory in the classpath.

The purpose of the persistence.xml file is to define one or more persistence units. A *persistence unit* is a grouping of one or more persistent classes that correspond to a single data source. In simple terms, persistence.xml enumerates one or more persistent classes along with any additional configuration such as data sources and XML-based mapping files. Here's a typical example of a persistence.xml file as it pertains to the Spittr application:

```
<persistence xmlns="http://java.sun.com/xml/ns/persistence"
     version="1.0">
  <persistence-unit name="spitterPU">
    <class>com.habuma.spittr.domain.Spitter</class>
    <class>com.habuma.spittr.domain.Spittle</class>
    <properties>
      <property name="toplink.jdbc.driver"
          value="org.hsqldb.jdbcDriver" />
      <property name="toplink.jdbc.url" value=
          "jdbc:hsqldb:hsql://localhost/spitter/spitter" />
      <property name="toplink.jdbc.user"
          value="sa" />
      <property name="toplink.jdbc.password"
          value="" />
    </properties>
  </persistence-unit>
</persistence>
```

Because so much configuration goes into a persistence.xml file, little configuration is required (or even possible) in Spring. The following <bean> declares a LocalEntity-ManagerFactoryBean in Spring:

```
@Bean
public LocalEntityManagerFactoryBean entityManagerFactoryBean() {
  LocalEntityManagerFactoryBean emfb
      = new LocalEntityManagerFactoryBean();
  emfb.setPersistenceUnitName("spitterPU");
  return emfb;
}
```

The value given to the persistenceUnitName property refers to the persistence unit name as it appears in persistence.xml.

The reason much of what goes into creating an application-managed Entity-ManagerFactory is contained in persistence.xml has everything to do with what it means to be application-managed. In the application-managed scenario (not involving Spring), an application is entirely responsible for obtaining an EntityManager-Factory through the JPA implementation's PersistenceProvider. The application code would become incredibly bloated if it had to define the persistence unit every time it requested an EntityManagerFactory. By specifying it in persistence.xml, JPA can look in this well-known location for persistence unit definitions.

But with Spring's support for JPA, you'll never deal directly with the Persistence-Provider. Therefore, it seems silly to extract configuration information into persistence.xml. In fact, doing so prevents you from configuring the EntityManager-Factory in Spring (so that, for example, you can provide a Spring-configured data source).

For that reason, we'll turn our attention to container-managed JPA.

CONFIGURING CONTAINER-MANAGED JPA

Container-managed JPA takes a different approach. When running in a container, an EntityManagerFactory can be produced using information provided by the container—Spring, in this case.

Instead of configuring data-source details in persistence.xml, you can configure this information in the Spring application context. For example, the following <bean> declaration shows how to configure container-managed JPA in Spring using Local-ContainerEntityManagerFactoryBean:

```
@Bean
public LocalContainerEntityManagerFactoryBean entityManagerFactory(
        DataSource dataSource, JpaVendorAdapter jpaVendorAdapter) {
  LocalContainerEntityManagerFactoryBean emfb =
      new LocalContainerEntityManagerFactoryBean();
  emfb.setDataSource(dataSource);
  emfb.setJpaVendorAdapter(jpaVendorAdapter);
  return emfb;
}
```

Here you configured the `dataSource` property with a Spring-configured data source. Any implementation of `javax.sql.DataSource` is appropriate. Although a data source may still be configured in persistence.xml, the data source specified through this property takes precedence.

You can use the `jpaVendorAdapter` property to provide specifics about the particular JPA implementation to use. Spring comes with a handful of JPA vendor adapters to choose from:

- `EclipseLinkJpaVendorAdapter`
- `HibernateJpaVendorAdapter`
- `OpenJpaVendorAdapter`
- `TopLinkJpaVendorAdapter` (deprecated in Spring 3.1)

In this case, you're using Hibernate as a JPA implementation, so you configure it with a `HibernateJpaVendorAdapter`:

```
@Bean
public JpaVendorAdapter jpaVendorAdapter() {
  HibernateJpaVendorAdapter adapter = new HibernateJpaVendorAdapter();
  adapter.setDatabase("HSQL");
  adapter.setShowSql(true);
  adapter.setGenerateDdl(false);
  adapter.setDatabasePlatform("org.hibernate.dialect.HSQLDialect");
  return adapter;
}
```

Several properties are set on the vendor adapter, but the most important is the `database` property, where you specify the Hypersonic database as the database you'll be using. Other values supported for this property include those listed in table 11.1.

Certain dynamic persistence features require that the class of persistent objects be modified with instrumentation to support the feature. Objects whose properties are lazily loaded (they won't be retrieved from the database until they're accessed) must have their class instrumented with code that knows to retrieve unloaded data on access. Some frameworks use dynamic proxies to implement lazy loading. Others, such as JDO, perform class instrumentation at compile time.

Table 11.1 The Hibernate JPA vendor adapter supports several databases. You can specify which database to use by setting its `database` property.

Database platform	Value for `database` property
IBM DB2	DB2
Apache Derby	DERBY
H2	H2
Hypersonic	HSQL
Informix	INFORMIX
MySQL	MYSQL
Oracle	ORACLE
PostgresQL	POSTGRESQL
Microsoft SQL Server	SQLSERVER
Sybase	SYBASE

Which entity manager factory bean you choose will depend primarily on how you'll use it. But here's a trick that may swing your favor in the direction of `Local-ContainerEntityManagerFactoryBean`.

The primary purpose of the persistence.xml file is to identify the entity classes in a persistence unit. But as of Spring 3.1, you can do that directly with `LocalContainer-EntityManagerFactoryBean` by setting the `packagesToScan` property:

```
@Bean
public LocalContainerEntityManagerFactoryBean entityManagerFactory(
        DataSource dataSource, JpaVendorAdapter jpaVendorAdapter) {
  LocalContainerEntityManagerFactoryBean emfb =
     new LocalContainerEntityManagerFactoryBean();
  emfb.setDataSource(dataSource);
  emfb.setJpaVendorAdapter(jpaVendorAdapter);
  emfb.setPackagesToScan("com.habuma.spittr.domain");
  return emfb;
}
```

As configured here, `LocalContainerEntityManagerFactoryBean` will scan the `com.habuma.spittr.domain` package for classes that are annotated with `@Entity`. Therefore, there's no need to declare them explicitly in persistence.xml. And because the `DataSource` is also injected into `LocalContainerEntityManagerFactoryBean`, there's no need to configure details about the database in persistence.xml. Therefore, there's no need for persistence.xml whatsoever! Delete it, and let `LocalContainer-EntityManagerFactoryBean` handle it for you.

PULLING AN ENTITYMANAGERFACTORY FROM JNDI

It's also worth noting that if you're deploying your Spring application in some application servers, an `EntityManagerFactory` may have already been created for you and may be waiting in JNDI to be retrieved. In that case, you can use the `<jee:jndi-lookup>` element from Spring's `jee` namespace to nab a reference to the `Entity-ManagerFactory`:

```
<jee:jndi-lookup id="emf" jndi-name="persistence/spitterPU" />
```

You can also configure the `EntityManagerFactory` bean with Java configuration by using

```
@Bean
public JndiObjectFactoryBean entityManagerFactory() {}
JndiObjectFactoryBean jndiObjectFB = new JndiObjectFactoryBean();
  jndiObjectFB.setJndiName("jdbc/SpittrDS");
  return jndiObjectFB;
}
```

Although this method doesn't return an `EntityManagerFactory`, it will result in an `EntityManagerFactory` bean. That's because it returns `JndiObjectFactoryBean`, which is an implementation of the `FactoryBean` interface that produces an `Entity-ManagerFactory`.

Regardless of how you get your hands on an `EntityManagerFactory`, once you have one, you're ready to start writing a repository. Let's do that now.

11.2.2 *Writing a JPA-based repository*

Just like all of Spring's other persistence integration options, Spring-JPA integration comes in template form with `JpaTemplate`. Nevertheless, template-based JPA has been set aside in favor of a pure JPA approach. This is analogous to the Hibernate contextual sessions you used in section 11.1.2.

Because pure JPA is favored over template-based JPA, this section focuses on building Spring-free JPA repositories. Specifically, `JpaSpitterRepository` in the following listing shows how you can develop a JPA repository without resorting to using Spring's `JpaTemplate`.

Listing 11.2   A pure JPA repository that doesn't use Spring templates

```
package com.habuma.spittr.persistence;
  import java.util.List;
  import javax.persistence.EntityManagerFactory;
  import javax.persistence.PersistenceUnit;
  import org.springframework.dao.DataAccessException;
  import org.springframework.stereotype.Repository;
  import org.springframework.transaction.annotation.Transactional;
  import com.habuma.spittr.domain.Spitter;
  import com.habuma.spittr.domain.Spittle;

  @Repository
  @Transactional
  public class JpaSpitterRepository implements SpitterRepository {

    @PersistenceUnit                                         Inject
    private EntityManagerFactory emf;                        EntityManagerFactory

    public void addSpitter(Spitter spitter) {
      emf.createEntityManager().persist(spitter);            Create and use
    }                                                        EntityManager

    public Spitter getSpitterById(long id) {
      return emf.createEntityManager().find(Spitter.class, id);
    }

    public void saveSpitter(Spitter spitter) {
      emf.createEntityManager().merge(spitter);
    }
  ...
  }
```

The main thing to notice in listing 11.2 is the `EntityManagerFactory` property. It's annotated with `@PersistenceUnit` so that Spring can inject the `EntityManager-Factory` into the repository. With an `EntityManagerFactory` in hand, `JpaSpitter-Repository`'s methods use it to create an `EntityManager` and then use that `EntityManager` to perform operations against the database.

The only gotcha with `JpaSpitterRepository` as it stands is that each method ends up calling `createEntityManager()`. Aside from presenting a troubling code-duplication situation, it also means a new `EntityManager` is created every time one of the repository methods is called. This complicates matters concerning transactions. Wouldn't it be handy if you just had the `EntityManager` up front?

The problem is that an `EntityManager` isn't thread-safe and generally shouldn't be injected into a shared singleton bean like your repository. But that doesn't mean you can't ask for an `EntityManager` anyway. The next listing shows how to use `@PersistenceContext` to give `JpaSpitterRepository` an `EntityManager`.

Listing 11.3 Injecting a repository with a proxy to the `EntityManager`

```java
package com.habuma.spittr.persistence;
import java.util.List;
import javax.persistence.EntityManager;
import javax.persistence.PersistenceContext;
import org.springframework.dao.DataAccessException;
import org.springframework.stereotype.Repository;
import org.springframework.transaction.annotation.Transactional;
import com.habuma.spittr.domain.Spitter;
import com.habuma.spittr.domain.Spittle;

@Repository
@Transactional
public class JpaSpitterRepository implements SpitterRepository {

  @PersistenceContext
  private EntityManager em;                    <--- Inject EntityManager

  public void addSpitter(Spitter spitter) {
    em.persist(spitter);                       <--- Use EntityManager
  }

  public Spitter getSpitterById(long id) {
    return em.find(Spitter.class, id);
  }

  public void saveSpitter(Spitter spitter) {
    em.merge(spitter);
  }
...
}
```

This new version of `JpaSpitterRepository` is now given an `EntityManager` directly; there's no need for it to create one from an `EntityManagerFactory` in each of its methods. Although this is much more convenient, you're probably wondering about the thread-safety issues of working with an injected `EntityManager`.

The truth is that `@PersistenceContext` doesn't inject an `EntityManager`—at least, not exactly. Instead of giving the repository a real `EntityManager`, it gives a proxy to a real `EntityManager`. That real `EntityManager` either is one associated with the current transaction or, if one doesn't exist, creates a new one. Thus, you know that you're always working with an entity manager in a thread-safe way.

It's important to understand that `@PersistenceUnit` and `@PersistenceContext` aren't Spring annotations; they're provided by the JPA specification. In order for Spring to understand them and inject an `EntityManagerFactory` or `EntityManager`,

Spring's PersistenceAnnotationBeanPostProcessor must be configured. If you're already using <context:annotation-config> or <context:component-scan>, then you're good to go because those configuration elements automatically register a PersistenceAnnotationBeanPostProcessor bean. Otherwise, you'll need to register that bean explicitly:

```
@Bean
public PersistenceAnnotationBeanPostProcessor paPostProcessor() {
  return new PersistenceAnnotationBeanPostProcessor();
}
```

You also may have noticed that JpaSpitterRepository is annotated with @Repository and @Transactional. @Transactional indicates that the persistence methods in this repository are involved in a transactional context.

@Repository serves the same purpose here as it did when you developed the Hibernate contextual session version of the repository. Without a template to handle exception translation, you need to annotate your repository with @Repository so PersistenceExceptionTranslationPostProcessor knows that this is a bean for which exceptions should be translated into one of Spring's unified data-access exceptions.

Speaking of PersistenceExceptionTranslationPostProcessor, you need to remember to wire it up as a bean in Spring just as you did for the Hibernate example:

```
@Bean
public BeanPostProcessor persistenceTranslation() {
  return new PersistenceExceptionTranslationPostProcessor();
}
```

Note that exception translation, whether with JPA or Hibernate, isn't mandatory. If you'd prefer that your repository throw JPA-specific or Hibernate-specific exceptions, you're welcome to forgo PersistenceExceptionTranslationPostProcessor and let the native exceptions flow freely. But if you do use Spring's exception translation, you'll be unifying all of your data-access exceptions under Spring's exception hierarchy, which will make it easier to swap out persistence mechanisms later.

11.3   *Automatic JPA repositories with Spring Data*

Even though the methods in listings 11.2 and 11.3 are fairly simple, they still interact directly with the EntityManager to query the database. And, on closer inspection, those methods start looking a bit boilerplate-ish. For example, let's reexamine the addSpitter() method:

```
public void addSpitter(Spitter spitter) {
    entityManager.persist(spitter);
  }
```

In any reasonably-sized application, you're likely to write that same method almost exactly the same way many times. In fact, aside from the fact that it's a Spitter that's being persisted, I'll bet you've written a similar method before. And the other methods in `JpaSpitterRepository` aren't too innovative, either. The domain types will be different, but those methods are fairly common across all kinds of repositories.

Why keep writing the same persistence methods over and over again, just because you're dealing with different domain types? Spring Data JPA brings an end to this boilerplate madness. Rather than write the same repository implementations again and again, Spring Data lets you stop at writing the repository interface. No implementation is required.

For instance, take a look at the following `SpitterRepository` interface.

Listing 11.4 Creating a repository from an interface definition with Spring Data

```
public interface SpitterRepository
        extends JpaRepository<Spitter, Long> {
}
```

At this point, `SpitterRepository` doesn't appear all that useful. But there's a lot more here than meets the eye.

The key to writing a Spring Data JPA repository is to extend one of a handful of interfaces. Here, `SpitterRepository` extends Spring Data JPA's `JpaRepository` (I'll mention a few of the other interfaces in a moment). In doing so, `JpaRepository` is parameterized such that it knows this is a repository for persisting `Spitter` objects and that `Spitters` have an ID of type `Long`. It also inherits 18 methods for performing common persistence operations, such as saving a `Spitter`, deleting a `Spitter`, and finding a `Spitter` by its ID.

At this point, you might be expecting that the next step is to write a class that implements `SpitterRepository` and its 18 methods. If that were true, then this chapter would be about to take a tedious turn. Fortunately, however, you won't be writing any implementations of `SpitterRepository`. Instead, you'll let Spring Data do it for you. All you need to do is ask.

To ask Spring Data to create an implementation of `SpitterRepository`, you need to add a single element to your Spring configuration. The following listing shows the XML configuration needed to put Spring Data JPA into motion.

Listing 11.5 Configuring Spring Data JPA

```
<?xml version="1.0" encoding="UTF-8"?>
<beans xmlns="http://www.springframework.org/schema/beans"
  xmlns:xsi="http://www.w3.org/2001/XMLSchema-instance"
  xmlns:jpa="http://www.springframework.org/schema/data/jpa"
  xsi:schemaLocation="http://www.springframework.org/schema/data/jpa
    http://www.springframework.org/schema/data/jpa/spring-jpa-1.0.xsd">

  <jpa:repositories base-package="com.habuma.spittr.db" />

  ...

</beans>
```

The <jpa:repositories> element holds all the magic of Spring Data JPA. Much like the <context:component-scan> element, <jpa:repositories> is given a base-package to scan. But where <context:component-scan> scans a package (and its sub-packages) for classes that are annotated with @Component, <jpa:repositories> scans its base package for any interfaces that extend Spring Data JPA's Repository interface. When it finds any interface extending Repository, it automatically (at application startup time) generates an implementation of that interface.

Instead of using the <jpa:repositories> element, you can use @EnableJpa-Repositories in your Java configuration class. What follows is a Java configuration class annotated with @EnableJpaRepositories to scan the com.habuma.spittr.db package:

```
@Configuration
@EnableJpaRepositories(basePackages="com.habuma.spittr.db")
public class JpaConfiguration {
  ...
}
```

Getting back to the SpitterRepository interface, it extends JpaRepository. JpaRepository extends the marker Repository interface (albeit indirectly). Therefore, SpitterRepository transitively extends the Repository interface that repository-scanning is looking for. When Spring Data finds it, it creates an implementation of SpitterRepository, including an implementation of all 18 methods inherited from JpaRepository, PagingAndSortingRepository, and CrudRepository.

It's important to understand that the repository implementation is generated at application startup time, as the Spring application context is being created. It isn't the product of build-time code generation. Nor is it created at the time any of the interface's methods are called.

Nifty, huh?

It's awesome that Spring Data JPA can give you 18 convenient methods for common JPA operations on Spitter objects without you having to write that persistence code. But what if you need something more than what those 18 methods offer? Fortunately, Spring Data JPA provides a few ways to add custom methods to a repository. Let's see how to define a custom query method using Spring Data JPA.

11.3.1 *Defining query methods*

One thing your SpitterRepository will need is a means of looking up a Spitter object given a username. For example, let's say you modify the SpitterRepository interface to look like this:

```
public interface SpitterRepository
      extends JpaRepository<Spitter, Long> {
    Spitter findByUsername(String username);
  }
```

The new findByUsername() method is simple enough and should satisfy your requirement. Now, how do you get Spring Data JPA to incorporate an implementation of that method?

Actually, nothing else needs to be done to implement `findByUsername()`. The method signature tells Spring Data JPA everything it needs to know in order to create an implementation for the method.

When creating the repository implementation, Spring Data will examine any methods in the repository interface, parse the method name, and attempt to understand the method's purpose in the context of the persisted object. In essence, Spring Data defines a sort of miniature domain-specific language (DSL) where persistence details are expressed in repository method signatures.

Spring Data knows that this method is intended to find `Spitters`, because you parameterized `JpaRepository` with `Spitter`. The method name, `findByUsername`, makes it clear that this method should find `Spitters` by matching their `username` property with the username passed in as a parameter to the method. Moreover, because the signature defines the method as returning a single `Spitter` and not a collection, it knows that it should look for only one `Spitter` whose username matches.

The `findByUsername()` method is simple enough, but Spring Data can handle even more interesting method names as well. Repository methods are composed of a verb, an optional subject, the word *By*, and a predicate. In the case of `findByUsername()`, the verb is *find* and the predicate is *Username*; the subject isn't specified and is implied to be a `Spitter`.

As another example of how to write repository method names, consider how the method parts are mapped to a method named `readSpitterByFirstnameOrLastname()`. Figure 11.1 illustrates how the method breaks down.

As you can see, the verb is *read*, as opposed to *find* from the previous example. Spring Data allows for four verbs in the method name: *get*, *read*, *find*, and *count*. The *get*, *read*, and *find* verbs are synonymous; all three result in repository methods that query for data and return objects. The *count* verb, on the other hand, returns a count of matching objects, rather than the objects themselves.

The subject of a repository method is optional. Its primary purpose is to allow you some flexibility in how you name the method. If it suits you to name a method `readSpittersByFirstnameOrLastname()` instead of `readByFirstnameOrLastname()`, you're welcome to do that.

The subject is ignored for the most part. `readSpittersByFirstnameOrLastname()` is no different from `readPuppiesByFirstnameOrLastname()`, which is no different from `readThoseThingsWeWantByFirstnameOrLastname()`. The type of object being retrieved is determined by how you parameterize the `JpaRepository` interface, not the subject of the method name.

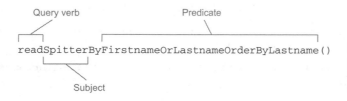

Figure 11.1 **Repository methods are named following a pattern that helps Spring Data generate queries against the database.**

There is one exception to the subject being ignored. If the subject starts with the word *Distinct*, then the generated query will be written to ensure a distinct result set.

The predicate is the most interesting part of the method name. It specifies the properties that will constrain the result set. In the case of `readByFirstnameOr-Lastname()`, the results are constrained by the value of either the `firstname` property or the `lastname` property.

Within the predicate, you'll find one or more conditions that constrain the results. Each condition must reference a property and may also specify a comparison operation. If the comparison operator is left off, it's implied to be an equals operation. But you may choose any other comparison operations, including the following:

- `IsAfter, After, IsGreaterThan, GreaterThan`
- `IsGreaterThanEqual, GreaterThanEqual`
- `IsBefore, Before, IsLessThan, LessThan`
- `IsLessThanEqual, LessThanEqual`
- `IsBetween, Between`
- `IsNull, Null`
- `IsNotNull, NotNull`
- `IsIn, In`
- `IsNotIn, NotIn`
- `IsStartingWith, StartingWith, StartsWith`
- `IsEndingWith, EndingWith, EndsWith`
- `IsContaining, Containing, Contains`
- `IsLike, Like`
- `IsNotLike, NotLike`
- `IsTrue, True`
- `IsFalse, False`
- `Is, Equals`
- `IsNot, Not`

The values that the properties will be compared against are the parameters of the method. The full method signature looks like this:

```
List<Spitter> readByFirstnameOrLastname(String first, String last);
```

When dealing with `String` properties, the condition may also include `IgnoringCase` or `IgnoresCase` to perform the comparison with no regard for whether the characters are uppercase or lowercase. For example, to ignore case on the `firstname` and `lastname` properties, you can write the method signature like this:

```
List<Spitter> readByFirstnameIgnoringCaseOrLastnameIgnoresCase(
                String first, String last);
```

Notice that `IgnoringCase` and `IgnoresCase` are synonymous. You may choose whichever one suits you best.

As an alternative to `IgnoringCase`/`IgnoresCase`, you may also use `AllIgnoring-Case` or `AllIgnoresCase` after all the conditions to ignore case for all conditions:

```
List<Spitter> readByFirstnameOrLastnameAllIgnoresCase(
                    String first, String last);
```

Note that the parameter names are irrelevant, but they must be ordered to match up with the method name's comparators.

Finally, you can sort the results by adding `OrderBy` at the end of the method name. For example, you can sort the results in ascending order by the `lastname` property:

```
List<Spitter> readByFirstnameOrLastnameOrderByLastnameAsc(
                    String first, String last);
```

To sort by multiple properties, add them to the `OrderBy` class. For example, this sorts by the `lastname` property in ascending order and then by the `firstname` property in descending order:

```
List<Spitter> readByFirstnameOrLastnameOrderByLastnameAscFirstnameDesc(
                    String first, String last);
```

As you've seen already, the conditional parts are separated by either `And` or `Or`.

It would be impossible (or at least *very* difficult) to offer a definitive list of the kinds of methods you can write with Spring Data's method-naming convention. But here are a few more method signatures that adhere to the method-naming conventions:

- `List<Pet> findPetsByBreedIn(List<String> breed)`
- `int countProductsByDiscontinuedTrue()`
- `List<Order> findByShippingDateBetween(Date start, Date end)`

This has been only a taste of the kinds of methods you can declare and have Spring Data JPA implement for you. For now, just know that by carefully constructing a repository method signature using a mix of property names and keywords, you can make Spring Data JPA generate an implementation method to query for *almost* anything you can imagine.

Nevertheless, Spring Data's mini-DSL has its limits, and sometimes it isn't convenient or even possible to express the desired query in a method name. When that happens, Spring Data has you covered with its `@Query` annotation.

11.3.2 Declaring custom queries

Suppose you want to create a repository method to find all `Spitters` whose email address is a Gmail address. One way to do this is to define a `findByEmailLike()` method and pass in `%gmail.com` any time you want to find Gmail users. But it would be nice to define a more convenient `findAllGmailSpitters()` method that doesn't require the partial email address to be passed in:

```
List<Spitter> findAllGmailSpitters();
```

Unfortunately, this method name doesn't adhere to Spring Data's method-naming conventions. When Spring Data attempts to generate an implementation for this method, it can't match the contents of the method name with the `Spitter` meta-model and throws an exception.

In situations where the desired data can't be adequately expressed in the method name, you can use the `@Query` annotation to provide Spring Data with the query that should be performed. For the `findAllGmailSpitters()` method, you might use `@Query` like this:

```
@Query("select s from Spitter s where s.email like '%gmail.com'")
List<Spitter> findAllGmailSpitters();
```

You still don't write the implementation of the `findAllGmailSpitters()` method. You only give the query, hinting to Spring Data JPA about how it should implement the method.

As you've seen here, `@Query` is useful when it's difficult to express the query you want using the method-naming convention. It can also be useful when, if you followed the naming convention, the method name would be incredibly long. For example, consider this finder method:

```
List<Order>
  findByCustomerAddressZipCodeOrCustomerNameAndCustomerAddressState();
```

Now *that's* a method name! I had to split it after the return type just to get it to fit in the margins of this book.

I'll grant that this is a contrived example. But there could be a real-world need to write a repository method to perform a query that could be defined using a long method name. In that situation, you'd probably rather come up with a shorter method name and use `@Query` to specify how the method should query the database.

The `@Query` annotation is handy for adding custom query methods to a Spring Data JPA-enabled interface. But it's limited to a single JPA query. What if you need to mix in something more complex than can be handled in a simple query?

11.3.3 *Mixing in custom functionality*

It's likely that at some point you'll want functionality in your repository that can't be described with Spring Data's method-naming conventions or even with a query given in the `@Query` annotation. As awesome as Spring Data JPA is, it still has its limits, and you may need to write a repository method the old-fashioned way: by working with the `EntityManager` directly. When that happens, do you give up on Spring Data JPA and go back to writing your repositories as you did in section 11.2.2?

In short, yes. When you need to do something that Spring Data JPA can't do, you'll have to work with JPA at a lower level than Spring Data JPA offers. But the good news is, you don't have to give up on Spring Data JPA completely. You only need to work at the lower level for those methods that require it. You can still let Spring Data JPA do the grunt work for the stuff it knows how to do.

When Spring Data JPA generates the implementation for a repository interface, it also looks for a class whose name is the same as the interface's name postfixed with

`Impl`. If the class exists, Spring Data JPA merges its methods with those generated by Spring Data JPA. For the `SpitterRepository` interface, the class it looks for is named `SpitterRepositoryImpl`.

To illustrate, suppose you need a method in your `SpitterRepository` that updates all `Spitters` who have posted 10,000 or more `Spittles`, setting them to Elite status. There's no good way to declare such a method using Spring Data JPA's method-naming conventions or with `@Query`. The most practical way to do it is using the following `eliteSweep()` method.

Listing 11.6 Repository that promotes frequent `Spitter` users to Elite status

```
public class SpitterRepositoryImpl implements SpitterSweeper {

  @PersistenceContext
  private EntityManager em;

  public int eliteSweep() {
    String update =
        "UPDATE Spitter spitter " +
        "SET spitter.status = 'Elite' " +
        "WHERE spitter.status = 'Newbie' " +
        "AND spitter.id IN (" +
        "SELECT s FROM Spitter s WHERE (" +
        "  SELECT COUNT(spittles) FROM s.spittles spittles) > 10000" +
        ")";
    return em.createQuery(update).executeUpdate();
  }

}
```

As you can see, the `eliteStatus()` method isn't much different from any of the repository methods you created earlier in section 11.2.2. There's nothing special about `SpitterRepositoryImpl`. It uses the injected `EntityManager` to do its work.

Notice that `SpitterRepositoryImpl` doesn't implement the `SpitterRepository` interface. Spring Data JPA is still responsible for implementing that interface. Instead, `SpitterRepositoryImpl` implements `SpitterSweeper`, which looks like this (the only thing that ties it into your Spring Data-enabled repository is its name):

```
public interface SpitterSweeper{
    int eliteSweep();
}
```

You should also make sure the `eliteSweep()` method is declared in the `Spitter-Repository` interface. The easy way to do that and avoid duplicating code is to change `SpitterRepository` so that it extends `SpitterSweeper`:

```
public interface SpitterRepository
        extends JpaRepository<Spitter, Long>,
                SpitterSweeper {
    ....
}
```

As I mentioned, Spring Data JPA associates the implementation class with the interface because the implementation's name is based on the name of the interface. The `Impl` postfix is only the default, though. If you'd prefer to use some other postfix, you need to specify it when configuring @EnableJpaRepositories by setting the repository-ImplementationPostfix attribute:

```
@EnableJpaRepositories(
  basePackages="com.habuma.spittr.db",
  repositoryImplementationPostfix="Helper")
```

Or, if you're configuring Spring Data JPA in XML using <jpa:repositories>, you can specify the postfix with the repository-impl-postfix attribute:

```
<jpa:repositories base-package="com.habuma.spittr.db"
    repository-impl-postfix="Helper" />
```

With the postfix set to Helper, Spring Data JPA will look for a class named Spitter-RepositoryHelper to match up with the SpitterRepository interface.

11.4 Summary

Relational databases have been the go-to data store for several applications and for many years. When working with JDBC and mapping objects to tables is too tedious, ORM options such as Hibernate and JPA enable a more declarative model for data persistence. Although Spring doesn't offer direct support for ORM, it does integrate with several popular ORM solutions, including Hibernate and the Java Persistence API.

In this chapter, we looked at how to use Hibernate's contextual sessions in a Spring application such that your repositories contain little or no Spring-specific code. Likewise, you saw how to write Spring-free JPA repositories by injecting an EntityManager-Factory or an EntityManager into your repository implementations.

You then got your first taste of Spring Data by seeing how to declare JPA repository interfaces while letting Spring Data JPA automatically generate implementations of those interfaces at runtime. And when you need more out of those repository methods than Spring Data JPA can handle on its own, you can help it out with the @Query annotation and by writing custom repository method implementations.

But you have just dipped your toe into the Spring Data pool. Coming up in the next chapter, we'll dig deeper into Spring Data's method-naming DSL and explore how Spring Data is good for more than just relational databases. That's right: you'll see how Spring Data also supports the new contingent of NoSQL databases that have become popular in the past few years.

Working with
NoSQL databases

12

This chapter covers

- Writing repositories backed by MongoDB and Neo4j
- Persisting data across multiple data stores
- Working with Spring and Redis

In his autobiography, Henry Ford is famous for having written "Any customer can have a car painted any color that he wants so long as it is black."[1] Some say this statement was arrogant and bull-headed. Others may think he was showing a bit of humor. The reality, however, may be found in the fact that at the time his biography was published, he was cutting costs by using a quick-drying paint that was only available in black.

Paraphrasing Ford's famous quote and applying it to database choice, we've been told for years that we can have any database we want, as long as it's a relational database. Relational databases have had a near-monopolistic hold on application development for a very long time.

---

[1] Henry Ford and Samuel Crowther, *My Life and Work* (Garden City, New York: Garden City Publishing Company, 1922).

But that hold is weakening now that some serious contenders have entered the database space. The so-called "NoSQL" databases are making inroads into production applications everywhere as we recognize that there's no one-size-fits-all database. We now have a greater choice and can choose the best database for the problem we're trying to solve.

Over the past couple of chapters, we've focused on relational databases, starting with Spring's JDBC support and then object-relational mapping. In the previous chapter, specifically, we looked at Spring Data JPA, one of several projects under the Spring Data umbrella project. We saw how Spring Data JPA can make working with JPA more pleasant by automatically generating repository implementations at runtime.

Spring Data also supports several NoSQL databases, including MongoDB, Neo4j, and Redis. This not only includes support for automatic repositories, but also template-based data access and mapping annotations. In this chapter, we're going to see how to write repositories that work with non-relational, NoSQL databases. We'll start with Spring Data MongoDB to see how to write repositories that deal with document-based data.

12.1 *Persisting documents with MongoDB*

Some kinds of data are best represented as *documents*. That is, rather than spread the data across multiple tables, nodes, or entities, it may make more sense to collect the information into denormalized structures (known as documents). Although two or more of these documents may be related to each other, generally documents are standalone entities. Databases that are finely tuned to work with documents in this way are known as document databases.

For example, suppose that you're writing an application that captures a college student's transcript. You'll need to be able to retrieve transcripts given a student's name or perhaps search across the transcripts for some common properties. But each student is evaluated individually, so it isn't necessary for any two transcripts to be related to each other. Although a relational database schema could be (and probably has been) designed to capture this transcript data, perhaps a document database is a better choice.

What document databases aren't good for

Knowing when to use a document database is important. But it's also important to know when document databases don't make sense. Document databases aren't general-purpose databases and they have a very narrow set of problems that they address well.

Document databases aren't well-tuned for storing data where there's any significant degree of relationships. A social network, for example, represents how different users of an application relate to each other and isn't best kept in a document database. Even though it's not impossible to store relation-rich data in a document database, you'll find more challenge than benefit in doing so.

The domain of the Spittr application isn't a good fit for a document database. In this chapter, we'll look at MongoDB in the context of a purchase order system.

MongoDB is one of the most popular open source document databases available. Spring Data MongoDB brings MongoDB to Spring applications in three ways:

- Annotations for object-to-document mapping
- Template-based database access with `MongoTemplate`
- Automatic runtime repository generation

We've already looked at how Spring Data JPA enabled automatic repository generation for JPA-based data access. Spring Data MongoDB offers the same feature for MongoDB-based data access.

Unlike Spring Data JPA, however, Spring Data MongoDB also offers annotations to map Java objects to documents. (Spring Data JPA doesn't need to offer such annotations for JPA because the JPA specification itself defines object-to-relational mapping annotations.) Moreover, Spring Data MongoDB provides for template-based MongoDB data access for several common document manipulation tasks.

Before we can use any of these features, however, we'll need to configure Spring Data MongoDB.

12.1.1 Enabling MongoDB

In order to effectively work with Spring Data MongoDB, you're going to need a few essential beans in your Spring configuration. First, you'll need to configure a `Mongo-Client` bean to be able to access the MongoDB database. You'll also need a `Mongo-Template` bean to be able to perform template-based data access against the database. Optionally, but desirably, you'll want to enable Spring Data MongoDB's automatic repository generation.

The following listing shows how to write a simple Spring Data MongoDB configuration class that addresses these needs.

Listing 12.1 An essential configuration for Spring Data MongoDB

```
package orders.config;
import org.springframework.context.annotation.Bean;
import org.springframework.context.annotation.Configuration;
import org.springframework.data.mongodb.core.MongoFactoryBean;
import org.springframework.data.mongodb.core.MongoOperations;
import org.springframework.data.mongodb.core.MongoTemplate;
import org.springframework.data.mongodb.repository.config.
                                        EnableMongoRepositories;
import com.mongodb.Mongo;

@Configuration
@EnableMongoRepositories(basePackages="orders.db")    ◁┐ Enable MongoDB
public class MongoConfig {                                │ repositories
```

```
@Bean
public MongoFactoryBean mongo() {                        <-- MongoClient bean
    MongoFactoryBean mongo = new MongoFactoryBean();
    mongo.setHost("localhost");
    return mongo;
}

@Bean
public MongoOperations mongoTemplate(Mongo mongo) {     <-- MongoTemplate bean
    return new MongoTemplate(mongo, "OrdersDB");
}

}
```

As you'll recall from the previous chapter, you enabled Spring Data's automatic JPA repository generation with the @EnableJpaRepositories annotation. Similarly, the @EnableMongoRepositories annotation does the same thing for MongoDB.

In addition to @EnableMongoRepositories, listing 12.1 also includes two @Bean methods. The first @Bean method uses MongoFactoryBean to declare a Mongo instance. This bean will bridge Spring Data MongoDB to the database itself (not unlike what a DataSource does when working with a relational database). Although you could create an instance of Mongo directly with MongoClient, you'd be forced to deal with the UnknownHostException that's thrown from MongoClient's constructor. It's easier to use Spring Data MongoDB's MongoFactoryBean here. As a factory bean, Mongo-FactoryBean will construct an instance of Mongo for you, without you needing to worry much about UnknownHostException.

The other @Bean method declares a MongoTemplate bean. It's constructed giving it a reference to the Mongo instance created by the other bean method and the name of the database. In a moment, you'll see how to use MongoTemplate to query the database. Even if you never use MongoTemplate directly, you'll need this bean because the automatically generated repositories will use it under the covers.

Rather than declare those beans directly, the configuration class could extend AbstractMongoConfiguration and override its getDatabaseName() and mongo() methods. The following listing shows how.

Listing 12.2 Enabling Spring Data MongoDB with the @EnableMongoRepositories

```
package orders.config;
import org.springframework.context.annotation.Configuration;
import org.springframework.data.mongodb.config.
                                        AbstractMongoConfiguration;
import org.springframework.data.mongodb.repository.config.
                                        EnableMongoRepositories;
import com.mongodb.Mongo;
import com.mongodb.MongoClient;

@Configuration
@EnableMongoRepositories("orders.db")
public class MongoConfig extends AbstractMongoConfiguration {

    @Override
```

```
  protected String getDatabaseName() {          <—— Specify database name
    return "OrdersDB";
  }

  @Override
  public Mongo mongo() throws Exception {        <—— Create a Mongo client
    return new MongoClient();
  }

}
```

This new configuration class is equivalent to the one in listing 12.1, albeit marginally simpler. The most noticeable difference is that this configuration doesn't directly declare a `MongoTemplate` bean, although one is implicitly created. Instead, you override `getDatabaseName()` to provide the name of the database. The `mongo()` method still creates an instance of `MongoClient`, but because it throws `Exception`, you can work with `MongoClient` directly without working with `MongoFactoryBean`.

As it stands, either listing 12.1 or 12.2 provide a working configuration for Spring Data MongoDB. That is, as long as the MongoDB server is running on localhost. If your MongoDB server is running on a different server, you can specify that when you create `MongoClient`:

```
public Mongo mongo() throws Exception {
  return new MongoClient("mongodbserver");
}
```

It's also possible that your MongoDB server is listening on a port other than the default (27017). In that case, you should also specify the port when creating `MongoClient`:

```
public Mongo mongo() throws Exception {
  return new MongoClient("mongodbserver", 37017);
}
```

And if your MongoDB server is running in a production setting, I'd hope that you have authentication enabled. In that case, you'll need to provide your application's credentials in order to access the database. Accessing an authenticated MongoDB server is a bit more involved, as you can see in the next listing.

Listing 12.3 Creating a MongoClient to access an authenticated MongoDB server

```
@Autowired
private Environment env;

@Override
public Mongo mongo() throws Exception {
  MongoCredential credential =
    MongoCredential.createMongoCRCredential(     <—— Create MongoDB credential
        env.getProperty("mongo.username"),
        "OrdersDB",
        env.getProperty("mongo.password").toCharArray());

  return new MongoClient(                         <—— Create MongoClient
      new ServerAddress("localhost", 37017),
    Arrays.asList(credential));
}
```

In order to access an authenticated MongoDB server, `MongoClient` must be instantiated with a list of `MongoCredentials`. In listing 12.3 a single `MongoCredential` is created for that purpose. In order to keep the credential details out of the configuration class, they're resolved from the injected `Environment`.

For what it's worth, Spring Data MongoDB can also be configured in XML. As you should know by now, I favor the Java configuration option. But if you've got a fondness for XML configuration, the following listing gives an example of how to configure Spring Data MongoDB using the `mongo` configuration namespace.

Listing 12.4   Spring Data MongoDB offers an XML configuration option

```xml
<?xml version="1.0" encoding="UTF-8"?>
<beans xmlns="http://www.springframework.org/schema/beans"      ◁─ Declare
  xmlns:xsi="http://www.w3.org/2001/XMLSchema-instance"              mongo
  xmlns:mongo="http://www.springframework.org/schema/data/mongo"  ◁─ namespace
  xsi:schemaLocation="
    http://www.springframework.org/schema/data/mongo
    http://www.springframework.org/schema/data/mongo/spring-mongo.xsd
    http://www.springframework.org/schema/beans
    http://www.springframework.org/schema/beans/spring-beans.xsd">

  <mongo:repositories base-package="orders.db" />    ◁─ Enable repository
                                                           generation
  <mongo:mongo />
                                                    Create
  <bean id="mongoTemplate"                          MongoTemplate bean
      class="org.springframework.data.mongodb.core.MongoTemplate">
    <constructor-arg ref="mongo" />
    <constructor-arg value="OrdersDB" />
  </bean>

</beans>
```

Declare MongoClient ▷ (points to `<mongo:mongo />`)

Now that Spring Data MongoDB has been configured, you're almost ready to start using it to save and retrieve documents. But first, you'll need to map your Java domain types for document persistence using Spring Data MongoDB's object-to-document mapping annotations.

12.1.2 *Annotating model types for MongoDB persistence*

When working with JPA, you had to map your Java entity types to relational tables and columns. The JPA specification provides for several annotations to support object-to-relational mapping, and some JPA implementations, such as Hibernate, add their own mapping annotations as well.

MongoDB, however, doesn't come with its own object-to-document mapping annotations. Spring Data MongoDB seized the opportunity to fill that gap with a handful of annotations that you can use to map your Java types to MongoDB documents. Table 12.1 describes these annotations.

Table 12.1 Spring Data MongoDB annotations for object-to-document mapping

Annotation	Description
@Document	Identifies a domain object to be mapped to a MongoDB document
@Id	Indicates that a field is the ID field
@DbRef	Indicates that a field is intended to reference another document, possibly in another database
@Field	Defines custom metadata for a document field
@Version	Identifies a property to be used as a version field

The `@Document` and `@Id` annotations are analogous to JPA's `@Entity` and `@Id` annotations. You'll use these two annotations often and on every Java type that will be stored as a document in the MongoDB database. For example, the next listing shows how you might annotate an `Order` class to be persisted in MongoDB.

Listing 12.5 Spring Data MongoDB annotations map Java types to documents.

```
package orders;
import java.util.Collection;
import java.util.LinkedHashSet;
import org.springframework.data.annotation.Id;
import org.springframework.data.mongodb.core.mapping.Document;
import org.springframework.data.mongodb.core.mapping.Field;

@Document                            ⟵— This is a document
 public class Order {

  @Id
  private String id;                 ⟵— Designate the ID

  @Field("client")
  private String customer;                    ⟵— Override the default field name

  private String type;

  private Collection<Item> items = new LinkedHashSet<Item>();

  public String getCustomer() {
    return customer;
  }

  public void setCustomer(String customer) {
    this.customer = customer;
  }

  public String getType() {
    return type;
  }

  public void setType(String type) {
    this.type = type;
  }
```

```
public Collection<Item> getItems() {
  return items;
}

public void setItems(Collection<Item> items) {
  this.items = items;
}

public String getId() {
  return id;
}

}
```

As you can see, `Order` is annotated with `@Document`, enabling it to be persisted using `MongoTemplate`, an automatically generated repository, or both. Its `id` property is annotated with `@Id` to designate it as the ID of the document. In addition, the `customer` property is annotated with `@Field` so that when the document is persisted, the `customer` property will be mapped to a field named `client`.

Notice that no other properties are annotated. Unless they're marked as transient, all fields of the Java object will be persisted as fields of the document. And unless otherwise indicated with `@Field`, the document fields will have the same names as their Java property counterparts.

Also, take note of the `items` property. It's clearly a collection of line items in this order. In a traditional relational database setting, those items would probably be kept in a separate database table, referenced with a foreign key, and the `items` field might be annotated for JPA with `@OneToMany`. But here that's not the case.

As I said earlier, documents can be related to other documents, but that's not what document databases are especially good at. In the case of the relationship between a purchase order and its line items, the line items are merely a nested part of the same order document (as shown in figure 12.1). Therefore, there's no need for any annotations to designate the relationship. In fact, the `Item` class itself isn't annotated at all:

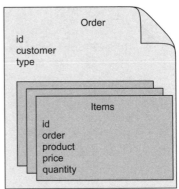

Figure 12.1 Documents represent related but denormalized data. Related concepts (such as items of an order) are embedded in the top-level document.

```
package orders;

public class Item {

  private Long id;
  private Order order;
  private String product;
  private double price;
  private int quantity;
```

```
    public Order getOrder() {
      return order;
    }

    public String getProduct() {
      return product;
    }

    public void setProduct(String product) {
      this.product = product;
    }

    public double getPrice() {
      return price;
    }

    public void setPrice(double price) {
      this.price = price;
    }

    public int getQuantity() {
      return quantity;
    }

    public void setQuantity(int quantity) {
      this.quantity = quantity;
    }

    public Long getId() {
      return id;
    }

}
```

It's not necessary to annotate `Item` with `@Document`, nor is it necessary to annotate one of its fields with `@Id`. That's because you'll never persist an `Item` as an independent document. It will always be a member of the `Order` document's `Item` list and a nested element in that document.

Of course, you could annotate one of `Item`'s properties with `@Field` if you wanted to dictate how that field should be stored in the document. It just wasn't necessary to do so in this example.

Now we have a Java domain type annotated for MongoDB persistence. Let's see how you can use `MongoTemplate` to store a few of them.

12.1.3 Accessing MongoDB with MongoTemplate

You've already configured a `MongoTemplate` bean, either explicitly or by extending `AbstractMongoConfiguration` in your configuration class. All you need to do is inject it wherever it will be used:

```
@Autowired
MongoOperations mongo;
```

Notice that here I'm injecting `MongoTemplate` into a property whose type is `Mongo-Operations`. `MongoOperations` is an interface that `MongoTemplate` implements, and it's good form to not work with the concrete implementation directly, especially when it's injected.

MongoOperations exposes several useful methods for working with a MongoDB document database. It'd be impossible for us to discuss all of them here, but we can take a look at a few of the most commonly used operations, such as counting how many documents are in a document collection. Using the injected MongoOperations, you get the order collection and then call count() to get a count:

```
long orderCount = mongo.getCollection("order").count();
```

Now let's suppose you want to save a new order. To do that, you can call the save() method:

```
Order order = new Order();
... // set properties and add line items
mongo.save(order, "order");
```

The first parameter to save() is the newly created Order; the second is the name of the document store to save it to.

You can also look up an order by its ID by calling findById():

```
String orderId = ...;
Order order = mongo.findById(orderId, Order.class);
```

More advanced queries require that you construct a Query object and pass it to the find() method. For example, to find all orders whose client field is equal to "Chuck Wagon", you can use this code:

```
List<Order> chucksOrders = mongo.find(Query.query(
    Criteria.where("client").is("Chuck Wagon")), Order.class);
```

In this case, the Criteria used to construct the Query only checks one field. But it can also be used for even more interesting queries. Perhaps you want to get all of Chuck's orders that were placed over the web:

```
List<Order> chucksWebOrders = mongo.find(Query.query(
    Criteria.where("customer").is("Chuck Wagon")
            .and("type").is("WEB")), Order.class);
```

And, should you wish to remove a document, the remove() method is what you're looking for:

```
mongo.remove(order);
```

As I've said, MongoOperations has several methods for working with document data. I encourage you to examine the JavaDoc to discover what else you can do with Mongo-Operations.

Typically, you'd inject MongoOperations into a repository class of your own design and use its operations to implement the repository methods. But if you don't want to bother writing the repository yourself, then Spring Data MongoDB can automatically generate a repository implementation for you at runtime. Let's see how.

12.1.4 *Writing a MongoDB repository*

To understand how to create repositories with Spring Data MongoDB, let's once again consider what you did in chapter 11 with Spring Data JPA. In listing 11.4, you created an interface named `SpitterRepository` that extends `JpaRepository`. In the same section, you also enabled Spring Data JPA repositories. As a result, Spring Data JPA was able to automatically create an implementation of that interface, including several built-in methods and any methods you added that followed a naming convention.

You've already enabled Spring Data MongoDB repositories with `@EnableMongo-Repositories`, so all that's left is to create an interface that you can generate the repository implementation from. Instead of extending `JpaRepository`, however, you'll need to extend `MongoRepository`. The `OrderRepository` interface in the following listing extends `MongoRepository` to provide basic CRUD operations for `Order` documents.

Listing 12.6 Spring Data MongoDB automatically implements repository interfaces

```
package orders.db;
import orders.Order;
import org.springframework.data.mongodb.repository.MongoRepository;

public interface OrderRepository
        extends MongoRepository<Order, String> {
}
```

Because `OrderRepository` extends `MongoRepository`, it transitively extends the `Repository` marker interface. As you'll recall from our exploration of Spring Data JPA, any interface that extends `Repository` will have an implementation automatically generated at runtime. In this case, however, instead of a JPA repository that interacts with a relational database, `OrderRepository` will be implemented to read and write data to a MongoDB document database.

The `MongoRepository` interface has two parameters. The first is the type of `@Document`-annotated object that this repository deals with. The second is the type of the `@Id`-annotated property.

Even though `OrderRepository` doesn't define any methods of its own, it inherits several methods, including several useful methods for CRUD operations on `Order` documents. Table 12.2 describes all of the methods that `OrderRepository` inherits.

The methods in table 12.2 refer to the generic types passed into and returned from the methods. Given that `OrderRepository` extends `MongoRepository<Order, String>`, this means that `T` maps to `Order`, `ID` maps to `String`, and `S` maps to any type that extends `Order`.

Table 12.2 By extending `MongoRepository`, a repository interface inherits several CRUD operations that are automatically implemented by Spring Data MongoDB.

Method	Description
`long count();`	Returns a count of the documents for the repository type
`void delete(Iterable<? extends T);`	Deletes all documents associated with the given objects
`void delete(T);`	Deletes the document associated with the given object
`void delete(ID);`	Deletes a document by its ID
`void deleteAll();`	Deletes all documents for the given repository type
`boolean exists(Object);`	Returns `true` if a document associated with the given object exists
`boolean exists(ID);`	Returns `true` if a document exists for the given ID
`List<T> findAll();`	Returns all documents for the repository type
`List<T> findAll(Iterable<ID>);`	Returns all documents for the given document IDs
`List<T> findAll(Pageable);`	Returns a paged and sorted list of documents for the repository type
`List<T> findAll(Sort);`	Returns a sorted list of all documents for the given document ID
`T findOne(ID);`	Returns a single document for the given ID
`save(Iterable<S>);`	Saves all documents in the given `Iterable`
`save(S);`	Saves a single document for the given object

ADDING CUSTOM QUERY METHODS

The CRUD operations are generally useful, but you may need the repository to provide methods beyond what comes out of the box.

In section 11.3.1, you learned that Spring Data JPA supports a method-naming convention that helps Spring Data to automatically generate implementations for the methods that follow that convention. As it turns out, the very same convention works with Spring Data MongoDB. That means you can add custom methods to `OrderRepository` like this:

```
public interface OrderRepository
        extends MongoRepository<Order, String> {
  List<Order> findByCustomer(String c);
  List<Order> findByCustomerLike(String c);
  List<Order> findByCustomerAndType(String c, String t);
  List<Order> findByCustomerLikeAndType(String c, String t);
}
```

Here you have four new methods, each one finding `Order` objects that match certain criteria. One method finds a list of `Order` where the `customer` property is equal to the value passed into the method. Another finds a list of `Order` where the `customer` property is like the value passed into the method. The next finds `Order` objects whose `customer` and `type` properties are equal to the values passed in. The final method is like the previous, except that the `customer` comparison is a *like* comparison instead of an *equals* comparison.

The `find` query verb is flexible. If you'd prefer, you can use `get` as the query verb:

```
List<Order> getByCustomer(String c);
```

Or if it suits you better, you can use `read`:

```
List<Order> readByCustomer(String c);
```

There's also another special query verb for counting the objects that match:

```
int countByCustomer(String c);
```

As with Spring Data JPA, there's a lot of flexibility in what can go in between the query verb and `By`. For example, you could state what it is you're finding:

```
List<Order> findOrdersByCustomer(String c);
```

There's nothing special about the word `Orders`, though. It has nothing to do with what is being fetched. You could name the method like this:

```
List<Order> findSomeStuffWeNeedByCustomer(String c);
```

You also don't need to return a `List<Order>`. If all you want is a single `Order`, you can simply return `Order`:

```
Order findASingleOrderByCustomer(String c);
```

Here, the first `Order` that would've been found if it were a `List` is what will be returned. If there isn't a match, the method will return `null`.

SPECIFYING QUERIES

As you saw in section 11.3.2, the `@Query` annotation can be used to specify a custom query for a repository method. `@Query` works equally well with MongoDB as it does with JPA. The only material difference is that for MongoDB, `@Query` takes a JSON query string instead of a JPA query.

For example, suppose you need a method that finds all orders of a given type for the customer whose name is "Chuck Wagon". The following method declaration in `OrderRepository` will give you what you need:

```
@Query("{'customer': 'Chuck Wagon', 'type' : ?0}")
List<Order> findChucksOrders(String t);
```

The JSON given to `@Query` is matched up against all `Order` documents, and any document that matches will be returned. Notice that the `type` property is mapped to `?0`. This indicates that the `type` property should be equal to the zeroth parameter to the query method. If there were more parameters, they could be referred to with ?1, ?2, and so forth.

MIXING IN CUSTOM REPOSITORY BEHAVIOR

In section 11.3.3, you learned how to mix fully custom methods into an otherwise automatically generated repository. For JPA, that involved creating an intermediary interface that declares the custom method(s), an implementation class for those custom methods, and changing the automatic repository interface to extend the intermediary interface. The steps are the same for a Spring Data MongoDB repository.

Suppose that you need a method that finds all Order objects where the document's type property matches a given value. You could easily create such a method by giving it a signature of List<Order> findByType(String t). But for the sake of this example, suppose that if the given type is NET, then it will query for Orders whose type is WEB. This would be hard to do, even with the @Query annotation. A mixin implementation, however, can make it work.

First, define the intermediary interface:

```
package orders.db;
import java.util.List;
import orders.Order;

public interface OrderOperations {
  List<Order> findOrdersByType(String t);
}
```

That's simple enough. Now you can write the mixin implementation. The following listing shows what the implementation might look like.

Listing 12.7 Mixing custom repository functionality into an automatic repository

```
package orders.db;
import java.util.List;
import orders.Order;
import org.springframework.beans.factory.annotation.Autowired;
import org.springframework.data.mongodb.core.MongoOperations;
import org.springframework.data.mongodb.core.query.Criteria;
import org.springframework.data.mongodb.core.query.Query;

public class OrderRepositoryImpl implements OrderOperations {
  @Autowired
  private MongoOperations mongo;                    ◁— Inject MongoOperations

  public List<Order> findOrdersByType(String t) {
    String type = t.equals("NET") ? "WEB" : t;

    Criteria where = Criteria.where("type").is(t);   ◁— Create query
    Query query = Query.query(where);

    return mongo.find(query, Order.class);           ◁— Perform query
  }
}
```

As you can see, the mixin implementation is injected with a `MongoOperations` (the interface that `MongoTemplate` implements). The `findOrdersByType()` method uses the `MongoOperations` to query the database for documents matching the constructed query.

All that's left is to change `OrderRepository` to extend the intermediary `Order-Operations` interface:

```
public interface OrderRepository
       extends MongoRepository<Order, String>, OrderOperations {
  ...
}
```

The thing that ties all of this together is the fact that the implementation class is named `OrderRepositoryImpl`. This is the same name as the `OrderRepository` interface, with an "Impl" suffix. When Spring Data MongoDB generates the repository implementation, it will look for this class and mix it into the automatically generated implementation.

If you don't care for the "Impl" suffix, you can configure Spring Data MongoDB to look for a class with a different suffix in its name. All you need to do is set the `repositoryImplementationPostfix` attribute of `@EnableMongoRepositories` (in the Spring configuration class).

```
@Configuration
@EnableMongoRepositories(basePackages="orders.db",
                         repositoryImplementationPostfix="Stuff")
public class MongoConfig extends AbstractMongoConfiguration {
  ...
}
```

Or, if you're using XML configuration, you can set the `repository-impl-postfix` attribute of `<mongo:repositories>`:

```
<mongo:repositories base-package="orders.db"
                    repository-impl-postfix="Stuff" />
```

Either way, if you configure Spring Data MongoDB this way, it will look for `Order-RepositoryStuff` instead of `OrderRepositoryImpl`.

Document databases such as MongoDB solve a certain class of problems. But just as relational databases aren't a one-size-fits-all solution, neither is MongoDB. And there are certain problems that neither a relational database nor a document database is well-suited for. Fortunately, those aren't the only two choices.

Let's have a look at how Spring Data supports Neo4j, a popular graph database.

12.2 *Working with graph data in Neo4j*

Whereas document databases store data in coarse-grained documents, graph databases store data in several fine-grained nodes that are connected with each other through relationships. A node in a graph database typically represents a concept in the database, having properties that describe the state of the node. Relationships connect two nodes and may carry properties of their own.

At their simplest, graph databases are more general purpose than document databases, potentially being a schemaless alternative to relational databases. But because data is structured as a graph, it's possible to traverse relationships to discover things about your data that would be difficult or even impossible with other kinds of databases.

Spring Data Neo4j offers many of the same capabilities as Spring Data JPA and Spring Data MongoDB, albeit targeting the Neo4j graph database. It provides annotations for mapping Java types to nodes and relationships, template-oriented Neo4j access, and automatic generation of repository implementations.

You'll see how to use these features to work with Neo4j. But first, you must configure Spring Data Neo4j.

12.2.1 *Configuring Spring Data Neo4j*

The key to configuring Spring Data Neo4j is to declare a `GraphDatabaseService` bean and enable automatic Neo4j repository generation. The following listing shows the basic Java configuration needed for Spring Data Neo4j.

Listing 12.8   Configuring Spring Data Neo4j with `@EnableNeo4jRepositories`

```
package orders.config;
import org.neo4j.graphdb.GraphDatabaseService;
import org.neo4j.graphdb.factory.GraphDatabaseFactory;
import org.springframework.context.annotation.Bean;
import org.springframework.context.annotation.Configuration;
import org.springframework.data.neo4j.config.EnableNeo4jRepositories;
import org.springframework.data.neo4j.config.Neo4jConfiguration;

@Configuration
@EnableNeo4jRepositories(basePackages="orders.db")          ◁─┐ Enable
public class Neo4jConfig extends Neo4jConfiguration {          │ automatic
                                                              │ repositories
  public Neo4jConfig() {
    setBasePackage("orders");             ◁─┐ Set model
  }                                          │ base package

  @Bean(destroyMethod="shutdown")
  public GraphDatabaseService graphDatabaseService() {
    return new GraphDatabaseFactory()
            .newEmbeddedDatabase("/tmp/graphdb");   ◁─ Configure embedded
  }                                                    databasepackage
}
```

The `@EnableNeo4jRepositories` annotation enables Spring Data Neo4j to automatically generate Neo4j repository implementations. Its `basePackages` is set so that it scans the `orders.db` package for interfaces that extend (directly or indirectly) the marker `Repository` interface.

`Neo4jConfig` extends `Neo4jConfiguration`, which provides convenient methods for configuring Spring Data Neo4j. Among those methods is `setBasePackage()`, which is called from `Neo4jConfig`'s constructor to tell Spring Data Neo4j that it can find model classes in the `orders` package.

The final piece of the puzzle is to define a `GraphDatabaseService` bean. In this case, the `graphDatabaseService()` method uses `GraphDatabaseFactory` to create an embedded Neo4j database. With Neo4j, an embedded database shouldn't be confused with an in-memory database. "Embedded" means that the database engine is running within the same JVM as a part of your application rather than as a separate server. The data is still persisted to the filesystem (at /tmp/graphdb in this case).

Alternatively, you might want to configure a `GraphDatabaseService` that references a remote Neo4j server. If you have the `spring-data-neo4j-rest` library in your application's classpath, you can configure `SpringRestGraphDatabase`, which accesses a remote Neo4j database over a RESTful API:

```
@Bean(destroyMethod="shutdown")
public GraphDatabaseService graphDatabaseService() {
  return new SpringRestGraphDatabase(
      "http://graphdbserver:7474/db/data/");
}
```

As shown here, `SpringRestGraphDatabase` is configured to assume that the remote database doesn't require authentication. In a production setting, however, it's likely that you'll want to secure the database server. In that case, you'll want to provide your application's credentials when creating the `SpringRestGraphDatabase`:

```
@Bean(destroyMethod="shutdown")
public GraphDatabaseService graphDatabaseService(Environment env) {
  return new SpringRestGraphDatabase(
      "http://graphdbserver:7474/db/data/",
      env.getProperty("db.username"), env.getProperty("db.password"));
}
```

Here, the credentials are obtained via the injected `Environment` to avoid hard-coding them in the configuration class.

Spring Data Neo4j also offers an XML configuration namespace. If you'd rather configure Spring Data Neo4j in XML, you can use the `<neo4j:config>` and `<neo4j:repositories>` elements from that namespace. Listing 12.9 shows an XML configuration that's equivalent to the Java configuration in listing 12.8.

> **Listing 12.9   Spring Data Neo4j can also be configured in XML.**

```
<?xml version="1.0" encoding="UTF-8"?>
<beans xmlns="http://www.springframework.org/schema/beans"
  xmlns:xsi="http://www.w3.org/2001/XMLSchema-instance"
  xmlns:neo4j="http://www.springframework.org/schema/data/neo4j"
  xsi:schemaLocation="
  http://www.springframework.org/schema/beans
  http://www.springframework.org/schema/beans/spring-beans.xsd
  http://www.springframework.org/schema/data/neo4j
  http://www.springframework.org/schema/data/neo4j/spring-neo4j.xsd">
```

```
<neo4j:config
    storeDirectory="/tmp/graphdb"
    base-package="orders" />
```
⟵┐ **Configure Neo4j**
   database details

```
<neo4j:repositories base-package="orders.db" />
```
⟵— **Enable repository generation**
```
</beans>
```

The `<neo4j:config>` element configures the details of how to access the database. In this case, it configures Spring Data Neo4j to work with an embedded database. Specifically, the `storeDirectory` attribute specifies the path in the filesystem where the data will be persisted. The `base-package` attribute sets the package where the model classes are defined.

As for `<neo4j:repositories>`, it enables Spring Data Neo4j to automatically generate repository implementations by scanning the `orders.db` package and looking for interfaces that extend the `Repository` interface.

To configure Spring Neo4j to access a remote Neo4j server, all you need to do is declare a `SpringRestGraphDatabase` bean and set `<neo4j:config>`'s `graphDatabase-Service` attribute:

```
<neo4j:config base-package="orders"
              graphDatabaseService="graphDatabaseService" />

<bean id="graphDatabaseService" class=
        "org.springframework.data.neo4j.rest.SpringRestGraphDatabase">
  <constructor-arg value="http://graphdbserver:7474/db/data/" />
  <constructor-arg value="db.username" />
  <constructor-arg value="db.password" />
</bean>
```

Whether you configure Spring Data Neo4j using Java or XML, you'll need to be sure that the domain types are under a package specified as a base package (`@EnableNeo4jRepositories`'s `basePackages` attribute or `<neo4j:config>`'s `base-package` attribute). They'll also need to be annotated as either node entities or relationship entities. That's what you'll do next.

12.2.2 Annotating graph entities

Neo4j defines two kinds of entities: nodes and relationships. Node entities typically represent the things in your application, whereas relationship entities define how those things are related.

Spring Data Neo4j provides several annotations that you can apply to domain types and their fields for persistence in Neo4j. Table 12.3 describes these annotations.

To see how a few of these annotations are used, let's apply these annotations to our order/item example.

One way you can model the data is to designate an order as a node that's related to one or more items. Figure 12.2 illustrates this model as a graph.

To designate orders as nodes, you'll need to annotate the `Order` class with `@Node-Entity`. The next listing shows the `Order` class annotated with `@NodeEntity`, as well as a few other annotations from table 12.3.

Table 12.3 Spring Data Neo4j annotations you can use to map domain types to nodes and relationships in a graph

Annotation	Description
@NodeEntity	Declares a Java type as a node entity
@RelationshipEntity	Declares a Java type as a relationship entity
@StartNode	Declares a property as the start node of a relationship entity
@EndNode	Declares a property as the end node of a relationship entity
@Fetch	Declares a property on an entity to be eagerly loaded
@GraphId	Declares a property as the ID field of an entity (the field must be a Long)
@GraphProperty	Explicitly declares a property
@GraphTraversal	Declares a property to automatically provide an iterable that's built by following a graph traversal
@Indexed	Declares a property to be indexed
@Labels	Declares the labels for an @NodeEntity
@Query	Declares a property to automatically provide an iterable that's built by executing a given Cypher query
@QueryResult	Declares a Java class or interface as being able to hold the results of a query
@RelatedTo	Declares a simple relationship between the current @NodeEntity and another @NodeEntity via a property
@RelatedToVia	Declares a field on an @NodeEntity as referencing an @RelationshipEntity that the node belongs to
@RelationshipType	Declares a field as the type of a relationship entity
@ResultColumn	Declares a property on an @QueryResult-annotated type to capture a specific field from a query result

Figure 12.2 A simple relationship connects two nodes but carries no properties of its own.

Listing 12.10 Order is annotated to be a node in the graph database

```
package orders;
import java.util.LinkedHashSet;
import java.util.Set;
import org.springframework.data.neo4j.annotation.GraphId;
```

```
import org.springframework.data.neo4j.annotation.NodeEntity;
import org.springframework.data.neo4j.annotation.RelatedTo;

@NodeEntity                              ◁— Orders are nodes
public class Order {

  @GraphId                                        ◁— The graph ID
  private Long id;
  private String customer;
  private String type;

  @RelatedTo(type="HAS_ITEMS")                      ◁— Relationship to items
  private Set<Item> items = new LinkedHashSet<Item>();

  ...

}
```

In addition to the `@NodeEntity` at the class level, notice that the `id` property is anno-tated with `@GraphId`. All entities in Neo4j must have a graph ID. This is roughly analo-gous to the `@Id`-annotated properties of a JPA `@Entity` or a MongoDB `@Document`. It's required that the `@GraphId`-annotated property be a `Long`.

The `customer` and `type` properties remain annotation-free. Unless they are tran-sient, they'll be properties on the node in the database.

The `items` property is annotated with `@RelatedTo`, indicating that an `Order` is related to a `Set` of `Item`. The `type` attribute essentially labels the relationship. It can be given any value, but it's commonly given human-readable text that briefly describes the nature of the relationship. Later you'll use this label in queries to query across relationships.

As for the `Item` class itself, the following listing shows how it's annotated for graph persistence.

Listing 12.11   Items are also represented as nodes in the graph database.

```
package orders;
import org.springframework.data.neo4j.annotation.GraphId;
import org.springframework.data.neo4j.annotation.NodeEntity;

@NodeEntity                              ◁— Items are nodes
public class Item {

  @GraphId                                ◁— The graph ID
  private Long id;
  private String product;
  private double price;
  private int quantity;

  ...

}
```

As with `Order`, `Item` is annotated as `@NodeEntity` to designate it as a node. It also has a `Long` property annotated to be the node's graph ID with `@GraphId`. The `product`, price, and `quantity` properties will also be persisted as node properties in the graph database.

The relationship between `Order` and `Item` is simple in that it doesn't carry any data of its own. Therefore, the `@RelatedTo` annotation is sufficient to define the relationship. But not all relationships are so simple.

Let's reconsider how we've modeled this data to see how to work with more complex relationships. In the current data model, we've combined the concepts of a line item and a product into the `Item` class. When you think about it, however, an order is related to one or more products. The relationship between an order and a product constitutes a line item of the order. Figure 12.3 illustrates an alternative way to model the data in a graph.

Figure 12.3 A relationship entity is a relationship that has properties of its own.

In this new model, the quantity of products in the order is a property of the line item, and a product is a different concept. As before, orders are nodes and so are products. Line items are relationships. But now that a line item must carry a quantity value, the relationship can't be simple. You're going to need to define a class that represents a line item, such as `LineItem` in the next listing.

Listing 12.12 A `LineItem` connects an `Order` node and a `Product` node.

```
package orders;
import org.springframework.data.neo4j.annotation.EndNode;
import org.springframework.data.neo4j.annotation.GraphId;
import org.springframework.data.neo4j.annotation.RelationshipEntity;
import org.springframework.data.neo4j.annotation.StartNode;

@RelationshipEntity(type="HAS_LINE_ITEM_FOR")      ⟵— LineItem is a relationship
public class LineItem {

    @GraphId                          ⟵— The graph ID
    private Long id;

    @StartNode                              ⟵— The start node
    private Order order;

    @EndNode                                   ⟵— The end node
    private Product product;

    private int quantity;

    ...

}
```

Whereas `Order` was annotated with `@NodeEntity` to designate it as a node, `LineItem` is annotated with `@RelationshipEntity`. `LineItem` also has an `id` property annotated with @GraphId. Again, all entities, both node entities and relationship entities, must have a graph ID and it must be of type Long.

What makes relationship entities special is that they connect two node entities. The @StartNode and @EndNode annotations are applied to properties that define each end of a relationship. In this case, the Order is the start node and the Product is the end node.

Finally, LineItem has a quantity property that will be persisted to the database when the relationship is created.

Now that the domain is annotated, you're ready to start saving and reading nodes and relationships. We'll start by looking at how you can use Spring Data Neo4j's template-oriented data access with Neo4jTemplate.

12.2.3   *Working with Neo4jTemplate*

Just as Spring Data MongoDB provides MongoTemplate for template-based MongoDB persistence, Spring Data Neo4j brings Neo4jTemplate to the table to work with nodes and relationships in the Neo4j graph database. If you've configured Spring Data Neo4j as shown earlier, then there's already a Neo4jTemplate bean in the Spring application context. All you need to do is inject it wherever you need it.

For example, you might autowire it directly into a bean property:

```
@Autowired
private Neo4jOperations neo4j;
```

Neo4jTemplate defines several dozen methods, including methods for saving nodes, deleting nodes, and creating relationships between nodes. There's not enough space to cover all of them, but let's have a look at a few of the most commonly used methods that Neo4jTemplate provides.

One of the first and most basic things you might want to do with Neo4jTemplate is to save an object as a node. Assuming that the object is annotated with @NodeEntity, you can use the save() method like this:

```
Order order = ...;
Order savedOrder = neo4j.save(order);
```

If you happen to know the object's graph ID, you can fetch it using the findOne() method:

```
Order order = neo4j.findOne(42, Order.class);
```

If there is no node with the given ID, then findOne() will throw a NotFoundException.

If you'd like to retrieve all objects of a given type, you can use the findAll() method:

```
EndResult<Order> allOrders = neo4j.findAll(Order.class);
```

The EndResult returned here is an Iterable, enabling it to be used in for-each looping and anywhere else an Iterable may be used. If no such nodes exist, findAll() will return an empty Iterable.

If all you need to know is a count of how many objects of a given type are in the Neo4j database, you can call the `count()` method:

```
long orderCount = count(Order.class);
```

The `delete()` method can be used to delete an object:

```
neo4j.delete(order);
```

One of the most interesting methods provided by `Neo4jTemplate` is the `create-RelationshipBetween()` method. As you might guess, it creates a relationship between two nodes. For example, you could create a `LineItem` relationship between an `Order` node and a `Product` node:

```
Order order = ...;
Product prod = ...;
LineItem lineItem = neo4j.createRelationshipBetween(
    order, prod, LineItem.class, "HAS_LINE_ITEM_FOR", false);
lineItem.setQuantity(5);
neo4j.save(lineItem);
```

The first two parameters to `createRelationshipBetween()` are the objects whose nodes will be at each end of the relationship. The next parameter specifies the `@RelationshipEntity`-annotated type that will represent the relationship. Next, you specify a `String` value that describes the nature of the relationship. The final parameter is a `boolean` that indicates whether or not duplicate relationships are allowed between the two node entities.

`createRelationshipBetween()` returns an instance of the relationship class. From there you can set any properties you'd like. The preceding example sets the `quantity` property. When you're done, you call `save()` to save the relationship to the database.

The `Neo4jTemplate` offers a straightforward way to work with nodes and relationships in a Neo4j graph database. But it requires that you write your own repository implementations that delegate to `Neo4jTemplate`. Let's see how Spring Data Neo4j can automatically generate repository implementations for you.

12.2.4 *Creating automatic Neo4j repositories*

One of the most awesome things that most Spring Data projects do is automatically generate implementations for a repository interface. You've already seen this with Spring Data JPA and Spring Data MongoDB. Not to be left out, Spring Data Neo4j also supports automatic repository generation.

You've already added `@EnableNeo4jRepositories` to your configuration, so Spring Data Neo4j is already set to generate repositories. All you need to do is write the interfaces. The following `OrderRepository` interface is a good start:

```
package orders.db;
import orders.Order;
import org.springframework.data.neo4j.repository.GraphRepository;

public interface OrderRepository extends GraphRepository<Order> {}
```

Just like the other Spring Data projects, Spring Data Neo4j triggers repository generation for interfaces that extend the Repository interface. In this case, OrderRepository extends GraphRepository, which indirectly extends Repository. Therefore, Spring Data Neo4j will generate an implementation for OrderRepository at runtime.

Notice that GraphRepository is parameterized with Order, the type of entity that the repository works with. Because Neo4j requires that graph IDs be of type Long, there's no need to specify the ID type when extending GraphRepository.

Out of the box, you get several common CRUD operations, much like what Jpa-Repository and MongoRepository provide. Table 12.4 describes the methods you get by extending GraphRepository.

Table 12.4 By extending `GraphRepository`, a repository interface inherits several CRUD operations that are automatically implemented by Spring Data Neo4j.

Method	Description
`long count();`	Returns a count of how many entities of the target type are in the database
`void delete(Iterable<? extends T>);`	Deletes several entities
`void delete(Long id);`	Deletes a single entity given its ID
`void delete(T);`	Deletes a single entity
`void deleteAll();`	Deletes all entities of the target type
`boolean exists(Long id);`	Checks for the existence of an entity given its ID
`EndResult<T> findAll();`	Retrieves all entities of the target type
`Iterable<T> findAll(Iterable<Long>);`	Retrieves all entities of the target type for the given IDs
`Page<T> findAll(Pageable);`	Retrieves a paged and sorted list of all entities of the target type
`EndResult<T> findAll(Sort);`	Retrieves a sorted list of all entities of the target type
`EndResult<T> findAllBySchemaPropertyValue(String, Object);`	Retrieves all entities where a given property matches the given value
`Iterable<T> findAllByTraversal(N, TraversalDescription);`	Retrieves all entities obtained by following a graph traversal starting at a given node
`T findBySchemaPropertyValue(String, Object);`	Finds a single entity where a given property matches a given value
`T findOne(Long);`	Finds a single entity given its ID
`EndResult<T> query(String, Map<String,Object>);`	Finds all entities that match a given Cypher query

Table 12.4 By extending `GraphRepository`, a repository interface inherits several CRUD operations that are automatically implemented by Spring Data Neo4j. *(continued)*

Method	Description
`Iterable<T> save(Iterable<T>);`	Saves several entities
`S save(S);`	Saves a single entity

There's not enough space to cover all of these methods, but there are a few methods that you'll get a lot of use out of. For example, the following line saves a single `Order` entity:

```
Order savedOrder = orderRepository.save(order);
```

When the entity is saved, the `save()` method returns the saved entity, which now should have its `@GraphId`-annotated property populated if it was `null` before.

You can look up a single entity by calling the `findOne()` method. For example, this line will look up an `Order` whose graph ID is 4:

```
Order order = orderRepository.findOne(4L);
```

Or, you can look up all orders:

```
EndResult<Order> allOrders = orderRepository.findAll();
```

Of course, you may want to delete an entity. In that case, you can use the `delete()` method:

```
delete(order);
```

This will delete the given `Order` node from the database. If you only have the graph ID, you can pass it to `delete()` instead of the node type itself:

```
delete(orderId);
```

If you want to do custom queries, you could use the `query()` method to execute an arbitrary Cypher query against the graph. But that's not much different than working with the `query()` method from `Neo4jTemplate`. Instead, you can add your own query methods to `OrderRepository`.

ADDING QUERY METHODS

You've already seen how to add query methods that follow a naming convention using Spring Data JPA and Spring Data MongoDB. It'd be awfully disappointing if Spring Data Neo4j didn't offer the same capability.

As the next listing shows, there's no need to be disappointed.

Listing 12.13 Defining query methods by following a naming convention.

```
package orders.db;
import java.util.List;
import orders.Order;
```

```
import org.springframework.data.neo4j.repository.GraphRepository;

public interface OrderRepository extends GraphRepository<Order> {
  List<Order> findByCustomer(String customer);
  List<Order> findByCustomerAndType(String customer, String type);
}
```

Query methods

Here you add two query methods. One finds all `Order` nodes where the `customer` property is equal to the given `String` value. The other method is similar, but in addition to matching the `customer` property, the `Order` nodes must also have a `type` property equal to the given type.

We've already discussed the naming convention for query methods, so there's no need to dwell on it any further. Refer to the previous chapter's discussion of Spring Data JPA for a refresher on how to write these methods.

SPECIFYING CUSTOM QUERIES

When the naming convention doesn't meet your needs, you also have the option of annotating a method with `@Query` to specify your own query. You've seen `@Query` before. With Spring Data JPA, you used it to specify a JPA query for a repository method. With Spring Data MongoDB, you used it to specify a JSON-matching query. When using Spring Data Neo4j, however, you must specify a Cypher query:

```
@Query("match (o:Order)-[:HAS_ITEMS]->(i:Item) " +
       "where i.product='Spring in Action' return o")
List<Order> findSiAOrders();
```

Here, the `findSiAOrders()` is annotated with `@Query` and given a Cypher query to find all `Order` nodes that are related to an `Item` whose `product` property is equal to "Spring in Action".

MIXING IN CUSTOM REPOSITORY BEHAVIOR

When neither the naming convention nor the `@Query` methods meet your needs, you always have the option of mixing in custom repository logic.

For example, suppose that you want to write the implementation of `find-SiAOrders()` yourself, instead of relying on the `@Query` annotation. You can start by defining an intermediary interface that carries the definition of the `findSiAOrders()` method:

```
package orders.db;
import java.util.List;
import orders.Order;

public interface OrderOperations {
  List<Order> findSiAOrders();
}
```

Then you can change `OrderRepository` to extend `OrderOperations` in addition to `GraphRepository`:

```
public interface OrderRepository
        extends GraphRepository<Order>, OrderOperations {

  ...

}
```

Finally, you need to write the implementation itself. As with Spring Data JPA and Spring Data MongoDB, Spring Data Neo4j will look for an implementation class whose name is the same as the repository interface with an "Impl" suffix. Therefore, you need to create an OrderRepositoryImpl class. The following listing shows Order-RepositoryImpl, which implements findSiAOrders().

Listing 12.14 Mixing custom functionality into OrderRepository

```
package orders.db;
import java.util.Collections;
import java.util.List;
import java.util.Map;
import orders.Order;
import org.neo4j.helpers.collection.IteratorUtil;
import org.springframework.beans.factory.annotation.Autowired;
import org.springframework.data.neo4j.conversion.EndResult;
import org.springframework.data.neo4j.conversion.Result;
import org.springframework.data.neo4j.template.Neo4jOperations;     ◁─┐ Implement
                                                                      │ intermediate
public class OrderRepositoryImpl implements OrderOperations {  ◁──────┘ interface

  private final Neo4jOperations neo4j;

  @Autowired                                                          ┐ Inject
  public OrderRepositoryImpl(Neo4jOperations neo4j) {   ◁─────────────┘ Neo4jOperations
    this.neo4j = neo4j;
  }

  public List<Order> findSiAOrders() {
    Result<Map<String, Object>> result = neo4j.query(      ◁── Perform query
            "match (o:Order)-[:HAS_ITEMS]->(i:Item) " +
            "where i.product='Spring in Action' return o",

    EndResult<Order> endResult = result.to(Order.class);   ◁─┐ Convert to
                                                              │ EndResult<Order>
    return IteratorUtil.asList(endResult);    ◁─┐ Convert to a
  }                                             │ List<Order>
}
```

OrderRepositoryImpl is injected with Neo4jOperations (specifically, an instance of Neo4jTemplate), which it uses to query the database. Because the query() method returns a Result<Map<String, Object>>, you'll need to convert it to a List<Order>. The first step is to call the to() method on the Result to produce an EndResult<Order>. Then you use Neo4j's IteratorUtil.asList() to convert the EndResult<Order> to a List<Order>, which is then returned.

Graph databases such as Neo4j are wonderful for capturing data that's represented well as nodes and relationships. When you consider that the world we live in is made up of all kinds of things that are related to each other, graph databases may be suitable for a wide range of domains. And, speaking personally, I'll admit that I have a strong fondness for Neo4j.

But sometimes your data needs are simpler. Sometimes you only need to store a value somewhere and be able to retrieve it later with a key. Let's see how Spring Data enables key-value data persistence using the Redis key-value store.

12.3 Working with key-value data in Redis

Redis is a special kind of database known as a key-value store. As the name implies, key-value stores keep key-value pairs. In fact, key-value stores share a lot in common with hash maps. To call them persistent hash maps would not be too great of an over-simplification.

When you think about it, there aren't too many kinds of queries that you can perform against a hash map ... or a key-value store. You can store a value at a particular key, and you can fetch the value for a particular key. That's about it. Consequently, Spring Data's automatic repository support doesn't make a lot of sense when applied to Redis. On the other hand, Spring Data's other key feature, template-oriented data access, can come in handy when working with Redis.

Spring Data Redis comes with a couple of template implementations for storing data to and fetching it from a Redis database. You'll see how to use them soon. But to create one of Spring Data Redis's templates, you'll need a Redis connection factory. Fortunately, Spring Data Redis offers four to choose from.

12.3.1 Connecting to Redis

A Redis connection factory produces connections to a Redis database server. Spring Data Redis comes with connection factories for four Redis client implementations:

- `JedisConnectionFactory`
- `JredisConnectionFactory`
- `LettuceConnectionFactory`
- `SrpConnectionFactory`

The choice is up to you. I encourage you to do your own testing and benchmarking to determine which Redis client and connection factory fits your needs best. From Spring Data Redis's perspective, all of these connection factories are equally suitable.

Once you've made your choice, you can configure the connection factory as a bean in Spring. For example, here's how you might configure the `JedisConnection-Factory` bean:

```
@Bean
public RedisConnectionFactory redisCF() {
  return new JedisConnectionFactory();
}
```

Instantiating the connection factory via its default constructor results in a connection factory that creates its connections for localhost, port 6379, and with no password. If your Redis server is running on a different host or port, you can set those properties when you create the connection factory:

```
@Bean
public RedisConnectionFactory redisCF() {
  JedisConnectionFactory cf = new JedisConnectionFactory();
  cf.setHostName("redis-server");
  cf.setPort(7379);
  return cf;
}
```

Similarly, if your Redis server is configured to require authorization from clients, you can set the password by calling setPassword():

```
@Bean
public RedisConnectionFactory redisCF() {
  JedisConnectionFactory cf = new JedisConnectionFactory();
  cf.setHostName("redis-server");
  cf.setPort(7379);
  cf.setPassword("foobared");
  return cf;
}
```

In all of these examples, I've been assuming the JedisConnectionFactory. If you've made a different choice, then any of the other connection factories can be a drop-in replacement. For example, if you'd rather use the LettuceConnectionFactory, you can configure it like this:

```
@Bean
public RedisConnectionFactory redisCF() {
  JedisConnectionFactory cf = new LettuceConnectionFactory();
  cf.setHostName("redis-server");
  cf.setPort(7379);
  cf.setPassword("foobared");
  return cf;
}
```

All of the Redis connection factories have setHostName(), setPort(), and set-Password() methods. This makes them virtually identical in terms of configuration.

Now that you have a Redis connection factory, you're ready to start working with Spring Data Redis's templates.

12.3.2 *Working with RedisTemplate*

As their names suggest, the Redis connection factories produce connections (as RedisConnection) to a Redis key-value store. Using RedisConnection, you can store and read data. For example, you might obtain a connection and use it to store a greeting like this:

```
RedisConnectionFactory cf = ...;
RedisConnection conn = cf.getConnection();
```

```
conn.set("greeting".getBytes(), "Hello World".getBytes());
```

Likewise, you could retrieve that greeting value using a RedisConnection like this:

```
byte[] greetingBytes = conn.get("greeting".getBytes());
String greeting = new String(greetingBytes);
```

No doubt, this will work. But do you really like working with arrays of bytes?

As with other Spring Data projects, Spring Data Redis offers a higher-level data access option with templates. In fact, Spring Data Redis offers two templates:

- RedisTemplate
- StringRedisTemplate

RedisTemplate is a class that greatly simplifies Redis data access, enabling you to persist keys and values of any type, not just byte arrays. In recognition of the fact that keys and values are frequently Strings, StringRedisTemplate extends RedisTemplate to have a String focus.

Assuming you have a RedisConnectionFactory available, you can construct a RedisTemplate like this:

```
RedisConnectionFactory cf = ...;
RedisTemplate<String, Product> redis =
    new RedisTemplate<String, Product>();
redis.setConnectionFactory(cf);
```

Note that RedisTemplate is parameterized with two types. The first type is that of the key, and the second is that of the value. In the RedisTemplate constructed here, Product objects will be stored as values assigned to String keys.

If you know that you'll be working with both String values and String keys, then you should consider using StringRedisTemplate instead of RedisTemplate:

```
RedisConnectionFactory cf = ...;
StringRedisTemplate redis = new StringRedisTemplate(cf);
```

Notice that, unlike RedisTemplate, StringRedisTemplate has a constructor that accepts a RedisConnectionFactory. Therefore, there's no need to call setConnection-Factory() after construction.

Although it's not required, if you'll be using RedisTemplate or StringRedis-Template frequently, you might consider configuring them as beans to be injected where they're needed. Here's a simple @Bean method declaring a RedisTemplate bean:

```
@Bean
public RedisTemplate<String, Product>
                            redisTemplate(RedisConnectionFactory cf) {
  RedisTemplate<String, Product> redis =
      new RedisTemplate<String, Product>();
  redis.setConnectionFactory(cf);
  return redis;
}
```

And here's a bean method to declare a StringRedisTemplate bean:

```
@Bean
public StringRedisTemplate
                    stringRedisTemplate(RedisConnectionFactory cf) {
  return new StringRedisTemplate(cf);
}
```

Once you have a `RedisTemplate` (or `StringRedisTemplate`), you can start saving, fetching, and deleting key-value entries. Most of the operations provided by `Redis-Template` are available via the sub-APIs listed in table 12.5.

Table 12.5 RedisTemplate offers much of its functionality via sub-APIs, which differentiate single values from collection values.

Method	Sub-API interface	Description
opsForValue()	ValueOperations<K, V>	Operations for working with entries having simple values
opsForList()	ListOperations<K, V>	Operations for working with entries having list values
opsForSet()	SetOperations<K, V>	Operations for working with entries having set values
opsForZSet()	ZSetOperations<K, V>	Operations for working with entries having ZSet (sorted set) values
opsForHash()	HashOperations<K, HK, HV>	Operations for working with entries having hash values
boundValueOps(K)	BoundValueOperations<K,V>	Operations for working with simple values bound to a given key
boundListOps(K)	BoundListOperations<K,V>	Operations for working with list values bound to a given key
boundSetOps(K)	BoundSetOperations<K,V>	Operations for working with set values bound to a given key
boundZSet(K)	BoundZSetOperations<K,V>	Operations for working with ZSet (sorted set) values bound to a given key
boundHashOps(K)	BoundHashOperations<K,V>	Operations for working with hash values bound to a given key

As you can see, the sub-APIs in table 12.5 are available through methods on `Redis-Template` (and `StringRedisTemplate`). Each one provides operations that work with entries based on whether the value is a simple value or a collection of values.

Across all of these sub-APIs, there are several dozen methods for saving and fetching data in Redis. We don't have space enough to cover them all, but we'll look at a handful of the most common operations you'll need.

WORKING WITH SIMPLE VALUES

Suppose that you want to save a `Product` to a `RedisTemplate<String, Product>` where the key is the value of the `sku` property. The following snippet of code will do that via `opsForValue()`:

```
redis.opsForValue().set(product.getSku(), product);
```

Similarly, if you wanted to fetch a product whose `sku` is `123456`, you could use this snippet:

```
Product product = redis.opsForValue().get("123456");
```

If no entry can be found with the given key, `null` will be returned.

WORKING WITH LISTS

Working with list values is similarly straightforward via `opsForList()`. For example, you can add a value to the end of a list entry like this:

```
redis.opsForList().rightPush("cart", product);
```

This adds a `Product` to the end of the list stored at the key `cart`. If a list doesn't already exist at that key, one will be created.

Whereas the `rightPush()` method adds an element to the end of a list entry, `left-Push()` inserts a value at the beginning:

```
redis.opsForList().leftPush("cart", product);
```

There are a number of ways you can fetch an item from a list. You can pop an entry off of either end using `leftPop()` or `rightPop()`:

```
Product first = redis.opsForList().leftPop("cart");
Product last = redis.opsForList().rightPop("cart");
```

Aside from fetching a value from the list, these two pop methods have the side effect of removing the popped items from the list. If you'd rather simply retrieve the value (perhaps even from the middle of the list), you can use the `range()` method:

```
List<Product> products = redis.opsForList().range("cart", 2, 12);
```

The `range()` method doesn't remove any values from the list entry, but it does retrieve one or more values given the key and a range of indexes. The preceding example fetches as many as eleven entries starting with the entry at index 2 and going through index 12 (inclusive). If the range exceeds the bounds of the list, then only the entries within those indexes will be returned. If no entries fall within the indexes, an empty list will be returned.

PERFORMING OPERATIONS ON SETS

In addition to lists, you can also work with sets via the `opsForSet()` method. The most basic thing you can do is add an item to a set entry:

```
redis.opsForSet().add("cart", product);
```

Once you have a few set entries created and populated with values, you can perform interesting operations against those sets, including difference, intersection, and union.

```
List<Product> diff = redis.opsForSet().difference("cart1", "cart2");
List<Product> union = redis.opsForSet().union("cart1", "cart2");
List<Product> isect = redis.opsForSet().isect("cart1", "cart2");
```

Of course, you can also remove items:

```
redis.opsForSet().remove(product);
```

And you can even fetch a random element from the set:

```
Product random = redis.opsForSet().randomMember("cart");
```

As sets don't have indexes or any implicit ordering, you can't pinpoint and fetch a single item from the set.

BINDING TO A KEY

Table 12.5 includes five sub-APIs for working with operations bound to a given key. These sub-APIs mirror the other sub-APIs, but focus on a given key.

As an example of how these are used, let's consider the case where you're storing `Product` objects in a list entry whose key is `cart`. In that scenario, suppose that you want to pop an item from the right end of the list and then add three new items to the end of the list. You can do that using the `BoundListOperations` returned from calling `boundListOps()`:

```
BoundListOperations<String, Product> cart =
        redis.boundListOps("cart");
Product popped = cart.rightPop();
cart.rightPush(product1);
cart.rightPush(product2);
cart.rightPush(product3);
```

Notice that the only time that the entry's key is mentioned is when calling `bound-ListOps()`. All of the operations performed against the returned `BoundList-Operations` will be applied to that entry.

12.3.3 *Setting key and value serializers*

When an entry is saved to the Redis key-value store, both the key and the value are serialized using a Redis serializer. Spring Data Redis comes with several such serializers, including these:

- `GenericToStringSerializer`—Serializes using a Spring conversion service
- `JacksonJsonRedisSerializer`—Serializes objects to JSON using Jackson 1
- `Jackson2JsonRedisSerializer`—Serializes objects to JSON using Jackson 2
- `JdkSerializationRedisSerializer`—Uses Java serialization
- `OxmSerializer`—Serializes using marshalers and unmarshalers from Spring's O/X mapping, for XML serialization

- StringRedisSerializer—Serializes `String` keys and values

All of these serializers implement the `RedisSerializer` interface, so if there's not one to suit your needs, you can always create your own serializer.

`RedisTemplate` uses `JdkSerializationRedisSerializer`, which means that keys and values are serialized through Java. As you might expect, `StringRedisTemplate` uses `StringRedisSerializer` by default, essentially converting the `String` values to and from `byte` arrays. These defaults are suitable for many cases, but you may find it helpful to plug in a different serializer.

For example, suppose that when using `RedisTemplate`, you want to serialize `Product` values to JSON with `String` keys. The `setKeySerializer()` and `setValue-Serializer()` methods of `RedisTemplate` are what you need:

```
@Bean
public RedisTemplate<String, Product>
       redisTemplate(RedisConnectionFactory cf) {
  RedisTemplate<String, Product> redis =
      new RedisTemplate<String, Product>();
  redis.setConnectionFactory(cf);
  redis.setKeySerializer(new StringRedisSerializer());
  redis.setValueSerializer(
      new Jackson2JsonRedisSerializer<Product>(Product.class));
  return redis;
}
```

Here, you set `RedisTemplate` to always use `StringRedisSerializer` when serializing key values. You also specify that it should use `Jackson2JsonRedisSerializer` only when serializing `Product` values.

12.4 *Summary*

Gone are the days when the only choice for data persistence was a relational database. Now there are several different kinds of databases, each representing data in different forms and offering capabilities to suit a variety of domain models. The Spring Data project enables developers to use these databases in their Spring applications and to use abstractions that are reasonably consistent across the various database choices.

In this chapter, we built on what you learned about Spring Data in the previous chapter when using JPA, applying it to the MongoDB document database and the Neo4j graph database. Just like their JPA counterpart, the Spring Data MongoDB and Spring Data Neo4j projects both offer automatic generation of repositories based on interface definitions. Additionally, you saw how to use the annotations provided by the Spring Data projects to map domain types to documents, nodes, and relationships.

Spring Data also enables data to be persisted to the Redis key-value store. Key-value stores are significantly simpler and thus do not require support for automatic repositories or mapping annotations. Nevertheless, Spring Data Redis offers two different template classes for working with the Redis key-value store.

No matter what kind of database you choose, fetching data from the database is a costly operation. In fact, database queries are often the biggest performance bottlenecks in any application. Now that you've seen how to store and fetch data from a variety of data sources, let's look at how to avoid that bottleneck. In the next chapter, you'll see how to apply declarative caching to prevent unnecessary database fetches.

Caching data

This chapter covers

- Enabling declarative caching
- Caching with Ehcache, Redis, and GemFire
- Annotation-oriented caching

Have you ever had someone ask you a question and then, moments after you reply, ask you the same thing again? Often, I'm asked this type of question by my children:

"Can I have some candy?"
"What time is it?"
"Are we there yet?"
"Can I have some candy?"

In many ways, the components of the applications we write are the same way. Stateless components tend to scale better, but they also tend to ask the same question over and over again. Because they're stateless, they discard any answer they were given once their current task is complete, and they have to ask the question again the next time that same answer is needed.

Sometimes it takes a little while to fetch or calculate the answer to the question being asked. Maybe you must fetch data from the database, invoke a remote service, or perform a complex calculation. That's time and resources spent arriving at the answer.

If that answer isn't likely to change frequently (or at all), then it's wasteful to go through the same channel to fetch it again. Moreover, doing so can and likely will have a negative impact on the performance of your application. Instead of asking the same question over and over, only to arrive at the same answer each time, it makes sense to ask once and remember that answer when it's needed later.

Caching is a way to store frequently needed information so that it's readily available when needed. In this chapter, we'll look at Spring's cache abstraction. Although Spring doesn't implement a cache solution, it offers declarative support for caching that integrates with several popular caching implementations.

13.1 *Enabling cache support*

Spring's cache abstraction comes in two forms:

- Annotation-driven caching
- XML-declared caching

The most common way to use Spring's cache abstraction is to annotate methods with annotations like @Cacheable and @CacheEvict. You'll spend most of this chapter working with that form of declarative caching. Then, in section 13.3, we'll look at how to declare cache boundaries in XML.

Before you can start applying caching annotations in your beans, you must enable Spring's support for annotation-driven caching. If you're using Java configuration, you can enable annotation-driven caching by adding @EnableCaching to one of your configuration classes. The following listing shows the @EnableCaching annotation in action.

> **Listing 13.1 Enabling annotation-driven caching with @EnableCaching**

```
package com.habuma.cachefun;
import org.springframework.cache.CacheManager;
import org.springframework.cache.annotation.EnableCaching;
import org.springframework.cache.concurrent.ConcurrentMapCacheManager;
import org.springframework.context.annotation.Bean;
import org.springframework.context.annotation.Configuration;

@Configuration
@EnableCaching                              <—— Enable caching
public class CachingConfig {

  @Bean
  public CacheManager cacheManager() {      <—— Declare a cache manager
    return new ConcurrentMapCacheManager();
  }

}
```

If you're configuring your application with XML, you can enable annotation-driven caching with the <cache:annotation-driven> element from Spring's cache namespace.

Listing 13.2 Enabling annotation-driven caching with `<cache:annotation-driven>`

```xml
<?xml version="1.0" encoding="UTF-8"?>
<beans xmlns="http://www.springframework.org/schema/beans"
  xmlns:xsi="http://www.w3.org/2001/XMLSchema-instance"
  xmlns:cache="http://www.springframework.org/schema/cache"
  xsi:schemaLocation="
    http://www.springframework.org/schema/beans
    http://www.springframework.org/schema/beans/spring-beans.xsd
    http://www.springframework.org/schema/cache
    http://www.springframework.org/schema/cache/spring-cache.xsd">

  <cache:annotation-driven />                              ⟵── Enable caching

  <bean id="cacheManager" class=
  "org.springframework.cache.concurrent.ConcurrentMapCacheManager" />   ⟵─┐

</beans>                                                 Declare a cache manager
```

Under the covers, `@EnableCaching` and `<cache:annotation-driven>` work the same way. They create an aspect with pointcuts that trigger off of Spring's caching annotations. Depending on the annotation used and the state of the cache, that aspect will fetch a value from the cache, add a value to the cache, or remove a value from the cache.

You've probably noticed that both listings 13.1 and 13.2 do more than enable annotation-driven caching. They also declare a cache-manager bean. Cache managers are the heart of Spring's cache abstraction, enabling integration with one of several popular caching implementations.

In this case, a `ConcurrentMapCacheManager` is declared. This simple cache manager uses a `java.util.concurrent.ConcurrentHashMap` as its cache store. Its simplicity makes it a tempting choice for development, testing, or basic applications. But because its cache storage is memory-based and thus tied to the lifecycle of the application, it's probably not an ideal choice for larger production applications.

Fortunately, several great cache-manager options are available. Let's look at a few of the most commonly used cache managers.

13.1.1 Configuring a cache manager

Out of the box, Spring 3.1 comes with five cache-manager implementations:

- `SimpleCacheManager`
- `NoOpCacheManager`
- `ConcurrentMapCacheManager`
- `CompositeCacheManager`
- `EhCacheCacheManager`

Spring 3.2 introduced another cache manager for working with JCache (JSR-107) based cache providers. Outside of the core Spring Framework, Spring Data offers two more cache managers:

- `RedisCacheManager` (from Spring Data Redis)
- `GemfireCacheManager` (from Spring Data GemFire)

As you can see, you have plenty of choices when it comes to selecting a cache manager for Spring's cache abstraction. Which one you select will depend on what underlying cache provider you want to use. Each will provide your application with a different flavor of caching, and some are more production-ready than others. Although the choice you make will have implications for how your data is cached, it will have no bearing on the way you declare caching rules in Spring.

You must select and configure a cache manager as a bean in your Spring application context. You've already seen how to configure a `ConcurrentMapCacheManager` and learned that it may not be the best choice for real-world applications. Now let's see how to configure some of Spring's other cache managers, starting with `EhCacheCacheManager`.

CACHING WITH EHCACHE

Ehcache is one of the most popular cache providers. The Ehcache website claims that it's "Java's most widely used cache." Given its wide adoption, it would make sense for Spring to offer a cache manager that integrates with Ehcache. `EhCacheCacheManager` is it.

Once you get past the name, which seems to stutter over the word *cache*, you'll find that `EhCacheCacheManager` is easily configured in Spring. The next listing shows how to configure it in Java.

> **Listing 13.3 Configuring `EhCacheCacheManager` in Java configuration**

```java
package com.habuma.cachefun;
import net.sf.ehcache.CacheManager;
import org.springframework.cache.annotation.EnableCaching;
import org.springframework.cache.ehcache.EhCacheCacheManager;
import org.springframework.cache.ehcache.EhCacheManagerFactoryBean;
import org.springframework.context.annotation.Bean;
import org.springframework.context.annotation.Configuration;
import org.springframework.core.io.ClassPathResource;

@Configuration
@EnableCaching
public class CachingConfig {

  @Bean
  public EhCacheCacheManager cacheManager(CacheManager cm) {       // Configure EhCacheCacheManager
    return new EhCacheCacheManager(cm);
  }

  @Bean
  public EhCacheManagerFactoryBean ehcache() {                     // EhCacheManagerFactoryBean
    EhCacheManagerFactoryBean ehCacheFactoryBean =
        new EhCacheManagerFactoryBean();
    ehCacheFactoryBean.setConfigLocation(
      new ClassPathResource("com/habuma/spittr/cache/ehcache.xml"));
```

```
      return ehCacheFactoryBean;
   }

}
```

The `cacheManager()` method in listing 13.3 creates an instance of `EhCacheCache-Manager` by passing in an instance of an Ehcache `CacheManager`. This particular bit of injection can be confusing because both Spring and Ehcache define a `CacheManager` type. To be clear, Ehcache's `CacheManager` is being injected into Spring's `EhCacheCacheManager` (which implements Spring's `CacheManager` implementation).

So that you'll have an Ehcache `CacheManager` to inject, you must also declare a `CacheManager` bean. To make that easy, Spring provides an `EhCacheManagerFactory-Bean` that generates an Ehcache `CacheManager`. The `ehcache()` method creates and returns an instance of `EhCacheManagerFactoryBean`. Because it's a factory bean (that is, it implements Spring's `FactoryBean` interface), the bean that is registered in the Spring application context isn't an instance of `EhCacheManagerFactoryBean` but rather is an instance of `CacheManager`, suitable for injection into `EhCacheCacheManager`.

There's more to Ehcache configuration than the beans you'll configure in Spring. Ehcache defines its own configuration schema for XML, and you'll configure caching specifics in an XML file that adheres to that schema. In the course of creating the `EhCacheManagerFactoryBean`, you need to tell it where the Ehcache configuration XML is located. Here you call the `setConfigLocation()` method, passing a `Class-PathResource` to specify the location of the Ehcache XML configuration relative to the root of the classpath.

The contents of the ehcache.xml file vary from application to application, but you need to declare at least a minimal cache. For example, the following Ehcache configuration declares a cache named `spittleCache` with 50 MB of maximum heap storage and a time-to-live of 100 seconds.

```
<ehcache>
  <cache name="spittleCache"
         maxBytesLocalHeap="50m"
         timeToLiveSeconds="100">
  </cache>
</ehcache>
```

Clearly, this is a basic Ehcache configuration. In your applications, you'll likely want to take advantage of the rich set of configuration options afforded by Ehcache. Consult Ehcache's documentation at http://ehcache.org/documentation/configuration for details on how to fine-tune your Ehcache configuration.

USING REDIS FOR CACHING

When you think about it, a cache entry is nothing more than a key-value pair where the key describes the operation and parameters from which the value was produced. Therefore, it isn't surprising to learn that Redis, which is a key-value store, is perfectly suited to be a cache store.

So that Redis can be used to store cache entries for Spring's caching abstraction, Spring Data Redis offers `RedisCacheManager`, an implementation of `CacheManager`. `RedisCacheManager` works with a Redis server via a `RedisTemplate` to store cache entries in Redis.

To use `RedisCacheManager`, you'll need a `RedisTemplate` bean and a bean that's an implementation of `RedisConnectionFactory` (such as `JedisConnectionFactory`). You saw how to configure those beans in chapter 12. With a `RedisTemplate` in place, it's a snap to configure a `RedisCacheManager`, as shown next.

Listing 13.4 Configuring a cache manager that stores cache entries in a Redis server

```java
package com.myapp;
import org.springframework.cache.CacheManager;
import org.springframework.cache.annotation.EnableCaching;
import org.springframework.context.annotation.Bean;
import org.springframework.data.redis.cache.RedisCacheManager;
import org.springframework.data.redis.connection.jedis
                                 .JedisConnectionFactory;
import org.springframework.data.redis.core.RedisTemplate;

@Configuration
@EnableCaching
public class CachingConfig {

  @Bean
  public CacheManager cacheManager(RedisTemplate redisTemplate) {
    return new RedisCacheManager(redisTemplate);      ◁─┐ Redis cache
  }                                                       manager bean

  @Bean
  public JedisConnectionFactory redisConnectionFactory() {  ◁─┐ Redis connection
    JedisConnectionFactory jedisConnectionFactory =              factory bean
            new JedisConnectionFactory();
    jedisConnectionFactory.afterPropertiesSet();
    return jedisConnectionFactory;
  }

  @Bean
  public RedisTemplate<String, String> redisTemplate(   ◁─┐ RedisTemplate
          RedisConnectionFactory redisCF) {                  bean
    RedisTemplate<String, String> redisTemplate =
            new RedisTemplate<String, String>();
    redisTemplate.setConnectionFactory(redisCF);
    redisTemplate.afterPropertiesSet();
    return redisTemplate;
  }

}
```

As you can see, you construct a `RedisCacheManager` by passing an instance of a `Redis-Template` as an argument to its constructor.

WORKING WITH MULTIPLE CACHE MANAGERS

There's no reason to think that you must choose one and only one cache manager. If you're having trouble pinning down which cache manager to use, or if you have valid technical reasons for choosing more than one cache manager, you can try Spring's CompositeCacheManager.

CompositeCacheManager is configured with one or more cache managers and iterates over them all as it tries to find a previously cached value. The following listing shows how to create a CompositeCacheManager bean that iterates over a JCacheCache-Manager, an EhCacheCacheManager, and a RedisCacheManager.

Listing 13.5 CompositeCacheManager iterates over a list of cache managers

```
@Bean
public CacheManager cacheManager(
      net.sf.ehcache.CacheManager cm,                          Create
      javax.cache.CacheManager jcm) {             CompositeCacheManager

  CompositeCacheManager cacheManager = new CompositeCacheManager();
  List<CacheManager> managers = new ArrayList<CacheManager>();
  managers.add(new JCacheCacheManager(jcm));
  managers.add(new EhCacheCacheManager(cm))
  managers.add(new RedisCacheManager(redisTemplate()));     Add individual
  cacheManager.setCacheManagers(managers);                  cache managers
  return cacheManager;
}
```

When it's time to look for a cache entry, CompositeCacheManager starts with JCacheCacheManager to check the JCache implementation, then turns to Ehcache by checking with EhCacheCacheManager, and finally consults with RedisCacheManager to check Redis for the cache entry.

Now that you have a cache manager configured and caching enabled, you're ready to start applying caching rules to your bean methods. Let's see how to use Spring's caching annotations to define cache boundaries.

13.2 Annotating methods for caching

As mentioned earlier, Spring's caching abstraction is largely built around aspects. When you enable caching in Spring, an aspect is created that triggers off one or more of Spring's caching annotations. Table 13.1 lists Spring's caching annotations.

Table 13.1 Spring provides four annotations for declaring caching rules.

Annotation	Description
@Cacheable	Indicates that Spring should look in a cache for the method's return value before invoking the method. If the value is found, the cached value is returned. If not, then the method is invoked and the return value is put in the cache.
@CachePut	Indicates that Spring should put the method's return value in a cache. The cache isn't checked prior to method invocation, and the method is always invoked.

Table 13.1   Spring provides four annotations for declaring caching rules.

Annotation	Description
@CacheEvict	Indicates that Spring should evict one or more entries from a cache.
@Caching	A grouping annotation for applying multiples of the other caching annotations at once.

All the annotations in table 13.1 can be placed either on a method or on a class. When placed on a single method, the caching behavior prescribed by the annotation applies only to that method. If the annotation is placed at the class level, however, the caching behavior is applied to all methods in that class.

13.2.1   *Populating the cache*

As you can see, the @Cacheable and @CachePut annotations can both populate a cache. They work in slightly different ways, though.

@Cacheable looks for an entry in the cache first, preempting the method invocation if a matching entry is found. If no matching entry is found, the method is invoked and the value returned is put in the cache. @CachePut, on the other hand, never checks for a matching value in the cache, always allows the target method to be invoked, and adds the returned value to the cache.

@Cacheable and @CachePut share a common set of attributes, which are listed in table 13.2.

Table 13.2   @Cacheable and @CachePut share a common set of attributes.

Attribute	Type	Description
value	String[]	The name(s) of the cache(s) to use
condition	String	A SpEL expression that, if it evaluates to false, results in caching not being applied to the method call
key	String	A SpEL expression to calculate a custom cache key
unless	String	A SpEL expression that, if it evaluates to true, prevents the return value from being put in the cache

In their simplest form, the @Cacheable and @CachePut attributes only specify one or more caches with the value attribute. For example, consider the findOne() method from SpittleRepository. Once it's initially saved, a Spittle isn't likely to change. If any particular Spittle is popular and is requested frequently, it's a waste of time and resources to fetch it from the database repeatedly. By annotating the findOne() method with @Cacheable, as shown in the following listing, you can make sure the Spittle is cached and avoid unnecessary trips to the database.

Listing 13.6   Using `@Cacheable` to store and fetch values in a cache

```
@Cacheable("spittleCache")                    <— Cache this method's results
public Spittle findOne(long id) {
  try {
    return jdbcTemplate.queryForObject(
        SELECT_SPITTLE_BY_ID,
        new SpittleRowMapper(),
        id);
  } catch (EmptyResultDataAccessException e) {
    return null;
  }
}
```

When `findOne()` is called, the caching aspect intercepts the call and looks for a previously returned value in the cache named `spittleCache`. The cache key is the `id` parameter passed to the `findOne()` method. If a value is found for that key, the found value will be returned and the method won't be invoked. On the other hand, if no value is found, then the method will be invoked and the returned value will be put in the cache, ready for the next time `findOne()` is called.

In listing 13.6, the `@Cacheable` annotation is placed on the implementation of `findOne()` in `JdbcSpittleRepository`. That will work, but the caching is confined to only the `JdbcSpittleRepository` implementation. Any other implementation of `SpittleRepository` won't have caching unless it's also annotated with `@Cacheable`. Therefore, you might consider placing the annotation on the method declaration in `SpittleRepository` instead of the implementation:

```
@Cacheable("spittleCache")
Spittle findOne(long id);
```

When you annotate the interface method, the `@Cacheable` annotation will be inherited by all implementations of `SpittleRepository`, and the same caching rules will be applied.

PUTTING VALUES IN THE CACHE

Whereas `@Cacheable` conditionally invokes a method, depending on whether the desired value is already in the cache, `@CachePut` applies a more linear flow to methods that it annotates. An `@CachePut`-annotated method is always invoked and its return value is placed in the cache. This offers a handy way to preload a cache before anyone comes asking.

For example, when a brand-new `Spittle` is saved via the `save()` method on `SpittleRepository`, there's a high likelihood that it will soon be asked for. It makes sense to toss the `Spittle` into the cache when `save()` is called, so it's ready to go when someone looks for it by calling `findOne()`. To do that, you can annotate the `save()` method with `@CachePut` like this:

```
@CachePut("spittleCache")
Spittle save(Spittle spittle);
```

When save() is called, it does whatever it needs to do to save the Spittle. Then the returned Spittle is placed in the spittleCache cache.

There's only one problem: the cache key. As I mentioned earlier, the default cache key is based on the parameters to the method. Because the only parameter to save() is a Spittle, it's used as the cache key. Doesn't it seem odd to place a Spittle in a cache where the key is the same Spittle?

Clearly, the default cache key isn't what you want in this case. You need the cache key to be the ID of the newly saved Spittle, not the Spittle itself. So, you need to specify a key other than the default key. Let's see how you can customize the cache key.

CUSTOMIZING THE CACHE KEY

Both @Cacheable and @CachePut have a key attribute that lets you replace the default key with one derived from a SpEL expression. Any valid SpEL expression will work, but you'll likely want to use an expression that evaluates to a key relevant to the value being stored in the cache.

For this particular case, you need the key to be the ID of the saved Spittle. The Spittle passed as a parameter to save() hasn't been saved yet and therefore doesn't have an ID. You need the id property of the Spittle that is returned from save().

Fortunately, Spring exposes several pieces of metadata that come in handy when you're writing SpEL expressions for caching. Table 13.3 lists the caching metadata available in SpEL.

Table 13.3   Spring offers several SpEL extensions specifically for defining cache rules.

Expression	Description
#root.args	The arguments passed in to the cached method, as an array
#root.caches	The caches this method is executed against, as an array
#root.target	The target object
#root.targetClass	The target object's class; a shortcut for #root.target.class
#root.method	The cached method
#root.methodName	The cached method's name; a shortcut for #root.method.name
#result	The return value from the method call (not available with @Cacheable)
#Argument	The name of any method argument (such as #argName) or argument index (such as #a0 or #p0)

For the save() method, you need the key to be the id property from the Spittle that is returned. The #result expression will give you the returned Spittle. From that, you can reference the id property by setting the key attribute to #result.id:

```
@CachePut(value="spittleCache", key="#result.id")
Spittle save(Spittle spittle);
```

With @CachePut specified this way, the cache isn't considered going into the save() method. But the Spittle that is returned will be put in the cache with a key equal to the Spittle's id property.

CONDITIONAL CACHING

By annotating a method with one of Spring's caching annotations, you indicate that you want Spring to create a caching aspect around that method. But there may be cases where you'd rather have caching turned off.

@Cacheable and @CachePut offer two attributes for conditional caching: unless and condition. Both are given a SpEL expression. If the unless attribute's SpEL expression evaluates to true, then the data returned from the cached method isn't placed in the cache. Similarly, if the condition attribute's SpEL expression evaluates to false, then caching is effectively disabled for the method.

On the surface, it may seem that unless and condition accomplish the same thing. There's a subtle difference, though. The unless attribute can only prevent an object from being placed in the cache. But the cache is still searched when the method is called, and if a match is found, it's returned. On the other hand, if condition's expression evaluates to false, then caching is disabled for the duration of the method invocation. The cache isn't searched, nor is the return value placed in the cache.

As an example (albeit a contrived one), suppose you don't want to cache any Spittle objects whose message property contains the text "NoCache". To prevent such Spittles from being cached, you can set the unless attribute like this:

```
@Cacheable(value="spittleCache"
    unless="#result.message.contains('NoCache')")
Spittle findOne(long id);
```

The SpEL expression given to unless considers the message property of the returned Spittle (identified in the expression as #result). If it contains the text "NoCache", then the expression evaluates to true and the Spittle isn't placed in the cache. Otherwise, the expression evaluates to false, the unless clause isn't satisfied, and the Spittle is cached.

The unless attribute prevents values from being written to the cache. But you may wish to disable caching altogether. That is, you may not want values added to the cache or fetched from the cache under certain conditions.

For instance, suppose you don't want caching to be applied to any Spittle whose ID is less than 10. In this scenario, those Spittles are test entries you use for debugging purposes, and there's no real value in caching them. To turn off caching when the Spittle ID is less than 10, you can use the condition attribute on @Cacheable like this:

```
@Cacheable(value="spittleCache"
    unless="#result.message.contains('NoCache')"
    condition="#id >= 10")
Spittle findOne(long id);
```

If `findOne()` is called with any value less than 10 as the parameter, the cache will not be searched, nor will the returned `Spittle` be placed in the cache. It will be as if there is no `@Cacheable` annotation on the method.

As you've seen in these examples, the `unless` attribute expression can refer to the return value by referring to `#result`. This is possible and useful because `unless` doesn't start doing its job until a value is returned from the cached method. On the other hand, `condition` has the job of disabling caching on the method. Therefore, it can't wait until the method has completed to decide if it needs to shut down caching. This means its expression must be evaluated on the way into the method and that you can't refer to the return value with `#result`.

You've added stuff to the cache, but can that stuff be removed? Let's see how to use the `@CacheEvict` annotation to tell cached data to hit the bricks.

13.2.2 *Removing cache entries*

`@CacheEvict` doesn't add anything to the cache. On the contrary, if an `@CacheEvict`-annotated method is called, one or more entries are removed from the cache.

Under what circumstances might you want to remove something from the cache? Any time a cached value is no longer valid, you should make sure it's removed from the cache so that future cache hits won't return stale or otherwise nonexistent data. One such case is when data is deleted. This makes the `remove()` method of `Spittle-Repository` a perfect candidate for `@CacheEvict`:

```
@CacheEvict("spittleCache")
void remove(long spittleId);
```

> **NOTE** Unlike `@Cacheable` and `@CachePut`, `@CacheEvict` can be used on `void` methods. `@Cacheable` and `@CachePut` require a non-void return value, which is the item to place in the cache. But because `@CacheEvict` is only removing items from the cache, it can be placed on any method, even a `void` one.

As shown here, a single entry is removed from the `spittleCache` cache when `remove()` is called. The entry to be removed is the one whose key is equal to the value passed in as the `spittleId` parameter.

`@CacheEvict` has several attributes, listed in table 13.4, that can influence its behavior beyond the defaults.

Table 13.4 The `@CacheEvict` annotation's attributes specify which cache entries should be removed.

Attribute	Type	Description
value	String[]	The name(s) of the cache(s) to use.
key	String	A SpEL expression to calculate a custom cache key.
condition	String	A SpEL expression that, if it evaluates to `false`, results in caching not being applied to the method call.

Table 13.4   The @CacheEvict annotation's attributes specify which cache entries should be removed. *(continued)*

Attribute	Type	Description
allEntries	boolean	If true, all entries in the specified cache(s) should be removed.
beforeInvocation	boolean	If true, the entries are removed from the cache before the method is invoked. If false (the default), the entries are removed after a successful method invocation.

As you can see, @CacheEvict shares some of the same attributes as @Cacheable and @CachePut, along with a couple of new attributes. Unlike @Cacheable and @CachePut, @CacheEvict doesn't offer an unless attribute.

Spring's caching annotations offer an elegant way to specify caching rules in your application code. But Spring also offers an XML namespace for caching. To close out this discussion on caching, let's take a quick look at how to configure caching rules in XML.

13.3   *Declaring caching in XML*

You may be wondering why you'd ever want to declare caching in XML. After all, the caching annotations we've looked at throughout this chapter are much more elegant.

I can think of two reasons:

- You don't feel comfortable putting Spring-specific annotations in your source code.
- You want to apply caching to beans for which you don't own the source code.

In either of those cases, it's better (or necessary) to keep the caching configuration separate from the code whose data is being cached. Spring's cache namespace offers a way to declare caching rules in XML as an alternative to annotation-oriented caching. Because caching is an aspect-oriented activity, the cache namespace is paired with Spring's aop namespace for declaring the pointcuts where caching should be applied.

To get started with XML-declared caching, you'll need to create a Spring configuration XML file that includes the cache and aop namespaces:

```
<?xml version="1.0" encoding="UTF-8"?>
<beans xmlns="http://www.springframework.org/schema/beans"
  xmlns:xsi="http://www.w3.org/2001/XMLSchema-instance"
  xmlns:cache="http://www.springframework.org/schema/cache"
  xmlns:aop="http://www.springframework.org/schema/aop"
  xsi:schemaLocation="http://www.springframework.org/schema/aop
    http://www.springframework.org/schema/aop/spring-aop.xsd
    http://www.springframework.org/schema/beans
    http://www.springframework.org/schema/beans/spring-beans.xsd
    http://www.springframework.org/schema/cache
    http://www.springframework.org/schema/cache/spring-cache.xsd">
```

```
    <!-- Caching configuration will go here -->
</beans>
```

The `cache` namespace defines the configuration elements for declaring caching in a Spring XML configuration file. Table 13.5 lists all the elements offered by the `cache` namespace.

Table 13.5 Spring's `cache` namespace offers elements for configuring caching rules in XML.

Element	Description
`<cache:annotation-driven>`	Enables annotation-driven caching. Equivalent to `@EnableCaching` in Java configuration.
`<cache:advice>`	Defines caching advice. Paired with `<aop:advisor>` to apply advice to a pointcut.
`<cache:caching>`	Defines a specific set of caching rules within the caching advice.
`<cache:cacheable>`	Designates a method as being cacheable. Equivalent to the `@Cacheable` annotation.
`<cache:cache-put>`	Designates a method as populating (but not considering) the cache. Equivalent to the `@CachePut` annotation.
`<cache:cache-evict>`	Designates a method as evicting one or more entries from the cache. Equivalent to the `@CacheEvict` annotation.

The `<cache:annotation-driven>` element, much like its Java configuration counterpart `@EnableCaching`, turns on annotation-oriented caching. We've already discussed this style of caching, so there's no need to dwell on it further.

The remaining elements in table 13.5 are for XML-based caching configuration. The next listing shows how to use these elements to configure caching around the `SpittleRepository` bean, equivalent to what you did earlier in this chapter using caching annotations.

Listing 13.7 Declaring caching rules around `SpittleRepository` using XML elements

```
<?xml version="1.0" encoding="UTF-8"?>
<beans xmlns="http://www.springframework.org/schema/beans"
  xmlns:xsi="http://www.w3.org/2001/XMLSchema-instance"
  xmlns:cache="http://www.springframework.org/schema/cache"
  xmlns:aop="http://www.springframework.org/schema/aop"
  xsi:schemaLocation="http://www.springframework.org/schema/aop
    http://www.springframework.org/schema/aop/spring-aop.xsd
    http://www.springframework.org/schema/beans
    http://www.springframework.org/schema/beans/spring-beans.xsd
    http://www.springframework.org/schema/cache
    http://www.springframework.org/schema/cache/spring-cache.xsd">

  <aop:config>
    <aop:advisor advice-ref="cacheAdvice"           ◁──┐ Bind cache advice
                                                         │ to a pointcut
```

```
          pointcut=
          "execution(* com.habuma.spittr.db.SpittleRepository.*(..))"/>
    </aop:config>

    <cache:advice id="cacheAdvice">
      <cache:caching>
        <cache:cacheable                        ⟵— Make cacheable
            cache="spittleCache"
            method="findRecent" />

        <cache:cacheable                                  ⟵— Make cacheable
            cache="spittleCache"            method="findOne" />
        <cache:cacheable                         ⟵— Make cacheable
            cache="spittleCache"
            method="findBySpitterId" />

        <cache:cache-put                ⟵— Populate cache on save
            cache="spittleCache"
            method="save"
            key="#result.id" />

        <cache:cache-evict              ⟵— Remove from cache
            cache="spittleCache"
            method="remove" />

      </cache:caching>
    </cache:advice>

    <bean id="cacheManager" class=
        "org.springframework.cache.concurrent.ConcurrentMapCacheManager"
    />

</beans>
```

The first thing you see declared in listing 13.7 is an <aop:advisor> that references the advice whose ID is cacheAdvice. This element matches the advice with a pointcut, thus establishing a complete aspect. In this case, the aspect's pointcut is triggered on the execution of any method of the SpittleRepository interface. If such a method is called on any bean in the Spring application context, the aspect's advice will be invoked.

The advice is declared with the <cache:advice> element. In the <cache:advice> element, you can have as many <cache:caching> elements as you need to fully define your application's caching rules. In this case, there's only one <cache:caching> element. It contains three <cache:cacheable> elements and one <cache:cache-put> element.

The <cache:cacheable> elements each declare a method from the pointcut as being cacheable. It's the XML equivalent to the @Cacheable annotation. Specifically, the findRecent(), findOne(), and findBySpitterId() methods are all declared as cacheable, and their return values will be cached in the spittleCache cache.

<cache:cache-put> is Spring's XML equivalent to the @CachePut annotation. It designates a method as one whose return value will populate a cache, but the method will never draw its return value from the cache. In this case, the save() method is

used to populate the cache. And, as with annotation-oriented caching, you need to override the default key to be the id property of the returned Spittle object.

Finally, the <cache:cache-evict> element is Spring's XML alternative to the @CacheEvict annotation. It removes an element from the cache so that it won't be found the next time someone looks for it. Here, when you delete a Spittle from the cache by calling remove(), the entry whose key is the same as the ID passed in to remove() will be evicted from the cache.

It's worth noting that the <cache:advice> element has a cache-manager attribute to specify the bean that serves as the cache manager. By default it's cacheManager, which coincides with the <bean> declared at the end of listing 13.7, so there's no need to explicitly set it. But if your cache manager bean has a different ID (as might be the case if you declared multiple cache managers), you can specify which cache manager to use by setting the cache-manager attribute.

Also notice that the <cache:cacheable>, <cache:cache-put>, and <cache:cache-evict> elements refer to the same cache named spittleCache. To remove that duplication, you can specify the cache name in the <cache:caching> annotation instead:

```
<cache:advice id="cacheAdvice">
  <cache:caching cache="spittleCache">

    <cache:cacheable method="findRecent" />

    <cache:cacheable method="findOne" />

    <cache:cacheable method="findBySpitterId" />

    <cache:cache-put
        method="save"
        key="#result.id" />

    <cache:cache-evict method="remove" />

  </cache:caching>
</cache:advice>
```

<cache:caching> shares several attributes with <cache:cacheable>, <cache:cache-put>, and <cache:cache-evict>, including these:

- cache—Specifies the cache to store values in and retrieve values from.
- condition—A SpEL expression that, if it evaluates to false, disables caching for the method.
- key—A SpEL expression used to derive the cache key. (Defaults to the method's parameters.)
- method—The name of the method to be cached.

In addition, <cache:cacheable> and <cache:cache-put> have an unless attribute. This optional attribute can be given a SpEL expression that, if it evaluates to true, prevents the return value from being cached.

The <cache:cache-evict> element offers a few unique attributes:

- all-entries—If true, all entries in the cache are removed. If false, only the entry matching the key is removed.
- before-invocation—If true, the cache entry (or entries) are removed before the method is invoked. If false, they're removed after the method is invoked.

Both all-entries and before-invocation default to false. This means that using <cache:cache-evict> without either of them will result in only a single entry being removed from the cache after the method is invoked. The item to be removed is identified by the default key (based on the method's parameter) or a key specified with a SpEL expression given to the key attribute.

13.4 *Summary*

Caching is a great way to keep your application code from having to derive, calculate, or retrieve the same answers over and over again for the same question. When a method is initially invoked with a given set of parameters, the return value can be stored in a cache and retrieved from that cache later when the same method is called with the same parameters. In many cases, looking up a value from a cache is a cheaper operation then looking it up otherwise (for example, performing a database query). Therefore, caching can have a positive impact on application performance.

In this chapter, you've seen how to declare caching in a Spring application. First you saw how to declare one or more of Spring's cache managers. Then you applied caching to the Spittr application by adding annotations such as @Cacheable, @CachePut, and @CacheEvict to the SpittleRepository.

We also looked at how to configure caching rules separate from the application code in XML. The <cache:cacheable>, <cache:cache-put>, and <cache:cache-evict> elements mirror the annotations you used earlier in the chapter.

Along the way, we discussed the fact that caching is an aspect-oriented activity. In fact, Spring implements caching as an aspect. This became apparent when you declared caching rules in XML: you had to bind your caching advice to a pointcut.

Spring also uses aspects when applying security rules to methods. In the next chapter, you'll see how to use Spring Security to enforce security on bean methods.

Securing methods

14

> **This chapter covers**
> - Securing method invocations
> - Defining security rules with expressions
> - Creating security expression evaluators

Before I leave my house or before I go to bed, one of the last things I do is make sure the doors to my house are locked. But just before that, I set the alarm. Why? Because although the locks on my doors are a good form of security, the alarm system gives a second line of defense, should any burglar make it past the locks.

In chapter 9, you saw how to use Spring Security to secure the web layer of your application. Web security is important, as it prevents users from accessing content that they're not authorized to access. But what if there's a hole in your application's web layer security? What if somehow a user is able to request content that they may not be allowed to see?

Although there's no reason to think that a user will be able to crack through your application's security, a security hole at the web layer can sneak in rather easily. Imagine, for instance, if a user makes a request for a page that they're allowed to see, but due to a lack of developer diligence, the controller that handles that request calls a method that fetches data that the user isn't allowed to see. It's an honest mistake. But security breaches are just as likely to arise from honest mistakes as they are from clever hacking.

By securing both the web layer of your application *and* the methods behind the scenes, you can be sure that no logic will be executed unless the user is authorized.

In this chapter, we'll look at how you can secure bean methods using Spring Security. In doing so, we'll declare security rules that prevent a method from being executed unless the user for whom it is being executed has the authority to execute it. We'll start by looking at a couple of simple annotations that can be placed on methods to lock them away from unauthorized access.

14.1 Securing methods with annotations

The most commonly used approach to method-level security with Spring Security is to apply special security annotations to the methods you want secured. This has several benefits, not the least of which is that the security rules for any given method are clearly visible when looking at the method in an editor.

Spring Security provides three different kinds of security annotations:

- Spring Security's own `@Secured`
- JSR-250's `@RolesAllowed`
- Expression-driven annotations, with `@PreAuthorize`, `@PostAuthorize`, `@PreFilter`, and `@PostFilter`

The `@Secured` and `@RolesAllowed` annotations are the simplest options, restricting access based on what authorities have been granted to the user. When you need more flexibility in defining security rules on methods, Spring Security offers `@PreAuthorize` and `@PostAuthorize`. And `@PreFilter`/`@PostFilter` filter elements out of collections returned from or passed into a method.

Before the end of this chapter, you'll have seen all of these annotations in action. To get the ball rolling, let's start by looking at the `@Secured` annotation, the simplest of the method-level security annotations offered by Spring Security.

14.1.1 Restricting method access with @Secured

The key to enabling annotation-based method security in Spring is to annotate a configuration class with `@EnableGlobalMethodSecurity`, like this:

```
@Configuration
@EnableGlobalMethodSecurity(securedEnabled=true)
public class MethodSecurityConfig
        extends GlobalMethodSecurityConfiguration {
}
```

In addition to being annotated with `@EnableGlobalMethodSecurity`, you'll notice that the configuration class extends `GlobalMethodSecurityConfiguration`. Much like the `WebSecurityConfigurerAdapter` class that your web security configuration class extended in chapter 9, this class offers you the opportunity to configure the finer points of method-level security.

For example, if you haven't already configured authentication in the web-layer security configuration, you may want to do that here by overriding the GlobalMethodSecurityConfiguration's configure() method:

```
@Override
protected void configure(AuthenticationManagerBuilder auth)
        throws Exception {
  auth
  .inMemoryAuthentication()
    .withUser("user").password("password").roles("USER");
}
```

A little later in this chapter, in section 14.2.2, you'll see how to override the GlobalMethodSecurityConfiguration's createExpressionHandler() method to provide some custom security expression-handling behavior.

Getting back to the @EnableGlobalMethodSecurity annotation, notice that its securedEnabled attribute is set to true. When securedEnabled is true, a pointcut is created such that the Spring Security aspects will wrap bean methods that are annotated with @Secured. For example, consider this addSpittle() method that's been annotated with @Secured:

```
@Secured("ROLE_SPITTER")
public void addSpittle(Spittle spittle) {
  // ...
}
```

The @Secured annotation takes an array of String as an argument. Each String value is an authorization, one of which is required to invoke the method. By passing in ROLE_SPITTER, you tell Spring Security to not allow the addSpittle() method to be invoked unless the authenticated user has ROLE_SPITTER as one of their granted authorities.

If more than one value is passed into @Secured, then the authenticated user must be granted at least one of those authorities to gain access to the method. For example, the following use of @Secured indicates that the user must have ROLE_SPITTER *or* ROLE_ADMIN privilege to invoke the method:

```
@Secured({"ROLE_SPITTER", "ROLE_ADMIN"})
public void addSpittle(Spittle spittle) {
  // ...
}
```

When the method is invoked by an unauthenticated user or by a user not possessing the required privileges, the aspect wrapping the method will throw one of Spring Security's exceptions (probably a subclass of AuthenticationException or AccessDeniedException). These are unchecked exceptions, but ultimately someone will need to catch it and handle it. If the secured method is invoked in the course of a web request, the exception will be automatically handled by Spring Security's filters. Otherwise, you'll need to write the code to handle the exception.

One drawback of the `@Secured` annotation is that it's a Spring-specific annotation. If you're more comfortable using annotations defined in Java standards, then perhaps you should consider using `@RolesAllowed` instead.

14.1.2 *Using JSR-250's @RolesAllowed with Spring Security*

The `@RolesAllowed` annotation is equivalent to `@Secured` in almost every way. The only substantial difference is that `@RolesAllowed` is one of Java's standard annotations as defined in JSR-250.

This difference carries more political consequence than technical. But using the standard `@RolesAllowed` annotation may have implications when used in the context of other frameworks or APIs that process that annotation.

Regardless, if you choose to use `@RolesAllowed`, you'll need to turn it on by setting `@EnableGlobalMethodSecurity`'s `jsr250Enabled` attribute to `true`:

```
@Configuration
@EnableGlobalMethodSecurity(jsr250Enabled=true)
public class MethodSecurityConfig
        extends GlobalMethodSecurityConfiguration {
}
```

Although here we've only enabled `jsr250Enabled`, it's good to note that it's not mutually exclusive with `securedEnabled`. These two annotation styles can both be enabled at the same time.

With `jsr250Enabled` set to `true`, a pointcut will be effected such that any methods annotated with `@RolesAllowed` will be wrapped with Spring Security's aspects. This makes it possible to use `@RolesAllowed` on your methods in much the same way that you might use `@Secured`. For example, here's the same `addSpittle()` method annotated with `@RolesAllowed` instead of `@Secured`:

```
@RolesAllowed("ROLE_SPITTER")
public void addSpittle(Spittle spittle) {
  // ...
}
```

Although `@RolesAllowed` has a slight political advantage over `@Secured` in that it's a standards-based annotation for method security, both annotations share a common shortcoming. They can restrict the invocation of a method based only on whether or not that user has been granted a specific privilege. No other factors can play a part in the decision to allow the method to execute or not. You saw in chapter 9, however, that SpEL expressions could be used to overcome a similar limitation when securing URLs. Let's see how you can use SpEL along with Spring Security's pre- and postinvocation annotations to perform expression-based method security.

14.2 Using expressions for method-level security

Although `@Secured` and `@RolesAllowed` seem to do the trick when it comes to keeping unauthorized users out, that's about all that they can do. Sometimes security constraints depend on more than just whether a user has privileges or not.

Spring Security 3.0 introduced a handful of new annotations that use SpEL to enable even more interesting security constraints on methods. These new annotations are described in table 14.1.

Table 14.1 Spring Security 3.0 offers four new annotations that can be used to secure methods with SpEL expressions.

Annotations	Description
`@PreAuthorize`	Restricts access to a method before invocation based on the result of evaluating an expression
`@PostAuthorize`	Allows a method to be invoked, but throws a security exception if the expression evaluates to `false`
`@PostFilter`	Allows a method to be invoked, but filters the results of that method based on an expression
`@PreFilter`	Allows a method to be invoked, but filters input prior to entering the method

Each of these annotations accepts a SpEL expression for its value parameter. The expression can be any valid SpEL expression and may include any of the Spring Security extensions to SpEL listed in table 9.5. If the expression evaluates to `true`, then the security rule passes; otherwise, it fails. The implications of a passing versus failing security rule differ depending on which annotation is in use.

We'll look at specific examples of each of these in a moment. But first, you'll need to enable them by setting `@EnableGlobalMethodSecurity`'s `prePostEnabled` attribute to true:

```
@Configuration
public class MethodSecurityConfig
        extends GlobalMethodSecurityConfiguration {
}
```

Now that the pre/post annotations are enabled, you can start using them. Let's start by seeing how you can restrict access to a method using the `@PreAuthorize` and `@PostAuthorize` annotations.

14.2.1 Expressing method access rules

Thus far you've seen how `@Secured` and `@RolesAllowed` prevent a method from being executed unless the user has the required authority. But their weakness is that they're only able to make their decisions based on the user's granted authorities.

Spring Security offers two more annotations, `@PreAuthorize` and `@PostAuthorize`, that restrict method access based on expression evaluation. Expressions add a tremendous amount of flexibility in defining security constraints. Using expressions, you can allow or disallow access to a method using almost any conditions you can imagine.

The key difference between @PreAuthorize and @PostAuthorize is in when their expressions are evaluated. @PreAuthorize is evaluated before the method executes and prevents method execution unless the expression evaluates to true. In contrast, @PostAuthorize waits until the method has returned before deciding whether or not to raise a security exception.

We'll first look at preauthorization, as it's the most commonly used of the expression-driven security annotations. After that, we'll see how to secure access to methods *after* the method executes.

PREAUTHORIZING METHOD ACCESS

At first glance, @PreAuthorize may appear to be nothing more than a SpEL-enabled equivalent to @Secured and @RolesAllowed. In fact, you could use @PreAuthorize to limit access based on the roles given to the authenticated user:

```
@PreAuthorize("hasRole('ROLE_SPITTER')")
public void addSpittle(Spittle spittle) {
  // ...
}
```

When used this way, @PreAuthorize has no tangible benefit over @Secured or @Roles-Allowed. If the user has the ROLE_SPITTER role, then the method will be allowed to execute. Otherwise, a security exception will be thrown and the method won't execute.

But there's a lot more to @PreAuthorize than is apparent in this simple example. The String argument to @PreAuthorize is a SpEL expression. With SpEL expressions guiding access decisions, far more advanced security constraints can be written. For example, suppose that the average Spittr user can only write spittles of 140 characters or less, but premium users are allowed unlimited spittle lengths.

The @Secured and @RolesAllowed annotations would be of no help here, but @PreAuthorize is on the case:

```
@PreAuthorize(
    "(hasRole('ROLE_SPITTER') and #spittle.text.length() <= 140)"
  +"or hasRole('ROLE_PREMIUM')")
public void addSpittle(Spittle spittle) {
  // ...
}
```

The #spittle portion of the expression refers directly to the method parameter of the same name. This enables Spring Security to examine the parameters passed to the method and use those parameters in its authorization decision making. In this example, you dig into the Spittle's text to make sure it doesn't exceed the length allowed for standard Spittr users. Or if the user is a premium user, then the length doesn't matter.

POSTAUTHORIZING METHOD ACCESS

A slightly less obvious way to authorize a method is to postauthorize it. Postauthorization typically involves making security decisions based on the object returned from the secured method. This of course means that the method must be invoked and given a chance to produce a return value.

For example, suppose that you wanted to secure the getSpittleById() method so that it only authorizes access if the Spittle object returned belongs to the authenticated user. There's no way of knowing if a Spittle belongs to the current user until you've already fetched it. Therefore, getSpittleById() must execute first. If, after fetching the Spittle, it turns out to not belong to the current user, then a security exception should be thrown.

Spring Security's @PostAuthorize works much the same way as @PreAuthorize, except that it waits to apply the security rule until after the method has already executed. At that point it has the opportunity to consider the return value in its decision-making.

For example, to secure the getSpittleById() method as previously described, you can use @PostAuthorize like this:

```
@PostAuthorize("returnObject.spitter.username == principal.username")
public Spittle getSpittleById(long id) {
  // ...
}
```

For easy access to the object returned from the secured method, Spring Security provides the returnObject variable in SpEL. Here you know that the returned object is a Spittle, so the expression digs into its spitter property and pulls the username property from that.

On the other side of the double-equal comparison, the expression digs into the built-in principal object to get its username property. principal is another one of Spring Security's special built-in names that represents the principal (typically the username) of the currently authenticated user.

If the Spittle object has a Spitter whose username property is the same as the principal's username, the Spittle will be returned to the caller. Otherwise, an AccessDeniedException will be thrown, and the caller won't get to see the Spittle.

It's important to keep in mind that, unlike methods annotated with @PreAuthorize, @PostAuthorize-annotated methods will be executed first and intercepted afterward. That means that care should be taken to make sure that the method doesn't have any side effects that would be undesirable if authorization fails.

14.2.2 *Filtering method inputs and outputs*

@PreAuthorize and @PostAuthorize are great if you're using expressions to secure a method. But sometimes restricting access to a method is too heavy-handed. Sometimes it's not the method that's being secured, but rather the data being passed into or returned from that method.

For instance, suppose that you have a method called `getOffensiveSpittles()` that returns a list of `Spittles` that have been flagged as offensive. This is a method that's primarily intended to be used by an administrator to help moderate the content on the Spittr application. But it could also be used by an individual user to see if any of their `Spittles` have been flagged as offensive. The method signature might look something like this:

```
public List<Spittle> getOffensiveSpittles() { ... }
```

As it is, the `getOffensiveSpittles()` method isn't concerned with any specific user. It merely returns a list of offensive `Spittles`, no matter who they belong to. That's perfect for the administrative use of the method, but it falls short of limiting the list to those `Spittles` that belong to the current user.

Certainly, you could overload `getOffensiveSpittles()` with another version that accepts a user ID as a parameter and uses that to fetch only the offensive `Spittles` for a given user. But as I stated in the outset of this chapter, there's always the possibility that the less restrictive version could be used in places where some restriction is needed.[1]

What's needed is a way to filter the collection of `Spittles` returned from `getOffensiveSpittles()`, narrowing it down to the list that the current user is allowed to see. That's precisely what Spring Security's `@PostFilter` does. Let's give it a try.

POSTFILTERING METHOD RETURN VALUES

Just like `@PreAuthorize` and `@PostAuthorize`, `@PostFilter` takes a SpEL expression as its value parameter. But instead of using that expression to restrict access to a method, `@PostFilter` evaluates that expression against each member of a collection being returned from the method, removing those members for whom the expression evaluates to `false`.

To demonstrate, let's apply `@PostFilter` to the `getOffensiveSpittles()` method:

```
@PreAuthorize("hasAnyRole({'ROLE_SPITTER', 'ROLE_ADMIN'})")
@PostFilter( "hasRole('ROLE_ADMIN') || "
        + "filterObject.spitter.username == principal.name")
public List<Spittle> getOffensiveSpittles() {
  ...
}
```

Here, the `@PreAuthorize` annotation only allows users with `ROLE_SPITTER` or `ROLE_ADMIN` authority to execute the method. If the user makes it through that checkpoint, the method will execute and a `List` of `Spittles` will be returned. But the `@PostFilter` annotation will filter that list, ensuring that the user only sees those `Spittle` objects that they're allowed to see. Specifically, administrators get to see all offensive `Spittles`, and non-administrators will only be given `Spittles` that belong to them.

---

[1] Besides that, if I overloaded `getOffensiveSpittles()` I'd have to dream up another example for showing you how to filter method output with SpEL.

The `filterObject` referenced in the expression refers to an individual element (which you know to be a `Spittle`) in the `List` returned from the method. If that `Spittle`'s `Spitter` has a username that's the same as the authenticated user (the `principal.name` in the expression) or if the user has the role of `ROLE_ADMIN`, then the element will end up in the filtered list. Otherwise, it'll be left out.

PREFILTERING METHOD PARAMETERS

In addition to postfiltering a method's return value, you also have the option of prefiltering the values passed into a method. This is a much less common technique, but it may come in handy on occasion.

For instance, suppose you have a list of `Spittles` that you want to delete as a batch. To accomplish that, you might write a method with a signature that looks a little like this:

```
public void deleteSpittles(List<Spittle> spittles) { ... }
```

Seems simple enough, right? But what if you want to apply some security rules to it, such that the `Spittles` can only be deleted by the user who owns them or by an administrator. In that case, you could write logic into the `deleteSpittles()` method to sift through each `Spittle` in the list and only delete those belonging to the current user (or all of them if the current user is an administrator).

While that would work, it means that you're embedding security logic directly into the logic of the method. And that security logic represents a separate (albeit related) concern from the concern of deleting `Spittles`. What would be better is if the list only contained `Spittles` that were actually going to be deleted. That would keep the logic for `deleteSpittles()` simpler and focused on the task of deleting `Spittles`.

Spring Security's `@PreFilter` seems to be a perfect fit for this problem. Much like `@PostFilter`, `@PreFilter` uses SpEL to filter a collection to only the elements that satisfy the SpEL expression. But instead of filtering the value returned from a method, `@PreFilter` filters those members of a collection going into the method.

Using `@PreFilter` is quite simple. Here's the `deleteSpittles()` method, now annotated with `@PreFilter`:

```
@PreAuthorize("hasAnyRole({'ROLE_SPITTER', 'ROLE_ADMIN'})")
@PreFilter( "hasRole('ROLE_ADMIN') || "
        + "targetObject.spitter.username == principal.name")
public void deleteSpittles(List<Spittle> spittles) { ... }
```

As before, `@PreAuthorize` will prevent this method from being called on behalf of any user who doesn't have either `ROLE_SPITTER` or `ROLE_ADMIN` authority. But also, `@PreFilter` will ensure that the list being passed into `deleteSpittles()` will contain only `Spittles` that the current user has permission to delete. The expression will be evaluated against each item in the collection, and only those items for whom the expression evaluates to `true` will remain in the list. The `targetObject` variable is another Spring Security–provided value that represents the current list item to evaluate against.

At this point, you've seen how to use all four of Spring Security's expression-driven annotations. Expressions are a much more powerful way to define security constraints than just specifying an authority that must be granted to the user.

Even so, you should take care not to get too clever with the expressions. Certainly you should avoid writing complex security expressions or trying to embed too much non-security business logic into the expressions. Ultimately, expressions are just String values that are given to the annotations. As such, they're difficult to test and difficult to debug.

If you find yourself thinking that maybe your security expressions are getting out of hand, you might want to look into writing a custom permission evaluator to help simplify your SpEL expressions. Let's see how you can create and use a custom permission evaluator to simplify the expressions you've used for filtering.

DEFINING A PERMISSION EVALUATOR

The expression we used with @PreFilter and @PostFilter certainly isn't that complex. But it's not trivial either, and it doesn't take much to imagine how you might keep growing that expression to accommodate other security rules. Before long, the expression could become unwieldy, complex, and difficult to test.

What if you replaced that entire expression with a much simpler one that looks a little something like this:

```
@PreAuthorize("hasAnyRole({'ROLE_SPITTER', 'ROLE_ADMIN'})")
@PreFilter("hasPermission(targetObject, 'delete')")
public void deleteSpittles(List<Spittle> spittles) { ... }
```

Now the expression given to @PreFilter is much tighter. It simply asks the question "Does the user have permission to delete the target object?" If so, the expression will evaluate to true and the Spittle will remain in the list passed to deleteSpittles(). If not, then it will be tossed out.

But where did hasPermission() come from? What does it mean? And more importantly, how does it know whether or not the user has permission to delete the Spittle in targetObject?

The hasPermission() function is a Spring Security–provided extension to SpEL, and it represents an opportunity for you, the developer, to plug in whatever logic you want to perform when it's evaluated. All you need to do is write and register a custom permission evaluator. Listing 14.1 shows SpittlePermissionEvaluator, a custom permission evaluator that contains the expression logic.

> ### Listing 14.1 A permission evaluator provides the logic behind `hasPermission()`

```
package spittr.security;
import java.io.Serializable;
import org.springframework.security.access.PermissionEvaluator;
import org.springframework.security.core.Authentication;
import spittr.Spittle;

public class SpittlePermissionEvaluator implements PermissionEvaluator {
```

```
    private static final GrantedAuthority ADMIN_AUTHORITY =
        new GrantedAuthorityImpl("ROLE_ADMIN");

    public boolean hasPermission(Authentication authentication,
            Object target, Object permission) {

        if (target instanceof Spittle) {
            Spittle spittle = (Spittle) target;
            String username = spittle.getSpitter().getUsername();
            if ("delete".equals(permission)) {
                return isAdmin(authentication) ||
                    username.equals(authentication.getName());
            }
        }

        throw new UnsupportedOperationException(
                "hasPermission not supported for object <" + target
                        + "> and permission <" + permission + ">");
    }

    public boolean hasPermission(Authentication authentication,
        Serializable targetId, String targetType, Object permission) {
        throw new UnsupportedOperationException();
    }

    private boolean isAdmin(Authentication authentication) {
        return authentication.getAuthorities().contains(ADMIN_AUTHORITY);
    }

}
```

SpittlePermissionEvaluator implements Spring Security's PermissionEvaluator interface, which demands that two different hasPermission() methods be implemented. One of the hasPermission() methods takes an Object as the object to evaluate against in the second parameter. The other hasPermission() is useful when only the ID of the target object is available, and it takes that ID as a Serializable in its second parameter.

For our purposes, we'll assume that you'll always have the Spittle object to evaluate permissions against, so the other method simply throws UnsupportedOperation-Exception.

As for the first hasPermission() method, it checks to see that the object being evaluated is a Spittle and that you're checking for delete permission. If so, it checks that the Spitter's username is equal to the authenticated user's name or that the current authentication has ROLE_ADMIN authority.

Once the permission evaluator is ready, you need to register it with Spring Security for it to back the hasPermission() operation in the expression given to @PostFilter. To do that, you'll need to replace the expression handler with one that's configured to use your custom permission evaluator.

By default, Spring Security is configured with a DefaultMethodSecurity-ExpressionHandler that's given an instance of DenyAllPermissionEvaluator. As its name suggests, DenyAllPermissionEvaluator always returns false from its has-

Permission() methods, denying all method access. But you can provide Spring Security with a DefaultMethodSecurityExpressionHandler configured with your custom SpittlePermissionEvaluator by overriding the createExpressionHandler method from GlobalMethodSecurityConfiguration:

```
@Override
protected MethodSecurityExpressionHandler createExpressionHandler() {
  DefaultMethodSecurityExpressionHandler expressionHandler =
      new DefaultMethodSecurityExpressionHandler();
  expressionHandler.setPermissionEvaluator(
      new SpittlePermissionEvaluator());
  return expressionHandler;
}
```

Now anytime you secure a method with an expression that uses hasPermission(), the SpittlePermissionEvaluator will be invoked and get to decide whether or not the user has permission to call the method.

14.3 Summary

Method-level security is an important complement to Spring Security's web-level security, which we discussed in chapter 9. For non-web applications, method-level security is the front line of defense. When applied in a web application, method-level security backs up the security rules declared to secure web requests.

In this chapter, we looked at six annotations that can be placed on methods to declare security constraints. For simple, authorities-oriented security, Spring Security's @Secured annotation or the standards-based @RolesAllowed come in handy. When the security rules get more interesting, @PreAuthorize and @PostAuthorize and SpEL provide more power. You also saw how to filter a method's inputs and outputs using SpEL expressions given to @PreFilter and @PostFilter.

Finally, we looked at how you can make your security rules easier to maintain, test, and debug by defining a custom expression evaluator that works behind the scenes of the hasPermission() function in SpEL.

Starting with the next chapter, we'll switch gears from developing the back end of the application to using Spring to integrate with other applications. Over the next several chapters, we'll look at all kinds of integration techniques, including remoting, asynchronous messaging, REST, and even sending emails. The first integration technique on tap will be working with Spring remoting, which we'll explore in the next chapter.

Part 4

Integrating Spring

No application is an island. These days, enterprise applications must coordinate with other systems to achieve their purpose. In part 4, you'll learn how to take your application beyond its own boundaries and integrate it with other applications and enterprise services.

In chapter 15, "Working with remote services," you'll learn how to expose your application objects as remote services. You'll learn how to transparently access remote services as though they're any other object in your application. In doing so, you'll explore various remoting technologies, including RMI, Hessian/Burlap, and SOAP web services with JAX-WS.

In contrast to RPC-style remote services presented in chapter 15, chapter 16, "Creating Rest APIs with Spring MVC," explores how to build RESTful services that are focused on application resources using Spring MVC.

Chapter 17, "Messaging with Spring," explores a different approach to application integration by showing how Spring can be used with the Java Message Service (JMS) and the Advanced Message Queuing Protocol (AMQP) to achieve asynchronous communication between applications.

Increasingly, web applications are expected to be responsive and show near real-time data. Chapter 18, "Messaging with WebSocket and STOMP," showcases Spring's new support for building asynchronous communication between a server and its web clients.

Another form of asynchronous communication isn't necessarily application-to-application. Chapter 19, "Sending email with Spring," shows how to send asynchronous messages to people in the form of email using Spring.

Management and monitoring of Spring beans is the subject of chapter 20, "Managing Spring beans with JMX." In this chapter, you'll learn how Spring can automatically expose beans configured in Spring as JMX MBeans.

Wrapping up the book is a late but necessary addition to the table of contents. Chapter 21, "Simplifying Spring development with Spring Boot," presents an exciting new game-changing development in Spring. You'll see how Spring Boot takes away the chore of writing much of the boilerplate configuration that is typical in Spring applications and leaves you to focus on implementing business functionality.

15

Working with
remote services

This chapter covers

- Accessing and exposing RMI services
- Using Hessian and Burlap services
- Working with Spring's HTTP invoker
- Using Spring with web services

Imagine for a moment that you're stranded on a deserted island. This may sound like a dream come true. After all, who wouldn't want some solitude on a beach, blissfully ignorant of the goings-on of the outside world?

But on a deserted island, it's not pina coladas and sunbathing all the time. Even if you enjoy the peaceful seclusion, it won't be long before you'll get hungry, bored, and lonely. You can only live on coconuts and spear-caught fish for so long. You'll eventually need food, fresh clothing, and other supplies. And if you don't get in contact with another human soon, you may end up talking to a volleyball!

Many applications that you'll develop are like island castaways. On the surface they might seem self-sufficient, but in reality, they probably collaborate with other systems, both within your organization and externally.

For example, consider a procurement system that needs to communicate with a vendor's supply-chain system. Maybe your company's human resources system needs to integrate with the payroll system. Or the payroll system may need to communicate with an external system that prints and mails paychecks. No matter what the circumstances, your application will need to communicate with other systems to access services remotely.

Several remoting technologies are available to you as a Java developer, including these:

- Remote Method Invocation (RMI)
- Caucho's Hessian and Burlap
- Spring's own HTTP-based remoting
- Web services with JAX-RPC and JAX-WS

Regardless of which remoting technology you choose, Spring provides broad support for accessing and creating remote services with several different technologies. In this chapter, you'll learn how Spring both simplifies and complements these remoting services. But first, let's set the stage for this chapter with an overview of how remoting works in Spring.

15.1 *An overview of Spring remoting*

Remoting is a conversation between a client application and a service. On the client side, some functionality is required that isn't within the scope of the application, so the application reaches out to another system that can provide the functionality. The remote application exposes the functionality through a remote service.

Suppose you'd like to make some of the Spittr application's functionality available as remote services for other applications to use. Perhaps in addition to the existing browser-based user interface, you'd like to make a desktop or mobile front end for Spittr, as illustrated in figure 15.1. To support that, you'll need to expose the basic functions of the SpitterService interface as a remote service.

The conversation between the other applications and Spittr begins with a *remote procedure call* (RPC) from the client applications. On the surface, an RPC is similar to a call to a method on a local object. Both are synchronous operations, blocking execution in the calling code until the called procedure is complete.

The difference is a matter of proximity, with an analogy to human communication. If you're at the proverbial water cooler at work discussing the outcome of the weekend's football game, you're conducting a local conversation—the conversation takes

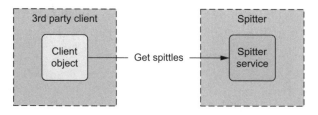

Figure 15.1   A third-party client can interact with the Spittr application by making remote calls to a service exposed by Spittr.

place between two people in the same room. Likewise, a local method call is one where execution flow is exchanged between two blocks of code in the same application.

On the other hand, if you were to pick up the phone to call a client in another city, your conversation would be conducted remotely over the telephone network. Similarly, during an RPC, execution flow is handed off from one application to another application, theoretically on a different machine in a remote location over the network.

As I mentioned, Spring supports remoting for several different RPC models, including RMI, Caucho's Hessian and Burlap, and Spring's HTTP invoker. Table 15.1 outlines each of these models and briefly discusses their usefulness in various situations.

Table 15.1 Spring supports RPC via several remoting technologies.

RPC model	Useful when...
Remote Method Invocation (RMI)	Accessing/exposing Java-based services when network constraints such as firewalls aren't a factor.
Hessian or Burlap	Accessing/exposing Java-based services over HTTP when network constraints are a factor. Hessian is a binary protocol, whereas Burlap is XML-based.
HTTP invoker	Accessing/exposing Spring-based services when network constraints are a factor and you desire Java serialization over XML or proprietary serialization.
JAX-RPC and JAX-WS	Accessing/exposing platform-neutral, SOAP-based web services.

Regardless of which remoting model you choose, you'll find that a common theme runs through Spring's support for each model. This means that once you understand how to configure Spring to work with one of the models, you'll have a modest learning curve if you decide to use a different model.

In all models, services can be configured into your application as Spring-managed beans. This is accomplished using a proxy factory bean that enables you to wire remote services into properties of your other beans as if they were local objects. Figure 15.2 illustrates how this works.

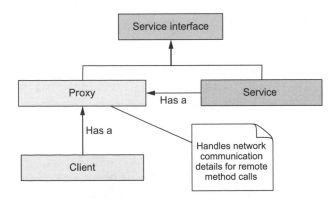

Figure 15.2 In Spring, remote services are proxied so that they can be wired into client code as if they were any other Spring bean.

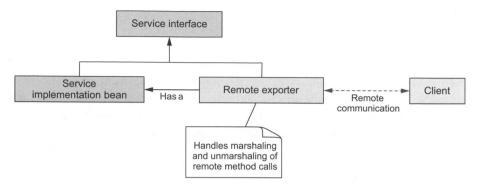

Figure 15.3   Spring-managed beans can be exported as remote services using remote exporters.

The client makes calls to the proxy as if the proxy were providing the service functionality. The proxy communicates with the remote service on behalf of the client. It handles the details of connecting and making remote calls to the remote service.

What's more, if the call to the remote service results in a `java.rmi.Remote-Exception`, the proxy handles that exception and rethrows it as an unchecked `RemoteAccessException`. Remote exceptions usually signal problems such as network or configuration issues that can't be gracefully recovered from. Because a client can usually do little to recover from a remote exception, rethrowing a `RemoteAccess-Exception` makes it optional for the client to handle the exception.

On the service side, you're able to expose the functionality of any Spring-managed bean as a remote service using any of the models listed in table 15.1. Figure 15.3 illustrates how remote exporters expose bean methods as remote services.

Whether you'll be developing code that consumes remote services, implements those services, or both, working with remote services in Spring is purely a matter of configuration. You won't have to write any Java code to support remoting. Your service beans don't have to be aware that they're involved in an RPC (although any beans passed to or returned from remote calls may need to implement `java.io.Serializable`).

Let's start our exploration of Spring's remoting support by looking at RMI, the original remoting technology for Java.

15.2   *Working with RMI*

If you've been working in Java for any length of time, you've no doubt heard of (and probably used) RMI. RMI—first introduced into the Java platform in JDK 1.1—gives Java programmers a powerful way to communicate between Java programs. Before RMI, the only remoting options available to Java programmers were CORBA (which at the time required the purchase of a third-party *object request broker* [ORB]) and handwritten socket programming.

But developing and accessing RMI services is tedious, involving several steps, both programmatic and manual. Spring simplifies the RMI model by providing a proxy factory bean that enables you to wire RMI services into your Spring application as if they were local JavaBeans. Spring also provides a remote exporter that makes short work of converting your Spring-managed beans into RMI services.

For the Spittr application, I'll show you how to wire an RMI service into a client application's Spring application context. But first, let's see how to use the RMI exporter to publish the SpitterService implementation as an RMI service.

15.2.1 *Exporting an RMI service*

If you've ever created an RMI service, you know that it involves the following steps:

1 Write the service implementation class with methods that throw java.rmi .RemoteException.

2 Create the service interface to extend java.rmi.Remote.

3 Run the RMI compiler (rmic) to produce client stub and server skeleton classes.

4 Start an RMI registry to host the services.

5 Register the service in the RMI registry.

Wow! That's a lot of work just to publish a simple RMI service. What's perhaps worse than all the steps required is that, as you may have noticed, RemoteExceptions and MalformedURLExceptions are thrown around a lot. These exceptions usually indicate a fatal error that can't be recovered from in a catch block, but you're still expected to write boilerplate code that catches and handles those exceptions—even if there's not much you can do to fix them.

Clearly a lot of code and manual work are involved in publishing an RMI service. Is there anything Spring can do to make this situation less knotty?

CONFIGURING AN RMI SERVICE IN SPRING

Fortunately, Spring provides an easier way to publish RMI services. Instead of writing RMI-specific classes with methods that throw RemoteException, you write a POJO that performs the functionality of your service. Spring handles the rest.

The RMI service that you'll create exposes the methods from the SpitterService interface. As a reminder, the following listing shows what that interface looks like.

> **Listing 15.1 SpitterService: defines the service layer of the Spittr application**

```java
package com.habuma.spittr.service;
import java.util.List;
import com.habuma.spittr.domain.Spitter;
import com.habuma.spittr.domain.Spittle;
public interface SpitterService {
  List<Spittle> getRecentSpittles(int count);
  void saveSpittle(Spittle spittle);
  void saveSpitter(Spitter spitter);
  Spitter getSpitter(long id);
  void startFollowing(Spitter follower, Spitter followee);
  List<Spittle> getSpittlesForSpitter(Spitter spitter);
  List<Spittle> getSpittlesForSpitter(String username);
```

```
Spitter getSpitter(String username);
Spittle getSpittleById(long id);
void deleteSpittle(long id);
List<Spitter> getAllSpitters();
}
```

If you were using traditional RMI to expose this service, all of those methods in SpitterService and in SpitterServiceImpl would need to throw java.rmi.Remote-Exception. But you're going to turn it into an RMI service using Spring's RmiService-Exporter, so the existing implementations will do fine.

RmiServiceExporter exports any Spring-managed bean as an RMI service. As shown in figure 15.4, RmiServiceExporter works by wrapping the bean in an adapter class. The adapter class is then bound to the RMI registry and proxies requests to the service class—SpitterServiceImpl, in this case.

The simplest way to use RmiServiceExporter to expose SpitterServiceImpl as an RMI service is to configure it in Spring with the following @Bean method:

```
@Bean
public RmiServiceExporter rmiExporter(SpitterService spitterService) {
  RmiServiceExporter rmiExporter = new RmiServiceExporter();
  rmiExporter.setService(spitterService);
  rmiExporter.setServiceName("SpitterService");
  rmiExporter.setServiceInterface(SpitterService.class);
  return rmiExporter;
}
```

Here the spitterService bean is wired into the service property to indicate that the RmiServiceExporter is to export the bean as an RMI service. The serviceName property names the RMI service. And the serviceInterface property specifies the interface that the service implements.

By default, RmiServiceExporter attempts to bind to an RMI registry on port 1099 of the local machine. If no RMI registry is found at that port, RmiServiceExporter will start one. If you'd rather bind to an RMI registry at a different port or host, you can specify that with the registryPort and registryHost properties. For example, the following RmiServiceExporter attempts to bind to an RMI registry on port 1199 on the host rmi.spitter.com:

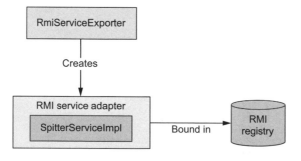

Figure 15.4 RmiServiceExporter turns POJOs into RMI services by wrapping them in a service adapter and binding the service adapter to the RMI registry.

```
@Bean
public RmiServiceExporter rmiExporter(SpitterService spitterService) {
  RmiServiceExporter rmiExporter = new RmiServiceExporter();
  rmiExporter.setService(spitterService);
  rmiExporter.setServiceName("SpitterService");
  rmiExporter.setServiceInterface(SpitterService.class);
  rmiExporter.setRegistryHost("rmi.spitter.com");
  rmiExporter.setRegistryPort(1199);
  return rmiExporter;
}
```

That's all you need to do to have Spring turn a bean into an RMI service. Now that the Spitter service has been exposed as an RMI service, you can create alternative user interfaces or invite third parties to create new clients for Spittr that use the RMI service. The developers of those clients will have an easy time connecting to the Spitter RMI service if they're using Spring.

Let's switch gears and see how to write a client of the Spitter RMI service.

15.2.2 *Wiring an RMI service*

Traditionally, RMI clients must use the RMI API's Naming class to look up a service from the RMI registry. For example, the following snippet of code might be used to retrieve the RMI Spitter service:

```
try {
  String serviceUrl = "rmi:/spitter/SpitterService";
  SpitterService spitterService =
          (SpitterService) Naming.lookup(serviceUrl);
  ...
}
catch (RemoteException e) { ... }
catch (NotBoundException e) { ... }
catch (MalformedURLException e) { ... }
```

Although this snippet of code would certainly retrieve a reference to the RMI Spitter service, it presents two problems:

- Conventional RMI lookups could result in any one of three checked exceptions (RemoteException, NotBoundException, and MalformedURLException) that must be caught or rethrown.
- Any code that needs the Spitter service is responsible for retrieving the service itself. That's plumbing code and probably is not directly cohesive with the client's functionality.

The exceptions thrown in the course of an RMI lookup are the kinds that typically signal a fatal and unrecoverable condition in the application. MalformedURLException, for instance, indicates that the address given for the service isn't valid. To recover from this exception, the application will, at a minimum, need to be reconfigured and may have to be recompiled. No try/catch block will be able to recover gracefully, so why should your code be forced to catch and handle it?

But perhaps more sinister is the fact that this code is in direct opposition to the principles of dependency injection (DI). Because the client code is responsible for looking up the Spitter service *and* the service is an RMI service, there's no opportunity to provide a different implementation of SpitterService from some other source. Ideally, you should be able to inject a SpitterService object into any bean that needs one, instead of having the bean look up the service itself. Using DI, any client of SpitterService can be ignorant of where that service comes from.

Spring's RmiProxyFactoryBean is a factory bean that creates a proxy to an RMI service. Using RmiProxyFactoryBean to reference an RMI SpitterService is as simple as adding the following @Bean method to the client's Spring configuration:

```
@Bean
public RmiProxyFactoryBean spitterService() {
  RmiProxyFactoryBean rmiProxy = new RmiProxyFactoryBean();
  rmiProxy.setServiceUrl("rmi://localhost/SpitterService");
  rmiProxy.setServiceInterface(SpitterService.class);
  return rmiProxy;
}
```

The URL of the service is set through RmiProxyFactoryBean's serviceUrl property. Here, the service is named SpitterService and is hosted on the local machine. Meanwhile, the interface that the service provides is specified with the serviceInterface property. The interaction between the client and the RMI proxy is illustrated in figure 15.5.

Now that you've declared the RMI service as a Spring-managed bean, you can wire it as a dependency into another bean just as you would a regular non-remote bean. For example, suppose the client needs to use the Spitter service to retrieve a list of Spittles for a given user. You might use @Autowired to wire the service proxy into the client:

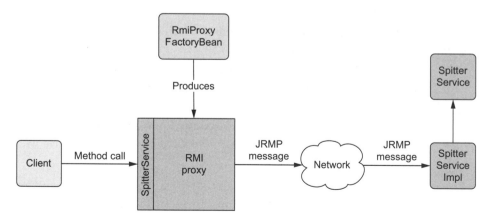

Figure 15.5 RmiProxyFactoryBean produces a proxy object that talks to remote RMI services on behalf of the client. The client talks to the proxy through the service's interface as if the remote service were a local POJO.

```
@Autowired
SpitterService spitterService;
```

Then you can invoke methods on it as if it were a local bean:

```
public List<Spittle> getSpittles(String userName) {
  Spitter spitter = spitterService.getSpitter(userName);
  return spitterService.getSpittlesForSpitter(spitter);
}
```

What's great about accessing an RMI service this way is that the client code doesn't even know it's dealing with an RMI service. It's given a `SpitterService` object via injection, without any concern for where it comes from. In fact, who's to say the client was even given an RMI-based implementation?

Furthermore, the proxy catches any `RemoteExceptions` that may be thrown by the service and rethrows them as unchecked exceptions that you may safely ignore. This makes it possible to easily swap out the remote service bean with another implementation of the service—perhaps a different remote service, or maybe a mock implementation used when unit-testing the client code.

Even though the client code isn't aware that the `SpitterService` it was given is a remote service, you may want to take care when you design the service's interface. Note that the client had to make two calls to the service: one to look up the `Spitter` by username, and another to retrieve the list of `Spittle` objects. That's two remote calls that are affected by network latency and that will impact the performance of the client. Knowing that this is how the service will be used, it may be worthwhile to revisit the service's interface to consolidate those two calls into a single method. But for now, you'll accept the service as is.

RMI is an excellent way to communicate with remote services, but it has some limitations. First, RMI has difficulty working across firewalls. That's because RMI uses arbitrary ports for communication—something that firewalls typically don't allow. In an intranet environment, this usually isn't a concern. But if you're working on the internet, you'll probably run into trouble with RMI. Even through RMI has support for tunneling over HTTP (which is usually allowed by firewalls), setting up RMI tunneling can be tricky.

Another thing to consider is that RMI is Java-based. That means both the client and the service must be written in Java. And because RMI uses Java serialization, the types of the objects being sent across the network must have the exact same version of the Java runtime on both sides of the call. These may or may not be issues for your application, but bear them in mind when choosing RMI for remoting.

Caucho Technology (the same company behind the Resin application server) has developed a remoting solution that addresses the limitations of RMI. Actually, Caucho has come up with two solutions: Hessian and Burlap. Let's see how to use Hessian and Burlap to work with remote services in Spring.

15.3 *Exposing remote services with Hessian and Burlap*

Hessian and Burlap are two solutions provided by Caucho Technology that enable lightweight remote services over HTTP. Each aims to simplify web services by keeping both its API and its communication protocols as simple as possible.

You may be wondering why Caucho has two solutions to the same problem. Hessian and Burlap are two sides of the same coin, but each serves slightly different purposes.

Hessian, like RMI, uses binary messages to communicate between client and service. But unlike other binary remoting technologies (such as RMI), the binary message is portable to languages other than Java, including PHP, Python, C++, and C#.

Burlap is an XML-based remoting technology, which automatically makes it portable to any language that can parse XML. And because it's XML, it's more easily human-readable than Hessian's binary format. Unlike other XML-based remoting technologies (such as SOAP and XML-RPC), Burlap's message structure is as simple as possible and doesn't require an external definition language (such as WSDL or IDL).

How do you choose between Hessian and Burlap? For the most part, they're identical. The only difference is that Hessian messages are binary and Burlap messages are XML. Because Hessian messages are binary, they're more bandwidth-friendly. If human readability is important to you (for debugging purposes), or if your application will be communicating with a language for which there's no Hessian implementation, Burlap's XML messages may be preferable.

To demonstrate Hessian and Burlap services in Spring, let's revisit the Spitter service example that we addressed with RMI in the previous section. This time, we'll look at how to solve the problem using Hessian and Burlap as the remoting models.

15.3.1 *Exposing bean functionality with Hessian/Burlap*

As before, suppose you want to expose the functionality of the `SpitterServiceImpl` class as a service—a Hessian service, this time. Even without Spring, doing this would be fairly trivial. You'd write a service class that extends `com.caucho.hessian.server.HessianServlet` and make sure all the service methods are `public` (all public methods are considered service methods to Hessian).

Because Hessian services are already easy to implement, Spring doesn't do much to simplify the Hessian model further. But when used with Spring, a Hessian service can take full advantage of the Spring Framework in ways that a pure Hessian service can't. This includes using Spring AOP to advise a Hessian service with system-wide services, such as declarative transactions.

EXPORTING A HESSIAN SERVICE

Exporting a Hessian service in Spring is remarkably similar to implementing an RMI service in Spring. To expose the Spitter service bean as an RMI service, you had to configure an `RmiServiceExporter` bean in the Spring configuration. Similarly, to expose the Spitter service as a Hessian service, you need to configure another exporter bean. This time it'll be a `HessianServiceExporter`.

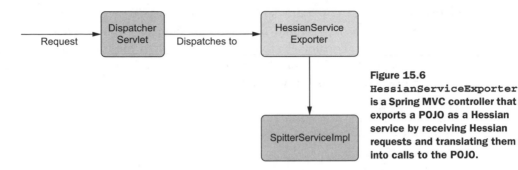

Figure 15.6
`HessianServiceExporter`
is a Spring MVC controller that exports a POJO as a Hessian service by receiving Hessian requests and translating them into calls to the POJO.

`HessianServiceExporter` performs the same function for a Hessian service as `RmiServiceExporter` does for an RMI service: it exposes the public methods of a POJO as methods of a Hessian service. But, as shown in figure 15.6, how it pulls off this feat is different from how `RmiServiceExporter` exports POJOs as RMI services.

`HessianServiceExporter` is a Spring MVC controller (more on that in a moment) that receives Hessian requests and translates them into method calls on the exported POJO. The following declaration of `HessianServiceExporter` in Spring exports the `spitterService` bean as a Hessian service:

```
@Bean
public HessianServiceExporter
    hessianExportedSpitterService(SpitterService service) {
  HessianServiceExporter exporter = new HessianServiceExporter();
  exporter.setService(service);
  exporter.setServiceInterface(SpitterService.class);
  return exporter;
}
```

Just as with `RmiServiceExporter`, the `service` property is wired with a reference to the bean that implements the service. Here, that's a reference to the `spitterService` bean. The `serviceInterface` is set to indicate that `SpitterService` is the interface the service implements.

Unlike `RmiServiceExporter`, you don't need to get a `serviceName` property. With RMI, the `serviceName` property is used to register a service in the RMI registry. Hessian doesn't have a registry, and, therefore, there's no need to name a Hessian service.

CONFIGURING THE HESSIAN CONTROLLER

Another major difference between `RmiServiceExporter` and `HessianService-Exporter` is that because Hessian is HTTP-based, `HessianServiceExporter` is implemented as a Spring MVC controller. This means that in order to use exported Hessian services, you'll need to perform two additional configuration steps:

- Configure a Spring `DispatcherServlet` in web.xml, and deploy your application as a web application.
- Configure a URL handler in your Spring configuration to dispatch Hessian service URLs to the appropriate Hessian service bean.

You first saw how to configure Spring's DispatcherServlet and URL handlers in chapter 5, so these steps should be somewhat familiar by now. First, you need a DispatcherServlet. Fortunately, you have one already configured in the Spittr application's web.xml file. But for the purposes of handling Hessian services, that DispatcherServlet needs a servlet mapping that catches *.service URLs:

```
<servlet-mapping>
  <servlet-name>spitter</servlet-name>
  <url-pattern>*.service</url-pattern>
</servlet-mapping>
```

If you're configuring DispatcherServlet in Java by implementing WebApplication-Initializer, you'll want to add that URL pattern as a mapping to the Servlet-Registration.Dynamic you got when adding DispatcherServlet to the container:

```
ServletRegistration.Dynamic dispatcher = container.addServlet(
        "appServlet", new DispatcherServlet(dispatcherServletContext));
    dispatcher.setLoadOnStartup(1);
    dispatcher.addMapping("/");
    dispatcher.addMapping("*.service");
```

Or, if you're configuring DispatcherServlet by extending AbstractDispatcher-ServletInitializer or AbstractAnnotationConfigDispatcherServletInitializer, you'll need to include the mapping when you override getServletMappings():

```
@Override
  protected String[] getServletMappings() {
    return new String[] { "/", "*.service" };
  }
```

Configured this way, any request whose URL ends with .service will be given to DispatcherServlet, which will in turn hand off the request to the Controller that's mapped to the URL. Thus, requests to /spitter.service will ultimately be handled by the hessianSpitterService bean (which is a proxy to SpitterServiceImpl).

How do you know the request will go to hessianSpitterService? Because you're also going to configure a URL mapping to have DispatcherServlet send the request to hessianSpitterService. The following SimpleUrlHandlerMapping bean will make that happen:

```
@Bean
public HandlerMapping hessianMapping() {
  SimpleUrlHandlerMapping mapping = new SimpleUrlHandlerMapping();
  Properties mappings = new Properties();
  mappings.setProperty("/spitter.service",
                       "hessianExportedSpitterService");
  mapping.setMappings(mappings);
  return mapping;
}
```

An alternative to Hessian's binary protocol is Burlap's XML-based protocol. Let's see how to export a service as a Burlap service.

EXPORTING A BURLAP SERVICE

`BurlapServiceExporter` is virtually identical to `HessianServiceExporter` in every way, except that it uses an XML-based protocol instead of a binary protocol. The following bean definition shows how to expose the Spitter service as a Burlap service using `BurlapServiceExporter`:

```
@Bean
public BurlapServiceExporter
      burlapExportedSpitterService(SpitterService service) {
  BurlapServiceExporter exporter = new BurlapServiceExporter();
  exporter.setService(service);
  exporter.setServiceInterface(SpitterService.class);
  return exporter;
}
```

As you can see, the only differences between this bean and its Hessian counterpart are the bean method and the exporter class. Configuring a Burlap service is otherwise the same as configuring a Hessian service. This includes the need to set up a URL handler and a `DispatcherServlet`.

Now let's look at the other side of the conversation and consume the service that you published using Hessian (or Burlap).

15.3.2 *Accessing Hessian/Burlap services*

As you'll recall from section 15.2.2, client code that consumes the Spitter service using `RmiProxyFactoryBean` has no idea the service is an RMI service. In fact, it has no clue that it's a remote service. It only deals with the `SpitterService` interface—all the RMI details are contained in the configuration of the beans in Spring's configuration. The good news is that because of the client's ignorance of the service's implementation, switching from an RMI client to a Hessian client is extremely easy, requiring no changes to the client's Java code.

The bad news is that if you love writing Java code, this section may be a letdown. That's because the only difference between wiring the client side of an RMI-based service and wiring the client side of a Hessian-based service is that you'll use Spring's `HessianProxyFactoryBean` instead of `RmiProxyFactoryBean`. A Hessian-based Spitter service can be declared in the client code like this:

```
@Bean
public HessianProxyFactoryBean spitterService() {
  HessianProxyFactoryBean proxy = new HessianProxyFactoryBean();
  proxy.setServiceUrl("http://localhost:8080/Spitter/spitter.service");
  proxy.setServiceInterface(SpitterService.class);
  return proxy;
}
```

Just as with an RMI-based service, the `serviceInterface` property specifies the interface that the service implements. And, as with `RmiProxyFactoryBean`, `serviceUrl` indicates the URL of the service. Because Hessian is HTTP-based, it's set to an HTTP URL here (determined in part by the URL mapping you defined earlier). Figure 15.7

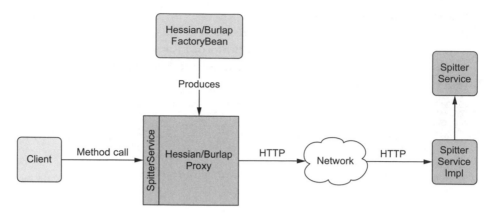

Figure 15.7 `HessianProxyFactoryBean` and `BurlapProxyFactoryBean` produce proxy objects that talk to a remote service over HTTP (Hessian in binary, Burlap in XML).

shows the interaction between a client and the proxy produced by HessianProxy-FactoryBean.

As it turns out, wiring a Burlap service into the client is equally uninteresting. The only difference is that you use BurlapProxyFactoryBean instead of HessianProxy-FactoryBean:

```
@Bean
public BurlapProxyFactoryBean spitterService() {
  BurlapProxyFactoryBean proxy = new BurlapProxyFactoryBean();
  proxy.setServiceUrl("http://localhost:8080/Spitter/spitter.service");
  proxy.setServiceInterface(SpitterService.class);
  return proxy;
}
```

Although I've made light of how uninteresting the configuration differences are among RMI, Hessian, and Burlap, this tedium is a benefit. It demonstrates that you can switch effortlessly between the various remoting technologies supported by Spring without having to learn a completely new model. Once you've configured a reference to an RMI service, it's short work to reconfigure it as a Hessian or Burlap service.

Because both Hessian and Burlap are based on HTTP, they don't suffer from the same firewall issues as RMI. But RMI has both Hessian and Burlap beat when it comes to serializing objects that are sent in RPC messages. Whereas Hessian and Burlap both use a proprietary serialization mechanism, RMI uses Java's own serialization mechanism. If your data model is complex, the Hessian/Burlap serialization model may not be sufficient.

There is, however, a best-of-both-worlds solution. Let's look at Spring's HTTP invoker, which offers RPC over HTTP (like Hessian/Burlap) while at the same time using Java serialization of objects (like RMI).

15.4 *Using Spring's HttpInvoker*

The Spring team recognized a void between RMI services and HTTP-based services such as Hessian and Burlap. On the one side, RMI uses Java's standard object serialization but is difficult to use across firewalls. On the other side, Hessian and Burlap work well across firewalls but use a proprietary object-serialization mechanism.

Thus Spring's HTTP invoker was born. The HTTP invoker is a new remoting model created as part of the Spring Framework to perform remoting across HTTP (to make the firewalls happy) and using Java's serialization (to make programmers happy). Working with HTTP invoker-based services is similar to working with Hessian/Burlap-based services.

To get started with the HTTP invoker, let's take another look at the Spitter service—this time implemented as an HTTP invoker service.

15.4.1 *Exposing beans as HTTP services*

To export a bean as an RMI service, you used `RmiServiceExporter`. To export it as a Hessian service, you used `HessianServiceExporter`. And to export it as a Burlap service, you used `BurlapServiceExporter`. Continuing this monotony over to Spring's HTTP invoker, it shouldn't surprise you that to export an HTTP invoker service, you'll need to use `HttpInvokerServiceExporter`.

To export the Spitter service as an HTTP invoker–based service, you need to configure an `HttpInvokerServiceExporter` bean like this:

```
@Bean
public HttpInvokerServiceExporter
      httpExportedSpitterService(SpitterService service) {
  HttpInvokerServiceExporter exporter =
          new HttpInvokerServiceExporter();
  exporter.setService(service);
  exporter.setServiceInterface(SpitterService.class);
  return exporter;
}
```

Feeling a sense of déjà vu? You may have a hard time spotting the difference between this bean declaration and the ones in section 15.3.2. The only material difference is the class name: `HttpInvokerServiceExporter`. Otherwise, this exporter isn't much different from the other remote service exporters.

As illustrated in figure 15.8, `HttpInvokerServiceExporter` works much like `HessianServiceExporter` and `BurlapServiceExporter`. It's a Spring MVC controller that receives requests from a client through `DispatcherServlet` and translates those requests into method calls on the service implementation POJO.

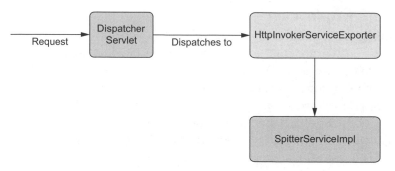

Figure 15.8   `HttpInvokerServiceExporter` works much like its Hessian and Burlap cousins, receiving requests from a Spring MVC `DispatcherServlet` and translating them into method calls on a Spring-managed bean.

Because `HttpInvokerServiceExporter` is a Spring MVC controller, you need to set up a URL handler to map an HTTP URL to the service, just like with the Hessian and Burlap exporters:

```
@Bean
public HandlerMapping httpInvokerMapping() {
  SimpleUrlHandlerMapping mapping = new SimpleUrlHandlerMapping();
  Properties mappings = new Properties();
  mappings.setProperty("/spitter.service",
                       "httpExportedSpitterService");
  mapping.setMappings(mappings);
  return mapping;
}
```

Also as before, you need to make sure you map `DispatcherServlet` such that it handles requests with a *.service extension. See the instructions in section 15.3.1 for details on how to set this mapping.

You've already seen how to consume remote services through RMI, Hessian, and Burlap. Now let's rework the Spitter client to use the service that you just exposed with HTTP invoker.

15.4.2   *Accessing services via HTTP*

At the risk of sounding like a broken record, I must tell you that consuming an HTTP invoker-based service is much like what you've already seen with the other remote service proxies. It's virtually identical. As you can see from figure 15.9, `HttpInvoker-ProxyFactoryBean` fills the same hole as the other remote service proxy factory beans you've seen in this chapter.

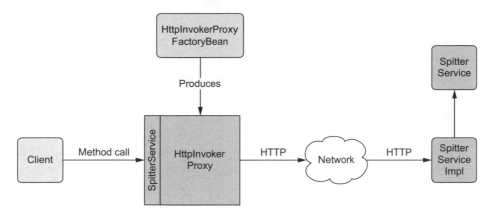

Figure 15.9 `HttpInvokerProxyFactoryBean` **is a proxy factory bean that produces a proxy for remoting with a Spring-specific HTTP-based protocol.**

To wire the HTTP invoker–based service into your client's Spring application context, you must configure a bean that proxies it using `HttpInvokerProxyFactoryBean`, as follows:

```
@Bean
public HttpInvokerProxyFactoryBean spitterService() {
  HttpInvokerProxyFactoryBean proxy = new HttpInvokerProxyFactoryBean();
  proxy.setServiceUrl("http://localhost:8080/Spitter/spitter.service");
  proxy.setServiceInterface(SpitterService.class);
  return proxy;
}
```

Comparing this bean definition to those in sections 15.2.2 and 15.3.2, you'll find that little has changed. The `serviceInterface` property is still used to indicate the interface implemented by the Spitter service. And the `serviceUrl` property is still used to indicate the location of the remote service. Because HTTP invoker is HTTP-based, like Hessian and Burlap, the `serviceUrl` can contain the same URL as with the Hessian and Burlap versions of the bean.

Don't you love the symmetry?

Spring's HTTP invoker presents a best-of-both-worlds remoting solution combining the simplicity of HTTP communication with Java's built-in object serialization. This makes HTTP invoker services an appealing alternative to either RMI or Hessian/Burlap.

`HttpInvoker` has one significant limitation that you should keep in mind: it's a remoting solution offered by the Spring Framework only. This means both the client and the service must be Spring-enabled applications. This also implies, at least for now, that both the client and the service must be Java-based. And because Java serialization is being used, both sides must have the same version of the classes as well as the same version of the Java runtime (much like RMI).

RMI, Hessian, Burlap, and the HTTP invoker are great remoting options. But when it comes to ubiquitous remoting, none hold a candle to web services. Next up, we'll look at how Spring supports remoting through SOAP-based web services.

15.5 *Publishing and consuming web services*

One of the most hyped TLAs (three-letter acronyms) in recent years is SOA (*service-oriented architecture*). SOA means many things to different people. But at the center of SOA is the idea that applications can and should be designed to lean on a common set of core services instead of reimplementing the same functionality for each application.

For example, a financial institution may have many applications, some of which need access to borrower account information. Rather than build account-access logic into each application (much of which would be duplicated), the applications can all rely on a common service to retrieve the account information.

Java and web services have a long history together, and various options are available for working with web services in Java. Many of those options integrate with Spring in some way. Although it would be impossible for me to cover every Spring-enabled web service framework and toolkit in this book, Spring comes with some capable support for publishing and consuming SOAP web services using the Java API for XML Web Services (JAX-WS).

In this section, we'll revisit the Spitter service example one more time. This time, you'll expose and consume the Spitter service as a web service using Spring's JAX-WS support. Let's start by seeing what it takes to create a JAX-WS web service in Spring.

15.5.1 *Creating Spring-enabled JAX-WS endpoints*

Earlier in this chapter, you created remote services using Spring's service exporters. These service exporters magically turn Spring-configured POJOs into remote services. You saw how to create RMI services using `RmiServiceExporter`, Hessian services using `HessianServiceExporter`, Burlap services using `BurlapServiceExporter`, and HTTP invoker services using `HttpInvokerServiceExporter`. Now you probably expect me to show you how to create web services using a JAX-WS service exporter in this section.

Spring does provide a JAX-WS service exporter, `SimpleJaxWsServiceExporter`, and you'll see it soon enough. But before you get there, you should know that it may not be the best choice in all situations. You see, `SimpleJaxWsServiceExporter` requires that the JAX-WS runtime support publishing of endpoints to a specified address. The JAX-WS runtime that ships with Sun's JDK 1.6 fits the bill, but other JAX-WS implementations, including the reference implementation of JAX-WS, may not.

If you'll be deploying to a JAX-WS runtime that doesn't support publishing to a specified address, you'll have write your JAX-WS endpoints in a more conventional way. That means the lifecycle of the endpoints will be managed by the JAX-WS runtime and not by Spring. But that doesn't mean they can't be wired with beans from a Spring application context.

AUTOWIRING JAX-WS ENDPOINTS IN SPRING

The JAX-WS programming model involves using annotations to declare a class and its methods as web service operations. A class that's annotated with @WebService is considered a web service endpoint, and its methods—annotated with @WebMethod—are the operations.

Just as with any other object in a sizable application, a JAX-WS endpoint will likely depend on other objects to do its work. That means JAX-WS endpoints could benefit from dependency injection. But if the endpoint's lifecycle is managed by the JAX-WS runtime and not by Spring, it would seem to be impossible to wire Spring-managed beans into a JAX-WS–managed endpoint instance.

The secret to wiring JAX-WS endpoints is to extend SpringBeanAutowiringSupport. By extending SpringBeanAutowiringSupport, you can annotate an endpoint's properties with @Autowired, and its dependencies will be met. SpitterServiceEndpoint in the following listing shows how this works.

Listing 15.2 SpringBeanAutowiringSupport on JAX-WS endpoints

```java
package com.habuma.spittr.remoting.jaxws;
import java.util.List;
import javax.jws.WebMethod;
import javax.jws.WebService;
import org.springframework.beans.factory.annotation.Autowired;
import
  org.springframework.web.context.support.SpringBeanAutowiringSupport;
import com.habuma.spittr.domain.Spitter;
import com.habuma.spittr.domain.Spittle;
import com.habuma.spittr.service.SpitterService;
@WebService(serviceName="SpitterService")
public class SpitterServiceEndpoint
    extends SpringBeanAutowiringSupport {          ←— Enable autowiring
  @Autowired
  SpitterService spitterService;                    ←— Autowire SpitterService
  @WebMethod
  public void addSpittle(Spittle spittle) {
    spitterService.saveSpittle(spittle);            ←┐
  }                                                  │  Delegate to
  @WebMethod                                         │  SpitterService
  public void deleteSpittle(long spittleId) {        │
    spitterService.deleteSpittle(spittleId);        ←┘
  }
  @WebMethod
  public List<Spittle> getRecentSpittles(int spittleCount) {
    return spitterService.getRecentSpittles(spittleCount);   ←┐
  }                                                            │  Delegate to
  @WebMethod                                                   │  SpitterService
  public List<Spittle> getSpittlesForSpitter(Spitter spitter) {│
    return spitterService.getSpittlesForSpitter(spitter);    ←┘
  }
}
```

You annotate the `spitterService` property with `@Autowired` to indicate that it should be automatically injected with a bean from the Spring application context. From there, this endpoint delegates to the injected `SpitterService` to do the real work.

EXPORTING STANDALONE JAX-WS ENDPOINTS

As I said, `SpringBeanAutowiringSupport` is useful when the object whose properties are being injected doesn't have its lifecycle managed by Spring. But under the right circumstances, it's possible to export a Spring-managed bean as a JAX-WS endpoint.

Spring's `SimpleJaxWsServiceExporter` works much like the other service exporters that you saw earlier in this chapter, in that it publishes Spring-managed beans as service endpoints in a JAX-WS runtime. Unlike those other service exporters, `SimpleJaxWsServiceExporter` doesn't need to be given a reference to the bean it's supposed to export. Instead, it publishes all beans that are annotated with JAX-WS annotations as JAX-WS services.

You can configure `SimpleJaxWsServiceExporter` using the following `@Bean` method:

```
@Bean
public SimpleJaxWsServiceExporter jaxWsExporter() {
  return new SimpleJaxWsServiceExporter();
}
```

As you can see, `SimpleJaxWsServiceExporter` needs nothing else to do its job. When it gets started, it digs through the Spring application context looking for beans that are annotated with `@WebService`. When it finds one, it publishes the bean as a JAX-WS endpoint with a base address of http://localhost:8080/. One such bean that it may find is `SpitterServiceEndpoint`.

Listing 15.3 `SimpleJaxWsServiceExporter` turns beans into JAX-WS endpoints

```
package com.habuma.spittr.remoting.jaxws;
import java.util.List;
import javax.jws.WebMethod;
import javax.jws.WebService;
import org.springframework.beans.factory.annotation.Autowired;
import org.springframework.stereotype.Component;
import com.habuma.spittr.domain.Spitter;
import com.habuma.spittr.domain.Spittle;
import com.habuma.spittr.service.SpitterService;
@Component
@WebService(serviceName="SpitterService")
public class SpitterServiceEndpoint {
  @Autowired
  SpitterService spitterService;          <--- Autowire SpitterService
   @WebMethod
  public void addSpittle(Spittle spittle) {
    spitterService.saveSpittle(spittle);   <--- Delegate to SpitterService
   }
  @WebMethod
  public void deleteSpittle(long spittleId) {
```

```
      spitterService.deleteSpittle(spittleId);
    }
  @WebMethod
  public List<Spittle> getRecentSpittles(int spittleCount) {
    return spitterService.getRecentSpittles(spittleCount);
    }
  @WebMethod
  public List<Spittle> getSpittlesForSpitter(Spitter spitter) {
    return spitterService.getSpittlesForSpitter(spitter);
    }
}
```

Delegate to SpitterService

Notice that this new implementation of `SpitterServiceEndpoint` no longer extends `SpringBeanAutowiringSupport`. As a full-fledged Spring bean, it qualifies for autowiring without extending a special support class.

Because `SimpleJaxWsServiceEndpoint`'s base address defaults to http://localhost:8080/, and because `SpitterServiceEndpoint` is annotated with `@WebService (serviceName="SpitterService")`, the matchup of these two beans results in a web service at http://localhost:8080/SpitterService. But you're in total control of the service URL, so if you'd like, you can set the base address to something else. For example, the following configuration of `SimpleJaxWsServiceEndpoint` publishes the same service endpoint to http://localhost:8888/services/SpitterService.

```
@Bean
public SimpleJaxWsServiceExporter jaxWsExporter() {
  SimpleJaxWsServiceExporter exporter =
          new SimpleJaxWsServiceExporter();
  exporter.setBaseAddress("http://localhost:8888/services/");
}
```

As simple as `SimpleJaxWsServiceEndpoint` seems, you should be aware that it only works with a JAX-WS runtime that supports publication of endpoints with an address. That includes the JAX-WS runtime that comes with Sun's 1.6 JDK. Other JAX-WS runtimes, such as the JAX-WS 2.1 reference implementation, don't support this type of endpoint publication and thus can't be used with `SimpleJaxWsServiceEndpoint`.

15.5.2 *Proxying JAX-WS services on the client side*

Publishing web services with Spring is different from the way you publish services in RMI, Hessian, Burlap, and the HTTP invoker. But as you'll soon see, consuming web services with Spring involves client-side proxies in much the same way that Spring-based clients consume those other remoting technologies.

Using `JaxWsPortProxyFactoryBean`, you can wire the Spitter web service in Spring as if it were any other bean. `JaxWsPortProxyFactoryBean` is a Spring `FactoryBean` that produces a proxy that knows how to talk to a SOAP web service. The proxy is created to implement the service's interface (see figure 15.10). Consequently, `JaxWsPortProxyFactoryBean` makes it possible to wire and use a remote web service as if it were any other local POJO.

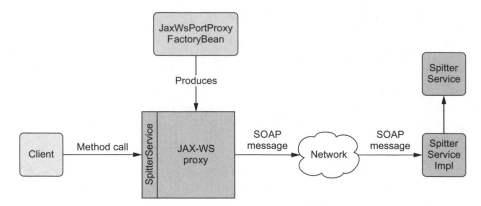

Figure 15.10 `JaxWsPortProxyFactoryBean` produces proxies that talk to remote web services. These proxies can then be wired into other beans as if they were local POJOs.

You configure JaxWsPortProxyFactoryBean to reference the Spitter web service like this:

```
@Bean
public JaxWsPortProxyFactoryBean spitterService() {
  JaxWsPortProxyFactoryBean proxy = new JaxWsPortProxyFactoryBean();
  proxy.setWsdlDocument(
          "http://localhost:8080/services/SpitterService?wsdl");
  proxy.setServiceName("spitterService");
  proxy.setPortName("spitterServiceHttpPort");
  proxy.setServiceInterface(SpitterService.class);
  proxy.setNamespaceUri("http://spitter.com");
  return proxy;
}
```

As you can see, several properties must be set for JaxWsPortProxyFactoryBean to work. The wsdlDocumentUrl property identifies the location of the remote web service's definition file. JaxWsPortProxyFactoryBean will use the WSDL available at that URL to construct a proxy to the service. The proxy that's produced by JaxWsPort-ProxyFactoryBean will implement the SpitterService interface, as specified by the serviceInterface property.

You can usually determine the values for the remaining three properties by looking at the service's WSDL. For illustration's sake, suppose the WSDL for the Spitter service looked like this:

```
<wsdl:definitions targetNamespace="http://spitter.com">
...
  <wsdl:service name="spitterService">
    <wsdl:port name="spitterServiceHttpPort"
            binding="tns:spitterServiceHttpBinding">
...
    </wsdl:port>
  </wsdl:service>
</wsdl:definitions>
```

Although not likely, it's possible for multiple services and/or ports to be defined in the service's WSDL. For that reason, `JaxWsPortProxyFactoryBean` requires that you specify the port and service names in the `portName` and `serviceName` properties. A quick glance at the `name` attributes of the `<wsdl:port>` and `<wsdl:service>` elements in the WSDL will help you figure out what these properties should be set to.

Finally, the `namespaceUri` property specifies the namespace of the service. Among other things, the namespace helps `JaxWsPortProxyFactoryBean` locate the service definition in the WSDL. As with the port and service names, you can find the correct value for this property by looking in the WSDL. It's usually available in the `target-Namespace` attribute of the `<wsdl:definitions>` element.

15.6 *Summary*

Working with remote services is usually a tedious chore. But Spring provides remoting support that makes working with remote services as simple as working with regular JavaBeans.

On the client side, Spring provides proxy factory beans that enable you to configure remote services in your Spring application. Regardless of whether you're using RMI, Hessian, Burlap, Spring's own HTTP invoker, or web services for remoting, you can wire remote services into your application as if they were POJOs. Spring even catches any `RemoteExceptions` that are thrown and rethrows runtime `RemoteAccess-Exceptions` in their place, freeing your code from having to deal with an exception that it probably can't recover from.

Even though Spring hides many of the details of remote services, making them appear as though they're local JavaBeans, you should bear in mind the consequences of remote services. Remote services, by their nature, are typically less efficient than local services. You should consider this when writing code that accesses remote services, limiting remote calls to avoid performance bottlenecks.

In this chapter, you saw how you can use Spring to expose and consume services based on basic remoting technologies. Although these remoting options are useful in distributing applications, this was just a taste of what's involved in working in a service-oriented architecture (SOA).

We also looked at how to export beans as SOAP-based web services. Although this is an easy way to develop web services, it may not be the best choice from an architectural standpoint. In the next chapter, we'll look at a different approach to building distributed applications by exposing portions of the application as RESTful resources.

Creating REST APIs
with Spring MVC

This chapter covers

- Writing controllers that serve REST resources
- Representing resources in XML, JSON, and other formats
- Consuming REST resources

Data is king.

As developers, we're often focused on building great software to solve business problems. Data is just the raw material that your software processes need to get their job done. But if you were to ask most business people which is most valuable to them, data or software, they'd likely choose data. Data is the lifeblood of many businesses. Software is often replaceable, but the data gathered over the years can never be replaced.

Don't you think it's odd that, given the importance of data, the way we develop software often treats data as an afterthought? Take the remote services from the previous chapter as an example. Those services were centered on actions and processes, not information and resources.

In recent years, *Representational State Transfer* (REST) has emerged as a popular information-centric alternative to traditional SOAP-based web services. Whereas SOAP typically focused on actions and processing, REST's concern is with the data being handled.

Starting with Spring 3.0, Spring introduced first-class support for creating REST APIs. And Spring's REST implementation has continued to evolve through Spring 3.1, 3.2, and now 4.0.

The good news is that Spring's REST support builds on Spring MVC, so we've already covered much of what you'll need for working with REST in Spring. In this chapter, you'll build on what you already know about Spring MVC to develop controllers that handle requests for RESTful resources. But before we get too carried away, let's examine what working with REST is all about.

16.1 Getting REST

I'll wager that this isn't the first time you've heard or read about REST. There's been a lot of talk about REST in recent years, and you'll find that it's fashionable in software development to speak ill of SOAP-based web services while promoting REST as an alternative.

Certainly, SOAP can be overkill for many applications, and REST brings a simpler alternative. Moreover, many modern applications have mobile and rich JavaScript clients that consume REST APIs running on a server.

The problem is that not everybody has a solid grasp of what REST really is. As a result, a lot of misinformation is floating about, and many things are labeled REST that don't fit the true REST intent. Before we can talk about how Spring supports REST, we need to establish a common understanding of what REST is all about.

16.1.1 The fundamentals of REST

A mistake that's often made when approaching REST is to think of it as "web services with URLs"—to think of REST as another remote procedure call (RPC) mechanism, like SOAP, but invoked through plain HTTP URLs and without SOAP's hefty XML namespaces.

On the contrary, REST has little to do with RPC. Whereas RPC is service oriented and focused on actions and verbs, REST is resource oriented, emphasizing the things and nouns that comprise an application.

To understand what REST is all about, it helps to break down the acronym into its constituent parts:

- *Representational*—REST resources can be represented in virtually any form, including XML, JavaScript Object Notation (JSON), or even HTML—whatever form best suits the consumer of those resources.
- *State*—When working with REST, you're more concerned with the state of a resource than with the actions you can take against resources.

- *Transfer*—REST involves transferring resource data, in some representational form, from one application to another.

Put more succinctly, REST is about transferring the state of resources—in a representational form that is most appropriate for the client or server—from a server to a client (or vice versa).

Resources in REST are identified and located with URLs. There are no strict rules regarding RESTful URL structure, but the URL should identify a resource, not bark a command to the server. Again, the focus is on things, not actions.

That said, there are actions in REST, and they're defined by HTTP methods. Specifically, GET, POST, PUT, DELETE, PATCH, and other HTTP methods make up the verbs in REST. These HTTP methods are often mapped to CRUD verbs as follows:

- *Create*—POST
- *Read*—GET
- *Update*—PUT or PATCH
- *Delete*—DELETE

Even though this is the common mapping of HTTP methods to CRUD verbs, it's not a strict requirement. There are cases where PUT can be used to create a new resource and POST can be used to update a resource. In fact, the non-idempotent nature of POST makes it a rogue method, capable of performing operations that don't easily fit the semantics of the other HTTP methods.

Given this view of REST, I try to avoid terms such as *REST service*, *RESTful web service*, and anything similar that incorrectly gives prominence to actions. Instead, I prefer to emphasize the resource-oriented nature of REST and speak of *RESTful resources*.

16.1.2 *How Spring supports REST*

Spring has long had some of the ingredients needed for exposing REST resources. Starting with version 3.0, however, Spring began adding enhancements to Spring MVC to provide first-class REST support. Now, at version 4.0, Spring supports the creation of REST resources in the following ways:

- Controllers can handle requests for all HTTP methods, including the four primary REST methods: GET, PUT, DELETE, and POST. Spring 3.2 and higher also supports the PATCH method.
- The @PathVariable annotation enables controllers to handle requests for parameterized URLs (URLs that have variable input as part of their path).
- Resources can be represented in a variety of ways using Spring views and view resolvers, including View implementations for rendering model data as XML, JSON, Atom, and RSS.
- The representation best suited for the client can be chosen using Content-NegotiatingViewResolver.

- View-based rendering can be bypassed altogether using the `@ResponseBody` annotation and various `HttpMethodConverter` implementations.
- Similarly, the `@RequestBody` annotation, along with `HttpMethodConverter` implementations, can convert inbound HTTP data into Java objects passed in to a controller's handler methods.
- Spring applications can consume REST resources using `RestTemplate`.

Throughout this chapter, we'll explore these features that make Spring more RESTful starting with how to produce REST resources using Spring MVC. Then in section 16.4, we'll switch to the client side of REST and see how to consume these resources. Let's start by looking at what goes into a RESTful Spring MVC controller.

16.2 *Creating your first REST endpoint*

One of the nice things about Spring's support for REST is that you already know a lot about what goes into creating RESTful controllers. What you learned in chapters 5–7 about creating web applications can now be used to expose resources in a REST API. Let's start by creating your first REST endpoint in a new controller named `Spittle-ApiController`.

The following listing shows the beginnings of a new REST controller that will serve `Spittle` resources. It's a small start, but you'll build on this controller throughout this chapter as you learn the ins and outs of Spring's REST programming model.

Listing 16.1   RESTful Spring MVC controller

```
package spittr.api;

import java.util.List;
import org.springframework.beans.factory.annotation.Autowired;
import org.springframework.stereotype.Controller;
import org.springframework.web.bind.annotation.RequestMapping;
import org.springframework.web.bind.annotation.RequestMethod;
import org.springframework.web.bind.annotation.RequestParam;
import spittr.Spittle;
import spittr.data.SpittleRepository;

@Controller
@RequestMapping("/spittles")
public class SpittleController {

  private static final String MAX_LONG_AS_STRING="9223372036854775807";

  private SpittleRepository spittleRepository;

  @Autowired
  public SpittleController(SpittleRepository spittleRepository) {
    this.spittleRepository = spittleRepository;
  }

  @RequestMapping(method=RequestMethod.GET)
  public List<Spittle> spittles(
      @RequestParam(value="max",
                    defaultValue=MAX_LONG_AS_STRING) long max,
```

```
        @RequestParam(value="count", defaultValue="20") int count) {

    return spittleRepository.findSpittles(max, count);
  }

}
```

Take a close look at listing 16.1. Can you see how it serves a REST resource instead of just a web page?

Probably not. Nothing about this controller, as it's written, makes it a RESTful, resource-serving controller. In fact, you may recognize the spittles() method; you've seen it before in chapter 5 (section 5.3.1).

As you'll recall, when a GET request comes in for /spittles, the spittles() method is called. It looks up and returns a Spittle list retrieved from the injected SpittleRepository. That list is placed into the model for a view to render. For a browser-based web application, this probably means the model data is rendered to an HTML page.

But we're talking about creating a REST API. In that case, HTML isn't the appropriate representation of the data.

Representation is an important facet of REST. It's how a client and a server communicate about a resource. Any given resource can be represented in virtually any form. If the consumer of the resource prefers JSON, then the resource can be presented in JSON format. Or if the consumer has a fondness for angle brackets, the same resource can be presented in XML. Meanwhile, a human user viewing the resource in a web browser will likely prefer seeing it in HTML (or possibly PDF, Excel, or some other human-readable form). The resource doesn't change—only how it's represented.

> **NOTE** Although Spring supports a variety of formats for representing resources, you aren't obligated to use them all when defining your REST API. JSON and XML are often sufficient representations expected by most clients.

Certainly, if you'll be presenting content to be consumed by a human, you should probably support HTML formatted resources. Depending on the nature of the resource and the requirements of your application, you may even choose to present the resource as a PDF document or an Excel spreadsheet.

For non-human consumers, such as other applications or code that invokes your REST endpoints, the leading choices for resource representation are XML and JSON. It's easy enough to support both of these options using Spring, so there's no need to make a choice.

With that said, I recommend that you *at minimum* support JSON. JSON is at least as easy to work with as XML (and many would argue that it's much easier). And if the client is JavaScript (which is increasingly common these days), JSON is a clear winner because essentially no marshaling/demarshaling is required to use JSON data in JavaScript.

It's important to know that controllers usually don't concern themselves with how resources are represented. Controllers deal with resources in terms of the Java objects that define them. But it's not until after the controller has finished its work that the resource is transformed into a form that best suits the client.

Spring offers two options to transform a resource's Java representation into the representation that's shipped to the client:

- *Content negotiation*—A view is selected that can render the model into a representation to be served to the client.
- *Message conversion*—A message converter transforms an object returned from the controller into a representation to be served to the client.

Because I discussed view resolvers in chapters 5 and 6, and you're already familiar with view-based rendering (from chapter 6), we'll start by looking at how to use content negotiation to select a view or view resolver that can render a resource into a form that's acceptable to the client.

16.2.1 *Negotiating resource representation*

As you'll recall from chapter 5 (and as depicted in figure 5.1), when a controller's handler method finishes, a logical view name is usually returned. If the method doesn't directly return a logical view name (if the method returns void, for example), the logical view name is derived from the request's URL. DispatcherServlet then passes the view name to a view resolver, asking it to help determine which view should render the results of the request.

In a human-facing web application, the view chosen is almost always rendered as HTML; view resolution is a one-dimensional activity. If the view name matches a view, then that's the view you go with.

When it comes to resolving view names into views that can produce resource representations, there's an additional dimension to consider. Not only does the view need to match the view name, but the view also needs to be chosen to suit the client. If the client wants JSON data, then an HTML-rendering view won't do—even if the view name matches.

Spring's ContentNegotiatingViewResolver is a special view resolver that takes the content type that the client wants into consideration. In it's simplest possible form, ContentNegotiatingViewResolver can be configured like this:

```
@Bean
public ViewResolver cnViewResolver() {
  return new ContentNegotiatingViewResolver();
}
```

A lot is going on in that simple bean declaration. Understanding how Content-NegotiatingViewResolver works involves getting to know the content-negotiation two-step:

1 Determine the requested media type(s).
2 Find the best view for the requested media type(s).

Let's dig deeper into each of these steps to see what makes `ContentNegotiatingView-Resolver` tick. You start by figuring out what kind of content the client wants.

DETERMINING THE REQUESTED MEDIA TYPES

The first step in the content-negotiation two-step is determining what kind of resource representation the client wants. On the surface, that seems like a simple job. Shouldn't the request's `Accept` header give a clear indication of what representation should be sent to the client?

Unfortunately, the `Accept` header can't always be deemed reliable. If the client in question is a web browser, there's no guarantee that what the client wants is what the browser sends in the `Accept` header. Web browsers typically only accept human-friendly content types (such as `text/html`), and there's no way (short of developer-oriented browser plugins) to specify a different content type.

`ContentNegotiatingViewResolver` considers the `Accept` header and uses what-ever media types it asks for, but only after it first looks at the URL's file extension. If the URL has a file extension on the end, `ContentNegotiatingViewResolver` tries to figure out the desired type based on that extension. If the extension is .json, then the desired content type must be `application/json`. If it's .xml, then the client is asking for `application/xml`. Of course, an .html extension indicates that the client wants the resource represented as HTML (`text/html`).

If the file extension doesn't produce any usable clues for the media type, then the `Accept` header in the request is considered. In that case, the `Accept` header's value indicates the MIME type(s) that the client wants; there's no need to look it up.

In the end, if there is no `Accept` header and the extension is no help, `Content-NegotiatingViewResolver` falls back to /as the default content type, meaning the client has to take whatever representation the server sends it.

Once a content type has been determined, it's time for `ContentNegotiatingView-Resolver` to resolve the logical view name into a `View` for rendering the model. Unlike Spring's other view resolvers, `ContentNegotiatingViewResolver` doesn't resolve views on its own. Instead, it delegates to other view resolvers, asking them to resolve the view.

`ContentNegotiatingViewResolver` asks the other view resolvers to resolve the logical view name into a view. Every view that's resolved is added to a list of candidate views. With the candidate view list assembled, `ContentNegotiatingViewResolver` cycles through all the requested media types, trying to find a view from among the candidate views that produces a matching content type. The first match found is the one that's used to render the model.

INFLUENCING HOW MEDIA TYPES ARE CHOSEN

The media-type selection process, as described so far, outlines the default strategy for determining the requested media types. But you can change how it behaves by giving it a `ContentNegotiationManager`. A few of the things you can do via a `Content-NegotiationManager` are as follows:

- Specify a default content type to fall back to if a content type can't be derived from the request.
- Specify a content type via a request parameter.
- Ignore the request's `Accept` header.
- Map request extensions to specific media types.
- Use the Java Activation Framework (JAF) as a fallback option for looking up media types from extensions.

There are three ways to configure a `ContentNegotiationManager`:

- Directly declare a bean whose type is `ContentNegotiationManager`.
- Create the bean indirectly via `ContentNegotiationManagerFactoryBean`.
- Override the `configureContentNegotiation()` method of `WebMvcConfigurerAdapter`.

Creating a `ContentNegotiationManager` directly is a bit involved and not something you'll want to do unless you have good reason to. The other two options exist to make the creation of a `ContentNegotiationManager` easier.

> ### ContentNegotiationManager added in Spring 3.2
>
> `ContentNegotiationManager` is relatively new to Spring, having been introduced in Spring 3.2. Prior to Spring 3.2, much of `ContentNegotiatingViewResolver`'s behavior was configured by setting properties on `ContentNegotiatingViewResolver` itself. As of Spring 3.2, most of the setter methods of `ContentNegotiatingViewResolver` have been deprecated, and you're encouraged to configure it via a `ContentNegotiationManager`.
>
> Although I won't cover the old way of configuring `ContentNegotiatingViewResolver` in this chapter, many of the properties you'll set when creating a `ContentNegotiationManager` have corresponding properties in `ContentNegotiatingViewResolver`. You should be able to easily map the new style of configuration to the old style if you're working with an older version of Spring.

Generally speaking, `ContentNegotiationManagerFactoryBean` is most useful when you're configuring the `ContentNegotiationManager` in XML. For example, you might configure a `ContentNegotiationManager` with a default content type of `application/json` in XML like this:

```
<bean id="contentNegotiationManager"
  class="org.springframework.http.ContentNegotiationManagerFactoryBean"
  p:defaultContentType="application/json">
```

Because `ContentNegotiationManagerFactoryBean` is an implementation of `FactoryBean`, this results in a `ContentNegotiationManager` bean being created. That `ContentNegotiationManager` can then be injected into `ContentNegotiatingViewResolver`'s contentNegotiationManager property.

For Java configuration, the easiest way to get a ContentNegotiationManager is to extend WebMvcConfigurerAdapter and override the configureContentNegotiation() method. Chances are you already extended WebMvcConfigurerAdapter when you started creating your Spring MVC application. In the Spittr application—for example, you already have an extension of WebMvcConfigurerAdapter called WebConfig, so all you need to do is override configureContentNegotiation(). Here's an implementation of configureContentNegotiation() that sets the default content type:

```
@Override
public void configureContentNegotiation(
    ContentNegotiationConfigurer configurer) {
  configurer.defaultContentType(MediaType.APPLICATION_JSON);
}
```

As you can see, configureContentNegotiation() is given a ContentNegotiation-Configurer to work with. ContentNegotiationConfigurer has several methods that mirror the setter methods of ContentNegotiationManager and enable you to set whatever content-negotiation behavior you'd like on the ContentNegotiation-Manager that will be created. In this case, you're calling the defaultContentType() method to set the default content type to application/json.

Now that you have a ContentNegotiationManager bean, all you need to do is inject it into the contentNegotiationManager property of ContentNegotiating-ViewResolver. That requires a small change to the @Bean method where you declare the ContentNegotiatingViewResolver:

```
@Bean
public ViewResolver cnViewResolver(ContentNegotiationManager cnm) {
  ContentNegotiatingViewResolver cnvr =
      new ContentNegotiatingViewResolver();
  cnvr.setContentNegotiationManager(cnm);
  return cnvr;
}
```

The @Bean method is injected with a ContentNegotiationManager and calls set-ContentNegotiationManager() with it. As a result, the ContentNegotiatingView-Resolver now takes on the behavior defined in the ContentNegotiationManager.

There are so many different twists on configuring ContentNegotiationManager that it would be impossible to cover them all here. The following listing is an example of a fairly simple configuration that I generally prefer when I use ContentNegotiating-ViewResolver: it defaults to HTML views but renders JSON output for certain view names.

> **Listing 16.2   Configuring a `ContentNegotiationManager`**

```
@Bean
public ViewResolver cnViewResolver(ContentNegotiationManager cnm) {
  ContentNegotiatingViewResolver cnvr =
      new ContentNegotiatingViewResolver();
  cnvr.setContentNegotiationManager(cnm);
  return cnvr;
}
```

```
@Override
public void configureContentNegotiation(
    ContentNegotiationConfigurer configurer) {
  configurer.defaultContentType(MediaType.TEXT_HTML);      ⟵ Default to HTML
}

@Bean
public ViewResolver beanNameViewResolver() {       ⟵ Look up views as beans
    return new BeanNameViewResolver();
}

@Bean
public View spittles() {
  return new MappingJackson2JsonView();      ⟵ "spittles" JSON view
}
```

In addition to what's shown in listing 16.2, there would also be an HTML-capable view resolver (such as `InternalResourceViewResolver` or `TilesViewResolver`). Under most circumstances, `ContentNegotiatingViewResolver` assumes that the client wants HTML, as configured in its `ContentNegotiationManager`. But if the client specifies that it wants JSON (either with a .json extension on the request path or via the `Accept` header), then `ContentNegotiatingViewResolver` attempts to find a view resolver that can serve a JSON view.

If the logical view name is "spittles", then the configured `BeanNameViewResolver` resolves the `View` declared in the `spittles()` method. That's because the bean name matches the logical view name. Otherwise, unless there's another matching `View`, `ContentNegotiatingViewResolver` falls back to the default, serving HTML.

Once `ContentNegotiatingViewResolver` knows what media types the client wants, it's time to find a view that can render that kind of content.

THE BENEFITS AND LIMITATIONS OF CONTENTNEGOTIATINGVIEWRESOLVER

The key benefit of using `ContentNegotiatingViewResolver` is that it layers REST resource representation on top of the Spring MVC with no change in controller code. The same controller method that serves human-facing HTML content can also serve JSON or XML to a non-human client.

Content negotiation is a convenient option when there's a great deal of overlap between your human and non-human interfaces. In practice, though, human-facing views rarely deal at the same level of detail as a REST API. The benefit of `ContentNegotiatingViewResolver` isn't realized when there isn't much overlap between the human and non-human interfaces.

`ContentNegotiatingViewResolver` also has a serious limitation. As a `ViewResolver` implementation, it only has an opportunity to determine how a resource is rendered to a client. It has no say in what representations a controller can consume from the client. If the client is sending JSON or XML, then `ContentNegotiatingViewResolver` isn't much help.

There's one more gotcha associated with using `ContentNegotiatingViewResolver`. The `View` chosen renders the model—not the resource—to the client. This is a subtle but important distinction. When a client requests a list of `Spittle` objects in JSON, the client is probably expecting a response that looks something like this:

```
[
  {
    "id": 42,
    "latitude": 28.419489,
    "longitude": -81.581184,
    "message": "Hello World!",
    "time": 1400389200000
  },
  {
    "id": 43,
    "latitude": 28.419136,
    "longitude": -81.577225,
    "message": "Blast off!",
    "time": 1400475600000
  }
]
```

But because the model is a map of key-value pairs, the response looks more like this:

```
{
    "spittleList": [
        {
            "id": 42,
            "latitude": 28.419489,
            "longitude": -81.581184,
            "message": "Hello World!",
            "time": 1400389200000
        },
        {
            "id": 43,
            "latitude": 28.419136,
            "longitude": -81.577225,
            "message": "Blast off!",
            "time": 1400475600000
        }
    ]
}
```

Although this isn't a terrible thing, it may not be what your client is expecting.

Because of these limitations, I generally prefer not to use `ContentNegotiating-VieWResolver`. Instead, I lean heavily toward using Spring's message converters for producing resource representations. Let's see how you can employ Spring's message converters in your controller methods.

16.2.2 *Working with HTTP message converters*

Message conversion is a more direct way to transform data produced by a controller into a representation that's served to a client. When using message conversion, `DispatcherServlet` doesn't bother with ferrying model data to a view. In fact, there is no model, and there is no view. There is only data produced by the controller and a resource representation produced when a message converter transforms that data.

Spring comes with a variety of message converters, listed in table 16.1, to handle the most common object-to-representation conversion needs.

Table 16.1 Spring provides several HTTP message converters that marshal resource representations to and from various Java types.

Message converter	Description
AtomFeedHttpMessageConverter	Converts Rome `Feed` objects to and from Atom feeds (media type `application/atom+xml`). *Registered if the Rome library is present on the classpath.*
BufferedImageHttpMessageConverter	Converts `BufferedImage` to and from image binary data.
ByteArrayHttpMessageConverter	Reads and writes byte arrays. Reads from all media types (`*/*`), and writes as `application/octet-stream`.
FormHttpMessageConverter	Reads content as `application/x-www-form-urlencoded` into a `MultiValueMap<String,String>`. Also writes `MultiValueMap<String,String>` as `application/x-www-form-urlencoded` and `MultiValueMap<String, Object>` as `multipart/form-data`.
Jaxb2RootElementHttpMessageConverter	Reads and writes XML (either `text/xml` or `application/xml`) to and from JAXB2-annotated objects. *Registered if JAXB v2 libraries are present on the classpath.*
MappingJacksonHttpMessageConverter	Reads and writes JSON to and from typed objects or untyped `HashMaps`. *Registered if the Jackson JSON library is present on the classpath.*
MappingJackson2HttpMessageConverter	Reads and writes JSON to and from typed objects or untyped `HashMaps`. *Registered if the Jackson 2 JSON library is present on the classpath.*
MarshallingHttpMessageConverter	Reads and writes XML using an injected marshaler and unmarshaler. Supported (un)marshalers include Castor, JAXB2, JIBX, XMLBeans, and XStream.
ResourceHttpMessageConverter	Reads and writes `org.springframework.core.io.Resource`.
RssChannelHttpMessageConverter	Reads and writes RSS feeds to and from Rome `Channel` objects. *Registered if the Rome library is present on the classpath.*
SourceHttpMessageConverter	Reads and writes XML to and from `javax.xml.transform.Source objects`.

Table 16.1   Spring provides several HTTP message converters that marshal resource representations to and from various Java types. *(continued)*

Message converter	Description
StringHttpMessageConverter	Reads all media types (*/*) into a String. Writes String to text/plain.
XmlAwareFormHttpMessageConverter	An extension of FormHttpMessageConverter that adds support for XML-based parts using a SourceHttpMessageConverter.

For example, suppose the client has indicated via the request's Accept header that it can accept application/json. Assuming that the Jackson JSON library is in the application's classpath, the object returned from the handler method is given to Mapping-JacksonHttpMessageConverter for conversion into a JSON representation to be returned to the client. On the other hand, if the request header indicates that the client prefers text/xml, then Jaxb2RootElementHttpMessageConverter is tasked with producing an XML response to the client.

Note that all but five of the HTTP message converters in table 16.1 are registered by default, so no Spring configuration is required to use them. But you may need to add additional libraries to your application's classpath to support them. For instance, if you want to use MappingJacksonHttpMessageConverter to convert JSON messages to and from Java objects, you'll need to add the Jackson JSON Processor library to the classpath. Similarly, the JAXB library is required for Jaxb2RootElement-HttpMessageConverter to convert messages between XML and Java objects. And the Rome library is required for AtomFeedHttpMessageConverter and RssChannel-HttpMessageConverter when the message comes in Atom or RSS format.

As you may have guessed, a slight twist to Spring MVC's programming model is required to support message conversion. Let's tweak the controller from listing 16.1 so that it will use message conversion.

RETURNING RESOURCE STATE IN THE RESPONSE BODY

Normally, when a handler method returns a Java object (anything other than String or an implementation of View), that object ends up in the model for rendering in the view. But if you're going to employ message conversion, you need to tell Spring to skip the normal model/view flow and use a message converter instead. There are a handful of ways to do this, but the simplest is to annotate the controller method with @ResponseBody.

Revisiting the spittles() method from listing 16.1, you can add @ResponseBody to have Spring convert the returned List<Spittle> to the body of the response:

```
@RequestMapping(method=RequestMethod.GET,
                produces="application/json")
public @ResponseBody List<Spittle> spittles(
    @RequestParam(value="max",
                defaultValue=MAX_LONG_AS_STRING) long max,
```

```
        @RequestParam(value="count", defaultValue="20") int count) {
    return spittleRepository.findSpittles(max, count);
}
```

The @ResponseBody annotation tells Spring that you want to send the returned object as a resource to the client, converted into some representational form that the client can accept. More specifically, DispatcherServlet considers the request's Accept header and looks for a message converter that can give the client the representation it wants.

For illustration's sake, if the client's Accept header specifies that the client will accept application/json, and if the Jackson JSON library is in the application's classpath, then either MappingJacksonHttpMessageConverter or MappingJackson2HttpMessageConverter will be chosen (depending on which version of Jackson is in the classpath). The message converter will convert the Spittle list returned from the controller into a JSON document that will be written to the body of the response. That response might look a little something like this:

```
[
  {
    "id": 42,
    "latitude": 28.419489,
    "longitude": -81.581184,
    "message": "Hello World!",
    "time": 1400389200000
  },
  {
    "id": 43,
    "latitude": 28.419136,
    "longitude": -81.577225,
    "message": "Blast off!",
    "time": 1400475600000
  }
]
```

Jackson uses reflection by default

Be aware that by default, the Jackson JSON libraries use reflection in producing the JSON resource representation from the returned object. For simple representations, this may be fine. But if you refactor the Java type by adding, removing, or renaming properties, then the produced JSON will be changed as well (which might break clients, depending on those properties).

You can, however, influence how the JSON is produced by applying Jackson's mapping annotations on the Java type. This gives you more control over what the resulting JSON looks like and prevents changes that could break your API and its clients.

Jackson's mapping annotations are well outside the scope of this book, but there's some useful documentation on the subject at http://wiki .fasterxml.com/Jackson-Annotations.

Speaking of the Accept header, note spittle()'s @RequestMapping. I've added a produces attribute to declare that this method will only handle requests where JSON output is expected. That is, this method will only handle requests whose Accept header includes application/json. Any other kind of request, even if it's a GET request whose URL matches the path specified, won't be handled by this method. Either it will be handled by some other handler method (if an appropriate one exists) or the client will be sent an HTTP 406 (Not Acceptable) response.

RECEIVING RESOURCE STATE IN THE REQUEST BODY

So far, we've been focused on REST endpoints that serve resources to the client. But REST isn't read-only. A REST API can also receive resource representations from the client. It'd be inconvenient if your controller had to convert a JSON or XML representation sent from a client into an object it can use. Spring's message converters were able to convert objects into representations on the way out of your controllers—can they do the same in reverse for representations coming in?

Just as @ResponseBody tells Spring to employ a message converter when sending data to a client, the @RequestBody tells Spring to find a message converter to convert a resource representation coming from a client into an object. For example, suppose that you need a way for a client to submit a new Spittle to be saved. You can write the controller method to handle such a request like this:

```
@RequestMapping(
    method=RequestMethod.POST
    consumes="application/json")
public @ResponseBody
    Spittle saveSpittle(@RequestBody Spittle spittle) {
  return spittleRepository.save(spittle);
}
```

If you disregard the annotations, saveSpittle() is a fairly straightforward method. It takes a single Spittle object as a parameter, saves it using the SpittleRepository, and then returns the Spittle returned from calling spittleRepository.save().

But by applying the annotations, it becomes much more interesting and powerful. The @RequestMapping indicates that it will only handle POST requests for /spittles (as declared in the class-level @RequestMapping). The body of the POST request is expected to carry a resource representation for a Spittle. Because the Spittle parameter is annotated with @RequestBody, Spring will look at the Content-Type header of the request and try to find a message converter that can convert the request body into a Spittle.

For example, if the client sent the Spittle data in a JSON representation, then the Content-Type header might be set to application/json. In that case, Dispatcher-Servlet will look for a message converter that can convert JSON into Java objects. If the Jackson 2 library is on the classpath, then MappingJackson2Http-MessageConverter will get the job and will convert the JSON representation into a Spittle that's passed into the saveSpittle() method. The method is also annotated with @ResponseBody so that the returned Spittle will be converted into a resource representation to be returned to the client.

Notice that the @RequestMapping has a consumes attribute set to application/json. The consumes attribute works much like the produces attribute, only with regard to the request's Content-Type header. This tells Spring that this method will only handle POST requests to /spittles if the request's Content-Type header is application/json. Otherwise, it will be up to some other method (if a suitable one exists) to handle the request.

DEFAULTING CONTROLLERS FOR MESSAGE CONVERSION

The @ResponseBody and @RequestBody annotations are succinct yet powerful ways to engage Spring's message converters when handling requests. But if you're writing a controller that has several methods, all of which should use message conversion, then those annotations get somewhat repetitive.

Spring 4.0 introduced the @RestController annotation to help with that. If you annotate your controller class with @RestController instead of @Controller, Spring applies message conversion to all handler methods in the controller. You don't need to annotate each method with @ResponseBody. SpittleController, as defined thus far, can look like the next listing.

> **Listing 16.3   Using the @RestController annotation**

```
package spittr.api;
import java.util.List;
import org.springframework.beans.factory.annotation.Autowired;
import org.springframework.web.bind.annotation.RestController;
import org.springframework.web.bind.annotation.RequestMapping;
import org.springframework.web.bind.annotation.RequestMethod;
import org.springframework.web.bind.annotation.RequestParam;
import spittr.Spittle;
import spittr.data.SpittleRepository;

@RestController                          ⟵── Default to message conversion
@RequestMapping("/spittles")
public class SpittleController {

  private static final String MAX_LONG_AS_STRING="9223372036854775807";

  private SpittleRepository spittleRepository;

  @Autowired
  public SpittleController(SpittleRepository spittleRepository) {
    this.spittleRepository = spittleRepository;
  }

  @RequestMapping(method=RequestMethod.GET)
  public List<Spittle> spittles(
      @RequestParam(value="max",
                    defaultValue=MAX_LONG_AS_STRING) long max,
      @RequestParam(value="count", defaultValue="20") int count) {

    return spittleRepository.findSpittles(max, count);
```

```
    }

    @RequestMapping(
        method=RequestMethod.POST
        consumes="application/json")
    public Spittle saveSpittle(@RequestBody Spittle spittle) {
      return spittleRepository.save(spittle);
    }
}
```

The key thing to notice in listing 16.3 is what's not in the code. Neither of the handler methods are annotated with `@ResponseBody`. But because the controller is annotated with `@RestController`, the objects returned from those methods will still go through message conversion to produce a resource representation for the client.

So far, you've seen how to use Spring MVC's programming model to publish RESTful resources in the body of responses. But there's more to a response than the payload. There are headers and status codes that can also provide useful information about the response to the client. Let's see how to populate response headers and set the status code when serving resources.

16.3 *Serving more than resources*

The `@ResponseBody` annotation is helpful in transforming a Java object returned from a controller to a resource representation to send to the client. As it turns out, serving a resource's representation to a client is only part of the story. A good REST API does more than transfer resources between the client and server. It also gives the client additional metadata to help the client understand the resource or know what has just taken place in the request.

16.3.1 *Communicating errors to the client*

For example, let's start by adding a new handler method to `SpittleController` to serve a single `Spittle`:

```
@RequestMapping(value="/{id}", method=RequestMethod.GET)
public @ResponseBody Spittle spittleById(@PathVariable long id) {
  return spittleRepository.findOne(id);
}
```

That ID is passed in to the `id` parameter and used to look up a `Spittle` from the repository by calling `findOne()`. The `Spittle` returned from `findOne()` will be returned from the handler method, and message conversion will take care of producing a resource representation consumable by the client.

Simple enough, right? This couldn't be made any better. Or could it?

What do you suppose will happen if there isn't a `Spittle` whose ID matches the given ID, and `findOne()` returns `null`?

The funny thing is that if `spittleById()` returns `null`, the body of the response is empty. No useful data is returned to the client. Meanwhile, the default HTTP status code carried on the response is 200 (OK), which means everything is fine.

But everything is not fine. The client asks for a `Spittle`, but it gets nothing. It receives neither a `Spittle` nor any indication that anything is wrong. The server is essentially saying, "Here's a useless response, but just know that everything's OK!"

Now consider what *should* happen in that scenario. At the least, the status code shouldn't be 200. It should be 404 (Not Found) to tell the client that what they asked for wasn't found. And it would be nice if the response body carried an error message instead of being empty.

Spring offers a few options for dealing with such scenarios:

- Status codes can be specified with the `@ResponseStatus` annotation.
- Controller methods can return a `ResponseEntity` that carries more metadata concerning the response.
- An exception handler can deal with the error cases, leaving the handler methods to focus on the happy path.

This is another area where Spring offers a lot of flexibility, and there's no one correct approach. Instead of trying to nail down a single strategy for dealing with these kind of errors or trying to cover all possible scenarios, I'll show you a couple of ways you could change `spittleById()` to handle the case where a `Spittle` can't be found.

WORKING WITH RESPONSEENTITY

As an alternative to `@ResponseBody`, controller methods can return a `Response-Entity`. `ResponseEntity` is an object that carries metadata (such as headers and the status code) about a response in addition to the object to be converted to a resource representation.

Because `ResponseEntity` allows you to specify the response's status code, it seems like a good choice for communicating an HTTP 404 error when the `Spittle` can't be found. Here's a new version of `spittleById()` that returns a `ResponseEntity`:

```
@RequestMapping(value="/{id}", method=RequestMethod.GET)
public ResponseEntity<Spittle> spittleById(@PathVariable long id) {
  Spittle spittle = spittleRepository.findOne(id);
  HttpStatus status = spittle != null ?
                    HttpStatus.OK : HttpStatus.NOT_FOUND;
  return new ResponseEntity<Spittle>(spittle, status);
}
```

As before, the ID from the path is used to retrieve a `Spittle` from the repository. If one is found, the status is set to `HttpStatus.OK` (which was the default before). But if the repository returns `null`, then the status is set to `HttpStatus.NOT_FOUND`, which translates to an HTTP 404. Finally, a new `ResponseEntity` is created to carry the `Spittle` and the status code to the client.

Notice that `spittleById()` isn't annotated with `@ResponseBody`. In addition to carrying response headers, a status code, and a payload, `ResponseEntity` implies the semantics of `@ResponseBody`, so the payload will be rendered into the response body just as if the method were annotated with `@ResponseBody`. There's no need to annotate the method with `@ResponseBody` if it returns `ResponseEntity`.

This is a step in the right direction, for sure. Now the client is given a proper status code if the `Spittle` it asks for can't be found. But the body of the response is still empty in that case. You'd like for the body to carry additional error information.

Let's try again. First, define an `Error` object to carry the error information:

```java
public class Error {
  private int code;
  private String message;

  public Error(int code, String message) {
    this.code = code;
    this.message = message;
  }

  public int getCode() {
    return code;
  }

  public String getMessage() {
    return message;
  }
}
```

Then you can change `spittleById()` to return the `Error`:

```java
@RequestMapping(value="/{id}", method=RequestMethod.GET)
public ResponseEntity<?> spittleById(@PathVariable long id) {
  Spittle spittle = spittleRepository.findOne(id);
  if (spittle == null) {
    Error error = new Error(4, "Spittle [" + id + "] not found");
    return new ResponseEntity<Error>(error, HttpStatus.NOT_FOUND);
  }
  return new ResponseEntity<Spittle>(spittle, HttpStatus.OK);
}
```

Now this controller method should behave as you wish. If the `Spittle` is found, it's returned, wrapped in a `ResponseEntity` with a status code of 200 (OK). On the other hand, if `findOne()` returns `null`, you construct an `Error` object and return it wrapped in a `ResponseEntity` with a status code of 404 (Not Found).

I suppose you could stop here. After all, the method works as you'd like it to. But a few things trouble me.

First, it's a bit more involved than when we started. There's a bit more logic involved, including a conditional statement. And the fact that the method returns `ResponseEntity<?>` feels wrong. The generic use of `ResponseEntity` leaves too much open for interpretation or mistake.

Fortunately, you can fix this with an error handler.

HANDLING ERRORS

The `if` block in `spittleById()` is handling an error. But that's what controller error handlers are good for. Error handlers deal with the ugly realities of what could go wrong, leaving the regular handler methods to blissfully focus on the happy path.

Let's refactor some of the code to take advantage of an error handler. Begin by defining an error handler that reacts to a `SpittleNotFoundException`:

```
@ExceptionHandler(SpittleNotFoundException.class)
public ResponseEntity<Error> spittleNotFound(
                                      SpittleNotFoundException e) {
  long spittleId = e.getSpittleId();
  Error error = new Error(4, "Spittle [" + spittleId + "] not found");
  return new ResponseEntity<Error>(error, HttpStatus.NOT_FOUND);
}
```

The `@ExceptionHandler` annotation can be applied to controller methods to handle specific exceptions. Here, it's indicating that if a `SpittleNotFoundException` is thrown from any of the handler methods in the same controller, the `spittleNot-Found()` method should be called to handle that exception.

As for `SpittleNotFoundException`, it's a fairly basic exception class:

```
public class SpittleNotFoundException extends RuntimeException {
  private long spittleId;
  public SpittleNotFoundException(long spittleId) {
    this.spittleId = spittleId;
  }

  public long getSpittleId() {
    return spittleId;
  }
}
```

Now you can remove most of the error handling from the `spittleById()` method:

```
@RequestMapping(value="/{id}", method=RequestMethod.GET)
public ResponseEntity<Spittle> spittleById(@PathVariable long id) {
  Spittle spittle = spittleRepository.findOne(id);
  if (spittle == null) { throw new SpittleNotFoundException(id); }
  return new ResponseEntity<Spittle>(spittle, HttpStatus.OK);
}
```

This cleans up `spittleById()` quite a bit. Aside from checking for a `null` return value, it's completely focused on the successful case where the requested `Spittle` is found. And you were able to get rid of the strange use of generics in the return type.

You can clean things up a little more, though. Now that you know that `spittle-ById()` will return a `Spittle` and that the HTTP status will always be 200 (OK), you no longer need to use `ResponseEntity` and can replace it with `@ResponseBody`:

```
@RequestMapping(value="/{id}", method=RequestMethod.GET)
public @ResponseBody Spittle spittleById(@PathVariable long id) {
  Spittle spittle = spittleRepository.findOne(id);
  if (spittle == null) { throw new SpittleNotFoundException(id); }
  return spittle;
}
```

Of course, if the controller class is annotated with `@RestController`, you don't even need `@ResponseBody`:

```
@RequestMapping(value="/{id}", method=RequestMethod.GET)
public Spittle spittleById(@PathVariable long id) {
  Spittle spittle = spittleRepository.findOne(id);
  if (spittle == null) { throw new SpittleNotFoundException(id); }
  return spittle;
}
```

Knowing that the error handler method always returns an `Error` and always responds with an HTTP status code of 404 (Not Found), you can apply a similar cleanup process to `spittleNotFound()`:

```
@ExceptionHandler(SpittleNotFoundException.class)
@ResponseStatus(HttpStatus.NOT_FOUND)
public @ResponseBody Error spittleNotFound(SpittleNotFoundException e) {
  long spittleId = e.getSpittleId();
  return new Error(4, "Spittle [" + spittleId + "] not found");
}
```

Because `spittleNotFound()` always returns an `Error`, the only reason to keep `Response-Entity` around is so you can set the status code. But by annotating `spittleNot-Found()` with `@ResponseStatus(HttpStatus.NOT_FOUND)`, you can achieve the same effect and get rid of `ResponseEntity`.

Again, if the controller class is annotated with `@RestController`, you can remove the `@ResponseBody` annotation and clean up the code a little more:

```
@ExceptionHandler(SpittleNotFoundException.class)
@ResponseStatus(HttpStatus.NOT_FOUND)
public Error spittleNotFound(SpittleNotFoundException e) {
  long spittleId = e.getSpittleId();
  return new Error(4, "Spittle [" + spittleId + "] not found");
}
```

In some ways, you've gone full circle. In order to set the response status code, you began using `ResponseEntity`. But then you were able to use an exception handler and `@ResponseStatus` to eliminate the need for `ResponseEntity` and tighten up the code.

It almost seems that you won't ever need `ResponseEntity`. But there's one more thing that `ResponseEntity` does well that can't be done with other annotations or exception handlers. Let's see how to set headers in the response.

16.3.2 *Setting headers in the response*

In the case of the `saveSpittle()` method, you're creating a new `Spittle` resource in the course of handling a `POST` request. But as it's currently written (refer to listing 16.3), you're not accurately communicating that to the client.

After `saveSpittle()` handles the request, the server responds to the client with a representation of the `Spittle` in the body and an HTTP status code of 200 (OK). That's not a horrible thing, but it's not entirely accurate.

Certainly, assuming that the request successfully creates the resource, the status can be thought of as OK. But there's more to be said than "OK." Something was just created, and an HTTP status code communicates that to the client. HTTP 201 says that the request completed successfully, but it also says that something was created. If you're trying to communicate completely and accurately to the client, shouldn't the response be a 201 (Created) and not just 200 (OK)?

Applying what you've learned so far, that's easy to fix. All you need to do is annotate `saveSpittle()` with `@ResponseStatus` like this:

```
@RequestMapping(
    method=RequestMethod.POST
    consumes="application/json")
@ResponseStatus(HttpStatus.CREATED)
public Spittle saveSpittle(@RequestBody Spittle spittle) {
  return spittleRepository.save(spittle);
}
```

That should do the trick. Now the status code accurately reflects what took place. It tells the client that a resource was created. Problem solved.

There's just one thing, though. The client knows that something was created, but don't you think it might be interested in knowing *where* the resource was created? After all, it's a new resource, and a new URL is associated with it. Must the client guess what the URL for the new resource should be? Or can you communicate that somehow?

When creating a new resource, it's considered good form to communicate the resource's URL to the client in the `Location` header of the response. Therefore, you need some way to populate the response headers. Your old friend `ResponseEntity` can help you with that.

The following listing shows a new version of `saveSpittle()` that returns a `ResponseEntity` to communicate that a new resource was created.

Listing 16.4 Setting headers in the response when returning a `ResponseEntity`

```
@RequestMapping(
    method=RequestMethod.POST
    consumes="application/json")
public ResponseEntity<Spittle> saveSpittle(
                    @RequestBody Spittle spittle) {

  Spittle spittle = spittleRepository.save(spittle);    <— Fetch spittle

  HttpHeaders headers = new HttpHeaders();    <— Set the location header
  URI locationUri = URI.create(
      "http://localhost:8080/spittr/spittles/" + spittle.getId());
  headers.setLocation(locationUri);

  ResponseEntity<Spittle> responseEntity =    <— Create a ResponseEntity
      new ResponseEntity<Spittle>(
          spittle, headers, HttpStatus.CREATED)
  return responseEntity;
}
```

In this new version, an instance of `HttpHeaders` is created to carry the header values you want on the response. `HttpHeaders` is a special implementation of `MultiValue-Map<String, String>` with some convenient setter methods (such as `setLocation()`)

for setting common HTTP headers. After calculating the URL of the newly created `Spittle` resource, the headers are used to create the `ResponseEntity`.

Wow! The simple `saveSpittle()` method suddenly put on weight. What's more concerning, however, is that it calculates the `Location` header value using hard-coded values. The localhost and 8080 portions of the URI are of particular concern, because those won't be applicable if this application is deployed anywhere other than your local system.

Rather than construct the URI manually, Spring offers some help in the form of `UriComponentsBuilder`. It's a builder class that lets you build up a `UriComponents` instance by specifying the various components of the URI (such as the host, port, path, and query) a piece at a time. From the `UriComponents` object that `UriComponents-Builder` builds, you can obtain a `URI` suitable for setting the `Location` header.

To use a `UriComponentsBuilder`, all you have to do is ask for it as a parameter to the handler method, as shown next.

Listing 16.5   Using a `UriComponentsBuilder` to construct the location URI

```
@RequestMapping(
    method=RequestMethod.POST
    consumes="application/json")
public ResponseEntity<Spittle> saveSpittle(
    @RequestBody Spittle spittle,
    UriComponentsBuilder ucb) {            <-- Given a UriComponentsBuilder ...

  Spittle spittle = spittleRepository.save(spittle);

  HttpHeaders headers = new HttpHeaders();   <-- ... calculate the location URI
  URI locationUri =
    ucb.path("/spittles/")
       .path(String.valueOf(spittle.getId()))
       .build()
       .toUri();
  headers.setLocation(locationUri);

  ResponseEntity<Spittle> responseEntity =
    new ResponseEntity<Spittle>(
        spittle, headers, HttpStatus.CREATED)
  return responseEntity;
}
```

The `UriComponentsBuilder` given to the handler method is preconfigured with known information such as the host, port, and servlet content. It obtains this foundational information from the request that the handler method is serving. From there, the code builds up the rest of the `UriComponents` by setting the path.

Notice that the path is built up in two steps. The first step calls `path()` to set it to `/spittles/`, the base path that the controller handles. Then the saved `Spittle` ID is given in a second call to `path()`. As you may surmise, each call to `path()` builds on the previous calls.

After the path is completely set, the `build()` method is called to construct a Uri-Components object. From that, a call to `toUri()` gives the URI of the newly created `Spittle` resource.

Exposing resources in a REST API represents only one side of the conversation. It does no good to publish an API if nobody comes along and uses it. Commonly, mobile and JavaScript applications are the clients of a REST API, but there's no reason a Spring application can't consume those resources, too. Let's shift gears and see how to write Spring code that works for the client side of a RESTful interaction.

16.4 Consuming REST resources

Writing code that interacts with a REST resource as a client can involve some tedium and boilerplate. For example, let's say you need to write a method to fetch someone's Facebook profile from Facebook's Graph API. But the code to fetch the profile data is a bit more involved, as shown in the following listing.

Listing 16.6 Fetching a Facebook profile using Apache HTTP Client

```
public Profile fetchFacebookProfile(String id) {
  try {
    HttpClient client = HttpClients.createDefault();        ⟵ Create the client
    HttpGet request = new HttpGet("http://graph.facebook.com/" + id);
      request.setHeader("Accept", "application/json");

    HttpResponse response = client.execute(request);         ⟵ Execute the request
    HttpEntity entity = response.getEntity();
    ObjectMapper mapper = new ObjectMapper();
      return mapper.readValue(entity.getContent(), Profile.class);
  } catch (IOException e) {
    throw new RuntimeException(e);
  }
}
```

Create the request points to the `HttpGet request` line. *Map response to object* points to the `ObjectMapper mapper` line.

As you can see, a lot goes into consuming a REST resource. And I'm even cheating by using Apache HTTP Client to make the request and the Jackson JSON processor to parse the response.

Looking closely at the `fetchFacebookProfile()` method, you'll realize that little is specific to the task of fetching a Facebook profile. Most of it is boilerplate code. If you were to write another method to consume a different REST resource, it would probably share a lot of code with `fetchFacebookProfile()`.

What's more, there are a few places along the way where an `IOException` could be thrown. Because `IOException` is a checked exception, you're forced to either catch it or throw it. In this case, I've chosen to catch it and throw an unchecked `Runtime-Exception` in its place.

With so much boilerplate involved in resource consumption, you'd think it would be wise to encapsulate the common code and parameterize the variations. That's precisely what Spring's `RestTemplate` does. Just as `JdbcTemplate` handles the ugly parts of working with JDBC data access, `RestTemplate` frees you from the tedium of consuming RESTful resources.

In a moment, you'll see how you can rewrite the `fetchFacebookProfile()` method, using `RestTemplate` to dramatically simplify it and eliminate the boilerplate. But first, let's take a high-level survey of all the REST operations that `RestTemplate` offers.

16.4.1 *Exploring RestTemplate's operations*

`RestTemplate` defines 36 methods for interacting with REST resources, and most of these methods map to HTTP methods. I don't have enough space to go over all 36 methods in this chapter, but as it turns out, there are only 11 unique operations. Ten of these are overloaded into 3 method variants, while an 11th is overloaded 6 times for a total of 36 methods. Table 16.2 describes the 11 unique operations provided by `RestTemplate`.

Table 16.2   `RestTemplate` defines 11 unique operations, each of which is overloaded for a total of 36 methods.

Method	Description
`delete()`	Performs an HTTP `DELETE` request on a resource at a specified URL
`exchange()`	Executes a specified HTTP method against a URL, returning a `ResponseEntity` containing an object mapped from the response body
`execute()`	Executes a specified HTTP method against a URL, returning an object mapped from the response body
`getForEntity()`	Sends an HTTP `GET` request, returning a `ResponseEntity` containing an object mapped from the response body
`getForObject()`	Sends an HTTP `GET` request, returning an object mapped from a response body
`headForHeaders()`	Sends an HTTP `HEAD` request, returning the HTTP headers for the specified resource URL
`optionsForAllow()`	Sends an HTTP `OPTIONS` request, returning the `Allow` header for the specified URL
`postForEntity()`	POSTs data to a URL, returning a `ResponseEntity` containing an object mapped from the response body
`postForLocation()`	POSTs data to a URL, returning the URL of the newly created resource
`postForObject()`	POSTs data to a URL, returning an object mapped from the response body
`put()`	PUTs resource data to the specified URL

With the exception of TRACE, RestTemplate has methods to cover all the HTTP verbs. In addition, execute() and exchange() offer lower-level, general-purpose methods for using any of the HTTP methods.

Most of the operations in table 16.2 are overloaded into three method forms:

- One that takes a java.net.URI as the URL specification with no support for parameterized URLs
- One that takes a String URL specification with URL parameters specified as a Map
- One that takes a String URL specification with URL parameters specified as a variable argument list

Once you get to know the 11 operations provided by RestTemplate and how each of the variant forms works, you'll be well on your way to writing resource-consuming REST clients. Let's survey RestTemplate's operations by looking at those that support the four primary HTTP methods: GET, PUT, DELETE, and POST. We'll start with get-ForObject() and getForEntity(), the GET methods.

16.4.2 GETting resources

You may have noticed that table 16.2 lists two kinds of methods for performing GET requests: getForObject() and getForEntity(). As described earlier, each of these methods is overloaded into three forms. The signatures of the three getForObject() methods look like this:

```
<T> T getForObject(URI url, Class<T> responseType)
                        throws RestClientException;
<T> T getForObject(String url, Class<T> responseType,
                Object... uriVariables)  throws RestClientException;
<T> T getForObject(String url, Class<T> responseType,
        Map<String, ?> uriVariables) throws RestClientException;
```

Similarly, the signatures of the getForEntity() methods are as follows:

```
<T> ResponseEntity<T> getForEntity(URI url, Class<T> responseType)
        throws RestClientException;
<T> ResponseEntity<T> getForEntity(String url, Class<T> responseType,
        Object... uriVariables) throws RestClientException;
<T> ResponseEntity<T> getForEntity(String url, Class<T> responseType,
        Map<String, ?> uriVariables) throws RestClientException;
```

Except for the return type, the getForEntity() methods are mirror images of the getForObject() methods. And they work much the same way. They both perform a GET request, retrieving a resource given a URL. And they both map that resource to an instance of some type specified by the responseType parameter. The only difference is that getForObject() returns an object of the type requested, whereas getForEntity() returns that object along with extra information about the response.

Let's first look at the simpler getForObject() method. Then you'll see how to get more information from a GET response by using the getForEntity() method.

16.4.3 *Retrieving resources*

The getForObject() method is a no-nonsense option for retrieving a resource. You ask for a resource, and you receive that resource mapped to a Java type of your choosing. As a simple example of what getForObject() can do, let's take another stab at implementing fetchFacebookProfile():

```
public Profile fetchFacebookProfile(String id) {
  RestTemplate rest = new RestTemplate();
  return rest.getForObject("http://graph.facebook.com/{spitter}",
    Profile.class, id);
}
```

Back in listing 16.6, fetchFacebookProfile() involved more than a dozen lines of code. Using RestTemplate, it's reduced to a handful of lines (and could be even less if I didn't have to wrap lines to fit within the margins of this book).

fetchFacebookProfile() starts by constructing an instance of RestTemplate (an alternate implementation might use an injected instance instead). Then it invokes the getForObject() method to retrieve a Facebook profile. In doing so, it asks for the result as a Profile object. Upon receiving that Profile object, the method returns it to the caller.

Note that in this new version of fetchFacebookProfile() you don't use String concatenation to produce the URL. Instead, you take advantage of the fact that RestTemplate accepts parameterized URLs. The {id} placeholder in the URL will ultimately be filled by the method's id parameter. The last argument of getForObject() is a variable-sized list of arguments, where each argument is inserted into a placeholder in the specified URL in the order it appears.

Alternatively, you could place the id parameter into a Map with a key of id and pass in that Map as the last parameter to getForObject():

```
public Spittle[] fetchFacebookProfile(String id) {
  Map<String, String> urlVariables = new HashMap<String, String();
  urlVariables.put("id", id);
  RestTemplate rest = new RestTemplate();
  return rest.getForObject("http://graph.facebook.com/{spitter}",
      Profile.class, urlVariables);
}
```

One thing that's absent here is any sort of JSON parsing or object mapping. Under the covers, getForObject() converts the response body into an object for you. It does this by relying on the same set of HTTP message converters from table 16.1 that Spring MVC uses for handler methods that are annotated with @ResponseBody.

What's also missing from this method is any sort of exception handling. That's not because getForObject() couldn't throw an exception, but because any exception it throws is unchecked. If anything goes wrong in getForObject(), an unchecked RestClientException (or some subclass thereof) will be thrown. You can catch it if you'd like—but you're not forced by the compiler to catch it.

16.4.4 *Extracting response metadata*

As an alternative to getForObject(), RestTemplate also offers getForEntity(). The getForEntity() methods work much the same as the getForObject() methods. But where getForObject() returns only the resource (converted into a Java object by an HTTP message converter), getForEntity() returns that same object carried in a ResponseEntity. The ResponseEntity also carries extra information about the response, such as the HTTP status code and response headers.

One thing you might want to do with a ResponseEntity is retrieve the value of one of the response headers. For example, suppose that in addition to retrieving the resource, you want to know when that resource was last modified. Assuming that the server provides that information in the LastModified header, you can use the get-Headers() method like this:

```
Date lastModified = new Date(response.getHeaders().getLastModified());
```

The getHeaders() method returns an HttpHeaders object that provides several convenience methods for retrieving response headers, including getLastModified(), which returns the number of milliseconds since January 1, 1970.

In addition to getLastModified(), HttpHeaders includes the following methods for retrieving header information:

```
public List<MediaType> getAccept() { ... }
public List<Charset> getAcceptCharset() { ... }
public Set<HttpMethod> getAllow() { ... }
public String getCacheControl() { ... }
public List<String> getConnection() { ... }
public long getContentLength() { ... }
public MediaType getContentType() { ... }
public long getDate() { ... }
public String getETag() { ... }
public long getExpires() { ... }
public long getIfNotModifiedSince() { ... }
public List<String> getIfNoneMatch() { ... }
public long getLastModified() { ... }
public URI getLocation() { ... }
public String getOrigin() { ... }
public String getPragma() { ... }
public String getUpgrade() { ... }
```

For more general-purpose HTTP header access, HttpHeaders includes a get() method and a getFirst() method. Both take a String argument that identifies the key of the desired header. The get() method returns a list of String values—one for each value assigned to the header. The getFirst() method returns only the first header value.

If you're interested in the response's HTTP status code, then you'll want to call the getStatusCode() method. For example, consider this method that fetches a Spittle:

```
public Spittle fetchSpittle(long id) {
  RestTemplate rest = new RestTemplate();
  ResponseEntity<Spittle> response = rest.getForEntity(
```

```
    "http://localhost:8080/spittr-api/spittles/{id}",
      Spittle.class, id);
  if(response.getStatusCode() == HttpStatus.NOT_MODIFIED) {
    throw new NotModifiedException();
  }
  return response.getBody();
}
```

Here, if the server responds with a status of 304, it indicates that the content on the server hasn't been modified since the client previously requested it. In that event, a custom NotModifiedException is thrown to indicate that the client should check its cache for the Spittle.

16.4.5 *PUTting resources*

For performing PUT operations on a resource, RestTemplate offers a simple set of three put() methods. As with all of RestTemplate's methods, the put() method comes in three forms:

```
void put(URI url, Object request) throws RestClientException;
void put(String url, Object request, Object... uriVariables)
      throws RestClientException;
void put(String url, Object request, Map<String, ?> uriVariables)
      throws RestClientException;
```

In its simplest form, the put() method takes a java.net.URI that identifies (and locates) the resource being sent to the server, and an object that's the Java representation of that resource.

For example, here's how you might use the URI-based version of put() to update a Spittle resource on the server:

```
public void updateSpittle(Spittle spittle) throws SpitterException {
  RestTemplate rest = new RestTemplate();
  String url = "http://localhost:8080/spittr-api/spittles/"
              + spittle.getId();
  rest.put(URI.create(url), spittle);
}
```

Here, although the method signature is simple, the implication of using a java.net.URI argument is evident. In order to create the URL for the Spittle object to be updated, you have to do String concatenation.

As you've already seen with getForObject() and getForEntity(), using one of the other String-based put() methods alleviates most of the discomfort associated with creating a URI. These methods enable you to specify the URI as a template, plugging in values for the variable parts. Here's a new updateSpittle() method rewritten to use one of the String-based put() methods:

```
public void updateSpittle(Spittle spittle) throws SpitterException {
  RestTemplate rest = new RestTemplate();
  rest.put("http://localhost:8080/spittr-api/spittles/{id}",
          spittle,  spittle.getId());
}
```

The URI is now expressed as a simple String template. When RestTemplate sends the PUT request, the URI template will be expanded to replace the {id} portion with the value returned from spittle.getId(). Just like getForObject() and getForEntity(), the last argument to this version of put() is a variable-sized list of arguments, each of which is assigned to the placeholder variables in the order they appear.

Optionally, you could pass in the template variables as a Map:

```
public void updateSpittle(Spittle spittle) throws SpitterException {
  RestTemplate rest = new RestTemplate();
  Map<String, String> params = new HashMap<String, String>();
  params.put("id", spittle.getId());
  rest.put("http://localhost:8080/spittr-api/spittles/{id}",
           spittle,  params);
}
```

When you use a Map to send the template variables, the key of each entry in the Map corresponds to the placeholder variable of the same name in the URI template.

In all versions of put(), the second argument is the Java object that represents the resource being PUT to the server at the given URI. In this case, it's a Spittle object. RestTemplate uses one of the message converters from table 16.1 to convert the Spittle into a representation to send to the server in the request body.

The content type into which the object will be converted depends largely on the type being passed in to put(). If given a String value, the StringHttpMessageConverter kicks in: the value is written directly to the body of the request, and the content type is set to text/plain. When given a MultiValueMap<String,String>, the values in the map are written to the request body in application/x-www-form-urlencoded form by FormHttpMessageConverter.

Because you're passing in a Spittle object, you need a message converter that can work with arbitrary objects. If the Jackson 2 library is in the classpath, then the MappingJackson2HttpMessageConverter writes the Spittle to the request as application/json.

16.4.6 DELETEing resources

When you don't want a resource to be kept around on the server anymore, you'll want to call RestTemplate's delete() methods. Much like the put() methods, the delete() methods have only three versions, whose signatures are as follows:

```
void delete(String url, Object... uriVariables)
        throws RestClientException;
void delete(String url, Map<String, ?> uriVariables)
        throws RestClientException;
void delete(URI url) throws RestClientException;
```

Hands down, the delete() methods are the simplest of all the RestTemplate methods. The only thing you need to supply them with is the URI of the resource to be deleted. For example, to get rid of a Spittle whose ID is given, you might call delete() like this:

```
public void deleteSpittle(long id) {
  RestTemplate rest = new RestTemplate();
  rest.delete(
      URI.create("http://localhost:8080/spittr-api/spittles/" + id));
}
```

That's easy enough, but here again you rely on String concatenation to create a URI object. Let's turn to one of the simpler versions of delete() to avoid doing so:

```
public void deleteSpittle(long id) {
  RestTemplate rest = new RestTemplate();
  rest.delete("http://localhost:8080/spittr-api/spittles/{id}", id));
}
```

There. I feel better about that. Don't you?

Now that I've shown you the simplest set of RestTemplate methods, let's look at RestTemplate's most diverse set of methods—those that support HTTP POST requests.

16.4.7 POSTing resource data

Looking back at table 16.2, you see that RestTemplate comes with three different kinds of methods for sending POST requests. When you multiply that by the three variants that each is overridden into, that's a total of nine methods for POSTing data to the server.

Two of those methods have names that look familiar. The postForObject() and postForEntity() methods work with POST requests in a way that's similar to how get-ForObject() and getForEntity() work for sending GET requests. The other method, postForLocation(), is unique for POST requests.

16.4.8 Receiving object responses from POST requests

Let's say that you're using RestTemplate to POST a new Spitter object to the Spittr application's REST API. Because it's a brand-new Spitter, the server doesn't know about it (yet). Therefore, it's not officially a REST resource and doesn't have a URL. Also, the client won't know the ID of the Spitter until it's created on the server.

One way of POSTing a resource to the server is to use RestTemplate's post-ForObject() method. The three varieties of postForObject() have the following signatures:

```
<T> T postForObject(URI url, Object request, Class<T> responseType)
        throws RestClientException;
<T> T postForObject(String url, Object request, Class<T> responseType,
        Object... uriVariables) throws RestClientException;
<T> T postForObject(String url, Object request, Class<T> responseType,
        Map<String, ?> uriVariables) throws RestClientException;
```

In all cases, the first parameter is the URL to which the resource should be POSTed, the second parameter is the object to post, and the third parameter is the Java type expected to be given in return. In the case of the two versions that take the URL as a

String, a fourth parameter identifies the URL variables (as either a variable arguments list or a Map).

When you POST new Spitter resources to the Spitter REST API, they should be
posted to http://localhost:8080/spittr-api/spitters, where a POST-handling controller
handler method is waiting to save the object. Because this URL requires no URL variables, you can use any version of postForObject(). But in the interest of keeping it
simple, let's make the call like this:

```
public Spitter postSpitterForObject(Spitter spitter) {
  RestTemplate rest = new RestTemplate();
  return rest.postForObject("http://localhost:8080/spittr-api/spitters",
        spitter, Spitter.class);
}
```

The postSpitterForObject() method is given a newly created Spitter object and
uses postForObject() to send it to the server. In response, it receives a Spitter object
and returns it to the caller.

As with the getForObject() methods, you may want to examine some of the metadata that comes back with the request. In that case, postForEntity() is the preferred
method. postForEntity() comes with a set of signatures that mirror those of post-
ForObject():

```
<T> ResponseEntity<T> postForEntity(URI url, Object request,
        Class<T> responseType) throws RestClientException;
<T> ResponseEntity<T> postForEntity(String url, Object request,
        Class<T> responseType, Object... uriVariables)
        throws RestClientException;
<T> ResponseEntity<T> postForEntity(String url, Object request,
        Class<T> responseType, Map<String, ?> uriVariables)
        throws RestClientException;
```

Suppose that, in addition to receiving the Spitter resource in return, you'd also like
to see the value of the Location header in the response. In that case, you can call
postForEntity() like this:

```
RestTemplate rest = new RestTemplate();
ResponseEntity<Spitter> response = rest.postForEntity(
    "http://localhost:8080/spittr-api/spitters",
    spitter, Spitter.class);
Spitter spitter = response.getBody();
URI url = response.getHeaders().getLocation();
```

Just like the getForEntity() method, postForEntity() returns a ResponseEntity<T>
object. From that object, you can call getBody() to get the resource object (a Spitter
in this case). And the getHeaders() method gives you an HttpHeaders from which you
can access the various HTTP headers returned in the response. Here, you're calling
getLocation() to retrieve the Location header as a java.net.URI.

16.4.9 *Receiving a resource location after a POST request*

The `postForEntity()` method is handy for receiving both the resource posted and any response headers. But often you don't need the resource to be sent back to you (after all, you sent it to the server in the first place). If the value of the `Location` header is all you need to know, then it's even easier to use `RestTemplate`'s `postForLocation()` method.

Like the other `POST` methods, `postForLocation()` sends a resource to the server in the body of a `POST` request. But instead of responding with that same resource object, `postForLocation()` responds with the location of the newly created resource. It has the following three method signatures:

```
URI postForLocation(String url, Object request, Object... uriVariables)
        throws RestClientException;
URI postForLocation(
        String url, Object request, Map<String, ?> uriVariables)
        throws RestClientException;
URI postForLocation(URI url, Object request) throws RestClientException;
```

To demonstrate `postForLocation()`, let's try POSTing a `Spitter` again. This time, you want the resource's URL in return:

```
public String postSpitter(Spitter spitter) {
  RestTemplate rest = new RestTemplate();
  return rest.postForLocation(
          "http://localhost:8080/spittr-api/spitters",
          spitter).toString();
}
```

Here, you're passing in the target URL as a `String`, along with the `Spitter` object to be POSTed (there are no URL variables in this case). If, after creating the resource, the server responds with the new resource URL in the response's `Location` header, then `postForLocation()` will return that URL as a `String`.

16.4.10 *Exchanging resources*

Up to this point, you've seen all manner of `RestTemplate` methods for GETting, PUTting, DELETEing, and POSTing resources. Among those you saw two special methods, `getForEntity()` and `postForEntity()`, that give you the resulting resource wrapped in a `RequestEntity` from which you can retrieve response headers and status codes.

Being able to read headers from the response is useful. But what if you want to set headers on the request sent to the server? That's what `RestTemplate`'s `exchange()` methods are good for.

Like all the other methods in `RestTemplate`, `exchange()` is overloaded into three signature forms. One takes a `java.net.URI` to identify the target URL, whereas the other two take the URL in `String` form with URL variables, as shown here:

```
<T> ResponseEntity<T> exchange(URI url, HttpMethod method,
        HttpEntity<?> requestEntity, Class<T> responseType)
        throws RestClientException;
```

```
<T> ResponseEntity<T> exchange(String url, HttpMethod method,
        HttpEntity<?> requestEntity, Class<T> responseType,
        Object... uriVariables) throws RestClientException;
<T> ResponseEntity<T> exchange(String url, HttpMethod method,
        HttpEntity<?> requestEntity, Class<T> responseType,
        Map<String, ?> uriVariables) throws RestClientException;
```

The exchange() method also takes an HttpMethod parameter to indicate the HTTP verb that should be used. Depending on the value given to this parameter, the exchange() method can perform the same jobs as any of the other RestTemplate methods.

For example, one way to retrieve a Spitter resource from the server is to use RestTemplate's getForEntity() method like this:

```
ResponseEntity<Spitter> response = rest.getForEntity(
        "http://localhost:8080/spittr-api/spitters/{spitter}",
        Spitter.class, spitterId);
Spitter spitter = response.getBody();
```

As you can see in the next snippet of code, exchange() is also up to the task:

```
ResponseEntity<Spitter> response = rest.exchange(
        "http://localhost:8080/spittr-api/spitters/{spitter}",
        HttpMethod.GET, null, Spitter.class, spitterId);
Spitter spitter = response.getBody();
```

By passing in HttpMethod.GET as the HTTP verb, you're asking exchange() to send a GET request. The third argument is for sending a resource on the request, but because this is a GET request, it can be null. The next argument indicates that you want the response converted into a Spitter object. And the final argument is the value to place into the {spitter} placeholder in the specified URL template.

Used this way, the exchange() method is virtually identical to the previously used getForEntity(). But unlike getForEntity()—or getForObject()—exchange() lets you set headers on the request sent. Instead of passing null to exchange(), you pass in an HttpEntity created with the request headers you want.

Without specifying the headers, exchange() sends the GET request for a Spitter with the following headers:

```
GET /Spitter/spitters/habuma HTTP/1.1
Accept: application/xml, text/xml, application/*+xml, application/json
Content-Length: 0
User-Agent: Java/1.6.0_20
Host: localhost:8080
Connection: keep-alive
```

Look at the Accept header. It says it can accept several different XML content types as well as application/json. That leaves a lot of room for the server to decide which format to send the resource back as. Suppose you want to demand that the server send the response back as JSON. In that case, you need to specify application/json as the only value in the Accept header.

Setting request headers is a simple matter of constructing the `HttpEntity` sent to exchange() with a `MultiValueMap` loaded with the desired headers:

```
MultiValueMap<String, String> headers =
    new LinkedMultiValueMap<String, String>();
headers.add("Accept", "application/json");
HttpEntity<Object> requestEntity = new HttpEntity<Object>(headers);
```

Here, you create a `LinkedMultiValueMap` and add an `Accept` header set to application/json. Then you construct an `HttpEntity` (with a generic type of `Object`), passing the `MultiValueMap` as a constructor argument. If this were a PUT or a POST request, you would also give the `HttpEntity` an object to send in the body of the request—but for a GET request, this isn't necessary.

Now you can call exchange(), passing in the `HttpEntity`:

```
ResponseEntity<Spitter> response = rest.exchange(
        "http://localhost:8080/spittr-api/spitters/{spitter}",
        HttpMethod.GET, requestEntity, Spitter.class, spitterId);
Spitter spitter = response.getBody();
```

On the surface, the results should be the same. You should receive the `Spitter` object that you asked for. Under the surface, the request is sent with the following headers:

```
GET /Spitter/spitters/habuma HTTP/1.1
Accept: application/json
Content-Length: 0
User-Agent: Java/1.6.0_20
Host: localhost:8080
Connection: keep-alive
```

And, assuming that the server can serialize the `Spitter` response into JSON, the response body should be represented in JSON format.

16.5   *Summary*

RESTful architecture uses web standards to integrate applications, keeping the interactions simple and natural. Resources in a system are identified by URLs, manipulated with HTTP methods, and represented in one or more forms suitable for the client.

In this chapter, you've seen how to write Spring MVC controllers that respond to requests to manipulate RESTful resources. By utilizing parameterized URL patterns and associating controller handler methods with specific HTTP methods, controllers can respond to GET, POST, PUT, and DELETE requests for the resources in an application.

In response to those requests, Spring can represent the data behind those resources in a format that's best for the client. For view-based responses, `Content-NegotiatingViewResolver` can select the best view produced from several view resolvers to satisfy the client's desired content type. Or a controller handler method can be annotated with `@ResponseBody` to completely bypass view resolution and have one of several message converters convert the returned value into a response for the client.

REST APIs expose an application's functionality to a client to build on, and they expose it in ways that maybe even the original API designers never dreamed of. Often, the clients of a REST API are mobile applications or JavaScript running in a web browser. But Spring applications can also consume those APIs using `RestTemplate`.

The REST resources defined in this chapter are part of a public API. That is, if you were to deploy them to an application somewhere on the internet, there'd be nothing stopping anyone from writing a client that uses them. Coming up in the next chapter, you'll start locking them down, as we look at ways to secure the REST resources so that only authorized clients are allowed to consume them.

17

This chapter covers

- Introduction to asynchronous messaging
- Messaging with JMS
- Sending messages with Spring and AMQP
- Message-driven POJOs

It's 4:55 p.m. on Friday. You're minutes away from starting a much-anticipated vacation. You have just enough time to drive to the airport and catch your flight. But before you pack up and head out, you need to be sure your boss and colleagues know the status of the work you've been doing so that on Monday they can pick up where you left off. Unfortunately, some of your colleagues have already skipped out for the weekend, and your boss is tied up in a meeting. What do you do?

You could call your boss's cell phone—but it's not necessary to interrupt him for a mere status report. Maybe you could stick around and wait until he returns. But it's anyone's guess how long the meeting will last, and you have a plane to catch. Perhaps you could leave a sticky note on his monitor … next to a hundred other sticky notes it will blend in with.

The most practical way to communicate your status and still catch your plane is to send a quick email to your boss and your colleagues, detailing your progress and promising to send a postcard. You don't know where they are or when they'll read the email, but you do know they'll eventually return to their desks and read it. Meanwhile, you're on your way to the airport.

Sometimes it's necessary to talk to someone directly. If you injure yourself and need an ambulance, you're probably going to pick up the phone—emailing the hospital just won't do. But often, sending a message is sufficient and offers some advantages over direct communication, such as letting you get on with your vacation.

A couple of chapters back, you saw how to use RMI, Hessian, Burlap, the HTTP invoker, and web services to enable communication between applications. All of these communication mechanisms employ synchronous communication in which a client application directly contacts a remote service and waits for the remote procedure to complete before continuing.

Synchronous communication has its place, but it's not the only style of inter-application communication available to developers. *Asynchronous messaging* is a way of indirectly sending messages from one application to another without waiting for a response. Asynchronous messaging has several advantages over synchronous messaging, as you'll soon see.

With Spring, you have a few options for asynchronous messaging. In this chapter, we'll look at how to send and receive messages in Spring using both the Java Message Service (JMS) and the Advanced Message Queuing Protocol (AMQP). In addition to basic sending and receiving of messages, we'll look at Spring's support for message-driven POJOs: a way to receive messages that resembles EJB's message-driven beans (MDBs).

17.1 A brief introduction to asynchronous messaging

Much like the remoting mechanisms and REST APIs we've covered so far in this part of the book, asynchronous messaging is all about applications communicating with one another. But it differs from those other communication mechanisms in how information is transferred between systems.

Remoting options such as RMI and Hessian/Burlap are synchronous. As illustrated in figure 17.1, when the client invokes a remote method, the client must wait for the method to complete before moving on. Even if the remote method doesn't return anything to the client, the client is put on hold until the service is done.

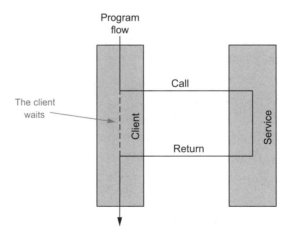

Figure 17.1 When communicating synchronously, the client must wait for the operation to complete.

On the other hand, when messages are sent asynchronously, as shown in figure 17.2, the client doesn't have to wait for the service to process the message or even for the message to be delivered. The client sends its message and then moves along, assuming that the service will eventually receive and process the message.

Asynchronous communication offers several advantages over synchronous communication. We'll take a closer look at these advantages in a moment, but first let's examine how the messages are sent asynchronously.

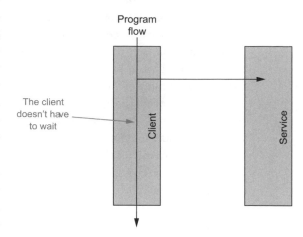

Figure 17.2   Asynchronous communication is a no-wait form of communication.

17.1.1 *Sending messages*

Most of us take the postal service for granted. Millions of times every day, people place letters, cards, and packages in the hands of postal workers, trusting that those items will reach the desired destinations. The world's too big for us to hand-deliver these things ourselves, so we rely on the postal system to handle them for us. We address our items, place the necessary postage on them, and then drop them in the mail to be delivered without giving a second thought to how they might get where they're going.

The key to the postal service is indirection. When Grandma's birthday comes around, it would be inconvenient if we had to deliver a card directly to her. Depending on where she lives, we'd have to set aside anywhere from a few hours to a few days to deliver a birthday card. Fortunately, the postal service will deliver the card to her while we go about our lives.

Similarly, indirection is the key to asynchronous messaging. When one application sends a message to another, there's no direct link between the two applications. Instead, the sending application places the message in the hands of a service that will ensure delivery to the receiving application.

There are two main actors in asynchronous messaging: *message brokers* and *destinations*. When an application sends a message, it hands it off to a message broker. A message broker is analogous to the post office. The message broker ensures that the message is delivered to the specified destination, leaving the sender free to go about other business.

When you send a letter through the mail, it's important to address it so that the postal service knows where it should be delivered. Likewise, asynchronously sent messages are addressed with a destination. Destinations are like mailboxes where the messages are placed until someone comes to pick them up.

But unlike mail addresses, which may indicate a specific person or street address, destinations are less specific. Destinations are only concerned about *where* messages will be picked up—not *who* will pick them up. In this way, a destination is like sending a letter addressed "To current resident."

Although different messaging systems may offer a variety of message-routing schemes, there are two common types of destinations: queues and topics. Each of these is associated with a specific messaging model: either point-to-point (for queues) or publish/subscribe (for topics).

POINT-TO-POINT MESSAGING

In the point-to-point model, each message has exactly one sender and one receiver, as illustrated in figure 17.3. When the message broker is given a message, it places the message in a queue. When a receiver comes along and asks for the next message in the queue, the message is pulled from the queue and delivered to the receiver. Because the message is removed from the queue as it's delivered, it's guaranteed that the message will be delivered to only one receiver.

Although each message in a message queue is delivered to only one receiver, this doesn't imply that only one receiver is pulling messages from the queue. It's likely that several receivers are processing messages from the queue. But they'll each be given their own messages to process.

This is analogous to waiting in line at the bank. As you wait, you may notice that multiple tellers are available to help you with your financial transaction. When a teller finishes helping a customer, the teller calls for the next person in line. When it's your turn at the front of the line, you're called to the counter and helped by one teller. The other tellers help other banking customers.

Another observation to be made at the bank is that when you get in line, you probably don't know which teller will eventually help you. You could count how many people are in line, match that with the number of available tellers, note which teller is fastest, and come up with a guess as to which teller will call you to their window. But chances are you'll be wrong and end up at a different teller's window.

Likewise, with point-to-point messaging, if multiple receivers are listening to a queue, there's no way of knowing which one will process a specific message. This uncertainty is a good thing, because it enables an application to scale up message processing by adding another listener to the queue.

Figure 17.3   A message queue decouples a message sender from the message receiver. Although a queue may have several receivers, each message is picked up by exactly one receiver.

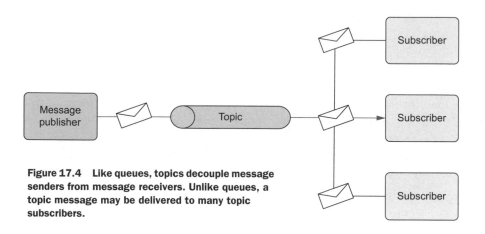

Figure 17.4   Like queues, topics decouple message senders from message receivers. Unlike queues, a topic message may be delivered to many topic subscribers.

PUBLISH-SUBSCRIBE MESSAGING

In the publish/subscribe messaging model, messages are sent to a topic. As with queues, many receivers may be listening to a topic. But unlike with queues, where a message is delivered to exactly one receiver, all subscribers to a topic receive a copy of the message, as shown in figure 17.4.

As you may have guessed from its name, the publish/subscribe message model is much like the model of a magazine publisher and its subscribers. The magazine (a message) is published and sent to the postal service, and all subscribers receive their own copy.

The magazine analogy breaks down when you realize that the publisher has no idea who its subscribers are. The publisher only knows that its message will be published to a particular topic—not who's listening to that topic. This also implies that the publisher has no idea how the message will be processed.

Now that we've covered the basics of asynchronous messaging, let's see how it compares to synchronous RPC.

17.1.2   *Assessing the benefits of asynchronous messaging*

Even though it's intuitive and simple to set up, synchronous communication imposes several limitations on the client of a remote service. These are the most significant:

- *Synchronous communication implies waiting.* When a client invokes a method on a remote service, the client must wait for the remote method to complete before continuing. If the client communicates frequently with the remote service or the remote service is slow to respond, this could negatively impact performance of the client application.
- *The client is coupled to the service through the service's interface.* If the interface of the service changes, all of the service's clients will need to change accordingly.
- *The client is coupled to the service's location.* A client must be configured with the service's network location so that it knows how to contact the service. If the

network topology changes, the client will need to be reconfigured with the new location.

- *The client is coupled to the service's availability.* If the service becomes unavailable, the client is effectively crippled.

Although synchronous communication has its place, these shortcomings should be taken into account when deciding what communication mechanism is a best fit for your application's needs. If these constraints are a concern for you, you may want to consider how asynchronous communication addresses them.

NO WAITING

When a message is sent asynchronously, the client doesn't need to wait for it to be processed or delivered. The client drops off the message with the message broker and moves along, confident that the message will make it to the appropriate destination.

Because it doesn't have to wait, the client is freed up to perform other activities. With all this free time, the client's performance can be dramatically improved.

MESSAGE ORIENTATION AND DECOUPLING

Unlike RPC communication, which is typically oriented around a method call, messages sent asynchronously are data-centric. This means the client isn't fixed to a specific method signature. Any queue or topic subscriber that can process the data sent by the client can process the message. The client doesn't need to be aware of any service specifics.

LOCATION INDEPENDENCE

Synchronous RPC services are typically located by their network address. The implication is that clients aren't resilient to changes in network topology. If a service's IP address changes or if it's configured to listen on a different port, the client must be changed accordingly, or the client will be unable to access the service.

In contrast, messaging clients have no idea what service will process their messages or where the service is located. The client only knows the queue or topic through which the messages will be sent. As a result, it doesn't matter where the service is located, as long as it can retrieve messages from the queue or topic.

In the point-to-point model, it's possible to take advantage of location independence to create a cluster of services. If the client is unaware of the service's location, and if the service's only requirement is that it must be able to access the message broker, there's no reason multiple services can't be configured to pull messages from the same queue. If the service is overburdened and falling behind in its processing, all you need to do is start a few more instances of the service to listen to the same queue.

Location independence takes on another interesting side effect in the publish/subscribe model. Multiple services could all subscribe to a single topic, receiving duplicate copies of the same message. But each service could process that message differently. For example, let's say you have a set of services that together process a message that details the new hire of an employee. One service might add the employee to the payroll system, another adds them to the HR portal, and yet another makes sure the employee is given access to the systems they'll need to do their job. Each service works independently on the same data that they all received from a topic.

GUARANTEED DELIVERY

In order for a client to communicate with a synchronous service, the service must be listening at the IP address and port specified. If the service were to go down or otherwise become unavailable, the client wouldn't be able to proceed.

But when sending messages asynchronously, the client can rest assured that its messages will be delivered. Even if the service is unavailable when a message is sent, the message will be stored until the service is available again.

Now that you have a feel for the basics of asynchronous messaging, let's see it in action. We'll start by using JMS to send and receive messages.

17.2 *Sending messages with JMS*

The Java Message Service (JMS) is a Java standard that defines a common API for working with message brokers. Before JMS, each message broker had a proprietary API, making an application's messaging code less portable between brokers. But with JMS, all compliant implementations can be worked with via a common interface in much the same way that JDBC has given database operations a common interface.

Spring supports JMS through a template-based abstraction known as `JmsTemplate`. Using `JmsTemplate`, it's easy to send messages across queues and topics from the producer side and also to receive those messages on the consumer side. Spring also supports the notion of message-driven POJOs: simple Java objects that react to messages arriving on a queue or topic in an asynchronous fashion.

We're going to explore Spring's JMS support, including `JmsTemplate` and message-driven POJOs. But before you can send and receive messages, you need a message broker ready to relay those messages between producers and consumers. Let's kick off our exploration of Spring JMS by setting up a message broker in Spring.

17.2.1 *Setting up a message broker in Spring*

ActiveMQ is a great open source message broker and a wonderful option for asynchronous messaging with JMS. As I'm writing this, the current version of ActiveMQ is 5.9.1. To get started with ActiveMQ, you'll need to download the binary distribution from http://activemq.apache.org. Once you've downloaded ActiveMQ, unzip it to your local hard drive. In the lib directory of the unzipped distribution, you'll find activemq-core-5.9.1.jar. This is the JAR file you'll need to add to the application's classpath to be able to use ActiveMQ's API.

Under the bin directory, you'll find subdirectories for various operating systems. In those, you'll find scripts that you can use to start ActiveMQ. For example, to start ActiveMQ on OS X, run `activemq start` from the bin/macosx directory. In moments, ActiveMQ will be ready and waiting to broker your messages.

CREATING A CONNECTION FACTORY

Throughout this chapter, you'll see different ways you can use Spring to both send and receive messages through JMS. In all cases, you'll need a JMS connection factory to be able to send messages through the message broker. Because you're using ActiveMQ as your message broker, you'll have to configure the JMS connection factory so that it knows how to connect to ActiveMQ. `ActiveMQConnectionFactory` is the JMS connection factory that comes with ActiveMQ. You can configure it in Spring like this:

```
<bean id="connectionFactory"
      class="org.apache.activemq.spring.ActiveMQConnectionFactory" />
```

By default, `ActiveMQConnectionFactory` assumes that the ActiveMQ broker is listening at port 61616 on `localhost`. That's fine for development purposes, but it's likely that your production ActiveMQ broker will be on a different host and/or port. In that case, you can specify the broker URL with the `brokerURL` property:

```
<bean id="connectionFactory"
      class="org.apache.activemq.spring.ActiveMQConnectionFactory"
      p:brokerURL="tcp://localhost:61616"/>
```

Optionally, because you know you're dealing with ActiveMQ, you can use ActiveMQ's own Spring configuration namespace (available with all versions of ActiveMQ since version 4.1) to declare the connection factory. First, be sure to declare the `amq` namespace in the Spring configuration XML file:

```
<?xml version="1.0" encoding="UTF-8"?>
  <beans xmlns="http://www.springframework.org/schema/beans"
   xmlns:xsi="http://www.w3.org/2001/XMLSchema-instance"
   xmlns:jms="http://www.springframework.org/schema/jms"
   xmlns:amq="http://activemq.apache.org/schema/core"
   xsi:schemaLocation="http://activemq.apache.org/schema/core
     http://activemq.apache.org/schema/core/activemq-core.xsd
     http://www.springframework.org/schema/jms
     http://www.springframework.org/schema/jms/spring-jms.xsd
     http://www.springframework.org/schema/beans
     http://www.springframework.org/schema/beans/spring-beans.xsd">
  ...
  </beans>
```

Then you can use the `<amq:connectionFactory>` element to declare the connection factory:

```
<amq:connectionFactory id="connectionFactory"
                       brokerURL="tcp://localhost:61616"/>
```

Note that the `<amq:connectionFactory>` element is specific to ActiveMQ. If you're using a different message-broker implementation, there may or may not be a Spring configuration namespace available. If not, you'll need to wire the connection factory as a `<bean>`.

Later in this chapter, you'll use this `connectionFactory` bean a lot. But for now, suffice it to say that `brokerURL` tells the connection factory where the message broker is located. In this case, the URL given to `brokerURL` tells the connection factory to connect to ActiveMQ on the local machine at port 61616 (which is the port that ActiveMQ listens to by default).

DECLARING AN ACTIVEMQ MESSAGE DESTINATION

In addition to a connection factory, you need a destination for the messages to be passed to. The destination can be either a queue or a topic, depending on the needs of the application.

Regardless of whether you're using a queue or a topic, you must configure the destination bean in Spring using a message broker–specific implementation class. For example, the following <bean> declaration declares an ActiveMQ queue:

```
<bean id="queue"
      class="org.apache.activemq.command.ActiveMQQueue"
      c:_="spitter.queue" />
```

Similarly, the following <bean> declares a topic for ActiveMQ:

```
<bean id="topic"
      class="org.apache.activemq.command.ActiveMQTopic"
      c:_="spitter.queue" />
```

In either case, the constructor is given the name of the queue, as it's known to the message broker—`spitter.topic` in this case.

As with the connection factory, the ActiveMQ namespace offers an alternative way to declare queues and topics. For queues, you can also use the <amq:queue> element:

```
<amq:queue id="spittleQueue" physicalName="spittle.alert.queue" />
```

Or, if it's a JMS topic that's in order, use the <amq:topic>:

```
<amq:topic id="spittleTopic" physicalName="spittle.alert.topic" />
```

Either way, the `physicalName` attribute sets the name of the message channel.

At this point you've seen how to declare the essential components of working with JMS. Now you're ready to start sending and receiving messages. For that, you'll use Spring's `JmsTemplate`, the centerpiece of Spring's JMS support. But first, let's gain an appreciation for what `JmsTemplate` provides by looking at what JMS is like without `JmsTemplate`.

17.2.2 *Using Spring's JMS template*

As you've seen, JMS gives Java developers a standard API for interacting with message brokers and for sending and receiving messages. Furthermore, virtually every message broker implementation supports JMS. So there's no reason to learn a proprietary messaging API for every message broker you deal with.

But although JMS offers a universal interface to all message brokers, its convenience comes at a cost. Sending and receiving messages with JMS isn't a simple matter of licking a stamp and placing it on an envelope. As you'll see, JMS demands that you also (figuratively) fuel the mail carrier's truck.

TACKLING RUNAWAY JMS CODE

In section 10.3.1, I showed you how conventional JDBC code can be an unwieldy mess when you need to handle connections, statements, result sets, and exceptions. Unfortunately, conventional JMS follows a similar model, as you'll observe in the following listing.

Listing 17.1 Sending a message using conventional (non-Spring) JMS

```
ConnectionFactory cf =
    new ActiveMQConnectionFactory("tcp://localhost:61616");
Connection conn = null;
Session session = null;
try {
  conn = cf.createConnection();
  session = conn.createSession(false, Session.AUTO_ACKNOWLEDGE);
  Destination destination = new ActiveMQQueue("spitter.queue");
  MessageProducer producer = session.createProducer(destination);
  TextMessage message = session.createTextMessage();

  message.setText("Hello world!");
  producer.send(message);                      <⎯ Send message
} catch (JMSException e) {
// handle exception?
} finally {
  try {
    if (session != null) {
      session.close();
    }
    if (conn != null) {
      conn.close();
    }
  } catch (JMSException ex) {
  }
}
```

At the risk of sounding repetitive—holy runaway code, Batman! As with the JDBC example, there are almost 20 lines of code here just to send a simple "Hello world!" message. Only a few of those lines actually send the message; the rest merely set the stage for sending the message.

It isn't much better on the receiving end, as you can see in the next listing.

Listing 17.2 Receiving a message using conventional (non-Spring) JMS

```
ConnectionFactory cf =
    new ActiveMQConnectionFactory("tcp://localhost:61616");
Connection conn = null;
Session session = null;
try {
  conn = cf.createConnection();
  conn.start();
  session = conn.createSession(false, Session.AUTO_ACKNOWLEDGE);
  Destination destination =
    new ActiveMQQueue("spitter.queue");
```

```
      MessageConsumer consumer = session.createConsumer(destination);
      Message message = consumer.receive();
      TextMessage textMessage = (TextMessage) message;
      System.out.println("GOT A MESSAGE: " + textMessage.getText());
      conn.start();
} catch (JMSException e) {
  // handle exception?
} finally {
  try {
    if (session != null) {
      session.close();
    }
    if (conn != null) {
      conn.close();
    }
  } catch (JMSException ex) {
  }
}
```

As in listing 17.1, that's a lot of code to do something so darn simple. If you take a line-by-line comparison, you'll find that the listings are almost identical. And if you were to look at a thousand other JMS examples, you'd find them all to be strikingly similar. Some may retrieve their connection factories from JNDI, and some may use a topic instead of a queue. Nevertheless, they all follow roughly the same pattern.

A consequence of this boilerplate code is that you repeat yourself every time you work with JMS. Worse still, you'll find yourself repeating other developers' JMS code.

You saw in chapter 10 how Spring's JdbcTemplate handles runaway JDBC boilerplate. Now let's look at how Spring's JmsTemplate can do the same thing for JMS boilerplate code.

WORKING WITH JMS TEMPLATES

JmsTemplate is Spring's answer to verbose and repetitive JMS code. JmsTemplate takes care of creating a connection, obtaining a session, and ultimately sending or receiving messages. This leaves you to focus your development efforts on constructing the message to send or processing messages that are received.

What's more, JmsTemplate can handle any clumsy JMSException that may be thrown along the way. If a JMSException is thrown in the course of working with Jms-Template, JmsTemplate will catch it and rethrow it as one of the unchecked subclasses of Spring's own JmsException. Table 17.1 shows how Spring maps standard JMS-Exceptions to Spring's unchecked JmsExceptions.

Table 17.1 Spring's JmsTemplate catches standard JMSExceptions and rethrows them as unchecked subclasses of Spring's own JmsException.

Spring (org.springframework.jms.*)	Standard JMS (javax.jms.*)
DestinationResolutionException	Spring-specific—thrown when Spring can't resolve a destination name
IllegalStateException	IllegalStateException

Table 17.1 Spring's `JmsTemplate` catches standard `JMSExceptions` and rethrows them as unchecked subclasses of Spring's own `JmsException`. *(continued)*

Spring (`org.springframework.jms.*`)	Standard JMS (`javax.jms.*`)
InvalidClientIDException	InvalidClientIDException
InvalidDestinationException	InvalidDestinationException
InvalidSelectorException	InvalidSelectorException
JmsSecurityException	JmsSecurityException
ListenerExecutionFailedException	Spring-specific—thrown when execution of a listener method fails
MessageConversionException	Spring-specific—thrown when message conversion fails
MessageEOFException	MessageEOFException
MessageFormatException	MessageFormatException
MessageNotReadableException	MessageNotReadableException
MessageNotWriteableException	MessageNotWriteableException
ResourceAllocationException	ResourceAllocationException
SynchedLocalTransactionFailedException	Spring-specific—thrown when a synchronized local transaction fails to complete
TransactionInProgressException	TransactionInProgressException
TransactionRolledBackException	TransactionRolledBackException
UncategorizedJmsException	Spring-specific—thrown when no other exception applies

In fairness to the JMS API, `JMSException` does come with a rich and descriptive set of subclasses that give you a better sense of what went wrong. Nevertheless, all these subclasses of `JMSException` are checked exceptions and thus must be caught. `JmsTemplate` attends to that for you by catching each exception and rethrowing an appropriate unchecked subclass of `JmsException`.

To use `JmsTemplate`, you'll need to declare it as a bean in the Spring configuration file. The following XML should do the trick:

```
<bean id="jmsTemplate"
      class="org.springframework.jms.core.JmsTemplate"
      c:_-ref="connectionFactory" />
```

Because `JmsTemplate` needs to know how to get connections to the message broker, you must set the `connectionFactory` property with a reference to the bean that implements JMS's `ConnectionFactory` interface. Here, you wire it with a reference to the `connectionFactory` bean that you declared earlier in section 17.2.1.

That's all you need to do to configure `JmsTemplate`—it's ready to go. Let's start sending messages!

SENDING MESSAGES

One of the features you'd like to build into the Spittr application is the option of alerting (perhaps by email) other users whenever a spittle has been created. You could build that feature directly into the application at the point where a spittle is added. But figuring out whom to send alerts to and sending those alerts may take a while, which could hurt the perceived performance of the application. When a new spittle is added, you want the application to be snappy and respond quickly.

Rather than taking the time to send a message the moment a spittle is added, it makes more sense to queue up that work and deal with it later, after the response has gone back to the user. The time it takes to send a message to a message queue or a topic is negligible, especially compared to the time it may take to send alerts to other users.

To support sending spittle alerts asynchronously with the creation of spittles, let's introduce `AlertService` to the Spittr application:

```
package com.habuma.spittr.alerts;
import com.habuma.spittr.domain.Spittle;

public interface AlertService {
  void sendSpittleAlert(Spittle spittle);
}
```

As you can see, `AlertService` is an interface that defines a single operation, `sendSpittleAlert()`.

`AlertServiceImpl`, shown in listing 17.3, is an implementation of the `AlertService` interface that uses an injected `JmsOperations` (the interface that `JmsTemplate` implements) to send `Spittle` objects to a message queue to be processed at some later time.

Listing 17.3 Sending a `Spittle` using `JmsTemplate`

```
package com.habuma.spittr.alerts;
import javax.jms.JMSException;
import javax.jms.Message;
import javax.jms.Session;
import org.springframework.beans.factory.annotation.Autowired;
import org.springframework.jms.core.JmsOperations;
import org.springframework.jms.core.MessageCreator;
import com.habuma.spittr.domain.Spittle;

public class AlertServiceImpl implements AlertService {

  private JmsOperations jmsOperations;

  @Autowired
  public AlertServiceImpl(JmsOperations jmsOperatons) {     <—— Inject JMS template
    this.jmsOperations = jmsOperations;
  }

  public void sendSpittleAlert(final Spittle spittle) {
```

```
jmsOperations.send(                                    <--- Send message
    "spittle.alert.queue",          <--- Specify destination
    new MessageCreator() {
     public Message createMessage(Session session)
             throws JMSException {
       return session.createObjectMessage(spittle);    <--- Create message
       }
     }
   );
  }
}
```

The first parameter to `JmsOperations`' `send()` method is the name of the JMS destination to which the message will be sent. When the `send()` method is called, `Jms-Template` deals with obtaining a JMS connection and session and sends the message on behalf of the sender (see figure 17.5).

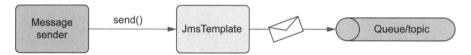

Figure 17.5 `JmsTemplate` deals with the complexities of sending a message on behalf of the sender.

The message is constructed using a `MessageCreator`, implemented here as an anonymous inner class. In `MessageCreator`'s `createMessage()` method, you ask for an object message from the session, giving it the `Spittle` object from which to build the object message.

And that's it! Note that the `sendSpittleAlert()` method is focused entirely on assembling and sending a message. There's no connection or session-management code; `JmsTemplate` handles all that for you. And there's no need to catch `JMS-Exception`; `JmsTemplate` will catch any `JMSException` that's thrown and then rethrow it as one of Spring's unchecked exceptions from table 17.1.

SETTING A DEFAULT DESTINATION

In listing 17.3, you explicitly specify a destination where the spittle message should be sent in the `send()` method. That form of `send()` comes in handy when you want to programmatically choose a destination. But in the case of `AlertServiceImpl`, you'll always be sending the spittle message to the same destination, so the benefits of that form of `send()` aren't as clear.

Instead of explicitly specifying a destination each time you send a message, you can opt for wiring a default destination into `JmsTemplate`:

```
<bean id="jmsTemplate"
    class="org.springframework.jms.core.JmsTemplate"
    c:_-ref="connectionFactory"
    p:defaultDestinationName="spittle.alert.queue" />
```

Here you set the destination name to `spittle.alert.queue`. But that's only a name: it doesn't say what kind of destination you're dealing with. If an existing queue or topic exists with that name, it will be used. If not, then a new destination (usually a queue) will be created. But if you want to be specific about what type of destination to create, you can instead wire in a reference to a queue or destination bean that you declared earlier:

```
<bean id="jmsTemplate"
      class="org.springframework.jms.core.JmsTemplate"
      c:_-ref="connectionFactory"
      p:defaultDestination-ref="spittleTopic" />
```

Now the call to `JmsOperations`' `send()` method can be simplified slightly by removing the first parameter:

```
jmsOperations.send(
  new MessageCreator() {
  ...
    }
);
```

This form of the `send()` method only takes a `MessageCreator`. There's no need to specify a destination, because the default destination is the one you want to send messages to.

Getting rid of the explicit destination in the call to `send()` made things a bit simpler. But sending messages can be even easier if you take advantage of a message converter.

CONVERTING MESSAGES WHEN SENDING

In addition to the `send()` method, `JmsTemplate` offers `convertAndSend()`. Unlike `send()`, the `convertAndSend()` method doesn't take a `MessageCreator` as an argument. That's because `convertAndSend()` uses a built-in message converter to create the message for you.

When you use `convertAndSend()`, the `sendSpittleAlert()` method can be reduced to a single line in its body:

```
public void sendSpittleAlert(Spittle spittle) {
  jmsOperations.convertAndSend(spittle);
}
```

Just like magic, the `Spittle` is converted into a `Message` before it's sent. But as with any magic trick, `JmsTemplate` has a little something up its sleeve. It uses an implementation of `MessageConverter` to do the dirty work of converting objects to `Message`s.

`MessageConverter` is a Spring-defined interface that has only two methods to be implemented:

```
public interface MessageConverter {
  Message toMessage(Object object, Session session)
                  throws JMSException, MessageConversionException;
  Object fromMessage(Message message)
                  throws JMSException, MessageConversionException;
}
```

Although this interface is simple enough to implement, you often won't need to create a custom implementation. Spring already offers a handful of implementations, such as those described in table 17.2.

Table 17.2 Spring offers several message converters for common conversion tasks. (All of these message converters are in the `org.springframework.jms.support.converter` package.)

Message converter	What it does
`MappingJacksonMessageConverter`	Uses the Jackson JSON library to convert messages to and from JSON
`MappingJackson2MessageConverter`	Uses the Jackson 2 JSON library to convert messages to and from JSON
`MarshallingMessageConverter`	Uses JAXB to convert messages to and from XML
`SimpleMessageConverter`	Converts Strings to/from `TextMessage`, byte arrays to/from `BytesMessage`, Maps to/from `MapMessage`, and `Serializable` objects to/from `ObjectMessage`

By default, `JmsTemplate` uses a `SimpleMessageConverter` when sending messages in `convertAndSend()`. But you can override that by declaring the message converter as a bean and injecting it into `JmsTemplate`'s `messageConverter` property. For example, if you want to work with JSON messages, you can declare a `MappingJacksonMessageConverter` bean:

```
<bean id="messageConverter"
      class="org.springframework.jms.support.converter.
                         ➥ MappingJacksonMessageConverter" />
```

Then you can wire it into `JmsTemplate` like this:

```
<bean id="jmsTemplate"
      class="org.springframework.jms.core.JmsTemplate"
      c:_-ref="connectionFactory"
      p:defaultDestinationName="spittle.alert.queue"
      p:messageConverter-ref="messageConverter" />
```

The various message converters may have additional configuration for finer-grained control of the conversion process. `MappingJacksonMessageConverter`, for instance, allows you to configure things such as encoding and a custom Jackson `ObjectMapper`. Consult the JavaDoc for each message converter for more details on how to configure the finer details of these message converters.

CONSUMING MESSAGES

Now you've seen how to send a message using `JmsTemplate`. But what if you're on the receiving end? Can `JmsTemplate` be used to receive messages, too?

Yes, it can. In fact, it's even easier to receive messages with `JmsTemplate` than it is to send them. All you need to do is call `JmsOperations`' `receive()` method, as shown in the following listing.

Listing 17.4   Receiving a message using `JmsTemplate`

```
public Spittle receiveSpittleAlert() {
  try {
    ObjectMessage receivedMessage =
        (ObjectMessage) jmsOperations.receive();          ←— Receive message

    return (Spittle) receivedMessage.getObject();          ←— Get object
  } catch (JMSException jmsException) {
    throw JmsUtils.convertJmsAccessException(jmsException); ←┐ Throw converted
  }                                                          │ exception
}
```

When the `JmsOperations`' `receive()` method is called, it attempts to retrieve a message from the message broker. If no message is available, `receive()` waits until a message becomes available. This interaction is illustrated in figure 17.6.

Because you know that the spittle message was sent as an object message, it can be cast to `ObjectMessage` on arrival. After that, you call `getObject()` to extract the `Spittle` object from the `ObjectMessage` and return it.

The one gotcha is that you have to do something about the `JMSException` that may be thrown. As I already mentioned, `JmsTemplate` is good about handling any checked `JMSExceptions` that are thrown and then rethrowing them as Spring unchecked `JmsExceptions`. But that's only applicable when you call one of `JmsTemplate`'s methods. `JmsTemplate` can't do much about the `JMSException` that may be thrown by the call to `ObjectMessage`'s `getObject()` method.

Therefore, you must either catch that `JMSException` or declare that the method throws it. In keeping with Spring's philosophy of avoiding checked exceptions, you don't want to let the `JMSException` escape this method, so you'll catch it instead. In the catch block, you can use the `convertJmsAccessException()` method from Spring's `JmsUtils` class to convert the checked `JMSException` to an unchecked `JmsException`. This is effectively the same thing `JmsTemplate` does for you in other cases.

One thing you can do to clear up the message in `receiveSpittleAlert()` is to take advantage of a message converter. You've seen how message converters can convert objects to `Messages` in `convertAndSend()`. But they can also be used on the receiving end with `JmsTemplate`'s `receiveAndConvert()`:

```
public Spittle retrieveSpittleAlert() {
  return (Spittle) jmsOperations.receiveAndConvert();
}
```

Figure 17.6   Receiving messages from a topic or queue using `JmsTemplate` is as simple as calling the `receive()` method. `JmsTemplate` takes care of the rest.

Now there's no need to cast the `Message` to `ObjectMessage`, retrieve the `Spittle` by calling `getObject()`, or muck about with the checked `JMSException`. This new `retrieveSpittleAlert()` is much cleaner. But there's still a small, not-so-obvious problem.

The big downside of consuming messages with `JmsTemplate` is that both the `receive()` and `receiveAndConvert()` methods are synchronous. This means the receiver must wait patiently for the message to arrive, because those methods will block until a message is available (or until a timeout condition occurs). Doesn't it seem odd to synchronously consume a message that was asynchronously sent?

That's where message-driven POJOs come in handy. Let's see how to receive messages asynchronously using components that react to messages rather than wait on them.

17.2.3 Creating message-driven POJOs

During one summer in college, I had the privilege of working at Yellowstone National Park. I didn't have a high-profile job like being a park ranger or the guy who turns Old Faithful on and off. Instead, I held a position in housekeeping at Old Faithful Inn, changing sheets, cleaning bathrooms, and vacuuming floors. Not glamorous, but at least I was working in one of the most beautiful places on Earth.

Every day after work, I'd head over to the local post office to see if I had any mail. I was away from home for several weeks, so it was nice to receive a letter or card from my friends back at school. I didn't have my own post box, so I'd walk up and ask the man sitting on the stool behind the counter if I had received any mail. That's when the wait would begin.

You see, the man behind the counter was approximately 195 years old. And like most people that age, he had a difficult time getting around. He'd drag his keister off the stool, slowly scoot his feet across the floor, and then disappear behind a partition. After a few moments, he'd emerge, shuffle his way back to the counter, and lift himself back up onto the stool. Then he'd look at me and say, "No mail today."

`JmsTemplate`'s `receive()` method is a lot like that aged postal employee. When you call `receive()`, it goes away and looks for a message in the queue or topic and doesn't return until a message arrives or until the timeout has passed. Meanwhile, your application is sitting there doing nothing, waiting to see if there's a message. Wouldn't it be better if your application could go about its business and be notified when a message arrives?

One of the highlights of the EJB 2 specification was the inclusion of the *message-driven bean* (MDB). MDBs are EJBs that process messages asynchronously. In other words, MDBs react to messages in a JMS destination as events and respond to those events. This is in contrast to synchronous message receivers, which block until a message is available.

MDBs were a bright spot in the EJB landscape. Even many of EJB's most rabid detractors would concede that MDBs were an elegant way of handling messages. The only blemish to be found in EJB 2 MDBs was that they had to implement `javax.ejb.MessageDrivenBean`. In doing so, they also had to implement a few EJB lifecycle callback methods. Put simply, EJB 2 MDBs were very un-POJO.

With the EJB 3 specification, MDBs were cleaned up to have a slightly more POJO feel to them. No longer must you implement the `MessageDrivenBean` interface. Instead, you implement the more generic `javax.jms.MessageListener` interface and annotate MDBs with `@MessageDriven`.

Spring 2.0 addresses the need for asynchronous consumption of messages by providing its own form of message-driven bean that's similar to EJB 3's MDBs. In this section, you'll learn how Spring supports asynchronous message consumption using message-driven POJOs (we'll call them *MDPs*, for short).

CREATING A MESSAGE LISTENER

If you were to build your spittle alert handler using EJB's message-driven model, it would need to be annotated with `@MessageDriven`. And although it's not strictly required, it's recommended that the MDB implement the `MessageListener` interface. The result would look something like this:

```
@MessageDriven(mappedName="jms/spittle.alert.queue")
public class SpittleAlertHandler implements MessageListener {
  @Resource
  private MessageDrivenContext mdc;

  public void onMessage(Message message) {
    ...
  }
}
```

For a moment, try to imagine a simpler world where message-driven components don't have to implement the `MessageListener` interface. In such a happy place, the sky would be the brightest of blues, the birds would always whistle your favorite song, and you wouldn't have to implement the `onMessage()` method or have a `Message-DrivenContext` injected.

Okay, maybe the demands placed on an MDB by the EJB 3 specification aren't that arduous. But the fact is that the EJB 3 implementation of `SpittleAlertHandler` is too tied to EJB's message-driven APIs and isn't as POJO-ish as you'd like. Ideally, you'd like the alert handler to be capable of handling messages, but not coded as if it knows that's what it will be doing.

Spring offers the ability for a method on a POJO to handle messages from a JMS queue or topic. For example, the following POJO implementation of `SpittleAlert-Handler` is sufficient.

> **Listing 17.5 Spring MDP that asynchronously receives and processes messages**

```
package com.habuma.spittr.alerts;
import com.habuma.spittr.domain.Spittle;

public class SpittleAlertHandler {
```

```
public void handleSpittleAlert(Spittle spittle) {     ⟵— Handler method
    // ... implementation goes here...
}
}
```

Although changing the color of the sky and training birds to sing are out of the scope of Spring, listing 17.5 shows that the dream world I described is much closer to reality. You'll fill in the details of the `handleSpittleAlert()` method later. For now, consider that nothing in `SpittleAlertHandler` shows any hint of JMS. It's a POJO in every sense of the term. It can nevertheless handle messages just like its EJB cousin. All it needs is some special Spring configuration.

CONFIGURING MESSAGE LISTENERS

The trick to empowering a POJO with message-receiving abilities is to configure it as a message listener in Spring. Spring's `jms` namespace provides everything you need to do that. First, you must declare the handler as a `<bean>`:

```
<bean id="spittleHandler"
      class="com.habuma.spittr.alerts.SpittleAlertHandler" />
```

Then, to turn `SpittleAlertHandler` into a message-driven POJO, you can declare the bean to be a message listener:

```
<jms:listener-container connection-factory="connectionFactory">
  <jms:listener destination="spitter.alert.queue"
      ref="spittleHandler" method="handleSpittleAlert" />
</jms:listener-container>
```

Here you have a message listener that's contained in a message-listener container. A *message-listener container* is a special bean that watches a JMS destination, waiting for a message to arrive. Once a message arrives, the bean retrieves the message and passes it on to any message listeners that are interested. Figure 17.7 illustrates this interaction.

To configure the message-listener container and message listener in Spring, you use two elements from Spring's `jms` namespace. The `<jms:listener-container>` is used to contain `<jms:listener>` elements. Here its `connectionFactory` attribute is configured with a reference to the `connectionFactory` that's to be used by each of the child `<jms:listener>`s as they listen for messages. In this case, the `connection-factory` attribute could have been left off, because it defaults to `connectionFactory`.

The `<jms:listener>` element is used to identify a bean and a method that should handle incoming messages. For the purposes of handling spittle alert messages, the `ref` element refers to your `spittleHandler` bean. When a message arrives on `spitter`

Figure 17.7   A message-listener container listens to a queue/topic. When a message arrives, it's forwarded to a message listener (such as a message-driven POJO).

.alert.queue (as designated by the destination attribute), the spittleHandler bean's handleSpittleAlert() method gets the call (per the method attribute).

It's also worth noting that if the bean identified by the ref attribute implements MessageListener, then there's no need to specify the method attribute. The onMessage() will be called by default.

17.2.4 *Using message-based RPC*

Chapter 15 explored several of Spring's options for exposing bean methods as remote services and for making calls on those services from clients. In this chapter, you've seen how to send messages between applications over message queues and topics. Now we'll bring those two concepts together and cover how to make remote calls that use JMS as a transport.

To support message-based RPC, Spring offers JmsInvokerServiceExporter for exporting beans as message-based services and JmsInvokerProxyFactoryBean for clients to consume those services. As you'll see, these two options are similar, but each has advantages and disadvantages. I'll show you both approaches and let you decide which works best for you. Let's start by looking at how to work with Spring's support for JMS-backed services.

As you'll recall from chapter 15, Spring provides several options for exporting beans as remote services. You used RmiServiceExporter to export beans as RMI services, HessianExporter and BurlapExporter for Hessian and Burlap services over HTTP, and HttpInvokerServiceExporter to create HTTP invoker services over HTTP. But Spring has one more service exporter that we didn't talk about in chapter 15.

EXPORTING JMS-BASED SERVICES

JmsInvokerServiceExporter is much like those other service exporters. In fact, note that there's some symmetry in the names of JmsInvokerServiceExporter and HttpInvokerServiceExporter. If HttpInvokerServiceExporter exports services that communicate over HTTP, then JmsInvokerServiceExporter must export services that converse over JMS.

To demonstrate how JmsInvokerServiceExporter works, consider AlertServiceImpl.

Listing 17.6 AlertServiceImpl: a JMS-free POJO to handle JMS messages

```
package com.habuma.spittr.alerts;
import org.springframework.mail.SimpleMailMessage;
import org.springframework.mail.javamail.JavaMailSender;
import org.springframework.stereotype.Component;
import com.habuma.spittr.domain.Spittle;

@Component("alertService")
public class AlertServiceImpl implements AlertService {

  private JavaMailSender mailSender;
  private String alertEmailAddress;
```

```
  public AlertServiceImpl(JavaMailSender mailSender,
                          String alertEmailAddress) {
    this.mailSender = mailSender;
    this.alertEmailAddress = alertEmailAddress;
  }

  public void sendSpittleAlert(final Spittle spittle) {      ⟵── Send Spittle alert
     SimpleMailMessage message = new SimpleMailMessage();
     String spitterName = spittle.getSpitter().getFullName();
     message.setFrom("noreply@spitter.com");
     message.setTo(alertEmailAddress);
     message.setSubject("New spittle from " + spitterName);
     message.setText(spitterName + " says: " + spittle.getText());
     mailSender.send(message);
  }

}
```

Don't concern yourself too much with the inner details of the sendSpittleAlert() method at this point. We'll talk more about how to send emails with Spring later, in chapter 20. The important thing to notice is that AlertServiceImpl is a simple POJO and has nothing that indicates it will be used to handle JMS messages. It does implement the AlertService interface, as shown here:

```
package com.habuma.spittr.alerts;
import com.habuma.spittr.domain.Spittle;
public interface AlertService {
  void sendSpittleAlert(Spittle spittle);
}
```

As you can see, AlertServiceImpl is annotated with @Component so that it will be automatically discovered and registered as a bean in the Spring application context with an ID of alertService. You'll refer to this bean as you configure a JmsInvokerService-Exporter:

```
<bean id="alertServiceExporter"
    class="org.springframework.jms.remoting.JmsInvokerServiceExporter"
    p:service-ref="alertService"
    p:serviceInterface="com.habuma.spittr.alerts.AlertService" />
```

This bean's properties describe what the exported service should look like. The service property is wired to refer to the alertService bean, which is the implementation of the remote service. Meanwhile, the serviceInterface property is set to the fully qualified class name of the interface that the service provides.

The exporter's properties don't describe the specifics of how the service will be carried over JMS. But the good news is that JmsInvokerServiceExporter qualifies as a JMS listener. Therefore, you can configure it as such in a <jms:listener-container> element:

```
<jms:listener-container connection-factory="connectionFactory">
  <jms:listener destination="spitter.alert.queue"
                ref="alertServiceExporter" />
</jms:listener-container>
```

The JMS listener container is given the connection factory so that it can know how to connect to the message broker. Meanwhile, the `<jms:listener>` declaration is given the destination on which the remote message will be carried.

CONSUMING JMS-BASED SERVICES

At this point, the JMS-based alert service should be ready and waiting for RPC messages to arrive on the `spitter.alert.queue` queue. On the client side, `JmsInvokerProxy-FactoryBean` will be used to access the service.

`JmsInvokerProxyFactoryBean` is a lot like the other remoting proxy factory beans that we looked at in chapter 15. It hides the details of accessing a remote service behind a convenient interface, through which the client interacts with the service. The big difference is that instead of proxying RMI- or HTTP-based services, `JmsInvokerProxyFactoryBean` proxies a JMS-based service that was exported by `JmsInvokerServiceExporter`.

To consume the alert service, you can wire the `JmsInvokerProxyFactoryBean` like this:

```
<bean id="alertService"
  class="org.springframework.jms.remoting.JmsInvokerProxyFactoryBean"
  p:connectionFactory-ref="connectionFactory"
  p:queueName="spittle.alert.queue"
  propp:serviceInterface="com.habuma.spittr.alerts.AlertService" />
```

The `connectionFactory` and `queueName` properties specify how RPC messages should be delivered—here, on the `spitter.alert.queue` queue at the message broker configured in the given connection factory. The `serviceInterface` specifies that the proxy should be exposed through the `AlertService` interface.

JMS has been the go-to messaging solution for Java applications for many years. But JMS isn't the only messaging choice available to Java and Spring developers. In the past few years, the *Advanced Message Queuing Protocol* (AMQP) has been getting a lot of attention. As it turns out, Spring has support for sending messages with AMQP, as you'll see next.

17.3 *Messaging with AMQP*

You may be wondering why you need another messaging specification. Isn't JMS good enough? What does AMQP bring to the table that is missing from JMS?

As it turns out, AMQP offers several advantages over JMS. First, AMQP defines a wire-level protocol for messaging, whereas JMS defines an API specification. JMS's API specification ensures that all JMS implementations can be used through a common API but doesn't mandate that messages sent by one JMS implementation can be consumed by a different JMS implementation. AMQP's wire-level protocol, on the other hand, specifies the format that messages will take when en route between the producer and consumer. Consequently, AMQP is more interoperable than JMS—not only across different AMQP implementations, but also across languages and platforms.[1]

---

[1] If you read this to mean that AMQP goes beyond the Java language and platform, then you're catching on quickly.

Another significant advantage of AMQP over JMS is that AMQP has a much more flexible and transparent messaging model. With JMS, there are only two messaging models to choose from: point-to-point and publish/subscribe. Both of those models are certainly possible with AMQP, but AMQP enables you to route messages in a number of ways, and it does this by decoupling the message producer from the queue(s) in which the messages will be placed.

Spring AMQP is an extension to the Spring Framework that enables AMQP-style messaging in Spring applications. As you'll see, Spring AMQP provides an API that makes working with AMQP remarkably similar to Spring's JMS abstraction. That means much of what you learned earlier in this chapter for JMS can be used to help you understand how to send and receive messages with Spring AMQP.

You'll see how to work with Spring AMQP soon enough. But before we dig deep into how to send and receive AMQP messages in Spring, let's take a quick look at what makes AMQP tick.

17.3.1 *A brief introduction to AMQP*

To understand the AMQP messaging model, it may help to briefly recall the JMS messaging model. In JMS, there are just three primary participants: the message producer, the message consumer(s), and a channel (either a queue or a topic) to carry the message between producers and consumers. These essentials of the JMS messaging model are illustrated in figures 17.3 and 17.4.

In JMS, the channel helps to decouple the producer from the consumer, but both are still coupled to the channel. A producer publishes messages to a specific queue or topic, and the consumer receives those message from a specific queue or topic. The channel has the double duty of relaying messages and determining how those messages will be routed; queues route using a point-to-point algorithm, and topics route in publish/subscribe fashion.

In contrast, AMQP producers don't publish directly to a queue. Instead, AMQP introduces a new level of indirection between the producer and any queues that will carry the message: the *exchange*. This relationship is illustrated in figure 17.8.

As you can see, a message producer publishes a message to an exchange. The exchange, which is bound to one or more queues, routes the message to the queue(s). Consumers pull messages from the queue and process them.

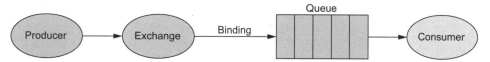

Figure 17.8 In AMQP, message producers are decoupled from message queues by an exchange that handles message routing.

What's not apparent from figure 17.8 is that the exchange isn't a pass-through mechanism to a queue. AMQP defines four different types of exchanges, each with a different routing algorithm that decides whether to place a message in a queue. Depending on an exchange's algorithm, it may consider the message's *routing key* and/or arguments and compare those with the routing key and arguments of the binding between the exchange and a queue. (A routing key can be loosely thought of as the To address in an email, specifying the intended recipient.) If the algorithm is satisfied with the comparison, the message will be routed to the queue. If not, then it won't be routed to the queue.

The four standard types of AMQP exchanges are as follows:

- *Direct*—A message will be routed to a queue if its routing key is a direct match for the routing key of the binding.
- *Topic*—A message will be routed to a queue if its routing key is a wildcard match for the routing key of the binding.
- *Headers*—A message will be routed to a queue if the headers and values in its table of arguments match those in the binding's table of arguments. A special header named `x-match` can specify whether `all` values must match or if `any` can match.
- *Fanout*—A message will be routed to all queues that are bound to the exchange, regardless of the routing key or headers/values in the table of arguments.

With these four types of exchanges, it's easy to imagine how you can define any number of routing schemes that go beyond simple point-to-point or publish/subscribe.[2] Fortunately, when it comes to sending and receiving messages, the routing algorithm(s) in play have little impact on how you develop the message producers and consumers. Put simply, producers publish to an exchange with a routing key; consumers retrieve from a queue.

This has been a quick overview of the basics of AMQP messaging—you should have just enough understanding to start sending and receiving messages using Spring AMQP. But I encourage you to dig deeper into AMQP by reading the specification and other materials at www.amqp.org or by reading *RabbitMQ in Action* by Alvaro Videla and Jason J.W. Williams (Manning, 2012, www.manning.com/videla/).

Now let's step away from the abstract discussion of AMQP so you can get your hands dirty writing code that sends and receives messages using Spring AMQP. You'll start by seeing some of the common Spring AMQP configuration needed for both producers and consumers.

---

[2] And I haven't even mentioned that it's possible to bind exchanges to other exchanges to create a nested hierarchy of routing.

17.3.2   *Configuring Spring for AMQP messaging*

When you first started working with Spring's JMS abstraction, you began by configuring a connection factory. Similarly, working with Spring AMQP starts with configuring a connection factory. But instead of configuring a JMS connection factory, you need to configure an AMQP connection factory. More specifically, you'll configure a RabbitMQ connection factory.

> **What is RabbitMQ?**
>
> RabbitMQ is a popular open source message broker that implements AMQP. Spring AMQP comes ready with RabbitMQ support, including a RabbitMQ connection factory, template, and Spring configuration namespace.
>
> You'll need to install RabbitMQ before you can send and receive messages with it. You can find installation instructions at www.rabbitmq.com/download.html. They vary depending on what OS you're running, so I'll leave it to you to follow the instructions appropriate for your environment.

The easiest way to configure a RabbitMQ connection factory is to use the `rabbit` configuration namespace provided by Spring AMQP. To use it, you need to be sure the schema is declared in your Spring configuration XML:

```
<?xml version="1.0" encoding="UTF-8"?>
<beans:beans xmlns="http://www.springframework.org/schema/rabbit"
  xmlns:beans="http://www.springframework.org/schema/beans"
  xmlns:xsi="http://www.w3.org/2001/XMLSchema-instance"
  xsi:schemaLocation="http://www.springframework.org/schema/rabbit
   http://www.springframework.org/schema/rabbit/spring-rabbit-1.0.xsd
    http://www.springframework.org/schema/beans
    http://www.springframework.org/schema/beans/spring-beans.xsd">

...

</beans:beans>
```

Although it's optional, in this case I've decided to declare the `rabbit` namespace as the primary namespace in the configuration and demote the `beans` namespace to being a secondary namespace. That's because I anticipate declaring more rabbits than beans in this configuration and would rather prefix the few bean elements with `beans:` and leave the rabbit elements prefix-less.

The `rabbit` namespace includes several elements for configuring RabbitMQ in Spring. But the one you're most interested in at this point is the `<connection-factory>` element. In its simplest form, you can configure a RabbitMQ connection factory with no attributes:

```
<connection-factory/>
```

This will work, but it leaves the resulting connection factory bean without a usable bean ID, which makes it hard to wire the connection factory into any other bean that needs it. Therefore, you'll probably want to give it a bean ID with the `id` attribute:

```
<connection-factory id="connectionFactory" />
```

By default, the connection factory will assume that the RabbitMQ server is listening on `localhost` at post 5672 and that the username and password are both *guest*. Those are reasonable defaults for development, but you'll probably want to change those for production. Here's a `<connection-factory>` with settings to override those defaults:

```
<connection-factory id="connectionFactory"
  host="${rabbitmq.host}"
  port="${rabbitmq.port}"
  username="${rabbitmq.username}"
  password="${rabbitmq.password}" />
```

You use placeholders to specify the values so that the configuration can be managed outside of the Spring configuration (most likely in a properties file).

In addition to the connection factory, there are a few more configuration elements that you may want to consider using. Let's see how to configure Spring AMQP to lazily create queues, exchanges, and bindings.

DECLARING QUEUES, EXCHANGES, AND BINDINGS

Unlike JMS, where the routing behavior of queues and topics is established by the specification, AMQP routing is richer and more flexible and thus depends on you to define the queues and exchanges and how they're bound to each other. One way of declaring queues, exchanges, and bindings is via a variety of methods on the RabbitMQ `Channel` interface. But working with RabbitMQ's `Channel` directly is involved. Can Spring AMQP help you declare your message-routing components?

Fortunately, the `rabbit` namespace includes several elements to help declare queues, exchanges, and the bindings that tie them together. These elements are listed in table 17.3.

Table 17.3   Spring AMQP's `rabbit` namespace includes several elements for lazily creating queues, exchanges, and the bindings between them.

Element	What it does
`<queue>`	Creates a queue.
`<fanout-exchange>`	Creates a fanout exchange.
`<header-exchange>`	Creates a headers exchange.
`<topic-exchange>`	Creates a topic exchange.
`<direct-exchange>`	Creates a direct exchange.

Table 17.3 Spring AMQP's `rabbit` namespace includes several elements for lazily creating queues, exchanges, and the bindings between them. *(continued)*

Element	What it does
`<bindings> <binding/> </bindings>`	The <bindings> element defines a set of one or more <binding> elements. The <binding> element creates a binding between an exchange and a queue.

These configuration elements are used alongside the <admin> element. The <admin> element creates a RabbitMQ administrative component that automatically creates (in the RabbitMQ broker, if they don't already exist) any queues, exchanges, and bindings declared using the elements in table 17.3.

For example, if you want to declare a queue named `spittle.alert.queue`, you only need to add the following two elements to your Spring configuration:

```
<admin connection-factory="connectionFactory"/
    > <queue id="spittleAlertQueue" name="spittle.alerts" />
```

For simple messaging, this may be all you need. That's because there's a default direct exchange with no name, and all queues are bound to that exchange with a routing key that's the same as the queue's name. With this simple configuration, you could send messages to the no-name exchange and specify a routing key of `spittle.alert.queue` to have messages routed to the queue. Essentially, this re-creates a JMS-style point-to-point model.

More interesting routing, however, will require that you declare one or more exchanges and bind them to queues. For example, to have a message routed to multiple queues with no regard for the routing key, you can configure a fanout exchange and several queues like this:

```
<admin connection-factory="connectionFactory" /
    > <queue name="spittle.alert.queue.1" > <queue name="spittle.alert.queue
    .2" > <queue name="spittle.alert.queue.3" > <fanout-
    exchange name="spittle.fanout">  <bindings>   <binding queue="spittle.al
    ert.queue.1" />   <binding queue="spittle.alert.queue.2" /
    >   <binding queue="spittle.alert.queue.3" />  </bindings> </fanout-
    exchange>
```

Using the elements in table 17.3, there are countless ways to configure routing in RabbitMQ. But I don't have countless pages to describe them all to you, so in the interest of keeping this discussion on track, I'll leave routing creativity as an exercise for you and move on to discussing how to send messages.

17.3.3 *Sending messages with RabbitTemplate*

As its name implies, the RabbitMQ connection factory is used to create connections with RabbitMQ. If you want to send messages via RabbitMQ, you *could* inject the `connectionFactory` bean into your `AlertServiceImpl` class, use it to create a

Connection, use that Connection to create a Channel, and use that Channel to publish a message to an exchange.

Yep, you *could* do that.

But that would be a lot of work and would involve a lot of boilerplate coding on your part. One thing that Spring abhors is boilerplate code. You've already seen several examples where Spring offers templates to eliminate boilerplate—including JmsTemplate, earlier in this chapter, which eliminates JMS boilerplate code. It should be no surprise that Spring AMQP provides RabbitTemplate to eliminate boilerplate associated with sending and receiving messages with RabbitMQ.

The simplest configuration for RabbitTemplate can be done using the <template> element from the rabbit configuration namespace as follows:

```
<template id="rabbitTemplate"
        connection-factory="connectionFactory" />
```

Now all you need to do to send a message is inject the template bean into Alert-ServiceImpl and use it to send a Spittle. The following listing shows a new version of AlertServiceImpl that uses RabbitTemplate instead of JmsTemplate to send a Spittle alert.

Listing 17.7   Sending a `Spittle` using `RabbitTemplate`

```
package com.habuma.spitter.alerts;

import org.springframework.amqp.rabbit.core.RabbitTemplate;
import org.springframework.beans.factory.annotation.Autowired;

import com.habuma.spitter.domain.Spittle;

public class AlertServiceImpl implements AlertService {

  private RabbitTemplate rabbit;

  @Autowired
  public AlertServiceImpl(RabbitTemplate rabbit) {
    this.rabbit = rabbit;
  }

  public void sendSpittleAlert(Spittle spittle) {
    rabbit.convertAndSend("spittle.alert.exchange",
                          "spittle.alerts",
                          spittle);
  }

}
```

As you can see, the sendSpittleAlert() method now calls the convertAndSend() method on the injected RabbitTemplate. It passes in three parameters: the name of the exchange, the routing key, and the object to be sent. Notice that what's *not* specified is how the message will be routed, what queues it will be sent on, or any consumers that are expected to receive the message.

RabbitTemplate has several overloaded versions of convertAndSend() to simplify its use. For example, using one of the overloaded convertAndSend() methods, you can leave out the exchange name when calling convertAndSend():

```
rabbit.convertAndSend("spittle.alerts", spittle);
```

Or, with another, you can leave out both the exchange name and routing key if you want:

```
rabbit.convertAndSend(spittle);
```

When the exchange name or the exchange name and routing key are left out of the parameter list, RabbitTemplate uses its default exchange name and routing key. As you have configured the template, the default exchange name is blank (or the default no-name exchange) and the default routing key is also blank. But you can configure different defaults using the exchange and routing-key attributes on the <template> element:

```
<template id="rabbitTemplate"
connection-factory="connectionFactory"
exchange="spittle.alert.exchange"
routing-key="spittle.alerts" />
```

No matter what you set the defaults to, you're always able to override them when calling convertAndSend() by explicitly specifying them as parameters.

You might be interested in considering one of RabbitTemplate's other methods for sending messages. For instance, you can use the lower-level send() method to send an org.springframework.amqp.core.Message object like this:

```
Message helloMessage =
    new Message("Hello World!".getBytes(), new MessageProperties());
rabbit.send("hello.exchange", "hello.routing", helloMessage);
```

As with convertAndSend(), the send() method is overloaded to not require the exchange name and/or routing key.

The trick to using the send() methods is constructing a Message object to send. In the Hello World example, you construct a Message instance by giving it the string's byte array. That's easy enough for String values but can get more complicated when the message payload is a complex object.

For that reason, convertAndSend() exists to automatically convert an object to a Message. It does this with the assistance of a message converter. The default message converter is SimpleMessageConverter, which is suitable for working with Strings, Serializable instances, and byte arrays. Spring AMQP provides a few other message converters that you might find useful, including some for working with JSON and XML data.

Now that you've sent a message, let's shift to the other side of the conversation and see how to retrieve the message.

17.3.4 *Receiving AMQP messages*

As you'll recall, Spring's JMS support offers two ways to fetch a message from a queue: synchronously via `JmsTemplate` and asynchronously with message-driven POJOs. Spring AMQP offers similar options for retrieving messages sent over AMQP. Because you already have a `RabbitTemplate` handy, let's first look at how to use it to synchronously fetch a message from a queue.

RECEIVING MESSAGES WITH RABBITTEMPLATE

`RabbitTemplate` offers a handful of methods for receiving messages. The simplest ones are the `receive()` methods, which are the consumer-side analogues to `Rabbit-Template`'s `send()` methods. Using the `receive()` methods, you can fetch a `Message` object from the queue:

```
Message message = rabbit.receive("spittle.alert.queue");
```

Or, if you prefer, you can configure a default queue for receiving messages by setting the `queue` attribute when configuring the template:

```
<template id="rabbitTemplate"
    connection-factory="connectionFactory"
    exchange="spittle.alert.exchange"
    routing-key="spittle.alerts"
    queue="spittle.alert.queue" />
```

This enables you to call the `receive()` method without any arguments to receive from the default queue:

```
Message message = rabbit.receive();
```

Once you have a `Message` object, you'll probably need to convert the array of bytes in its `body` property to whatever object you want. Just as it was tricky to convert domain objects into `Message`s for sending, it's messy to convert received `Message`s to domain objects. Therefore, consider using `RabbitTemplate`'s `receiveAndConvert()` method instead:

```
Spittle spittle =
    (Spittle) rabbit.receiveAndConvert("spittle.alert.queue");
```

Or you can leave the queue name out of the call parameters to fall back on the template's default queue name:

```
Spittle spittle = (Spittle) rabbit.receiveAndConvert();
```

The `receiveAndConvert()` method uses the same message converters as `sendAndConvert()` to turn a `Message` object into the type it originated as.

Calls to both `receive()` and `receiveAndConvert()` return immediately, possibly with a `null` if no messages are waiting in the queue. That leaves it up to you to manage any polling and threading necessary to monitor the queue.

Instead of synchronously polling and waiting for messages to arrive, Spring AMQP offers message-driven POJO support that's reminiscent of the same feature in Spring JMS. Let's see how to consume messages with message-driven AMQP POJOs.

DEFINING MESSAGE-DRIVEN AMQP POJOS

The first thing you'll need in order to consume a `Spittle` object asynchronously in a message-driven POJO is the POJO itself. Here's `SpittleAlertHandler`, which fills that role:

```
package com.habuma.spittr.alerts;
import com.habuma.spittr.domain.Spittle;

public class SpittleAlertHandler {

  public void handleSpittleAlert(Spittle spittle) {
    // ... implementation goes here ...
  }

}
```

Notice that this is exactly the same `SpittleAlertHandler` that you used when consuming `Spittle` messages using JMS. You can get away with reusing the same POJO because nothing about it is dependent on JMS or AMQP. It's just a POJO and is ready to process a `Spittle` regardless of what messaging mechanism it's carried over.

You also need to declare `SpittleAlertHandler` as a bean in the Spring application context:

```
<bean id="spittleListener"
      class="com.habuma.spittr.alert.SpittleAlertHandler" />
```

But again, you already did this when you were working with JMS-based MDPs. There's no difference.

Finally, you need to declare a listener container and a listener to call on `Spittle-AlertHandler` when a message arrives. You did this for JMS-based MDPs, but there is a slight difference in the configuration for AMQP-based MDPs:

```
<listener-container connection-factory="connectionFactory">
    <listener ref="spittleListener"
          method="handleSpittleAlert"
          queue-names="spittle.alert.queue" />
</listener-container>
```

Do you see the difference? I'll agree that it's not obvious. The `<listener-container>` and `<listener>` elements appear to be similar to their JMS counterparts. These elements, however, come from the `rabbit` namespace instead of the JMS namespace.

I said it wasn't obvious.

Well, there is one other slight difference. Instead of specifying a queue or topic to listen on through the `destination` attribute (as you did for JMS), here you specify the queue on which to listen for messages via the `queue-names` attribute. But otherwise, AMQP-based MDPs and JMS-based MDPs work similarly.

In case you're wondering, yes: the `queue-names` attribute name indicates plurality. Here you only specify a single queue to listen on, but you can list as many queue names as you want, separated with commas.

Another way of specifying the queues to listen on is to reference the queue beans you declared with the <queue> element. You can do this via the `queues` attribute:

```
<listener-container connection-factory="connectionFactory">
    <listener ref="spittleListener"
        method="handleSpittleAlert"
        queues="spittleAlertQueue" />
</listener-container>
```

Again, this attribute can take a comma-separated list of queue IDs. This, of course, requires that you declare the queues with IDs. For example, here's the alert queue redeclared, this time with an ID:

```
<queue id="spittleAlertQueue" name="spittle.alert.queue" />
```

Note that the `id` attribute is used to assign a bean ID for the queue in the Spring application context. The `name` attribute specifies the queue's name in the RabbitMQ broker.

17.4 *Summary*

Asynchronous messaging presents several advantages over synchronous RPC. Indirect communication results in applications that are loosely coupled with respect to one another and thus reduces the impact of any one system going down. Additionally, because messages are forwarded to their recipients, there's no need for a sender to wait for a response. In many circumstances, this can be a boost to application performance and scalability.

Although JMS provides a standard API for all Java applications wishing to participate in asynchronous communication, it can be cumbersome to use. Spring eliminates the need for JMS boilerplate code and exception-handling code and makes asynchronous messaging easier to use.

In this chapter, you've seen several ways that Spring can help establish asynchronous communication between two applications by way of message brokers and JMS. Spring's JMS template eliminates the boilerplate that's commonly required by the traditional JMS programming model. And Spring-enabled message-driven beans make it possible to declare bean methods that react to messages that arrive in a queue or topic. We also looked at using Spring's JMS invoker to provide message-based RPC with Spring beans.

You've seen how to use asynchronous communication between applications in this chapter. Coming up in the next chapter, we'll continue this theme by looking at how to enable asynchronous communication between a browser-based client and a server using WebSocket.

Messaging with WebSocket and STOMP

This chapter covers

- Sending messages between the browser and the server
- Handling messages in Spring MVC controllers
- Sending user-targeted messages

In the previous chapter, you saw ways to send messages between applications using JMS and AMQP. Asynchronous messaging is a common form of communication between applications. But when one of those applications is running in a web browser, something a little different is needed.

WebSocket is a protocol providing full-duplex communication across a single socket. It enables, among other things, asynchronous messaging between a web browser and a server. Being full-duplex means that the server can send messages to the browser as well as the browser sending messages to the server.

Spring 4.0 introduced support for WebSocket communication, including

- A low-level API for sending and receiving messages
- A higher-level API for handling messages in Spring MVC controllers
- A messaging template for sending messages

- SockJS support to cope with the lack of WebSocket support in browsers, servers, and proxies

In this chapter, you'll learn how to achieve asynchronous communication between a server and a browser-based application using Spring's WebSocket features. We'll start by looking at how to work with Spring's low-level WebSocket API.

18.1 *Working with Spring's low-level WebSocket API*

In its simplest form, a WebSocket is just a communication channel between two applications. An application on one end of the WebSocket sends a message, and the other end handles that message. Because it's full-duplex, either end can send messages and either end can handle messages. This is illustrated in figure 18.1.

WebSocket communication can be used between any kinds of applications, but the most common use of WebSocket is to facilitate communication between a server and a browser-based application. A JavaScript client in the browser opens a connection to the server, and the server sends updates to the browser on that connection. This is generally more efficient and more natural than the historically common alternative of polling the server for updates.

To demonstrate Spring's low-level WebSocket API, let's write a simple WebSocket example where a JavaScript-based client plays a never-ending game of Marco Polo with the server. The server-side application will handle a text message ("Marco!") and will react by sending a text message ("Polo!") back on the same connection. To handle messages in Spring with low-level WebSocket support, you must write a class that implements `WebSocketHandler`:

```
public interface WebSocketHandler {
  void afterConnectionEstablished(WebSocketSession session)
                                                  throws Exception;
  void handleMessage(WebSocketSession session,
                  WebSocketMessage<?> message) throws Exception;
  void handleTransportError(WebSocketSession session,
                         Throwable exception) throws Exception;
  void afterConnectionClosed(WebSocketSession session,
                            CloseStatus closeStatus) throws Exception;
  boolean supportsPartialMessages();
}
```

As you can see, the `WebSocketHandler` interface requires that you implement five methods. Rather than implement `WebSocketHandler` directly, it's easier to extend

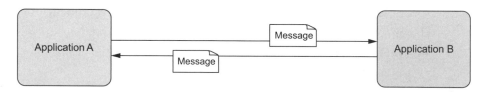

Figure 18.1   A WebSocket is a full-duplex communication channel between two applications.

AbstractWebSocketHandler, an abstract implementation of WebSocketHandler. The following listing shows MarcoHandler, a subclass of AbstractWebSocketHandler that will handle messages on the server.

Listing 18.1 `MarcoHandler` handles text messages sent via a WebSocket.

```
package marcopolo;

import org.slf4j.Logger;
import org.slf4j.LoggerFactory;
import org.springframework.web.socket.TextMessage;
import org.springframework.web.socket.WebSocketSession;
import org.springframework.web.socket.handler.AbstractWebSocketHandler;

public class MarcoHandler extends AbstractWebSocketHandler {

  private static final Logger logger =
      LoggerFactory.getLogger(MarcoHandler.class);          Handle text
                                                            message
  protected void handleTextMessage(                    ◁─┘
      WebSocketSession session, TextMessage message) throws Exception {
    logger.info("Received message: " + message.getPayload());

    Thread.sleep(2000);                              ◁── Simulate delay

    session.sendMessage(new TextMessage("Polo!"));   ◁── Send text message
  }

}
```

Although it's an abstract class, AbstractWebSocketHandler doesn't require that you override any specific method. Instead, it leaves it up to you to decide which methods you want to override. In addition to the five methods defined in WebSocketHandler, you may also override three additional methods defined by AbstractWebSocket-Handler:

- handleBinaryMessage()
- handlePongMessage()
- handleTextMessage()

These three methods are merely specializations of the handleMessage() method, each tuned to a specific kind of message.

Because MarcoHandler will be handling the textual "Marco!" message, it makes sense for it to override handleTextMessage(). When a text message comes in, that message is logged and, after a simulated 2-second delay, another text message is sent back on the same connection.

All of the other methods that MarcoHandler doesn't override are implemented by AbstractWebSocketHandler with no-op implementations. This means that Marco-Handler will also handle binary and pong messages, but will do nothing with those messages.

Alternatively, you could extend TextWebSocketHandler instead of AbstractWeb-SocketHandler:

```
public class MarcoHandler extends TextWebSocketHandler {
  ...
}
```

`TextWebSocketHandler` is a subclass of `AbstractWebSocketHandler` that refuses to handle binary messages. It overrides `handleBinaryMessage()` to close the WebSocket connection if a binary connection is received. In a similar way, Spring also offers `BinaryWebSocketHandler`, a subclass of `AbstractWebSocketHandler` that overrides `handleTextMessage()` to close the connection if a text message is received.

Regardless of whether you handle text messages, binary messages, or both, you might also be interested in handling the establishment and closing of connections. In that case, you can override `afterConnectionEstablished()` and `afterConnection-Closed()`:

```
public void afterConnectionEstablished(WebSocketSession session)
    throws Exception {
  logger.info("Connection established");
}

@Override
public void afterConnectionClosed(
    WebSocketSession session, CloseStatus status) throws Exception {
  logger.info("Connection closed. Status: " + status);
}
```

Connections are bookended with the `afterConnectionEstablished()` and `after-ConnectionClosed()` methods. When a new connection is established, the `after-ConnectionEstablished()` method is called. Likewise, `afterConnectionClosed()` will be called whenever a connection is closed. In this example, the connection events are only logged, but these methods could be useful for setup and teardown of any resources used during the life of the connection.

Notice that these methods both start with the word "after." That means that these methods are only able to react to those events after the event occurs and can't change the outcome.

Now that you have a message handler class, you must configure it so that Spring will dispatch messages to it. In Spring's Java configuration, this involves annotating a configuration class with `@EnableWebSocket` and implementing the `WebSocketConfigurer` interface, as shown in the next listing.

Listing 18.2   Enabling WebSocket and mapping a message handler in Java configuration

```
package marcopolo;

import org.springframework.context.annotation.Bean;
import org.springframework.web.socket.config.annotation.
                                        EnableWebSocket;
import org.springframework.web.socket.config.annotation.
                                        WebSocketConfigurer;
import org.springframework.web.socket.config.annotation.
                                        WebSocketHandlerRegistry;
```

```
@EnableWebSocket
public class WebSocketConfig implements WebSocketConfigurer {

  @Override
  public void registerWebSocketHandlers(
                              WebSocketHandlerRegistry registry) {
    registry.addHandler(marcoHandler(), "/marco");      ◁─┐  Map MarcoHandler
  }                                                         │  to "/marco"

  @Bean
  public MarcoHandler marcoHandler() {    ◁─┐  Declare
    return new MarcoHandler();               │  MarcoHandler bean
  }

}
```

The registerWebSocketHandlers() method is the key to registering a message handler. By overriding it, you're given a WebSocketHandlerRegistry through which you can call addHandler() to register a message handler. In this case, you register the MarcoHandler (declared as a bean) and associate it with the /marco path.

Alternatively, if you'd rather configure Spring in XML, you can take advantage of the websocket namespace, as follows.

Listing 18.3 The websocket namespace enables XML configuration for WebSockets.

```
<?xml version="1.0" encoding="UTF-8"?>
<beans xmlns="http://www.springframework.org/schema/beans"
 xmlns:xsi="http://www.w3.org/2001/XMLSchema-instance"
 xmlns:websocket="http://www.springframework.org/schema/websocket"
 xsi:schemaLocation="
  http://www.springframework.org/schema/websocket
  http://www.springframework.org/schema/websocket/spring-websocket.xsd
  http://www.springframework.org/schema/beans
  http://www.springframework.org/schema/beans/spring-beans.xsd">

  <websocket:handlers>
    <websocket:mapping handler="marcoHandler" path="/marco" />   ◁─┐  Map
  </websocket:handlers>                                              │  MarcoHandler
                                                                     │  to "/marco"
  <bean id="marcoHandler"
        class="marcopolo.MarcoHandler" />    ◁─┐  Declare
                                                │  MarcoHandler bean
</beans>
```

Whether you use Java or XML configuration, that's the only configuration you'll need.

Now we can turn our attention to the client that will send a "Marco!" text message to the server and listen for text messages coming from the server. The following listing shows some JavaScript that opens a native WebSocket and uses it to volley messages to the server.

Listing 18.4 A JavaScript client that connects to the "marco" websocket

```
var url = 'ws://' + window.location.host + '/websocket/marco';
var sock = new WebSocket(url);              ◁──────────────── Open WebSocket

sock.onopen = function() {                  ◁──────────────── Handle open event
```

```
    console.log('Opening');
  sayMarco();
};

sock.onmessage = function(e) {                    ◁──────────── Handle message
    console.log('Received message: ', e.data);
  setTimeout(function(){sayMarco()}, 2000);
};

sock.onclose = function() {                    ◁──────────── Handle close event
    console.log('Closing');
};

function sayMarco() {
  console.log('Sending Marco!');
  sock.send("Marco!");                    ◁──────────── Send message
  }
```

The first thing that the code in listing 18.4 does is create an instance of WebSocket. This type is native to browsers that support WebSocket. By creating a WebSocket instance, it effectively opens the WebSocket to the URL it's given. In this case, the URL is prefixed with "ws://", indicating a basic WebSocket connection. If it were a secure WebSocket connection, the protocol prefix would have been "wss://".

Once the WebSocket instance is created, the next several lines set up the WebSocket with event-handling functions. Notice that the WebSocket's onopen, onmessage, and onclose events mirror MarcoHandler's afterConnectionEstablished(), handleText-Message(), and afterConnectionClosed() methods. The onopen event is given a function that calls sayMarco() to send the "Marco!" message on the WebSocket. By sending "Marco!", the never-ending game of Marco Polo begins, because Marco-Handler on the server will react by sending "Polo!" back. When the client receives the message from the server, the onmessage event will result in another "Marco!" message being sent to the server.

And it goes on and on like that until the connection is closed. It's not shown in listing 18.4, but a call to sock.close() will put an end to the madness. The server could also close the connection, or the browser could navigate away from the page, and the connection will be closed. In any case, once the connection goes down, the onclose event will be fired. Here, that occasion will be marked with a simple message to the console log.

At this point, you've written everything that goes into enabling Spring's low-level WebSocket support, including a handler class that receives and sends messages and a simple JavaScript client to do the same in the browser. If you were to build the code and deploy it to a servlet container, it *might* even work.

Did you sense some pessimism in my choice of the word "might"? That's because I can't guarantee that it will work. In fact, there's a really good chance that it won't work. Even if we do everything correctly, the odds are stacked against us.

Let's look at what will prevent WebSocket code from working and take steps to improve our chances.

18.2 *Coping with a lack of WebSocket support*

WebSocket is a relatively new specification. Even though it was standardized by the end of 2011, it still doesn't have consistent support in web browsers and application servers. Firefox and Chrome have had full support for WebSocket for quite a while, but other browsers have only recently started to support WebSocket. Here's a brief list of the minimum versions of several popular browsers that support WebSocket:

- Internet Explorer: 10.0
- Firefox: 4.0 (partial), 6.0 (full)
- Chrome: 4.0 (partial), 13.0 (full)
- Safari: 5.0 (partial), 6.0 (full)
- Opera: 11.0 (partial), 12.10 (full)
- iOS Safari: 4.2 (partial), 6.0 (full)
- Android Browser: 4.4

Unfortunately, many web surfers don't recognize or understand the features of new web browsers and are slow to upgrade. Moreover, many corporations standardize on a specific version of a browser, making it hard (or impossible) for their employees to use anything newer. Given those circumstances, it's very likely that your application's audience will not be able to use your application if it employs WebSocket.

It's the same song, second verse, when it comes to server-side support for WebSocket. GlassFish has had some form of WebSocket support for a couple of years, but many other application servers have only just started supporting WebSocket in their most recent versions. For example, I had to test the previous example using a release candidate build of Tomcat 8.

Even if the browser and application server versions align and WebSocket is supported on both ends, there might be trouble in the middle. Firewall proxies generally block anything but HTTP traffic. They're not capable or not configured (yet) to allow WebSocket communication.

I realize that I've painted a rather bleak picture of the current WebSocket landscape. But don't let a little thing like lack of support stop you from trying to use WebSockct. When it works, WebSocket is fantastic. When it doesn't, all you need is a fallback plan.

Fortunately, WebSocket fallback is the specialty of SockJS. SockJS is a WebSocket emulator that mirrors the WebSocket API as closely as possible on the surface, but under the covers is clever enough to choose another form of communication when WebSocket isn't available. SockJS will always favor WebSocket first, but if WebSocket isn't an option, it will determine the best available option from the following:

- XHR streaming
- XDR streaming
- iFrame event source
- iFrame HTML file

- XHR polling
- XDR polling
- iFrame XHR polling
- JSONP polling

The good news is that you don't need to fully understand all of those options to be able to use SockJS. SockJS lets you develop to a consistent programming model as if Web-Socket support were ubiquitous, and it handles the fallback plans under the covers.

For example, to enable SockJS communication on the server side, you can simply ask for it in the Spring configuration. Revisiting the `registerWebSocketHandlers()` method from listing 18.2, you can enable WebSocket with a small addition:

```
@Override
public void registerWebSocketHandlers(
                                WebSocketHandlerRegistry registry) {
  registry.addHandler(marcoHandler(), "/marco").withSockJS();
}
```

By simply calling `withSockJS()` on the `WebSocketHandlerRegistration` returned from the call to `addHandler()`, you're saying that you want SockJS to be enabled, and for its fallbacks to go into effect if WebSocket can't be used.

If you're using XML to configure Spring, enabling SockJS is a simple matter of adding the `<websocket:sockjs>` element to the configuration:

```
<websocket:handlers>
  <websocket:mapping handler="marcoHandler" path="/marco" />
  <websocket:sockjs />
</websocket:handlers>
```

To use SockJS on the client, you'll need to be sure to load the SockJS client library. The exact way you do that depends largely on whether you're using a JavaScript module loader (such as require.js or curl.js) or are simply loading your JavaScript libraries with a `<script>` tag. The simplest way to load the SockJS client library is to load it from the SockJS CDN with a `<script>` tag like this:

```
<script src="http://cdn.sockjs.org/sockjs-0.3.min.js"></script>
```

Resolving web resources with WebJars

In my example code, I'm using WebJars to resolve JavaScript libraries as part of the project's Maven or Gradle build, just like any other dependency. To support that, I've set up a resource handler in the Spring MVC configuration to resolve requests where the path starts with /webjars/** from the WebJars standard path:

```
@Override
public void addResourceHandlers(ResourceHandlerRegistry registry) {
  registry.addResourceHandler("/webjars/**")
      .addResourceLocations("classpath:/META-INF/resources/webjars/");
}
```

With that resource handler in effect, I can load the SockJS library in a web page with the following `<script>` tag:

```
<script th:src="@{/webjars/sockjs-client/0.3.4/sockjs.min.js}">
</script>
```

Notice that this particular `<script>` tag comes from a Thymeleaf template and takes advantage of the `@{...}` expression to calculate the full context-relative URL path for the JavaScript file.

Aside from loading the SockJS client library, there are only two lines from listing 18.4 that must be changed to use SockJS:

```
var url = 'marco';
var sock = new SockJS(url);
```

The first change you can make is to the URL. SockJS deals in URLs with the http:// or https:// scheme instead of ws:// and wss://. Even so, you can use relative URLs, keeping you from having to derive the fully qualified URL. In this case, if the page containing the JavaScript was at http://localhost:8080/websocket, the simple `marco` path given will result in a connection to http://localhost:8080/websocket/marco.

The key change you must make, however, is to create an instance of `SockJS` instead of `WebSocket`. Because `SockJS` mimics `WebSocket` as closely as possible, the rest of the code from listing 18.4 can remain the same. The same `onopen`, `onmessage`, and `onclose` event-handler functions will still respond to their respective events. And the same `send()` function will still send "Marco!" to the server.

You didn't change too many lines of code, and yet you've made a huge difference in how the client-server messaging works. You can be reasonably confident that WebSocket-like communication will work between the browser and the server, even if WebSocket isn't supported by the browser, server, or any proxy that sits in the middle.

WebSocket enables browser-server communication, and SockJS offers fallback communication when WebSocket isn't supported. But in either case, this form of communication is too low-level for practical use. Let's see how you can layer STOMP (Simple Text Oriented Messaging Protocol) on top of WebSocket to add proper messaging semantics to browser-server communication.

18.3 *Working with STOMP messaging*

If I were to suggest that you write a web application, you'd probably already have a good idea of the base technologies and frameworks you might use, even before we discussed requirements. Even for a simple Hello World web application, you might be thinking of writing a Spring MVC controller to handle a request and a JSP or Thymeleaf template for the response. At the very least, you might create a static HTML page and let the web server deal with serving it to any web browser that requests it. You'd probably not concern yourself with exactly how a browser would request the page or how the page would be delivered.

Now let's suppose I suggested we pretend that HTTP doesn't exist and that you write a web application using nothing but TCP sockets. You'd probably think I was out of my mind. Certainly, it would be possible to pull off this feat, but you'd need to devise your own wire protocol that both the client and server could agree upon to facilitate effective communication. In short, it'd be non-trivial.

Thankfully, the HTTP protocol addresses the minute details of how a web browser makes a request and how a web server responds to that request. As a result, most developers never write code that deals with low-level TCP socket communication.

Working directly with WebSocket (or SockJS) is a lot like developing a web application using only TCP sockets. Without a higher-level wire protocol, it's up to you to define the semantics of the messages being sent between applications. And you'd need to be sure that both ends of the connection agreed on those semantics.

Fortunately, you don't have to work with raw WebSocket connections. Just as HTTP layers a request-response model on top of TCP sockets, STOMP layers a frame-based wire format to define messaging semantics on top of WebSocket.

At a quick glance, STOMP message frames look very similar in structure to HTTP requests. Much like HTTP requests and responses, STOMP frames are comprised of a command, one or more headers, and a payload. For example, here's a STOMP frame that sends data.

```
SEND
destination:/app/marco
content-length:20

{\"message\":\"Marco!\"}
```

In this simple example, the STOMP command is `SEND`, indicating that something is being sent. It's followed by two headers: one indicates the destination where the message should be sent, and the other communicates the size of the payload. Following a blank line, the frame concludes with the payload; in this case, a JSON message.

The `destination` header is probably the most interesting thing about the STOMP frame. It's a clue that STOMP is a messaging protocol, very much like JMS or AMQP. Messages are published to destinations that may, in fact, be backed by real message brokers. On the other end, message handlers can listen to those destinations to receive the messages sent.

In the context of WebSocket communication, a browser-based JavaScript application may publish a message to a destination that's handled by a server-side component. And it works the other way around, too. A server-side component may publish a message to a destination to be received by the JavaScript client.

Spring provides for STOMP-based messaging with a programming model based on Spring MVC. As you'll see, handling STOMP messages in a Spring MVC controller isn't much different from handling HTTP requests. But first, you must configure Spring to enable STOMP-based messaging.

18.3.1 Enabling STOMP messaging

In a moment, you'll see how to annotate controller methods with @MessageMapping to handle STOMP messages within Spring MVC in a way very similar to how @Request-Mapping-annotated methods handle HTTP requests. Unlike @RequestMapping, however, @MessageMapping isn't enabled by the @EnableWebMvc annotation. Spring's web messaging is built around a message broker, so there's more to configure than just telling Spring that you'd like to handle messages. You must also configure a message broker and some basic destination details.

The following listing shows the basic Java configuration required to enable broker-based web messaging.

Listing 18.5 @EnableWebSocketMessageBroker enables STOMP over WebSocket.

```
package marcopolo;
import org.springframework.context.annotation.Configuration;
import org.springframework.web.socket.config.annotation.
                                AbstractWebSocketMessageBrokerConfigurer;
import org.springframework.web.socket.config.annotation.
                                      EnableWebSocketMessageBroker;
import org.springframework.web.socket.config.annotation.
                                       StompEndpointRegistry;


@Configuration
@EnableWebSocketMessageBroker                     ←— Enable STOMP messaging
 public class WebSocketStompConfig
      extends AbstractWebSocketMessageBrokerConfigurer {

  @Override
  public void registerStompEndpoints(StompEndpointRegistry registry) {
    registry.addEndpoint("/marcopolo").withSockJS();      ←┐ Enable SockJS over
  }                                                        │ /marcopolo

  @Override
  public void configureMessageBroker(MessageBrokerRegistry registry) {
    registry.enableSimpleBroker("/queue", "/topic");
    registry.setApplicationDestinationPrefixes("/app");
  }

}
```

In contrast to the configuration class in listing 18.2, WebSocketStompConfig is annotated with @EnableWebSocketMessageBroker. This indicates that this configuration class is not only configuring WebSocket, but it's configuring broker-based STOMP messaging. It overrides the registerStompEndpoints() method to register /marcopolo as a STOMP endpoint. This path is distinct from any destination path that you might send or receive messages from. It's the endpoint that a client would connect to before subscribing to or publishing to a destination path.

WebSocketStompConfig also configures a simple message broker by overriding the configureMessageBroker() method. This method is optional. If you don't override it, you'll get a simple in-memory message broker configured to handle messages prefixed with /topic. But in this example, you override it so that the message broker is

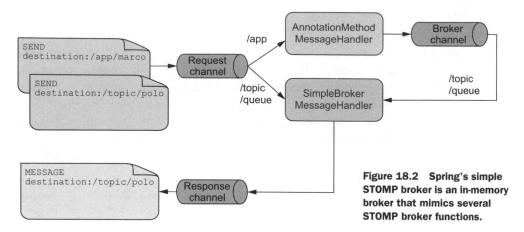

Figure 18.2   Spring's simple STOMP broker is an in-memory broker that mimics several STOMP broker functions.

responsible for messages prefixed with /topic and /queue. In addition, any messages destined for the application will be prefixed with /app. Figure 18.2 illustrates how messages flow in this setup.

When a message arrives, the destination prefix will determine how the message is handled. In figure 18.2 the application destinations are prefixed with /app and the broker destinations are prefixed with either /topic or /queue. A message headed for an application destination is routed directly to an @MessageMapping-annotated controller method. Messages destined for the broker, including any messages resulting from values returned by @MessageMapping-annotated methods, are routed to the broker and are ultimately sent out to clients subscribed to those destinations.

ENABLING A STOMP BROKER RELAY

The simple broker is great for getting started, but it has a few limitations. Although it mimics a STOMP message broker, it only supports a subset of STOMP commands. And because it's memory-based, it's not suitable for clusters where each node would be managing its own broker and set of messages.

For a production application, you'll probably want to back your WebSocket messaging with a real STOMP-enabled broker, such as RabbitMQ or ActiveMQ. Such brokers will offer more scalable and robust messaging, not to mention the complete set of STOMP commands. You'll need to be sure to set up your broker for STOMP according to their documentation. Once the broker is ready, you can replace the default in-memory broker with a STOMP broker relay by overriding the configureMessage-Broker() method like this:

```
@Override
public void configureMessageBroker(MessageBrokerRegistry registry) {
  registry.enableStompBrokerRelay("/topic", "/queue");
  registry.setApplicationDestinationPrefixes("/app");
}
```

The first line of configureMessageBroker() shown here enables the STOMP broker relay and sets its destination prefixes to /topic and /queue. This is a clue to Spring

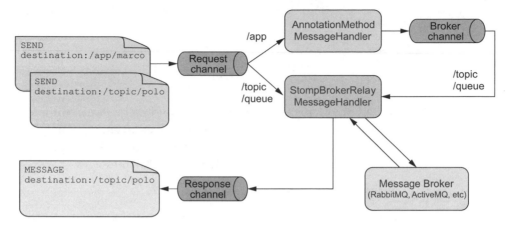

Figure 18.3 **The STOMP broker relay delegates to a real message broker for handling STOMP messages.**

that any messages whose destination begins with /topic or /queue should go to the STOMP broker. Depending on which STOMP broker you choose, you may be limited in your choices for the destination prefix. RabbitMQ, for instance, only allows destinations of type /temp-queue, /exchange, /topic, /queue, /amq/queue, and /reply-queue/. Consult your broker's documentation for supported destination types and their purposes.

In addition to the destination prefix, the second line in `configureMessage-Broker()` sets an application prefix to /app. Any messages whose destination begins with /app will be routed to an `@MessageMapping` method and not published to a broker queue or topic.

Figure 18.3 illustrates how the broker relay fits into Spring's STOMP message handling. As you can see, the key difference is that rather than mimicking a STOMP broker's functionality, the broker relay hands messages off to a real message broker for handling.

Note that both `enableStompBrokerRelay()` and `setApplicationDestination-Prefixes()` accept a variable-length `String` argument, so you can configure multiple destination and application prefixes. For example:

```
@Override
public void configureMessageBroker(MessageBrokerRegistry registry) {
  registry.enableStompBrokerRelay("/topic", "/queue");
  registry.setApplicationDestinationPrefixes("/app", "/foo");
}
```

By default, the STOMP broker relay assumes that the broker is listening on port 61613 of localhost and that the client username and password are both "guest". If your STOMP broker is on another server or is configured with different client credentials, you can configure those details when enabling the STOMP broker relay:

```
@Override
public void configureMessageBroker(MessageBrokerRegistry registry) {
```

```
registry.enableStompBrokerRelay("/topic", "/queue")
        .setRelayHost("rabbit.someotherserver")
        .setRelayPort(62623)
        .setClientLogin("marcopolo")
        .setClientPasscode("letmein01");
  registry.setApplicationDestinationPrefixes("/app", "/foo");
}
```

This bit of configuration adjusts the server, port, and credentials. But it's not necessary to configure them all. For instance, if you only need to change the relay host, you can call `setRelayHost()` and leave out the other setter methods in the configuration.

Now Spring is configured and ready to handle STOMP messages.

18.3.2 *Handling STOMP messages from the client*

As you learned in chapter 5, Spring MVC offers an annotation-oriented programming model for handling HTTP web requests. `@RequestMapping`, the star annotation in Spring MVC, maps HTTP requests to methods that will process those requests. That same programming model extends to serving RESTful resources as you saw in chapter 16.

STOMP and WebSocket are more about synchronous messaging as opposed to HTTP's request-response approach. Nevertheless, Spring offers a programming model that's very similar to Spring MVC for handling STOMP messages. It's so similar, in fact, that the handler methods for STOMP are members of `@Controller`-annotated classes.

Spring 4.0 introduced `@MessageMapping`, STOMP messaging's analog to Spring MVC's `@RequestMapping`. A method annotated with `@MessageMapping` can handle messages as they arrive at a specified destination. For example, consider the simple controller class in the following listing.

> **Listing 18.6   `@MessageMapping` handles STOMP messages in a controller.**

```
package marcopolo;
import org.slf4j.Logger;
import org.slf4j.LoggerFactory;
import org.springframework.messaging.handler.annotation.MessageMapping;
import org.springframework.stereotype.Controller;

@Controller
public class MarcoController {

  private static final Logger logger =
      LoggerFactory.getLogger(MarcoController.class);        Handle messages
                                                             for /app/marco
  @MessageMapping("/marco")                              ◁── destination
   public void handleShout(Shout incoming) {
    logger.info("Received message: " + incoming.getMessage());
  }

}
```

At first glance, this looks like any other Spring MVC controller class. It's annotated with @Controller, so it will be picked up and registered as a bean by component-scanning. And it has a handler method, just like any @Controller class would have.

But the handler method is a little different than those we've looked at before. Instead of @RequestMapping, the handleShout() method is annotated with @Message-Mapping. This signifies that handleShout() should handle any messages that arrive at the specified destination. In this case, the destination is /app/marco (the "/app" pre-fix is implied as it is the prefix we configured as the application destination prefix).

Because handleShout() accepts a Shout parameter, the payload of the STOMP message will be converted into a Shout using one of Spring's message converters. The Shout class is just a simple one-property JavaBean that carries a message:

```
package marcopolo;

public class Shout {
  private String message;

  public String getMessage() {
    return message;
  }

  public void setMessage(String message) {
    this.message = message;
  }
}
```

Since you're not working with HTTP here, it won't be one of Spring's HttpMessage-Converter implementations that handles the conversion to a Shout object. Instead, Spring 4.0 offers only a few message converters as part of its messaging API. Table 18.1 describes the message converters that might come into play when handling STOMP messages.

Table 18.1   Spring can convert message payloads to Java types using one of a few message converters.

Message converter	Description
ByteArrayMessageConverter	Converts a message with a MIME type of application/octet-stream to and from byte[]
MappingJackson2MessageConverter	Converts a message with a MIME type of application/json to and from a Java object
StringMessageConverter	Converts a message with a MIME type of text/plain to and from String

Assuming that the message handled by handleShout() has a content type of application/json (which is probably a safe guess given that Shout is neither a byte[] nor a String), the MappingJackson2MessageConverter will be tasked with converting the JSON message into a Shout object. Just like its HTTP-oriented counterpart,

MappingJackson2HttpMessageConverter, MappingJackson2MessageConverter delegates much of its work to the underlying Jackson 2 JSON processor. By default, Jackson will use reflection to map JSON properties to Java object properties. Although it's unnecessary in this example, you can influence how the conversion takes place by annotating the Java type with Jackson annotations.

PROCESSING SUBSCRIPTIONS

In addition to the @MessagingMapping annotation, Spring also offers an @SubscribeMapping annotation. Any method that's annotated with @SubscribeMapping will be invoked, much like @MessagingMapping methods, when a STOMP subscription message arrives.

It's important to understand that just like @MessageMapping methods, @SubscribeMapping methods receive their messages via AnnotationMethodMessage-Handler (as illustrated in figures 18.2 and 18.3). Per the configuration in listing 18.5, that means that @SubscribeMapping methods can only handle messages for destinations that are prefixed with /app.

This may seem odd, knowing that outgoing messages tend to go to broker destinations prefixed with /topic or /queue. Clients subscribe to those destinations and probably won't subscribe to destinations prefixed with /app. If the clients are subscribing to /topic and /queue destinations, there's no way that an @SubscribeMapping method can handle those subscriptions. And if that's true, then what good is @SubscribeMapping?

The primary use case for @SubscribeMapping is to implement a request-reply pattern. In the request-reply pattern, the client subscribes to a destination expecting a one-time response at that destination.

For example, consider the following @SubscribeMapping-annotated method:

```
@SubscribeMapping({"/marco"})
public Shout handleSubscription() {
  Shout outgoing = new Shout();
  outgoing.setMessage("Polo!");
  return outgoing;
}
```

As you can see, the handleSubscription() method is annotated with @SubscribeMapping to handle subscriptions to /app/marco. (As with @MessageMapping, the "/app" prefix is implied). When handling the subscription, handleSubscription() produces an outgoing Shout object and returns it. The Shout object is then converted into a message and sent back to the client at the same destination to which the client subscribed.

If you're thinking that this request-reply pattern isn't much different than an HTTP GET request-response pattern, then you're mostly correct. The key difference, however, is that where an HTTP GET request is synchronous, a subscription request-reply is asynchronous, allowing the client to deal with the reply whenever it's available and not have to wait for it.

WRITING THE JAVASCRIPT CLIENT

The handleShout() method is ready to process messages as they're sent. Now all you need is a client to send those messages.

The following listing shows some JavaScript client code that might connect to the /marcopolo endpoint and send a "Marco!" message.

Listing 18.7 Messages can be sent from JavaScript using the STOMP library

```
var url = 'http://' + window.location.host + '/stomp/marcopolo';
var sock = new SockJS(url);                        ⟵— Create SockJS connection

var stomp = Stomp.over(sock);                      ⟵— Create STOMP client

var payload = JSON.stringify({ 'message': 'Marco!' });

stomp.connect('guest', 'guest', function(frame) {  ⟵— Connect to STOMP endpoint
  stomp.send("/marco", {}, payload);               ⟵— Send message
});
```

As with our previous JavaScript client example, this one starts by creating an instance of SockJS for a given URL. The URL in this case references the STOMP endpoint configured in listing 18.5 (not including the application's context path, /stomp).

What's different here, however, is that you never use SockJS directly. Instead you construct an instance of the STOMP client by calling Stomp.over(sock). This effectively wraps SockJS to send STOMP messages over the WebSocket connection.

Next, you use the STOMP client to connect to and, assuming that the connection succeeds, send a message with a JSON payload to the destination named /marco. The second parameter passed to send() is a map of headers to be included in the STOMP frame; although in this case you're not contributing any headers and the map is empty.

Now you have a client that sends a message to the server, and a handler method on the server ready to process it. It's a good start. But you may have noticed that it's a bit one-sided. Let's give the server a voice and see how to send messages to the client.

18.3.3 Sending messages to the client

So far, the client is doing all of the message sending and the server is forced to listen for those messages. While that's a valid use of WebSocket and STOMP, it's not the use case that you probably think of when you think of WebSocket. WebSocket is often viewed as a way that a server can send data to the browser without being in response to an HTTP request. How can you communicate with the browser-based client using Spring and WebSocket/STOMP?

Spring offers two ways to send data to a client:

- As a side-effect of handling a message or subscription
- Using a messaging template

You already know about some methods to handle messages and subscriptions, so we'll first look at how to send messages to the client as a side-effect of those methods. Then we'll look at Spring's `SimpMessagingTemplate` for sending messages from anywhere in the application.

SENDING A MESSAGE AFTER HANDLING A MESSAGE

The `handleShout()` method from listing 18.6 simply returns `void`. Its job is to simply handle a message, not reply to the client.

Even so, if you want to send a message in response to receiving a message, all you need to do is return something other than `void`. For example, if you want to send a "Polo!" message in reaction to a "Marco!" message, you could change the `handle-Shout()` message to look like this:

```
@MessageMapping("/marco")
public Shout handleShout(Shout incoming) {
  logger.info("Received message: " + incoming.getMessage());

  Shout outgoing = new Shout();
  outgoing.setMessage("Polo!");
  return outgoing;
}
```

In this new version of `handleShout()`, a new `Shout` object is returned. By simply returning an object, a handler method can also be a sender method. When an `@MessageMapping`-annotated method has a return value, the returned object will be converted (via a message converter) and placed into the payload of a STOMP frame and published to the broker.

By default, the frame will be published to the same destination that triggered the handler method, but with /topic as the prefix. In the case of `handleShout()`, that means that the returned `Shout` object will be written to the payload of a STOMP frame and published to the /topic/marco destination. But you can override the destination by annotating the method with `@SendTo`:

```
@MessageMapping("/marco")
@SendTo("/topic/shout")
public Shout handleShout(Shout incoming) {
  logger.info("Received message: " + incoming.getMessage());

  Shout outgoing = new Shout();
  outgoing.setMessage("Polo!");
  return outgoing;
}
```

With this `@SendTo` annotation in place, the message will be published to /topic/shout. Any application that's subscribed to that topic (such as the client), will receive that message.

The `handleShout()` method now sends a message in response to having received a message. In a similar way, an `@SubscribeMapping`-annotated method can send a message in reply to a subscription. For example, you could send a `Shout` message when the client subscribes by adding this method to the controller:

```
@SubscribeMapping("/marco")
public Shout handleSubscription() {
```

```
  Shout outgoing = new Shout();
  outgoing.setMessage("Polo!");
  return outgoing;
}
```

The @SubscribeMapping annotation designates the handleSubscription() method to be invoked whenever a client subscribes to the /app/marco destination (with the /app application destination prefix). The Shout object it returns will be converted and sent back to the client.

What's different with @SubscribeMapping is that the Shout message is sent directly to the client without going through the broker. If you annotate the method with @SendTo, the message will be sent to the destination specified, going through the broker.

SENDING A MESSAGE FROM ANYWHERE

@MessageMapping and @SubscribeMapping offer a simple way to send messages as a consequence of receiving a message or handling a subscription. But Spring's SimpMessagingTemplate makes it possible to send messages from anywhere in an application, even without having received a message first.

The easiest way to use a SimpMessagingTemplate is to autowire it (or its interface, SimpMessageSendingOperations) into the object that needs it.

To put this into practice, let's revisit the Spittr application's home page to offer a live Spittle feed. As it is currently written, the controller handling the home page request fetches the most recent list of Spittles and places them into the model to be rendered into the user's browser. Although this works fine, it doesn't offer a live feed of Spittle updates. If the user wants to see an updated Spittle feed, they'll have to refresh the page in their browser.

Rather than force the user to refresh the page, you can have the home page subscribe to a STOMP topic to receive a live feed of Spittle updates as they're created. Within the home page, you need to add the following JavaScript chunk:

```
<script>
  var sock = new SockJS('spittr');
  var stomp = Stomp.over(sock);

  stomp.connect('guest', 'guest', function(frame) {
    console.log('Connected');
    stomp.subscribe("/topic/spittlefeed", handleSpittle);
  });

  function handleSpittle(incoming) {
    var spittle = JSON.parse(incoming.body);
    console.log('Received: ', spittle);
    var source = $("#spittle-template").html();
    var template = Handlebars.compile(source);
    var spittleHtml = template(spittle);
    $('.spittleList').prepend(spittleHtml);
  }
</script>
```

As in previous examples, you're creating an instance of `SockJS` and then an instance of `Stomp` over that `SockJS` instance. After connecting to the STOMP broker, you subscribe to /topic/spittlefeed and designate the `handleSpittle()` function to handle the `Spittle` updates as they arrive. The `handleSpittle()` function parses the incoming message's body into a proper JavaScript object and then uses the Handlebars library to render the `Spittle` data into HTML prepended to the list. The Handlebars template is defined in a separate `<script>` tag as follows:

```
<script id="spittle-template" type="text/x-handlebars-template">
  <li id="preexist">
  <div class="spittleMessage">{{message}}</div>
  <div>
   <span class="spittleTime">{{time}}</span>
   <span class="spittleLocation">({{latitude}}, {{longitude}})</span>
  </div>
  </li>
</script>
```

On the server, you can use `SimpMessagingTemplate` to publish any newly created `Spittle` as a message to the /topic/spittlefeed topic. The following listing shows `SpittleFeedServiceImpl`, a simple service that does exactly that.

Listing 18.8 `SimpMessagingTemplate` publishes messages from anywhere

```
package spittr;
import org.springframework.beans.factory.annotation.Autowired;
import org.springframework.messaging.simp.SimpMessageSendingOperations;
import org.springframework.stereotype.Service;

@Service
public class SpittleFeedServiceImpl implements SpittleFeedService {

  private SimpMessageSendingOperations messaging;

  @Autowired
  public SpittleFeedServiceImpl(
      SimpMessageSendingOperations messaging) {      <-- Inject messaging template
    this.messaging = messaging;
  }

  public void broadcastSpittle(Spittle spittle) {
    messaging.convertAndSend("/topic/spittlefeed", spittle);   <-- Send message
   }

}
```

As a side-effect of configuring Spring's STOMP support, there's already a `SimpMessage-Template` bean in the Spring application context. Therefore, there's no need to create a new instance here. Instead, the `SpittleFeedServiceImpl` constructor is annotated with `@Autowired` to inject the existing `SimpMessagingTemplate` (as `SimpMessage-SendingOperations`) when `SpittleFeedServiceImpl` is created.

The `broadcastSpittle()` method is where the `Spittle` message is sent. It calls `convertAndSend()` on the injected `SimpMessageSendingOperations` to convert the

`Spittle` into a message and send it to the /topic/spittlefeed topic. If the `convertAnd-Send()` method seems familiar, that's because it mimics the methods of the same name offered by both `JmsTemplate` and `RabbitTemplate`.

When you publish a message to a STOMP topic with `convertAndSend()` or as a result of a handler method, any client subscribed to that topic will receive the message. For a situation where you want to keep all clients up to date with a live `Spittle` feed, that's perfect. But sometimes you might want to send a message to a specific user and not to all clients.

18.4 Working with user-targeted messages

Up to this point, the messages you've sent and received were between a client (in a web browser) and the server. The user of that client hasn't been taken into account. When an `@MessageMapping`-annotated method is invoked, you know that a message has been received, but not who it's from. Similarly, if you don't know who the user is, then any messages sent will go to all clients that have subscribed to the topic that the message is carried on; there's no way to send that message to a specific user.

If you know who the user is, however, it becomes possible to deal with messages associated with a user, not just those associated with a client. The good news is that you already know how to identify the user. Using the same authentication mechanism applied in chapter 9, you can use Spring Security to authenticate the user and work with user-targeted messages.

There are three ways to take advantage of an authenticated user when messaging with Spring and STOMP:

- The `@MessageMapping` and `@SubscribeMapping` methods can receive a `Principal` for the authenticated user.
- Values returned from the `@MessageMapping`, `@SubscribeMapping`, and `@Message-Exception` methods can be sent as messages to the authenticated user.
- The `SimpMessagingTemplate` can send messages to a specific user.

Let's start by looking at the first two ways, both of which enable a controller's message-handling methods to work with user messages.

18.4.1 Working with user messages in a controller

As mentioned before, there are two ways that a controller's `@MessageMapping` or `@SubscribeMapping` method can be user-aware in processing messages. By simply asking for a `Principal` as a parameter to a handler method, the handler method can know who the user is and use that information to focus its work on that user's data. In addition, a handler method can be annotated with `@SendToUser` to indicate that its return value should be sent in a message to the authenticated user's client (and to that client only).

To demonstrate, let's write a controller method that creates a new `Spittle` object from an incoming message and sends a reply indicating that the `Spittle` has been saved. If this use-case sounds familiar, it's because you already implemented this as a REST endpoint in chapter 16. Certainly, REST is one way of implementing that functionality. But REST requests are synchronous by nature, and the client must wait while the server processes them. By posting the `Spittle` as a STOMP message, you can take full advantage of the asynchronous nature of STOMP messaging.

Consider the following `handleSpittle()` method, which handles an incoming message and saves it as a `Spittle`:

```
@MessageMapping("/spittle")
@SendToUser("/queue/notifications")
public Notification handleSpittle(
      Principal principal, SpittleForm form) {

  Spittle spittle = new Spittle(
      principal.getName(), form.getText(), new Date());

  spittleRepo.save(spittle);

  return new Notification("Saved Spittle");
}
```

As you can see, `handleSpittle()` accepts both a `Principal` object as well as a `SpittleForm` object. It uses those to create an instance of `Spittle` and then uses the `SpittleRepository` to save it. Finally, it returns a new `Notification` indicating that the `Spittle` was saved.

Of course, what happens inside the method isn't nearly as interesting as what's going on outside. Because this method is annotated with `@MessageMapping`, it will be invoked whenever a message arrives on the /app/spittle destination. The `Spittle-Form` will be created from that message and, assuming that the user is authenticated, the `Principal` will also be derived from headers in the STOMP frame.

The big thing to pay attention to, however, is where the returned `Notification` goes. The `@SendToUser` annotation specifies that the returned `Notification` should be sent as a message to the /queue/notifications destination. On the surface, /queue/ notifications doesn't appear to be specific to a given user. But because this is the `@SendToUser` annotation and not the `@SendTo` annotation, there's more to the story.

To understand how Spring will publish the message, let's step back a bit and see how a client would subscribe to the destination that this controller method publishes a `Notification` to. Consider this line of JavaScript that subscribes to a user-specific destination:

```
stomp.subscribe("/user/queue/notifications", handleNotifications);
```

Notice that the destination is prefixed with /user. Internally, destinations that are prefixed with /user are handled in a special way. Rather than flowing through `AnnotationMethodMessageHandler` (like an application message), or through `Simple-BrokerMessageHandler` or `StompBrokerRelayMessageHandler` (like a broker message), /user messages flow through `UserDestinationMessageHandler`, as illustrated in figure 18.4.

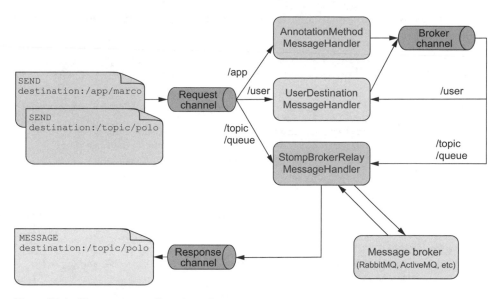

Figure 18.4 User messages flow through `UserDestinationMessageHandler`, which reroutes them to a destination that's unique to a user.

`UserDestinationMessageHandler`'s primary job is to reroute user messages to a destination that's unique to the user. In the case of a subscription, it derives the target destination by removing the /user prefix and adding a suffix that's based on the user's session. For instance, a subscription to /user/queue/notifications may end up being rerouted to a destination named /queue/notifications-user6hr83v6t.

In our example, `handleSpittle()` is annotated with `@SendToUser("/queue/notifications")`. This new destination is prefixed with /queue, which is one of the prefixes that your `StompBrokerRelayMessageHandler` (or `SimpleBrokerMessageHandler`) is configured to handle, so the message will go there next. As it turns out, the client subscribed to that destination, so the client will receive the `Notification` message.

The `@SendToUser` annotation and a `Principal` parameter are very useful when working within a controller method. But in listing 18.8 you saw how to send messages from anywhere in an application using a messaging template. Let's see how you can use `SimpMessagingTemplate` to send messages to a specific user.

18.4.2 Sending messages to a specific user

In addition to `convertAndSend()`, `SimpMessagingTemplate` also offers `convertAndSendToUser()`. As its name suggests, the `convertAndSendToUser()` method enables you to send messages that target a specific user.

To demonstrate, let's add a feature to the Spittr application that notifies a user when some other user posts a `Spittle` that mentions them. For example, if the `Spittle` text includes "@jbauer", then you should send a message to the client where a user with the username "jbauer" is logged in. The `broadcastSpittle()` method in the following listing uses `convertAndSendToUser()` to notify a user that they're being talked about.

Listing 18.9   `convertAndSendToUser()` can send a message to a specific user

```
package spittr;
import java.util.regex.Matcher;
import java.util.regex.Pattern;
import org.springframework.beans.factory.annotation.Autowired;
import org.springframework.messaging.simp.SimpMessagingTemplate;
import org.springframework.stereotype.Service;

@Service
public class SpittleFeedServiceImpl implements SpittleFeedService {

  private SimpMessagingTemplate messaging;
  private Pattern pattern = Pattern.compile("\\@(\\S+)");     ← Regex pattern for user mention

  @Autowired
  public SpittleFeedServiceImpl(SimpMessagingTemplate messaging) {
    this.messaging = messaging;
  }

  public void broadcastSpittle(Spittle spittle) {

    messaging.convertAndSend("/topic/spittlefeed", spittle);

    Matcher matcher = pattern.matcher(spittle.getMessage());
    if (matcher.find()) {
      String username = matcher.group(1);
      messaging.convertAndSendToUser(                          ← Send notification to user
          username, "/queue/notifications",
          new Notification("You just got mentioned!"));
    }
  }

}
```

Within `broadcastSpittle()`, if the given `Spittle` object's message contains what appears to be a username (that is, any text that begins with "@"), a new `Notification` will be sent to a destination named /queue/notifications. Therefore, if the `Spittle` has a message that contains "@jbauer", the `Notification` will be published to the /user/jbauer/queue/notifications destination.

18.5 *Handling message exceptions*

Sometimes things don't work out the way you expected. When handling a message, something could go wrong and an exception could be thrown. Due to the asynchronous nature of STOMP messaging, the sender may never know that anything went wrong. Aside from being logged by Spring, the exception could be lost with no recourse or opportunity to recover.

In Spring MVC, if an exception occurs during request handling, an `@Exception-Handler` method will be given an opportunity to deal with the exception. Similarly, you can annotate a controller method with `@MessageExceptionHandler` to handle exceptions thrown in an `@MessageMapping` method.

For example, consider this method that handles exceptions thrown from message-handling methods:

```
@MessageExceptionHandler
public void handleExceptions(Throwable t) {
  logger.error("Error handling message: " + t.getMessage());
}
```

In its simplest form, `@MessageExceptionHandler` will handle any exception thrown from a message-handling method. But you can declare a specific exception type that it should handle as a parameter:

```
@MessageExceptionHandler(SpittleException.class)
public void handleExceptions(Throwable t) {
  logger.error("Error handling message: " + t.getMessage());
}
```

Or you can specify several exception types to be handled as an array parameter:

```
@MessageExceptionHandler(
        {SpittleException.class, DatabaseException.class})
public void handleExceptions(Throwable t) {
  logger.error("Error handling message: " + t.getMessage());
}
```

Although it only logs that an error occurred, this method could do much more. For instance, it could reply with an error:

```
@MessageExceptionHandler(SpittleException.class)
@SendToUser("/queue/errors")
public SpittleException handleExceptions(SpittleException e) {
  logger.error("Error handling message: " + e.getMessage());
  return e;
}
```

Here, if a `SpittleException` is thrown, that exception will be logged and then returned. As you learned in section 18.4.1, `UserDestinationMessageHandler` will reroute the message to a destination unique to the user.

18.6 *Summary*

WebSocket is an exciting way to send messages between applications, especially when one of those applications is running within a web browser. It's critical for writing highly interactive web applications that seamlessly transfer data to and from the server.

Spring's WebSocket support includes a low-level API that lets you work with raw WebSocket connections. Unfortunately, WebSocket support is not ubiquitous among web browsers, servers, and proxies. Therefore, Spring also supports SockJS, a protocol that falls back to alternative communication schemes when WebSocket doesn't work.

Spring also offers a higher-level programming model for handling WebSocket messages using the STOMP wire-level protocol. In this higher-level model, STOMP messages are handled in Spring MVC controllers, similarly to how HTTP messages are handled.

In the past couple of chapters, you've seen a few ways to send messages asynchronously between applications. But there's another kind of asynchronous messaging that Spring can do. In the next chapter, you'll see how to use Spring to send emails.

19

Sending email with Spring

This chapter covers

- Configuring Spring's email abstraction
- Sending rich email messages
- Using templates to construct email messages

It's no secret that email has become a common form of communication, displacing many traditional means of communication such as postal mail, telephone calls, and, to some degree, face-to-face communication. Email offers many of the same asynchronous benefits as the messaging options we discussed in chapter 17, only with humans as the senders and receivers. As soon as you click Send in your email client, you can move on to some other task, knowing that the recipient will eventually receive and (hopefully) read your email.

But humans aren't always the senders of email. Frequently, email messages are sent by applications to users. Perhaps it's an email confirmation of an order that a user placed on an eCommerce site, or maybe it's an automated notification of an activity involving someone's bank account. Whatever the subject, it's likely that you'll develop applications that need to send email messages. Fortunately, Spring is ready to help.

In chapter 17, you used Spring's messaging support to asynchronously queue up jobs to send spittle alerts to other Spittr application users. But you left that task unfinished, because no email messages were sent. Let's finish what you started by looking at how Spring abstracts the problem of sending email, and then use that abstraction to send spittle alert email messages.

19.1 *Configuring Spring to send email*

At the heart of Spring's email abstraction is the `MailSender` interface. As its name implies, and as illustrated in figure 19.1, a `MailSender` implementation sends email by connecting with an email server.

Spring comes with one implementation of the `MailSender` interface, `JavaMail-SenderImpl`, which uses the JavaMail API to send email. Before you can send email messages from your Spring application, you must wire `JavaMailSenderImpl` as a bean in the Spring application context.

19.1.1 *Configuring a mail sender*

In its simplest form, `JavaMailSenderImpl` can be configured as a bean with only a few lines in an `@Bean` method:

```
@Bean
public MailSender mailSender(Environment env) {
  JavaMailSenderImpl mailSender = new JavaMailSenderImpl();
  mailSender.setHost(env.getProperty("mailserver.host"));
  return mailSender;
}
```

The `host` property is optional (it defaults to the host of the underlying JavaMail session), but you'll probably want to set it. It specifies the hostname for the mail server that will be used to send the email. Here it's configured by fetching the value from the injected `Environment` so that you can manage the mail-server configuration outside of Spring (for example, in a properties file).

By default, `JavaMailSenderImpl` assumes that the mail server is listening on port 25 (the standard SMTP port). If your mail server is listening on a different port, specify the correct port number using the `port` property. For example,

```
@Bean
public MailSender mailSender(Environment env) {
  JavaMailSenderImpl mailSender = new JavaMailSenderImpl();
  mailSender.setHost(env.getProperty("mailserver.host"));
  mailSender.setPort(env.getProperty("mailserver.port"));
  return mailSender;
}
```

Figure 19.1   Spring's `MailSender` interface is the primary component of Spring's email abstraction API. It sends email to a mail server for delivery.

Likewise, if the mail server requires authentication, you'll want to set values for the username and password properties:

```
@Bean
public MailSender mailSender(Environment env) {
  JavaMailSenderImpl mailSender = new JavaMailSenderImpl();
  mailSender.setHost(env.getProperty("mailserver.host"));
  mailSender.setPort(env.getProperty("mailserver.port"));
  mailSender.setUsername(env.getProperty("mailserver.username"));
  mailSender.setPassword(env.getProperty("mailserver.password"));
  return mailSender;
}
```

Thus far, JavaMailSenderImpl has been configured to create its own mail session. But you may already have a javax.mail.MailSession configured in JNDI (or perhaps one was placed there by your application server). If so, it doesn't make much sense to configure JavaMailSenderImpl with the full server details. Instead, you can configure it to use the MailSession you have ready to use from JNDI.

Using JndiObjectFactoryBean, you can configure a bean that looks up the Mail-Session from JNDI with the following @Bean method:

```
@Bean
public JndiObjectFactoryBean mailSession() {
  JndiObjectFactoryBean jndi = new JndiObjectFactoryBean();
  jndi.setJndiName("mail/Session");
  jndi.setProxyInterface(MailSession.class);
  jndi.setResourceRef(true);
  return jndi;
}
```

You've also seen how to retrieve objects from JNDI using Spring's <jee:jndi-lookup> element. You can use <jee:jndi-lookup> to create a bean that references a mail session in JNDI:

```
<jee:jndi-lookup id="mailSession"
  jndi-name="mail/Session" resource-ref="true" />
```

With the mail session bean configured, you can now wire it into the mailSender bean like this:

```
@Bean
public MailSender mailSender(MailSession mailSession) {
  JavaMailSenderImpl mailSender = new JavaMailSenderImpl();
  mailSender.setSession(mailSession);
  return mailSender;
}
```

By wiring the mail session into the session property of JavaMailSenderImpl, you replace the explicit server (and username/password) configuration from before. Now the mail session is completely configured and managed in JNDI. JavaMailSenderImpl can focus on sending email messages and not worry about the details of how to connect with the mail server.

19.1.2 *Wiring and using the mail sender*

With the mail sender configured, it's time to wire it into the bean that will use it. In
the Spittr application, the `SpitterEmailServiceImpl` class is the most appropriate
place from which to send email. This class has a `mailSender` property that's annotated
with `@Autowired`:

```
@Autowired
JavaMailSender mailSender;
```

When Spring creates `SpitterEmailServiceImpl` as a bean, it will try to find a bean
that implements `MailSender` that it can wire in to the `mailSender` property. It should
find your `mailSender` bean and use that. With the `mailSender` bean wired in, you're
ready to construct and send email messages.

Because you want to send email to a Spitter user to alert them about new spittles that
their friends may have written, you'll need a method that, given an email address and
a `Spittle` object, will send that email message. The following `sendSimpleSpittle-`
`Email()` method uses the mail sender to do just that.

Listing 19.1 Sending email with Spring using a `MailSender`

```
public void sendSimpleSpittleEmail(String to, Spittle spittle) {
    SimpleMailMessage message = new SimpleMailMessage();       ◁─ Construct
    String spitterName = spittle.getSpitter().getFullName();       message
    message.setFrom("noreply@spitter.com");
    message.setTo(to);
    message.setSubject("New spittle from " + spitterName);
    message.setText(spitterName + " says: " +        ◁─ Set message text
            spittle.getText());

    mailSender.send(message);        ◁─ Send email
}
```

Address email →

The first thing that `sendSimpleSpittleEmail()` does is construct an instance of
`SimpleMailMessage`. This mail-message object, as its name implies, is perfect for sending no-nonsense email messages.

Next, the details of the message are set. The sender and recipient are specified via
the `setFrom()` and `setTo()` methods on the email message. After you set the subject
with `setSubject()`, the virtual "envelope" has been addressed. All that's left is to call
`setText()` to set the message's content.

The last step is to pass the message to the mail sender's `send()` method, and the
email is on its way.

Now you've configured a mail sender and used it to send a simple email message.
And as you've seen, working with Spring's email abstraction is easy. We could call it
good at this point and move on to the next chapter. But then you'd miss out on the
fun stuff in Spring's email abstraction. Let's kick it up a notch and see how to add
attachments and create rich email messages.

19.2 *Constructing rich email messages*

Plaintext email messages are fine for simple things like asking your friends over to watch the big game. But they're less than ideal when you need to send photos or documents. And they're ineffective for capturing the recipient's attention, as in marketing email.

Fortunately, Spring's email capabilities don't end with plaintext email. You have the option of adding attachments and even dressing up the body of the message with HTML. Let's start with the basic task of adding attachments. Then you'll go a step further and make your email messages look good with HTML.

19.2.1 *Adding attachments*

The trick to sending email with attachments is to create multipart messages—email messages composed of multiple parts, one of which is the body and the other parts being the attachments.

The `SimpleMailMessage` class is too ... well ... simple for sending attachments. To send multipart email messages, you need to create a *Multipurpose Internet Mail Extensions* (MIME) message. The mail sender object's `createMimeMessage()` method can get you started:

```
MimeMessage message = mailSender.createMimeMessage();
```

There you go. You now have a MIME message to work with. It seems that all you need to do is give it To and From addresses, a subject, some text, and an attachment. Although that's true, it's not as straightforward as you might think. The `javax.mail.internet.MimeMessage` class has an API that's too cumbersome to use on its own. Fortunately, Spring provides `MimeMessageHelper` to lend a hand.

To use `MimeMessageHelper`, instantiate an instance of it, passing in the `Mime-Message` to its constructor:

```
MimeMessageHelper helper = new MimeMessageHelper(message, true);
```

The second parameter to the constructor, a Boolean `true` as shown here, indicates that this is to be a multipart message.

From the `MimeMessageHelper` instance, you're ready to assemble your email message. The only major difference is that you'll provide the email specifics through methods on the helper instead of on the message itself:

```
String spitterName = spittle.getSpitter().getFullName();
helper.setFrom("noreply@spitter.com");
helper.setTo(to);
helper.setSubject("New spittle from " + spitterName);
helper.setText(spitterName + " says: " + spittle.getText());
```

The only thing needed before you can send the message is to add the attachment: in this case, a coupon image. To do that, you'll need to load the image as a resource and then pass that resource in as you call the helper's `addAttachment()` method:

```
FileSystemResource couponImage =
    new FileSystemResource("/collateral/coupon.png");
helper.addAttachment("Coupon.png", couponImage);
```

Here, you're using Spring's `FileSystemResource` to load coupon.png from within the application's classpath. From there, you call `addAttachment()`. The first parameter is the name to be given to the attachment in the message. The second parameter is the image's resource.

The multipart email message has been constructed, and you're ready to send it. The complete `sendSpittleEmailWithAttachment()` method is shown next.

Listing 19.2   Sending email messages with attachments using `MimeMessageHelper`

```
public void sendSpittleEmailWithAttachment(
        String to, Spittle spittle) throws MessagingException {
  MimeMessage message = mailSender.createMimeMessage();
  MimeMessageHelper helper =                            ⟵─┐ Construct
      new MimeMessageHelper(message, true);             ⟵─┘ message helper
   String spitterName = spittle.getSpitter().getFullName();
  helper.setFrom("noreply@spitter.com");
  helper.setTo(to);
  helper.setSubject("New spittle from " + spitterName);
  helper.setText(spitterName + " says: " + spittle.getText());
  FileSystemResource couponImage =
      new FileSystemResource("/collateral/coupon.png");
  helper.addAttachment("Coupon.png", couponImage);     ⟵── Add attachment
   mailSender.send(message);
}
```

Adding attachments is only one thing you can do with multipart email messages. In addition, by specifying that the body of the message is HTML, you can produce polished email messages that look much nicer than flat text. Let's see how to send attractive-looking email using Spring's `MimeMessageHelper`.

19.2.2 *Sending email with rich content*

Sending rich email isn't much different than sending plaintext email messages. The key is to set the message's text as HTML. Doing that is as simple as passing in an HTML string to the helper's `setText()` method and `true` as the second parameter:

```
helper.setText("<html><body><img src='cid:spitterLogo'>" +
  "<h4>" + spittle.getSpitter().getFullName() + " says...</h4>" +
  "<i>" + spittle.getText() + "</i>" +
      "</body></html>", true);
```

The second parameter indicates that the text passed in to the first parameter is HTML, so that the message part's content type will be set accordingly.

Note that the HTML passed in has an `<img>` tag to display the Spittr application's logo as part of the message. The `src` attribute could be set to a standard `http:` URL to pull the Spittr logo from the web. But here, you embed the logo image in the email message. The value `cid:spitterLogo` indicates that there will be an image in one of the message's parts identified as `spitterLogo`.

Adding the embedded image to the message is much like adding an attachment. Instead of calling the helper's `addAttachment()` method, you call the `addInline()` method:

```
ClassPathResource image =
              new ClassPathResource("spitter_logo_50.png");
helper.addInline("spitterLogo", image);
```

The first parameter to `addInline` specifies the identity of the inline image—which is the same as was specified by the `<img>`'s src attribute. The second parameter is the resource reference for the image, created here using Spring's `ClassPathResource` to retrieve the image from the application's classpath.

Aside from the slightly different call to `setText()` and the use of the `addInline()` method, sending email with rich content is much like sending a plaintext message with attachments. For sake of comparison, here's the new `sendRichSpitterEmail()` method.

```
public void sendRichSpitterEmail(String to, Spittle spittle)
                              throws MessagingException {
MimeMessage message = mailSender.createMimeMessage();
MimeMessageHelper helper = new MimeMessageHelper(message, true);
helper.setFrom("noreply@spitter.com");
helper.setTo("craig@habuma.com");
helper.setSubject("New spittle from " +
        spittle.getSpitter().getFullName());
helper.setText("<html><body><img src='cid:spitterLogo'>" +        ⟵┐ Set HTML
    "<h4>" + spittle.getSpitter().getFullName() + " says...</h4>" +    │ body
    "<i>" + spittle.getText() + "</i>" +
        "</body></html>", true);
ClassPathResource image =
    new ClassPathResource("spitter_logo_50.png");
helper.addInline("spitterLogo", image);                  ⟵── Add inline image
 mailSender.send(message);
}
```

And now you're sending email messages with rich content and embedded images! You could stop here and call your email code complete. But it bugs me that the email's body is created by using string concatenation to construct an HTML message. Before we put the email topic to rest, let's see how to replace that string-concatenated message with a template.

19.3 *Generating email with templates*

The problem with constructing an email message using string concatenation is that it's not clear what the resulting message will look like. It's hard enough to mentally parse HTML markup to imagine how it might appear when rendered. But mixing up that HTML in Java code compounds the issue. Moreover, it might be nice to extract the email layout into a template that a graphic designer (who probably has an aversion to Java code) can produce.

What you need is a way to express the email layout in something close to what the resulting HTML will look like, and then transform that template into a `String` to be passed into the `setText()` method on the message helper. When it comes to transforming templates into strings, there are several templating options to choose from, including Apache Velocity and Thymeleaf. Let's look at how to create rich email messages using each of these options, starting with Velocity.

19.3.1 *Constructing email messages with Velocity*

Apache Velocity is a general-purpose templating engine from Apache. Velocity has been around for quite a while and has been used for all kinds of things, including code generation and as an alternative to JSP. It can also be used to format rich email messages, as you'll do here.

To use Velocity to lay out your email messages, you'll first need to wire a `Velocity-Engine` into `SpitterEmailServiceImpl`. Spring provides a handy factory bean called `VelocityEngineFactoryBean` that produces a `VelocityEngine` in the Spring application context. The declaration for `VelocityEngineFactoryBean` looks like this:

```
@Bean
public VelocityEngineFactoryBean velocityEngine() {
  VelocityEngineFactoryBean velocityEngine =
        new VelocityEngineFactoryBean();

  Properties props = new Properties();
  props.setProperty("resource.loader", "class");
  props.setProperty("class.resource.loader.class",
        ClasspathResourceLoader.class.getName());
  velocityEngine.setVelocityProperties(props);
  return velocityEngine;
}
```

The only property that needs to be set on `VelocityEngineFactoryBean` is `velocity-Properties`. In this case, you're configuring it to load Velocity templates from the classpath (see the Velocity documentation for more details on how to configure Velocity).

Now you can wire the Velocity engine into `SpitterEmailServiceImpl`. Because `SpitterEmailServiceImpl` is automatically registered with the component scanner, you can use `@Autowired` to automatically wire a `velocityEngine` property:

```
@Autowired
VelocityEngine velocityEngine;
```

Next, you can use the `velocityEngine` property to transform a Velocity template into a `String` to send as your email text. To help with that, Spring comes with `Velocity-EngineUtils` to make simple work of merging a Velocity template and some model data into a `String`. Here's how you might use it:

```
Map<String, String> model = new HashMap<String, String>();
model.put("spitterName", spitterName);
model.put("spittleText", spittle.getText());
String emailText = VelocityEngineUtils.mergeTemplateIntoString(
        velocityEngine, "emailTemplate.vm", model );
```

In preparation for processing the template, you start by creating a `Map` to hold the model data used by the template. In the previous string-concatenated code, you needed the full name of the spitter and the text of their spittle, so you'll need that here as well. To produce the merged email text, you then call `VelocityEngineUtils`'s `mergeTemplateIntoString()` method, passing in the Velocity engine, the path to the template (relative to the root of the classpath), and the model map.

All that's left to be done in the Java code is to hand off the merged email text to the message helper's `setText()` method:

```
helper.setText(emailText, true);
```

The template is sitting at the root of the classpath in a file called emailTemplate.vm, which looks like this:

```
<html>
<body>
  <img src='cid:spitterLogo'>
  <h4>${spitterName} says...</h4>
  <i>${spittleText}</i>
</body>
</html>
```

As you can see, the template file is a lot easier to read than the string-concatenated version from before. Consequently, it's also easier to maintain and edit. Figure 19.2 gives a sample of the kind of email message it might produce.

Looking at the figure, I see a lot of opportunity to dress up the template so the message looks much nicer. But, as they say, I'll leave that as an exercise for the reader.

Figure 19.2   A Velocity template and some embedded images can dress up an otherwise ho-hum email message.

Velocity has been used for years as the templating engine of choice for many tasks. But as you saw in chapter 6, a new templating option is becoming popular. Let's see how you can use Thymeleaf to construct spittle email messages.

19.3.2 *Using Thymeleaf to create email messages*

As we discussed in chapter 6, Thymeleaf is an attractive templating engine for HTML because it enables you to create WYSIWYG templates. Unlike JSP and Velocity, Thymeleaf templates don't contain any special tag libraries or unusual markup. This makes it easy for template designers to use any HTML tools they like in their work without worrying about a tool's inability to deal with special markup.

When you convert an email template to a Thymeleaf template, the WYSIWYG nature of Thymeleaf is apparent:

```
<!DOCTYPE html>
<html xmlns:th="http://www.thymeleaf.org">
<body>
  <img src="spitterLogo.png" th:src='cid:spitterLogo'>
  <h4><span th:text="${spitterName}">Craig Walls</span> says...</h4>
  <i><span th:text="${spittleText}">Hello there!</span></i>
</body>
</html>
```

Notice that there are no custom tags (as you might see in JSP). And although model attributes are referenced with ${} notation, it's confined to values of attributes instead of being out in the open as with Velocity. This template could easily be opened in a web browser and viewed in its complete form without relying on the Thymeleaf engine to process it.

Using Thymeleaf to generate and send HTML email messages is similar to what you did with Velocity:

```
Context ctx = new Context();
ctx.setVariable("spitterName", spitterName);
ctx.setVariable("spittleText", spittle.getText());
String emailText = thymeleaf.process("emailTemplate.html", ctx);
...
helper.setText(emailText, true);
mailSender.send(message);
```

The first thing to do is create a Thymeleaf Context instance and populate it with model data. This is analogous to populating a Map with model data, as you did with Velocity. Then you ask Thymeleaf to process your template, merging the model data in the context into the template by calling the process() method on the Thymeleaf engine. Finally, you set the resulting text on the message using the message helper and send the message using the mail sender.

That seems simple enough. But where does the Thymeleaf engine (represented by the thymeleaf variable) come from?

The Thymeleaf engine here is the same `SpringTemplateEngine` bean that you configured for constructing web views in chapter 6. But now you're injecting it into `SpitterEmailServiceImpl` via constructor injection:

```
@Autowired
private SpringTemplateEngine thymeleaf;

@Autowired
public SpitterEmailServiceImpl(SpringTemplateEngine thymeleaf) {
  this.thymeleaf = thymeleaf;
}
```

You must make one small tweak to the `SpringTemplateEngine` bean, however. As you left it in chapter 6, it's only configured to resolve templates from the servlet context. Your email templates will need to be resolved from the classpath. So in addition to `ServletContextTemplateResolver`, you'll also need a `ClassLoaderTemplate-Resolver`:

```
@Bean
public ClassLoaderTemplateResolver emailTemplateResolver() {
  ClassLoaderTemplateResolver resolver =
          new ClassLoaderTemplateResolver();
  resolver.setPrefix("mail/");
  resolver.setTemplateMode("HTML5");
  resolver.setCharacterEncoding("UTF-8");
  setOrder(1);
  return resolver;
}
```

For the most part, you'll configure the `ClassLoaderTemplateResolver` bean just as you did `ServletContextTemplateResolver`. Note, though, that the `prefix` property is set to `mail/`, indicating that it expects to find Thymeleaf templates in the mail directory rooted at the classpath root. Therefore, your email template file must be named email-Template.html and reside in the mail directory relative to the root of the classpath.

Also, because you'll now have two template resolvers, you need to indicate which one takes precedence, using the `order` property. The `ClassLoaderTemplateResolver` bean has its `order` as 1. Tweak the `ServletContextTemplateResolver` configuration, setting its order to 2:

```
@Bean
public ServletContextTemplateResolver webTemplateResolver() {
  ServletContextTemplateResolver resolver =
          new ServletContextTemplateResolver();
  resolver.setPrefix("/WEB-INF/templates/");
  resolver.setTemplateMode("HTML5");
  resolver.setCharacterEncoding("UTF-8");
  setOrder(2);
  return resolver;
}
```

All that's left to do is change the `SpringTemplateEngine` bean's configuration to use both of your template resolvers:

```
@Bean
public SpringTemplateEngine templateEngine(
     Set<ITemplateResolver> resolvers) {
  SpringTemplateEngine engine = new SpringTemplateEngine();
  engine.setTemplateResolvers(resolvers);
  return engine;
}
```

Before, you only had one template resolver, so you injected it into `SpringTemplate-Engine`'s `templateResolver` property. But now you have two template resolvers, so you must inject them as members of a `Set` into the `templateResolvers` (plural) property.

19.4   *Summary*

Email is an important form of human-to-human communication and frequently a crucial form of application-to-human communication as well. Spring builds on the email capabilities provided in Java, abstracting JavaMail for simpler use and configuration in a Spring application.

In this chapter, you've seen how to use Spring's email abstraction to send simple email messages, and you've taken it further by sending rich messages that contain attachments and that are formatted with HTML. We also looked at using templating engines like Velocity and Thymeleaf to generate rich email text without resorting to creating HTML via string concatenation.

Coming up in the next chapter, you'll see how to add management and notification capabilities to your Spring beans using Java Management Extensions (JMX).

Managing Spring beans
with JMX

This chapter covers
- Exposing Spring beans as managed beans
- Remotely managing Spring beans
- Handling JMX notifications

Spring's support for DI is a great way to configure bean properties in an application. But once the application has been deployed and is running, DI alone can't do much to help you change that configuration. Suppose you want to dig into a running application and change its configuration on the fly. That's where *Java Management Extensions* (JMX) comes in.

JMX is a technology that enables you to instrument applications for management, monitoring, and configuration. Originally available as a separate extension to Java, JMX is now a standard part of the Java 5 distribution.

The key component of an application that's instrumented for management with JMX is the *managed bean* (MBean). An MBean is a JavaBean that exposes certain methods that define the management interface. The JMX specification defines four types of MBeans:

- *Standard MBeans*—MBeans whose management interface is determined by reflection on a fixed Java interface that's implemented by the bean class.
- *Dynamic MBeans*—MBeans whose management interface is determined at runtime by invoking methods of the `DynamicMBean` interface. Because the management interface isn't defined by a static interface, it can vary at runtime.
- *Open MBeans*—A special kind of dynamic MBean whose attributes and operations are limited to primitive types, class wrappers for primitive types, and any type that can be decomposed into primitives or primitive wrappers.
- *Model MBeans*—A special kind of dynamic MBean that bridges a management interface to the managed resource. Model MBeans aren't written as much as they are declared. They're typically produced by a factory that uses some meta-information to assemble the management interface.

Spring's JMX module enables you to export Spring beans as model MBeans so that you can see inside your application and tweak the configuration—even while the application is running. Let's see how to JMX-enable your Spring application so that you can manage the beans in the Spring application context.

20.1 *Exporting Spring beans as MBeans*

There are several ways you can use JMX to manage the beans in the Spittr application. In the interest of keeping things simple, let's start by making a modest change to `SpittleController` as it appeared in listing 5.10. We'll add a new `spittlesPerPage` property:

```
public static final int DEFAULT_SPITTLES_PER_PAGE = 25;
private int spittlesPerPage = DEFAULT_SPITTLES_PER_PAGE;

public void setSpittlesPerPage(int spittlesPerPage) {
  this.spittlesPerPage = spittlesPerPage;
}

public int getSpittlesPerPage() {
  return spittlesPerPage;
}
```

Before this change, when `SpittleController` called `findSpittles()` on the `SpitterService`, it passed in 20 for the second argument, asking for only the most recent 20 `Spittles`. Now, rather than commit to that decision at build time with a hard-coded value, you're going to use JMX to leave the decision open to change at runtime. The new `spittlesPerPage` property is the first step toward enabling that.

But on its own, the `spittlesPerPage` property can't enable external configuration of the number of spittles displayed on the page. It's just a property on a bean, like any other property. What you need to do next is expose the `SpittleController` bean as an MBean. Then the `spittlesPerPage` property will be exposed as the MBean's *managed attribute*, and you'll be able to change its value at runtime.

Spring's `MBeanExporter` is the key to JMX-ifying beans in Spring. `MBeanExporter` is a bean that exports one or more Spring-managed beans as model MBeans in an

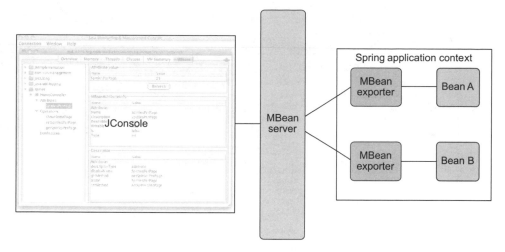

Figure 20.1 Spring's `MBeanExporter` exports the properties and methods of Spring beans as JMX attributes and operations in an MBean server. From there, a JMX management tool such as JConsole can look inside the running application.

MBean server. An MBean server (sometimes called an *MBean agent*) is a container where MBeans live and through which the MBeans are accessed.

As illustrated in figure 20.1, exporting Spring beans as JMX MBeans makes it possible for a JMX-based management tool such as JConsole or VisualVM to peer inside a running application to view the beans' properties and invoke their methods.

The following `@Bean` method declares an `MBeanExporter` in Spring to export the `spittleController` bean as a model MBean:

```
@Bean
public MBeanExporter mbeanExporter(SpittleController spittleController) {
  MBeanExporter exporter = new MBeanExporter();
  Map<String, Object> beans = new HashMap<String, Object>();
  beans.put("spitter:name=SpittleController", spittleController);
  exporter.setBeans(beans);
  return exporter;
}
```

In its most straightforward form, `MBeanExporter` can be configured through its beans property by injecting a `Map` of one or more beans that you'd like to expose as model MBeans in JMX. The key of each <entry> is the name to be given to the MBean (composed of a management domain name and a key-value pair—`spitter:name=Spittle-Controller` in the case of the `SpittleController` MBean). The value of entry is a reference to the Spring-managed bean that's to be exported. Here, you're exporting the `spittleController` bean so that its properties can be managed at runtime through JMX.

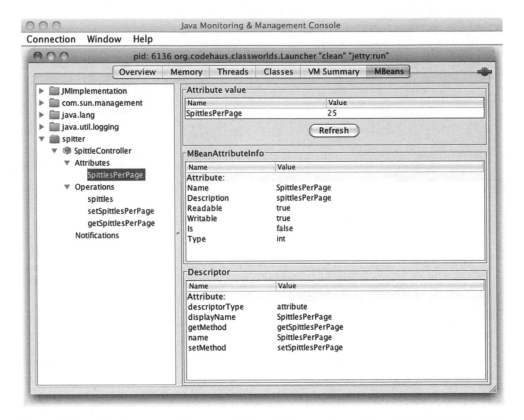

Figure 20.2   `SpittleController` exported as an MBean and seen through the eyes of JConsole

With the `MBeanExporter` in place, the `spittleController` bean is exported as a model MBean to the MBean server for management under the name `Spittle-Controller`. Figure 20.2 shows how the `SpittleController` MBean appears when viewed through JConsole.

As you can see on the left side of figure 20.2, all public members of the `Spittle-Controller` are exported as MBean operations and attributes. This probably isn't what you want. All you really want to do is configure the `spittlesPerPage` property. You don't need to invoke the `spittles()` method or muck about with any other part of `SpittleController`. Thus, you need a way to select which attributes and operations are available.

To gain finer control over an MBean's attributes and operations, Spring offers a few options, including the following:

- Declaring bean methods that are to be exposed/ignored by name
- Fronting the bean with an interface to select the exposed methods
- Annotating the bean to designate managed attributes and operations

Let's try each of these options to see which best suits the `SpittleController` MBean. You'll start by selecting the bean methods to expose by name.

From whence the MBean server?

As configured, `MBeanExporter` assumes that it's running in an application server (such as Tomcat) or some other context that provides an MBean server. But if your Spring application will be running standalone or in a container that doesn't provide an MBean server, you'll want to configure an MBean server in the Spring context.

In XML configuration, the `<context:mbean-server>` element can handle that for you. In Java configuration, you'll need to take a more direct approach and configure a bean of type `MBeanServerFactoryBean()` (which is what `<context:mbean-server>` does for you in XML).

`MBeanServerFactoryBean` creates an MBean server as a bean in the Spring application context. By default, that bean's ID is `mbeanServer`. Knowing this, you can wire it into `MBeanExporter`'s `server` property to specify which MBean server an MBean should be exposed through.

20.1.1 Exposing methods by name

An *MBean info assembler* is the key to constraining which operations and attributes are exported in an MBean. One such MBean info assembler is `MethodNameBasedMBean-InfoAssembler`. This assembler is given a list of names of methods to export as MBean operations. For the `SpittleController` bean, you want to export `spittlesPerPage` as a managed attribute. How can a method name–based assembler help you export a managed attribute?

Recall that per JavaBean rules (not necessarily Spring bean rules), what makes `spittlesPerPage` a property is that it has corresponding accessor methods named `setSpittlesPerPage()` and `getSpittlesPerPage()`. To limit your MBean's exposure, you need to tell `MethodNameBasedMBeanInfoAssembler` to include only those methods in the MBean's interface. The following declaration of a `MethodNameBasedMBean-InfoAssembler` bean singles out those methods:

```
@Bean
public MethodNameBasedMBeanInfoAssembler assembler() {
  MethodNameBasedMBeanInfoAssembler assembler =
          new MethodNameBasedMBeanInfoAssembler();
  assembler.setManagedMethods(new String[] {
    "getSpittlesPerPage", "setSpittlesPerPage"
  });
  return assembler;
}
```

The `managedMethods` property takes a list of method names. Those are the methods that will be exposed as the MBean's managed operations. Because they're property accessor methods, they will also result in a `spittlesPerPage` managed attribute on the MBean.

To put the assembler into action, you need to wire it into the `MBeanExporter`:

```
@Bean
public MBeanExporter mbeanExporter(
      SpittleController spittleController,
      MBeanInfoAssembler assembler) {
  MBeanExporter exporter = new MBeanExporter();
  Map<String, Object> beans = new HashMap<String, Object>();
  beans.put("spitter:name=SpittleController", spittleController);
  exporter.setBeans(beans);
  exporter.setAssembler(assembler);
  return exporter;
}
```

Now, if you fire up the application, `SpittleController`'s `spittlesPerPage` is available as a managed attribute, but the `spittles()` method isn't exposed as a managed operation. Figure 20.3 shows what this looks like in JConsole.

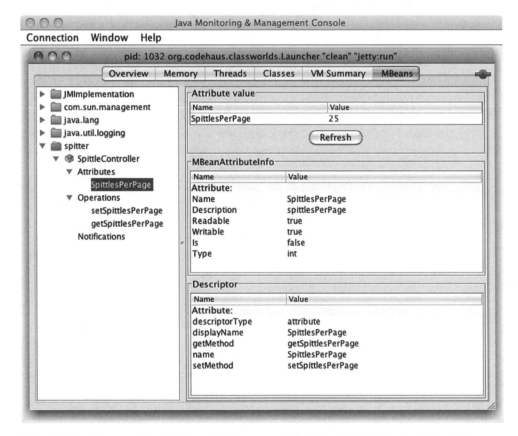

Figure 20.3   After specifying which methods are exported in the `SpittleController` MBean, the `spittles()` method is no longer a managed operation.

Another method name–based assembler to consider is `MethodExclusionMBeanInfo-Assembler`. This MBean info assembler is the inverse of `MethodNameBasedMBean-InfoAssembler`. Rather than specifying which methods to expose as managed operations, `MethodExclusionMBeanInfoAssembler` is given a list of methods to *not* reveal as managed operations. For example, here's how to use `MethodExclusion-MBeanInfoAssembler` to keep `spittles()` out of consideration as a managed operation:

```
@Bean
public MethodExclusionMBeanInfoAssembler assembler() {
  MethodExclusionMBeanInfoAssembler assembler =
        new MethodExclusionMBeanInfoAssembler();
  assembler.setIgnoredMethods(new String[] {
      "spittles"
  });
  return assembler;
}
```

Method name–based assemblers are straightforward and easy to use. But can you imagine what would happen if you were to export several Spring beans as MBeans? After a while, the list of method names given to the assembler would be huge. And there's also a possibility that you may want to export a method from one bean while another bean has a same-named method that you don't want to export.

Clearly, in terms of Spring configuration, the method-name approach doesn't scale well when exporting multiple MBeans. Let's see if using interfaces to expose MBean operations and attributes is any better.

20.1.2 *Using interfaces to define MBean operations and attributes*

Spring's `InterfaceBasedMBeanInfoAssembler` is another MBean info assembler that lets you use interfaces to pick and choose which methods on a bean are exported as MBean-managed operations. It's similar to the method name–based assemblers, except that instead of listing method names to be exported, you list interfaces that define the methods to be exported.

For example, suppose I define an interface named `SpittleControllerManaged-Operations` like this:

```
package com.habuma.spittr.jmx;

public interface SpittleControllerManagedOperations {
  int getSpittlesPerPage();
  void setSpittlesPerPage(int spittlesPerPage);
}
```

Here I've selected the `setSpittlesPerPage()` and `getSpittlesPerPage()` methods as the operations I want to export. Again, these accessor methods will indirectly export the `spittlesPerPage` property as a managed attribute. To use this assembler, I just need to use the following `assembler` bean instead of the method name–based assemblers from before:

```
@Bean
public InterfaceBasedMBeanInfoAssembler assembler() {
  InterfaceBasedMBeanInfoAssembler assembler =
        new InterfaceBasedMBeanInfoAssembler();
  assembler.setManagedInterfaces(
     new Class<?>[] { SpittleControllerManagedOperations.class }
  );
  return assembler;
}
```

The `managedInterfaces` property takes a list of one or more interfaces that serve as the MBean-managed operation interfaces—in this case, the `SpittleController-ManagedOperations` interface.

What may not be apparent, but is certainly interesting, is that `SpittleController` doesn't have to explicitly implement `SpittleControllerManagedOperations`. The interface is there for the sake of the exporter, but you don't need to implement it directly in any of your code. `SpittleController` probably should implement the interface, though, if for no other reason than to enforce a consistent contract between the MBean and the implementation class.

The nice thing about using interfaces to select managed operations is that you can collect dozens of methods into a few interfaces and keep the configuration of `InterfaceBasedMBeanInfoAssembler` clean. This goes a long way toward keeping the Spring configuration tidy even when exporting multiple MBeans.

Ultimately, those managed operations must be declared somewhere, whether in Spring configuration or in an interface. Moreover, the declaration of the managed operations represents a duplication in code: method names declared in an interface or Spring context and method names in the implementation. This duplication exists for no other reason than to satisfy the `MBeanExporter`.

One of the things that Java annotations are good at is helping to eliminate such duplication. Let's see how to annotate a Spring-managed bean so that it can be exported as an MBean.

20.1.3 *Working with annotation-driven MBeans*

In addition to the MBean info assemblers you've seen thus far, Spring provides another assembler known as `MetadataMBeanInfoAssembler` that can be configured to use annotations to appoint bean methods as managed operations and attributes. I could show you how to use that assembler, but I won't. That's because wiring it up manually is burdensome and not worth the trouble just to be able to use annotations. Instead, I'm going to show you how to use the `<context:mbean-export>` element from Spring's `context` configuration namespace. This handy element wires up an MBean exporter and all the appropriate assemblers to turn on annotation-driven MBeans in Spring. All you have to do is use it instead of the `MBeanExporter` bean that you've been using:

```
<context:mbean-export server="mbeanServer" />
```

Now, to turn any Spring bean into an MBean, all you must do is annotate it with `@ManagedResource` and annotate its methods with `@ManagedOperation` or `@Managed-Attribute`. For example, the following listing shows how to alter `SpittleController` to be exported as an MBean using annotations.

Listing 20.1 Annotating `SpittleController` to be an MBean

```
package com.habuma.spittr.mvc;
import java.util.Map;
import org.springframework.beans.factory.annotation.Autowired;
import org.springframework.jmx.export.annotation.ManagedAttribute;
import org.springframework.jmx.export.annotation.ManagedResource;
import org.springframework.stereotype.Controller;
import org.springframework.web.bind.annotation.RequestMapping;
import com.habuma.spittr.service.SpittrService;
@Controller
@ManagedResource(objectName="spitter:name=SpittleController") //       Export
public class SpittleController {                                       SpittleController
  ...                                                                   as an MBean
  @ManagedAttribute   //
  public void setSpittlesPerPage(int spittlesPerPage) {        Expose
    this.spittlesPerPage = spittlesPerPage;                    spittlesPerPage
  }                                                            as a managed
                                                               attribute
  @ManagedAttribute   //
  public int getSpittlesPerPage() {
    return spittlesPerPage;
  }
}
```

The `@ManagedResource` annotation is applied at the class level to indicate that this bean should be exported as an MBean. The `objectName` attribute indicates the domain (`spitter`) and name (`SpittleController`) of the MBean.

The accessor methods for the `spittlesPerPage` property are both annotated with `@ManagedAttribute` to indicate that it should be exposed as a managed attribute. Note that it's not strictly necessary to annotate both accessor methods. If you choose to only annotate the `setSpittlesPerPage()` method, then you can still set the property through JMX, but you won't be able to see what its value is. Conversely, annotating `getSpittlesPerPage()` enables the property's value to be viewed as read-only via JMX.

Also note that it's possible to annotate the accessor methods with `@Managed-Operation` instead of `@ManagedAttribute`. For example,

```
@ManagedOperation
public void setSpittlesPerPage(int spittlesPerPage) {
  this.spittlesPerPage = spittlesPerPage;
}

@ManagedOperation
public int getSpittlesPerPage() {
  return spittlesPerPage;
}
```

This exposes those methods through JMX, but it doesn't expose the `spittlesPerPage` property as a managed attribute. That's because methods annotated with `@Managed-Operation` are treated strictly as methods and not as JavaBean accessors when it comes to exposing MBean functionality. Thus, `@ManagedOperation` should be reserved for exposing methods as MBean operations, and `@ManagedAttribute` should be used when exposing managed attributes.

20.1.4 *Handling MBean collisions*

So far you've seen how to publish an MBean into an MBean server using several approaches. In all cases, you've given the MBean an object name that's made up of a management domain name and a key-value pair. Assuming that there's not already an MBean published with the name you've given your MBean, you should have no trouble publishing your MBean. But what happens if there's a name collision?

By default, `MBeanExporter` throws an `InstanceAlreadyExistsException` if you try to export an MBean that's named the same as an MBean that's already in the MBean server. But you can change that behavior by specifying how the collision should be handled via the `MBeanExporter`'s `registrationBehaviorName` property or through `<context:mbean-export>`'s `registration` attribute.

There are three ways to handle an MBean name collision via the `registration-Policy` property:

- `FAIL_ON_EXISTING`—Fail if an existing MBean has the same name (this is the default behavior).
- `IGNORE_EXISTING`—Ignore the collision and don't register the new MBean.
- `REPLACING_EXISTING`—Replace the existing MBean with the new MBean.

For example, if you're using `MBeanExporter`, you can configure it to ignore collisions by setting the `registrationPolicy` property to `RegistrationPolicy.IGNORE _EXISTING`, like this:

```
@Bean
public MBeanExporter mbeanExporter(
      SpittleController spittleController,
      MBeanInfoAssembler assembler) {
  MBeanExporter exporter = new MBeanExporter();
  Map<String, Object> beans = new HashMap<String, Object>();
  beans.put("spitter:name=SpittleController", spittleController);
  exporter.setBeans(beans);
  exporter.setAssembler(assembler);
  exporter.setRegistrationPolicy(RegistrationPolicy.IGNORE_EXISTING);
  return exporter;
}
```

The `registrationPolicy` property accepts a value from the `RegistrationPolicy` enum representing one of the three collision-handling behaviors available.

Now that you've registered your MBeans using MBeanExporter, you need a way to access them for management. As you've seen already, you can use tools like JConsole to access a local MBean server to view and manipulate MBeans. But a tool such as JConsole doesn't lend itself to programmatic management of MBeans. How can you manipulate MBeans in one application from within another application? Fortunately, there's another way to access MBeans as remote objects. Let's explore how Spring's support for remote MBeans enables you to access your MBeans in a standard way through a remote interface.

20.2 Remoting MBeans

Although the original JMX specification referred to remote management of applications through MBeans, it didn't define the actual remoting protocol or API. Consequently, it fell to JMX vendors to define their own, often proprietary, remoting solutions for JMX.

In response to the need for a standard for remote JMX, the Java Community Process produced JSR-160, the Java Management Extensions Remote API Specification. This specification defines a standard for JMX remoting, which at a minimum requires an RMI binding and optionally the *JMX Messaging Protocol* (JMXMP).

In this section, you'll see how Spring enables remote MBeans. You'll start by configuring Spring to export the `SpittleController` MBean as a remote MBean. Then you'll see how to use Spring to manipulate that MBean remotely.

20.2.1 Exposing remote MBeans

The simplest thing you can do to make your MBeans available as remote objects is to configure Spring's `ConnectorServerFactoryBean`:

```
@Bean
public ConnectorServerFactoryBean connectorServerFactoryBean() {
  return new ConnectorServerFactoryBean();
}
```

`ConnectorServerFactoryBean` creates and starts a JSR-160 `JMXConnectorServer`. By default, the server listens for the JMXMP protocol on port 9875—thus, it's bound to `service:jmx:jmxmp://localhost:9875`. But you're not limited to exporting MBeans using only JMXMP.

Depending on the JMX implementation, you may have several remoting protocol options to choose from, including Remote Method Invocation (RMI), SOAP, Hessian/Burlap, and even Internet InterORB Protocol (IIOP). To specify a different remote binding for your MBeans, you need to set the `serviceUrl` property of `Connector-ServerFactoryBean`. For example, if you want to use RMI for MBean remoting, you'd set `serviceUrl` like this:

```
@Bean
public ConnectorServerFactoryBean connectorServerFactoryBean() {
  ConnectorServerFactoryBean csfb = new ConnectorServerFactoryBean();
  csfb.setServiceUrl(
      "service:jmx:rmi://localhost/jndi/rmi://localhost:1099/spitter");
  return csfb;
}
```

Here, you're binding the `ConnectorServerFactoryBean` to an RMI registry listening on port 1099 of the localhost. That means you also need an RMI registry running and listening at that port. As you'll recall from chapter 15, `RmiServiceExporter` can start an RMI registry automatically for you. But in this case, you're not using `RmiService-Exporter`, so you need to start an RMI registry by declaring an `RmiRegistryFactory-Bean` in Spring with the following `@Bean` method:

```
@Bean
public RmiRegistryFactoryBean rmiRegistryFB() {
  RmiRegistryFactoryBean rmiRegistryFB = new RmiRegistryFactoryBean();
  rmiRegistryFB.setPort(1099);
  return rmiRegistryFB;
}
```

And that's it! Now your MBeans are available through RMI. But there's little point in doing this if nobody will ever access the MBeans over RMI. Let's turn our attention to the client side of JMX remoting and see how to wire up a remote MBean in the Spring context of a JMX client.

20.2.2 *Accessing remote MBeans*

Accessing a remote MBean server involves configuring an `MBeanServerConnection-FactoryBean` in the Spring context. The following bean declaration sets up an `MBean-ServerConnectionFactoryBean` that can be used to access the RMI-based remote server you created in the previous section:

```
@Bean
public MBeanServerConnectionFactoryBean connectionFactoryBean() {
  MBeanServerConnectionFactoryBean mbscfb =
          new MBeanServerConnectionFactoryBean();
  mbscfb.setServiceUrl(
      "service:jmx:rmi://localhost/jndi/rmi://localhost:1099/spitter");
  return mbscfb;
}
```

As its name implies, `MBeanServerConnectionFactoryBean` is a factory bean that creates an `MBeanServerConnection`. The `MBeanServerConnection` produced by `MBean-ServerConnectionFactoryBean` acts as a local proxy to the remote MBean server. It can be wired into a bean property as an `MBeanServerConnection`:

```
@Bean
public JmxClient jmxClient(MBeanServerConnection connection) {
  JmxClient jmxClient = new JmxClient();
  jmxClient.setMbeanServerConnection(connection);
  return jmxClient;
}
```

`MBeanServerConnection` provides several methods that let you query the remote MBean server and invoke methods on the MBeans contained therein. For example, say that you'd like to know how many MBeans are registered in the remote MBean server. The following code snippet prints that information:

```
int mbeanCount = mbeanServerConnection.getMBeanCount();
System.out.println("There are " + mbeanCount + " MBeans");
```

You can also query the remote server for the names of all the MBeans using the queryNames() method:

```
java.util.Set mbeanNames = mbeanServerConnection.queryNames(null, null);
```

The two parameters passed to queryNames() are used to refine the results. Passing in null for both parameters indicates that you're asking for the names of all the registered MBeans.

Querying the remote MBean server for bean counts and names is fun, but doesn't get much work done. The real value of accessing an MBean server remotely is found in accessing attributes and invoking operations on the MBeans that are registered in the remote server.

For accessing MBean attributes, you'll want to use the getAttribute() and setAttribute() methods. For example, to retrieve the value of an MBean attribute, you'd call the getAttribute() method like so:

```
String cronExpression = mbeanServerConnection.getAttribute(
    new ObjectName("spitter:name=SpittleController"), "spittlesPerPage");
```

Similarly, you can change the value of an MBean attribute using the setAttribute() method:

```
mbeanServerConnection.setAttribute(
    new ObjectName("spitter:name=SpittleController"),
    new Attribute("spittlesPerPage", 10));
```

If you'd like to invoke an MBean's operation, the invoke() method is what you're looking for. Here's how you might invoke the setSpittlesPerPage() method on the SpittleController MBean:

```
mbeanServerConnection.invoke(
    new ObjectName("spitter:name=SpittleController"),
    "setSpittlesPerPage",
    new Object[] { 100 },
    new String[] {"int"});
```

You can do dozens of other things with remote MBeans by using the methods available through MBeanServerConnection. I'll leave it to you to explore the possibilities. But invoking methods and setting attributes on remote MBeans is awkward when done through MBeanServerConnection. Doing something as simple as calling the setSpittlesPerPage() method involves creating an ObjectName instance and passing several other parameters to the invoke() method. This isn't nearly as intuitive as a normal method invocation would be. For a more direct approach, you need to proxy the remote MBean.

20.2.3 *Proxying MBeans*

Spring's `MBeanProxyFactoryBean` is a proxy factory bean in the same vein as the remoting proxy factory beans we examined in chapter 15. But instead of providing proxy-based access to remote Spring-managed beans, `MBeanProxyFactoryBean` lets you access remote MBeans directly (as if they were any other locally configured bean). Figure 20.4 illustrates how this works.

For example, consider the following declaration of `MBeanProxyFactoryBean`:

```
@Bean
public MBeanProxyFactoryBean remoteSpittleControllerMBean(
        MBeanServerConnection mbeanServerClient) {
  MBeanProxyFactoryBean proxy = new MBeanProxyFactoryBean();
  proxy.setObjectName("");
  proxy.setServer(mbeanServerClient);
  proxy.setProxyInterface(SpittleControllerManagedOperations.class);
  return proxy;
}
```

The `objectName` property specifies the object name of the remote MBean that's to be proxied locally. Here it's referring to the `SpittleController` MBean that you exported earlier.

The `server` property refers to an `MBeanServerConnection` through which all communication with the MBean is routed. Here you've wired in the `MBeanServer-ConnectionFactoryBean` that you configured earlier.

Finally, the `proxyInterface` property specifies the interface that will be implemented by the proxy. In this case, you're using the same `SpittleControllerManaged-Operations` interface that you defined in section 20.1.2.

With the `remoteSpittleControllerMBean` bean declared, you can now wire it into any bean property whose type is `SpittleControllerManagedOperations` and use it to access the remote MBean. From there, you can invoke the `setSpittlesPerPage()` and `getSpittlesPerPage()` methods.

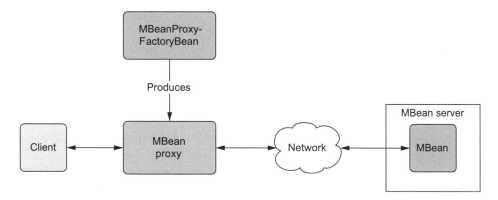

Figure 20.4 `MBeanProxyFactoryBean` produces a proxy to a remote MBean. The proxy's client can then interact with the remote MBean as if it were a locally configured POJO.

You've seen several ways that you can communicate with MBeans, and you can now view and tweak your Spring bean configuration while the application is running. But thus far it's been a one-sided conversation. You've talked to the MBeans, but the MBeans haven't been able to get a word in edgewise. It's time for you to hear what they have to say by listening for notifications.

20.3 Handling notifications

Querying an MBean for information is only one way of keeping an eye on the state of an application. But it's not the most efficient way to be informed of significant events within the application.

For example, suppose the Spittr application were to keep a count of how many spittles have been posted. And suppose you want to know every time the count has increased by one million spittles (the one millionth spittle, the two millionth, the three millionth, and so on). One way to handle this

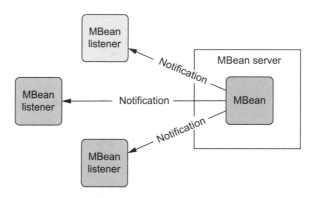

Figure 20.5 JMX notifications enable MBeans to communicate proactively with the outside world.

would be to write some code that periodically queried the database, counting the number of spittles. But the process that performed that query would keep itself and the database busy as it constantly checked for the spittle count.

Instead of repeatedly querying the database to get that information, a better approach may be to have an MBean notify you when the momentous occasion takes place. JMX notifications, as illustrated in figure 20.5, are a way that MBeans can communicate with the outside world proactively, instead of waiting for some external application to query them for information.

Spring's support for sending notifications comes in the form of the `Notification-PublisherAware` interface. Any bean-turned-MBean that wishes to send notifications should implement this interface. For example, consider `SpittleNotifierImpl` in the next listing.

Listing 20.2 Using a `NotificationPublisher` to send JMX notifications

```
package com.habuma.spittr.jmx;
import javax.management.Notification;
import org.springframework.jmx.export.annotation.ManagedNotification;
import org.springframework.jmx.export.annotation.ManagedResource;
import
org.springframework.jmx.export.notification.NotificationPublisher;
import
org.springframework.jmx.export.notification.NotificationPublisherAware;
```

```
import org.springframework.stereotype.Component;
@Component                                                    Implement
@ManagedResource("spitter:name=SpitterNotifier")    NotificationPublisherAware
@ManagedNotification(
        notificationTypes="SpittleNotifier.OneMillionSpittles",
        name="TODO")
public class SpittleNotifierImpl
    implements NotificationPublisherAware, SpittleNotifier {  ◁——

  private NotificationPublisher notificationPublisher;       Inject notification
                                                             publisher
  public void setNotificationPublisher(            ◁—┘
          NotificationPublisher notificationPublisher) {
    this.notificationPublisher = notificationPublisher;
  }

  public void millionthSpittlePosted() {
    notificationPublisher.sendNotification(        ◁—— Send notification
            new Notification(
                    "SpittleNotifier.OneMillionSpittles", this, 0));
  }

}
```

As you can see, `SpittleNotifierImpl` implements `NotificationPublisherAware`. This isn't a demanding interface. It requires only that a single method be implemented: `setNotificationPublisher`.

`SpittleNotifierImpl` also implements a single method from the `SpittleNotifier` interface, `millionthSpittlePosted()`. This method uses the `NotificationPublisher` that's automatically injected via the `setNotificationPublisher()` method to send a notification that another million spittles have been posted.

Once the `sendNotification()` method has been called, the notification is on its way to … hmm … it seems that you haven't yet decided who will receive the notification. Let's set up a notification listener to listen to and react to the notification.

20.3.1 *Listening for notifications*

The standard way to receive MBean notifications is to implement the `javax .management.NotificationListener` interface. For example, consider `Paging-NotificationListener`:

```
package com.habuma.spittr.jmx;
import javax.management.Notification;
import javax.management.NotificationListener;
public class PagingNotificationListener
        implements NotificationListener {

  public void handleNotification(
          Notification notification, Object handback) {
    // ...
  }

}
```

PagingNotificationListener is a typical JMX notification listener. When a notification is received, its handleNotification() method is invoked to react to the notification. Presumably, PagingNotificationListener's handleNotification() method will send a message to a pager or cell phone about the fact that another million spittles have been posted. (I've left the actual implementation to your imagination.)

The only thing left to do is register PagingNotificationListener with the MBean-Exporter:

```
@Bean
public MBeanExporter mbeanExporter() {
  MBeanExporter exporter = new MBeanExporter();
  Map<?, NotificationListener> mappings =
          new HashMap<?, NotificationListener>();
  mappings.put("Spitter:name=PagingNotificationListener",
              new PagingNotificationListener());
  exporter.setNotificationListenerMappings(mappings);
  return exporter;
}
```

MBeanExporter's notificationListenerMappings property is used to map notification listeners to the MBeans they will be listening to. In this case, you set up Paging-NotificationListener to listen to any notifications published by the SpittleNotifier MBean.

20.4 *Summary*

With JMX, you can open a window into the inner workings of your application. In this chapter, you saw how to configure Spring to automatically export Spring beans as JMX MBeans so that their details can be viewed and manipulated through JMX-ready management tools. You also learned how to create and use remote MBeans for times when those MBeans and tools are distant from each other. Finally, you saw how to use Spring to publish and listen for JMX notifications.

By now you've probably noticed that the number of remaining pages in this book is dwindling fast. Your journey through Spring is almost complete. But before we conclude, we have one more quick stop to make. In the next chapter, we'll look at Spring Boot, an exciting new way to build Spring applications with little or no explicit configuration.

21

Simplifying Spring development with Spring Boot

This chapter covers

- Adding project dependencies with Spring Boot starters
- Automatic bean configuration
- Groovy and the Spring Boot CLI
- The Spring Boot Actuator

I recall the first few days of my first calculus course where we learned about derivatives of functions. We performed some rather hairy computations using limits to arrive at the derivatives of several functions. Even though the functions were simple, the work involved in calculating the derivatives was nightmarish.

After several homework assignments, study groups, and an exam, most everyone in the class was able to do the work. But the tedium of it was nearly unbearable. If this was the first thing we'd learn in a class named "Calculus I," then what monstrosity of mathematics awaited us mid-semester in "Calculus II"?

Then the instructor clued us in on a trick. Applying a simple formula made quick work of calculating derivatives (if you've ever taken calculus, you'll know what

I'm talking about). With this newfound trick, we were able to compute derivatives for dozens of functions in the time it would've previously taken for a single function.

At this point, one of my classmates spoke up and said what the rest of us were thinking: "Why didn't you show us this on the first day?!?!"

The instructor replied that the hard way helped us appreciate the derivatives for what they mean, told us it built character, and said something about putting hair on our chests.

Now that we've gone through an entire book on Spring, I find myself in the same position as that calculus instructor. Although Spring's chief benefit is to make Java development easy, this chapter will show you how Spring Boot can make it even easier. Spring Boot is arguably the most exciting thing to happen to Spring since the Spring Framework was first created. It layers a completely new development model on top of Spring, taking away much of the tedium of developing applications with Spring.

We'll get started with an overview of the tricks that Spring Boot employs to simplify Spring. Before this chapter concludes, you'll have developed a complete (albeit simple) application using Spring Boot.

21.1 Introducing Spring Boot

Spring Boot is an exciting (dare I say "game-changing"?) new project in the Spring family. It offers four main features that will change the way you develop Spring applications:

- *Spring Boot starters*—Spring Boot starters aggregate common groupings of dependencies into single dependencies that can be added to a project's Maven or Gradle build.
- *Autoconfiguration*—Spring Boot's autoconfiguration feature leverages Spring 4's support for conditional configuration to make reasonable guesses about the beans your application needs and automatically configure them.
- *Command-line interface (CLI)*—Spring Boot's CLI takes advantage of the Groovy programming language along with autoconfiguration to further simplify Spring application development.
- *Actuator*—The Spring Boot Actuator adds certain management features to a Spring Boot application.

Throughout this chapter, you'll build a small application using all of these features of Spring Boot. But first, let's take a quick look at each to get a better feel for how they contribute to a simpler Spring programming model.

21.1.1 Adding starter dependencies

There are two ways to bake a cake. The ambitious baker will mix flour, eggs, sugar, baking powder, salt, butter, vanilla, and milk into a batter. Or you can buy a prepackaged box of cake mix that includes most of the ingredients you'll need and only mix in a few wet ingredients like water, eggs, and vegetable oil.

Much as a prepackaged cake mix aggregates many of the ingredients of a cake recipe into a single ingredient, Spring Boot starters aggregate the various dependencies of an application into a single dependency.

To illustrate, let's suppose you're starting a new Spring project from scratch. This will be a web project, so you'll need Spring MVC. There will also be a REST API, exposing resources as JSON, so you'll need the Jackson JSON library in your build.

Because your application will use JDBC to store and fetch data from a relational database, you'll want to be sure to include Spring's JDBC module (for `JdbcTemplate`) and Spring's transaction module (for declarative transaction support). As for the database itself, the H2 database will do fine.

And, oh yeah, you want to use Thymeleaf for Spring MVC views.

If you're building your project with Gradle, you'll need (at least) the following dependencies in build.gradle:

```
dependencies {
  compile("org.springframework:spring-web:4.0.6.RELEASE")
  compile("org.springframework:spring-webmvc:4.0.6.RELEASE")
  compile("com.fasterxml.jackson.core:jackson-databind:2.2.2")
  compile("org.springframework:spring-jdbc:4.0.6.RELEASE")
  compile("org.springframework:spring-tx:4.0.6.RELEASE")
  compile("com.h2database:h2:1.3.174")
  compile("org.thymeleaf:thymeleaf-spring4:2.1.2.RELEASE")
}
```

Fortunately, Gradle makes it possible to express dependencies succinctly. (For the sake of brevity, I won't bother showing you what this list of dependencies would look like in a Maven pom.xml file.) Even so, a lot of work went into creating this list, and more will go into maintaining it. How can you know if these dependencies will play well together? As the application grows and evolves, dependency management will become even more challenging.

But if you're using the prepackaged dependencies from Spring Boot starters, the Gradle dependency list can be a little shorter:

```
dependencies {
  compile("org.springframework.boot:spring-boot-starter-web:
          1.1.4.RELEASE")
  compile("org.springframework.boot:spring-boot-starter-jdbc:
          1.1.4.RELEASE")
  compile("com.h2database:h2:1.3.174")
  compile("org.thymeleaf:thymeleaf-spring4:2.1.2.RELEASE")
}
```

As you can see, Spring Boot's web and JDBC starters replaced several of the finer-grained dependencies. You still need to include the H2 and Thymeleaf dependencies, but the other dependencies are rolled up into the starter dependencies. Aside from making the dependency list shorter, you can feel confident that the versions of dependencies provided by the starters are compatible with each other.

The web and JDBC starters are just two of the starters that Spring Boot has to offer. Table 21.1 lists all of the starters available at the time I was writing this chapter.

Table 21.1   Spring Boot starter dependencies aggregate commonly needed dependency groupings into single project dependencies.

Starter	Provides
spring-boot-starter-actuator	spring-boot-starter, spring-boot-actuator, spring-core
spring-boot-starter-amqp	spring-boot-starter, spring-boot-rabbit, spring-core, spring-tx
spring-boot-starter-aop	spring-boot-starter, spring-aop, AspectJ Runtime, AspectJ Weaver, spring-core
spring-boot-starter-batch	spring-boot-starter, HSQLDB, spring-jdbc, spring-batch-core, spring-core
spring-boot-starter-elasticsearch	spring-boot-starter, spring-data-elasticsearch, spring-core, spring-tx
spring-boot-starter-gemfire	spring-boot-starter, Gemfire, spring-core, spring-tx, spring-context, spring-context-support, spring-data-gemfire
spring-boot-starter-data-jpa	spring-boot-starter, spring-boot-starter-jdbc, spring-boot-starter-aop, spring-core, Hibernate EntityManager, spring-orm, spring-data-jpa, spring-aspects
spring-boot-starter-data-mongodb	spring-boot-starter, MongoDB Java driver, spring-core, spring-tx, spring-data-mongodb
spring-boot-starter-data-rest	spring-boot-starter, spring-boot-starter-web, Jackson annotations, Jackson databind, spring-core, spring-tx, spring-data-rest-webmvc
spring-boot-starter-data-solr	spring-boot-starter, Solrj, spring-core, spring-tx, spring-data-solr, Apache HTTP Mime
spring-boot-starter-freemarker	spring-boot-starter, spring-boot-starter-web, Freemarker, spring-core, spring-context-support
spring-boot-starter-groovy-templates	spring-boot-starter, spring-boot-starter-web, Groovy, Groovy Templates spring-core
spring-boot-starter-hornetq	spring-boot-starter, spring-core, spring-jms, Hornet JMS Client

Table 21.1   Spring Boot starter dependencies aggregate commonly needed dependency groupings into single project dependencies. *(continued)*

Starter	Provides
spring-boot-starter-integration	spring-boot-starter, spring-aop, spring-tx, spring-web, spring-webmvc, spring-integration-core, spring-integration-file, spring-integration-http, spring-integration-ip, spring-integration-stream
spring-boot-starter-jdbc	spring-boot-starter, spring-jdbc, tomcat-jdbc, spring-tx
spring-boot-starter-jetty	jetty-webapp, jetty-jsp
spring-boot-starter-log4j	jcl-over-slf4j, jul-to-slf4j, slf4j-log4j12, log4j
spring-boot-starter-logging	jcl-over-slf4j, jul-to-slf4j, log4j-over-slf4j, logback-classic
spring-boot-starter-mobile	spring-boot-starter, spring-boot-starter-web, spring-mobile-device
spring-boot-starter-redis	spring-boot-starter, spring-data-redis, lettuce
spring-boot-starter-remote-shell	spring-boot-starter-actuator, spring-context, org.crashub.**
spring-boot-starter-security	spring-boot-starter, spring-security-config, spring-security-web, spring-aop, spring-beans, spring-context, spring-core, spring-expression, spring-web
spring-boot-starter-social-facebook	spring-boot-starter, spring-boot-starter-web, spring-core, spring-social-config, spring-social-core, spring-social-web, spring-social-facebook
spring-boot-starter-social-twitter	spring-boot-starter, spring-boot-starter-web, spring-core, spring-social-config, spring-social-core, spring-social-web, spring-social-twitter

Table 21.1 Spring Boot starter dependencies aggregate commonly needed dependency groupings into single project dependencies. *(continued)*

Starter	Provides

`spring-boot-starter-social-linkedin`	`spring-boot-starter,`
	`spring-boot-starter-web, spring-core,`
	`spring-social-config,`
	`spring-social-core,`
	`spring-social-web,`
	`spring-social-linkedin`

`spring-boot-starter`	`spring-boot,`
	`spring-boot-autoconfigure,`
	`spring-boot-starter-logging`

`spring-boot-starter-test`	`spring-boot-starter-logging,`
	`spring-boot, junit, mockito-core,`
	`hamcrest-library, spring-test`

`spring-boot-starter-thymeleaf`	`spring-boot-starter,`
	`spring-boot-starter-web, spring-core,`
	`thymeleaf-spring4,`
	`thymeleaf-layout-dialect`

`spring-boot-starter-tomcat`	`tomcat-embed-core,` `tomcat-embed-logging-juli`

`spring-boot-starter-web`	`spring-boot-starter,`
	`spring-boot-starter-tomcat,`
	`jackson-databind, spring-web,`
	`spring-webmvc`

`spring-boot-starter-websocket`	`spring-boot-starter-web,`
	`spring-websocket, tomcat-embed-core,`
	`tomcat-embed-logging-juli`

`spring-boot-starter-ws`	`spring-boot-starter,`
	`spring-boot-starter-web, spring-core,`
	`spring-jms, spring-oxm,`
	`spring-ws-core, spring-ws-support`

If you were to look under the covers of these starter dependencies, you'd realize that there's not much mystery to how the starters work. Taking advantage of Maven's and Gradle's transitive dependency resolution, the starters declare several dependencies in their own pom.xml file. When you add one of these starter dependencies to your Maven or Gradle build, the starter's dependencies are resolved transitively. And those dependencies may have dependencies of their own. A single starter could transitively pull in dozens of other dependencies.

Notice that many of the starters reference other starters. The mobile starter, for instance, references the web starter, which in turn references the Tomcat starter. And most of the starters reference `spring-boot-starter`, which is essentially a base starter (although it references the logging starter). The dependencies are transitively applied; adding the mobile starter as a dependency will effectively add dependencies from all of the starters down the line.

21.1.2 *Autoconfiguration*

Whereas Spring Boot starters cut down the size of your build's dependency list, Spring Boot autoconfiguration cuts down on the amount of Spring configuration. It does this by considering other factors in your application and making assumptions about what Spring configuration you'll need.

As an example, recall from chapter 6 (listing 6.4) that you'll need at least three beans to enable Thymeleaf templates as views in Spring MVC: a `ThymeleafView-Resolver`, a `SpringTemplateEngine`, and a `TemplateResolver`. With Spring Boot autoconfiguration, however, all you need to do is add Thymeleaf to the project's classpath. When Spring Boot detects that Thymeleaf is on the classpath, it will assume that you want to use Thymeleaf for Spring MVC views and will automatically configure those three beans.

Spring Boot starters can trigger autoconfiguration. For instance, all you need to do to use Spring MVC in your Spring Boot application is to add the web starter as a dependency in the build. When you add the web starter to your project's build, it will transitively pull in Spring MVC dependencies. When Spring Boot's web autoconfiguration detects Spring MVC in the classpath, it will automatically configure several beans to support Spring MVC, including view resolvers, resource handlers, and message converters (among others). All that's left for you to do is write the controller classes to handle the requests.

21.1.3 *The Spring Boot CLI*

The Spring Boot CLI takes the magic provided by Spring Boot starters and autoconfiguration and spices it up a little with Groovy. It reduces the Spring development process to the point where you can run one or more Groovy scripts through a CLI and see it run. In the course of running the application, the CLI will also automatically import Spring types and resolve dependencies.

One of the most interesting examples used to illustrate Spring Boot CLI is contained in the following Groovy script:

```
@RestController
class Hi {
  @RequestMapping("/")
  String hi() {
        "Hi!"
  }
}
```

Believe it or not, that is a complete (albeit simple) Spring application that can be executed through the Spring Boot CLI. Including whitespace, it's 82 characters in length. You can paste it into your Twitter client and tweet it to your friends.

Eliminate the unnecessary whitespace and you get this 64-character one-liner:

```
@RestController class Hi{@RequestMapping("/")String hi(){"Hi!"}}
```

This version is so brief that you can paste it *twice* into a single tweet on Twitter. But it's still a complete and runnable (if feature-poor) Spring application. If you have the Spring Boot CLI installed, you can run it with the following command line:

```
$ spring run Hi.groovy
```

Although it's fun to show off a tweetable example of Spring Boot CLI's capabilities, there's much more to it than meets the eye. In section 21.3 we'll look at how you can build a more complete application with Groovy and the CLI.

21.1.4 *The Actuator*

The Spring Boot Actuator brings a handful of useful features to a Spring Boot project, including

- Management endpoints
- Sensible error handling and a default mapping for an /error endpoint
- An /info endpoint that can communicate information about an application
- An audit events framework when Spring Security is in play

All of these features are useful, but the management endpoints are the most immediately useful and interesting features of the Actuator. In section 21.4 we'll look at a few examples of how Spring Boot's Actuator opens a window into the inner workings of your application.

Now that you've had a glimpse of each of the four main features of Spring Boot, let's put them to work and build a small but complete application.

21.2 *Building an application with Spring Boot*

Throughout the rest of this chapter, I aim to show you how to build complete, real-world applications using Spring Boot. Of course, the qualities that define a "real-world" application are subject to debate and would likely exceed the space and scope of this chapter. Therefore, rather than build a real-world application here, we'll scale it back a little and develop something a little less real-world, but representative of the kinds of bigger applications you might build with Spring Boot.

Our application will be a simple contact-list application. It will allow a user to enter contact information (name, phone number, email address) and to list all of the contacts that the user has previously entered.

You have the choice of building your application with either Maven or Gradle. I prefer Gradle, but I'll show you what's needed for Maven in case that's your preference. The following listing shows the starter build.gradle file. The dependencies block is empty to start, but we'll fill it in with dependencies along the way.

Listing 21.1   The Gradle build file for the Contacts application

```
buildscript {
  repositories {
    mavenLocal()
  }
  dependencies {
    classpath("org.springframework.boot:spring-boot-gradle-plugin:
          1.1.4.RELEASE")
  }
}

apply plugin: 'java'                              Use the Spring
apply plugin: 'spring-boot'          ⟵┘          Boot plugin

jar {                        ⟵── Build a JAR file
  baseName = 'contacts'
  version =  '0.1.0'
}

repositories {
  mavenCentral()
}

dependencies {              ⟵── Dependencies will go here

}

task wrapper(type: Wrapper) {
  gradleVersion = '1.8'
}
```

Notice that the build includes a `buildscript` dependency on the Spring Boot Gradle plugin. As you'll see later, this will help produce an executable uber-JAR file that contains all of the application's dependencies.

Alternatively, if you prefer Maven, the following listing shows the complete pom.xml file.

Listing 21.2   The Maven build file for the Contacts application

```
<?xml version="1.0" encoding="UTF-8"?>
<project xmlns="http://maven.apache.org/POM/4.0.0"
    xmlns:xsi="http://www.w3.org/2001/XMLSchema-instance"
    xsi:schemaLocation="http://maven.apache.org/POM/4.0.0
    http://maven.apache.org/xsd/maven-4.0.0.xsd">

  <modelVersion>4.0.0</modelVersion>
  <groupId>com.habuma</groupId>
  <artifactId>contacts</artifactId>
  <version>0.1.0</version>
  <packaging>jar</packaging>          ⟵── Build a JAR file

  <parent>
    <groupId>org.springframework.boot</groupId>          ⟵┐  Inherit from
    <artifactId>spring-boot-starter-parent</artifactId>        Spring Boot
                                                               starter parent
```

```
      <version>1.1.4.RELEASE</version>
   </parent>

   <dependencies>                        ⊲── Dependencies will go here

   </dependencies>

   <build>
      <plugins>
         <plugin>                                    ⊲── Use the Spring Boot plugin
            <groupId>org.springframework.boot</groupId>
         <artifactId>spring-boot-maven-plugin</artifactId>
         </plugin>
      </plugins>
   </build>

</project>
```

Similar to the Gradle build, this Maven pom.xml file makes use of the Spring Boot Maven plugin. This plugin is the Maven counterpart to the Gradle plugin and enables the build to produce an executable uber-JAR file.

Also notice that unlike the Gradle build, this Maven build has a parent project. By basing your project's Maven build on the Spring Boot starter parent, you get the benefit of Maven dependency management, and you won't have to explicitly declare version numbers for many of your project dependencies. The versions will be inherited from the parent.

Following the standard project structure for Maven- and Gradle-based projects, the project will be structured like this when you're finished:

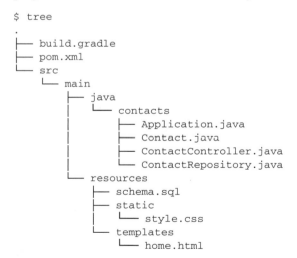

```
$ tree
.
├── build.gradle
├── pom.xml
└── src
    └── main
        ├── java
        │   └── contacts
        │       ├── Application.java
        │       ├── Contact.java
        │       ├── ContactController.java
        │       └── ContactRepository.java
        └── resources
            ├── schema.sql
            ├── static
            │   └── style.css
            └── templates
                └── home.html
```

Don't worry about those missing Java files and other resource files. You'll create those over the next few sections as we develop the Contacts application. In fact, we'll start right now by developing the web layer of the application.

21.2.1 *Handling requests*

Since you're going to develop the web layer of the application with Spring MVC, you're going to need to add Spring MVC as a dependency in your build. As we've already discussed, Spring Boot's web starter is the one-stop-shop for adding everything needed for Spring MVC to a build. This is the Gradle dependency you'll need:

```
compile("org.springframework.boot:spring-boot-starter-web")
```

If you're using Maven to do the build, those dependencies will look like this:

```
<dependency>
  <groupId>org.springframework.boot</groupId>
  <artifactId>spring-boot-starter-web</artifactId>
</dependency>
```

Note that because the Spring Boot parent project specifies the version for the web starter dependency, there's no need to explicitly specify it in the project's build.gradle or pom.xml.

With the web starter dependency in place, all of the dependencies you'll need to work with Spring MVC will be available to your project. Now you're ready to write a controller class for the application.

The controller will be relatively simple, presenting a contact form for an HTTP GET request and processing the form submission for a POST request. It won't do any of the real work itself, but will delegate to a ContactRepository (which you'll create soon) for persisting contacts. The ContactController class in listing 21.3 captures these requirements.

Listing 21.3   ContactController handles basic web requests for the Contacts application

```java
package contacts;
import java.util.List;
import java.util.Map;
import org.springframework.beans.factory.annotation.Autowired;
import org.springframework.stereotype.Controller;
import org.springframework.web.bind.annotation.RequestMapping;
import org.springframework.web.bind.annotation.RequestMethod;

@Controller
@RequestMapping("/")
public class ContactController {
  private ContactRepository contactRepo;                    Inject
                                                  ContactRepository
  @Autowired
  public ContactController(ContactRepository contactRepo) {   ⊲┈┄
    this.contactRepo = contactRepo;
  }

  @RequestMapping(method=RequestMethod.GET)        ⊲┈┄ Handle GET /
   public String home(Map<String,Object> model) {
    List<Contact> contacts = contactRepo.findAll();
    model.put("contacts", contacts);
    return "home";
  }
```

```
@RequestMapping(method=RequestMethod.POST)              ⟵ Handle POST /
  public String submit(Contact contact) {
   contactRepo.save(contact);
   return "redirect:/";
  }
}
```

The first thing you should notice about `ContactController` is that it's a typical Spring MVC controller. Although Spring Boot gets involved when it comes to managing build dependencies and minimizing Spring configuration, the programming model is the same when it comes to writing much of your application logic.

In this case, `ContactController` follows the typical pattern for a Spring MVC controller that displays and handles form submission. The `home()` method uses the injected `ContactRepository` to retrieve a list of all `Contact` objects, placing them into the model before handing the request off to the `home` view. That view will render the list of contacts along with a form to add a new `Contact`. The `submit()` method will handle the `POST` request resulting from the form submission, save the `Contact`, and redirect to the home page.

And because `ContactController` is annotated with `@Controller`, it's subject to component scanning. Therefore, you won't have to explicitly configure it as a bean in the Spring application context.

As for the `Contact` model type, it's just a simple POJO with a handful of properties and accessor methods, as shown in the following listing.

> **Listing 21.4 Contact is a simple domain type.**

```
package contacts;

public class Contact {
  private Long id;                        ⟵ Properties
  private String firstName;
  private String lastName;
  private String phoneNumber;
  private String emailAddress;

  public void setId(Long id) {            ⟵ Accessor methods
    this.id = id;
  }

  public Long getId() {
    return id;
  }

  public void setFirstName(String firstName) {
    this.firstName = firstName;
  }

  public String getFirstName() {
    return firstName;
  }

  public void setLastName(String lastName) {
    this.lastName = lastName;
  }
```

```
  public String getLastName() {
    return lastName;
  }

  public void setPhoneNumber(String phoneNumber) {
    this.phoneNumber = phoneNumber;
  }

  public String getPhoneNumber() {
    return phoneNumber;
  }

  public void setEmailAddress(String emailAddress) {
    this.emailAddress = emailAddress;
  }

  public String getEmailAddress() {
    return emailAddress;
  }
}
```

The web layer of your application is almost finished. All that's left is to create a Thymeleaf template that defines the home view.

21.2.2 *Creating the view*

Traditionally, Java web applications use JSP as the view-layer technology. But as we discussed in chapter 6, there's a new kid in town. Thymeleaf's natural templates are much more pleasant to work with than JSP, and they make it possible for you to write your templates as HTML. Because of that, we're going to use Thymeleaf to define the home view for the Contacts application.

First, you need to add Thymeleaf to your project's build. In this example I'm working with Spring 4, so I need to add Thymeleaf's Spring 4 module to the build. In Gradle, the dependency would look like this:

```
compile("org.thymeleaf:thymeleaf-spring4")
```

If you're using Maven, this is the dependency you'll need:

```
<dependency>
  <groupId>org.thymeleaf</groupId>
  <artifactId>thymeleaf-spring4</artifactId>
</dependency>
```

Keep in mind that by simply adding Thymeleaf to the project's classpath, you're setting Spring Boot autoconfiguration in motion. When the application is run, Spring Boot will detect that Thymeleaf is in the classpath and will automatically configure the view resolver, template resolver, and template engine beans necessary to use Thymeleaf with Spring MVC. Therefore, there's no explicit Spring configuration required to use Thymeleaf in your application.

Aside from adding the Thymeleaf dependency to the build, the only thing you need to do is define the view template. Listing 21.5 shows home.html, a Thymeleaf template that defines the home view.

Listing 21.5 The home view renders a form to create new contacts and to list contacts

```
<!DOCTYPE html>
<html xmlns:th="http://www.thymeleaf.org">
  <head>
    <title>Spring Boot Contacts</title>
    <link rel="stylesheet" th:href="@{/style.css}" />       ⟵— Load stylesheet
  </head>
<body>
  <h2>Spring Boot Contacts</h2>

  <form method="POST">                                        ⟵— New contact form
     <label for="firstName">First Name:</label>
      <input type="text" name="firstName"></input><br/>
    <label for="lastName">Last Name:</label>
      <input type="text" name="lastName"></input><br/>
    <label for="phoneNumber">Phone #:</label>
      <input type="text" name="phoneNumber"></input><br/>
    <label for="emailAddress">Email:</label>
      <input type="text" name="emailAddress"></input><br/>
    <input type="submit"></input>
  </form>

  <ul th:each="contact : ${contacts}">         ⟵— Render list of contacts
    <li>
      <span th:text="${contact.firstName}">First</span>
    <span th:text="${contact.lastName}">Last</span> :
      <span th:text="${contact.phoneNumber}">phoneNumber</span>,
    <span th:text="${contact.emailAddress}">emailAddress</span>
  </li>
  </ul>
  </body>
</html>
```

This is a fairly basic Thymeleaf template. It has two parts: a form and then a list of contacts. The form will POST data back to the submit() method of ContactController to create a new Contact. The list cycles through the list of Contact objects in the model.

In order for this template to be used, you need to be careful to name and place it correctly in your project. Because the logical view name returned from the home() method in ContactController is home, the template file should be named home.html. And because the autoconfigured template resolver will look for Thymeleaf templates under a directory named *templates* relative to the root of the classpath, you'll need to place home.html in the Maven or Gradle project at src/main/resources/templates.

There's only one loose end that needs to be tied up with regard to this Thymeleaf template. The HTML it produces will reference a stylesheet named style.css. Therefore, you need to add that stylesheet to the project.

21.2.3 *Adding static artifacts*

Normally, stylesheets and images are things that I avoid discussing in the context of writing Spring applications. Certainly, those kind of artifacts go a long way toward making any application (including Spring applications) more aesthetically pleasing to a user. But static artifacts aren't critical to the discussion of writing server-side Spring code.

In the case of Spring Boot, however, it's worth mentioning how Spring Boot deals with static content. When Spring Boot's web autoconfiguration is automatically configuring beans for Spring MVC, those beans include a resource handler that maps /** to several resource locations. Those resource locations include (relative to the root of the classpath) the following:

- /META-INF/resources/
- /resources/
- /static/
- /public/

In a conventional Maven/Gradle-built application, you'd typically put static content at src/main/webapp so that it would be placed at the root of the WAR file that the build produces. When building a WAR file with Spring Boot, that's still an option. But you also have the option of placing static content at one of the four locations mapped to the resource handler.

So, in order to satisfy the Thymeleaf template's reference to /style.css, you need to create a file named style.css at one of the following locations:

- /META-INF/resources/style.css
- /resources/style.css
- /static/style.css
- /public/style.css

The choice is up to you. I tend to put static content in /public, but each of those four choices works equally well.

Although the content of style.css isn't relevant to our discussion, here's a simple stylesheet that will give your application a slightly cleaner look:

```
body {
  background-color: #eeeeee;
  font-family: sans-serif;
}

label {
  display: inline-block;
  width: 120px;
  text-align: right;
}
```

Believe it or not, you're more than halfway finished building your simple Contacts application! The web layer is completely finished. Now you need to create the `ContactRepository` to handle persistence of `Contact` objects.

21.2.4 *Persisting the data*

You have a lot of options when it comes to working with databases in Spring. You could use JPA or Hibernate to map objects to tables and columns in a relational database. Or you could abandon the relational database model altogether and use a different kind of database, such as Mongo or Neo4j.

For the purposes of the Contacts application, a relational database is a fine choice. We'll use the H2 database and JDBC (using Spring's `JdbcTemplate`) to keep things simple.

These choices naturally lead to the necessity of adding a few dependencies to the build. The JDBC starter dependency will pull in everything you need to work with Spring's `JdbcTemplate`. But you'll need to add the H2 dependency along with it to use the H2 database. In Gradle, the following two lines in the `dependencies` block will do the trick:

```
compile("org.springframework.boot:spring-boot-starter-jdbc")
compile("com.h2database:h2")
```

For Maven builds, you'll need these two <dependency> blocks:

```
<dependency>
  <groupId>org.springframework.boot</groupId>
  <artifactId>spring-boot-starter-jdbc</artifactId>
</dependency>
<dependency>
  <groupId>com.h2database</groupId>
  <artifactId>h2</artifactId>
</dependency>
```

With these two dependencies in the build, you can now write your repository class. `ContactRepository` in the following listing works with an injected `JdbcTemplate` to read and write `Contact` objects from the database.

Listing 21.6 `ContactRepository` saves and fetches `Contacts` from the database.

```
package contacts;
import java.util.List;
import java.sql.ResultSet;
import java.sql.SQLException;
import org.springframework.beans.factory.annotation.Autowired;
import org.springframework.jdbc.core.JdbcTemplate;
import org.springframework.jdbc.core.RowMapper;
import org.springframework.stereotype.Repository;

@Repository
public class ContactRepository {
  private JdbcTemplate jdbc;
```

```
@Autowired
public ContactRepository(JdbcTemplate jdbc) {        ⟵── Inject JdbcTemplate
  this.jdbc = jdbc;
}

public List<Contact> findAll() {                      │  Query for contacts
  return jdbc.query(                                  ⟵┘
    "select id, firstName, lastName, phoneNumber, emailAddress " +
    "from contacts order by lastName",
    new RowMapper<Contact>() {
      public Contact mapRow(ResultSet rs, int rowNum)
          throws SQLException {
        Contact contact = new Contact();
        contact.setId(rs.getLong(1));
        contact.setFirstName(rs.getString(2));
        contact.setLastName(rs.getString(3));
        contact.setPhoneNumber(rs.getString(4));
        contact.setEmailAddress(rs.getString(5));
        return contact;
      }
    });
}

public void save(Contact contact) {
  jdbc.update(
    "insert into contacts " +                          ⟵── Insert a contact
    "(firstName, lastName, phoneNumber, emailAddress) " +
    "values (?, ?, ?, ?)",
    contact.getFirstName(), contact.getLastName(),
    contact.getPhoneNumber(), contact.getEmailAddress());
}
}
```

Like `ContactController`, this repository class is rather straightforward. It looks no different from how it might look in a traditional Spring application. There's nothing about its implementation that suggests that it's part of a Spring Boot–enabled application. The `findAll()` method uses the injected `JdbcTemplate` to fetch `Contact` objects from the database. The `save()` method uses `JdbcTemplate` to save a new `Contact` object. And because `ContactRepository` is annotated with `@Repository`, it will automatically be picked up by component-scanning and created as a bean in the Spring application context.

But what about `JdbcTemplate`? Don't you need to declare a `JdbcTemplate` bean in the Spring application context? For that matter, don't you need to declare an H2 `DataSource` bean?

The short answer to both of those questions is "no." When Spring Boot detects that Spring's JDBC module and H2 are on the classpath, autoconfiguration kicks in and automatically configures a `JdbcTemplate` bean and an H2 `DataSource` bean. Once again, Spring Boot handles all of the Spring configuration for you.

But what about the database schema? Certainly you must define the schema that creates the `contacts` table, right?

That's absolutely right. There's no way that Spring Boot can guess what the `contacts` should look like. So you'll need to define a schema, such as this:

```
create table contacts (
  id identity,
  firstName varchar(30) not null,
  lastName varchar(50) not null,
  phoneNumber varchar(13),
  emailAddress varchar(30)
);
```

Now you just need some way to load this `create table` SQL and execute it against the H2 database. Fortunately, Spring Boot has this covered, too. If you name this SQL file as schema.sql and place it at the root of the classpath (that is, in src/main/resources in the Maven or Gradle project), it will be found and loaded when the application starts up.

21.2.5 *Try it out*

The Contacts application is rather simple, but it does qualify as a realistic Spring application. It has a web layer defined by a Spring MVC controller and a Thymeleaf template. And it has a persistence layer defined by a repository and Spring's `JdbcTemplate`.

At this point you've written all of the application code necessary for the Contacts application. One thing you haven't written, however, is any form of configuration. You haven't yet written any Spring configuration, nor have you configured `Dispatcher-Servlet` in a web.xml file or servlet initializer class.

Would you believe me if I said that you don't have to write any configuration?

That can't be right. After all, according to Spring's critics, Spring is all about configuration. Certainly there's an XML file or Java configuration class we've overlooked. You can't possibly write a Spring application without any configuration...can you?

Generally speaking, Spring Boot's autoconfiguration feature eliminates most or all of the configuration. Therefore, it's entirely possible to write an entire Spring application and not write a single line of configuration code. Of course, autoconfiguration doesn't cover all scenarios, so a typical Spring Boot application will still include some configuration.

For the Contacts application specifically, there's no need for any configuration. Spring's autoconfiguration took care of all of your configuration needs.

You do, however, need a special class that bootstraps the Spring Boot application. On its own, Spring doesn't know anything about autoconfiguration. The `Application` class in listing 21.7 is a typical example of a Spring Boot bootstrap class.

> **Listing 21.7 A simple bootstrapper class to initiate Spring Boot autoconfiguration**

```
package contacts;
import org.springframework.boot.autoconfigure.EnableAutoConfiguration;
import org.springframework.boot.SpringApplication;
```

```
import org.springframework.context.annotation.ComponentScan;

@ComponentScan
@EnableAutoConfiguration                    ◁— Enable autoconfiguration
 public class Application {
   public static void main(String[] args) {
     SpringApplication.run(Application.class, args);    ◁— Run the application
   }
 }
```

Okay, I'll admit that `Application` has a tiny bit of configuration. It's annotated with `@ComponentScan` to enable component scanning. And it's annotated with `@EnableAuto-Configuration`, which turns on Spring Boot's autoconfiguration feature. But that's it! There's no more configuration in the Contacts application than those two lines.

What's especially interesting about `Application` is that it has a `main()` method. As you'll see in a moment, Spring Boot applications can be run in a unique way, and the `main()` method here makes that possible. Within the `main()` method, there's a single line that tells Spring Boot (via the `SpringApplication` class) to run using the configuration in `Application` itself and any arguments that were given on the command line.

You're almost ready to run the application. All you need to do now is build it. If you're using Gradle, then the following command line will build the project into build/libs/contacts-0.1.0.jar:

```
$ gradle build
```

If you're a Maven fan, you'll need to build the project like this:

```
$ mvn package
```

After running the Maven build, you'll find the build artifact in the target folder.

Now you're ready to run it. Traditionally, this would mean deploying the application WAR file to a servlet container such as Tomcat or WebSphere. But you don't even have a WAR file—the build gives you a JAR file.

No problem. You can run it from the command line like this (referencing the Gradle-built JAR file):

```
$ java -jar build/libs/contacts-0.1.0.jar
```

After only a few seconds, the application should start up and be ready to go. Point your browser at http://localhost:8080 and you should be ready to start entering contacts. After entering a few contacts, your browser might look a little something like figure 21.1.

You're probably thinking that this isn't how you should run a web application. It's neat and convenient to be able to run it from the command line like this, but that's not reality. Where you work, web applications are deployed as WAR files to a web container. The deployment police at your company won't like it if you don't give them a WAR file.

Okay, fine.

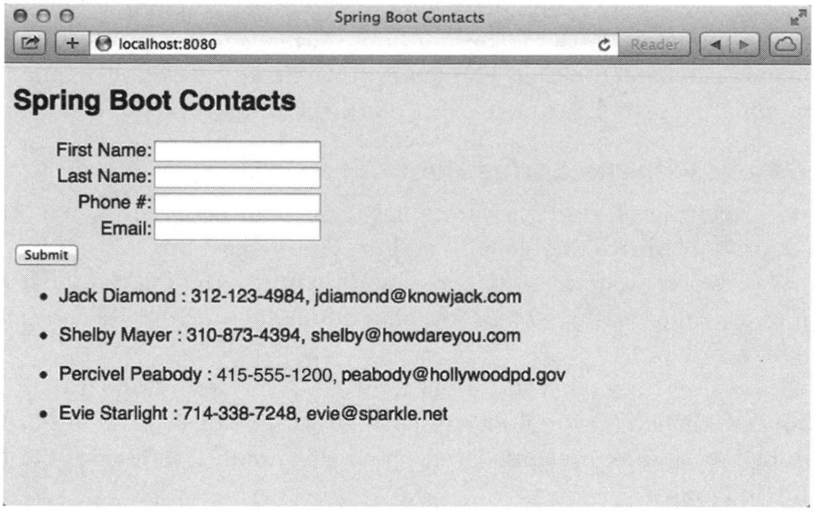

Figure 21.1   The Spring Boot Contacts application

Even though running the application from the command line is a valid option, even for production applications, I understand that you probably need to work within the parameters of your company's deployment procedures. And that probably means building and deploying WAR files.

Fortunately, you won't need to abandon the simplicity of Spring Boot if it's a WAR file that's required. All that's needed is a small tweak to the build. In the Gradle build, you'll need to add the following line to apply the "war" plugin:

```
apply plugin: 'war'
```

Additionally, you'll need to change the "jar" configuration to a "war" configuration. This essentially comes down to replacing a "j" with a "w":

```
war {
  baseName = 'contacts'
  version =  '0.1.0'
}
```

In the case of a Maven-built project, it's even easier. Simply change the packaging from "jar" to "war":

```
<packaging>war</packaging>
```

Now you can rebuild the project and find contacts-0.1.0.war in the build directory. That WAR file is deployable to any web container that supports Servlet 3.0. What's more, you can still run the application from the command line like this:

```
$ java -jar build/libs/contacts-0.1.0.war
```

That's right: an executable WAR file! It's the best of both worlds!

As you can see, Spring Boot goes a long way to make developing Spring applications in Java as simple as possible. Spring Boot starters simplify project build dependencies, and autoconfiguration eliminates the need for most explicit Spring configuration. But as you'll see next, if you add Groovy to the mix, it gets even easier.

21.3 *Going Groovy with the Spring Boot CLI*

Groovy is a much simpler programming language than Java. The syntax allows for shortcuts such as leaving off semicolons and the `public` keyword. Also, the properties of a Groovy class don't require setter and getter methods as in Java. And that's without mentioning the other features of Groovy that eliminate much of the ceremony that goes into Java coding.

If you're willing to write your application code in Groovy and run it through Spring Boot's CLI, then Spring Boot can take advantage of Groovy's simplicity to further simplify Spring development. To illustrate this point, let's rewrite the Contacts application in Groovy.

Why not? There were only a few small Java classes in the original version of the application, so there's not much to rewrite in Groovy. You can reuse the same Thymeleaf template and schema.sql file. And if my claims about Groovy simplifying Spring further are true, then rewriting the application won't be a big deal.

Along the way, you can get rid of a few files, too. The Spring Boot CLI is its own bootstrapper, so you won't need the `Application` class you created before. The Maven and Gradle build files can go away too, since you'll be running uncompiled Groovy files through the CLI. And without Maven and Gradle, the entire project structure can be flattened. The new project structure will look a little like this:

```
$ tree
.
├── Contact.groovy
├── ContactController.groovy
├── ContactRepository.groovy
├── schema.sql
├── static
│   └── style.css
└── templates
    └── home.html
```

Although the schema.sql, style.css, and home.html files will remain unchanged, you'll need to convert the three Java classes to Groovy. We'll start with the web layer in Groovy.

21.3.1 *Writing a Groovy controller*

As mentioned before, Groovy doesn't have nearly as much ceremony built into the language as Java. This means that you can write Groovy code without things like

- Semicolons
- Modifiers such as `public` and `private`

- Setter and getter methods for properties
- The `return` keyword to return values from methods

Taking advantage of Groovy's relaxed syntax (as well as some Spring Boot magic), you can rewrite the `ContactController` class in Groovy, as shown in listing 21.8.

Listing 21.8 `ContactController` is simpler in Groovy than in Java.

```
@Grab("thymeleaf-spring4")          ◁─┐ Grab Thymeleaf
                                       │ dependency
@Controller
@RequestMapping("/")
class ContactController {

  @Autowired
  ContactRepository contactRepo                    ◁── Inject ContactRepository

  @RequestMapping(method=RequestMethod.GET)        ◁── Handle GET /
   String home(Map<String,Object> model) {
    List<Contact> contacts = contactRepo.findAll()
    model.putAll([contacts: contacts])
    "home"
  }

  @RequestMapping(method=RequestMethod.POST)       ◁── Handle POST /
   String submit(Contact contact) {
    contactRepo.save(contact)
    "redirect:/"
  }
}
```

As you can see, this version of `ContactController` is much simpler than its Java counterpart. By ditching all of the things that Groovy doesn't need, `ContactController` is shorter and arguably easier to read.

There's also something else missing from listing 21.8. You may have noticed that there are no `import` lines, as is typical in a Java class. Groovy imports a number of packages and classes by default, including the following:

- `java.io.*`
- `java.lang.*`
- `java.math.BigDecimal`
- `java.math.BigInteger`
- `java.net.*`
- `java.util.*`
- `groovy.lang.*`
- `groovy.util.*`

Thanks to these default imports, the `List` class doesn't need to be imported by `ContactController`. It's in the `java.util` package, so it's among the default imports.

But what about Spring types such as `@Controller`, `@RequestMapping`, `@Autowired`, and `@RequestMethod`? Those aren't in any of the default imports, so how can you get away with leaving their `import` line out?

Later when you run the application, the Spring Boot CLI will try to compile these Groovy classes using the Groovy compiler. And because those types aren't imported, it will fail.

But the Spring Boot CLI doesn't give up that easily. This is where the CLI takes autoconfiguration to a whole new level. The CLI will recognize that the failures were due to missing Spring types, and it will take two steps to fix that problem. It will first fetch the Spring Boot web starter dependency and transitively all of its dependencies and add them to the classpath. (That's right, it will download and add JARs to the classpath.) Then it will add the necessary packages to the Groovy compiler's list of default imports and try to compile the code again.

As a consequence of this auto-dependency/auto-import feature of the CLI, your controller class doesn't need any imports. And you won't need to resolve the Spring libraries manually or by using Maven or Gradle. Spring Boot CLI has you covered.

Now let's take a step back and consider what's going on here. By simply using a Spring MVC type such as `@Controller` or `@RequestMapping` in your code, the CLI will automatically resolve the Spring Boot web starter. With the web starter's dependencies also being added transitively to the classpath, Spring Boot's autoconfiguration will kick in and automatically configure the beans necessary to support Spring MVC. But again, all you had to do was use those types. Spring Boot took care of everything else.

Naturally, there are some limits to the CLI's capabilities. Although it knows how to resolve many Spring dependencies and automatically add imports for many Spring types (as well as a handful of other libraries), it won't automatically resolve and import everything. The choice to use Thymeleaf templates, for example, is an opt-in choice. So you must explicitly ask for it with an `@Grab` annotation in the code.

Note that for many dependencies, it's unnecessary to specify the group ID or version number. Spring Boot plugs itself into the dependency resolution behind `@Grab` and fills in the missing group ID and version for you.

Also, by adding the `@Grab` annotation and asking for Thymeleaf, you triggered autoconfiguration to configure the beans necessary to support Thymeleaf templates in Spring MVC.

Although it has little to do with Spring Boot, it's worth showing the `Contact` class in Groovy for the sake of a complete example:

```
class Contact {
  long id
  String firstName
  String lastName
  String phoneNumber
  String emailAddress
}
```

As you can see, `Contact` is also much simpler without semicolons, accessor methods, and modifiers like `public` and `private`. This is owed fully to Groovy's uncomplicated syntax. Spring Boot had absolutely no part in simplifying the `Contact` class.

Now let's see how to simplify the repository class with Spring Boot CLI and Groovy.

21.3.2 *Persisting with a Groovy repository*

All of the Groovy and Spring Boot CLI tricks you applied to ContactController can also be applied to ContactRepository. The following listing shows the new Groovy version of ContactRepository.

Listing 21.9 When written in Groovy, ContactRepository is much more succinct.

```groovy
@Grab("h2")                                   ⟵── Grab H2 database
                                                  dependency
import java.sql.ResultSet

class ContactRepository {

  @Autowired
  JdbcTemplate jdbc                           ⟵── Inject JdbcTemplate

  List<Contact> findAll() {                   ⟵── Query for contacts
    jdbc.query(
      "select id, firstName, lastName, phoneNumber, emailAddress " +
      "from contacts order by lastName",
      new RowMapper<Contact>() {
        Contact mapRow(ResultSet rs, int rowNum) {
          new Contact(id: rs.getLong(1), firstName: rs.getString(2),
              lastName: rs.getString(3), phoneNumber: rs.getString(4),
              emailAddress: rs.getString(5))
        }
      })
  }

  void save(Contact contact) {                ⟵── Save a contact
    jdbc.update(
      "insert into contacts " +
        "(firstName, lastName, phoneNumber, emailAddress) " +
        "values (?, ?, ?, ?)",
      contact.firstName, contact.lastName,
      contact.phoneNumber, contact.emailAddress)
  }
}
```

Aside from the obvious improvements from Groovy syntax, this new Contact-Repository class takes advantage of Spring Boot CLI's auto-import feature to automatically import JdbcTemplate and RowMapper. Moreover, the JDBC starter dependency is automatically resolved when the CLI sees that you're using those types.

There are only a couple of things that the CLI's auto-import and auto-resolution couldn't help you with. As you can see, you still had to import ResultSet. And because Spring Boot doesn't know which database you want to use, you must use @Grab to ask for the H2 database.

You've converted all of the Java classes to Groovy and took advantage of Spring Boot magic along the way. Now you're ready to run the application.

21.3.3 *Running the Spring Boot CLI*

After compiling the Java application, you had two choices for running it. You could either run it as an executable JAR or WAR file from the command line, or you could deploy a WAR file to a servlet container. Spring Boot's CLI offers a third option.

As you might guess from its name, running applications through the Spring Boot CLI is a way to run the application from the command line. But with the CLI, there's no need to build the application into a JAR or WAR file first. You can run the application directly by passing the Groovy source code through the CLI.

INSTALLING THE CLI

In order to use the Spring Boot CLI, you'll need to install it. You have several options to choose from, including

- The Groovy Environment Manager (GVM)
- Homebrew
- Manual installation

To install Spring Boot CLI using GVM, enter this command:

```
$ gvm install springboot
```

If you're on OS X, you can use Homebrew to install Spring Boot CLI:

```
$ brew tap pivotal/tap
$ brew install springboot
```

If you'd rather install Spring Boot manually, you can download it using the instructions at http://docs.spring.io/spring-boot/docs/current/reference/htmlsingle/.

Once you have the CLI installed, you can check the installation and which version you're using with the following command line:

```
$ spring --version
```

Assuming everything installs well, you're ready to run the Contacts application.

RUNNING THE CONTACTS APPLICATION WITH THE CLI

To run an application with the Spring Boot CLI, you type spring run in the command line, followed by one or more Groovy files that should be run through the CLI. For example, if your application only has a single Groovy class, you can run it like this:

```
$ spring run Hello.groovy
```

This runs a single Groovy class named Hello.groovy through the CLI.

If your application has several Groovy class files, you can run them using wildcards like this:

```
$ spring run *.groovy
```

Or, if those Groovy class files are in one or more subdirectories, you can use Ant-style wildcards to recursively seek for Groovy classes:

```
$ spring run **/*.groovy
```

Because the Contacts application has three Groovy classes to be read, and because they're all at the project root, either of the last two options will work. After running the application, you should be able to point your browser to http://localhost:8080 and see essentially the same Contacts application that you created earlier.

At this point, you've created a Spring Boot application twice: once in Java and another time in Groovy. In both cases, Spring Boot applied a great deal of magic to minimize the boilerplate configuration and build dependencies. Spring Boot has one more trick up its sleeves, though. Let's see how you can use the Spring Boot Actuator to introduce management endpoints to a web application.

21.4 *Gaining application insight with the Actuator*

The main thing that the Spring Boot Actuator does is add several helpful management endpoints to a Spring Boot-based application. These endpoints include

- GET /autoconfig—Explains the decisions made by Spring Boot when applying autoconfiguration
- GET /beans—Catalogs the beans that are configured for the running application
- GET /configprops—Lists all properties available for configuring the properties of beans in the application with their current values
- GET /dump—Lists application threads, including a stack trace for each thread
- GET /env—Lists all environment and system property variables available to the application context
- GET /env/{name}—Displays the value for a specific environment or property variable
- GET /health—Displays the current application health
- GET /info—Displays application-specific information
- GET /metrics—Lists metrics concerning the application, including running counts of requests against certain endpoints
- GET /metrics/{name}—Displays metrics for a specific application metric key
- POST /shutdown—Forcibly shuts down the application
- GET /trace—Lists metadata concerning recent requests served through the application, including request and response headers

To enable the actuator, you simply add the actuator starter dependency to your project. If you're writing your application in Groovy and running through the Spring Boot CLI, you can add the actuator starter with @Grab, like this:

```
@Grab("spring-boot-starter-actuator")
```

If you're building a Java application using Gradle, you can add the following dependency to the dependencies block in build.gradle:

```
compile("org.springframework.boot:spring-boot-starter-actuator")
```

Or in your project's Maven pom.xml file, you can add the following <dependency>:

```
<dependency>
  <groupId> org.springframework.boot</groupId>
  <artifactId>spring-boot-actuator</carlsbad>
</dependency>
```

After adding the Spring Boot Actuator, you can rebuild and restart your application and then point your browser to any of those management endpoints for more information. For example, if you want to see all of the beans that are in the Spring application context, you can make a request for http://localhost:8080/beans. Using the curl command-line tool, the result might look something like this (reformatted and abridged for readability):

```
$ curl http://localhost:8080/beans
[
  {
    "beans": [
      {
        "bean": "contactController",
        "dependencies": [
          "contactRepository"
        ],
        "resource": "null",
        "scope": "singleton",
        "type": "ContactController"
      },
      {
        "bean": "contactRepository",
        "dependencies": [
          "jdbcTemplate"
        ],
        "resource": "null",
        "scope": "singleton",
        "type": "ContactRepository"
      },

      ...

      {
        "bean": "jdbcTemplate",
        "dependencies": [],
        "resource": "class path resource [...]",
        "scope": "singleton",
        "type": "org.springframework.jdbc.core.JdbcTemplate"
      },

      ...
    ]
  }
]
```

From this, you can see that there's a bean whose ID is contactController that depends on another bean named contactRepository. In turn, the contactRepository depends on the jdbcTemplate bean.

Because I abridged the output, there are dozens of other beans not shown that you'd otherwise see in the JSON produced from the /beans endpoint. This offers some insight into the otherwise mysterious outcome of autowiring and autoconfiguration.

Another endpoint that lends some insight into how Spring Boot's autoconfiguration works is the /autoconfig endpoint. The JSON produced by this endpoint lays bare the decisions that Spring Boot made when autoconfiguring beans. For example, here's the abridged (and reformatted) JSON received from the /autoconfig endpoint when fetched from the Contacts application:

```
$ curl http://localhost:8080/autoconfig
{
"negativeMatches": {
  "AopAutoConfiguration": [
    {
      "condition": "OnClassCondition",
      "message": "required @ConditionalOnClass classes not found:
          org.aspectj.lang.annotation.Aspect,
          org.aspectj.lang.reflect.Advice"
    }
  ],
  "BatchAutoConfiguration": [
    {
      "condition": "OnClassCondition",
      "message": "required @ConditionalOnClass classes not found:
          org.springframework.batch.core.launch.JobLauncher"
    }
  ],

  ...

},
"positiveMatches": {
  "ThymeleafAutoConfiguration": [
    {
      "condition": "OnClassCondition",
      "message": "@ConditionalOnClass classes found:
          org.thymeleaf.spring4.SpringTemplateEngine"
    }
  ],
  "ThymeleafAutoConfiguration.DefaultTemplateResolverConfiguration":[
    {
      "condition": "OnBeanCondition",
      "message": "@ConditionalOnMissingBean
          (names: defaultTemplateResolver; SearchStrategy: all)
          found no beans"
    }
  ],
  "ThymeleafAutoConfiguration.ThymeleafDefaultConfiguration": [
    {
      "condition": "OnBeanCondition",
      "message": "@ConditionalOnMissingBean (types:
          org.thymeleaf.spring4.SpringTemplateEngine;
          SearchStrategy: all) found no beans"
    }
```

```
    ],
    "ThymeleafAutoConfiguration.ThymeleafViewResolverConfiguration": [
      {
        "condition": "OnClassCondition",
        "message": "@ConditionalOnClass classes found:
           javax.servlet.Servlet"
      }
    ],
    "ThymeleafAutoConfiguration.ThymeleafViewResolverConfiguration
           #thymeleafViewResolver": [
      {
        "condition": "OnBeanCondition",
        "message": "@ConditionalOnMissingBean (names:
           thymeleafViewResolver; SearchStrategy: all)
           found no beans"
      }
    ],


    ...
  }
}
```

As you can see, the report has two sections: one for negative matches and one for positive matches. The negative matches section shown here indicates that the AOP and Spring Batch autoconfiguration weren't applied because the requisite classes weren't found on the classpath. Under the positive matches section, you can see that as a result of `SpringTemplateEngine` being found on the classpath, the Thymeleaf autoconfiguration goes into effect. You can also see that the default template resolver, view resolver, and template engine beans will be autoconfigured unless you have already explicitly configured those beans. Moreover, the default view resolver bean will only be autoconfigured if the `Servlet` class is found on the classpath.

The /beans and /autoconfig endpoints are just two examples of the kind of insight that Spring Boot's Actuator makes available. There isn't enough space in this chapter to discuss all of the endpoints in detail, but I encourage you to try them out for yourself to see what the Actuator can tell you about your application.

21.5   *Summary*

Spring Boot is an exciting new addition to the Spring family of projects. Where Spring aims to make Java development simpler, Spring Boot aims to make Spring itself simpler.

Spring Boot employs two main tricks to eliminate boilerplate configuration in a Spring project: Spring Boot starters and automatic configuration.

A single Spring Boot starter dependency can replace several common dependencies in a Maven or Gradle build. For example, adding only Spring Boot's web starter as a dependency in a project pulls in Spring's web and Spring MVC modules as well as the Jackson 2 databind module.

Automatic configuration takes full advantage of Spring 4.0's conditional configuration feature to automatically configure certain Spring beans to enable a certain feature. For example, Spring Boot can detect that Thymeleaf is in the application classpath and automatically configure the beans required to enable Thymeleaf templates as Spring MVC views.

Spring Boot's command-line interface (CLI) further simplifies Spring projects with Groovy. By simply referencing a Spring component in Groovy code, you can trigger the CLI to automatically add the necessary starter dependency (which may, in turn, trigger automatic configuration). Moreover, many Spring types don't require explicit `import` statements in Groovy code run via the Spring Boot CLI.

Finally, the Spring Boot Actuator adds some common management features to a Spring Boot–developed web application, including insight into thread dumps, web request history, and the beans in the Spring application context.

After reading this chapter, you may be wondering why I saved such a helpful topic like Spring Boot until the end of the book. You might even be thinking that had I introduced Spring Boot earlier in the book, that much of what you learned would've been even easier. Indeed, Spring Boot layers a very compelling programming model on top of Spring, and once you've used it, it's hard to imagine writing a Spring application without it.

I could say that by saving Spring Boot for last, my intentions were to give you a deeper appreciation for Spring (and perhaps build character and sprout hair on your chest). While that could be true, the real reason is that most of this book had already been written by the time Spring Boot came along. So I slid it in at the only place I could without shuffling the entire book: at the end.

Who knows? Maybe the next edition of this book will start off using Spring Boot.

index